MANAGEMENT

For

UGC-NET/JRF/ SET

&

Other Competitive Examinations
(With Multiple Choice Question-Answer and Explanation)

Mr. Nilesh S Ugemuge
UGC-NET(HRM), UGC-NET(IR), UGC-NET(LW), UGC-NET(PM),SET(SW),
PGDHRM, MIRPM, M.Sc. (Physics), MSW,
MA (Economics), MA(Public Admin),B.Ed.
Assistant Professor
Priyadarshini College of Engineering,
Nagpur, Maharashtra.

Er. Moreshwar N Kudkilwar
BE (Fire), LLB,PGDIS, MIRPM
Sr. Fire Officer
Neelam Process Complex
ONGC, Bombay High, Mumbai.

Er. Prachita A Patil
BE(Electronics & Telecommunication), MBA
Former Assistant Professor
ITM College of Engineering, Nagpur,
Maharashtra.

Foreword By
Dr. Vivek Nanoti, Ph.D.
Principal
Priyadarshini Indira Gandhi College of Engineering,
Nagpur, Maharashtra.

HPH

Himalaya Publishing House

MUMBAI • NEW DELHI • NAGPUR • BENGALURU • HYDERBAD • CHENNAI • PUNE • LUCKNOW
• AHMEDABAD • ERNAKULAM • BHUBANESWAR • KOLKATA • GUWAHATI

First Edition : 2014

Published by : Mrs. Meena Pandey for **Himalaya Publishing House Pvt. Ltd.,**
"Ramdoot", Dr. Bhalerao Marg, Girgaon, **Mumbai - 400 004.**
Phone: 022-23860170/23863863, Fax: 022-23877178
E-mail: himpub@vsnl.com; Website: www.himpub.com

Branch Offices :

New Delhi : "Pooja Apartments", 4-B, Murari Lal Street, Ansari Road, Darya Ganj, New Delhi - 110 002. Phone: 011-23270392, 23278631; Fax: 011-23256286

Nagpur : Kundanlal Chandak Industrial Estate, Ghat Road, Nagpur - 440 018. Phone: 0712-2738731, 3296733; Telefax: 0712-2721215

Bengaluru : No. 16/1 (Old 12/1), 1st Floor, Next to Hotel Highlands, Madhava Nagar, Race Course Road, Bengaluru - 560 001. Phone: 080-32919385; Telefax: 080-22286611

Hyderabad : No. 3-4-184, Lingampally, Besides Raghavendra Swamy Matham, Kachiguda, Hyderabad - 500 027. Phone: 040-27560041, 27550139; Mobile: 09390905282

Chennai : No. 8/2, 2nd Madley Street, Ground Floor, T. Nagar, Chennai - 600 017. Mobile: 09345345055

Pune : First Floor, "Laksha" Apartment, No. 527, Mehunpura, Shaniwarpeth (Near Prabhat Theatre), Pune - 411 030. Phone: 020-24496323/24496333; Mobile: 09370579333

Lucknow : House No 731, Shekhupura Colony, Near B.D. Convent School, Aliganj, Lucknow - 226 022. Mobile: 09307501549

Ahmedabad : 114, "SHAIL", 1st Floor, Opp. Madhu Sudan House, C.G. Road, Navrang Pura, Ahmedabad - 380 009. Phone: 079-26560126; Mobile: 09377088847

Ernakulam : 39/176 (New No: 60/251) 1st Floor, Karikkamuri Road, Ernakulam, Kochi - 682011, Phone: 0484-2378012, 2378016; Mobile: 09344199799

Bhubaneswar : 5 Station Square, Bhubaneswar - 751 001 (Odisha). Phone: 0674-2532129, Mobile: 09338746007

Kolkata : 108/4, Beliaghata Main Road, Near ID Hospital, Opp. SBI Bank, Kolkata - 700 010, Phone: 033-32449649, Mobile: 09883055590, 07439040301

Guwahati : House No. 15, Behind Pragjyotish College, Near Sharma Printing Press, P.O. Bharalumukh, Guwahati - 781009, (Assam). Mobile: 09883055590, 09883055536

DTP by : HPH, Nagpur **(Prasad)**

Printed at : Geetanjali Press Pvt. Ltd., Nagpur, on behalf of HPH.

This Book is dedicated to

My Uncle (Naresh) and Aunty (Nilima)

Who encourage me in all steps of life.

-Nilesh

Dr. Vivek Nanoti

Principal, Priyadarshini Indira Gandhi College of Engineering, Nagpur
National Exe. Council Member, ISTE, New Delhi

FOREWORD

It's indeed a great pleasure and matter of pride to write the foreword to the first edition of Management for UGC-NET/JRF/SET by Prof. Nilesh S. Ugemuge , Er. Moreshwar N. Kudkilwar & Prachita A.Patil for several reasons.

The book is developed on the basis of need analysis of the aspirants as well as the survey of most important and probable set of questions for the UGC-NET/JRF/SET in Management. This book includes comprehensive concepts about every topics and objective question answer for the detail preparation ideally suited for the readers. It also contains several solved questions with explanation.

Prof. Nilesh S. Ugemuge ,Er. Moreshwar N. Kudkilwar & Prachita A.Patil are unusual and unique blend of talent which make them an excellent textbook author. They are academically well trained and recognized Management Scholar. In addition they have adequate academic and industry experience.

Therefore I am happy to foreword this book for the aspirants of UGC-NET/JRF/SET in Management for the desiourus students as well as teachers of Management.

(Dr. Vivek Nanoti)

Preface

The work of giving an introduction to this effort of bringing a marvel in the form of book is come up keeping in mind the selective approach of students and those who many are involved into the tangible and intangible understanding of the subject (Management).

The idea come and crop up to bring this master piece in the form of text book only for those thousands and lakhs of students who are in search of their desired objective and career in the field of Management. The aim of this work is to provide a textbook distinctly covering the basics and intricacies of the topics laid down into the content of this book.

While preparing for academic and different kind of competitive examinations pertaining to the subject relevance, adequate and legible study material is required which may give elaborate idea about the topic in short period of time. An attempt is being made to bring this all requirements of the readers at one platform at the same time in form of this book. This book provide the extensive material in the form of more than two thousand objective type question for the aspirants of various competitive examination in the field of Management.

Also an attempt has been made to cover wide spectrum of contents with illustrations and associated objective type questions followed by their answers. Each section of chapter begins with an outline of contents and learning objectives.

In preparing this edition, a sincere effort has been made towards the clarity in explanation and legibility of the words. Keeping in view the extensive practice to answer objective questions large number of associated objective type questions on respective topics is incorporated.

We wish to express our heartfelt gratitude to our family member and colleagues of Department for their constant support and encouragement during this project. We would like to express our heartfelt thanks to the Management of LTJSS, Principal Dr. M. P. Singh and Dr. R. V. Kshirsagar, Vice Principal and Dean, Faculty of Engineering, RTM Nagpur University,Dr.Vivek Nanoti, Principal, PIGCE, Nagpur for their encouragement. We would also like to express our gratitude to all those who helped us, in every way in our endeavor.

An untiring help rendered by Mr. **Gokulji Pandey** is sincerely acknowledged. We wish to particularly thank the entire team of Himalaya Publishing House for their continuous help of all kind.

We are grateful to and in particular thank the Himalaya Publishing House for their constant support in all kind.

Constructive criticism and suggestions will be most welcome.

Nilesh S.Ugemuge

Moreshwar N. Kudkilwar

Prachita A. Patil

Acknowledgements

A large number of works were consulted while preparing the present book. The authors do not claim originality in content or presentation of the material included in this book. The authors record here their indebtedness to the authors of those original works from where much of the information is liberally drawn.

We offer our thanks to **Shri Gokulji Pandey,** Director, Himalaya Publishing House Nagpur and **Mr. Dinesh Dhawne**, Area Manager and entire team of HPH for constant support during entire work and giving the opportunity to publish this book.

I also thanks to editorial staff of HPH for designing and arranging text in an appropriate manner.

Syllabus

MANAGEMENT (Including Business Administration Management / Marketing Management /Industrial Relations and Personnel Management)

Managerial Economics

Demand Analysis; Production Function; Cost-output relations; Market structures; Pricing theories; Advertising; Macro-economics; National Income concepts; Infrastructure-Management and Policy; Business Environment; Capital Budgeting.

Organizational behavior

The concept and significance of organizational behavior; Skills and roles in an organization; Classical, Neo-classical and modern theories of organisational structure; Organisational design-Understanding and Managing individual behaviour personality-Perception-Values-Attitudes-Learning-Motivation. Understanding and managing group behavior;Processes-Inter-personal and group dynamics; Communication-Leadership-Managing change-Managing conflicts; Organisational development.

Human Resource Management and Industrial Relation

Concepts and perspectives in HRM; HRM in changing environment Human resource planning-Objectives, Process and Techniques Job analysis-Job description Selecting human resources;Induction, Training and Development; Exit policy and implications; Performance appraisal and evaluation; Potential assessment; Job evaluation; Wage determination; Industrial Relations and Trade Unions; Dispute resolution and Grievance management; Labour Welfare and Social security measures.

Financial Management

Nature and Scope; Valuation concepts and valuation of securities; Capital budgeting decisions-Risk analysis; Capital structure and Cost of capital; Dividend policy-Determinants; Long-term and short-term financing instruments Mergers and Acquisitions.

Marketing Management

Marketing environment and Environment scanning; Marketing Information Systems and Marketing research; Understanding consumer and industrial markets; Demand Measurement and Forecasting; Market Segmentation-. Targeting and Positioning: Product decisions, Product mix, Product Life Cycle; New product development; Branding and Packaging; Pricing methods and strategies.

Promotion decisions-Promotion mix; Advertising; Personal selling; Channel management; Vertical marketing systems; Evaluation and control of marketing effort; Marketing of services; Customer relation management; Uses of internet as a marketing medium-other related issues like branding. market development, Advertising and retailing on the net; New issues in Marketing.

Production management and Operations Research

Role and scope of production management; Facility location; Layout planning and analysis; Production _planning and control-production process analysis; Demand forecasting for operations; Deterininants of product mix; Production scheduling; Work measurement; Time and motion study; Statistical Quality Control.

Role and scope of Operations Research; Linear Programming; Sensitivity analysis; Duality; Transportation model; Inventory control; Queueing theory; , Decision theory; Markov analysis; PERT */CPM.*

Research Methodology and Information Technology

Probability theory; Probability distributions-Binomial, Poisson, Normal and Exponential; Correlation and Regression analysis; Sampling theory; Sampling distributions; Tests of Hypothesis; Large and small samples; t, z, F, Chi-square tests. Use of Computers in Managerial ,applications; Technology issues and Data processing in organizations; Information systems; MIS and Decision making; System analysis and design; Trends in Information Technology; Internet and Internet-based applications.

Strategic Management

Concept of corporate strategy; Components of strategy formulation; Ansoff,s growth vector; BCG Model; Porter's generic strrategies; Competitor analysis; Strategic dimensions and group mapping; Industry analysis; Strategies in industry evolution, fragmentation, maturity, and decline; Competitive strategy and corporate strategy; Transnationalization of world economy; Managing cultural diversity; Global Entry strategies; Globalisation of financial system and services; Managing international business; Competitive advantage of nations; RTP and WTO.

Enterpreneurship Development

Concepts-Types-Characteristics; Motivation; Competencies and its development; Innovation and Entrepreneurship; Small business-Concepts Government policy for promotion of small and tiny enterprises; Process of business opportunity identification; detailed business plan. preparation; Managing small enterprises; Planning for growth; Sickness in Small Enterprises; Rehabilitation of sick enterprises; Intrapreneurship (organisational entrepreneurship).

Ethics and Corporate Governance

Ethics and Management system; Ethical issues and analysis in management; Value based organisations; Personal framework for ethical choices; Ethical pressure on individual in organisations; Gender issues; Ecological consciousness; Environmental ethics; Social responsibilities of business; Corporate governance and ethics.

Contents

UNIT-I

MANAGERIAL ECONOMICS

1. The Kinky demand curve hypothesis predicts:

(A)Stable costs for the firms

(B)Sticky prices in the market

(C)More advertising by the firms

(D)None of the above

2. In the case of Veblen goods, demand curve will slope :

(A) Upwards (B) Downwards

(C) Horizontal (D) Vertical

3. Consider a demand curve which takes the form of a straight-line cutting both axes. Elasticity at the mid-point of the line would be:

(A) 0 (B) 1.0

(C) 1.5 (D)2.0

4. The demand for Rice from farm A is perfectly elastic because Rice from farm A is

(A)a perfect complement for Rice from farm B.

(B)a normal good.

(C)a perfect substitute for Rice from farm B.

(D)an inferior good.

5. Match the following:

LIST-I

(a)Percentage change in quantity demanded to percentage change in price.

(b)Percentage change in demand to percentage change in the price of some other commodity.

(c)Homogeneous products

(d)Relationship between quantity of the product demanded and factors that affect the quantity.

LIST-II

(i)Perfect competition

(ii)Market demand

(iii)Price elasticity

(iv)Cross elasticity

Codes:

(a) (b) (c) (d)

(A)(iii) (iv) (i) (ii)

(B)(iv) (iii) (i) (ii)

(C)(iii) (ii) (i) (iv)

(D)(iv) (ii) (i) (iii)

6. Demand curve under monopolistic competition is :

(A)Downward sloping and flat

(B)Downward sloping and steep

(C)Parallel to 'X' axis

(D)Parallel to 'Y' axis

7. For a perfectly competitive firm,

(A)marginal revenue equals total revenue

(B)total revenue always exceeds total cost

(C)price always exceeds average total cost

(D)the marginal revenue curve and the demand curve are the same

8. Other things being equal an increase in income leads to a decrease in demand for

(A)Superior Goods (B) Inferior Goods

(C)Both (A) and (B) (D) None of the above

9. If for a demand process suited to a = 0.1 we try to fit a forecasting procedure with a = 0.3, the forecast will

(A)Show large swings up and down

(B)Follow the demand better, consequently reducing forecast errors

(C)Show a pronounced behaviour

(D)None of the above

10. Match the following :

List – I

(a)Responsiveness of demand to change in price

(b)Responsiveness of demand to change in tastes

(c)Responsiveness of demand to change in income

(d)Responsiveness of demand to change in price of related goods

List – II

(i)Income elasticity of demand

(ii)Price elasticity of demand

(iii)Cross elasticity of demand

(iv)Taste elasticity of demand

Codes:

	(a)	(b)	(c)	(d)
(A)	(i)	(ii)	(iii)	(iv)
(B)	(iv)	(iii)	(i)	(ii)
(C)	(iii)	(iv)	(ii)	(i)
(D)	(ii)	(iv)	(i)	(iii)

11. If both supply and demand increase by the same proportion,

(A)Quantity remains constant

(B)Price remains constant

(C)Price increases

(D)Quantity increases

12. When marginal propensity to consumption (MPC) is one, then multiplier value (K) is:

(A) Zero (B) One

(C) Infinity (D) None of the above

13. The demand curve facing the pure monopolist is :

(A)Positively sloped (B) Negatively sloped

(C)Horizontal (D) None of the above

14. "Supply creates its own demand" is known as :

(A)Keynesian law (B) Veblen law

(C)Say's law (D) None of the above

15. In the typical demand schedule, quantity demanded :

(A)varies directly with price

(B)varies indirectly with price

(C)varies inversely with price

(D)is independent of price

16. In demand forecasting important method used in trend projection is :

(A)Scientific method (B)Bax-Jenkin method

(C)Delphi method (D) Logistics method

17. The elasticity of demand indicates

(A)The rate of response of demand to a change in price.

(B)The rate of change of demand to a change in income.

(C)The change in the tastes of consumers at different prices.

(D)The rate of response of demand to a change in supply.

18. A rightward shift in supply curve indicates

(A)A decrease in supply

(B)An increase in quantity demanded

(C)An increase in supply

(D)Law of variable proportion

19. Production can be measured in terms of which of the following?

(A)Total productivity

(B)Marginal productivity

(C)Average productivity

(D)All of the above

20. The demand curve faced by a monopolist is

(A)perfectly elastic

(B)perfectly inelastic

(C)undefined

(D)the market demand curve

21. The positive cross elasticity of demand between two products means:

(A)two products are substitutes

(B)two products are complementary

(C)two products are neither substitutes nor complementary

(D)none of the above

22. The price elasticity of demand for any product in the long run

(A)is more than it's short run value.

(B)is less than its short run value.

(C)is same as its short run value.

(D)None of the above.

23. During the 3rd stage of Law of variable proportions:

(A)MP is negative (B) AP is negative

(C)AP is rising (D)TP is constant

24. A firm is a price takes under:

(A)Monopoly

(B)Duopoly

(C)Monopolistic competition

(D)Perfect competition

25. The law of Demand does ***not*** assume constancy of:

(A)Price of the concern commodity

(B)Price of other commodity

(C)Consumers income level

(D)Tastes and preferences

26. Which of the following statements is true?

(A)MC is a subset of incremental cost

(B)Incremental cost is a subset of MC

(C)MC is a subset of sunk cost

(D)Sunk cost is a subset of incremental cost

27. Which concept shows the overall output generated at a given level of input?

(A)Cost function

(B)Production function

(C)Marginal rate of technical substitution

(D)Isocost

28. A demand curve suggesting unitary elasticity throughout shall be:

(A)a rectangular hyperbola

(B)a straight line parallel to X-axis

(C)a straight line parallel to Y-axis

(D)a negatively sloping straight line of 45° angle

29. Demand pull inflation is the result of

(A)Increase in production.

(B)Increase in the supply of goods.

(C)Increase in money supply.

(D)Increase in the cost of production.

30. In a perfectly competitive industry, there are:

(A)many buyers and many sellers.

(B)many buyers, but there might be only one or two sellers.

(C)many sellers, but there might be only one or two buyers.

(D)one firm that sets the price for the others to follow.

31. Managerial Economics as a specialized branch of Economics

(A)Provide ready-made solutions to business problems.

(B)Provide logic and methodology to find solutions to business problems.

(C)Provide theoretical background to analyze business problems.

(D)Provide alternative answers to specific business problems.

32. Managerial economics as a new branch of Economics

(A)Highlights on analyzing business problems.

(B)Acts totally independent of other subjects.

(C)Uses new techniques to identify business and management problems.

(D)Applies economic theories and concepts to solve business and management problems.

33. The relationship between price and demand is :

(A)Direct. (B) Inverse.

(C)Proportionate (D) positive.

34. Demand for a product refers to

(A)Various quantities that are demanded by consumers.

(B)Various amounts desired by consumers.

(C)Total quantity of a product demanded during a given period of time.

(D)Total quantity of a product demanded at a particular price in the market during a given period of time.

35. The prices statutorily determined by the government for certain important goods like steel, cement, etc., is called:

(A)Mark-up pricing. (B)Customary pricing.

(C)Full cost pricing. (D)Administered prices.

36. If a shortage exists in a market, the natural tendency is for:

(A)demand to increase.

(B)price to increase.

(C)quantity supplied to decrease.

(D)no change in the market.

37. An increase in supply demand remaining constant will change the equilibrium

(A)Causing a fall in price.

(B)Causing a backward shift in supply curve.

(C)Causing no change in price.

(D)Causing a rise in price.

38. Suppose you produce wooden desks, and government legislation protecting the spotted owl has made it more expensive for you to purchase wood. What do you expect to happen to the equilibrium price and quantity of wooden desks?

(A)price and quantity will increase.

(B)price will increase but quantity will decrease.

(C)price and quantity will decrease.

(D)price will decrease but quantity will increase.

39. Suppose that supply increases and demand decreases. What effect will this have on price and quantity?

(A)price will increase and quantity may rise or fall.

(B)price will decrease and quantity will increase.

(C)price will decrease and quantity will decrease.

(D)none of the above.

40. Suppose both supply and demand decrease. What effect will this have on price?

(A)it will fall.

(B)it will rise.

(C)it may rise or fall.

(D)it will remain the same.

41. Suppose that good X is a substitute for good Y. Then an increase in the price of good Y leads to:

(A)an increase in the demand of good X.

(B)a decrease in the demand of good X.

(C)a decrease in the supply of good X.

(D)an increase in the supply of good X.

42. If consumers expect future prices to be higher

(A)they substitute current purchases for future purchases of perishable products.

(B)stockpiling will happen when products are durable in nature.

(C)the position of the demand will not change.

(D)the demand for automobiles today will not change.

43. The demand function :

(A)describes how much of good X will be purchased at the alternative price of good X, given all the other variables being constant.

(B)recognizes that the quantity of a good consumed depends on its price and demand shifters.

(C)shows the relationship between the quantity demanded of X and variables other than its price.

(D)does not include expectations.

44. Which of the assumptions on which the demand is based are

(A)Production Costs.

(B)Technology.

(C)Prices of Inputs.

(D)Prices of other related goods and tastes and preferences.

45. In case of increase in demand, the demand curve

(A)Shifts backwards.

(B)Shifts forward.

(C)Will have upward slope.

(D)Will be horizontal.

46. Demand forecasting is made - for the

(A)For the existing products only.

(B)New products only.

(C)For both the existing products & for the new products.

(D)For the substitutes only.

47. Nilesh prefers a three pack of soda to a six-pack. What properties does this preference violate?

(A)Completeness. (B) Transitivity.

(C)More is better. (D) Diminishing MRS.

48. When the price of substitute of a commodity X falls, the demand for X

(A)rises (B) remains unchanged

(C)falls (D) any of the above

49. An individual's demand for good is:

(A)the amount he will buy at any given price

(B)the total amount he is able to buy

(C)his ability to buy a given quantity

(D)the satisfaction he obtains from a given quantity

50. Usually the demand for necessities is:

(A)Highly elastic (B) Highly inelastic

(C)Slightly elastic (D) Slightly inelastic

51. When the greater the elasticity of supply the change in the new equilibrium price will:

(A)Be higher

(B)Be higher than previous price

(C)Be lower

(D)Be lower than previous price

52. The area which lies under the demand curve for a given good measures:

(A)Marginal utility (B) Total utility

(C)Disutility (D) Marginal cost of production

53. In the case of an inferior commodity, the income elasticity of demand is

(A) Positive (B) Unitary

(C) Negative (D) Infinity

54. Supply curve slopes backward towards left, when :

(A) More quantity is supplied at higher prices.

(B) Less quantity is supplied at higher prices.

(C) Same quantity is supplied at higher prices

(D) None of the above

55. Match the following

List – I

(a) For a given 10 per cent change in price, demand changes by zero percent

(b) For a given 10 per cent change in price, demand changes by 5 percent

(c) For a given 10 percent change in price demand changes by 10 percent

(d) For a given 10 percent change in price, demand changes by 20 percent

List – II

(i) $e > 1$

(ii) $e = 1$

(iii) $e < 1$

(iv) $e = 0$

Code:

(a) (b) (c) (d)

(A) (iii) (i) (ii) (iv)

(B) (iv) (iii) (ii) (i)

(C) (i) (ii) (iii) (iv)

(D) (ii) (iii) (i) (iv)

56. If the demand curve is rectangular hyperbola the elasticity is :

(A) One (B) Zero

(C) Infinity (D) Less than one

57. In the short run firm considers the minimum of its average variable cost curve as:

(A) Break-even point (B) Shutdown point

(C) Economies of scope (D) None of the above

58. Match List – I with List – II and select the correct answer using the codes given below the lists :

List – I

(a) Cost Function

(b) Supply Function

(c) Production Function

(d) Oligopoly

List – II

(i) Kinky Demand Curve

(ii) Isoquants

(iii) Engineering Method

(iv) Factor Prices

Codes:

(a) (b) (c) (d)

(A) (iii) (iv) (ii) (i)

(B) (iv) (iii) (i) (ii)

(C) (iii) (ii) (i) (iv)

(D) (i) (ii) (iii) (iv)

59. The marginal revenue curve for a perfectly competitive firm is

(A) Downward sloping (B) Upward sloping

(C) Horizontal (D) Vertical

60. Consumer's Willingness to pay minus (-) actual payment is called :

(A) Producer's surplus

(B) Consumer's surplus

(C) Supplier's surplus

(D) Utility cost

61. The Cobb Dauglass Production function is often used as :

(A) $\varphi = AK^a L^b$

(B) $\varphi = AK^a L^{1-a}$

(C) $\log\varphi = a\log K + \log C$

(D) $\varphi = Ab^a - L^a$

62. In a competitive industry with identical firms, long run equilibrium is characterized by:

(A) P = AC. (B) P = MC.

(C) MR = MC. (D) All of the above.

63. If a production function is homogenous of degree one it implies that

(A)There is decreasing return to scale.

(B)There is increasing return to scale.

(C)There is constant return to scale.

(D)None of these

64. Firms that are price takers

(A)produce differentiated products.

(B)can charge a price above the market price for some of its output.

(C)cannot decide what price to charge for their products.

(D)must be large relative to the total market.

65. Firms that are price takers:

(A)are small relative to the total market.

(B)produce products that are different than their competitors.

(C)can sell only a portion of their output at the market price.

(D)have downward-sloping demand curves.

66. Average revenue curve of the firm is the same as the demand curve of the consumer except in the context of

(A)Perfect competition.

(B)Monopolistic competition.

(C)Monopoly.

(D)Discriminatory monopoly.

67. The marginal revenue of a price taker is

(A)equal to price. (B) less than price.

(C)more than price. (D) unrelated to price.

68. In the long-run, monopolistically competitive firms:

(A)charge prices equal to marginal cost.

(B)have excess capacity.

(C)produce at the minimum of average total cost.

(D)Both (B) and (C).

69. Total revenue will increase with the reduction in price when the price elasticity of demand for the product is

(A)Relatively elastic (B)Relatively inelastic

(C)Unitary elastic (D)Perfectly elastic

70. Which of the following market structures would you expect to yield the greatest product variety?

(A)Monopoly

(B)Monopolistic Competition

(C)Bertrand Oligopoly

(D) Perfect Competition

71. Which of the following statements concerning monopoly is ***not*** true?

(A)A market may be monopolistic because there are some legal barriers.

(B)A monopoly has market power.

(C)A monopoly is always undesirable.

(D)There is some deadweight loss in a monopolistic market.

72. Which of the following features is common to both perfectly competitive markets and monopolistically competitive markets?

(A)Firms produce homogeneous goods.

(B)There is free entry.

(C)Long run profits are zero.

(D)both (B) and (C).

73. In case of long run production

(A)The Quantity of both fixed and variable inputs are changed.

(B)The Quantity of both fixed and variable inputs are kept constant.

(C)The Quantity of both fixed and variable inputs are changed in the same proportions.

(D)The Quantity of both fixed and variable inputs are changed in different proportions.

74. A production function:

(A)defines the minimum amount of output that can be produced with inputs such as capital and labor.

(B)defines the average amount of output that can be produced with inputs such as capital and labor.

(C)represents the technology available for turning inputs into output.

(D)is determined only by the expenditures on R&D.

75. The short-run is defined as the time-frame

(A)in which there are no fixed factors of production.

(B)in which there are fixed factors of production.

(C)less than one year.

(D)less than three years.

76. Marris model is an example for

(A)Profit- maximizing model.

(B)Non-profit maximizing model.

(C)Behavioral model.

(D)Growth maximizing model.

77. The long-run is defined as

(A)the horizon in which the manager can adjust all

(B)the horizon in which there are only fixed factors of production.

(C)the horizon in which there are both fixed and variable factors of production.

(D)greater than one year.

78. What is MR?

(A)MR=TRn-TRn-1. (B) MR=TR/TQ.

(C)MR=TR/TC. (D) MR=TR/AC.

79. In case of short run production function Quantity of fixed input remains constant and

(A)Quantity of either one or two variable inputs change.

(B)Quantity of one or two variable inputs are kept constant as Quantity of fixed inputs change.

(C)The Quantity of both fixed as well as variable inputs remains constant.

(D)The Quantity of both variable and fixed input change.

80. Production function explains

(A)The relationship between Quantity of inputs employed and the corresponding total production cost.

(B)The relationship between the firms total revenue and total production cost.

(C)The relationship between Quantity of inputs used and the corresponding output obtained.

(D)The relationship between market price charged and quantity supplied.

81. If income increases, then:

(A)the budget line rotates counter-clockwise.

(B)the budget line rotates clockwise.

(C)the budget line shifts to the right.

(D)the opportunity set contracts.

82. In case the two commodities are complements, cross elasticity will be:

(A) Positive (B) Unitary

(C) Negative (D) Infinite

83. MU curve will he below X-axis when:

(A)MU is positive (B)MU is negative

(C)MU is zero (D)MU is constant

84. If the proportionate change in supply is exactly equal and proportionate to the change in price than elasticity of supply is

(A)Equal to zero (B) Greater than one.

(C)Less than one (D) Equal to one.

85. If an increase in income causes a decrease in the consumption of good Y we know that good Y is:

(A) a normal good. (B)a substitute.

(C)a complement (D) an inferior good.

86. Which of the following is ***not*** an economic activity?

(A)A chartered accountant doing his own activity

(B)A teacher teaching in a college

(C)A son looking after his ailing mother

(D)A manager managing his organization

87. The Law of Diminishing Returns depends on the assumption that:

(A)Total output is constant

(B)The state of technical knowledge is unchanged'

(C)Land is the factor kept constant

(D)Average output declines faster than marginal output

88. If the quantity demanded remains unchanged as its price changes , the coefficient of price elasticity of demand is:

(A)greater than 1 (B) smaller than 1

(C)equal to 1 (D) zero

89. Cross elasticity of demand between two perfect substitutes will be:

(A)very high (B) very low

(C)zero (D) infinity

90. If the income elasticity of demand is greater than 1, the commodity is

(A)a necessary (B) a luxury

(C)an inferior good (D)a non related good

91. A stable equilibrium position is one in which:

(A)There are never any departures from the equilibrium position

(B)There are only two forces influencing equilibrium

(C)Any departure from the equilibrium position calls into play forces which end to restore that position

(D)There are endless oscillations

92. If two goods are complements:

(A) they are consumed independently.

(B)an increase in the price of one will increase the demand for the other.

(C)a decrease in the price of one will increase the demand for the other.

(D)they are necessarily inferior goods.

93. Which of the following is a flow variable?

(A)Income (B) Product

(C)Capital Formation (D) Wealth

94. The Law of Diminishing Returns is applied to all fields of production was stated by

(A)Walras (B) A. C. Pigou

(C)Alfred Marshall (D) David Ricardo

95. Which of the following conditions is true when a producer minimizes the cost of producing a given level of output?

(A)The MRTS is equal to the ratio of input prices.

(B)The marginal product per dollar spent on all inputs are equal.

(C)The marginal products of all inputs are equal.

(D)Both (A) and (B).

96. Williamson's model is an example for

(A)Profit maximization model

(B)Non- Profit maximization model

(C)Managerial utility model.

(D)Behavioral model.

97. For 'make or buy decision', which cost is to be considered?

(A)Marginal cost (B) Total cost

(C)Fixed cost (D) None of the above

98. A perfectly competitive firm maximizes its profit by producing the output at which its marginal cost equals its

(A)marginal revenue

(B)average total cost.

(C)average variable cost

(D)average fixed cost.

99. When Average cost (AC) is at its minimum, then:

(A)Marginal cost is equal to Average cost

(B)Marginal cost is less than Average cost

(C)Marginal cost is more than Average cost

(D)None of the above

100. The term opportunity cost refers to:

(A)Cost related to an optimum level of production

(B)Variable cost

(C)Short - run cost

(D)Cost of one product in terms of production of others forgone / sacrificed

101. The difference in return between a chosen investment and one that is necessarily passed up. In the law of variable proportions, phase "two" indicates :

(A)Increasing returns (B) Constant returns

(C)Diminishing returns (D) Negative returns

102. Total cost is calculated as:

(A)the sum of total fixed cost and total variable cost.

(B)the product of average total cost and price.

(C)the sum of all the firms explicit costs.

(D)the sum of average fixed cost and average variable cost.

103. Which statement is ***not*** true regarding the total variable cost curve?

(A)increases as output increases.

(B)shows the variable cost of production given current factor prices.

(C)starts at the origin.

(D)is a horizontal line.

104. Marginal cost is equal to average variable cost when:

(A)equal to; average total cost is minimized

(B)less than; total cost is maximized

(C)greater than; average fixed cost is minimized

(D) average variable cost is minimized

105. In the short run, as output increases,

(A)the difference between average total cost and average variable cost decreases.

(B)the difference between total cost and average variable cost decreases.

(C)marginal cost eventually decreases.

(D)All of the above are correct.

106. Anil□s Grain Shop is producing where *MR* = *MC*, Anil□s Grain Shop must be

(A)earning a zero economic profit.

(B)incurring a loss.

(C)maximizing profits.

(D)maximizing revenue but ***not*** maximizing profits.

107. The break-even point is defined as occurring at an output rate at which

(A)total revenue equals total opportunity cost.

(B)economic profit is maximized.

(C)total cost is minimized.

(D)marginal revenue equals marginal cost.

108. ISO cost line is also called as :

(A) Profit line (B) Budget line

(C) Production line (D) Return line

109. An ISQ cost line represents:

(A)Combinations of two inputs which yield the same amount of output

(B)Combinations of two inputs which cost the same amount to a firm

(C) Combinations of two inputs which yields varying amounts of output

(D)Combination of two inputs which Cost different amounts of outlay to a firm

110. Quadratic cost function is written as :

(A)TC=a+bQ (B)TC=a+bQ+Q^2

(C)TC=a+bQ+cQ (D)TC+a+b+c

111. The difference between price and average total cost is

(A)a tax write off

(B)total economic profit (or loss)

(C)fixed cost

(D)the profit (or loss) per unit of output

112. What is the shape of short run average cost curve?

(A)'L' shape (B) 'U' shape

(C)Horizontal (D) Vertical

113. Which of the following statements is incorrect:

(A)Fixed costs do not vary with output.

(B)Sunk costs are those costs that are forever lost after they have been paid.

(C)Fixed costs are always greater than sunk costs.

(D)Fixed costs could be positive when sunk costs are zero.

114. The average fixed cost curve of a firm is

(A)parallel to the horizontal axis

(B)parallel to the vertical axis.

(C)a 'U' shaped curve

(D)a downward sloping curve from left to right

115. If total cost function of a firm :TC=1050+10Q2+8Q, find the marginal cost of the firm when the quantity produced is 15 units

(A)105 (B) 225

(C)308 (D) 247

116. The prime cost may be considered as:

(A)Variable cost (B) Direct cost

(C)Sunk cost (D) Fixed cost

117. The optimum is the one which is produced:

(A)By the optimum firm

(B)At the maximum average cost

(C)At the minimum average cost

(D)At zero marginal cost

118. Match the following:

List-I

(a)Increasing cost industry

(b)Decreasing cost industry

(c)Constant cost industry

List-II

(i)Horizontal long run supply curve

(ii)Positively sloped long run supply curve

(iii)Negatively sloped long run supply curve industry

Codes:

(a) (b) (c)

(A) (i) (ii) (iii)

(B) (iii) (ii) (i)

(C) (ii) (iii) (i)

(D) (ii) (i) (iii)

119. The slope of the iso-cost line is determined by:

(A) Prices of the two factors

(B) Productivity of the two factors

(C)Degree of substitutability of the two factors

(D) None of these

120. Cost advantage is referred as:

(A)A firm achieving a lower cumulative cost of performing value activities than its competitors

(B)Firm trying to outsource all relative products from one company to gain economies of scale

(C)Firm trying to restrict the cost control measure relative to its nearer competitor

(D)None of the above

121. At the point of inflexion, the marginal utility is:

(A)Increasing (B) Maximum

(C)Decreasing (D) Negative

122. A monopolist always operates in the

(A)Inelastic segment of its demand curve

(B)Elastic segment of its demand curve

(C)Unitary elastic segment of its demand curve

(D)None of the above

123. A monopolist…

(A)always charges a price that is higher than marginal revenue.

(B)can earn a greater than normal rate of return in the long run.

(C)can raise its price without losing any sales because it is the only supplier in the market.

(D)both (A) and (B)

124. In perfect competition, the elasticity of demand for the product of a single firm is

(A)zero, because the firm produces a unique product.

(B)zero, because many other firms produce identical products.

(C)infinite, because the firm produces a unique product.

(D)infinite, because many other firms produce identical products.

125. In perfect competition, an individual firm

(A)faces unitary elasticity of demand.

(B)has a price elasticity of supply equal to one.

(C)faces a perfectly elastic demand.

(D)has perfectly elastic supply.

126. In perfect competition, the elasticity of demand for the product of a single firm is

(A)0. (B) between 0 and 1.

(C)1. (D) infinite.

127. In perfect competition,

(A)each firm can influence the price of the good.

(B)there are few buyers.

(C)there are significant restrictions on entry.

(D)all firms in the market sell their product at the same price.

128. What is the characteristic of a purely competitive market?

(A)Large number of buyers and sellers

(B)A few sellers

(C)A few buyers

(D)Abnormal profit

129. Under perfect competition in the long run:

(A)All firms earn normal profits

(B)Few firms earn super normal profits

(C)All firms are at break even

(D)None of the above

130. What leads to rationing and black marketing under perfect competition?

(A)Price support (B) Excess demand

(C)Decrease in supply (D) Price control

131. Which of the following is the condition of equilibrium for the monopolist?

(A)MR = MC (B) MC = AR

(C)AR = MC = Price (D) AC = AR

132. Monopolist can decide :

(A)Price (B) Quantity

(C)Both (D)Either price or quantity

133. The economic profit of a perfectly competitive firm

(A)is less than its total revenue.

(B)is greater than its total revenue.

(C)equals its total revenue.

(D) is less than its total revenue if its supply curve is inelastic and is greater than its total revenue if its supply curve is elastic.

134. In the short run, profit maximizing firm produces additional units of production, as long as :

(A)Elasticity of demand is infinite

(B)Total revenue is increasing

(C)Price covers at least average fixed cost

(D)Additional revenue per unit exceeds additional cost per unit

135. Under monopoly market structure, the degree of freedom in pricing decision is :

(A)Very low (B) Quite good

(C)Very high (D) Zero

136. In perfect competition, a firm that maximizes its economic profit will sell its good:

(A)below the market price.

(B)at the market price.

(C)above the market price.

(D)below the market price if its supply curve is inelastic and above the market price if its supply curve is elastic.

137. Which one is ***not*** the pre-requisite of a perfect market?

(A)Existence of large number of buyers and sellers in the market

(B)Free flow of market information among the players

(C)Free entry and free exit

(D)Intervention of the Government

138. A perfectly competitive firm

(A)can increase total revenue by raising its price

(B)can sell more goods by lowering its price

(C)can sell more goods by raising its price

(D)cannot increase sales or total revenue by changing its price.

139. In a perfectly competitive market, the

(A)market demand curve is horizontal

(B)short-run market supply curve is horizontal

(C)short-run market demand curve slopes upward

(D)market demand curve slopes downward

140. A market structure which consists of one buyer and one seller is referred as

(A)Monopsony (B) Bilateral monopoly

(C)Monopoly (D) Duopoly

141. If there is a single buyer, it is called:

(A) Monopoly (B) Oligopoly

(C) Monopsony (D) None of the above

142. The situation where the market consists of only two buyers, then it is called :

(A)Monopsony (B) Duopsony

(C)Monopoly (D) Duopoly

143. A natural monopoly is based on

(A)diseconomies of scale

(B)diseconomies of scope

(C)external diseconomies

(D)economies of scale

144. In which type of market situation competitors offer same type of products and services for the same price with no differentiation?

(A)Monopolistic competition

(B) Monopoly

(C)Oligopoly

(D)Perfect competition

145. A market is competitive if:

(A) firms have the flexibility to price their own product.

(B)each firm sells slightly different products

(C)each firm is small compared to the entire industry.

(D)All of the above are correct.

146. If two commodities are complementary, then a rise in the price of one commodity will induce:

(A)A rise in the price of the other commodity

(B)An upward shift of demand curve

(C)No shift in demand for the other commodity

(D)A backward shift in demand for the other commodity

147. A firm operating under conditions of perfect competitions can

(A)Determine the price of its product.

(B)Determine only the size of its output.

(C)Promote the sales through effective advertisement.

(D)Capture the market by cutting down the price.

148. Pure monopoly exists:

(A)When there is a single producer

(B)When there is a single producer without any close substitutes

(C)When there is a single producer with close substitutes

(D)When a few producers control the industry

149. Under bilateral monopoly the price is higher if:

(A)The monopolist has his way

(B)The monopolist acts as a competitor

(C)The monopolist has not his way

(D)The monopolist sells his own product in a monopoly market

150. Dumping is an example of:

(A)Monopolistic practice in international trade

(B) Monopoly in international trade

(C) Oligopoly in international trade

(D) Perfect competition in international trade

151. Which of the following creates time utility?

(A) Farmer (B) Carpenter

(C) Trader (D) Driver

152. In the short run, the monopolist:

(A)Incurs a loss (B) Breaks down

(C)Makes a profit (D) Any of the above

153. Product differentiation is a common feature of

(A)Perfect Competition (B)Monopoly

(C)Monopolistic Competition (D)Oligopoly

154. Under perfect competition, a firm will be in equilibrium when its AC is:

(A)At a maximum

(B)At a minimum

(C)Covering only prime costs of production

(D)Covering wages and salaries only

155. In the long run a firm under perfectly competitive market earns :

(A)Economic profit (B)Normal profit

(C)Super normal profit(D)Sub-normal profit

156. Which one of the following statements is correct or more nearly correct?

(A)An increase in the price of commodity represents a fall in its value

(B)Value has nothing to do with the price

(C)If the price of a commodity falls, its value relative to other goods does not change

(D)The price of a good is its value measured in terms of money

157. A linear demand function exhibits:

(A)constant demand elasticity.

(B)more elastic demand as output increases.

(C)less elastic demand as output increases.

(D)insufficient information to determine.

158. Which of the following is ***not*** a basic feature of a monopolistically competitive industry?

(A)There are many buyers and sellers in the industry.

(B)Each firm in the industry produces a differentiated product.

(C)There is free entry and exit into the industry.

(D)Each firm owns a patent on its product.

159. Which of the following statements is not correct about monopoly?

(A)A monopolist generally faces a downward sloping demand curve.

(B)Monopolists always make positive profits in the long-run.

(C)A monopoly may make negative profits in the short-run.

(D)There is no close substitute for a monopoly's product.

160. Which of the following features is common to both perfectly competitive markets and monopolistically competitive markets?

(A)Firms produce homogeneous goods.

(B)Prices are equal to marginal costs in the long-run.

(C)Long run profits are zero.

(D)Prices are above marginal costs in the long-run.

161. Perfect competition is an industry with

(A)a few firms producing identical goods.

(B)a few firms producing goods that differ somewhat in quality.

(C)many firms producing identical goods.

(D)many firms producing goods that differ somewhat.

162. In perfect competition, the product of a single firm

(A)has many perfect substitutes produced by other firms.

(B)has many perfect complements produced by other firms.

(C)is sold under many differing brand names.

(D)is sold to different customers at different prices.

163. In perfect competition, restrictions on entry into an industry

(A)apply to both capital and labor.

(B)apply to labor but not to capital.

(C)apply to capital but not to labor.

(D)do not exist.

164. When average cost is declining

(A)Marginal cost must be declining.

(B)Marginal cost must be above average cost

(C)Marginal cost must be below average cost

(D)Marginal cost must be rising.

165. Income and Expenditure Account of non-profit organisation is a

(A)Real Account

(B)Nominal Account

(C)Personal Account

(D)Representative Personal Account

166. 'Kinked' demand curve is related with

(A)Monopoly

(B)Discriminating monopoly

(C)Oligopoly

(D)Perfect competition

167. In perfect competition, the demand curve of a firm is

(A)Vertical (B) Horizontal

(C)Positively sloped (D) Negatively sloped

168. If price of any commodity decreases by 20% and the demand for that commodity increases by 40%, then elasticity of demand would be:

(A)perfectly elastic (B) perfectly inelastic

(C)unit elastic (D) highly elastic

169. Which of the following statements is true?

(A)In case of inferior goods, the income effect is negative, although the substitution effect is positive.

(B)In inferior goods, the income and substitution effects are positive.

(C)In inferior goods, the income and substitution effects are negative.

(D)In case of inferior goods, the income effect is positive although the substitution effect is negative.

170. The Comparative Cost Advantage Theory was given by:

(A)David Ricardo (B) Adam Smith

(C)Raymond Vernon (D) Michael E. Porter

171. Which of the following denote the structural changes in Indian economy?

(A)Primary sector contribution has gone down.

(B)Service sector contribution has gone up.

(C)Secondary sector has not changed much.

(D)All of the above

172. Which of the following refers to Perfect Competition?

(i)There are restrictions on buyers and sellers

(ii)There are no restrictions on movement of goods

(iii)There are no restrictions on factors of production Correct one is

(A)only (i) and (ii) (B)only (ii) and (iii)

(C)only (i) and (iii) (D)only (i)

173. The price elasticity of demand for any particular perfectly competitive firm's output is:

(A)less than 1. (B) 1.

(C) equal to zero. (D) infinite.

174. A firm is having increasing returns to scale means:

(A)It is having increasing costs.

(B)It is having constant costs.

(C)It is having decreasing costs.

(D)None of the above

175. Total economic profit is:

(A)total revenue minus total opportunity cost

(B)marginal revenue minus marginal cost.

(C)marginal revenue divided by marginal cost

(D)total revenue divided by total cost.

176. Output under price discrimination will:

(A)Generally be larger than under simple Monopoly

(B)Be indeterminate because, we cannot know what prices can be charged

(C)Usually be the same as under perfect competition

(D)Be produced at higher average cost than under simple monopoly

177. Total consumer expenditure on a good falls as its price falls, this indicates that its price elasticity is :

(A)One (B) Less than one

(C)More than one (D) None of the above

178. Price elasticity of demand for luxury goods will be :

(A)Relatively elastic (B) Relatively inelastic

(C)Infinitely elastic (D) Infinitely inelastic

179. Skimming price for a new product is :

(A)Low initial price (B) Average price

(C)High initial price (D) Moderate price

180. Margin of safety is :

(A)Above the Break even point

(B)Below the Break even point

(C)Equals to Break even point

(D)Not related to Break even point

181. Profit is maximized when :

(A)MC=MR (B) MC>MR

(C)MC<MR (D) MR ≤ MC

182. In case of Giffen goods, price effect is:

(A)Negative (B) Zero

(C)Positive (D) 21

183. Price elasticity of demand is best defined as :

(A)The change in the tastes of consumers at different prices

(B)The rate of response of demand to a change in supply

(C)The rate of response of demand to a change in price

(D)The rate of change of demand to a change in price

184. Giffen goods are those goods :

(A)For which demand increases as price increases

(B)Which are in short supply

(C)Which have high income elasticity of demand

(D)Which give rise to a decrease in demand

185. When AR is falling, MR will be:

(A)Equal to AR

(B)Less than AR

(C)More than AR

(D)Either more or equal to AR

186. Price control is one of the monopoly regulations which is most advantageous for:

(A) The producer (B) The consumer

(C) The government (D) The seller

187. A fall in the price of commodity leads to:

(A)a shift in demand

(B)reduce the demand

(C)a rise in the consumers real income

(D) a fall in the consumers real income

188. In case of a Giffen good, like wheat, a fall in its price tends to:

(A)increase the demand

(B)reduce the demand

(C)change demand in an abnormal way

(D)make the demand remain constant

189. If ten goods are compliments, this means that a rise in the price of one commodity will induce:

(A) an upward shift in demand for the other commodity

(B)a rise in the price of the other commodity

(C)a downward shift in the demand for the other commodity

(D)no shift in demand for the other commodity

190. If A and B are complements, an increase in the price of good A would:

(A)have no effect on the quantity demanded of B.

(B) lead to an increase in demand for B.

(C) lead to a decrease in demand for B.

(D) none of the above.

191. Match List-I with List-II and select the correct answer using the codes given below the lists.

List – I (Demand Estimation Method)

(a)Customer Interview Method

(b)Market Experiment Method

(c)Regression Method

(d)Demand Forecasts

List – II (Steps involved)

(i)Consumers Interview

(ii)Time series or Cross Section Data

(iii)Market Stimulation

(iv)Market Experiments' Survey

Codes:

	(a)	(b)	(c)	(d)
(A)	(i)	(iii)	(iv)	(ii)
(B)	(i)	(iii)	(ii)	(iv)
(C)	(ii)	(iv)	(iii)	(i)
(D)	(iv)	(ii)	(i)	(iii)

192. Cardinal measure of utility is required

(A)Utility Theory

(B)Indifference Curve Analysis

(C)Revealed Preference

(D)Inferior Goods

193. Economists assume that a perfectly competitive firm's objective is to maximize its:

(A)quantity sold. (B) economic profit.

(C)revenue. (D) output price.

194. Marginal Revenue will be negative if the demand is:

(A) Relatively elastic (B) Unitary elastic

(C) Relatively inelastic (D) Perfectly elastic

195. The theory which deals with the comparative statistics and positive equilibrium is called:

(A)Macro Economics(B) Modern Economics

(C)Micro Economics (D) None of the above

196. The important macro-economic aggregates are

(A)Aggregate Consumption

(B)Gross Domestic Capital Formation

(C) Gross Domestic Savings and GNP

(D) All of the above

197. In India, which method is used to measure National Income in service sector?

(A)Expenditure method (B)Income method

(C)Output method (D)Value added method

198. Which is the method applied for measuring GNP?

(A)Income method

(B)Expenditure method

(C)Value Added method

(D)All of the above

199. National income is :

(A)NDP at factor cost

(B)NNP at factor cost

(C)NNP at market price

(D)GNP at factor cost

200. Which is not an instrument of monitory policy?

(A)Bank rate

(B)Tax policy

(C)Reserve ratio

(D)Buying/selling securities in open market

201. National Income at market prices is equal to:

(A)Gross national product at market prices

(B)Gross domestic product at market prices

(C)Net national product at factor cost

(D)None of the above

202. During last five years per capita income of India is increasing, that means:

(A)National income growth of India is more than growth of population.

(B)Growth in population is more than the growth in National income of India.

(C)National income of India & population of India have grown at the uniform rate.

(D)All of the above

203. When national income of a country is calculated in terms of constant prices, it is called as:

(A) Nominal GNP

(B) GNP at current prices.

(C) GNP at constant prices.

(D) GDP at constant prices.

204. We can separate the income effect from the substitution effect of the price fall of reducing the consumers:

(A)Money income sufficiently to keep his real income constant

(B)Money income to make his real income higher

(C)Money income to make his real income lower

(D)None of these

205. National income at current prices is equal to :

(A)Gross National Product at market prices

(B)Net National Product at market prices

(C)Net national product at factor cost

(D)Gross domestic product at market prices

206. The most appropriate measure of a country's economic growth is its :

(A)GDP (B)NDP

(C)NNP (D)Per capita real income

207. Shut down point is that point where price is :

(A)Less than variable cost

(B)Equal to variable cost

(C)Equal to average cost

(D)None of the above

208. At the shut down point:

(A)P = AVC

(B)TR + TVC

(C)The total losses of the firm equal TFC

(D)All the above

209. Earnings foregone in the context of the best alternative is termed as

(A)Past cost (B) Historical cost

(C)Opportunity cost (D) Sunk cost

210. Cost incurred in the past and is not affected by a current decision is referred to as :

(A)Sunk cost (B) Marginal cost

(C)Incremental cost (D) Replacement cost

211. Bath tub curve is encountered in

(A)Process control

(B)Acceptance sampling

(C)Both (A) and (B)

(D)Maintenance management

212. OPEC is an example of the type of producer's organization known as a:

(A)Marketing board (B) Trust

(C)Producer's cooperative (D) Cartel

213. When analysing your business and its environment, it is useful to carefully inspect:

(A)Threats

(B) Strengths and weaknesses

(C)Opportunities

(D) All of the above

214. Which of the following is an example of an external threat?

(A)Decreased competition

(B)New Trade Regulations

(C)Global Sales Potential

(D)Economies of Scale

215. If steak is a normal good, what do you suppose would happen to price and quantity during an economic recession?

(A)price would increase and quantity decrease.

(B)price and quantity would both increase.

(C)price and quantity would both decrease.

(D)price would decrease and quantity increase

216. Which is the first export processing zone declared as free trade in India:

(A)Santaçruz (B) Kandla

(C) Falta (D) Noida

217. Economies of scale exist whenever:

(A)average total costs decline as output increases

(B)average total costs increase as output increases

(C)average total costs are stationary as output increases.

(D)both(B) and(C).

218. Match the following :

List-I

(a) Wealth of Nations

(b) Income and Substitution effect

(c) Kinked Demand Curve

(d) Production function

List-II

(i)Robert Giffen

(ii)Paul M. Sweezy

(iii) Cobb-Douglas

(iv)Adam Smith

Codes:

	(a)	(b)	(c)	(d)
(A)	(iv)	(ii)	(i)	(iii)
(B)	(iv)	(i)	(iii)	(ii)
(C)	(iv)	(ii)	(iii)	(i)
(D)	(iv)	(i)	(ii)	(iii)

219. The economic order quantity is that quantity for which :

(A)the fixed cost is equal to the variable cost

(B)the ordering cost is equal to the carrying cost

(C)the economic cost is less than economic value

(D)the value of the product is equal to the operating cost

220. The EOQ inventory model attempts to minimize:

(A) The number of items ordered

(B) The number of orders placed

(C) The total inventory costs

(D) The safety stock

221. Opportunity costs are also known as:

(A) Spillover costs (B) Money-costs

(C) Alternative costs (D) External costs

222. If unit item cost = Rs. 10, monthly carrying charge = 3 per cent, monthly demand = 100 units and ordering cost = Rs. 20 per order, the EOQ is :

(A) 11.45 (B) 400

(C) 115.4 (D) 33.3

223. In case where the investment can be made in stages and is dependent on the future outcomes, the capital budgeting technique that can be adopted will be

(A) Simulation technique

(B) Hiller model

(C) Decision-tree analysis

(D) Scenario analysis

224. Which of the following is to be considered by an investor while exercising the option?

(A) Exercise price

(B) Spot price

(C) Exercise price and spot price

(D) None of the above

225. How can the government of a country reduce its deficit in the BOP for arresting imports and stimulating exports?

(A)Depreciation (B) Deflation

(C)Devaluation (D) Inflation

226. Privatization in India has initially be adopted from:

(A) U.S.A. (B) U.K.

(C) Germany (D) France

227. Which combination of the following factors led to Globalisation in the recent past?

(A) Growth of Multinational Corporations

(B) Internationalisation of Finance

(C) Increased International Trade

(D)All of the above

228. All the following curves are 'U' shaped except:

(A) AC Curve (B) AFC Curve

(C) AVC Curve (D) MC Curve

229. Match items of List-I, with those of List–II

List – I

(i) Utility theory

(ii) Indifference

(iii) Revealed

List – II

(a) Stating the preference

(b) Constant Curve marginal utility

(c) Convexity Preference

(A) (i) – (a), (ii) – (b), (iii) – (c)

(B) (i) –(c), (ii) – (b), (iii) – (a)

(C) (i) –(b), (ii) –(c), (iii)– (a)

(D) (i) –(b), (ii)– (a), (iii) – (c)

230. Statements :

Assertion (X): Monopolistic competition is a market structure similar to perfect competition.

Reason (Y): There is a large number of sellers and no scope for free entry & free exit from the industry.

(A) Both X and Y are true and Y is the correct explanation

(B) Both X and Y are true, but Y is not the correct explanation

(C) X is true, but Y is false

(D) X is false, but Y is true

231. Following is the example for convenience goods

(A) Furniture (B) Soaps

(C) Cars (D) LIC Policy

232. Which of the following statements is correct?

(A) BEP is the point at which total revenue is equal to total cost

(B) Contribution margin= Sales x P/V ratio

(C) At BEP, the firm yields neither profit nor loss

(D) All of the above

233. During the 3rd stage of Law of variable proportions:

(A)MP is negative (B)AP is negative

(C)AP is rising (D)TP is constant

234. A firm is a price takes under:

(A)Monopoly (B)Monopolistic competition

(C) Duopoly (D)Perfect competition

235. The law of Demand does not assume constancy of:

(A)Price of the concern commodity

(B) Price of other commodity

(C) Consumers income level

(D)Tastes and preferences

236. The hypothesis that 'consumption in one period would be a function of income in that period and the returns on savings of the previous period' is given by:

(A)Irving Fisher (B) Franco Modigilani

(C)Duesenberry (D) Robert Hall

237. From the following identify one which is ***not*** a property of Indifference curve?

(A)Indifference curves are downward sloping

(B)Indifference curves are concave to the origin

(C)Indifference curves are convex to the origin

(D)Indifference curves do not intersect each other

238. Which of the following statements is true?

(A)Business decisions cannot be taken without a sound knowledge of Macro Economic Theories.

(B)Knowledge of Economic Theory is misleading in making Business decisions.

(C)With the help of Economic Theories, it is always possible to predict the future accurately.

(D)Every Economic Theory is based on realistic facts which are common to all societies.

239. Arrange the following in the proper order for decision under capital budgeting.

(i)Estimating the cost and benefits of proposals.

(ii)Deciding the investment objective.

(iii)Selecting the best investment proposal.

(iv)Applying the capital budgeting technique.

Codes:

(A) (ii) (iv) (i) (iii)

(B) (ii) (iv) (iii) (i)

(C) (ii) (i) (iv) (iii)

(D) (ii) (i) (iii) (iv)

240. Match the following items in List-I with the most appropriate options from List-II:

List-I

(a)A lender buys securities to protect himself from a falling interest rate

(b)A borrower buys securities to protect himself from rising interest rate

(c)A combination of interest rate cap and floor

(d)A combination of two or more interest rate caps.

List-II

(i)Interest rate collar

(ii)Interest rate cap

(iii)Interest rate corridor

(iv)Interest rate floor

Codes:

(a)(b)(c)(d)

(A) (ii) (iv) (iii) (i)

(B) (iv) (ii) (i) (iii)

(C) (iv) (ii) (iii) (i)

(D)(iii) (ii) (i) (iv)

241. From the following identify one which is ***not*** a collusive oligopoly model

(A)Cartels (B)Edgeworth Model

(C)Price Leadership (D)Market Share model

242. The rate at which the consumer can trade one good for another is termed as marginal rate of substitution in

(A)Exchange (B) Consumption

(C)Production (D) The distribution

243. If demand equation is given by D=1000-P and the supply equation is given by S=100+4P, price will be:

(A)160 (B) 180

(C)170 (D) 200

244. Arrange the following steps, involved in the estimation of a demand function using econometric analysis, in the proper order

(i)Collection of data

(ii)Estimating the parameters of the model

(iii)Mathematical specification of the relationship among the variables

(iv)Using the estimates to arrive at the estimates of variables.

(v)Identification of variables

Codes:

(A) (v) (i) (iii) (iv) (ii)

(B) (i) (ii) (iii) (iv) (v)

(C) (i) (ii) (iv) (iii) (v)

(D) (v) (i) (iii) (ii) (iv)

245. Match the following items in List-I with the most appropriate options from List-II:

List-I

(a) Maximization of society's welfare even when individuals behave selfishly to further their own economic status.

(b) State of balance from which there is no tendency to change.

(c) Best possible state within a given set of constraints.

(d) A situation wherein a customer always prefer more of goods to less of goods.

List-II

(i) Equilibrium

(ii) Non-Sanitation

(iii)The invisible hand

(iv)Optimization

Codes:

(a) (b) (c) (d)

(A) (iv) (i) (iii)(ii)

(B)(ii) (i) (iv)(iii)

(C) (iii)(i)(iv) (ii)

(D)(iv) (i) (ii) (iii)

---000---

UNIT-I

MANAGERIAL ECONOMICS

1. (D)None of the above

Explanation: The Kinked demand curve theory of oligopoly predicts that if there are large changes in a firm's marginal costs, the price the firm sets does change.

2. (A)Upwards

Explanation: Veblen Good:

- Goods that are perceived to be exclusive as long as prices remain high or increase.
- Veblen goods get their name from economist ***Thorstein Veblen***, who was one of the first to look into and write about conspicuous consumption and the concept of seeking status through consumption.
- Veblen goods are often referred to as "status symbols".
- High-status items such as luxury cars, expensive shoes or pricey watches remain appealing to certain consumers as long as prices remain high or increase.
- A decrease in the price of a Veblen good could cause it to become less exclusive, which may reduce consumers' fondness for it.

3. (B)1.0

4. (C)a perfect substitute for Rice from farm B.

5. (A)(iii) (iv) (i) (ii)

6. (A)Downward sloping and flat

7. (D)the marginal revenue curve and the demand curve are the same

8. (B) Inferior Goods

Explanation: Inferior Good:

- A type of good for which demand declines as the level of income or real GDP in the economy increases.
- This occurs when a good has more costly substitutes that see an increase in demand as the society's economy improves.
- An inferior good is the opposite of a normal good, which experiences an increase in demand along with increases in the income level.

9. (A)Show large swings up and down

10. (D) (ii) (iv) (i) (iii)

11. (D)Quantity increases

12. (C)Infinity

Explanation:

Marginal Propensity to Consume (MPC):

- A component of Keynesian theory, MPC represents the proportion of an aggregate raise in pay that is spent on the consumption of goods and services, as opposed to being saved.
- The marginal propensity to consume (MPC) is the share of a change in disposable income (ΔY-ΔT) that is composed of changes in consumption (ΔC).
- The formula can be expressed as:

$$MPC = \frac{\Delta C}{\Delta Y - \Delta T}$$

- All disposable income is either consumed or saved; thus, the MPC is a fraction greater than zero and less than 1.
- The marginal propensity to save (MPS) is the difference between 1 and the MPC; that is, MPS = 1 − MPC.
- The MPC is an important component of the multiplier in Keynesian models that articulate the link between events or government policy and changes in the level of economic activity.
- If the MPC is large, the multiplier effect is

large as well because income changes lead to immediate changes in spending.

13. (B)Negatively sloped

14. (C)Say's law

Explanation:

- **Keynesian law** is the view that in the short run, especially during recessions, economic output is strongly influenced by aggregate demand (total spending in the economy).
- In the Keynesian view, aggregate demand does not necessarily equal the productive capacity of the economy; instead, it is influenced by a host of factors and sometimes behaves erratically, affecting production, employment, and inflation.
- **Veblen Law:** Goods that are perceived to be exclusive as long as prices remain high or increase.
- Veblen goods are often referred to as "status symbols".
- **Say's law**, or the law of market, is an economic principle of classical economics stated that "products are paid for with products".
- According to Say's Law, when an individual produces a product or service, he or she gets paid for that work, and is then able to use that pay to demand other goods and services.

15.(C)varies inversely with price

16.(B)Bax-Jenkin method

Explanation: Bax-Jenkins Forecasting Method: The univariate version of this methodology is a self- projecting time series forecasting method.

17.(A)The rate of response of demand to a change in price.

Explanation: Price Elasticity of Demand (PED):

- A measure of the relationship between a change in the quantity demanded of a particular good and a change in its price.
- Price elasticity of demand is a term in economics often used when discussing price sensitivity.
- The formula for calculating price elasticity of demand is:
- Price Elasticity of Demand=% Change in Quantity Demanded / % Change in Price
- If a small change in price is accompanied by a large change in quantity demanded, the product is said to be elastic (or responsive to price changes).
- Conversely, a product is inelastic if a large change in price is accompanied by a small amount of change in quantity demanded.

18. (C)An increase in supply

19.(D)All of the above

20.(D)the market demand curve

21.(A)two products are substitutes

22.(A)is more than it's short run value.

23.(A)MP is negative

24.(D)Perfect competition

Explanation: Perfect Competition:

A market structure in which the following five criteria are met:

1) All firms sell an identical product;

2) All firms are price takers - they cannot control the market price of their product;

3) All firms have a relatively small market share;

4) Buyers have complete information about the product being sold and the prices charged by each firm; and

5) The industry is characterized by freedom of entry and exit.

Perfect competition is sometimes referred to as ***"pure competition"***.

25.(A)Price of the concern commodity

26.(A)MC is a subset of incremental cost

27.(B)Production function

Explanation:Production function

- A production function shows the relationship between inputs of capital and labor and other factors and the outputs of goods and services.
- Production of goods requires resources or inputs. These inputs are called factors of production named as land, labour, capital and organization.
- The relationship between the inputs and the resulting output is described as production function in Economics.
- A production function shows the relationship between the amounts of factors used and the amount of output generated per period of time.

28.(A)a rectangular hyperbola

29.(C)Increase in money supply.

30.(A)many buyers and many sellers.

31.(B)Provide logic and methodology to find solutions to business problems.

32.(D)Applies economic theories and concepts to solve business and management problems.

33.(B)Inverse.

34.(D)Total quantity of a product demanded at a particular price in the market during a given period of time.

35.(D)Administered prices.

Explanation: Administered Price:

- The price of a good or service as dictated by a governmental or other governing agency.
- Administered prices are not determined by regular market forces of supply and demand.
- Examples of administered prices included price controls and rent controls.
- Administered prices are often imposed to maintain the affordability of certain goods and to prevent price gouging during periods of shortages (such as gas prices).
- Rent controls are intended to stabilize rent in certain cities, where rents are reviewed by a standard of reasonableness.

36.(B)price to increase.

37.(A)Causing a fall in price.

38.(B)price will increase but quantity will decrease.

39.(D)none of the above.

40.(C)it may rise or fall.

41.(A)an increase in the demand of good X.

42.(B)stockpiling will happen when products are durable in nature.

43.(B)recognizes that the quantity of a good consumed depends on its price and demand shifters.

44.(D)Prices of other related goods and tastes and preferences.

45.(B)Shifts forward.

46.(C)For both the existing products & for the new products.

47.(C)More is better.

48.(C)falls

49.(A)the amount he will buy at any given price

Explanation: Determinants of individual demand

- The determinants of individual demand of a particular good, service or commodity refer to all the factors that determine the quantity demanded of an individual or household for the particular commodity.

The main determinants of demand are:

- The (unit) price of the commodity.
- The tastes and preferences of the individual or household.
- The prices and nature of substitute goods, i.e., goods whose consumption can replace the consumption of the given good. The cheaper and better the substitute goods, the less the demand, ceteris paribus. This is termed the substitution effect.
- The prices and nature of complementary goods, i.e., goods for which increased consumption makes the consumption of the given good more worthwhile. A drop in the price of complementary goods leads to an

increase in demand, ceteris paribus.

- An increase in income leads to an increase (or at any rate, no decrease) in demand for most goods. This is termed the income effect. Goods for which the income effect is reversed are typically inferior goods. For these good, demand may drop with a rise in income.
- The demand curve (specifically, the individual demand curve) is a plot with quantity demanded on the horizontal axis and price on the vertical axis, keeping all other parameters constant (i.e., ceteris paribus).

50.(B)Highly inelastic

51.(C)Be lower

52.(B) Total utility

Explanation:

Marginal Utility:

- The additional satisfaction a consumer gains from consuming one more unit of a good or service.
- Marginal utility is use to determine how much of an item a consumer will buy.
- Positive marginal utility is when the consumption of an additional item increases the total utility.
- Negative marginal utility is when the consumption of an additional item decreases the total utility.

Total Utility:

- The aggregate level of satisfaction or fulfillment that a consumer receives through the consumption of a specific good or service.
- Each individual unit of a good or service has its own marginal utility, and the total utility is simply the sum of all the marginal utilities of the individual units.
- In order to maximize total utility, consumers will look to combine different combinations of goods and services.
- Given their limited resources (money), consumers will make choices in an attempt to increase their total utility with each additional unit of consumption.

Disutility:

- The shortcomings of a commodity or activity in satisfying human wants
- The degree to which a commodity or activity fails to satisfy human wants.

Marginal Cost of Production:

- The change in total cost that comes from making or producing one additional item.
- The purpose of analyzing marginal cost is to determine at what point an organization can achieve economies of scale.

53.(C)Negative

54.(B)Less quantity is supplied at higher prices.

55.(B) (iv) (iii) (ii) (i)

56.(A)One

Explanation: It is possible to have a demand curve in the shape of *a* rectangular hyperbola for which the elasticity at every point would be equal to one.

57. (B)Shutdown point

Explanation:

Breakeven Point (BEP):

- In general, the point at which gains equal losses.
- In options, the market price that a stock must reach for option buyers to avoid a loss if they exercise.
- For a call, it is the strike price plus the premium paid.
- For a put, it is the strike price minus the premium paid.
- For businesses, reaching the break-even point is the first major step towards profitability.

Shutdown Point:

- A point of operations where a firm is indifferent between continuing operations and shutting down temporarily.

- The shutdown point is the combination of output and price where a firm earns just enough revenue to cover its total variable costs.
- If a firm is operating at its shutdown point, it is usually operating at a loss.
- The concept is that if a firm can produce revenue greater or equal to its total variable costs, it can use the additional revenue to pay down its fixed costs.
- In other words, when a firm can earn a positive contribution margin, it should remain in operations, despite an overall loss.

Economies of Scope:

- An economic theory stating that the average total cost of production decreases as a result of increasing the number of different goods produced.
- For example, McDonalds can produce both hamburgers and French fries at a lower average cost than what it would cost two separate firms to produce the same goods.
- This is because McDonalds hamburgers and French fries share the use of food storage, preparation facilities, and so forth during production.

58.(A) (iii) (iv) (ii) (i)

59.(C)Horizontal

Explanation: Marginal revenue curve:

- A curve that graphically represents the relation between the marginal revenue received by a firm for selling its output and the quantity of output sold.
- A firm maximizes profit by producing the quantity of output found at the intersection of the marginal revenue curve and marginal cost curve.
- The marginal revenue curve for a firm with no market control is horizontal.
- The marginal revenue curve for a firm with market control is negatively sloped and lies below the average revenue curve.
- The marginal revenue curve reflects the degree of market control held by a firm.
- For a perfectly competitive firm with no market control, the marginal revenue curve is a horizontal line. Because a perfectly competitive firm is a price taker and faces a horizontal demand curve, its marginal revenue curve is also horizontal and coincides with its average revenue (and demand) curve.

60.(B)Consumer's surplus

Explanation:

Producer Surplus:

- An economic measure of the difference between the amount that a producer of a good receives and the minimum amount that he or she would be willing to accept for the good.
- The difference, or surplus amount, is the benefit that the producer receives for selling the good in the market.
- This is shown graphically above as the area (Producer Surplus) above the producer's supply curve that it receives at the price point (P(i)).
- The size of this area increases as the price for the good increases.

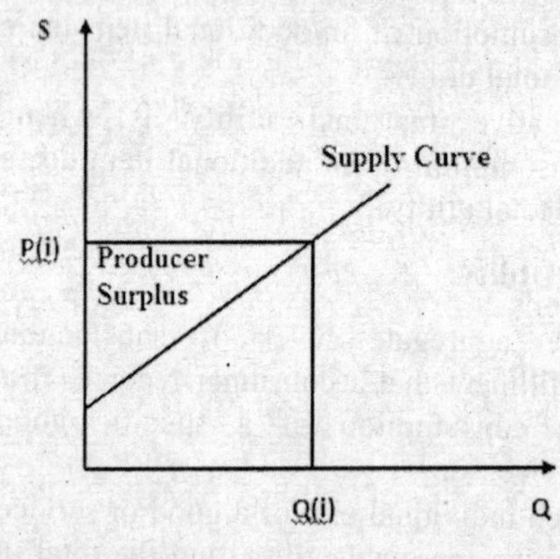

Consumer Surplus:

- An economic measure of consumer satisfaction, which is calculated by analyzing the difference between what consumers are willing to pay for a good or service relative to its market price.

- A consumer surplus occurs when the consumer is willing to pay more for a given product than the current market price.

Utility:

- An economic term referring to the total satisfaction received from consuming a good or service.
- A consumer's utility is hard to measure. However, we can determine it indirectly with consumer behavior theories, which assume that consumers will strive to maximize their utility.
- Utility is a concept that was introduced by ***Daniel Bernoulli.***
- Since consumer demand for utilities does not change dramatically with a change in price, these companies are regulated by the state or provincial and federal governments.

61.(B) $\varphi = AK^{a}L^{1-a}$

Explanation:

- In economics, the Cobb-Douglas functional form of production functions is widely used to represent the relationship of an output to inputs.
- It was proposed by ***Knut Wicksell*** and tested against statistical evidence by ***Charles Cobb and Paul Douglas*** in 1928.
- The function they used to model production was of the form:

$$P(L,K)=bL^{\alpha}K^{\beta}$$

Where:

P = total production (the monetary value of all goods produced in a year)

L = labor input (the total number of person-hours worked in a year)

K = capital input (the monetary worth of all machinery, equipment, and buildings)

b = total factor productivity

α and β are the output elasticities of labor and capital, respectively. These values are constants determined by available technology.

62.(D) All of the above.

Explanation:

- Long run equilibrium is basically the same as short run equilibrium, except that in the long run all inputs are variable, including plant size; in the long run, each firm can change its level of output by changing plant size.
- For both short run and long run equilibrium, P=AC; P=MC; and MR=MC for each firm.
- In equilibrium, no economic profits exist, which makes P = MC true.
- In a perfectly competitive industry, the price is given for each firm, which makes MC = AC, and since P = MC, it follows that P = AC.
- And as always, the profit maximizing point is the level where MR = MC.

63.(C)There is constant return to scale.

64.(C)cannot decide what price to charge for their products.

Explanation: Price taker:

- An individual or company which is not influential enough to affect the price of an item.
- For example, most investors are price takers, because their individual actions in buying and selling stocks are not enough to change the price of the security.
- A company is considered to be a price taker if the price it sets and quantity of goods it produces do not have any effect on the market price, and therefore the company is usually forced to go with the market price if they want to sell its goods.
- An individual consumer is also considered to be a price taker, because the purchases of one consumer do not affect the price a company sets for its products.
- Companies or individuals can exert varying degrees of influence, so it is not always easy to classify someone as a price taker.
- It is opposite of price maker.

65.(A)are small relative to the total market.

66.(D)Discriminatory monopoly.

Explanation: Discriminating Monopoly

- A single entity that charges different prices, which are not associated with the cost to provide the product or service, for its products or services for different consumers.
- A discriminating monopoly, by using its monopolistic position, can do this as long as there are differences in price elasticity of demand between consumers or markets, and barriers to prevent consumers from making an arbitrage profit by selling among themselves.
- By catering to each type of customer the monopoly makes more profit.

67.(A)equal to price.

68.(B)have excess capacity.

69.(A)Relatively elastic

70.(B)Monopolistic Competition

71.(C)A monopoly is always undesirable.

72.(D)both (B) and (C).

73.(A)The Quantity of both fixed and variable inputs are changed.

74.(C)represents the technology available for turning inputs into output.

75.(B)in which there are fixed factors of production.

76.(D)Growth maximizing model.

77.(A)the horizon in which the manager can adjust all

78.(A)MR=TRn-TRn-1.

79.(A)Quantity of either one or two variable inputs change.

80.(C)The relationship between Quantity of inputs used and the corresponding output obtained.

81.(C)the budget line shifts to the right.

82.(C) Negative

83.(B)MU is negative

84.(D)Equal to one.

85.(D)an inferior good.

86.(C)A son looking after his ailing mother.

87.(B)The state of technical knowledge is unchanged'

Explanation:

Law of Diminishing Marginal Returns: A law of economics stating that, as the number of new employees increases, the marginal product of an additional employee will at some point be less than the marginal product of the previous employee.

88.(D)zero

89. (D)infinity

Explanation: Cross Elasticity of Demand:

- An economic concept that measures the responsiveness in the quantity demand of one good when a change in price takes place in another good.
- The measure is calculated by taking the percentage change in the quantity demanded of one good, divided by the percentage change in price of the substitute good.
- Cross elasticity of demand is synonomous to "cross price elasticity of demand".

90.(B)a luxury

Explanation: Income Elasticity of Demand:

- A measure of the relationship between a change in the quantity demanded for a particular good and a change in real income.
- Income elasticity of demand is an economics term that refers to the sensitivity of the quantity demanded for a certain product in response to a change in consumer incomes.
- The formula for calculating income elasticity of demand is:
- ***Income Elasticity of Demand = % change in quantity demanded / % change in income***
- For example, if the quantity demanded for a good increases for 15% in response to a 10%increase in income, the income elasticity

of demand would be 15% / 10% = 1.5.

- The degree to which the quantity demanded for a good changes in response to a change in income depends on whether the good is a necessity or a luxury.

91.(C)Any departure from the equilibrium position calls into play forces which end to restore that position

92.(C)a decrease in the price of one will increase the demand for the other.

93.(A)Income

94.(A)Walras

Explanation: Law of Diminishing Marginal Returns:

- A law of economics stating that, as the number of new employees increases, the marginal product of an additional employee will at some point be less than the marginal product of the previous employee.
- A concept in economics that if one factor of production (number of workers, for example) is increased while other factors (machines and workspace, for example) are held constant, the output per unit of the variable factor will eventually diminish.
- Although the marginal productivity of the workforce decreases as output increases, diminishing returns do not mean negative returns until (in this example) the number of workers exceeds the available machines or workspace.
- In everyday experience, this law is expressed as "the gain is not worth the pain."

95. (D)Both (A) and (B).

96.(C)Managerial utility model.

Explanation: The Williamson model was developed by Professor Oliver Williamson. His theory states that when a merger creates a monopoly power, productivity efficiencies can outweigh the loss in welfare. Meaning that cost saving from an efficiency- enhancing merger may offset the dead weight loss from the output restriction

97.(A)Marginal cost

Explanation:

Marginal cost:

- Marginal costs are variable costs consisting of labor and material costs, plus an estimated portion of fixed costs (such as administration overheads and selling expenses).
- In companies where average costs are fairly constant, marginal cost is usually equal to average cost. However, in industries that require heavy capital investment (automobile plants, airlines, mines) and have high average costs, it is comparatively very low.
- The concept of marginal cost is critically important in resource allocation because, for optimum results, management must concentrate its resources where the excess of marginal revenue over the marginal cost is maximum.
- It is also called choice cost, differential cost, or incremental cost.

Total cost:

- Total costs is the sum of fixed costs and variable costs. In the Cost-Volume-Profit Analysis model, total costs are linear in volume.
- The total cost curve, if non-linear, can represent increasing and diminishing marginal returns.
- Total cost (TC) describes the total economic cost of production and is made up of variable costs, which vary according to the quantity of a good produced and include inputs such as labor and raw materials, plus fixed costs, which are independent of the quantity of a good produced and include inputs (capital) that cannot be varied in the short term, such as buildings and machinery.
- Total cost in economics includes the total opportunity cost of each factor of production as part of its fixed or variable costs.
- The rate at which total cost changes as the amount produced changes is called marginal cost.
- This is also known as the marginal unit variable cost.

Fixed Cost:

- A cost that does not change with an increase or decrease in the amount of goods or services produced.
- Fixed costs are expenses that have to be paid by a company, independent of any business activity.
- It is one of the two components of the total cost of a good or service, along with variable cost.

98.(A)marginal revenue

Explanation: Marginal Revenue(MR):

- The increase in revenue that results from the sale of one additional unit of output.
- Marginal revenue is calculated by dividing the change in total revenue by the change in output quantity.
- While marginal revenue can remain constant over a certain level of output, it follows the law of diminishing returns and will eventually slow down, as the output level increases.
- Perfectly competitive firms continue producing output until marginal revenue equals marginal cost.

99.(A)Marginal cost is equal to Average cost

Explanation: Average Cost (AC):

- The average cost is the total cost divided by the number of units produced.
- Firms maximize profits by considering the marginal cost, not the average cost.
- The difference between the average cost and the sales price does determine the profits per unit once the profit maximizing quantity is determined, but the profit maximizing quantity generally does not maximize profits per unit.
- Perfect Competition and Monopoly emphasize the roles of average cost and marginal cost curves.

100. (D)Cost of one product in terms of production of others forgone / sacrificed

Explanation: Opportunity Cost: The cost of an alternative that must be forgone in order to pursue a certain action.

101. (D) Negative returns

Explanation:

- The law of variable proportions states that in all productive processes, adding more of one factor of productions while others are held constant will at some point yield lower per-unit returns.
- It does not imply that adding more of a factor will decrease the total production.
- It is the generalized form of Law of Diminishing marginal return.
- The law of variable proportion is the study of short run production function with some factors fixed and some factors variable.
- In the short run the volume of production can be changed by altering variable factors only.
- In the study of production function (variable proportion) the effect on output is examined by varying factor proportions.
- The law of variable proportion is also called as non-proportional returns.
- "As the proportion of one factor in a combination of factors is increased, after a point, first the marginal and then the average production of that factor will diminishing".
- The behaviour of these total, average and marginal products of the variable factor as a result of the increase in its amount is generally divided into three stages.

  Stage-I: Increasing Return

  Stage-II: Diminishing Return

  Stage-Ill: Negative Return

Assumptions of the Law:

(i) The state of technology is assumed be given and unchanged.

(ii)The law specially operates in the short run because some factors are fixed and the proportion between factors is disturbed.

(iii)Variable factor units are homogeneous or identical in amount and quality.

(iv)The law is based on the possibility of varying the proportions in which the various factors can be combined to produce a product.

102. (A)the sum of total fixed cost and total variable cost.

Explanation: Total cost:

- Total cost (TC) describes the total economic cost of production and is made up of variable costs, which vary according to the quantity of a good produced and include inputs such as labor and raw materials, plus fixed costs, which are independent of the quantity of a good produced and include inputs (capital) that cannot be varied in the short term, such as buildings and machinery.
- Total cost in economics includes the total opportunity cost of each factor of production as part of its fixed or variable costs.
- The rate at which total cost changes as the amount produced changes is called marginal cost. This is also known as the marginal unit variable cost.
- The sum of fixed costs, variable costs, and semi-variable costs.
- The addition of all costs-direct and indirect, or how much an investor paid to acquire an investment. The cost includes commissions and trading fees.

103.(D)is a horizontal line.

Explanation: Total variable cost:

- The overall expense associated with producing a good or providing a service that change in direct proportion to the quantity produced or provided.
- The total variable cost of producing an item will typically include the cost of labor and raw materials used in the process.
- Cost of production that does change with changes in the quantity of output produced by a firm in the short run.
- Total variable cost is one part of total cost. The other is total fixed cost.
- Variable cost depends on the level of output. If a firm produces more output, then variable cost is greater.
- If a firm produces no output, then variable cost is zero.
- A cost measure directly related to total variable cost is average variable cost.
- Total variable cost is the opportunity cost incurred in the short-run production that depends on the quantity of output.
- If a firm produces a little output, then total variable cost is less.
- If a firm produces a lot of output, then total variable cost is more.
- The firm can avoid variable cost in the short run by reducing production to zero.

104.(D) average variable cost is minimized

Explanation:

Marginal Cost of Production:

- The change in total cost that comes from making or producing one additional item.
- The purpose of analyzing marginal cost is to determine at what point an organization can achieve economies of scale.
- The calculation is most often used among manufacturers as a means of isolating an optimum production level.

Average Variable Cost (AVC):

- Average variable cost refers to the variable expenses per unit of output average variable cost is obtained by dividing the total variable cost by the total output.

105. (A)the difference between average total cost and average variable cost decreases.

Explanation: Short Run:

- It is the concept that within a certain period of time, in the future, at least one input is fixed while others are variable.
- The short run is not a definite period of time, but rather varies based on the length of the firm's contracts.
- For example, a firm may have entered into lease contracts which fix the amount of rent over the next month, year or several years. Or the firm may have wage contracts with certain workers which cannot be changed until the contract renewal.

106. (C)maximizing profits.

107. (A)total revenue equals total opportunity cost.

Explanation: Breakeven Point (BEP):

- In general, the point at which gains equal losses.
- In options, the market price that a stock must reach for option buyers to avoid a loss if they exercise.
- For a call, it is the strike price plus the premium paid. For a put, it is the strike price minus the premium paid.
- For businesses, reaching the break-even point is the first major step towards profitability.

108. (C)Production line

Explanation:

- An isocost line is also called outlay line or price line or factor cost line.
- An isocost line shows all the combinations of labour and capital that are available for a given total cost to the producer.
- Just as there are infinite number of isoquants, there are infinite number of isocost lines, one for every possible level of a given total cost.
- The greater the total cost, the further from origin is the isocost line.

109. (B)Combinations of two inputs which cost the same amount to a firm

110. (B)$TC=a+bQ+Q^2$

111. (D)the profit (or loss) per unit of output

112. (B)'U' shape

Explanation:

- The short run AC curve is a U-shaped because as output increases, AC falls and reaches a minimum point and rises beyond that.
- The reason behind the U-shape of AC is attributed to the law of variable proportions. In the initial stages, due to the increasing returns to a factor, the average cost falls, as marginal product of labour (MPL) is rising.
- However, at minimum point, owing to constant returns to labour, AC tends to stabilise and after the minimum point, as the firm is employing more units of labour with the constant unit of fixed input, the MPL falls and consequently cost rises and therefore, AC starts rising up due to higher cost at the latter stages of production due to decreasing returns to labour. Therefore, AC is 'U-shaped' curve.

113. (C)Fixed costs are always greater than sunk costs.

114. (D)a downward sloping curve from left to right

Explanation: Average fixed cost curve:

- A curve that graphically represents the relation between average fixed cost incurred by a firm in the short-run product of a good or service and the quantity produced.
- This curve is constructed to capture the relation between average fixed cost and the level of output, holding other variables, like technology and resource prices, constant.
- The average fixed cost curve is negatively sloped.
- Average fixed cost is relatively high at small quantities of output, then declines as production increases.

- For the geometrically inclined, this average fixed cost curve is a ***rectangular hyperbola***.
- This declining average fixed cost curve is a major reason that the average total curve is negatively sloped for relatively small output quantities.

115.(C)308

116. (D)Fixed cost

Explanation: Prime Cost:

- A business's expenses for the materials and labor it uses in production. Prime cost is a way of measuring the total cost of the production inputs needed to create a given output.
- By analyzing its prime costs, a company can determine how much it must charge for its finished product in order to make a profit.
- By lowering its prime costs, a company can increase its profit margin and/or undercut its competitors' prices.

117.(C)At the minimum average cost

118.(C) (ii) (iii) (i)

119.(A) Prices of the two factors

120.(A)A firm achieving a lower cumulative cost of performing value activities than its competitors

Explanation: Cost advantage: Superiority achieved through factors such as access to cheaper inputs, efficient processes, favorable location, skilled workforce, superior technology, and/or waste reduction or elimination.

121. (C)Decreasing

122. (B)Elastic segment of its demand curve

123. (D)both (A) and (B)

124. (D)infinite, because many other firms produce identical products.

125. (C)faces a perfectly elastic demand.

126. (D)infinite.

127. (D)all firms in the market sell their product at the same price.

128. (A)Large number of buyers and sellers

Explanation: The characteristic of a purely competitive firm:

- **Homogeneous Product:** The products are identical between firms.
- No barriers to entry or exit from the market.
- **Perfect Knowledge:** Both consumers and suppliers.
- **Firms are Price Takers**: The market sets the price and firms will just produce output until P=MC (due to P=MR because of the price taker concept).
- Many sellers.

129. (A)All firms earn normal profits

130. (D) Price control

131. (A)MR = MC

Explanation: Marginal Revenue = Marginal Cost; mark-up price to the demand curve.

132.(D) Either price or quantity

Explanation: Monopolistic Competition:

A type of competition within an industry where:

- All firms produce similar yet not perfectly substitutable products.
- All firms are able to enter the industry if the profits are attractive.
- All firms are profit maximizers.
- All firms have some market power, which means none are price takers.

133.(A)is less than its total revenue.

Explanation: Perfectly competitive firm:

- A firm in a perfect competition is a price taker. It is not a Price maker or price breaker.
- The price of a good is determined in a perfectly competitive market by the demand and supply in the market.
- It has no influence over the price of the goods. Also a firm in a perfect competition

earns Normal profit that is No Profit No Loss.

134. (D)Additional revenue per unit exceeds additional cost per unit

135. (B)Quite good

Explanation:

Monopoly Market Structure:

- This single seller may be in the form of an individual owner or a single partnership or a Joint Stock Company. Such a single firm in market is called ***monopolist.***
- Monopolist is price maker and has a control over the market supply of goods. But it does not mean that he can set both price and output level.
- A monopolist can do either of the two things i.e. price or output. It means he can fix either price or output but not both at a time.

Characteristics of Monopoly:

- A single seller has complete control over the supply of the commodity.
- There are no close substitutes for the product.
- There is no free entry and exit because of some restrictions.
- There is a complete negation of competition.
- Monopolist is a price maker.
- Since there is a single firm, the firm and industry are one and same i.e. firm coincides the industry.
- Monopoly firm faces downward sloping demand curve. It means he can sell more at lower price and vice versa. Therefore, elasticity of demand factor is very important for him.

Types of Monopoly

1. **Perfect Monopoly:** It is also called as absolute monopoly. In this case, there is only a single seller of product having no close substitute; not even remote one. There is absolutely zero level of competition. Such monopoly is practically very rare.
2. **Imperfect Monopoly:** It is also called as relative monopoly or simple or limited monopoly. It refers to a single seller market having no close substitute. It means in this market, a product may have a remote substitute.
3. **Private Monopoly:** When production is owned, controlled and managed by the individual, or private body or private organization, it is called private monopoly. e.g. Tata, Reliance, Bajaj, etc. groups in India. Such type of monopoly is profit oriented.
4. **Public Monopoly:** When production is owned, controlled and managed by government, it is called public monopoly. It is welfare and service oriented. So, it is also called as 'Welfare Monopoly' e.g. Railways, Defence, etc.
5. **Simple Monopoly:** Simple monopoly firm charges a uniform price or single price to all the customers. He operates in a single market.
6. **Discriminating Monopoly:** Such a monopoly firm charges different price to different customers for the same product. It prevails in more than one market.
7. **Legal Monopoly:** When monopoly exists on account of trade marks, patents, copy rights, statutory regulation of government etc., it is called legal monopoly. Music industry is an example of legal monopoly.
8. **Natural Monopoly:** It emerges as a result of natural advantages like good location, abundant mineral resources, etc. e.g. Gulf countries are having monopoly in crude oil exploration activities because of plenty of natural oil resources.
9. **Technological Monopoly:** It emerges as a result of economies of large scale production, use of capital goods, new production methods, etc. e.g. engineering goods industry, automobile industry, software industry, etc.

10. Joint Monopoly: A number of business firms acquire monopoly position through amalgamation, cartels, syndicates, etc, it becomes joint monopoly. e.g. Actually, pizza making firm and burger making firm are competitors of each other in fast food industry. But when they combine their business, that leads to reduction in competition. So they can enjoy monopoly power in market.

136. (B)at the market price.

Explanation: Perfect Competition: A market structure in which the following five criteria are met:

- All firms sell an identical product.
- All firms are price takers.
- All firms have a relatively small market share.
- Buyers know the nature of the product being sold and the prices charged by each firm.
- The industry is characterized by freedom of entry and exit.
- Sometimes referred to as "pure competition".

137. (D)Intervention of the Government

Explanation: Essential features of a perfectly competitive market:

- Large number of buyers and sellers
- Homogeneous Products
- Uniform price
- Free entry and free exit
- Perfect knowledge about the market
- Perfect mobility
- Absence of transport cost.

138. (D)cannot increase sales or total revenue by changing its price.

Explanation:

- A firm in a perfect competition is a price taker. It is not a Price maker or price breaker.
- The price of a good is determined in a perfectly competitive market by the demand and supply in the market.
- It has no influence over the price of the goods.
- Also a firm in a perfect competition earns Normal profit that is No Profit No Loss.

139. (D)market demand curve slopes downward

140. (B)Bilateral monopoly

Explanation: Bilateral Monopoly:

- A market that has only one supplier and one buyer.
- The one supplier will tend to act as a monopoly power, and look to charge high prices to the one buyer.
- The one buyer will look towards paying a price that is as low as possible.
- Since both parties have conflicting goals, the two sides must negotiate based on the relative bargaining power of each, with a final price settling in between the two sides's points of maximum profit.

Duopoly:

- A situation in which two companies own all or nearly all of the market for a given product or service.
- A duopoly is the most basic form of oligopoly, a market dominated by a small number of companies.
- A duopoly can have the same impact on the market as a monopoly if the two players collude on prices or output.

141. (C)Monopsony

Explanation:

Monopoly:

- A situation in which a single company or group owns all or nearly all of the market for a given type of product or service.
- By definition, monopoly is characterized by an absence of competition, which often results in high prices and inferior products.
- A monopoly is a market containing a single firm. In such instances where a single firm holds monopoly power, the company will typically be forced to divest its assets.
- Monopoly is the extreme case in capitalism.

Oligopoly:

- A situation in which a particular market is controlled by a small group of firms.
- An oligopoly is much like a monopoly, in which only one company exerts control over most of a market. In an oligopoly, there are at least two firms controlling the market.
- The retail gas market is a good example of an oligopoly because a small number of firms control a large majority of the market.

Monopsony:

- A market similar to a monopoly except that a large buyer not seller controls a large proportion of the market and drives the prices down. Sometimes referred to as the buyer's monopoly.

142. (B)Duopsony

Explanation: Duopsony: Market situation in which only two buyers create the entire demand for a commodity supplied by many sellers a mirror image of duopoly.

143. (D)economies of scale

Explanation: Natural Monopoly: A type of monopoly that exists as a result of the high fixed or start-up costs of operating a business in a particular industry. Because it is economically sensible to have certain natural monopolies, governments often regulate those in operation, ensuring that consumers get a fair deal.

144. (D)Perfect competition

145. (C)each firm is small compared to the entire industry.

146. (D)A backward shift in demand for the other commodity

147. (B)Determine only the size of its output.

148. (B)When there is a single producer without any close substitutes

149. (A)The monopolist has his way

Explanation: Bilateral Monopoly:

- A market that has only one supplier and one buyer. The one supplier will tend to act as a monopoly power, and look to charge high prices to the one buyer.
- The lone buyer will look towards paying a price that is as low as possible.
- Since both parties have conflicting goals, the two sides must negotiate based on the relative bargaining power of each, with a final price settling in between the two sides's points of maximum profit.

150. (A)Monopolistic practice in international trade

Explanation: Dumping:

- In international trade, the export by a country or company of a product at a price that is lower in the foreign market than the price charged in the domestic market.
- As dumping usually involves substantial export volumes of the product, it often has the effect of endangering the financial viability of manufacturers or producers of the product in the importing nation.
- Dumping is also a colloquial term that refers to the act of offloading a stock with little regard for its price.

151. (C)Trader

152. (D)Any of the above

153. (C)Monopolistic Competition

Explanation: Product Differentiation:

- A marketing process that showcases the differences between products.
- Differentiation looks to make a product more attractive by contrasting its unique qualities with other competing products.
- Successful product differentiation creates a competitive advantage for the seller, as customers view these products as unique or superior.

154. (B)At a minimum

155. (B)Normal profit

Explanation:

Economic Profit:

- The difference between the revenue received from the sale of an output and the opportunity cost of the inputs used. This can be used as another name for "economic value added" (EVA).
- It is important to note that zero economic profit does not mean that the company is not earning any money (accounting profit).
- It is simply a measure of how well resources are being used relative to all possible options.
- In the long period, economic profit cannot be sustained.
- The arrival of new firms or expansion of existing firms (if returns to scale are constant) in the market causes the (horizontal) demand curve of each individual firm to shift downward, bringing down at the same time the price, the average revenue and marginal revenue curve.
- The final outcome is that, in the long run, the firm will make only normal profit (zero economic profit).
- When economic profit is equal to zero; this occurs when the difference between total revenue and total cost (explicit and implicit costs) equals zero.

Normal Profit:

- Normal profit is different than accounting profit because opportunity cost is taken into consideration.
- Normal profit is the minimum level of profit needed for a company to remain competitive in the market.
- It is also known as "economic profit".
- Normal profit occurs at the point at which the resources available to the firm are being efficiently used and could not be put to better use elsewhere.

Supernormal profit:

- The total revenue exceeding total costs for a company that holds a monopoly in a market.
- Supernormal profits are the profits earned by the entrepreneur in excess of normal profits which form a part of the cost of production.
- Supernormal profit or otherwise called abnormal profit arises due to risks and uncertainty bearing in the business.
- It also arises because of monopoly advantage and chance factors.
- According to ***Hawley*** an entrepreneur earns abnormal profit because of risks in the business.
- Abnormal profit arises on account of non-insurable risks.

Abnormal profit:

- It arises because of the introduction of innovation.
- An entrepreneur earns constant windfall profit so long as the same innovation is not introduced by others.
- Abnormal profits disappear when the innovation is universalized. Chance factors also fetch abnormal profit.
- No amount of human effort is made to earn this abnormal profit.
- Abnormal profit arising out of chance factors is short-lived.
- Abnormal profit also arises due to the nature of market. Under monopoly abnormal profit emerges because of the entrepreneurs' exclusive power on the production. The entries of others are strictly prohibited.

Sub-normal profit: - profit less than normal profit (P < average cost).

156.(B)Value has nothing to do with the price

157.(C)less elastic demand as output increases.

158.(D)Each firm owns a patent on its product.

159.(B)Monopolists always make positive profits in the long-run.

160.(C)Long run profits are zero.

161.(C)many firms producing identical goods.

162.(A)has many perfect substitutes produced by other firms.

163.(D)do not exist.

164.(C)Marginal cost must be below average cost

165.(B)Nominal Account

Explanation: Nominal account:

- Revenue or expense account that is a subdivision of the owners' equity account, and which is closed to a zero balance at the end of each accounting period.
- It starts with a zero balance at the beginning of a new accounting period, accumulates balances during the period, and returns to zero at the yearend by means of closing entries.
- Nominal accounts are income statement accounts and are also called 'temporary accounts' in contrast to balance sheet (asset, liability, and owners' equity) accounts which are called 'permanent accounts' or 'real accounts.'

166.(C)Oligopoly

Explanation: Oligopoly:

- A situation in which a particular market is controlled by a small group of firms.
- An oligopoly is much like a monopoly, in which only one company exerts control over most of a market.
- In an oligopoly, there are at least two firms controlling the market.

167.(B)Horizontal

168.(D)highly elastic

169.(A)In case of inferior goods, the income effect is negative, although the substitution effect is positive.

170.(A)David Ricardo

171.(D)All of the above

172.(B)only (ii) and (iii)

173.(D)infinite.

174.(C)It is having decreasing costs.

175.(A)total revenue minus total opportunity cost

Explanation: Economic profit:

- The difference between the revenue received from the sale of an output and the opportunity cost of the inputs used.
- This can be used as another name for "economic value added" (EVA).
- Economic profit is a measure of performance that compares net operating profit to total cost of capital.
- Economic profit is also referred to as economic value added (EVA), which is a trademarked concept originally devised by ***Stern Stewart & Co.***
- The formula for economic profit is:

Economic Profit = Net operating profit after tax − [Capital invested x weighted average cost of capital (WACC)].

- The net operating profit after tax (NOPAT) can be found on the corporation's income statement, or calculated if preferred.
- Capital invested is the amount of money used to fund a particular project.
- The purpose of multiplying WACC and capital investment is to assess a charge for using the invested capital.

176.(B)Be indeterminate because, we cannot know what prices can be charged

Explanation: Price Discrimination:

- A pricing strategy that charges customers different prices for the same product or service.
- In pure price discrimination, the seller will charge each customer the maximum price that he or she is willing to pay.
- In more common forms of price discrimination, the seller places customers in

groups based on certain attributes and charges each group a different price.

177.(B)Less than one

178.(C)Infinitely elastic

Explanation:

- Luxury goods are products and services that are not considered essential and are associated with affluence.
- With the clear differences between social classes in earlier civilizations, the consumption of luxury was originally limited to the elite classes.
- **Price elasticity of demand(PED):**

$$PED = \frac{\%\,Change\,in\,demand\,of\,good\,X}{\%\,Change\,in\,price\,of\,good\,X}$$

- If the PED is greater than one, the good is price elastic. Demand is responsive to a change in price.
- If for example a 15% fall in price leads to a 30% increase in quantity demanded, the price elasticity = 2.0
- If the PED is less than one, the good is inelastic. Demand is not very responsive to changes in price.
- If for example a 20% increase in price leads to a 5% fall in quantity demanded, the price elasticity = 0.25.
- If the PED is equal to one, the good has unit elasticity. The percentage change in quantity demanded is equal to the percentage change in price. Demand changes proportionately to a price change.
- If the PED is equal to zero, the good is perfectly inelastic. A change in price will have no influence on quantity demanded.
- The demand curve for such a product will be vertical.
- If the PED is infinity, the good is perfectly elastic. Any change in price will see quantity demanded fall to zero.
- This demand curve is associated with firms operating in perfectly competitive markets.
- Factors that determine the value of price elasticity of demand:
    - Number of close substitutes within the market
    - Luxuries and necessities
    - Percentage of income spent on a good
    - Habit forming goods
    - Time period under consideration.

179.(C) High initial price

Explanation: Price Skimming:

- A product pricing strategy by which a firm charges the highest initial price that customers will pay.
- As the demand of the first customers is satisfied, the firm lowers the price to attract another, more price-sensitive segment.
- Therefore, the skimming strategy gets its name from skimming successive layers of "cream," or customer segments, as prices are lowered over time.

180. (A)Above the Break even point

Explanation:

- Margin of safety is used in break-even analysis to indicate the amount of sales that are above the break-even point.
- An excess of a company's actual sales revenue over the breakeven sales revenue, expressed usually as a percentage. The greater this margin, the less sensitive the company to any abrupt fall in revenue.

Formula:

Margin of safety=(Actual sales revenue - Breakeven sales revenue) x 100 ÷ Actual sales revenue

181. (A) MC=MR

Explanation:

- Profits are maximized when marginal costs equals marginal revenue because fixed costs are now spread over a larger amount of revenue.
- This means that total cost per unit declines and profits increase.
- This is that this is the effect of scale.When marginal revenue equals marginal costs, in a growing revenue situation, you gain economies of scale and higher profits.

182. (C)Positive

Explanation:

- Giffen good is one which people consume more of as price rises, violating the law of demand.
- In normal situations, as the price of a good rises, the substitution effect causes consumers to purchase less of it and more of substitute goods.
- In the Giffen good situation, cheaper close substitutes are not available.

183. (C)The rate of response of demand to a change in price

Explanation: Price Elasticity of Demand:

- A measure of the relationship between a change in the quantity demanded of a particular good and a change in its price.
- Price elasticity of demand is a term in economics often used when discussing price sensitivity.
- It is a measure of responsiveness of the quantity of a good or service demanded to changes in its price.
- The formula for calculating price elasticity of demand is:

Price Elasticity of Demand = % Change in Quantity Demanded / % Change in Price

- If a small change in price is accompanied by a large change in quantity demanded, the product is said to be elastic (or responsive to price changes).
- Conversely, a product is inelastic if a large change in price is accompanied by a small amount of change in quantity demanded.

184.(A)For which demand increases as price increases

Explanation:

- A consumer good for which demand rises when the price increases, and demand falls when the price decreases.
- This phenomenon is notable because it violates the law of demand, whereby demand should increase as price falls and decrease as price rises.
- To be a Giffen good, the item must lack easy subsitutes and it must be an inferior good, or a good for which demand declines as the level of income in the economy increases.
- Economists disagree on whether Giffen goods exist and how common they are.

185.(B)Less than AR

186.(B) The consumer

Explanation: Price Controls:

- Government mandated minimum or maximum prices that can be charged for specified goods.
- Governments sometimes implement price controls when prices on essential items, such as food or oil, are rising rapidly.
- It is also known as "price floors" or "price ceilings".

187.(C)a rise in the consumers real income

188.(B)reduce the demand

Explanation: Giffen Good:

- A consumer good for which demand rises when the price increases, and demand falls when the price decreases.
- This phenomenon is notable because it violates the law of demand, whereby demand should increase as price falls and decrease as

price rises.

- To be a Giffen good, the item must lack easy substitutes and it must be an inferior good, or a good for which demand declines as the level of income in the economy increases.

189.(C)a downward shift in the demand for the other commodity

190.(C) lead to a decrease in demand for B.

191.(B) (i) (iii) (ii) (iv)

192.(A)Utility Theory

Explanation: Cardinal utility:

- A measure of utility, or satisfaction derived from the consumption of goods and services that can be measured using an absolute scale.
- Cardinal utility exists if the utility derived from consumption is measurable in the same way that other physical characteristics--height and weight--are measured using a scale that is comparable between people.
- Cardinal utility, however, is often employed as a convenient teaching device for discussing such concepts as marginal utility and utility maximization.

193.(B)economic profit.

Explanation: Economic Profit:

- The difference between the revenue received from the sale of an output and the opportunity cost of the inputs used.
- This can be used as another name for "economic value added" (EVA).

194.(C) Relatively inelastic

Explanation: Marginal Revenue:

- The increase in revenue that results from the sale of one additional unit of output.
- Marginal revenue is calculated by dividing the change in total revenue by the change in output quantity.
- While marginal revenue can remain constant over a certain level of output, it follows the law of diminishing returns and will eventually slow down, as the output level increases.
- Perfectly competitive firms continue producing output until marginal revenue equals marginal cost

195.(B) Modern Economics

Explanation:

Macroeconomics:

- The field of economics that studies the behavior of the aggregate economy.
- Macroeconomics examines economy-wide phenomena such as changes in unemployment, national income, rate of growth, gross domestic product, inflation and price levels.

Microeconomics:

- The branch of economics that analyzes the market behavior of individual consumers and firms in an attempt to understand the decision-making process of firms and households.
- It is concerned with the interaction between individual buyers and sellers and the factors that influence the choices made by buyers and sellers.
- In particular, microeconomics focuses on patterns of supply and demand and the determination of price and output in individual markets (e.g. coffee industry).

Modern economics:

- It builds on neoclassical economics but with many refinements that either supplement or generalize earlier analysis, such as econometrics, game theory, analysis of market failure and imperfect competition, and the neoclassical model of economic growth for analyzing long-run variables affecting national income.

196.(D) All of the above

197.(C)Output method

Explanation: Methods of measuring national income.

Product method: Dr. Alfred Marshall: According to product method, the total value of final goods and services produced in a country during a year is calculated at market prices. According to this method only the final goods and services are included and the intermediary goods and services are not taken into account.

The product method is used at the product level.

Income method: A.C. Pigou: According to income method, the net income payments received by all citizens of a country in a particular year are added up. The net incomes earned by the factors of production in the form of rent, wage, interest and profit aggregated but incomes in the form of transfer payments are not included in the national income.

Income method is used at income level and expenditure method is used at expenditure level.

Expenditure method: Dr. Iriving Fisher: According to the expenditure method, the total expenditure incurred by the society in a particular year is added together. There expenditures include personal consumption expenditure, net domestic investment, Govt, expenditure on goods and-services, and net foreign investments, Govt, expenditure and net foreign investment. According to these methods total expenditure equals the national income.

The use of the above three methods depends on the level at which the national income is calculated.

As all the three methods are used to measure the same physical output at three phases, namely production, distributions and expenditure, they will provide the same national income.

The formula for computing value added GNP is as under:

GNP by value added =
Gross value added + Net income overseas

198.(D)All of the above

199.(B)NNP at factor cost

Explanation: National income:

- National income is the total value a country's final output of all new goods and services produced in one year.
- **J.M. Keynes:** "National Income is the money value of all goods and services produced in a country during a year"
- National income measures the money value of the flow of output of goods and services produced within an economy over a period of time.
- The level and rate of growth of national income provide various purposes regarding economy, production, trade, consumption, policy formulation, etc.

The Importance of National Income:

- It allows measuring the size of the economy and level of country's economic performance; tracing the trend or the speed of the economic growth in relation to previous year also in other countries; knowing the composition and structure of the national income in terms of various sectors and the periodical variations in them.
- It allows making projection about the future development trend of the economy.
- Help government to formulate suitable development plans and policies to increase growth rates and fix various development targets for different sectors of the economy on the basis of the earlier performance.
- Help to business firms in forecasting future demand for their products.
- Make international comparison of people's living standards.

Methods of Measuring National Income:

- Product or Output Method
- Income Method
- Expenditure Method

200.(B)Tax policy

Explanation: Instruments of Monetary Policy:

(A)Quantitative Instruments or General Tools

- These tools are related to the Quantity or Volume of the money.
- The Quantitative Tools of credit control are also called as General Tools for credit control.
- They are designed to regulate or control the total volume of bank credit in the economy.
- These tools are indirect in nature and are employed for influencing the quantity of credit in the country.
- The general tool of credit control comprises of following instruments:

1. Bank Rate Policy (BRP):

- This technique is used in the monetary policy for influencing the volume or the quantity of the credit in a country.
- The bank rate refers to rate at which the central bank (i.e RBI) rediscounts bills and prepares of commercial banks or provides advance to commercial banks against approved securities.

2. Open Market Operation (OMO):

- The open market operation refers to the purchase and/or sale of short term and long term securities by the RBI in the open market.
- This is very effective and popular instrument of the monetary policy.
- The OMO is used to wipe out shortage of money in the money market, to influence the term and structure of the interest rate and to stabilize the market for government securities, etc.

3. Variation in the Reserve Ratios (VRR):

- The Commercial Banks have to keep a certain proportion of their total assets in the form of Cash Reserves.
- Some part of these cash reserves are their total assets in the form of cash.
- Apart from these cash reserves are also to be kept with the ***RBI for the purpose of maintaining liquidity and controlling credit in an economy.***
- These reserve ratios are named as Cash Reserve Ratio (CRR) and a Statutory Liquidity Ratio (SLR).
- The CRR refers to some percentage of commercial bank's net demand and time liabilities which commercial banks have to maintain with the central bank and SLR refers to some percent of reserves to be maintained in the form of gold or foreign securities.

(B)Qualitative Instruments or Selective Tools :

- They are used for discriminating between different uses of credit.
- It can be discrimination favoring export over import or essential over non-essential credit supply.
- This method can have influence over the lender and borrower of the credit.
- The Selective Tools of credit control comprises of following instruments:

1. Fixing Margin Requirements:

- The margin refers to the "proportion of the loan amount which is not financed by the bank".
- It is that part of a loan which a borrower has to raise in order to get finance for his purpose.
- A change in a margin implies a change in the loan size.
- ***This method is used to encourage credit supply for the needy sector and discourage it for other non-necessary sectors.***
- This can be done by increasing margin for the non-necessary sectors and by reducing it for other needy sectors.

2. Consumer Credit Regulation:

- Under this method, consumer credit supply is regulated through hire-purchase and installment sale of consumer goods.

- Under this method the down payment, installment amount, loan duration, etc is fixed in advance.
- This can help in checking the credit use and then inflation in a country.

3.Publicity:

- This is method of selective credit control.
- Through it Central Bank (RBI) publishes various reports stating what is good and what is bad in the system.
- This published information can help commercial banks to direct credit supply in the desired sectors.
- Through its weekly and monthly bulletins, the information is made public and banks can use it for attaining goals of monetary policy.

4. Credit Rationing:

- Central Bank fixes credit amount to be granted. Credit is rationed by limiting the amount available for each commercial bank.
- This method controls even bill rediscounting.
- For certain purpose, upper limit of credit can be fixed and banks are told to stick to this limit.
- This can help in lowering banks credit exposure to unwanted sectors.

5. Moral Suasion:

- It implies to pressure exerted by the RBI on the indian banking system without any strict action for compliance of the rules.
- It is a suggestion to banks. It helps in restraining credit during inflationary periods.
- Commercial banks are informed about the expectations of the central bank through a monetary policy.
- Under moral suasion central banks can issue directives, guidelines and suggestions for commercial banks regarding reducing credit supply for speculative purposes.

6. Control through Directives:

- Under this method the central bank issue frequent directives to commercial banks.
- These directives guide commercial banks in framing their lending policy.
- Through a directive the central bank can influence credit structures, supply of credit to certain limit for a specific purpose.
- The RBI issues directives to commercial banks for not lending loans to speculative sector such as securities, etc beyond a certain limit.

7. Direct Action:

- Under this method the RBI can impose an action against a bank.
- If certain banks are not adhering to the RBI's directives, the RBI may refuse to rediscount their bills and securities.
- Secondly, RBI may refuse credit supply to those banks whose borrowings are in excess to their capital.
- Central bank can penalize a bank by changing some rates.
- At last it can even put a ban on a particular bank if it dose not follow its directives and work against the objectives of the monetary policy.

201. (C)Net national product at factor cost

202. (A)National income growth of India is more than growth of population.

203.(C) GNP at constant prices.

204.(A)Money income sufficiently to keep his real income constant

205.(B)Net National Product at market prices

Explanation: The national income is equal to the NNP at mp minus revenue.

206.(A)GDP

Explanation: Gross Domestic Product (GDP):

- The monetary value of all the finished goods and services produced within a country's borders in a specific time period, though GDP is usually calculated on an annual basis.
- It includes all of private and public consumption, government outlays, investments and exports less imports that occur within a defined territory.

$$\mathbf{GDP = C + G + I + NX}$$

Where:

"C" is equal to all private consumption, or consumer spending, in a nation's economy

"G" is the sum of government spending

"I" is the sum of all the country's businesses spending on capital

"NX" is the nation's total net exports, calculated as total exports minus total imports. (NX = Exports - Imports).

207. (B)Equal to variable cost

Explanation: Shutdown Point:

- A point of operations where a firm is indifferent between continuing operations and shutting down temporarily.
- The shutdown point is the combination of output and price where a firm earns just enough revenue to cover its total variable costs.

208. (A)P = AVC

209. (C)Opportunity cost

Explanation:

Historical Cost:

- A measure of value used in accounting in which the price of an asset on the balance sheet is based on its nominal or original cost when acquired by the company.
- The historical-cost method is used for assets in the U.S. under generally accepted accounting principals (GAAP).
- Based on the historical-cost principle, under U.S. GAAP, most assets held on the balance sheet are to be recorded at the historical cost even if they have significantly changed in value over time.

Opportunity Cost:

- The cost of an alternative that must be forgone in order to pursue a certain action.
- Put another way, the benefits you could have received by taking an alternative action.
- The difference in return between a chosen investment and one that is necessarily passed up.

210. (A)Sunk cost

Explanation: Sunk cost:

- costs incurred in the past whose total will not be affected by any decision made now or in the future.
- Sunk costs are usually past or historical costs.

211. (C)Both (A) and (B)

212. (D) Cartel

Explanation: OPEC is the Organization of the Petroleum Exporting Countries. It is an oil cartel whose mission is to coordinate the policies of the oil-producing countries.

213. (D) All of the above

214. (B)New Trade Regulations

215. (C)price and quantity would both decrease.

216. (B)Kandla

Explanation: Export processing zone (EPZ):

- Type of free trade zone (FTZ), set up generally in developing countries by their governments to promote industrial and commercial exports.
- In addition to providing the benefits of a FTZ, these zones offer other incentives such as exemptions from certain taxes and business regulations.
- Also called development economic zone or special economic zone.

217. (A)average total costs decline as output increases

218. (D)(iv) (i) (ii) (iii)

219. (B)the ordering cost is equal to the carrying cost

Explanation: Economic Order Quantity (EOQ):

- An inventory-related equation that determines the optimum order quantity that a company should hold in its inventory given a set cost of production, demand rate and other variables.

- This is done to minimize variable inventory costs.
- Economic Order Quantity (EOQ) is:

$$EOQ = \sqrt{\frac{2SD}{PI}}$$

Where:

S = Setup costs

D = Demand rate

P = Production cost

I = Interest rate (considered an opportunity cost, so the risk-free rate can be used).

220. (C) The total inventory costs

221. (C) Alternative costs

Explanation:

Opportunity Cost: The cost of an alternative that must be forgone in order to pursue a certain action. Put another way, the benefits you could have received by taking an alternative action.

Spillover cost: It is also known as "negative externality," is a term used to describe some loss or damage that a market transaction causes a third party. The third party ends up paying for the transaction in some way, even though it was neither the buyer nor the seller and had no part in the original decision.

Cost of money: The interest that could be earned if the amount invested in a business or security was instead invested in government bonds or in time deposits.

Alternative Cost: Opportunity Cost or Alternative Cost is the value of what certain resources could have produced have they been used in the best alternative way.

Since economic resources are scarce, only a limited amount of goods and services can be produced from them and there arise the necessity of choice.

External costs: An external costs occurs when producing or consuming a good or service imposes a cost upon a third party. If there are external costs in consuming a good (negative externalities), the social cost will be greater than the private cost. The existence of external costs can lead to market failure. This is because the free market generally ignores the existence of external costs. Any cost that is impose to other without any agreement is called external cost.

222. (C) 115.4

223. (C) Decision-tree analysis

224. (C) Exercise price and spot price

225. (C)Devaluation

Explanation: Devaluation:

- A deliberate downward adjustment to a country's official exchange rate relative to other currencies.
- In a fixed exchange rate regime, only a decision by a country's government (i.e central bank) can alter the official value of the currency.

226. (B) U.K.

227. (D)All of the above

228. (B) AFC Curve

229. (C) (i) –(b), (ii) –(c), (iii)– (a)

230. (C) X is true, but Y is false

231. (B) Soaps

232. (D) All of the above

233. (A)MP is negative

234. (D)Perfect competition

235. (A)Price of the concern commodity

236. (A)Irving Fisher

237. (B)Indifference curves are concave to the origin

Explanation: Properties of Indifference Curves

- Indifference curves are negatively sloped.

- Indifference curves are nonintersecting.
- A higher indifference curve represents a higher utility level.
- Indifference curves are convex to the origin.

238. (B)Knowledge of Economic Theory is misleading in making Business decisions.

239. (C) (ii) (i) (iv) (iii)

Explanation: Capital Budgeting Process

The following procedure may be considered in the process of capital budgeting decisions:

(1) Identification of profitable investment proposals.

(2) Screening and selection of right proposals.

(3) Evaluation of measures of investment worth on the basis of profitability and uncertainty or risk.

(4) Establishing priorities, i.e., uneconomical or unprofitable proposals may be rejected.

(5) Final approval and preparation of capital expenditure budget.

(6) Implementing proposal, i.e., project execution.

(7) Review the performance of projects.

240. (B) (iv) (ii) (i) (iii)

241. (B)Edgeworth Model

Explanation:

- Collusion is an agreement between two or more parties, sometimes illegal and therefore secretive, to limit open competition by deceiving, misleading, or defrauding others of their legal rights, or to obtain an objective forbidden by law typically by defrauding or gaining an unfair advantage.
- It is an agreement among firms or individuals to divide a market, set prices, limit production or limit opportunities.
- It can involve "wage fixing, kickbacks, or misrepresenting the independence of the relationship between the colluding parties".
- In legal terms, all acts affected by collusion are considered void.

242. (A)Exchange

Explanation: Marginal Rate of Substitution

- The rate at which an individual must give up "good A" in order to obtain one more unit of "good B", while keeping their overall utility (satisfaction) constant.
- The marginal rate of substitution is calculated between two goods placed on an indifference curve, which displays a frontier of equal utility for each combination of "good A" and "good B".
- As such, the marginal rate of substitution is always changing for a given point on the indifference curve, and mathematically represents the slope of the curve at that point.
- The rate at which a consumer is willing to trade one good for another.
- The rate at which a consumer is willing to trade one good for the other depends on the amounts of the goods he is already consuming.

243.(B) 180

244.(D) (v) (i) (iii) (ii) (iv)

Explanation: Steps involved in the estimation of a demand function using econometric analysis:

1. Identification of the variables.
2. Collection of the data
3. Formulation of the demand model
4. Estimation of the parameters
5. Development of forecasts (estimates) based on the model.

245. (C) (iii)(i)(iv) (ii)

---000---

UNIT-II

ORGANIZATION BEHAVIOR (OB)

1. OB is concerned with study of :

(A)Individuals, groups and organization system

(B)Individuals, groups and their institutions

(C)Organization, its roles and performance and behaviour

(D)Organization, its environment, its strategies and performance

2. Organization Behavior offers:

(A)Technical skills

(B) People skills

(C)Communication skills

(D)Wide knowledge

3. Organizational behaviour was popularized by:

(A) F.W. Taylor (B) Keith Davis

(C) Elton Mayo (D) David Cock

4. According to the integrative model of organizational behavior, the two organizational-level variables that impact individual-level attitudes and behaviors are:

(A)Job performance and organizational commitment

(B)Culture and structure

(C)Team processes and team characteristics

(D)Personality and ability

5. According to the integrative model of organizational behavior, •which of the following is an individual outcome?

(A) Job satisfaction

(B)Ability

(C)Personality

(D)Organizational commitment

6. According to the integrative model of organizational behavior, trust, justice, and ethics are:

(A)Individual mechanisms

(B)Organizational mechanisms.

(C)Group mechanisms.

(D)Individual outcomes.

7. While guiding organization members in appropriate directions, a manager exhibits:

(A)Consideration behavior

(B) Authoritarian behavior

(C)Theory Y behavior

(D)Leadership behavior

8. The change in specialization and integration in organization context is called:

(A)Co-ordination

(B)Co-operation

(C)Organizational restructuring

(D)Feedback

9. ________ means willingness to exert high levels of effort on behalf of the organization.

(A)Organizational commitment

(B)Organization Effectiveness

(C)Organizational Control

(D)None of the above

10. Organizational Effectiveness is :

(A)Input - Output ratio

(B)Target achievement

(C)Doing right things

(D)Doing things right

11. Organizational commitment is an example of :

(A)Job satisfaction (B) Work attitude

(C)Personality (D)Perception

12. The process of selecting, organising and interpreting or attaching meaning to events happening in the environment is called :

(A) Perception (B) Attitude

(C) Personality (D) Learning

13. OB can be contrasted with two other courses commonly offered in management departments_____ and strategic management.

(A) project management

(B) business management

(C) human resource management

(D) operations management

14. An OB study might explore the relationship between pay and motivation, whereas a _______ study might examine the best way to structure compensation programs.

(A)Strategic management

(B)Anthropology

(C)Organizational development

(D)Human resource management

15. Factors contributing to unethical behaviour are :

(A)Poor leadership

(B)Poor internal communication

(C)Lack of management support

(D)All of the above

16. The Neo - classical theory of organizational structure was propounded by :

(A) Henry Fayol (B) Elton Mayo

(C) Peter Drucker (D) J.T. Dunlop

17. Research on satisfaction, emotions, and team processes found in OB draws heavily from studies in:

(A) Sociology

(B) Organizational psychology

(C)Industrial psychology

(D)Social psychology

18. Study of organization culture is called:

(A)Organization Behaviour

(B)Organization Development

(C)Social Psychology

(D)Anthropology

19. Organization culture mostly effected by:

(A) Technology (B) Market place

(C) Employees (D) Top management

20. Which of the practice will ***not*** create an ethical culture in an organization?

(A)Visible role models from an organization

(B)Clearly communicating ethical expectations

(C)Provide ethical training

(D)Punishing whistle blowers

21. The primary outcomes of interest to organizational behavior researchers are

(A)Job performance and organizational commitment.

(B)Organizational culture and organizational structure.

(C)Team processes and team characteristics.

(D) Personality and ability.

22. Models from _______ are used to understand motivation, learning, and decision making in OB.

(A)Marketing (B) Economics

(C)Sociology (D)Strategic management

23. Cross-functional groups that operate across space, time and organizational boundaries with members who communicate mainly through information technologies are:

(A) Telecomputers (B) Virtual teams

(C) Teleworkers (D) Telemarketers

24. Which of these mechanisms dictate how the units within the firm link to other units?

(A) Organizational culture

(B) Organizational ability

(C) Organization size

(D) Organizational structure

25. Which of the following mechanism captures "the way things are" in an organization?

(A) Organizational structure

(B) Organizational ability

(C) Organizational leadership

(D) Organizational culture

26. According to resource-based view, a resource is more valuable when it is rare and

(A) Complex. (B) Simple.

(C) Inimitable. (D) Transparent.

27. An organizational memory includes the following except

(A) Information that employees possess

(B) Knowledge embedded in the organisation's systems and structures

(C) Documents

(D) Knowledge that is not documented

28. Nominal group technique is:

(A) a consensus planning tool, generally used by groups to discuss, debate and decide on issues of strength- identification, problems and solutions.

(B) a consensus planning tool to arrive at decisions on issues, for instance man-power requirement, by involving group of experts through blind rounds of communication

(C) a majority based decision making tool

(D) None of the above

29. Which of these mechanisms capture shared knowledge about the rules, norms, and values that shape employee attitudes and behaviors?

(A) Organizational structure

(B) Organizational ability

(C) Organizational culture

(D) Job performance

30. Which pattern reflects a pure executive form of management?

(A) Functional (B) Line

(C) Line and Staff (D) Committee

31. 'Appreciative Enquiry' is :

(A) Psychological Theory

(B) Training Method

(C) Business etiquette

(D) Problem Solving Method

32. Graphical representation of Manpower in the organization is known as :

(A) Replacement chart

(B) Placement chart

(C) Organization structure

(D) Manpower inventory

33. Which of the following is a method of indicating the feeling of acceptance or rejection among members of a group?

(A) Mutuality (B) Simulation

(C) T – group (D) Sociometry

34. Group dynamics is the systematic study of :

(A) the forces operating outside the organization

(B) the forces operating within the group

(C) the forces operating between management and union

(D) the forces operating inside the organization

35. The group to which a person would like to belong is known as:

(A)Primary Group

(B)Membership Group

(C)Reference Group

(D)None of the above

36. Sequence the following stages of group development :

(A)Forming-Norming-Storming-Performing

(B)Forming-Storming-Norming- Performing

(C)Norming-Forming-Storming- Performing

(D)Storming-Norming-Performing-Forming

37. Sensitivity training evolved from the group dynamics concept of

(A)French and Bell (B) Eric Bernie

(C)Moreno (D) Kurt Lewin

38. The theory which explains affiliation in Group formation and dynamics is called :

(A)Proximity theory (B) Balance theory

(C)Exchange theory(D)Propinquity theory

39. Group norms are strongly enforced by groups if they

(A) Aid in group survival

(B) Simplify expected behaviour of members

(C) Express central values of the group

(D) All the above

40. Which of the following is ***not*** a correct statement?

(A) Informal groups always hamper the performance of formal groups.

(B) Informal groups do not have prescribed goals and relationships.

(C) Informal and formal groups co-exist in organizations.

(D) Informal groups provide safety valve for employee emotions.

41. The process of grouping activities into units for the purpose of administration may be referred to as__________.

(A)Departmentation (B) Decentralisation

(C)Coordination (D) Specialisation

42. One method of bringing a group to agreement is called:

(A)proportional values (B)consensus

(C)accordance (D)conformance

43. Groups created by managerial decision in order to accomplish stated goals of the organization are called:

(A) formal groups (B) informal groups

(C) task groups (D) interest groups

44. Continued membership in a group will usually require:

(A)supporting the group leader

(B)conforming to group norms

(C)encouraging cohesiveness in the group

(D)developing a status system

45. Which of the following decreases group cohesiveness?

(A)Agreement on group goals

(B)Frequency of interaction

(C)Large group size

(D)All the above

46. The way teams are formed, staffed, and composed, and the way members depend on one another is summarized by:

(A)Team processes (B) Team innovation.

(C)Team characteristics(D)Team policies

47. The Cricket team at a local school has attributed their poor performance to the following: the team's coordination; inability to resolve conflict and cohesion. Which of the following is represented by the above scenario?

(A)Team responsibilities

(B)Team innovation

(C)Team characteristics

(D)Team processes

48. Organization structures

(A)Affect group behavior more than individual behavior

(B)Change rapidly to meet environmental and market changes

(C)Contribute positively to organizational performance

(D)Can be defined simply as activities that occur regularly

49. Organization structure primarily refers to:

(A)How activities are coordinated and controlled

(B)How resources are allocated

(C)The location of departments and office space

(D)The policy statements developed by the firm

50. What is the key word in understanding organization structure?

(A)Control (B)Change

(C)Process (D)Delegation

51. 'Unity of Command' is violated under :

(A) Line and staff organization

(B) Line organization

(C) Matrix organization

(D) Staff organization

52. In a line organization, authority flows from:

(A)Top to bottom (B)Bottom to top

(C)Side by side (D)None of these

53. Which of the following organizations is generally a combination of functional and project patterns of departmentation?

(A)Line and staff organization

(B)Matrix organisation

(C)Functional organization

(D)All the above

54. Functional managers are responsible:

(A)for a single area of activity

(B)to the upper level of management and staff

(C)for complex organizational sub-units

(D)for obtaining copyrights and patents for newly developed processes and equipment

55. The line organization structure is also called as:

(A)Matrix Organization

(B)Scalar Organization

(C)Functional Organization

(D)Horizontal Organization

56. The main advantage of functional organization is :

(A)Simplicity (B)Hierarchical level

(C)Experience (D)Specialization

57. When the chain of command is longer than the span of control, the resultant organization structure is :

(A) Balanced (B) Flat

(C) Tall (D)None of the above

58. Role of staff in 'line and staff' organization is

(A) Authoritative (B) Managerial

(C) Superior (D)Advisory

59. Which principle of management is violated by matrix organization structure?

(A)Division of Labour

(B)Unity of Direction

(C)Unity of Command

(D)None of the above

60. Feeling arising out of inadequate definition of roles is known as

(A)Role ambiguity (B) Role conflict

(C)Role perception (D)Role expectation

61. A type of group discussion process in which members of the group are encouraged to generate as many imaginative and creative ideas in a relatively short period of time is known as:

(A) Brain storming (B) Group working

(C) Simulation (D) Group effect

62. __________ is the third person acting as a catalyst, who assists in the achievement of the smooth introduction and implementation of change.

(A)Change manager

(B)Change supervisor

(C)Change player

(D)Change agent

63. The right sequence of steps in Kurt Lewin's change procedure is:

(A) Unfreezing – Moving – Freezing

(B) Moving – Unfreezing – Freezing

(C) Unfreezing – Freezing – Moving

(D)Freezing – Moving – Unfreezing

64. Where do the following activities fall in Kurt Lewin's model of change process? 'Reinforcing the newly learned behaviour, finding 'fits' between organizational components, and maintaining 'fits' between organizational components'

(A) Unfreezing (B) Moving

(C) Refreezing (D) None of the above

65. The change procedure of unfreezing, moving and refreezing was given by:

(A) Kurt Lewin (B) P.F. Drucker

(C) French and Bell (D) Katz and Kahn

66. Lewin's theory is consistent with which view of organizational change?

(A) continuous (B) contemporary

(C) Mayo's (D)"calm waters"

67. According to Kurt Lewin, which of the following is ***not*** a stage in the change process?

(A) unfreezing (B) changing

(C) refreezing (D)restraining

68. According to Kurt Lewin, increasing the driving forces, which direct behavior away from the status quo, is a means of doing which of the following?

(A)unfreezing (B) changing

(C)restraining forces (D)refreezing

69. The unfreezing step of the change process can be thought of as __________.

(A)thawing the organization loose from the current status to the new status

(B)making the move to the new organizational condition

(C)loosening the organization from the old condition and moving it to the new condition

(D)preparing for the needed change

70. According to Lewin, which of the following is the objective of refreezing?

(A)directs behavior away from the status quo

(B)hinders movement away from existing equilibrium

(C)eliminates the need for future change

(D)stabilizes the new situation

71. The ______________ is consistent with uncertain and dynamic environments.

(A) calm waters metaphor

(B) white-water rapids metaphor

(C) contemporary metaphor

(D) continuous metaphor

72. In the white-water rapids metaphor, change is a natural state, and managing change is:

(A) an accepted practice

(B) an expected practice

(C) a continual process

(D) a maintenance process

73. Changes in population characteristics such as age, gender, race, marital status, income and education are examples of change :

(A) Demographic (B) Cultural

(C) Geographic (D) Diversity

74. Managing change is an integral part of:

(A) Top management's job

(B) Middle-level management's job

(C) The first-line manager's job

(D) Every manager's job

75. Changing human resource management activities to attract and retain health care specialists due to increased needs for those workers is an example of what kind of environmental change factor?

(A) marketplace (B) technology

(C) labor markets (D) economic

76. Which of the following is ***not*** an internal force of change?

(A) technology (B) strategy

(C) workforce (D) employee attitudes

77. Which of the following is ***not*** an external force of change?

(A) marketplace

(B) government laws and regulations

(C) economic changes

(D) workforce

78. Internal forces that stimulate the need for change tend to originate primarily from the impact of external forces or from _______.

(A) the forces of competition

(B) change in technology

(C) customer demand for the products the company produces

(D) the internal operations of the organization

79. What change factor did Steve Bennett address in his turnaround of Intuit, Inc?

(A) technology (B) workforce

(C) equipment (D) strategy

80. Increasing the numbers of employed women and minorities forces managers to pay attention to what change factor?

(A) strategy (B) workforce

(C) equipment (D) technology

81. Labor strikes are an example of what change factor that may encourage a change in management thinking and practices?

(A) workforce (B) equipment

(C) employee attitudes (D) strategy

82. One of the primary views of the change process is ___, while the other view is___.

(A) problematic; encouraged

(B) occasional; continuous

(C) costly; conservative

(D) optimistic; pessimistic

83. In organizations, people who act as catalysts and assume the responsibility for managing the change process are called ________.

(A) change masters

(B) change agents

(C) operations managers

(D) charismatic leaders

84. In spurring organizational change, outside consultants are usually more____, whereas internal managers may be more____.

(A) drastic; thoughtful

(B) highly paid; risky

(C) resistant; bold

(D) cautious; friendly

85. As change agents, managers should be motivated to initiate change because they are committed to _______.

(A) promoting the welfare of their employees

(B) managing and want to do the best they can for everyone

(C) improving their organization's performance

(D) meeting the competition head-on in the market

86. Initiating change involves identifying what organizational areas might need to be changed and _______.

(A) discussing it with the board of directors

(B) hiring a consultant to confirm that the change is needed

(C) forming a committee to determine that the need for change is real

(D) putting the change process in motion

87. Managers' options for change essentially fall into what three categories?

(A) environment, technology, and mission

(B) structure, technology, and people

(C) mission, structure, and people

(D) mission, environment, and process

88. What category of change involves work processes, methods, and equipment?

(A) technology (B) people

(C) competitors (D) structure

89. A company that decides to decentralize its sales procedures is managing what change category?

(A) technology (B) people

(C) competitors (D) structure

90. What type of change might include a shift from a functional to a product structure?

(A) a structural design change

(B) a structural component change

(C) automation

(D) computerization

91. Competitive factors or new innovations within an industry often require managers to introduce all of the following ***except*** new __.

(A) equipment (B) tools

(C) operating methods (D) employees

92. When grocery stores installed scanners to read the product price, this was an example of managing what change category?

(A) technology (B) people

(C) competitors (D) structure

93. If Kraft Foods hired a consultant to decrease group friction and enhance cooperative work relationships, this would be an example of managing what change category?

(A) technology (B) people

(C) competitors (D) structure

94. An individual is likely to resist change because of all of the following reasons ***except:***

(A) uncertainty

(B) increased productivity

(C) concern over personal loss

(D) belief that the change is not in the organization's best interest

95. To cope with the complexity of life, individuals rely on habits or _________.

(A) programmed responses

(B) the status quo

(C) beliefs

(D) certainties

96. Which of the reasons for resistance to change expressed by an employee may be beneficial to the organization?

(A) uncertainty

(B) freezing

(C) change is incompatible with the interests of the organization

(D) refreezing

97. All of the following are mentioned as actions that managers can use to deal with resistance to change except __________.

(A) education and communication

(B) diversification

(C) participation

(D) facilitation and support

98. For ________ to be effective, there must be mutual trust and credibility between managers and employees.

(A) education (B) coercion

(C) negotiation (D) participation

99. _______ may be necessary when resistance comes from a powerful source.

(A) Education and communication

(B) Coercion

(C) Facilitation and support

(D) Negotiation

100. _____________ is using direct threats or force on those who resist change.

(A) Negotiation (B) Coercion

(C) Cooptation (D) Education

101. Which of the following represents the relationship between organizational culture and change?

(A) Culture and change are naturally compatible.

(B) Culture tends to be very resistant to change.

(C) Culture can change in months but not weeks.

(D) Culture can never be purposely changed.

102. Which of the following is ***not*** a favorable situational condition that may facilitate change in an organizational culture?

(A) a dramatic crisis occurs

(B) the culture is weak

(C) stock prices remain constant

(D) the organization is young and small

103. Cultural change is most likely to take place when ________________.

(A) the organization is old

(B) the organization is large

(C) the culture is strong

(D) there is a leadership change

104. What is a strategy for managing cultural change?

(A) Support employees who remain devoted to the old values.

(B) Redesign socialization processes to align with the new values.

(C) Keep the reward system the same.

(D) Terminate top managers who are positive role models.

105. A dynamic and uncertain organizational environment has created a large number of employees who are ____________.

(A) old enough to retire, but can't afford to retire

(B) young and energetic about the "next day's work"

(C) over worked and stressed out

(D) over worked, but paid very well

106. An important potential environmental source of change is

(A) a new competitive product

(B) dissatisfied employee attitudes

(C) employee grievances

(D) a wildcat strike

107. Organizational change should be managed by:

(A) Top management (B) Employees

(C) All mangers (D) Consultants

108. The categories of human process, techno structural, human resources management and strategic applications are related to :

(A)Change management

(B)O. D. application

(C)Training

(D)Action research

109. Which of the following is ***not*** among the actions for change?

(A) Changing (B) Forcing

(C) Unfreezing (D) Refreezing

110. If the change is plotted on two axis of 'Time and difficulty involved in change ' then which of the following would be the correct sequence of change taking place in shortest time and difficulty to maximum period and difficulty ?

(i) Group Behaviour

(ii) Individual Behaviour

(iii) Organizational Behaviour

(iv) Knowledge

(v) Attitude

(A) (iv) (v) (iii) (ii) (i)

(B) (i) (ii) (iv) (iii) (v)

(C) (ii) (iii) (i) (v) (iv)

(D) (iv) (v) (ii) (i) (iii)

111. A person who will initiate change in the organization is called :

(A) Consultant (B) Trainer

(C) Change Agent (D) Counselor

112. An organisation that has developed capacity to adapt and change is described as :

(A) Virtual organisation

(B) Learning organisation

(C) Developing organisation

(D) Changing organization

113. Global economic pressures force organizations to become more _____.

(A)price competitive (B)quality conscious

(C)cost efficient (D)conservative

114. How can managers increase the likelihood of making change happen successfully?

(A)focus on how they want to change the organization

(B)understand the difficult task at hand

(C)increase the role of individual employees

(D)observe how competitors are changing

115. What is a characteristic of a change-capable organization?

(A)separates the present and the future

(B)makes controlling a way of life

(C)discourages mavericks

(D)shelters breakthroughs

116. What organizational development (OD) technique is a technique for assessing attitudes and perceptions, identifying discrepancies in these, and resolving the differences by using survey information in feedback groups?

(A) team building

(B) intergroup development

(C) survey feedback

(D) sensitivity training

117. Which of the following is ***not*** a traditional method of organizational development?

(A)Survey feedback (B) Sensitivity training

(C)Process consultation (D)Managerial grid

118. What OD technique involves changing the attitudes, stereotypes, and perceptions that work groups have about each other?

(A) team building

(B) intergroup development

(C) survey feedback

(D) sensitivity training

119. Before using the same OD techniques to implement behavioral changes, especially across different countries, managers need to be sure that they've taken into account:

(A)cultural characteristics

(B)organizational differences

(C)employee attitudes

(D)societal differences

120. Techniques to change people and the quality of interpersonal work relationships are termed ______.

(A) operations

(B) organizational development

(C) downsizing

(D) robotics

121. Which of the following is correct about Organizational Development?

(A) It is a planned change

(B) It aims at problem solving

(C) It is focused primarily on human and social relationships

(D) All the above

122. Among the following which is *not* OD technique

(A) Sensitivity training

(B) MBO

(C) Delphi technique

(D) Grid training and development

123. Which of the following is *not* correct about Organization Development?

(A)It is not a top management led and supported process.

(B)It is a process of planned change.

(C)It is an ongoing collaborative management of organization culture.

(D)It is a problem solving process.

124. Action research, as a methodology for behavioural science was proposed by:

(A) Wendell L. French (B)P. F. Drucker

(C) Kurt Lewin (D) Reddin

125. Which of the following is *not* an OD intervention?

(A) Grid Training

(B) Transactional Analysis

(C) Process Consultation

(D) None of the above

126. Arrange the following phases of Grid training in OD in the sequence in which they are held.

(a)Team development

(b)Organizational goal setting and attainment

(c)Inter-group development

(d)Laboratory-Seminar Training

(A) (d) (a) (c) (b)

(B) (a) (d) (b) (c)

(C) (c) (d) (b) (a)

(D) (d) (c) (b) (a)

127. Systematic collection of data on a problem, analysis, feedback and helping organization to take action to address the problem is called :

(A)Process Research (B) Field Research

(C)Action Research (D)Business Research

128. Who propounded Self Theory of Personality?

(A) Kretschmer (B) Allport

(C) Eysenck (D) Carl Roger

129. Individual psychology of personality was given by:

(A) A. Adler (B) Jung

(C) Eysenck (D) None of these

130. Among the best known trait approaches to personality measurement – column A gives Traits and column B states the name of authority defining them. Match the correct combination:

Traits	Author
(A) 20 + needs	Murray
(B) 16 traits	Eysenck
(C) 3 traits	Cattell
(D) 5 traits	Costa & Merree

131. People's behavior at work, the kinds of tasks they are interested in, and how they react to events that happen on the job are associated with their _____.

(A) Ability.

(B) Trust, justice, and ethics.

(C) Learning and decision making.

(D) Personality and cultural values.

132. Which of the following describes the cognitive abilities, emotional skills, and physical abilities that employees bring to a job?

(A) Ability

(B) Personality and cultural values

(C) Trust, justice, and ethics

(D) Individual's characteristics

133. Which of the following influences the kinds of tasks an employee is good at and those with which an employee may struggle?

(A) Personality

(B) Ability

(C) Trust, justice, and ethics

(D) Learning and decision making

134. The personality theory that emphasises the unconscious determinants of behaviour is known as :

(A) Cognitive theory

(B) Psychodynamic theory

(C) Perpetual theory

(D) Refreezing

135. The assumptions about human nature:

(i)work is inherently distasteful to most people

(ii)most people would like to be directed, and

(iii)most people have little or no creativity are propounded by :

(A)Hygiene Theory (B) Maslow's Theory

(C)Theory- X (D) Theory- Y

136. In the theory of Mc Gregor following assumptions have been made about human nature, under theory X those are:

(A) Self-centered (B) Lacks ambitions

(C) Gullible (D) All the above

137. The usual tendency with negative feedback is to find the reason to explain one's own behaviour. This tendency is termed as :

(A) Mutuality (B) Displacement

(C) Rationalisation (D) Projection

138. In which of the following inter - personal styles, people are critical of other's behaviour, develop rules and regulations and impose them on others :

(A)Rescuing style (B) Prescriptive style

(C)Normative style (D)Supportive style

139. A personality characteristic indicating one's willingness to do whatever it takes to get one's own way is known as:

(A) Locus of control

(B) Machiavellism

(C) Job characteristic model

(D) Personality legitimacy

140. Emotional Intelligence includes :

(A) Self awareness, self management and self motivation

(B) Self awareness, self knowledge and self understanding

(C) Knowledge, belief, culture and perception

(D) All the above

141. Transactional Analysis (TA) is related to

(A) Learning (B) Attitudes

(C) Perception (D) Personality

142. In ______, a person is perceived on the basis of a single trait.

(A) Halo Effect (B)Hawthorne Effect

(C) Stereotyping (D)None of the above

143. Figure – Ground Theory explains the process of

(A) Cognition (B) Sensation

(C) Perception (D) Motivation

144. The process selecting, organizing and interpreting or attaining meaning to events happening in the environment is called:

(A) Perception (B) Attitude

(C) Personality (D) Learning

145. Organization value refers to :

(A) Individual belief

(B) Group belief

(C) Corporate believes and ethos

(D) None of the above

146. Dependability, predictability and faith are the three elements that constitute :

(A) Values (B) Moral principles

(C) Trust (D) Justice

147. ______ reflect the various traits and tendencies that describe how people act, with commonly studied traits including extraversion, conscientiousness, and collectivism.

(A)Leadership

(B)Motivation

(C)Social values

(D)Personality and cultural values

148. Shared organizational values are

(A)unconscious, affective desires or wants that guide society's behavior

(B)influenced by international values

(C)different for the various components of a diverse work force

(D)a myth

149. Instrumental values are :

(A)Hardworking, sincerity, rationality and self-discipline

(B)Free of conflict, quality, happiness and self-esteem

(C)Social recognition, contentment and harmony

(D)All the above

150. A common method of measuring attitudes is by using:

(A) in-depth interviews

(B) observing people's behaviour

(C)systematic differential scales

(D)a lie detector

151. The conditioned - learning theory was propounded by :

(A) Thoradike (B) Pavlov

(C) Maslow (D) Luther Gullick

152. Classical conditioning is associated with:

(A) Repetition (B) Generalization

(C) Discrimination (D) All the above

153. Match the following expressions with the ego states mentioned against them :

Expressions	**Ego states**
(a)Rationality	(i) Parent
(b)Fantasising	(ii) Child
(c)Demonstrating	(iii) Adult

Codes:

	(a)	(b)	(c)
(A)	(i)	(ii)	(iii)
(B)	(ii)	(i)	(iii)
(C)	(iii)	(ii)	(i)
(D)	(iii)	(i)	(ii)

154. The tools and techniques used in learning organizations are

(A) Creativity &Brainstorming

(B) Observing outcomes

(C) Reframing knowledge

(D) All the above

155. According to Freud, Super Ego is properly developed during

(A)latency period (B) anal period

(C)phallic period (D) none of these

156. Which of the following theories is most quantitatively measurable?

(A) Pavlov's (B) Skinner's

(C) Hull's (D) None of these

157. Match the following List – I with List – II in correct order :

List – I	**List – II**
(a)Classical conditioning	(i)Kohler
(b)Drive reduction	(ii)Hull
(c)Sign Gestalt learning	(iii)Pavlov
(d)Learning by insight	(iv)Skinner
	(v)Tolman

Codes:

	(a)	(b)	(c)	(d)
(A)	(iv)	(ii)	(v)	(i)
(B)	(iii)	(ii)	(v)	(i)
(C)	(iv)	(ii)	(i)	(v)
(D)	(iii)	(ii)	(i)	(v)

158. "Assistant Manager, after observing the style of conducting a meeting of Senior Manager on number of occasions started conducting the meeting in similar manner" is an example of :

(A)Classical conditioning

(B)Social learning

(C)Insight learning

(D)Operant conditioning

159. In a learning organization

(A)Vision is provided by top management

(B)Conflicts are resolved through power and hierarchical influence

(C)Formulation and implementation of ideas takes place at all levels of organization

(D) All the above

160. Who has advanced the single loop and double loop learning models?

(A)Albert Bandura (B) Robert Blake

(C)Robert Katz (D)Chris Argyris

161. Match the following :

Contributor

(a)Ivan Pavlor

(b)B.F. Skinner

(c)Albert Bandura

(d)Edward Tolman

Behavioural Models

(i)social learning model

(ii)cognitive framework

(iii)classical conditioning

(iv)operant conditioning

	(a)	(b)	(c)	(d)
(A)	(iii)	(iv)	(ii)	(i)
(B)	(ii)	(iii)	(i)	(iv)
(C)	(iii)	(iv)	(i)	(ii)
(D)	(iii)	(ii)	(iv)	(i)

162. Reinforcement given by removing a noxious or undesirable stimulus from the environment is known as :

(A) Positive Reinforcement

(B) Negative Reinforcement

(C) Punishment

(D) None of the above

163. As employees gain experience, they obtain job knowledge and use this knowledge to make accurate judgments on the job. Which of the following is represented by this statement?

(A) Team processes

(B) Trust, justice, and ethics

(C) Learning and decision making

(D) Personality and ability

164. Match the following :

List – I (Propagators)

(a) Ivan Pavlov

(b) B.F. Skinner

(c) Albert Bandura

(d) Freud Luthans

List – II (Contributions)

(i) Social Learning Thoery

(ii) S-O-B-C.Model

(iii)Classical Conditioning

(iv)Operant Conditioning

Codes:

	(a)	(b)	(c)	(d)
(A)	(iii)	(iv)	(ii)	(i)
(B)	(ii)	(iii)	(i)	(iv)
(C)	(iii)	(iv)	(i)	(ii)
(D)	(iii)	(ii)	(iv)	(i)

165. Which of the following statements correctly describe 'extinction'? When a previously reinforced behaviour :

(A) is reinforced immediately

(B) is reinforced for a short period

(C) is not reinforced for a long time

(D) both (B) and (C) above

166. In which of the following transactions, stimulus and response are parallel?

(A) Cross Transactions

(B) Complementary Transactions

(C) Ulterior Transactions

(D) All the above

167. Need-Hierarchy Theory was propounded by:

(A)Peter F. Drucker (B)Abraham Maslow

(C)Mc – Fraland (D)Elton Mayo

168. Arrange Maslow's Hierarchy of Needs in descending order :

(i) Social Needs

(ii) Self-actualisation Needs

(iii) Physiological Needs

(iv) Ego Needs

(v)Security Needs

Codes:

(A) (iii), (v), (i), (iv) and (ii)

(B) (iii), (v), (i), (ii) and (iv)

(C) (ii), (iv), (i), (iii) and (v)

(D) (ii), (iv), (i), (v) and (iii)

169. Which is the correct sequence in Maslow's need hierarchy theory?

(A) Security, Affiliation, Esteem

(B) Affiliation, Security, Esteem

(C) Security, Esteem, Affiliation

(D) None of the above are correct

170. In order from lowest to highest, what are Maslow's five classes of needs?

(A) Social.esteem.physiological.safety.self-actualization

(B) Physiological.safety.social.self-actualization.esteem

(C) Physiological.safety.social.esteem.self-actualization

(D) Self-actualization. esteem. safety. social. physiological

171. In Maslow's need hierarchy theory, which of the following are ***not*** high order needs?

(A) Safety (B) Social

(C) Esteem (D) Self-Actualisation

172. Who propounded the Two - Factor Theory?

(A)Frederick Herberg (B)Mc Gregor

(C)J. S. Mill (D)Adam Smith

173. 'X' and 'Y' theory was prepared by

(A)Herzbeg (B) Maslow

(C)Porter and Lawler (D) McGregor

174. According to Herzberg, which of the following is a maintenance factor?

(A) Salary (B) Work itself

(C) Responsibility (D)Recognition

175. Which of the following is Herzberg's hygiene factor?

(A) Recognition at work place

(B) Reasonable salary

(C) Responsibility for work

(D) Sense of achievement

176. Which one of the following is a motivating factor according to Herzberg?

(A)Job itself (B) Working conditions

(C)Salary (D) Size of the organization

177. Among of following which is a hygiene factor

(A) Salary (B) Reorganization

(C) Growth (D) Self actualization

178. Which of the following is hygiene factor?

(A) Advancement (B) Growth

(C) Job Security (D)Achievement

179. Assertion:"All hygiene factors put together do ***not*** motivate a person on the job".

Reason: "A satisfied need is ***not*** a motivator of behaviour."

(A)The Assertion is right but Reason is wrong

(B)The Assertion is wrong but Reason is right

(C)The Assertion distinguishes hyegiene factors from motivational factors thereby justifying the Reason.

(D)Neither the Assertion nor the Reason is right.

180. Under Alderfer's ERG theory, the three core needs are

(A) Emotional, Relational, and Growth

(B) Emotional, Rational and Growth

(C) Existence, Reliability and Gain

(D) Existence, Relatedness and Growth

181. Clayton Alderfer attempted to rework Maslow's need hierarchy to align it more closely with empirical research. His revised need hierarchy is labeled as:

(A)Theory of Needs (B) ERG theory

(C) Self efficiency theory (D) Equity theory

182. Which of the following theories was propounded by McClelland?

(A)Achievement motivation

(B)Need hierarchy

(C)Two factor theory

(D)ERG theory

183. What are the motives identified by David C Mc Celland?

(A) Affiliation (B) Power

(C) Achievement (D) All the above

184. Need for achievement goes with

(A) F.W. Taylor (B) Hertzberg

(C) McGregor (D) McClelland

185. Which of the following is ***not*** a content theory of motivation?

(A) Maslow's Need Hierarchy Theory

(B) Alderfer's ERG Theory

(C) Vroom's Expectancy Theory

(D) Herzberg's Two Factor Theory

186. Which of the following is one of the process Theories of motivation?

(A) Alderfer's E R G Theory

(B) Achievement motivation Theory

(C) Manifest need Theory

(D) None of the above

187. Expectancy Theory of Motivation was propounded by:

(A)Porter and Lawler (B) McGregor

(C)Vroom (D)J. Stacy Adams

188. In Vroom's theory, motivation is expressed as

(A) Valence + Expectancy

(B) Valence – Expectancy

(C) Valence × Expectancy

(D) Valence /Expectancy

189. Who has given the 'expectancy theory' of Motivation?

(A) Abraham Maslow (B) Victor Vroom

(C) Frederick Herzberg (D) Clayton Adler

190. Which of the following is ***not*** the process theory of motivation?

(A)Vroom's expectancy model

(B)Adam's equity theory

(C)Porter's performance satisfaction theory

(D)Alderfer's ERG theory

191. Prachita is a new employee at a company. She feels very energetic and this drives her to perform well. Which of these individual mechanisms captures the energetic forces that drive employees' work efforts?

(A) Motivation (B) Ability

(C)Job performance (D) Personality

192. 'Hot-Stove' rule was given by :

(A)Douglas Mc Gregor (B)Mc Clleland

(C)Dale S. Beach (D)Dale Yoder

193. The 'Cognitive Dissonance' theory of motivation was advanced by :

(A)Parter and Lawler

(B)Kelly and Rolter

(C)Lewin and Tolman

(D)Festinger and Homans

194. Match the following :

List-I

(a) Frederick Herzberg

(b) F.W. Taylor

(c) Blake and Monton

(d) Abraham Maslow

List-II

(i) Scientific Management

(ii) Two Factor Theory

(iii) Need Hierarchy Theory

(iv) Managerial Grid

	(a)	(b)	(c)	(d)
(A)	(ii)	(i)	(iv)	(iii)
(B)	(i)	(iii)	(ii)	(iv)
(C)	(i)	(ii)	(iii)	(iv)
(D)	(iv)	(iii)	(ii)	(i)

195. The subjective probability of efforts resulting in the outcome (the first level outcomes), is known as :

(A)Expectancy (B) Instrumentality

(C)Incentive (D) None of the above

196. Competency theory is given by

(A) Maslow (B) McClendon

(C)Mc duologues (D) Frederick Herzberg

197. Motivation is important to managers because:

(A)it is a significant contributor to high performance

(B)it does not explain the differences in intensity of behavior

(C)it explains the differences in attitude and personality

(D)not all employees know how to use it effectively

198. Considering extrinsic rewards:

(A)money modifies behavior irrespective of the perceptions and preferences of the person being rewarded

(B)recognition is a powerful motivating reward for everyone

(C)upper management compensation is a strong incentive for lower-level employees to work harder

(D)benefits are usually based on longevity, not performance

199. Employees with relatively weak higher-order needs are _______ concerned with variety and autonomy.

(A)less (B) more

(C)very (D) extremely

200. What are the negative types of motivators?

(A) Fear (B) Force

(C)Reprimands (D) All the above

201. Some of the general motivators are:

(A) job security

(B) freedom at workplace

(C) interesting work

(D) All the above

202. Certain important motivational techniques are:

(A) Monetary incentives

(B) Job-based techniques

(C) MBO techniques

(D) All the above

203. Which theory of motivation places a premium on the effort - reward relationship?

(A) Vroom's (B) McClelland's

(C) Equity (D) Herzberg

204. The assumption that employees like work, are creative and can exercise self direction is known as :

(A) Theory X (B) Theory Y

(C) Theory Z (D) None of these

205. The amount of satisfaction an individual anticipates from a particular outcome is known as:

(A) Theory Y (B) Theory Z

(C) Valence (D) Stress

206. Employees with high self-esteem set

(A) Higher goals for others

(B) Higher goals for themselves and lower goals for others

(C) Higher goals for themselves

(D) None of the above

207. ________ is a predisposition to behave in a certain way and to take particular point of view.

(A) Motivation (B) Behaviour

(C) Perception (D) Attitude

208. Theory " Z " has been propounded by :

(A) Mc Gregor (B) Ouchi

(C) Maslow (D) Skinner

209. Match the following :

List-I	List-II
(a)Z – Theory	(i) Herzberg
(b)Y – Theory	(ii) Maslow
(c)Hierarchy Needs Theory	(iii)McGregor
(d)Hygiene Theory	(iv) Urwick

Codes:

	(a)	(b)	(c)	(d)
(A)	(iv)	(i)	(iii)	(ii)
(B)	(iii)	(ii)	(iv)	(i)
(C)	(iv)	(iii)	(ii)	(i)
(D)	(iii)	(iv)	(i)	(ii)

210. Porter and Lawler model is related to

(A) Perception (B) Attitudes

(C) Motivation (D) Leadership

211. Emotional intelligence is said to be the ability to sense, understand and effectively apply the power and acumen of emotions as a source of:

(A) Information (B) Trust

(C) Human energy (D) All the above

212. Who among the following has advanced the Power, Affiliation and Achievement motivation concepts?

(A) J. Stacey Adams (B) B.F. Skinner

(C) Victor Vroom (D) David

213. Who among the following has advanced Transactional Analysis as an explanation of interpersonal communication strategy?

(A) Thomas A Harris (B) Eric Frank

(C) Muriel James (D) Eric Beme

214. Match List-I with List- II and select the correct answer using the code given below the Lists:

List -I (Theory of Motivation)

(a) X, Y theory

(b) Expectancy theory

(c) Two factor theory

(d) Equity theory

List-II (Contributor)

(i) Frederick Herzberg

(ii) J Stacey Adams

(iii) Douglas McGregor

(iv) Victor Vroom

Code:

	(a)	(b)	(c)	(d)
(A)	(iii)	(i)	(iv)	(ii)
(B)	(ii)	(iv)	(i)	(iii)
(C)	(ii)	(i)	(iv)	(iii)
(D)	(iii)	(iv)	(i)	(ii)

215. The four systems of Management in terms of Leadership styles are related to

(A) Blake and Mouton (B) Philip Kotler

(C) Peter F. Drucker (D) Rensis Likert

216. Who developed the Two-Dimensional Managerial Grid?

(A)Blake and Mouton (B) Howthorne

(C) McCarthy (D) W. A. Taylor

217. What is the most important attribute of an effective leader?

(A) Behaviour (B) Character

(C) Drive (D) Influence

218. Match the names of the Behavioural scientists and their contributions given in the List–A and B

List–A

(a) Mayo E. and Roethlisberger F. J.

(b) Mc. Gregar D.

(c) Likert R.

(d) Kelly J.

List–B

(i) Theory X and Y

(ii) Michigan study an leadership style

(iii)Trait Theory of leadership

(iv) Hawthorne effect

	(a)	(b)	(c)	(d)
(A)	(iv)	(i)	(ii)	(iii)
(B)	(ii)	(i)	(iv)	(iii)
(C)	(iii)	(i)	(ii)	(iv)
(D)	(iv)	(i)	(iii)	(ii)

219. The process by which individuals attain authority over others is summarized by

(A) Leader cultural values.

(B) Leader personality.

(C) Leader styles and behaviors.

(D) Leader power and influence.

220. It appears that

(A) successful leaders tend to be more intelligent than followers

(B) there is no link between intelligence of the leader and success

(C) intelligence is the most important "ability" trait in leaders

(D) persons with creativity make the best leaders

221. Concerning leadership concepts,

(A)leader roles are unnecessary in organizations like Gore-Tex, where a self-leadership approach is used

(B)it is likely that a particular set of leader characteristics and behaviors do suit specific situations and groups

(C)it is likely that the need for leaders will decline in the 21st century due to more decentralized structures

(D)the military model of leadership will become more popular in the 21st century

222. Which of the following captures the specific actions that leaders take to influence others at work?

(A) Leader styles and behaviors

(B) Leader cultural values

(C) Leader personality

(D)Leader influence

223. Match List – I with List – II. Select the correct answer from the codes given below:

List – I

(a) R. Blake and J. Mouton

(b) Fred Fiedler

(c) Robert House

(d) P. Herseyand K.Blanchard

List – II

(i) Path-goal Theory

(ii) Managerial grid

(iii) Life Cycle Theory

(iv) Theory of Leadership Effectiveness

Codes:

(a) (b) (c) (d)

(A)(ii) (iv) (i) (iii)

(B) (iv) (iii) (ii) (i)

(C) (ii) (iv) (iii) (i)

(D) (i) (ii) (iv) (iii)

224. People of Theory of Y belongs to:

(A) They are self motivated

(B) They are lazy

(C) Work oriented & Dedicated

(D) Need close supervision

225. Which of the following is ***not*** the assumption of theory X?

(A) Most people must be corrected and controlled.

(B) The average human being prefers to be directed.

(C) Most of the people do not dislike work inherently.

(D) People have relatively little ambitions and wants.

226. The power vested in a leader by a virtue of accepting organizational authority is known as :

(A)Legitimate Power (B) Coercive Power

(C)Democratic Power(D)None of the above

227. The concept of task - oriented and people oriented leadership was developed by :

(A)Blake and Monton (B) John Berry

(C)Maxwell (D) Hertzberg

228. The "Tri-dimensional grid" was developed by :

(A) Fayol (B) Gullick

(C) F. W. Taylor (D) Reddin

229. Autocratic leadership :

(A) Requires task completion

(B) Works with consensus of all

(C) Does not accept views and suggestions of all

(D) Demands obedience from authorities

230. A leader may use the following methods :

(a) Use criticism

(b) Encourage growth

(c) Set objectives

(d) Give orders and directions

Which of these methods are used by a democratic leader?

(A) (a) and (b) (B)(c) and (d)

(C) (b) and (c) (D)(a), (b) and (d)

231. In the 'Managerial grid' 9, 1 style is termed as:

(A) Team Management

(B) Country Club Management

(C) Authority Obedience

(D) Improvised Management

232. Which of the following is ***not*** one of the ego-states of transactional analysis?

(A) Child (B) Young

(C) Adult (D)Parent

233. Match the following:

Group (A)

(a) Douglas M. Mc Gregor

(b) William Ouchi

(c) Joseph Lufth and Harry Inghams

(d) Kurt Lewin

Group (B)

(i) Johari Window

(ii) Force Field Theory

(iii) Theory 'X' and 'Y'

(iv) Theory Z

Code:

(a) (b) (c) (d)

(A) (iii) (ii) (iv) (i)

(B) (ii) (iii) (i)(iv)

(C) (iii) (iv) (i)(ii)

(D) (iv) (ii) (i)(iii)

234. Managers subscribing to ______ assumptions attempt to structure, control and closely supervise their employees.

(A) Theory 'X'

(B) Theory 'Y'

(C) Both Theory 'X' and Theory 'Y'

(D) Neither Theory 'X' nor Theory 'Y'

235. According to Fiedler's Contingency Model of Leadership, which one of the following is a situational variable?

(A)Leader – Member relationship

(B)Organisational System

(C) Degree of task structure

(D) Leader's position power

236. Theory X represents

(A) Democratic style of leadership

(B) Autocratic style of leadership

(C) Laissez-faire style of leadership

(D) Humanistic style of leadership

237. In Black and Mouton's "Managerial Grid", the 'task style' represents :

(A) High concern for people and low concern for production.

(B) High concern for people and high concern for production.

(C) Low concern for people and low concern for production.

(D) High concern for production and low concern for people.

238. Who had advanced the '3-D' theory of Leadership Effectiveness?

(A) Robert Blake & Jane S. Mouton

(B) William J. Reddin

(C) Fred E. Fiedler

(D) Rensis Likert

239. Match the following :

Leadership Theory

(a) Contingency Theory

(b) Trait Theory

(c) Charismatic Theory

Leadership Factors

(i)Personal vision and energy

(ii)Personal drive, desire to lead, Personal integrity

(iii) Leader's Position power, task structure and leader member relations

	(a)	(b)	(c)
(A)	(i)	(iii)	(ii)
(B)	(iii)	(ii)	(i)
(C)	(ii)	(iii)	(i)
(D)	(i)	(ii)	(iii)

240. How many dimensions are there in Blake and Moutoni Managerial Grid?

(A) Two (B) Three

(C) Four (D) Five

241. Who developed the 'Managerial Grid' Theory?

(A) Sydney and Beatrice Webbs

(B) Robert Blake & Jane S. Mouton

(C) W.J. Reddin

(D) Rensis Likert

242. The concept of task oriented and people oriented leadership was developed by :

(A)John Berry (B) Maxwell

(C)Blake and Mouton(D) Hertzberg

243. Arrange the following systems in the right order on continuum suggested by Rensis Likert

(a) Consultative

(b) Benevolent Authoritative

(c) Exploitative Authoritative

(d) Joint decision-making

(A) c, b, a, d (B) c, a, b, d

(C) b, a, c, d (D) c, d, b, a

244. The different leadership styles are :

(A) Autocratic (B) Democratic

(C) laissez - faire (D) All the above

245. The internal environment factors that influence management are:

(A) Labour (B) Machines

(C) place (D) All the above

246. A responsible leader does ***not*** limit:

(A) Discussions

(B)Development of alternatives

(C)Interactions

(D)All the above

247. Some of the traits of leaderships are as follows

(A) Emotional stability

(B) Communication skill

(C) Knowledge of human relations

(D) All the above

248. Under hard boiled type of autocratic leadership, the employees tend to become

(A) Resentful (B) quarrelsome

(C) Both (D) None of them

249. Which of the following is ***not*** considered as a leadership style?

(A) Task oriented leadership style.

(B) Society oriented leadership style.

(C) Employee oriented leadership style.

(D) Autocratic leadership style

250. In Transactional Analysis the "I am ok, you are ***not*** ok" life position is also referred to as :

(A) Bossing (B) Avoidant

(C) Diffident (D) Bohemian

251. Match List I with List II and select the correct answer using the code given below the Lists:

List- I (Contributor)

(a) Robert Blake and Jane Mouton

(b) W.J. Reddin

(c) Rensis Likert

(d) Vroom and Yetton

List- II (Leadership Style)

(i) Four-system model

(ii)Normative model

(iii)Managerial grid

(iv)The 3-D theory

Code:

	(a)	(b)	(c)	(d)
(A)	(iii)	(iv)	(i)	(ii)
(B)	(iii)	(i)	(iv)	(ii)
(C)	(ii)	(i)	(iv)	(iii)
(D)	(ii)	(iv)	(i)	(iii)

252. Which one of the following is ***not*** a dimension of the managerial grid theory of leadership?

(A) Country club management

(B) Impoverished management

(C) Team management

(D) Entrepreneurship management

253. The first stage of conflict resolution is to

:

(A) Analyze the problem

(B) Choose a solution

(C) Think through possible solutions

(D) Define the problem

254. Which term is ***not*** used in transactional analysis

(A) Ego states (B) Life position

(C)Child states (D) Stroking

255. The term 'Blind Spot' in Johari window model refers to :

(A) The self that is known to others as well as to oneself

(B) The self which is known to others but not to oneself

(C) The self which is known neither to others nor to oneself

(D) The motives, feelings etc, which are known to one's own self

256. Conflict is a :

(A) Natural disagreement arising between two people

(B) Disliking for each other

(C)Lack of understanding of one party

(D) Lack of understanding of the problem

257. The view that the conflict should be accepted and encouraged, corresponds to which of the following views :

(A) Traditional view

(B) Interactionist view

(C) Behavioural view

(D) Both (A) and (C) above

258. What can drive conflict?

(A)Environment (B) Angry people

(C)Unreasonable rules (D) Goals

259. Which of the following is true of managers in relationship to conflict?

(A)Managers generally encourage low levels of conflict because it improves performance, up to a certain point.

(B)Managers generally ignore conflict.

(C)Managers attempt to eliminate conflict because the organization rewards them for keeping conflict out of their area of responsibility.

(D)Managers show no consistent attitude toward conflict.

260. Which of the following concepts are related to constructive conflict as suggested by Mary Parker Follet?

(i) Domination

(ii) Compromise

(iii) Integration

(iv) Delegation

Select the correct answer from the codes given below:

Codes:

(A) (i), (ii) (B) (iii), (iv)

(C) (i), (ii), (iii) (D) (ii), (iii), (iv)

261. _____________ is the adverse reaction people have to excessive pressure placed on them from extraordinary demands, constraints, or opportunities.

(A) Stereotyping (B) Stress

(C) A halo effect (D) Creativity

262. Stress, in and of itself, is _____________.

(A) not necessarily bad

(B) healthy in most cases

(C)harmful, especially if not managed by exercise

(D)beneficial to those who use it

263. ________ prevent you from doing what you desire; __________ refer to the loss of something desired.

(A) Constraints; demands

(B) Demands; constraints

(C) Fears; stressors

(D) Stressors; fears

264. Which of the following is true concerning stress?

(A) Stress is a static condition.

(B) Stress is a negative reaction to an outside force.

(C) Stress can be caused by change of any kind.

(D) Stress limits performance.

265. _______ there must be uncertainty over the outcome, and the outcome must be important.

(A) For uncertainty to become fear

(B) For anxiety to become stress

(C) For potential stress to become actual stress

(D) For anxiety to become fear

266. Stress symptoms can be grouped under any of the following three general categories except ______________.

(A) Physiological (B) Cultural

(C) Psychological (D) Behavioral

267. Which of the following is an example of a psychological symptom of stress?

(A) changes in metabolism

(B) increased heart and breathing rate

(C) irritability

(D) changes in productivity

268. Changes in eating habits are a ____ symptom of stress.

(A) Physical (B) psychological

(C) Behavioral (D) inertial

269. Managers need to make sure that employees' abilities ________.

(A) match the job requirements

(B) are being maximized

(C) are not being affected by their stress

(D) are not causing them stress

270. ____ that increase opportunities for employees to participate in decisions and to gain social support have been found to lessen stress.

(A) Improved organizational communications

(B) Time management programs

(C) Wellness programs

(D) Job redesigns

271. Stress from an employee's personal life __.

(A) is difficult for the manager to control directly

(B) should never concern the manager

(C) indicates that the employee needs counseling

(D) always affects work behavior, so the manager should always intervene

272. Managers might want to offer ______ to employees who want to talk to someone about their problems.

(A) wellness programs

(B) time management programs

(C) employee counseling

(D) performance planning programs

273. Find out the one which is ***not*** an element of employee empowerment :

(A) Belief system and trust

(B) Purposefulness

(C) Arbitrariness

(D) Self sufficiency or Competency

274. Which of the following is ***not*** a factor of emotional intelligence?

(A)Ability (B) Reason

(C)Emotion (D) Thinking without feeling

275. Employees' psychological responses to job demands that tax or exceed their capacities come under which of the following mechanisms?

(A) Job satisfaction (B) Ability

(C) Job performance (D) Stress

276. All of these are individual mechanisms as reflected in the integrative model of organizational behavior except:

(A) Stress. (B) Motivation.

(C) Job satisfaction (D)Job performance.

277. Which of the following is the outcome of job satisfaction?

(A) High employee turn3over

(B) High productivity

(C) Absenteeism

(D) All the above

278. What Suzie feels when thinking about her job and doing her day-to-day work is captured in her

(A) ability (B) job satisfaction

(C) personality (D)leadership style

279. The term job satisfaction refers to :

(A)A collection of feelings that an individual has towards his/her job

(B)The degree to which an individual identifies himself/herself with job

(C)The degree to which an individual identifies himself/herself with the organization

(D)None of the above

280. The factors measuring the morale of the workers and ascertain whether it is increasing or diminishing can be listed as :

(A)Absenteeism (B) Number of accidents

(C)Grievances (D) All the above

281. Morale largely depends on:

(A) Physical well-being

(B) Monetary well-being

(C) Mental well-being

(D) Sociological well-being

282. Which of the following is a group phenomenon?

(A) Perception (B) Attitude

(C) Morale (D) Motivation

283. The different factors that affect morale are

(A) Supervision received

(B) Nature of work

(C) Employees occupational level

(D) All the above

284. The factors measuring the morale of the workers and ascertain whether it is increasing or diminishing can be listed as:

(A) Absenteeism (B) No. of accidents

(C) Grievances (D) All the above

285. Any morale improvement programme of management must embrace the following rules.

(A)Respect individual (B) Be fair and just

(C)Encourage initiative (D) All the above

286. The factors measuring the morale of the workers and ascertain whether it is increasing or diminishing can be listed as:

(A)Grievances (B)Absenteeism

(C) No. of accidents (D)All the above

287. The term emotion refers to:

(A)A broad range of feelings that a person experiences

(B)A broad and intense feeling that is directed at someone or something

(C)A broad range of feelings in the form of anger that a person experiences

(D)None of the above

288. Characteristics of all formal and informal communication are:

(A) Same (B) Unstructured

(C) Structured (D) Different

289. A good communicator needs to be good at:

(A) Listening (B) Speaking

(C) Using language (D) Witty

290. Which step should a communicator take as the starting point?

(A)Select the channels of communication

(B)Set up feedback process

(C)Specify the objectives of communication

(D)Identify the tools of communication

291. The best way to ensure that what a person has communicated has reached receiver is:

(A)To use simple words

(B)To communicate when there is no disturbance

(C)To communicate when the receiver is attentive

(D)To ask the receiver to tell what they have received

292. An effective communication does ***not*** require:

(A) Change in speech pattern

(B) Appropriate gestures

(C) Mastery of content

(D) Handsome personality

293. Communication will be effective if:

(A)It is delivered slowly and clearly

(B)It is delivered in a calm situation

(C)It reaches the receiver completely

(D)It reaches the receiver as intended by the sender

294. A good manager is a___ communicator.

(A) Poor (B) Bad

(C) Good (D) Least

295. Communication is a:

(A)One way process (B) Two way process

(C)Multi way process (D) None of the above

296. Effective communication is measured through

(A) Feed Back (B) Encoding

(C) Decoding (D) None of the above

297. Communication helps to

(A)Increase productions

(B)Decrease production

(C)Increase Labor turnover

(D)None of the above

298. What are the basic elements of communication?

(A)Sender and receiver

(B)Message and channel of communication

(C)Response and feedback

(D)All of the above

299. A person who sends the message is known as:

(A)Communitee (B) Receiver

(C)Communicator (D) None of the above

300. The direction in which the formal communication flows is always

(A) Upward (B) Downward

(C) Horizontal (D) All of these

301. Communication involves:

(A) Information (B) Understanding

(C) Both A and B (D) None of the above

302. Grapevine is also known as:

(A) Informal communication

(B) Horizontal communication

(C) Upward communication

(D) Downward communication

303. Communication in an organization should ideally flow

(A)From top to bottom(B)from bottom to top

(C)Both ways (D)None of these

304. Telephone, radio inter communicating system are the media used for

(A)Formal communication

(B)Downward communication

(C)Oral communication

(D)None of these

305. Which of the following steps would you consider first for an effective communication?

(A)Select the channel of communication

(B)Plan the evaluation procedure

(C)Specify the objectives of communication

(D)Identify various media of communication

306. Principles of effective communication would be

(A)clear in use of language

(B)attentive listening

(C)use of right medium

(D)All the above

307. Under principle of effective communication what should be fully understood by all concerned.

(A) Tasks (B) Policies

(C) Responsibilities (D) All the above

308. The different types of psychological barriers to communication will be:

(A)Ego (B)Status consciousness

(C)Closed mind (D)All the above

309. The activities of the communicator while communicating a message will include

(A) Ideation (B) Encoding

(C) Transmission (D) All the above

310. Process of communication :

(A) Sender, Medium, Recipient, Feedback

(B) Sender, Feedback, Medium, Recipient

(C) Recipient, Medium, Sender, Feedback

(D) Sender, Medium, Feedback, Recipient

311. One of the main purposes of horizontal communication is :

(A)Problem-Solving

(B)Morale booster

(C)Give feedback to the top

(D)Provide job instructions and information

312. Premature evaluation takes place due to:

(A) Semantic Barriers

(B) Psychological Barriers

(C) Organizational Barriers

(D) None of the above

313. Which of the following is correct about 'Grapevine'?

(A)It tends to exist when members of formal group know another well.

(B)It is the result of social forces at work place.

(C)It is more common in times of high organizational excitement.

(D)All the above.

314. Grapevine is :

(A) Officially created

(B) Formal method of information

(C) Informal communication

(D) None of the above

315. Gangplank theory of communication advanced by Henry Fayol is an example of:

(A) Downward Communication

(B) Lateral Communication

(C) Upward Communication

(D) Network Communication

316. Which among the following are barriers to communication?

(A) Noise and Wrong Medium

(B) time and distance

(C) Semantic barriers

(D) All the above

317. Semantic barriers in communication occur due to :

(A) Personality problems

(B) Language problems

(C) Attitude problems

(D) All the Above

318. Which of the following is ***not*** a semantic barrier of communication?

(A) Faulty translation (B) Ambiguous words

(C) Specialist's language (D) Inattention

319. The definition of communication implies that:

(A) Communication is mostly verbal

(B)Communication is mostly written

(C)Most communication is in a vertical direction

(D)Understanding must occur to have communication

320. The LEAST-used communication channel in an organization is usually

(A) Upward (B) Downward

(C) Diagonal (D) Horizontal

321. One of the most helpful mechanisms for refining a spoken or written communication is called the

(A) Grapevine (B)Counseling service

(C) Five C.s (D)Complaint system

322. Communication begins with

(A) Encoding (B) idea origination

(C) Decoding (D) channel selection

323. The process of any communication will include

(A) Communicator (B) Medium

(C) Message (D) All the above

324. The lack of communication leads to:

(A) information gap

(B) disintegration

(C) deviation from performance

(D) All the above

325. What are the Communication barriers in the international environment?

(A) Loss by transmission

(B) Loss by poor retention

(C) Poor listening

(D) All the above

326. Objectives of communication

(i)to seek compliance and ensure uniformity in action

(ii)to meet deadlines and production targets

(iii)to disseminate information to a larger number of people, and

(iv)save cost in terms of time and money refers to :

(A) One-way communication

(B) Two-way communication

(C) Grapevine

(D) Non-verbal communication

327. The obstruction in communication caused due to differences in individual's interpretation of words and symbols, is known as :

(A) Psychological Barrier

(B) Social Barrier

(C) Organisational Barrier

(D) Semantic Barrier

328. The communication taking place among members of the same work group or among members or work groups at the same level is described as :

(A) Downward Communication

(B) Upward Communication

(C) Lateral Communication

(D) Parallel Communication

329. The final link in the communication process that puts the message back into the system as a check against misunderstandings is described as:

(A) Decoding (B) Feedback

(C) Encoding (D) None of these

330. Communication can be

(A) Oral (B) Oral and Written

(C) Written (D) None of the above

331. Which communication component is ***not*** a paid form of communication?

(A) Advertising (B) Sales promotion

(C) Personal selling (D) Publicity

332. Downward communication means:

(A) Transmission of ideas or information from executives to the subordinates

(B) Transmission of information from manager to manager

(C) Transmission of ideas or information from worker to worker

(D) Transmission of ideas or information from worker to superior

333. Who of the following was instrumental in developing a framework for classifying countries based on the work-related values (Dimension of Cultures) that predominate in respective countries, globally?

(A) W.Chan Kin (B) Renee Monborgue

(C) G.Hofstede (D) C.K.Prahlad

334. In order to predict human behaviour, it is best to supplement your intuitive opinions with information derived in what fashion?

(A) Common sense

(B) Systematic inquiry

(C) Direct observation

(D) Organisational theory

335. Role playing is often used to:

(A) Change attitudes (B) Learn skills

(C) Change results (D) Model behaviour

336. Which roles in a group-setting contributes to the socio-emotional bonding of a members and the groups overall success?

(A) Facilitative or building role

(B) Individualizing

(C) Maintenance

(D) Blocking

337. Which is the part of every interpersonal relationship?

(A) Conflict (B) Love

(C) Stress (D) Communication

338. Ethical values are derived from:

(A) Corporate objectives

(B) Organizational culture

(C) The Bible, the Kuran and the Geeta

(D) Corporative philosophy

339. Match the following :

List – I

(a) Three needs theory

(b) ERG theory

(c) XY theory

(d) Hygiene theory

List – II

(i) Mclelland

(ii) Clayton Alderfer

(iii) Mc Gregor

(iv) F.Herzberg

(a) (b) (c) (d)

(A) (iii) (i) (iv) (ii)

(B) (i) (ii) (iii) (iv)

(C) (ii) (i) (iv) (iii)

(D) (iv) (iii) (ii) (i)

340. Which is the correct sequence of needs, in hierarchy of Abraham Maslow's needs theory? (Arrange among them in hierarchical order)

(A) Self→actualisation→Social→Security→Physiological → Esteem

(B)Esteem→Self→actualisation→Social→Security→Physiological

(C) Physiological→Security→Social→Esteem→Self→actualisation

(D)Security→Social→Physiological→Esteem→Self→actualization

---000---

UNIT-II

ORGANIZATION BEHAVIOR (OB)

1. (A)Individuals, groups and organization system

Explanation:

- **Robbins:** "Organisation Behaviour is concerned with the study of what people do in an organisation and how that behaviour affects the performance of the organisation."
- OB refers to the behavior of individuals and groups within organization and the interaction between organizational members and their external environments.

2. (B) People skills

Explanation:

Technical Skills:

- The knowledge and abilities needed to accomplish mathematical, engineering, scientific or computer-related duties, as well as other specific tasks.
- Technical skills could also refer to the ability of a certain type of stock trader which uses technical analysis to buy and sell stocks.

People skills:

- According to the Portland Business Journal, people skills are described as: understanding ourselves and moderating our responses talking effectively and empathizing accurately building relationships of trust, respect and productive interactions.
- A British definition is "the ability to communicate effectively with people in a friendly way, especially in business."

3. (A)F.W. Taylor

Explanation:

- ***Frederic Taylor*** was one of the first to attempt to systematically analyze human behavior at work.
- His model was the machine with its cheap, interchangeable parts, each of which does one specific function.
- Taylor attempted to do to complex organizations what engineers had done to machines and this involved making individuals into the equivalent of machine parts.
- Just as machine parts were easily interchangeable, cheap, and passive, so too should the human parts be the same in the Machine model of organizations. "

4. (B)Culture and structure

Explanation: Organizational culture and organizational structure are the two variables at the organizational level that impact individual-level attitudes and behaviors.

5. (D)Organizational commitment

Explanation: According to the integrative model of organizational behavior, the two individual outcomes are Job performance and Organizational commitment.

6. (A)Individual mechanisms

Explanation: According to the integrative model of organizational behavior, trust, justice, and ethics are part of the Individual mechanism.

7. (D)Leadership behavior

Explanation:

Consideration: It is defined as the degree to which a leader shows concern and respect for followers, looks out for their welfare, and expresses appreciation and support. This is a people-oriented leadership style.

Authoritarianism: Practice of management in which orders are issued with threats of punishment for disobedience, and which is based on the belief that status and power differences in an organization are appropriate and must be maintained.

Theory X and theory Y

Assumptions of Theory-X:

- Most people dislike work and will avoid it to the extent possible.
- They must be continually coerced, controlled, and threatened with punishment to get the work done.
- They have little or no ambition, prefer to avoid responsibility, and choose security above everything else.
- Management that believes in theory-X assumptions, creates stick-and-carrot approach based firms with restrictive discipline and pervasive controls.

Assumptions of Theory-Y:

- Physical and mental efforts are natural and most people (depending on the work environment) find work to be a source of satisfaction.
- They generally, on their own motivation, exercise self-control, self-direction, creativity, and ingenuity in pursuit of individual and collective (company) goals.
- They either seek responsibility or learn to accept it willingly.
- Their full potential is not tapped in most organizations.
- Theory-Y believers create trust based firms with empowered employees.
- These concepts were introduced by the Douglas McGregor in his book ***'The Human Side of Enterprise.'***

Leadership & Human Behavior

- Leader should interact with followers, peers, seniors, and others; whose support needed in order to accomplish the goals.
- To gain their support, leader must be able to understand and motivate them.
- To understand and motivate people, leader must know human nature. Human nature is the common qualities of all human beings.
- Values, beliefs, and customs differ from country to country and even within group to group, but in general, all people have a few basic needs.
- Leader must understand these needs because they can be powerful motivators.

8. (C)Organizational restructuring

Explanation: Organizational restructuring:

- Organization restructuring happens when the reporting hierarchy of a company changes.
- After organization restructuring certain groups will report to different departments, and some departments may be newly created or disappear altogether.
- If the organization chart has changed shape then organization restructuring has occurred.
- There is no need for people to be hired or fired for a organization restructuring to happen, though organization restructuring is often a result of large layoffs.
- Often, organization restructuring is simply a euphemism for large-scale layoffs.

9. (A)Organizational commitment

Explanation:

Organizational commitment: Strength of the feeling of responsibility that an employee has towards the mission of the organization.

10.(A)Input - Output ratio

Explanation: Organizational effectiveness: It is the concept of how effective an organization is in achieving the outcomes the organization intends to produce.

11.(A)Job satisfaction

Explanation:

Job satisfaction: It is how content an individual is with his or her job. Scholars and human resource professionals generally make a distinction between affective job satisfaction and cognitive job satisfaction. Affective job satisfaction is the extent of pleasurable emotional feelings individuals have about their jobs overall, and is different to cognitive job satisfaction which is the extent of individuals' satisfaction with particular facets of their jobs, such as pay, pension arrangements, working hours, and numerous other aspects of their jobs.

Personality: It is the particular combination of emotional, attitudinal, and behavioral response patterns of an individual. Different personality theorists present their own definitions of the word based on their theoretical positions.

12. (A)Perception

Explanation: Perception:

It is the organization, identification, and interpretation of sensory information in order to represent and understand the environment. All perception involves signals in the nervous system, which in turn result from physical stimulation of the sense organs.

13.(C) Human Resource management

Explanation:

- Organizational behavior (OB) is a field of study devoted to understanding, explaining, and ultimately improving the attitudes and behaviors of individuals and groups in organizations.
- OB can be contrasted with two other courses: human resource management and strategic management.

14.(D)Human resource management

Explanation: Human resource management takes the theories; principles studied in OB and explore the practical applications of those principles in organizations.

15.(D)All of the above

Explanation:

Unethical behaviour: Unethical behavior is any action that is aimed at taking advantage of another without their knowledge or consent. Most define this as manipulating someone without their permission. Unethical actions are not necessarily illegal.

16.(B)Elton Mayo

Explanation:

Neo - classical theory of organizational structure:

- The human relations movement evolved as a reaction to the tough, authoritarian structure of classical theory.
- It addressed many of the problems inherent in classical theory.
- The most serious objections to classical theory are that it created over conformity and rigidity, thus squelching creativity, individual growth, and motivation.
- Neo-classical theory displayed genuine concern for human needs.

17.(D)Social psychology

Explanation: The theories and concepts found in OB are actually drawn from a wide variety of disciplines. Research on satisfaction, emotions, and team processes draws heavily from social psychology.

18.(A)Organization Behaviour

Explanation: Organization culture:

- The values and behaviors that contribute to the unique social and psychological environment of an organization.
- Organizational culture includes an organization's expectations, experiences, philosophy, and values that hold it together, and is expressed in its self-image, inner workings, interactions with the outside world, and future expectations.
- It is based on shared attitudes, beliefs, customs, and written and unwritten rules that have been developed over time and are considered valid.
- Also called corporate culture, it's shown in: the ways the organization conducts its business, treats its employees, customers, and the wider community, the extent to which freedom is allowed in decision making,

developing new ideas, and personal expression, how power and information flow through its hierarchy, and how committed employees are towards collective objectives.

- It affects the organization's productivity and performance, and provides guidelines on customer care and service, product quality and safety, attendance and punctuality, and concern for the environment.
- It also extends to production-methods, marketing and advertising practices, and to new product creation.
- Organizational culture is unique for every organization and one of the hardest things to change.

19.(C)Employees

20.(D)Punishing whistle blowers

21. (A)Job performance and organizational commitment.

Explanation: The two primary outcomes of interest to organizational behavior researchers (and employees and managers in organizations) are job performance and organizational commitment.

22.(B) Economics

Explanation: The theories and concepts found in OB are actually drawn from a wide variety of disciplines. Models from economics are used to understand motivation, learning, and decision making.

23.(A)Telecomputers

Explanation:

Cross-functional groups: A cross-functional team helps communicate more broadly, gain alignment more easily, and builds better products. As an added benefit, the team helps product managers spend more time in the market, figuring out what should be developed next year and the year after.

24.(D)Organizational structure

Explanation: Organizational structure dictates how the units within the firm link to other units.

25.(D)Organizational culture

Explanation: Organizational culture captures "the way things are" in an organization.

26.(C)Inimitable.

Explanation: The resource-based view suggests that a resource is more valuable when it is inimitable.

27.(A)Information that employees possess

Explanation: Organizational memory is the accumulated body of data, information, and knowledge created in the course of an individual organization's existence. It has two repositories: an organization's archives, including its electronic data bases; and individuals' memories.

28.(A)a consensus planning tool, generally used by groups to discuss, debate and decide on issues of strength-identification, problems and solutions.

Explanation: Nominal group technique (NGT) is a structured method for group brainstorming that encourages contributions from everyone.

29.(C)Organizational culture

Explanation: Organizational culture captures shared knowledge about the rules, norms, and values that shape employee attitudes and behaviors.

30.(A)Functional

31.(D)Problem Solving Method

Explanation: Appreciative Inquiry is a method of problem solving that was pioneered by ***David Cooperrider.*** It is primarily an organizational development method which focuses on increasing what an organization does well rather than on eliminating what it does badly.

32.(C)Organization structure

Explanation: Replacement chart:

- Replacement charts are a human resource forecasting technique that describes a firm's organization structure in terms of individuals who occupy various managerial and professional positions.

- For each position the incumbent and potential replacements are identified along with information such as potential for advancement, experience or skills needed to qualify for next position, gender (for aid in diversity planning), and age (only for retirement planning).
- Replacement charts should be computerized and provide a description of how vacancies can be filled by a firm's internal labor markets.
- They should be updated annually or when changes in strategic directions occur.
- Updates should be guided by ongoing assessments of potential replacements – matching their current knowledge, skills, abilities, and other characteristics against not only present position requirements but also those needed to meet anticipated future needs of the position.
- Assessments should include KSAOs needed for horizontal as well as vertical moves. The former require more broad-based experience and responsibilities, often of a cross-functional nature, to meet the needs of today's flatter structures.
- Before the number of qualified replacements for a current or future position can be determined, a method of comparing potential replacement candidates with the position's requirements is needed.

Organization structure:

- The typically hierarchical arrangement of lines of authority, communications, rights and duties of an organization.
- Organizational structure determines how the roles, power and responsibilities are assigned, controlled, and coordinated, and how information flows between the different levels of management.
- A structure depends on the organization's objectives and strategy.
- In a centralized structure, the top layer of management has most of the decision making power and has tight control over departments and divisions.
- In a decentralized structure, the decision making power is distributed and the departments and divisions may have different degrees of independence.
- An organizational chart illustrates the organizational structure.

Manpower inventory : Manpower inventory is the record of staffs in a commercial organisation.

33.(C)T – group

Explanation:

- **A T-group** or training group also referred to as **sensitivity-training group, human relations training group** or **encounter group** is a form of group psychotherapy where participants themselves learn about themselves through their interaction with each other.
- They use feedback, problem solving, and role play to gain insights into themselves, others, and groups.
- **Mutuality:** Having the same relationship each to the other.
- **Sociometry:** It is a quantitative method for measuring social relationships. It was developed by psychotherapist ***Jacob L. Moreno.***
- **Simulation** is the imitation of the operation of a real-world process or system over time.

34.(B) the forces operating within the group

Explanation:

- Group dynamics means the action of a group engaged in a common endeavor.
- The word dynamics comes from the Greek word meaning force.
- The phrase Group Dynamics thus means a study of cohesive and disruptive force operating within a group.
- The group dynamics will be structured around the three key elements such as basic

element of group behaviour, group cohesiveness and the group structure. These three basic elements generally of use in understanding the behavior of a group are activities, interactions and sentiments.

35.(D)None of the above

Explanation: When discussing ***social groups***, a group is said to be in a state of cohesion when its members possess bonds linking them to one another and to the group as a whole. Members of strongly cohesive groups are more inclined to participate readily and to stay with the group.

36.(B)Forming-Storming-Norming-Performing

Explanation: Stages of Group development: Bruce W. Tuckman

1. **Forming:** Group members learn about each other, and the task at hand. Indicators of this stage might include: unclear objectives, confusion, and low morale.
2. **Storming:** As group members continue to work, they will engage each other in arguments about the structure of the group which often are significantly emotional and illustrate a struggle for status in the group. Lack of cohesion marks this phase.
3. **Norming:** Group members establish implicit or explicit rules about how they will achieve their goal. They address the types of communication that will or will not help with the task. Indicators include: Questioning performance, Reviewing/ clarify objective, Changing/confirming roles, Opening risky issues, Assertiveness, Listening, Testing new ground, Identifying strengths and weaknesses.
4. **Performing:** Groups reach a conclusion and implement the conclusion. Indicators include: Creativity, Initiative, Flexibility, and Open relationships.
5. **Adjourning:** This, the final stage of team development, is sometimes called 'mourning'. The process of "unforming" the group, that is, letting go of the group structure and moving on.

Remember: FSNPA

37.(D)Kurt Lewin

Explanation:

Sensitivity training: Training designed to make people more aware of group dynamics and their own behavior, interpersonal traits, and role within a group. Based on the work of ***Kurt Levin and Ronald Lippit***, it also forms a part of the 'human potential development' movement.

38.(B)Balance theory

Explanation:

Balance theory:

- The theory as proposed by ***Theodore Newcomb*** states that "persons are attracted to one another on the basis of similar attitudes towards commonly relevant objects and goals.
- Once a relationship is formed, it strives to maintain a symmetrical balance between the attraction and the common attitudes.
- If an imbalance occurs, attempts are made to restore the balance.
- If the balance cannot be restored, the relationship dissolves".

Exchange theory:

- This theory is based on reward -cost outcomes of interaction between people.
- To be attracted towards a group, a person thinks in terms of what he will get in exchange of interaction with the group members.
- Thus, there is an exchange relationship in terms of rewards and costs of associating with the group.

Propinquity theory: The propinquity theory explains a basic factor, i.e., proximity of people at the workplace, which leads to formation of groups.

39.(D)All the above

Explanation:

Group norms: Unspoken and often unwritten set of informal rules that govern individual behaviors in a group. Group norms vary based on the group and issues important to the group. Without group norms, individuals would have no understanding of how to act in social situations.

40.(D)Informal groups provide safety valve for employee emotions.

Explanation:

Formal Groups:

- Formal groups are created and maintained to fulfill needs or tasks which are related to the total organisation mission.
- These are consciously and deliberately created.
- Such groups may be either permanent in the form of top management team such as board of directors or management committees, work units in the various departments of the organisation, staff groups providing specialised services to the organisation, and so on; or the formal groups may be constituted on temporary basis for fulfilling certain specified objectives.
- The working of formal groups is regulated by organisational rules and regulations.

Informal Group:

- Informal groups are created in the organisation because of operation of social and psychological forces operating at the work-place.
- Members create such groups for their own satisfaction and their working is not regulated by the general framework of organisational rules and regulations.
- Groups which emerge naturally due to the response and common interests of the members of an organization who can easily identify with the goals or independent activities of the group.

41.(B)Decentralisation

Explanation: Decentralization is the process of redistributing or dispersing functions, powers, people or things away from a central location or authority.

42.(B)consensus

Explanation: Consensus planning tool, generally used by groups to discuss, debate and decide on issues of strength-identification, problems and solutions.

43.(A)formal groups

Explanation:

- **Formal groups:** Deliberately created to perform a specific task.
- **Informal groups:** Also called a **clique,** is a neither formally structured, nor organizationally determined. This may be a group of friends, like-minded people, etc. created by themselves.
- **A task group:** Temporarily formal group that is created to solve specific problems.
- **An interest group:** It is made up of individuals who affiliate to achieve an objective of mutual interest that may have nothing to do with their formal task group memberships.

44.(B)conforming to group norms

45.(C)Large group size

Explanation: Group cohesiveness:

- "The resultant of all the forces acting on members to remain in the group."
- Group cohesiveness is the 'stick togetherness' of the group, its peanut butter.
- Group cohesiveness provides the bonds that hold a group together.
- It is a stumbling block to change.

46.(C)Team characteristics

Explanation: Team characteristics summarize the qualities that teams possess, such as their norms, their roles, and the way members depend on one another.

47.(D)Team processes

Explanation: Team processes summarize how teams behave, including their coordination, conflict, and cohesion.

48.(D) Can be defined simply as activities that occur regularly

Explanation: Organizational structure:

- An organizational structure consists of activities such as task allocation, coordination and supervision, which are directed towards the achievement of organizational aims.
- It can also be considered as the viewing glass or perspective through which individuals see their organization and its environment.

49.(A)How activities are coordinated and controlled

50. (A)Control

Explanation: Organizational structure

- The typically hierarchical arrangement of lines of authority, communications, rights and duties of an organization.
- Organizational structure determines how the roles, power and responsibilities are assigned, controlled, and coordinated, and how information flows between the different levels of management.
- A structure depends on the organization's objectives and strategy.
- In a centralized structure, the top layer of management has most of the decision making power and has tight control over departments and divisions.
- In a decentralized structure, the decision making power is distributed and the departments and divisions may have different degrees of independence.
- An organizational chart illustrates the organizational structure.

51. (C)Matrix organization

Explanation:

Line organization:

- This is the oldest form of organization.
- This is known by different names, i.e. military, vertical, scalar, departmental, organization.
- All other types of organization structure have mostly been either modifications of this organization.
- The concept of line organization holds that in any organization derived from a scalar process, there must be a single head who commands it.

Line and staff organization

- A manager today cannot hope to think of all possible factors in a given situation. Therefore, he has a set of expert advisers.
- Those functions which have direct responsibility for accomplishing the major objectives of the firm are called line functions.
- The staff functions are supposed to help and assist the line in discharging their responsibility.
- The staff position established as a measure of support for the line organization may be of personal staff, specialized staff and general staff.

Functional Organization

- Whole task of management and direction of subordinates should be divided according to the type of the work involved.
- The functional management carries this idea to its logical limit and divides up management into a number of functions such as production, sales, finance and personae, and research and development etc.
- Each of these departments would serve its best for the organization.

Formal organization and Informal Organization:

- "A Network of personal and social relation not established or required by the formal organization but arising spontaneously as people associate with one another."

Matrix organization:

- Developed at the US National Aeronautics & Space Administration (NASA) in association with its suppliers, this structure gets its name from its resemblance to a table (matrix) where every element is included in a row as well as a column.
- An organizational structure that facilitates the horizontal flow of skills and information.
- It is used mainly in the management of large projects or product development processes, drawing employees from different functional disciplines for assignment to a team without removing them from their respective positions.
- Employees in a matrix organization report on day-to-day performance to the project or product manager whose authority flows sideways (horizontally) across departmental boundaries.
- They also continue to report on their overall performance to the head of their department whose authority flows downwards (vertically) within his or her department.
- In addition to a multiple command and control structure, a matrix organization necessitates new support mechanisms, organizational culture, and behavior patterns.

52. (A)Top to bottom

53.(B)Matrix organisation

54.(A)for a single area of activity

Explanation:

- A functional manager is a person who has management authority over an organizational unit - such as a department - within a business, company, or other organization.
- For functional management, communication generally occurs within a single department.
- Functional managers have ongoing responsibilities, and are not usually directly affiliated with project teams, other than ensuring that goals and objectives are aligned with the organization's overall strategy and vision.
- In both traditional and matrix organizations, the control of the resources is centered around the functional managers, essentially putting project managers at a disadvantage when bargaining about staffing arrangements.
- Additionally, in such organizations, Project managers usually report to functional managers, who report to senior management.

55.(B)Scalar Organization

56.(D)Specialization

Explanation: Advantages of functional organization:

- It ensures a greater division of labour
- It improves the efficiency of the organization.
- It brings specialization and innovations.
- It facilitates mass production.

57.(C)Tall

58.(D)Advisory

59.(C)Unity of Command

60.(B)Role conflict

Explanation:

Role ambiguity:

- A lack of clarity about expected behavior from a job or position.
- Role Ambiguity - norms for a specific position are vague, unclear and ill-defined.
- Actors disagree on role expectations, not because there is role conflict but because role expectations are unclear.
- Examples: job descriptions, clinical objectives.

Role conflict:

- A situation in which a person is expected to play two incompatible roles.
- For example, a boss will suffer role conflict if forced to fire an employee who is also a close friend.
- Demands placed by an employee's job/role that are incompatible with his or her personality or skills.

Role perception:

- The absence of a distinctly defined role of employees and an amorphous perception of their roles and responsibilities in the organization may have a downturn effect on the employees' morale and self-esteem.
- Role Perception of the employees acts as one of the most critical components in the workplaces today.
- It also plays a key role in an individual's performance.
- A misty perception of the role may also lead to underperformance by and underutilization of the potential of the individual.
- Consequently, the organization may lose not only some vital man-hours but also some of the most competent employees, in the long run.
- It is, therefore, in the organization's interest to provide a clearly-defined role to every employee as a step towards combating the ever-increasing competition in the global milieu.

Role expectation:

- A role expectation is what you are expected to do depending on what role you obtain.
- Every role has expectations.

61.(A)Brain storming

Explanation: Brainstorming is a group or individual creativity technique by which efforts are made to find a conclusion for a specific problem by gathering a list of ideas spontaneously contributed by its members. The term was popularized by ***Alex Faickney Osborn*** in the book "Applied Imagination".

62. (D)Change agent

Explanation: A change agent is an event, organization, material thing or, more usually, a person that acts as a catalyst for change. In business terms, a change agent is a person chosen to bring about organizational change. Corporations often hire senior managers or even chief executives because of their ability to effect change.

63.(A) Unfreezing – Moving – Freezing

Explanation: Kurt Lewin's change model:

- **Unfreezing:** Process by which people become aware of the need for change. Unfreezing can be achieved by Increasing driving forces that direct behavior away from the status quo and decrease restraining forces that hinder movement from the existing equilibrium.
- **Moving or Changing:** Developing new attitudes, values and behaviors. Movement from the old way of doing things to a new way.
- **Refreezing:** Reinforcing new values, attitudes and behaviors. Process of making new behaviors relatively permanent and resistant to further change.

64.(C)Refreezing

65.(A)Kurt Lewin

66.(D)"calm waters"

Explanation:

- The calm waters view of organizational change envisions the organization as a large ship crossing a calm sea.
- The ship's captain and crew know exactly where they are going because they have made the trip many times before. Change comes in the form of an occasional storm, a brief distraction in an otherwise calm and predictable trip.
- In the calm waters metaphor, change is seen as an occasional disruption in the normal flow of events.
- It is best illustrated by Kurt Lewin's 3-step description of the change process.

- According to Lewin, successful change can be planned and requires unfreezing the status quo, changing to a new state, and refreezing to make the change permanent.
- The status quo can be considered an equilibrium state.
- To move from this equilibrium, unfreezing is necessary.
- Lewin's 3-step process treats change as a move away from the organization's current equilibrium state.
- It is a calm waters scenario where an occasional disruption means changing to deal with the disruption.
- Once the disruption has been dealt with, however, things can continue on under the new changed situation.

67.(D)restraining

68.(A)unfreezing

69.(D)preparing for the needed change

70.(D)stabilizes the new situation

71.(B)white-water rapids metaphor

Explanation:

- White-water rapids metaphor takes into consideration the fact that environments are both uncertain and dynamic.
- The stability and predictability of the calm waters do not exist. Many of today's managers never get out of the rapids.
- They are facing constant change, bordering on chaos.
- Many of today's managers are being forced to play a game that they have never played before that is governed by rules created as the game progresses.
- White-water rapids metaphor is not merely an overstatement because many of today's managers are facing it.
- Managers who are working for companies in industries like computer software and women's fashion have long confronted with a world of white-water rapids.

72. (C)a continual process

73.(A)Demographic

Explanation: Demographic change as a statistic characterizing human populations (or segments of human populations broken down by age or sex or income etc.)

74.(D)Every manager's job

75.(C)labor markets

76.(A)technology

77.(D)workforce

78.(D)the internal operations of the organization

79.(D)strategy

80. (B)workforce

81. (C)employee attitudes

82.(B)occasional; continuous

83. (B)change agents

84. (A)drastic; thoughtful

85. (C)improving their organization's performance

86.(D)putting the change process in motion

87.(D)mission, environment, and process

88. (A)technology

89.(D)structure

90. (A)a structural design change

91. (D)employees

92. (A)technology

93.(B)people

94.(B)increased productivity

95. (A)programmed responses

96.(C)change is incompatible with the interests of the organization

97.(B)diversification

Explanation:

Diversification: Diversification strives to smooth out unsystematic risk events in a portfolio so that the positive performance of some investments will neutralize the negative performance of others. Therefore, the benefits of diversification will hold only if the securities in the portfolio are not perfectly correlated.

98.(A) education

99.(D) Negotiation

Explanation:

- Negotiation is a dialogue between two or more people or parties, intended to reach an understanding, resolve point of difference, or gain advantage in outcome of dialogue, to produce an agreement upon courses of action, to bargain for individual or collective advantage, to craft outcomes to satisfy various interests of two people/parties involved in negotiation process.
- Negotiation is a process where each party involved in negotiating tries to gain an advantage for themselves by the end of the process.
- Negotiation is intended to aim at compromise.

100. (B)Coercion

101. (B)Culture tends to be very resistant to change.

102. (C)stock prices remain constant

103. (D)there is a leadership change

104. (B)Redesign socialization processes to align with the new values.

105. (C)overworked and stressed out

106. (A)a new competitive product

107. (C)All mangers

108. (A)Change management

Explanation:

Change management: Change management is an approach to transitioning individuals, teams, and organizations to a desired future state. In some project management contexts, change management refers to a project management process wherein changes to a project are formally introduced and approved.

109. (B)Forcing

110. (D)(iv) (v) (ii) (i) (iii)

111. (C)Change Agent

112. (B)Learning organisation

Explanation: A learning organization is the term given to a company that facilitates the learning of its members and continuously transforms itself. Learning organizations develop as a result of the pressures facing modern organizations and enables them to remain competitive in the business environment.

113. (C)cost efficient

114. (C)increase the role of individual employees

115. (D)shelters breakthroughs

116. (C)survey feedback

Explanation:

Team building:

- Team building is a philosophy of job design in which employees are viewed as members of interdependent teams instead of as individual workers.

Intergroup development:

- Inter-group Team building intervention intends to increase communications and interactions between work related groups to reduce the amount of dysfunctional competition and to replace a parochial independent point of view with an awareness of the necessity for interdependence of action calling on the best efforts of both the groups.
- Inter-group interventions are integrated into Organizational Development programs to facilitate cooperation and efficiency between different groups within an organization.
- Conflict resolution meetings are one common inter-group intervention.

Survey feedback:

- The intervention provides data and information to the managers.

- Information on Attitudes of employees about wage level, and structure, hours of work, working conditions and relations are collected and the results are supplied to the top executive teams.
- They analyse the data, find out the problem, evaluate the results and develop the means to correct the problems identified.
- The team are formed with the employees at all levels in the organization hierarchy i.e, from the rank and file to the top level.

117. (C)Process consultation

Explanation: Process Consultation:

- The process consultant meets the members of the department and work teams observes this interaction, problem identification skills, solving procedures etc.
- He feeds back the team with the information collected through observations, coaches and counsels individuals & groups in moulding their behavior.

Goal setting and planning:

- Each division in an organization sets the goals or formulates the plans for profitability.
- These goals are sent to the top management which in turn sends them back to the divisions after modification.
- A set of organization goals thus emerge thereafter.

Managerial grid:

- This identifies a range of management behavior based on the different ways that how production/service oriented and employee oriented states interact with each other.
- Managerial grid is also called as instrumental laboratory training as it is a structured version of laboratory training.
- It consists of individual and group exercises with a view to developing awareness of individual managerial style interpersonal competence and group effeciveness.
- Thus grid training is related to the leadership styles.
- The managerial grid focuses on the observations of behaviour in exercises specifically related to work.
- Participants in this training are encouraged and helped to appraise their own managerial style.

Sensitivity training:

- The most commonly used Organizational Development intervention is sensitivity training.
- It is called laboratory training as it is conducted by creating an experimental laboratory situation in which employees are brought together, in groups, to interact in an unstructured environment.
- The members are encouraged to interact with new members and new individual behaviors.

118. (B)intergroup development

119. (A)cultural characteristics

120. (B)organizational development

121. (A) It is a planned change

Explanation: Organization Development

- Organization Development (OD) is a planned process of change in an organization's culture through the utilization of behavioral science technology, research, and theory.
- OD refers to a long-range effort to improve an organization's problem-solving capabilities and its ability to cope with changes in its external environment with the help of external or internal behavioral-scientist consultants.
- OD is an effort: Planned, organization-wide, and managed from the top, to increase organization effectiveness and health through planned interventions in the organization's "processes," using behavioral science knowledge.

- Organization Development is a system wise application and transfer of behavioral science knowledge to the planned development, improvement, and reinforcement of the strategies, structures, and processes that lead to organization effectiveness.

122. (B)MBO

Explanation: Management by Objective:

- The process of setting objectives in the organization to give a sense of direction to the employees is called as Management by Objectives.
- It refers to the process of setting goals for the employees so that they know what they are supposed to do at the workplace.
- Management by Objectives defines roles and responsibilities for the employees and help them chalk out their future course of action in the organization.
- Management by objectives guides the employees to deliver their level best and achieve the targets within the stipulated time frame.

123. (A)It is not a top management led and supported process.

124. (C)Kurt Lewin

Explanation: Action research:

- Action research is a research initiated to solve an immediate problem or a reflective process of progressive problem solving led by individuals working with others in teams or as part of a "community of practice" to improve the way they address issues and solve problems.
- There are two types of action research: participatory action research, and practical action research.
- Action research involves the process of actively participating in an organization change situation whilst conducting research.
- Action research can also be undertaken by larger organizations or institutions, assisted or guided by professional researchers, with the aim of improving their strategies, practices and knowledge of the environments within which they practice.
- As designers and stakeholders, researchers work with others to propose a new course of action to help their community improve its work practices.
- ***Kurt Lewin*** coined the term "action research" in his paper "Action Research and Minority Problems" he described action research as "a comparative research on the conditions and effects of various forms of social action and research leading to social action" that uses "a spiral of steps, each of which is composed of a circle of planning, action and fact-finding about the result of the action".

125. (B)Transactional Analysis

126. (A)(d)(a) (c)(b)

127. (C)Action Research

128. (D)Carl Roger

Explanation: Carl Rogers Self Theory of Personality is a part of the Humanist School of Psychological Thought. It is based on the idea that human beings need a genuine environment where they can open, unconditionally accepted, and understood in order to fully realize their potential.

129. (A)A. Adler

130. (A)20 + needs:Murray

Explanation: 3 traits given by Eysenck and 16 traits given by Cattel and 20 traits by Murray.

131. (D)Personality and cultural values.

Explanation: Personality and cultural values affect the way people behave at work, the kinds of tasks they're interested in, and how they react to events that happen on the job.

132. (A)Ability

Explanation: Ability describes the cognitive abilities, emotional skills, and physical abilities that employees bring to a job.

133. (B)Ability

Explanation: Ability influences the kinds of tasks an employee is good at and those with which an employee may struggle.

134. (B)Psychodynamic theory

Explanation: Psychodynamic Theory:

- In psychology, a psychodynamic theory is a view that explains personality in terms of conscious and unconscious forces, such as unconscious desires and beliefs.
- Sigmund Freud proposed a psychodynamic theory according to which personality consists of the id (responsible for instincts and pleasure-seeking), the superego (which attempts to obey the rules of parents and society), and the ego (which mediates between them according to the demands of reality).
- Psychodynamic theories commonly hold that childhood experiences shape personality. Such theories are associated with psychoanalysis, a type of therapy that attempts to reveal unconscious thoughts and desires.

135. (C)Theory- X

136. (D)All the above

137. (C)Rationalisation

138. (B)Prescriptive style

Explanation:

Prescriptive Leadership style:

- Leaders with a notably forceful personality who have the time and energy to micromanage will likely be inclined towards prescriptive leadership.
- Prescriptive leadership theories describe what a leader must do to become effective and have a rather formulaic approach to effective management.
- Prescriptive leaders determine what kind of behavior is best for a situation and stick with it.

139. (B)Machiavellism

140. (B)Self awareness, self knowledge and self understanding

Explanation: Emotional Intelligence:

- Emotional intelligence (EI) is the ability to identify, assess, and control the emotions of oneself, of others, and of groups.
- It can be divided into ability EI and trait EI.
- Criticisms have centered on whether EI is a real intelligence and whether it has incremental validity over IQ and the Big Five personality traits.

141. (D)Personality

Explanation: Transactional Analysis (TA):

- Transactional analysis is an integrative approach to the theory of psychology and psychotherapy.
- It is described as integrative because it has elements of psychoanalytic, humanist and cognitive approaches. TA was first developed by Eric Berne.

142. (A)Halo Effect

Explanation: Halo Effect:

- The halo effect is a term used in marketing to explain the bias shown by customers towards certain products because of a favorable experience with other products made by the same manufacturer or maker.
- Basically, the halo effect is driven by brand equity. The opposite of the halo effect is "cannibalization".

143. (C)Perception

Explanation: Figure – Ground Theory:

- Figure–ground organization is a type of perceptual grouping which is a vital necessity for recognizing objects through vision.
- In Gestalt psychology it is known as identifying a figure from the background.

144. (A)Perception

Explanation: Perception :

- "The study of perception is concerned with identifying the process through which we interpret and organize sensory information to produce our conscious experience of objects and object relationship."
- "Perception is the process of receiving information about and making sense of the world around us. It involves deciding which information to notice, how to categorize this information and how to interpret it within the framework of existing knowledge.
- "A process by which individuals organize and interpret their sensory impressions in order to give meaning to their environment.
- Perception is the act of seeing what is there to be seen.

145. (B)Group belief

Explanation: Organization value:

- Values are the standards that guide our conduct in a variety of settings.
- An organization's values might be thought of as a moral compass for its business practices.
- While circumstances may change, ideally values do not.
- Vision and mission statements provide direction, focus, and energy to accomplish shared goals.
- Values express the integrity that individuals and organizations believe in.
- They serve as a decision-making tool in daily interactions that guide behavior.

146. (C)Trust

147. (D)Personality and cultural values

Explanation: Personality and cultural values reflect the various traits and tendencies that describe how people act, with commonly studied traits including extraversion, conscientiousness, and collectivism.

148. (C)different for the various components of a diverse work force

149. (A)Hardworking, sincerity, rationality and self-discipline.

Explanation:

- Instrumental Values are core values, permanent in nature, comprise personal characteristics and character traits.
- Instrumental values refer to preferable modes of behaviour and include values like honesty, sincerity, ambition, independence, obedience, imaginativeness, courageousness, competitiveness.

150. (B) observing people's behaviour

151. (B)Pavlov

Explanation: Classical Conditioning (Pavlov)

- Classical conditioning is a reflexive or automatic type of learning in which a stimulus acquires the capacity to evoke a response that was originally evoked by another stimulus.
- Originators and Key Contributors: First described by Ivan Pavlov in 1903, and studied in infants by John B. Watson.
- ***Keywords:*** stimulus-response, psychic reflexes, unconditioned stimulus, conditioned response, respondent conditioning
- In Classical Conditioning (Ivan Pavlov) Several types of learning exist. The most basic form is associative learning, i.e., making a new association between events in the environment.
- There are two forms of associative learning: classical conditioning (made famous by Ivan Pavlov's experiments with dogs) and operant conditioning.

152. (A)Repetition

Explanation: Classical conditioning :

A process of behavior modification by which a subject comes to respond in a desired manner to a previously neutral stimulus that has been repeatedly presented along with an unconditioned stimulus that elicits the desired response.

153. (C) (iii) (ii) (i)

154. (D)All the above

155. (A)latency period

156. (C)Hull's

157. (B)(iii) (ii) (v) (i)

158. (A)Classical conditioning

159. (C)Formulation and implementation of ideas takes place at all levels of organization

Explanation: Learning organization:

- Organization that acquires knowledge and innovates fast enough to survive and thrive in a rapidly changing environment.
- Learning organizations create a culture that encourages and supports continuous employee learning, critical thinking, and risk taking with new ideas.
- Allow mistakes, and value employee contributions.
- Learn from experience and experiment.
- Disseminate the new knowledge throughout the organization for incorporation into day-to-day activities.

160. (D)Chris Argyris

Explanation: The single loop and double loop learning models:

- The work of Chris Argyris describes the concept of double-loop learning (DLL) in which an individual, organization or entity is able, having attempted to achieve a goal on different occasions, to modify the goal in the light of experience or possibly even reject the goal.
- Single-loop learning (SLL) is the repeated attempt at the same problem, with no variation of method and without ever questioning the goal.

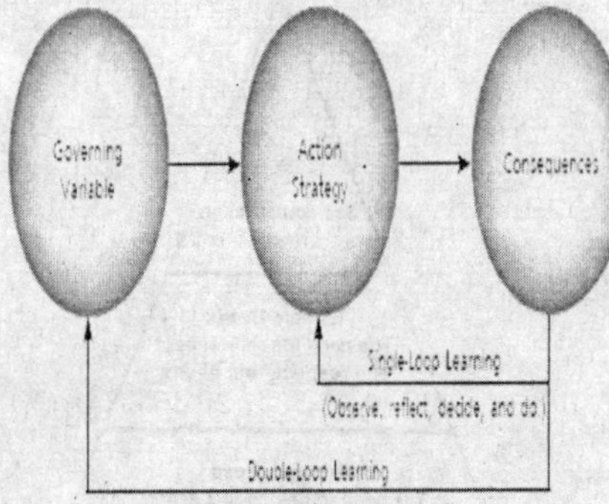

161. (C)(iii) (iv) (i) (ii)

162. (B)Negative Reinforcement

163. (C) Learning and decision making

Explanation: Learning and decision making deals with how employees gain job knowledge and how they use that knowledge to make accurate judgments on the job.

164. (C)(iii) (iv) (i) (ii)

165. (C)is not reinforced for a long time

Explanation:

- Extinction is observed in both operantly conditioned and classically conditioned behavior.
- When operant behavior that has been previously reinforced no longer produces reinforcing consequences the behavior gradually stops occurring.

166. (B)Complementary Transactions

167. (B)Abraham Maslow

Explanation:

- Abraham Maslow's book on motivation and personality emphasizes multiplicity of human needs are arranged in an order.
- Maslow's theory consisted of two parts:

  (1) The classification of human needs, and

  (2) Workers are not just motivated by money but also by having their human/social needs met.

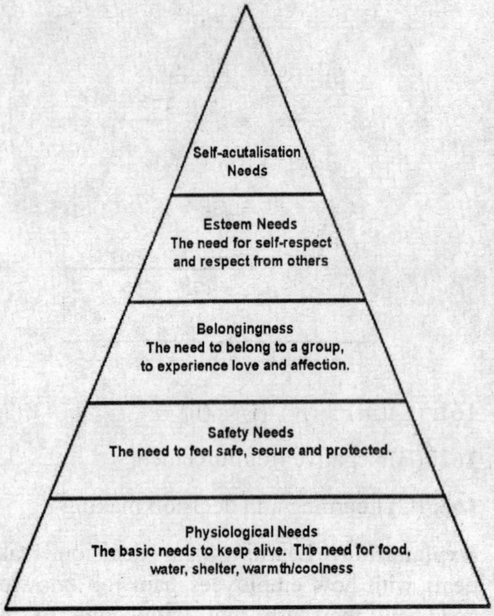

168. (D)(ii), (iv), (i), (v) and (iii)

169. (A)Security, Affiliation, Esteem

170. (C)Physiological.safety.social.esteem.self-actualization

171. (B) Social

172. (A)Frederick Herberg

Explanation:

- Herzberg's Two Factor Theory is a "content theory" of motivation"
- Needs priority, to a great extent, characterizes the types of behavior.

Hygien or Maintenance factors:

1. Fair co-policy and administration
2. Supervisor knows the work
3. Supervisors relationship
4. Peers relationship
5. Fair salary
6. Job security
7. Subordinates relationship
8. Personal life
9. Status
10. Good working condition

- Concerned basically with job environment.
- Extrinsic to the work itself.
- Leads to High Job dissatisfaction
- The maintenance seekers tend to be more concerned with factors surrounding the job such as supervision; working conditions, pay etc.

Motivators:

- Factors that give satisfaction (feeling of achievement, significance of growth).

1. Opportunity to accomplish something significant.
2. Recognition.
3. Chance for development
4. Opportunity to grow
5. Chance for increased responsibility
6. The job/work itself

- Motivators or Growth Factors - concerned with job content. Intrinsic to the work itself.
- Leads to High Job satisfaction
- The motivation seekers generally are individuals who are primarily motivated by the satisfier's such as advancement, achievement and other factors associated with work itself.

173. (D)McGregor

Explanation:

- **McGregor** argued that the style of Management adopted is a function of the manager's attitudes towards human nature and behaviour at work.
- He put forward two suppositions called Theory X and Theory Y which are based on popular assumptions about work and people.
- Douglas Mc. Gregore has classified the prevalent theories into two groups:

1. Traditional or Theory-X

2. Modern or Theory-Y.

Traditional or Theory-X

- It completely excludes workers from the process of managerial decision making the theory stress that would here only when forced to do so through ruthless exercise of managerial authority over them through constant rebuking scolding reprimanding.
- Decisions whether right or wrong have to be made by managers only, the only rule assigned to workers being to mainly incline the decision.

Assumptions of Theory-X

1. Lack of inclination to work.
2. Fears can alone force action.
3. Inbuilt dislike for responsibility
4. Living – off others.
5. Obession with security.
6. Money alone can make the people to work.
7. Labour is only a factor of production.
8. Authority is synonymous with control.

Modern theory or Theory-Y

- It is the exact opposite of theory X, it gives workers a pride of place in the process of management.
- It emphasis fuel and active cooperation, between workers and management to accomplish the enterprise objectives as per theory if workers are properly maturated, they would willingly accept responsibility and show the sense of creativity and imagination in their work performance.
- It can be said to be positive and optimistic outlook.
- Managers take a more positive approach and assume that employees are able to achieve organizational objectives out of their own accord and initiative.
- They believe that workers can gain satisfaction from work and that they are able to take on responsibility.

Assumptions of Theory- Y

1. Work is reward in itself
2. Inherent sense of responsibility
3. Recognition.
4. Sense of security.
5. Financial reward is not the only inspiration.
6. Decision – making ability is not the monopoly
7. Democratically inclined

174. (A)Salary

175. (B)Reasonable salary

Explanation: Hygiene Factors:

- Hygiene factors are based on the need to for a business to avoid unpleasantness at work.
- If these factors are considered inadequate by employees, then they can cause dissatisfaction with work.
- Hygiene factors include:
  - Company policy and administration
  - Wages, salaries and other financial remuneration
  - Quality of supervision
  - Quality of inter-personal relations
  - Working conditions
  - Feelings of job security

176. (B) Working conditions

Explanation: Motivator Factors

- Motivator factors are based on an individual's need for personal growth.
- When they exist, motivator factors actively create job satisfaction. If they are effective, then they can motivate an individual to achieve above-average performance and effort.
- Motivator factors include:
  - Status
  - Opportunity for advancement
  - Gaining recognition

- Responsibility
- Challenging / stimulating work
- Sense of personal achievement & personal growth in a job

177. (A)Salary

178. (C)Job Security

179. (C)The Assertion distinguishes hygiene factors from motivational factors thereby justifying the Reason.

180. (D)Existence, Relatedness and Growth

Explanation: Alderfer's ERG theory

- To bring Maslow's need hierarchy theory of motivation in synchronization with empirical research, ***Clayton Alderfer*** redefined it in his own terms.
- His rework is called as ERG theory of motivation.
- He re-categorized Maslow's hierarchy of needs into three simpler and broader classes of needs:

1. **Existence needs:** Desire for physiological and material well-being. These include need for basic material necessities. In short, it includes an individual's physiological and physical safety needs.
2. **Relatedness needs:** Desire for satisfying interpersonal relationships. These include the aspiration individual's have for maintaining significant interpersonal relationships (be it with family, peers or superiors), getting public fame and recognition.

   Maslow's social needs and external component of esteem needs fall under this class of need.
3. **Growth needs:** Desire for continued personal growth and development. These include need for self-development and personal growth and advancement. Maslow's self-actualization needs and intrinsic component of esteem needs fall under this category of need.

181. (B) ERG theory

182. (A)Achievement motivation

Explanation: McClelland Achievement theory

- Employees with a high need for achievement derive satisfaction from achieving goals.
- The employees exhibiting the need for power derive satisfaction from the ability to control others.
- Individuals exhibiting need for affiliation derive satisfaction from social and interpersonal activities.
- The essence of McClelland's model is that individual needs along with congential work environment can create motivation and satisfaction.

1. **Need for achievement:** The desire to do something better or more efficiently, to solve problems, or to master complex tasks. Need for achievement must be given challenging tasks.
2. **Need for affiliation:** The desire to establish and maintain friendly and warm relations with others. Need for affiliation should be given opportunities to manage and lead a team of people. It should be provided with a cooperative working environment in order to gain their:

   Work Preferences: Prefers moderately challenging goals, Prefers performance feedback, Prefers individual responsibility
3. **Need for power:** The desire to control others, to influence their behavior, or to be responsible for others.

   Conclusion: McClelland's main contribution is that people with different kinds of needs are motivated differently.

183. (D)All the above

184. (D)McClelland

185. (C)Vroom's Expectancy Theory

Explanation:

- **Content theories:** Focus on profiling the needs that people seek to fulfill.
- **Process theories:** Focus on people's thought or cognitive processes. Emphasize controlling behavior by manipulating its consequences.

186. (D)None of the above

Explanation:

Process theories: Focus on people's thought or cognitive processes. Emphasize controlling behavior by manipulating its consequences.

- Goal Setting theory
- Vroom's Expectancy theory
- Porters Performance satisfaction model
- Adams Equity theory

187. (C)Vroom

Explanation: Vroom's Expectancy theory

- The expectancy theory of motivation given by ***Victor H. Vroom.***
- People will be motivated to do things to reach a goal if they believe in the worth of that goal and if they can see that what they do will help them in achieve it.
- Vroom makes the point that motivate is a product of the anticipated worth that an individual places on a goal and the chances of achieving that goal.
- This theory states that workers will only act when they have a reasonable expectation that their work will lead to the desired outcome.
- They need to believe that they possess the necessary ability and skill to achieve the given goal.
- Expectancy theory predicts that employees in an organization will be motivated when they believe that: putting in more effort will yield better job performance
- Better job performance will lead to organizational rewards, such as an increase in salary or benefits these predicted organizational rewards are valued by the employee in question.

FORCE=VALENCE X EXPECTANCY

- **Force:** Strength of the person motivation.
- **Valence:** Strength of an individual preference for an outcome.
- **Expectancy**: Probability that a particular action will lead to a desired outcomes.

Merits of Vroom's Theory

- It recognizes the importance of various individual needs and motivations.
- It fits the concept of harmony of objectives
- It is completely consistent with the system of management by objectives.

Demerits of Vroom's Theory

- Perception of value varies among individuals at different times and in various places.
- Difficulty to apply the practice.

Conclusion

- The relationship between people's behavior at work and their goals was not as simple as was first imagined by other scientists.
- Vroom realized that an employee's performance is based on individuals factors such as personality, skills, knowledge, experience and abilities.
- In order to enhance performance managers should use reward systems that tie rewards very closely to performance.

188. (C) Valence × Expectancy

189. (B) Victor Vroom

190. (C)Porter's performance satisfaction theory

191. (A) Motivation

Explanation: Motivation captures the energetic forces that drive employees' work effort.

192. (A)Douglas Mc Gregor

Explanation: Hot-Stove Rule

- The "Hot-Stove Rule" of Douglas McGregor gives a good illustration of how to impose disciplinary action without generating resentment.
- This rule draws an analogy between touching a hot stove, and undergoing discipline.

193. (D)Festinger and Homans

Explanation: Cognitive Dissonance' theory of motivation:

- Festinger's (1957) cognitive dissonance theory suggests that we have an inner drive to hold all our attitudes and beliefs in harmony and avoid disharmony (or dissonance).
- Cognitive dissonance refers to a situation involving conflicting attitudes, beliefs or behaviors.
- This produces a feeling of discomfort leading to an alteration in one of the attitudes, beliefs or behaviors to reduce the discomfort and restore balance etc.

194. (A) (ii) (i) (iv) (iii)

195. (A)Expectancy

196. (A) Maslow

197. (A) it is a significant contributor to high performance

198. (D)benefits are usually based on longevity, not performance

199. (A)less

200. (D)All the above

Explanation: Negative motivation is the type of feeling a person gets when he expects punishment.

201. (D)All the above

202. (D)All the above

203. (A) Vroom's

204. (B)Theory Y

205. (C)Valence

Explanation: Valence – a measure of attraction a given outcome holds for an individual or the satisfaction the person anticipates receiving from a particular outcome. Valence can be positive, negative or zero.

206. (C)Higher goals for themselves

Explanation:

- Self-esteem is the degree to which a person has overall positive feelings about himself or herself.
- People with high self-esteem view themselves in a positive light, are confident, and respect themselves. In contrast, people with low self-esteem experience high levels of self-doubt and question their self-worth.
- High self-esteem is related to higher levels of satisfaction with one's job and higher levels of performance on the job.
- People with low self-esteem are attracted to situations where they will be relatively invisible, such as large companies.

207. (D)Attitude

208. (B)Ouchi

Explanation: Theory " Z ":

- Japanese consensus management style based on the assumptions that:
- (1) employees want to build cooperative relationships with their employers, peers, and other employees in the firm;
- (2)for this they require high degree of support in the form of secure employment and facilities for development of multiple skills through training and job rotation,
- (3) they value family life, culture and traditions, and social institutions as much as material success,
- (4) they have well-developed sense of dedication, moral obligations, and self-discipline, and
- (5) they can make collective decisions through consensus.
- Introduced by the author ***William Ouchi*** in his book 'Theory Z.'

209. (C) (iv) (iii) (ii) (i)

210. (C) Motivation (D) Leadership

Explanation:

- Porter and Lawler used Victor Vroom's expectancy theory as a foundation to develop their expectancy model.
- Similar to Vroom's theory Porter and Lawler concluded that an individual's motivation to complete a task is affected by the reward they expect to receive for completing the task.
- However Porter and Lawler introduced additional aspects to the expectancy theory.
- Porter and Lawler categorised the reward as intrinsic and extrinsic
- Intrinsic rewards are the positive feelings that the individual experiences from completing the task e.g. satisfaction, sense of achievement.
- Extrinsic rewards are rewards emanating from outside the individual such as bonus, commission and pay increases.
- Porter and Lawler's model suggested that an individual's view regarding the attractiveness and fairness of the rewards will affect motivation.

211. (D) All the above

Explanation:

- Emotional intelligence (EI) is the ability to identify, assess, and control the emotions of oneself, of others, and of groups.
- It can be divided into ability EI and trait EI. Criticisms have centered on whether EI is a real intelligence and whether it has incremental validity over IQ and the Big Five personality traits.

212. (D)David

213. (D)Eric Beme

214. (D)(iii) (iv) (i) (ii)

215. (D) Rensis Likert

216. (A)Blake and Mouton

Explanation: Two-Dimensional Managerial Grid:

- A two-dimensional graph or grid that measures the relative importance a leader attaches to the task (measured along the horizontal axis) and the people (measured along the vertical axis).
- A leader who attaches great importance to the task and little importance to the people involved is considered authoritarian.
- A leader who attaches great importance to both the task and the people is considered a good team leader.

217. (C)Drive

218. (C)(iii) (i) (ii) (iv)

219. (D) Leader power and influence.

Explanation: Leader power and influence summarizes the process by which individuals attain authority over others.

220. (A) successful leaders tend to be more intelligent than followers

221. (B)it is likely that a particular set of leader characteristics and behaviors do suit specific situations and groups

222. (A) Leader styles and behaviors

Explanation: Leader styles and behaviors capture the specific actions that leaders take to influence others at work.

223. (A)(ii) (iv) (i) (iii)

224. (C) Work oriented & Dedicated

225. (C)Most of the people do not dislike work inherently.

Explanation: Assumptions of Theory-X:

- Lack of inclination to work.
- Fears can alone force action.
- Inbuilt dislike for responsibility
- Living – off others.
- Obsession with security.
- Money alone can make the people to work.

- Labour is only a factor of production.
- Authority is synonymous with control.

226. (A)Legitimate Power

Explanation:

- **Legitimate Power:** Power derived from a job, position, or status and held as belonging to the person in such a position. Legitimate power refers to actual power to control a country or events. You have the position and authority to maintain control unlike assumed power where you just think you have control but actually do not.
- **Coercive Power:** Authority or power that is dependent on fear, suppression of free will, and/or use of punishment or threat, for its existence.

227. (A)Blake and Monton

Explanation: Task - oriented and people oriented leadership:

- Task-oriented leadership is a behavioral approach in which the leader focuses on the tasks that need to be performed in order to meet certain goals, or to achieve a certain performance standard.
- Relationship-oriented leadership is a behavioral approach in which the leader focuses on the satisfaction, motivation and the general well-being of the team members.

228. (D)Reddin

Explanation: Tridimensional Grid:

- ***Reddin*** conceptualized a three-dimensional grid. It is also known as 3-D management.
- This leadership style borrows some of the ideas from managerial grid.
- Three-dimensional axes represent task-orientation, relationship-orientation and effectiveness.
- By adding an effectiveness dimension to the task-oriented and relationship-oriented behavior dimensions, Reddin has integrated the concept of leadership styles with the situational demand of a specific environment.

229. (C)Does not accept views and suggestions of all

Explanation:

- Autocratic leadership, also known as authoritarian leadership, is a leadership style characterized by individual control over all decisions and little input from group members.
- Autocratic leaders typically make choices based on their own ideas and judgments and rarely accept advice from followers.
- Autocratic leadership involves absolute, authoritarian control over a group.

230. (C)(b) and (c)

231. (C)Authority Obedience

Explanation:

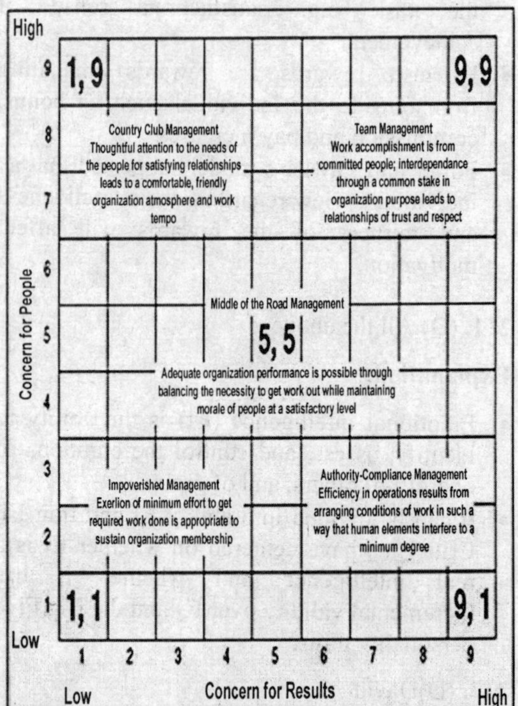

232. (B)Young

233. (C) (iii) (iv) (i)(ii)

234. (A) Theory 'X'

235. (B)Organisational System

Explanation:

- ***Fred E. Fiedler's*** contingency theory of leadership effectiveness was based on studies of a wide range of group effectiveness, and concentrated on the relationship between leadership and organizational performance.
- This is one of the earliest situation-contingent leadership theories given by Fiedler.
- According to him, if an organization attempts to achieve group effectiveness through leadership, then there is a need to assess the leader according to an underlying trait, assess the situation faced by the leader, and construct a proper match between the two.

236. (B) Autocratic style of leadership

237. (D)High concern for production and low concern for people.

238. (B)William J. Reddin

Explanation: Reddin's 3-D Leadership model:

- ***Bill Reddin*** introduced a model of leadership style containing four basic types, namely:

  1. High relationship orientation & high task orientation is called as ***integrated type***.

  2. High relationship orientation & low task orientation is called as ***related type.***

  3. Low relationship orientation & high task orientation is called as ***dedicated type***.

  4. Low relationship orientation & low task orientation is called as ***separated type***.

239. (B) (iii) (ii) (i)

240. (D) Five

241. (B) Robert Blake & Jane S. Mouton

242. (C)Blake and Mouton

243. (A)c, b, a, d

244. (D) All the above

Explanation: Autocratic Leadership

- Autocratic leadership is an extreme form of transactional leadership, where leaders have a lot of power over their people.
- Staff and team members have little opportunity to make suggestions, even if these would be in the team's or the organization's best interest.
- The benefit of autocratic leadership is that it's incredibly efficient. Decisions are made quickly, and work gets done efficiently.

Bureaucratic Leadership:

- Bureaucratic leaders work "by the book." They follow rules rigorously, and ensure that their people follow procedures precisely.
- This is an appropriate leadership style for work involving serious safety risks (such as working with machinery, with toxic substances, or at dangerous heights) or where large sums of money are involved.
- Bureaucratic leadership is also useful in organizations where employees do routine tasks (as in manufacturing).

Charismatic Leadership

- A charismatic leadership style can resemble transformational leadership because these leaders inspire enthusiasm in their teams and are energetic in motivating others to move forward.
- This ability to create excitement and commitment is an enormous benefit.
- The difference between charismatic leaders and transformational leaders lies in their intention.
- Transformational leaders want to transform their teams and organizations.
- Charismatic leaders are often focused on themselves, and may not want to change anything.

Democratic/Participative Leadership

- Democratic leaders make the final decisions, but they include team members in the decision-making process.
- They encourage creativity, and team members are often highly engaged in projects and decisions.
- There are many benefits of democratic leadership.
- Team members tend to have high job satisfaction and are productive because they're more involved in decisions.
- This style also helps develop people's skills. Team members feel in control of their destiny, so they're motivated to work hard by more than just a financial reward.
- Because participation takes time, this approach can slow decision-making, but the result is often good.
- The approach can be most suitable when working as a team is essential, and when quality is more important than efficiency or productivity.

Laissez-Faire Leadership

- This French phrase means "leave it be," and it describes leaders who allow their people to work on their own.
- This type of leadership can also occur naturally, when managers don't have sufficient control over their work and their people.
- Laissez-faire leaders may give their teams complete freedom to do their work and set their own deadlines.
- They provide team support with resources and advice, if needed, but otherwise don't get involved.
- This leadership style can be effective if the leader monitors performance and gives feedback to team members regularly.
- It is most likely to be effective when individual team members are experienced, skilled, self-starters.
- The main benefit of laissez-faire leadership is that giving team members so much autonomy can lead to high job satisfaction and increased productivity.
- The downside is that it can be damaging if team members don't manage their time well or if they don't have the knowledge, skills, or motivation to do their work effectively.

People-Oriented/Relations-Oriented Leadership

- With people-oriented leadership, leaders are totally focused on organizing, supporting, and developing the people on their teams.
- This is a participatory style and tends to encourage good teamwork and creative collaboration.
- This is the opposite of task-oriented leadership.
- People-oriented leaders treat everyone on the team equally.
- They're friendly and approachable, they pay attention to the welfare of everyone in the group, and they make themselves available whenever team members need help or advice.
- The benefit of this leadership style is that people-oriented leaders create teams that everyone wants to be part of.
- Team members are often more productive and willing to take risks, because they know that the leader will provide support if they need it.

Servant Leadership

- This term, created by Robert Greenleaf in the 1970s, describes a leader often not formally recognized as such.
- When someone at any level within an organization leads simply by meeting the needs of the team, he or she can be described as a "servant leader."
- Servant leaders often lead by example. They have high integrity and lead with generosity.

- In many ways, servant leadership is a form of democratic leadership because the whole team tends to be involved in decision making.
- However, servant leaders often "lead from behind," preferring to stay out of the limelight and letting their team accept recognition for their hard work.
- Supporters of the servant leadership model suggest that it's a good way to move ahead in a world where values are increasingly important, and where servant leaders can achieve power because of their values, ideals, and ethics.
- This is an approach that can help to create a positive corporate culture and can lead to high morale among team members.

Task-Oriented Leadership:

- Task-oriented leaders focus only on getting the job done and can be autocratic.
- They actively define the work and the roles required, put structures in place, and plan, organize, and monitor work.
- These leaders also perform other key tasks, such as creating and maintaining standards for performance.
- The benefit of task-oriented leadership is that it ensures that deadlines are met, and it's especially useful for team members who don't manage their time well.

Transactional Leadership:

- This leadership style starts with the idea that team members agree to obey their leader when they accept a job.
- The "transaction" usually involves the organization paying team members in return for their effort and compliance.
- The leader has a right to "punish" team members if their work doesn't meet an appropriate standard.
- Although this might sound controlling and paternalistic, transactional leadership offers some benefits.
- For one, this leadership style clarifies everyone's roles and responsibilities. Another benefit is that, because transactional leadership judges team members on performance, people who are ambitious or who are motivated by external rewards – including compensation – often thrive.

Transformational Leadership:

- Transformation leadership is often the best leadership style to use in business situations.
- Transformational leaders are inspiring because they expect the best from everyone on their team as well as themselves.
- This leads to high productivity and engagement from everyone in their team.
- The downside of transformational leadership is that while the leader's enthusiasm is passed onto the team, he or she can need to be supported by "detail people."
- It's also important to use other leadership styles when necessary – this will depend on the people you're leading and the situation that you're in.

245. (D) All the above

246. (D)All the above

247. (D)All the above

248. (C)Both

249. (B)Society oriented leadership style.

250. (A)Bossing

251. (A)(iii) (iv) (i) (ii)

252. (B) Impoverished management

253. (D)Define the problem

254. (D) Stroking

255. (B)The self which is known to others but not to oneself

256. (A) Natural disagreement arising between two people

257. (B)Interactionist view

Explanation:

- **Traditional view:** Conflict is dysfunctional, destructive and irrational. Usually caused by poor communication, a lack of trust, or a failure to be responsible to the needs of others.
- **Human relations view:** Conflict is natural in groups and organizations. It may even be beneficial on occasion.
- **Interactionist view:** Without conflict, we become static and non-responsive. Conflict keeps us viable and creative, but there are two kinds of conflict: ***Functional and dysfunctional:*** Functional conflict improves long-term group performance.

258. (D) Goals

Explanation: Conflict: Friction or opposition 9resulting from actual or perceived differences or incompatibilities.

259. (C)Managers attempt to eliminate conflict because the organization rewards them for keeping conflict out of their area of responsibility.

260. (C) (i), (ii), (iii)

261. (B) Stress

262. (A) not necessarily bad

Explanation:

- Stress is a general term applied to various mental and physiological pressures experienced by people feel in their lives.
- Stress may be defined as "a state of psychological and / or physiological imbalance resulting from the disparity between situational demand and the individual's ability and / or motivation to meet those demands."
- ***Dr. Hans Selye***, one of the leading authorities on the concept of stress, described stress as "the rate of all wear and tear caused by life."
- Stress can be positive or negative. Stress can be positive when the situation offers an opportunity for a person to gain something.
- It acts as a motivator for peak performance. Stress can be negative when a person faces social, physical, organisational and emotional problems.

263. (A)Constraints; demands

264. (C)Stress can be caused by change of any kind.

265. (C)For potential stress to become actual stress.

266. (B) Cultural

267. (C)irritability

268. (C)Behavioral

269. (A)match the job requirements

270. (D)Job redesigns

271. (A)is difficult for the manager to control directly

272. (C)employee counseling

273. (C)Arbitrariness

274. (D) Thinking without feeling

275. (D)Stress

Explanation: Stress reflects employees' psychological responses to job demands that tax or exceed their capacities.

276. (D)Job performance.

Explanation: Job performance belongs to the Individual outcomes according to the integrated model of OB.

277. (B)High productivity

278. (B) job satisfaction

Explanation: Job satisfaction captures what employees feel when thinking about her job and doing her day-to-day work.

279. (A)A collection of feelings that an individual has towards his/her job

280. (D)All the above

281. (C) Mental well-being

Explanation:

- Morale (also known as esprit de corps) is the capacity of a group's members to maintain belief in an institution or goal, particularly in the face of opposition or hardship.
- Morale is often referenced by authority figures as a generic value judgment of the willpower, obedience, and self-discipline of a group tasked with performing duties assigned by a superior.
- According to ***Alexander H. Leighton***, "morale is the capacity of a group of people to pull together persistently and consistently in pursuit of a common purpose".

282. (C)Morale

283. (D)All the above

284. (D) All the above

285. (D) All the above

286. (D)All the above

287. (B)A broad and intense feeling that is directed at someone or something

288. (A)Same

Explanation: Formal communication

- A type of verbal presentation or document intended to share information and which conforms to established professional rules, standards and processes and avoids using slang terminology.
- The main types of formal communication within a business are:
- (1) downward where information moves from higher management to subordinate employees,
- (2) upward where information moves from employees to management and
- (3) horizontal where information is shared between peers.

Informal communication

- A casual form of information sharing typically used in personal conversations with friends or family members.
- Within a business environment, informal communication is sometimes called the grapevine and might be observed occurring in conversations, electronic mails, text messages and phone calls between socializing employees.

289. (C)Using language

290. (C)Specify the objectives of communication

291. (D)To ask the receiver to tell what they have received

292. (D)Handsome personality

293. (D)It reaches the receiver as intended by the sender

294. (C)Good

295. (B)Two way process

296. (A)Feed Back

297. (D)None of the above

298. (D)All of the above

Explanation: The elements of communication are approach which involves the choice of medium, tone and timing. Another element is development, clarity, style in terms of word choice and correctness or accuracy. The feedback is also important since it portrays the reactions of the receiver.

299. (C)Communicator

300. (D)All of these

301. (C)Both A and B

302. (A)Informal communication

Explanation:

- The grapevine is a communication system or process which is barely informal communication system.
- It is comprised of gossip and rumor. More and wide information can be transmitted through grapevine communication system.
- In the real world, it exists together with the formal communication system.
- According to ***Prof. Keith Davis***, "Grapevine arises from social interaction, It is as fickle, dynamic and varied as people are. It is the exercise of their freedom of speech and is a natural, normal activity".

303. (C)Both ways

304. (C)Oral communication

305. (C)Specify the objectives of communication

306. (D)All the above

Explanation: Principles of effective communication

- Principle of clarity
- Principle of objective
- Principle of understanding the receiver
- Principle of consistency
- Principle of completeness
- Principle of feedback
- Principle of time

307. (D)All the above

308. (D)All the above

309. (D)All the above

310. (A) Sender, Medium, Recipient, Feedback

311. (B)Morale booster

Explanation: Horizontal communication: Information exchange between departments or functional units as means of coordinating their activities.

312. (D) None of the above

Explanation: Barriers in communication

- Physical barriers
- Perceptual barriers
- Emotional barriers
- Cultural barriers
- Language barriers
- Gender barriers
- Interpersonal barriers

313. (D)All the above.

314. (C)Informal communication

315. (B)Lateral Communication

316. (D) All the above

317. (B)Language problems

318. (D) Inattention

319. (D)Understanding must occur to have communication

320. (D)Horizontal

321. (C)Five C.s

322. (B)idea origination

323. (D)All the above

324. (D)All the above

325. (D)All the above

326. (D)Non-verbal communication

327. (D)Semantic Barrier

328. (C)Lateral Communication

329. (B)Feedback

330. (B)Oral and Written

331. (D) Publicity

332. (A)Transmission of ideas or information from executives to the subordinates.

Explanation: Downward communication:

- The flow of information from higher levels of management to subordinate individuals working within an organization.
- Business managers often need to be very skilled at downward communication in order to properly motivate the staff working under them at their company.

333. (C)G.Hofstede

334. (B)Systematic inquiry

335. (A)Change attitudes

336. (C)Maintenance

337. (A)Conflict

Explanation: Interpersonal Relationship:

- A strong bond between two or more people refers to interpersonal relationship.
- Attraction between individuals brings them close to each other and eventually results in a strong interpersonal relationship.

Forms of Interpersonal relationship

An interpersonal relationship can develop between any of the following:

- Individuals working together in the same organization.
- People working in the same team.
- Relationship between a man and a woman (Love, Marriage).
- Relationship with immediate family members and relatives.
- Relationship of a child with his parents.
- Relationship between friends.

338. (D)Corporative philosophy

339. (B) (i) (ii) (iii) (iv)

340. (C) Physiological→Security→ Social →Esteem →Self →actualisation

---000---

UNIT-III

HUMAN RESOURCE MANAGEMENT (HRM)

1. Human Resource Management is improving quality of employees as well as:

(A)Performance (B) Effectiveness

(C)Efficiency (D) Outputs

2. Human Resource Management is the management of :

(A)Man (B) Machine

(C)Material (D) All the above

3. Which of the following objective of human resource management?

(A)Productivity (B) Quality of work life

(C)Organizational change (D) All the above

4. Human Resource Management is primarily concerned with :

(A)Sales

(B)Dimension of People

(C)External Environment

(D)Internal Environment

5. The following concept is developed on unitarism, individualism, commitment and strategic alignment.

(A)Personnel Management

(B)Human Resource Management

(C)Industrial Relations

(D)Personnel Administration

6. Which of the following is ***not*** an element of People?

(A) Motivation (B) Flow of activities

(C) Teamwork (D) Customer training

7. Which of the following is ***not*** a function of human resource management?

(A) Planning (B) Organizing

(C) Directing (D) Accounting

8. People should be regarded as assets rather than variable costs was emphasized in:

(A) Personnel Management

(B) Human Resource Management

(C) Personnel Administration

(D) Public Administration

9. What are the operative functions of HRM?

(A)Organizing (B) Directing

(C)Controlling (D) All of the above

10. Which of the following is ***not*** an operative function of Personnel/Human Resource Management?

(A)Procuring (B) Planning

(C)Developing (D) Maintaining

11. Reducing the number of employees at operational level and reorganizing the work system in order to attain greater productivity.

(A)Downsizing (B) Manpower inventory

(C)Manpower forecasting (D) All the above

12. Dramatic reduction of manpower is called:

(A) Termination (B) Retrenchment

(C) Downsizing (D) Right sizing

13. Which of the following is/are new challenge/s in the field of human resource management?

(A)Rightsizing (B) Outsourcing

(C)Diversity Management (D) All the above

14. Selection of persons in an organization is the responsibility of :

(A)Security Department

(B)Personnel Department

(C)Trade Unions

(D)Canteen Department

15. The book "HR Champions" is authored by :

(A) Mintzberg (B) J. Pfeffer

(C) M. Porter (D) Dave Ulrich

16. Reduction of Labour Force is called:

(A) Termination (B) Retrenchment

(C) Lay-off (D) Right sizing

17. Which of the following is ***not*** a fringe benefit?

(A) Transport

(B) Subsidized canteen facilities

(C) Free education to the children

(D) Dearness Allowance

18. The policy of introducing "New Blood" is

(A) Steriotypic

(B) Bureacratic as well as redtapic

(C) Innovative and challenging, making the corporate dynamic

(D) Innovative, challenging, but often resisted

19. Human Resource Management (HRM) is a part of the broad Human Resource Development (HRD) System, as this focus to

(A) Selection, Induction, Training and Development

(B) Operational and Organizational Options

(C) (A) and (B) above

(D) None of the above

20. Exit Policy primarily emphasizes in the broad sense, for policy makers as

(A) Removing employees

(B) Down sizing

(C) Retiring people and rehabilitating them

(D) Bringing new blood to the Corporate

21. The development of a performance-appraisal system is primarily the concern of:

(A) Financial management

(B) Human resources management.

(C) Production and operations management.

(D) Marketing management

22. Having good human relations skills means that a manager is able to:

(A) Use a computer

(B) Train employees and solve problems

(C) Think creatively

(D) Work with others

23. In which company 'Six Sigma' was first experimented?

(A) Toyota (B) Motorola

(C) Sony (D) Ford

24. The word 'Kaizen', which refers to improvement in performance and productivity has been borrowed from :

(A) Japan (B) Germany

(C) Korea (D) Sweden

25. Kanban is associated with all of the following except:

(A) signaling when it is time for the next batch

(B) reducing setup time

(C) reducing batch size

(D) increasing material handling

26. The word "kanban" means:

(A) low inventory

(B) employee empowerment

(C) card

(D) continuous improvement

27. The word "Kanban" refers to :

(A) A means of effective dialogue

(B)A meaning of effective communication and visual control

(C)A means of potential appraisal

(D)All the above

28. Which one is ***not*** a general concept of T.Q.M.?

(A) Continuous Improvement

(B) Team Work

(C) Strategy

(D) Quality Education

29. Match the following contributions to TQM with the contributors :

List – I (Contributors)

(a) Walter A. Shewart

(b) Joseph M. Juran

(c) Kaoru Ishikawa

(d) Genichi Taguchi

List – II (Contributions)

(i) Concept of Internal Customer

(ii) Product Design Quality

(iii) Statistical control charts

(iv) Quality as 'fitness for use'

Codes:

	(a)	(b)	(c)	(d)
(A)	(ii)	(i)	(iii)	(iv)
(B)	(iv)	(iii)	(i)	(ii)
(C)	(ii)	(iii)	(i)	(iv)
(D)	(iii)	(iv)	(i)	(ii)

30. The total dedication of continuous improvement so that customers' needs are met is known as :

(A)Theory X (B) Total Quality Management

(C) Theory Y (D)Change Management

31. The philosophy of 'never-ending improvement' in total quality management is called:

(A)Kanaban

(B)Business Process Re-engineering

(C)Benchmarking

(D)Kaizan

32. Which one of the following is ***not*** a step in planning?

(A) Establishing objectives

(B) Developing premises

(C) Determining alternative courses

(D) Identifying needs of employees

33. Which one of the following refers to plan of action:

(A) Objectives (B) Policy

(C) Principle (D) Strategy

34. Planning is looking ahead and control is:

(A) Scanning environment

(B) Looking back

(C) Setting targets

(D) Defining objectives

35. The ultimate mission or purpose is to relate human resources to future enterprise needs, so as to maximize the future return on investment in human resources. It is referred as:

(A) Demand and Supply

(B) Forecasting

(C) Human Resource Planning

(D) Human Resource Development

36. Human Resource Planning include:

(A) Scenario planning

(B)Action planning

(C)Demand and Supply forecasts

(D)All the above

37. Human Resource Planning is the __________ step in the management function.

(A) Primary (B) Middle

(C) Final (D) None of the above

38. Arrange the steps in Manpower Planning in the order in which they occur.

(a) Identifying sources of manpower supply.

(b) Manpower forecasting.

(c) Determining manpower requirements.

(d) Manpower Inventory

(e) Selection

(f) Recruitment

(g) Placement

(A) (c) (b) (d) (a) (f) (e) (g)

(B) (a) (c) (b) (d) (e) (f) (g)

(C) (d) (a) (b) (c) (f) (e) (g)

(D) (c) (d) (a) (b) (f) (e) (g)

39. Which of the following is the meaning of Human Resource Planning?

(A) Evaluation of job

(B) Satisfaction of the employees on the job

(C) Appraising the performance of employees

(D) It is the process by which an organisation ensures that it has the right number and kind of people at the right place, at the right time.

40. In which order the following aspects of Manpower planning operate in established organizations?

(i) Recruitment

(ii) Job analysis

(iii) Manpower Inventory

(iv) Manpower Forecasting

(A) (iii), (ii), (iv), (i)

(B) (ii), (iv), (iii), (i)

(C) (iv), (iii), (ii), (i)

(D) (iii), (ii), (i), (iv)

41. Which of the following are the techniques of the Human Resource Demand Forecasting?

(A) Ratio-Trend Analysis

(B) Work-Study method

(C) Managerial Judgement

(D) All of the above

42. Human Resource Planning is the process of :

(A) Managing people at work

(B) Stimulating people to work effectively

(C) Getting maximum out of employee

(D) Demand and supply forecasting of manpower

43. Which of the following is ***not*** true in case of manpower planning?

(A) It is a process by which an organization should move from its current manpower position to its desired manpower position.

(B) It is an integrated approach to performing the personnel function required to meet organizational and individual objectives.

(C) It involves forecasting human resource requirements.

(D) It is a process to discover the sources of manpower.

44. One of the following is training provided to enhance decision making skills:

(A) On the job training

(B) Behavioural modeling

(C) Management games

(D) Action learning

45. Which one of the following are the functions of personnel management?

(A) Planning, Organising, Staffing, Directing and Controlling

(B)Planning, Organising, Coordinating, Budgeting and Controlling

(C)Procurement, Development, Compensation, Integration and Maintenance

(D) Perception, Development, Learning, Organization and Behaviour

46. Recruitment is concerned with

(A) Selecting the right candidate

(B) Developing a pool of job candidates

(C) Getting applications

(D) None of the above

47. Which of the following are the internal sources of recruitment?

(A) Advertisement (B) Selection

(C) Both (A) and (B) (D) None of the above

48. Which of the following is the process of searching for perspective employees and stimulating them to apply for the jobs in the organizations:

(A) Recruitment (B) Selection

(C) Promotion (D) Retrenchment

49. When an organization outsources the responsibilities for the end-to-end delivery of the recruitment/selection process covering all vacancies is:

(A)Recruitment process and screening

(B)Business process and screening

(C)Knowledge process and screening

(D)All the above

50. Which one is ***not*** a part of recruitment process?

(A)Determining requirements

(B)Planning recruitment campaign

(C)Attracting candidates

(D)Selecting candidates

51. Which one is the appropriate sequence in recruitment and selection process?

(A)Recruitment, Job analysis, Manpower planning

(B)Manpower planning, Job analysis, Recruitment

(C)Manpower planning, Recruitment, Job analysis

(D)Job analysis, Manpower planning, Recruitment

52. An organization secretly tries to lure the employee of another organization. It is called:

(A)Consulting (B) Poaching

(C)Negotiating (D) Persuading

53. Recruitment Refers to :

(A)Process of searching for prospective employee

(B)Basis for selecting the right candidate

(C)Solicit necessary information from prospective applicant

(D)Know thc suitability of candidates

54. Which of the following is ***not*** a method of recruitment?

(A)Scouting (B) Employment exchanges

(C)Advertisement (D) Application Blank

55. Which of the following method of recruiting is from external sources?

(A)Personnel Consultants (B) Advertisement

(C)Employment exchanges (D) All the above

56. Which of the following source is the most relevant for recruitment of managerial personnel?

(A)Employment Exchange (B)Advertisement

(C)Gate Hiring (D) Trade Unions

57. Promotion means:

(i) Elevation to higher position.

(ii)Elevation to higher position with financial benefits.

(iii)Elevation to higher position with more power.

(A) (i) and (ii) only (B) (i) and (iii) only

(C) (ii) and (iii) only (D) All the above

58. What are benefits of external recruitment?

(A)Easy and heap method

(B)Acquiring new skills and talent

(C)To save training cost

(D)To increase production

59. (1)Recruitment is influenced by the internal labour market conditions

(2) Recruitment is influenced by the external labour market conditions

Which option is correct?

(A)Statement (1) (B) Statement (2)

(C)Both of the above (D) None of the above

60. Which of the following is ***not*** a method of selection?

(A)Advertisement (B) Interview

(C)Tests (D) Reference checking

61. Match the following :

List-I

(a) Interest Tests

(b) Voluntary Retirement rating

(c) Disposition

(d) Deputation

List-II

(i) Recruitment

(ii) Interview

(iii) Separation

(iv) Selection

	(a)	(b)	(c)	(d)
(A)	(i)	(ii)	(iii)	(iv)
(B)	(ii)	(i)	(iii)	(iv)
(C)	(iv)	(iii)	(ii)	(i)
(D)	(iv)	(ii)	(i)	(iii)

62. Which of the following is ***not*** a model of selection?

(A) Multiple Choice Models

(B) Multiple Cut-off Models

(C) Multiple Hurdles Model

(D) Predictor Criterion Model

63. Tests devised to assess a person's ability to undertake a particular type of work or to learn a particular skill are called

(A)Aptitude Test (B) Knowledge Test

(C)Intelligence Test (D) Attitude Test

64. Which of the following is ***not*** a type of test pertaining to selection procedure?

(A)Aptitude Test (B) Achievement Test

(C)Situational Test (D) Statistical Test

65. Achievement Test is also known as:

(A)Proficiency Test (B) Interest Test

(C)Aptitude Test (D) Personality Test

66. Which of the following is Psychological Test?

(A)Aptitude Test (B) Physical Test

(C)Ability Test (D) Knowledge Test

67. Which of the following test is used to measure the mental ability or mental alertness of the applicant:

(A)Performance Test (B) Intelligence Test

(C)Aptitude Test (D) Personality Test

68. Arrange the following in a proper sequence to show selection procedure :

(a)Medical Test

(b)Screening of applications

(c)Interview

(d)Application of Psychological Test

(e)Written Test

(f)Checking of references

(g)Issuance of Appointment letter

(A) (b), (e), (d), (c), (f), (a), (g)

(B) (e), (d), (b), (c), (a), (g), (f)

(C) (d), (b), (e), (c), (a), (g), (f)

(D) (f), (a), (g), (b), (c), (d), (e)

69. Technique of drawing conclusions from a candidate's hand writing about future performance in a role is:

(A)Graphology (B)Physiognomy

(C)Phrenology (D) Astronomy

70. What is ***not*** an advantage of seniority principle of promotion?

(A) It is more objective and easier in application.

(B) It eliminates internal strife for advancement.

(C) It promotes general morale of the personnel.

(D) It affects the self-improvement efforts of personnel.

71. The art of judging, character of a person from appearance specially the face, based on the assumption that face is an index of mind, is known as :

(A)Graphology (B) Physiognomy

(C)Phrenology (D) None of the above

72. An interview process must be:

(A)Direct questions (B) Open Ended

(C) FAQ (D)Personal Questions

73. Excess & Deficiency of employees is generally observed in which of following

(A)Recruitment (B) Selection

(C)H.R.P (D) Wages and admin

74. Interviews conducted for knowing why an employee is leaving the organization is called

(A)Exit Interview

(B)Separation interview

(C)Termination interview

(D)Retrenchment interview

75. Selection is the process in which candidates for employment are divided into two classes – those who are to be offered employment and those who are ***not***." This is stated by

(A) Dale Yoder (B) Milton M. Mandell

(C) R.D. Agarwal (D) Edwin Flippo

76. The use of predesigned set of questions used in an interview process leads to :

(A)Behavioural interview

(B)Situational interview

(C)Non-directional interview

(D)Structured interview

77. One of the following is training provided to enhance decision making skills:

(A) On the job training

(B) Behavioural modeling

(C) Action learning

(D) Management games

78. An "Assessment Centre" is

(A)A place (B) A technique

(C)Both (A) and (B) (D) None of the above

79. The following are the three components of creativity:

(A)Expertise, creativity skills and task motivation

(B)Expertise, innovation and rationality

(C)Expertise, rationality and relevance

(D)Expertise, novelty and performance

80. While considering promotion of an employee, the following is the most important consideration :

(A)Seniority (B) Competence

(C)Loyalty (D) Only (A) and (B)

81. Which type of promotion described by W. R. Spiegel?

(i)Departmental Promotion

(ii)Inter-departmental Promotion

(iii)Inter-plant Promotion

(iv)Inter-company Promotion

(A)(i), (ii), (iii)

(B)(ii), (iii), (iv)

(C)(i), (ii), (iv)

(D)(i), (iii), (iv)

82. Induction means :

(A)The determination of the job to which an accepted candidate is to be assigned

(B)Introducing the new employee who is designated as a probationer to the job

(C)Measuring the efficiency of labour

(D)Absorbing human resources as organs of the company

83. Introducing the new employee to the job, location, surroundings is called

(A) Placement (B) Job design

(C) Recruitment (D) Induction

84. What is the term used to describe the process of helping a new employee to settle quickly into their job so they become efficient and productive workers?

(A) Action learning (B) discovery learning

(C) Sitting by Nellie (D) induction

85. Induction training is also called as:

(A) Orientation (B) Refresher

(C) Indoctrination (D) Both A and C

86. Giving general information's regarding organization to the newly appointed personnel is called :

(A) Training (B) Development

(C) Induction (D) Promotion

87. Induction refers to

(A) Giving training to the employees.

(B) Giving incentive to the employees.

(C) Introducing employees to the organization culture and situation.

(D) Increasing the morale of the employees.

88. Consider the following:

(i)Measurement (ii)Projection

(iii)Selection (iv) Observation

(v)Comparison(vi) Decision making

The correct sequence of the above ingredients of management by exception (MBE) is:

(A) (i) (ii) (iii) (iv) (v) (vi)

(B) (i) (ii) (iii) (v) (iv) (vi)

(C) (i) (ii) (iii) (vi) (iv) (v)

(D) (i) (ii) (iii) (vi) (v) (iv)

89. The sequence of human resource development activities according to Leonard Nadler are

(A)Education, training and development

(B)Development, training and education

(C)Training, education and development

(D)Training, development and education

90. Which of the following is the focus of the Human Resource Development System?

(A) Individuals and Dyads

(B)Collectives and Organization

(C) Both (A) and (B)

(D)None of the above

91. Which of the following are the sub systems of HRD?

(A)Training

(B)Performance appraisal

(C)Career development and counseling

(D)All the above

92. Which of the following is ***not*** a sub-system of HRD?

(A) Training and Development

(B) Career Planning

(C) Performance Appraisal

(D) None of the above

93. Match the following :

List-I

(a)Fish-Bone Analysis

(b)Balance Score Card

(c)Learning and Performance Cycle

(d)Job Enrichment

List-II

(i) Paul Branthal et. Al

(ii) Frederick Herzberg

(iii) Ishikawa

(iv) Kaplan and Norton

Codes:

	(a)	(b)	(c)	(d)
(A)	(ii)	(iv)	(iii)	(i)
(B)	(iii)	(i)	(iv)	(ii)
(C)	(iv)	(ii)	(i)	(iii)
(D)	(iii)	(iv)	(i)	(ii)

94. Who is associated with 'The Human Capital Approach' of HRD?

(A)Dalton E. McFarland (B)T.W. Schultz

(C)T.V. Rao (D)Rensis Likert

95. The goal of HRD system is to develop the capabilities of each employee:

(A)as an individual and in relation to his or her present role

(B)in relation to his or her expected future role and dyadic relationship between employee and his/her supervisor.

(C)Both (A) and (B)

(D)None of the above

96. The HRD matrix linking HRD sub-systems with development dimensions has been evolved by

(A) Dharani P. Sinha (B) D.M. Pestonjee

(C) T.V. Rao (D)Udai Pareek

97. Who is ***not*** associated with development of human development index?

(A) Mahabub-ul-Haq (B)Manmohan Singh

(C) Meghnad Desai (D)Sudhir Anand

98. Which of the following factors are included in the calculation of human development index?

(A)Life expectancy

(B)Adult literacy

(C)Decent standard of living

(D)All the above

99. The concept of HRD scorecard was introduced in India by

(A) Udai Pareek (B) Rao and Pareek

(C) T.V. Rao (D) Arun Honappa

100. Which of the following is most important for HRD?

(A)to be clearly related to the organization's objectives

(B)to be clearly related to the expertise in the department

(C) to be flexible to be able to respond to sudden crisis

(D)to operate as an extension of the HRM department

101. Who has given the concept of OCTAPACE culture:

(A)Dharni P. Sinha (B)T. V. Rao

(C)D. M. Pestonjee (D)Udai Pareek

102. In OCTAPACE instrument of HRD culture , the words O, T, and P stand for :

(A) Openness, Team, and Performance

(B) Organisation, Training, and Potential

(C) Opinion, T-Group, and Probability

(D) Openness, Trust, and Pro-action

103. OCTAPACE culture means

(A)Openness-cooperation-Truth-Authenticity-Proaction-Autonomy-Collaboration-Experimentation

(B)Openness-Confrontation-Trust-Autonomy-Proaction-Authority-Collaboration-Experimentation

(C)Openness-Confrontation-Trust-Authority-Proaction-Autonomy-cooperation-Experimentation

(D)Openness-Confrontation-Trust-Authenticity-Proaction-Autonomy-Collaboration-Experimentation

104. Empowerment means authority to make decisions in ones area of operation

(A) by taking approval from the senior

(B)without having to get approval from anyone else

(C) without caring for the consequences

(D) All the above

105. Who has advanced the Bottom of the Pyramid concept?

(A) Garry Dessler (B) Peter Drucker

(C) C.K. Prahlad (D) Michael Porter

106. Which one is ***not*** a part of Mc. Kinsy's 7's frame work?

(A) Standards (B) Structure

(C) Skills (D) Strategy

107. Under McKinsey's 7 S model, the soft S's are:

(A)Style (B) Staff

(C)Skills (D) All the above

108. Which one is ***not*** a part of Mc Kinsy's 7's' framework?

(A)Systems (B) Strategy

(C)Standards (D) Style

109. Which of the following is ***not*** one of the 5s of housekeeping?

(A)Sort (B)Systemize

(C)Specialize (D)Shine

110. "A place for everything, everything in its place" is

(A)American Management (B) 5S Practice

(C)Peter Principle (D)A Chinese Practice

111. Robert Kaplan is associated with

(A)A Benchmark Practice

(B) Balanced Score Card

(C) Kaizen

(D) Quality of Life

112. Who has given the 'Balance Score Card' as a measurement based performance management strategy?

(A)Robert S. Kaplan and David P.Norton

(B)Hammel and Prahallad

(C)Stablein and Nord

(D)Pascale and Athos

113. Who has advance the PDCA cycle of Quality Management?

(A)Joseph M. Juran (B)W.Edwards Deming

(C)Kaoru Ishikawa (D)Phillip Crosby

114. The components of Marvin Weisbord's six box model are:

(A) Purposes, structure, rewards, mechanisms, relationships and leadership

(B) Processes, structure, resources, mechanisms, relationships and leadership.

(C) Performance, structure, rewards, machines, relationships and leadership

(D) Purposes, structure, resources, machines, relationships and Leadership

115. The process of comparing work and service methods against the best practices and outcomes in industry is known as

(A) Benchmarking (B) Kaizens

(C) Quality Circles (D)None of the above

116. HRD Matrix was conceptualized by :

(A)Leonard Nadler (B)Leon C. Megginson

(C)T. V. Rao (D)Udai Pareekh

117. Which of the following explain the HRD concept?

(A)It is competence building exercise

(B)It is a subprocess of OD

(C)It brings about attitudinal changes in people

(D)All of the above

118. Which of the following is (are) the goal(s) of HRD?

(A)Attracting people to organisation and retaining them

(B)Maximising performance in assigned roles

(C)Maximising performance in future roles

(D)All the above

119. HRD develops competencies at which level (s)?

(A)Individual level (B) Group level

(C)Organization level (D) All the above

120. Moonlighting means:

(A)Working simultaneously in two organizations

(B) Working under moonlight.

(C) Working in the night.

(D)Encouraging employee to improve productivity

121. Training refers to:

(A)An act of increasing the knowledge and skill of an employee for doing a particular job.

(B)A short term educational process and utilizing systematic and organized procedure by which employees learn technical knowledge and skills for a definite purpose.

(C)It bridges the differences between job requirements and employee's present specifications

(D)All of the above

122. Which of the following is the correct sequence of training evaluation?

(A)Reaction, learning, behaviour and results

(B)Learning, reaction, behaviour and results

(C)Learning, behaviour, reaction and results

(D)Reaction, learning, results and behaviour

123. Training Evaluation at Reaction, Learning, Job behaviour and results levels is the model advanced by:

(A) Donald Kirkpatrick (B) Goldstein

(C) Brinkerhoff (D) Phillips

124. The following is the right process of training :

(A) Instructional design, validation, need analysis, implementation and evaluation

(B) Need analysis, instructional design, validation, implementation and evaluation

(C) Need analysis, validation, instructional design, implementation and evaluation

(D) Instructional design, need analysis, implementation, validation and evaluation

125. Sensitivity Training is known as___.

(A)T - group training

(B)Operative training

(C)In - basket exercise

(D)Problem solving Training

126. 'Cousin Lab', 'Stranger lab' and 'Family lab' are terms associated with which OD technique?

(A)Survey Feedback

(B)Managerial Grid

(C)Sensitivity Training

(D)Process Consultation

127. Which of the following labs are in use in the sensitivity training?

(A)Stranger lab (B) Cousin lab

(C)Family lab (D) All of the above

128. Identify the factors which do ***not*** help organization in dealing with knowledge management:

(A)Improve the returns

(B)Improve competency

(C)Do not exploit opportunity

(D)Great value for core business

129. Which of the following is ***not*** an objectives of sensitivity training?

(A) Awareness of behavioural pattern of oneself and others

(B)Increased openness and greater concern for others

(C)Increased tolerance and less ethnic prejudice

(D)Potentialities for the next level job

130. Off the job training does ***not*** include :

(A)Role playing (B) Lecture method

(C)Coaching (D) Conference or discussion

131. Arrange the following steps of training procedure in proper sequence:

(i)Preparing the trainee

(ii)Preparing the instructor

(iii)Presenting the operation

(iv)Getting ready to teach

(v)Tryout the trainee's performance

(vi)Follow up

(A) (i) (ii) (iii) (iv) (v) (vi)

(B)(ii) (i) (iv) (iii) (v) (vi)

(C)(vi) (v) (iv) (iii) (i) (ii)

(D) (i) (iv) (iii) (v) (ii) (vi)

132. Which of the following is ***not*** a method of operative training?

(A) Grid Training

(B) Vestibule Training

(C) Apprenticeship Training

(D) Demonstration

133. Match the following :

(Training Programmes)

(a)Inbasket Exercize

(b)Role Playing

(c)Sensiticity Training

(d)Understudy

(Skills Imparted)

(i)Problem solving

(ii)Skills required for promotion

(iii)Time Management

(iv)Group Skills

Code:

	(a)	(b)	(c)	(d)
(A)	(iii)	(i)	(iv)	(ii)
(B)	(ii)	(iii)	(i)	(iv)
(C)	(iii)	(ii)	(iv)	(i)
(D)	(iv)	(iii)	(ii)	(i)

134. Which of the following is ***not*** on the job training programme?

(A)Vestibule Training (B)Role Playing

(C)Simulation (D)All the above

135. Arrange the following in the sequence in which they occur in a training and development programe.

(a) training programmes

(b) training evaluation

(c) determining training needs

(d) feedback

(A) (a)(d) (b) (c)

(B) (b)(a) (c) (d)

(C) (c) (a) (b) (d)

(D) (c) (b) (a) (d)

136. The training analysis is required to :

(A)Find out the training needs

(B)Find out additional requirement of manpower.

(C)Find out working problems

(D)Maintain industrial democracy at work

137. What is the correct order of the following phases of training?

(i)Development Phase

(ii)Design Phase

(iii)Need Analysis Phase

(iv) Implementation Phase

(v)Evaluation Phase

(A) (iii) (ii) (i) (iv) (v)

(B) (ii) (i) (iii) (v) (iv)

(C) (iii) (iv) (i) (ii) (v)

(D) (iv) (ii) (i) (iii) (v)

138. On–the–job training does ***not*** include :

(A)Coaching (B) Job rotation

(C)Under study (D) The case study

139. When situation is duplicated in such a way that it carries a closer resemblance to the actual job setting, it is called:

(A) Sensitivity Training (B) Simulation

(C) Managerial Grid (D) In Basket Method

140. What may be particularly necessary as part of the training process where people are working in another country?

(A) e-learning (B) Cross-cultural training

(C) discovery learning (D) Activist learning

141. Which of the following is ***not*** a stage in the systematic training cycle?

(A) evaluation

(B) assessing training needs

(C) planning the training

(D) job instruction on a one to one basis

142. Sensitivity Training is

(A) Sensitization of an employee for organization

(B)Kind of group for discussing the interpersonal behavior

(C)Related with organization change

(D)Induction training

143. One of the following is a Training provided to enhance decision making skills

(A)On the job training

(B)Behavioural modeling

(C)Management games

(D)Action learning

144. Group-building training techniques are most effective for:

(A)Developing specific skills or dealing with interpersonal issues on the job.

(B)Teaching new facts or alternative problem-solving solutions.

(C)Continuously attempting to learn new things to apply for quality improvements.

(D)Sharing ideas and experiences and getting to know one's strengths and weaknesses.

145. One of the acceptable methods for obtaining feedback of training is called

(A) Structured Interview

(B) Performance after Training

(C) Improvement after Training

(D) Employee Turnover Rate

146. Match the following :

List-I

(i) Sensitivity training

(ii) Hygiene factors

(iii) Number of subordinates

(iv) Likert's management system

List-II

(a) Leadership

(b) Organizational Development

(c) Motivation

(d) Span of management

Codes:

(i)(ii)(iii) (iv)

(A) (b) (c) (d) (a)

(B) (a)(c) (d) (b)

(C) (d) (c) (a) (b)

(D) (a) (b) (c) (d)

147. Sensitivity training method is a part of:

(A) On-the-job training method

(B) Off-the-job training method

(C) Vestibule training method

(D) None of the above

148. Which of the following techniques may be used for management development?

(A)Planned progression

(B)Creation of 'Assistants to' position

(C)Sensitivity training

(D)All the above

149. Human values in regard to Management Development do ***not*** include

(A) Dignity and forgiveness

(B) Arrogance and anger

(C) Gratitude and gentleness

(D) Humility and Honesty

150. Management development is concerned with learning of

(A) Mechanical skills

(B) Specific job skills

(C) Conceptual and creative skills

(D) All the above

151. Management Development Programmes are required :

(A) To increase production

(B) To increase effectiveness and personality of a manager

(C) To increase morale

(D) To increase team work

152. The following definition "development of awareness and sensitivity to behavioural patterns of oneself and others" refers to which of the following methods of training?

(A)In-Basket (B) Case study

(C)Management games (D) T-Group

153. In organizing an Executive Development Programme, how would you arrange the following steps?

(i)Actual conduct of the programme.

(ii)Evaluation of the programme.

(iii)Inventory of Management Talent.

(iv) Analysis of Developmental Needs

(A) (i) (iii) (ii) (iv)

(B) (iv) (iii) (i) (ii)

(C) (i) (iv) (iii) (ii)

(D) (i) (ii) (iii) (iv)

154. Which of the following is the correct sequence of management development process?

(i) Designing Development Programmes

(ii)Conducting Development Programmes

(iii)Evaluating Development Programmes

(iv)Defining Parameters to Development

(v)Identifying Development needs

(A) (ii), (iii), (i), (iv), (v)

(B) (iii), (ii), (iv), (i), (v)

(C) (iv), (iii), (ii), (v), (i)

(D) (v), (iv), (i), (ii), (iii)

155. Which of the following is ***not*** a simulation technique of development?

(A)In – Basket (B)Case study

(C)T – group (D)Management games

156. The term human resource development reflects the fact that it is no longer appropriate in modern organizations to focus on just the development of which group?

(A)Workers (B) employees

(C)Consultants (D) part timers

157. The method of management development which purports to develop awareness and sentiments to one's own and others' behavioural patterns, is known as :

(A)Structured Insight

(B)The syndicate system

(C)Business games

(D)Sensitivity training

158. When the career progression stagnates at a point, it is called

(A)Career Resilience (B) Career Anchor

(C)Career Insight (D) Career Plateau

159. Which of the following is the correct sequence of career development stages?

(i)Mid career (ii) late career

(iii)Exploration (iv) Decline

(v)Establishment

(A)	(i)	(ii)	(iii)	(iv)	(v)
(B)	(ii)	(iii)	(i)	(v)	(iv)
(C)	(i)	(iv)	(v)	(ii)	(iii)
(D)	(iii)	(v)	(i)	(ii)	(iv)

160. Career planning linked with multi skilling results into :

(A)linear career planning

(B)protean career planning

(C)Vertical career planning

(D)none of the above

161. Which of the following factors may be leveled as career anchor?

(A) Managerial competence

(B) Creativity

(C) Functional competence

(D) All the above

162. Self perceived talents, motives and values that influence career of an individual are known as:

(A) career anchors (B) career plans

(C) career aims (D) none of the above

163. Arrange the following steps involved in establishing a career development system in proper sequence:

(a)Vision (b)Needs

(c)Action plan (d)Results

(A) (d) (c) (b) (a)

(B) (b) (a) (c) (d)

(C) (b) (d) (a), (c)

(D) (c) (a) (b) (d)

164. Which of the following provides direction, serves as standards for evaluating performance and motivates members of the organization?

(A) Mission (B) Values

(C) Objectives (D) Goals

165. Which of the following is ***not*** one of the career anchors :

(A)Managerial competence

(B) Technical - functional competence

(C)Personal competence

(D) Security

166. Career resilience means

(A)Ability to switch careers

(B)Ability to remain with same competencies refining suitably for organizations

(C)Lack of capacity to remain in career

(D)None of the above

167. The process of retaining suitable successors is called :

(A)Alternative staffing

(B)Succession planning

(C)Position replacement

(D)Promotion

168. Monitoring employees through a preplanned series of position is called:

(A) Promotion (B) Succession planning

(C)Job reporting (D) Job rotation

169. All of the following are phases of career development except:

(A)Performance Phase

(B)Direction Phase

(C)Assessment Phase

(D)Development Phase

170. Performance Appraisal is a double edged tool to:

(A)Create space for the employee to organizationally survive.

(B) Offering challenges for promotion.

(C)Accompanying the course of demotion

(D)All of the above

171. The process of evaluating an employee's current and/or past performance relative to his or her performance standards is called:

(A) Recruitment (B) Employee selection

(C)Performance appraisal (D) Training

172. Which one is a part of performance measurement?

(A)Trait (B)Behaviour

(C)Outcome (D)All the above

173. Which one is ***not*** a performance appraisal error arising from rater?

(A)Halo error (B) Content error

(C)Contrast error (D)Recency error

174. Every evaluator has his/her own value system that acts as a standard against which appraisals are made. Relative to the true or actual performance an individual exhibits, some evaluators mark high and others low. Such errors are known as:

(A) Similarity errors

(B) Central tendency

(C) Strictness/Leniency error

(D) Recency Vs Primacy effect

175. The influence of rater's general impression on ratings of specific rate qualities is called

(A)Halo effect (B) Central tendency

(C)Leniency (D) Hawthorne Effect

176. Performance appraisal helps in :

(A)Training (B) Career planning

(C)Promotion (D) All the above

177. Which of the following is ***not*** a method of Performance Appraisal?

(A)Paired comparison method

(B) 360^0 Appraisal

(C)Assessment centers

(D)None of the above

178. BARS stand for :

(A)Behaviourally Anchored Ranking Scales

(B)Behaviour Aptitude Reaction Syndrome

(C)Behaviourally Anchored Rating Scales

(D)Behavioural Alternative Reaction Syndrome

179. 360^0 Appraisal refers to the appraisal to be done by :

(A) Superiors and Subordinates

(B) Superiors Subordinates and Customers

(C) Superiors Subordinates, Customers and Peers

(D) None of the above

180. Assertion: Management of performance is a better substitute to the performance appraisal.

Reason: Appraisal of performance is affected by many errors as in human processes biases are bound to occur.

(A) Both asseration and reason are wrong

(B) Assertion is wrong but reason is right

(C)Assertion is right and it will control reason

(D)None of the above

181. Arrange the following aspects of performance appraisal objectives in the proper sequence:

(i) to identify potential for promotion

(ii) to help develop individuals

(iii) to assess training needs

(iv) to review past performance

(v) to set targets for future performance

(vi) to audit the skills within an organisation

(A)(i)(iii) (iv) (vi) (v) (ii)

(B)(i)(ii)(iii) (v)(vi) (iv)

(C)(iv) (v) (vi) (iii) (ii) (i)

(D)(iv) (iii) (ii) (vi) (v) (i)

182. Which of the following would be the correct sequence of various phases in performance coaching?

(i)Report building

(ii)Exploration

(iii)Action Planning

(A) (iii) (ii) (i)

(B) (i) (iii) (ii)

(C) (i) (ii) (iii)

(D) (ii) (iii) (i)

183. Consider following steps in performance appraisal process and arrange them in proper sequence :

(i)Comparison of actual performance with performance standards

(ii)Communicate performance expectations

(iii) Initiate corrective action, if any

(iv) Establish performance standards

(v) Measurement of actual performance

(A) (iv), (ii), (v), (iii), (i)

(B) (i), (ii), (iii), (iv), (v)

(C) (iv), (ii), (v), (i), (iii)

(D) (i), (iv), (iii), (ii), (v)

184. Match the following :

List - I

(a)Forced Distribution method

(b)Critical Incident method

(c)Alternation Ranking method

(d)Management by objectives

List - II

(i)Keeping record of uncommonly examples of work related behaviour

(ii)Predetermined percentages of employees placed in various performance categories

(iii)Ranking employees from best to worst on a particular trait until all are ranked

(iv)Setting goals and periodically measuring performance

Codes:

	(a)	(b)	(c)	(d)
(A)	(ii)	(i)	(iii)	(iv)
(B)	(i)	(ii)	(iii)	(iv)
(C)	(iii)	(i)	(ii)	(iv)
(D)	(iii)	(ii)	(i)	(iv)

185. Which of the following is the correct sequence of Performance Appraisal Process?

(i) Setting standards for performance.

(ii) Measuring the performance.

(iii)Comparing the actual performance with the standard set.

(iv)Communicating the standards set to the employees.

(A)	(i)	(ii)	(iii)	(iv)
(B)	(i)	(ii)	(iv)	(iii)
(C)	(i)	(iv)	(ii)	(iii)
(D)	(ii)	(iii)	(iv)	(i)

186. Which of the following is ***not*** a method of Performance Appraisal?

(A) Behaviorally Anchored Rating Scales.

(B) Critical Incidence Method

(C) Grading Method

(D) Weighted Check List Method

187. Which of the following statements is ***not*** true about Performance Appraisal?

(A) Key performance areas are developed for role clarity.

(B) Key result areas are developed for accountability.

(C) KSA stands for knowledge, skill and attitude.

(D) Attributes and traits are of no importance in Performance Appraisal.

188. Behaviourally Anchored Rating Scale is associated with

(A) Training and Development

(B) Performance Appraisal

(C) Career Planning

(D)Workers'Participation in Management

189. Performance Appraisal is a primary human resource management process that links employees and organizations and provides input for other processes through these means :

(A) Identification, measurement, management

(B) Assessment,direction, development.

(C) Recruitment, Selection, onboarding

(D) Skill, effort, responsibility

190. Who has advanced the Goal setting theory of Performance Management?

(A) E.A. Locke & Gary Lutham

(B) F. Trompenaavs and Charles Hamp

(C) R. Tung and Arthur Anderson

(D) J.C. Usunier and P.N. Gharvi

191. Performance appraisal by all the following parties is called 360^0performance appraisal

(A) Supervisors and Peers

(B)Subordinates and Employees themselves

(C) Users of Service and Consultants

(D) All the above

192. The term BARS stands for :

(A)Behavioural Abnormality Rating Scales

(B)Behavioural Abnormality Response Scale

(C)Behaviourally Anchored Response Scales

(D)Behaviourally Anchored Rating Scales

193. When goal setting, performance appraisal, and development are consolidated into a single, common system designed to ensure that employee performance supports a company's strategy, it is called _____.

(A)strategic organizational development

(B)performance management

(C) performance appraisal

(D)human resource management

194. Performance management combines performance appraisal with _____ to ensure that employee performance is supportive of corporate goals.

(A)goal setting (B)training

(C)incentive systems (D)all of the above

195. Managers following a performance management approach to appraisals will usually meet with employees on a__ basis.

(A)Weekly (B)monthly

(C)bi-annual (D)yearly

196. Managers following a traditional performance appraisal system will typically meet with employees on a_ basis.

(A)Daily (B)weekly

(C)Monthly (D)yearly

197. The component of an effective performance management process that communicates the organization's higher level goals throughout the organization and then translates these goals into departmental goals is called _____.

(A)role clarification

(B)goal alignment

(C) developmental goal setting

(D)direction sharing

198. The component of an effective performance management process that explains each employee's role in terms of his or her day-to-day work is called _____.

(A)role clarification

(B)goal alignment

(C)developmental goal setting

(D)direction sharing

199. Which of the following is ***not*** one of the guidelines for effective goal setting?

(A)assign specific goals

(B)assign measurable goals

(C)assign challenging but doable goals

(D)assign consequences for performance

200. The S in the acronym for SMART goals stands for _____.

(A)Specific (B)straightforward

(C)Strategic (D)source

201. Participatively set goals result in higher performance than assigned goals when __.

(A) participatively set goals are more difficult

(B) assigned goals are more difficult

(C) the rewards are also higher

(D)participatively set goals are used consistently

202. When using goal setting in performance management, the goals should be _____.

(A)Difficult (B) challenging

(C)Doable (D) all of the above

203. Who is the primary person responsible for doing the actual appraising of an employee's performance?

(A)the employee's direct supervisor

(B)the company appraiser

(C)the human resource manager

(D)the EEO contact person

204. Which of the following is ***not*** a role played by the HR department regarding performance appraisals?

(A)Training of supervisors

(B)Monitoring the appraisal system

(C)Appraising of employees

(D)Ensuring compliance with EEO laws

205. When designing an actual appraisal method, the two basic considerations are:

(A)who should measure and when to measure

(B)when to measure and what to measure

(C)what to measure and who should measure

(D)what to measure and how to measure

206. The most popular technique for appraising performance is the ______ method.

(A)alternation ranking (B)Likert

(C) graphic rating scale (D)MBO

207. Which performance appraisal technique lists traits and a range of performance?

(A)alternation ranking (B) Likert

(C) graphic rating scale (D)MBO

208. What do performance appraisals measure?

(A)generic dimensions of performance

(B)performance of actual duties

(C)employee competency

(D)all of the above

209. If a performance appraisal focuses on an employee's quality and quantity of wok, then the performance appraisal is focused on measuring _____.

(A)generic dimensions of performance

(B)performance of actual duties

(C)employee competency

(D)achievement of objectives

210. The _____ method of performance appraisal involves listing all the subordinates to be rated, crossing out the names of any not known well enough to rank, indicating the employee who is the highest on each characteristic being measured and who is the lowest, and then alternating between the next highest and lowest until all employees have been ranked.

(A)alternation ranking (B) Likert

(C) graphic rating scale (D)MBO

211. Alternation ranking refers to an appraisal method, which ______.

(A)is based on progress made toward the accomplishment of measurable goals

(B)combines the benefits of narratives, critical incidents, and quantified scales by assigning scale points with specific examples of good or poor performance

(C)requires that the supervisor keep a log of positive and negative examples of a subordinate's work-related behavior

(D)involves listing all the subordinates to be rated, crossing out the names of any not known well enough to rank, indicating the employee who is the highest on each characteristic being measured and who is the lowest, and then alternating between the next highest and lowest until all employees have been ranked.

212. The most popular method for ranking employees is the _____ method.

(A)graphic ranking scale

(B)constant sum ranking scale

(C)alternation ranking

(D)paired comparison

213. Suppose you have five employees to rate. You make a chart of all possible pairs of employees for each trait being evaluated. Then, you indicate the better employee of the pair for each pair. Finally, you add up the number of positives for each employee.

In this case, you have used the _____ method of performance appraisal.

(A)graphic ranking scale

(B)constant sum ranking scale

(C)alternation ranking

(D)paired comparison

214. Forced distribution refers to an appraisal method, which _____.

(A)is based on progress made toward the accomplishment of measurable goals

(B)combines the benefits of narratives, critical incidents, and quantified scales by assigning scale points with specific examples of good or poor performance

(C)requires that the supervisor keep a log of positive and negative examples of a subordinate's work-related behavior

(D)involves listing all the subordinates to be rated, crossing out the names of any not known well enough to rank, indicating the employee who is the highest on each characteristic being measured and who is the lowest, and then alternating between the next highest and lowest until all employees have been ranked.

215. When a supervisor evaluates performance by assigning predetermined percentages of ratees into performance categories, he or she has used the _____ method of performance appraisal.

(A)graphic ranking scale

(B)constant sum ranking scale

(C)alternation ranking

(D)forced distribution

216. Anil, the supervisor of the manufacturing department, is in the process of evaluating his staff's performance. He has determined that 15% of the group will be identified as high performers, 20% as above average performers, 30% as average performers, 20% as below average performers, and 15% as poor performers. Anil is using a _____ method.

(A)graphic rating scale

(B)constant sum ranking scale

(C) forced distribution

(D) alternation ranking

217. Which of the following measurement methods rates employee performance relative to other employees?

(A)graphic rating scale (B)forced distribution

(C) likert scale (D)constant sums rating

218. With the _____ method, the supervisor keeps a log of positive and negative examples of a subordinate's work-related behavior.

(A)alternation ranking

(B)constant sums rating

(C)forced distribution

(D) critical incident

219. The critical incident technique refers to an appraisal method, which _____.

(A)is based on progress made toward the accomplishment of measurable goals

(B)combines the benefits of narratives, critical incidents, and quantified scales by assigning scale points with specific examples of good or poor performance

(C)requires that the supervisor keep a log of positive and negative examples of a subordinate's work-related behavior.

(D)requires a supervisor to evaluate performance by assigning predetermined percentages of those being rated into performance categories.

220. All of the following are advantages of using the critical incident method for appraising performance except that _____.

(A)it provides examples of good performance

(B)it does not include a numerical rating

(C)it provides examples of poor performance

(D)it reflects performance from throughout the appraisal period

221. Which appraisal method combines the benefits of narratives, critical incidents, and quantified scales by assigning scale points with specific examples of good or poor performance?

(A)behaviorally anchored rating scale

(B)graphic rating scale

(C)constant sums rating scale

(D)alternation ranking

222. Behaviorally anchored rating scale (BARS) refers to an appraisal method, which _____.

(A)is based on progress made toward the accomplishment of measurable goals

(B)combines the benefits of narratives, critical incidents, and quantified scales by assigning scale points with specific examples of good or poor performance

(C)requires that the supervisor keep a log of positive and negative examples of a subordinate's work-related behavior

(D)requires a supervisor to evaluate performance by assigning predetermined percentages of those being rated into performance categories

223. The first step in developing a behaviorally anchored rating scale is to _____.

(A)develop performance dimensions

(B)generate critical incidents

(C)reallocate incidents

(D)scale incidents

224. Which step in developing a behaviorally anchored rating scale involves clustering critical incidents into a smaller set of performance dimensions?

(A)First (B)Second

(C)Third (D)Fourth

225. Which step in developing a behaviorally anchored rating scale involves clustering definitions and critical incidents, reassigning each incident to the cluster where it fits best and then determining the level of agreement among the group as to the allocation of incidents?

(A)First (B) second

(C)Third (D) fourth

226. All of the following are advantages of behaviorally anchored rating scales (BARS) ***except*** that they _____.

(A)are more accurate

(B)provide clearer standards

(C) are time consuming

(D)are reliable

227. Management by objectives (MBO) refers to an appraisal method, which _____.

(A)is based on progress made toward the accomplishment of measurable goals

(B)combines the benefits of narratives, critical incidents, and quantified scales by assigning scale points with specific examples of good or poor performance

(C)requires that the supervisor keep a log of positive and negative examples of a subordinate's work-related behavior

(D)requires a supervisor to evaluate performance by assigning predetermined percentages of those being rated into performance categories

228. Which of the following is a problem with using MBO?

(A)a tendency to set unclear objectives

(B)a tendency to set unmeasurable objectives

(C)it is time consuming

(D)all of the above

229. Graphic rating scales are subject to all of the following problems ***except*** :

(A)unclear standards (B)halo effects

(B)complexity (D)central tendency

230. When different supervisors define levels of performance (good, fair, poor) differently, unfair appraisals could result due to a problem with _____.

(A)unclear standards (B)halo effects

(C) complexity (D)central tendency

231. _____ is defined as the influence of a rater's general impression on ratings of specific ratee qualities.

(A)Impression management (B)Halo effect

(C)Central tendency (D) Stereotyping

232. Neeraj is generally considered unfriendly at work. His supervisor rates him low on the trait "gets along well with others" but also rates him lower on other traits unrelated to socialization at work. Neeraj's performance appraisal may be unfair due to:

(A) impression management (B) bias

(C) stereotyping (D) halo effects

233. Some supervisors, when filling in rating scales, tend to avoid the highs and lows on the scale and rate most people in the middle. This _____ means that all employees may be rated average.

(A)halo effect (B)stereotyping

(C)central tendency (D)strictness

234. The best way of reducing the problem of central tendency in performance appraisals is to:

(A)rank employees

(B)be aware of the problem

(C)train supervisors to avoid it

(D)impose a distribution for performance

235. The _____ problem occurs when supervisors tend to rate all their subordinates consistently high.

(A)central tendency (B)leniency

(C) strictness (D)bias

236. The _____ problem occurs when supervisors tend to rate all their subordinates consistently low.

(A)central tendency (B)leniency

(C) strictness (D)bias

237. Which big five personality trait is associated with performance appraisal ratings that are too strict?

(A)Agreeableness (B)extraversion

(C)conscientiousness (D)openness

238. Which big five personality trait is associated with performance appraisal ratings that are too lenient?

(A)Agreeableness (B)extraversion

(C)Conscientiousness (D)openness

239. The best way of reducing the problems of leniency or strictness in performance appraisals is to _____.

(A)rank employees

(B)be aware of the problem

(C) train supervisors to avoid it

(D)impose a distribution for performance

240. When an employee's personal characteristics such as age, race, and gender influence a supervisor's evaluation of his or her performance, the problem of _____ has occurred.

(A)Bias (B) stereotyping

(C) central tendency (D)halo affect

241. Which of the following could result in a legally questionable appraisal process?

(A)conduct a job analysis to establish criteria and standards for successful performance

(B)base appraisals on subjective supervisory observations

(C)administer and score appraisals in a standardized fashion

(D)use clearly defined job performance dimensions

242. Who is in the best position to observe and evaluate an employee's performance for the purposes of a performance appraisal?

(A)Peers (B) rating committees

(C) customers (D)immediate supervisor

243. Performance appraisals may be conducted by:

(A)the immediate supervisor (B)peers

(C)rating committees (D)all of the above

244. Rating committees, made up of an employee's immediate supervisor along with other supervisors, usually have _____ members.

(A)2-3 (B)4-5

(C)6-7 (D)8-9

245. While peer appraisals have many benefits, one problem is _____, when several peers collaborate to rate each other highly.

(A)social loafing (B)group think

(C)logrolling (D)alliance forging

246. Peer appraisals have been shown to result in a(n)_____.

(A)reduction of social loafing in the team

(B)reduction of group cohesion

(C)decrease in satisfaction with the group

(D)lower task motivation

247. What usually occurs when employees rate themselves in a performance appraisal?

(A)interrater reliability is higher

(B)appraisals are subject to halo effects

(C)logrolling could occur

(D)ratings are higher than when rated by supervisors or peers

248. Firms that use _____ let subordinates anonymously rate their supervisor's performance.

(A)downward feedback (B)upward feedback

(C)MBO (D) narratives

249. What process allows top management to diagnose the management styles of supervisors, identify potential "people" problems, and take corrective action with individual supervisors as necessary?

(A)strategic performance appraisal

(B)organizational development

(C) upward feedback

(D)MBO

250. When subordinates provide feedback for supervisors, the comments should be anonymous because identifiable responses tend to result in _____.

(A)more critical ratings

(B)increased comfort with the process on the part of the subordinate

(C)more negative attitudes from managers receiving the feedback

(D)more inflated ratings

251. What is another term for 360-degree feedback?

(A)feedback loop (B)multi source assessment

(C)upward feedback (D)circle feedback

252. You are conducting an appraisal interview with an employee who is satisfactory, but ***not*** promotable. Which incentive listed below would likely be the least effective for maintaining satisfactory performance in this situation?

(A)time off

(B)small bonus

(C)compliments

(D)additional professional development

253. Which is the easiest type of appraisal interview to conduct?

(A)satisfactory-not promotable

(B)satisfactory-promotable

(C)unsatisfactory-correctable

(D)unsatisfactory-uncorrectable

254. When conducting an appraisal interview, supervisors should do all of the following ***except***

(A)talk in terms of objective work data

(B)compare the person's performance to a standard

(C)encourage the employee to talk

(D)compare the person's performance to that of other employees

255. Which of the following responses is ***not*** typical during a negative appraisal interview?

(A)Denial (B)anger

(C)Relief (D)aggression

256. When a supervisor must criticize a subordinate in an appraisal interview, it is best to _____.

(A)hold the meeting with other people who can diffuse the negative situation

(B)provide examples of critical incidents

(C)acknowledge the supervisor's personal biases in the situation

(D)provide feedback once per year

257. Subordinates may feel dissatisfied with their appraisal interview when they _____.

(A)feel threatened during the interview

(B) have an opportunity to express their ideas

(C)have an opportunity to influence the course of the interview

(D)have a constructive interviewer conduct the interview

258. When an employee's performance is so poor that a written warning is required, the warning should _____.

(A)identify the standards by which the employee is judged

(B)provide examples of employees who met the standards

(C)provide examples of times when the employee did meet the standards

(D)be sent to the employee in question, to the manager's superior, and to the EEO office.

259. If a performance appraisal focuses on an employee's ability to "identify and analyze problems" or to "maintain harmonious and effective working relationships," then the performance appraisal is focused on measuring _____.

(A)generic dimensions of performance

(B)performance of actual duties

(C) employee competency

(D)achievement of objectives

260. Self-assessment is a part of :

(A)Interview followed by written test

(B)Competency mapping

(C)Induction

(D)Performance Appraisal System

261. Which of the following is called a negative process?

(A) Recruitment (B) Selection

(C) Induction (D) Performance Appraisal

262. Which of the following provides directions, serves as standard for evaluating performance and motivates members of the organization?

(A) Mission (B) Values

(C) Objectives (D) Goals

263. The systematic collection and feedback of performance data on an individual or group derived from a number of stake holders in their performance is called :

(A)180^0Appraisal (B)360^0 Appraisal

(C)Confidential reports (D)None of these

264. When the water allows one aspect of a person's character or performance to influence the enitre evaluation, the error will be :

(A)Constant error (B)Halo effect

(C)Central tendency (D)Similar to me

265. The main objective of 360^0Appraisal is to bring :

(A)Subjectivity (B) Objectivity

(C)Uniformity of standards (D)None of these

266. Who introduced the concept of M B O ?

(A)Mary Parker Foilet (B)Keith Davice

(C)Peter Drucker (D)F. W. Taylor

267. The concept of management by objectives was given by

(A)Peter F. Drucker (B)Luther Gulick

(C)Rensis Likert (D)Blake and Mouton

268. MBO was popularised as an approach to planning by :

(A)P.F. Drucker (B)Henry Fayol

(C) F. W. Taylor (D)None of the above

269. MBO ***cannot*** be implemented effectively in an organisation which is prone to rapid changes, either internal or environmental, because :

(A)It becomes difficult to set objectives in a changing environment

(B)It becomes difficult to assign responsibilities in a changing situation

(C) Unforeseen changes may refer most objectives unachievable

(D) None of the above

270. Which one is ***not*** a performance appraisal method?

(A) 360^0 performance appraisal

(B) Balanced score card

(C) Rank method

(D) Interview method

271. Who had given the 'Work linked democracy' explanation of Quality of Work Life.

(A) Evic Tryst (B)Evic Frank

(C) Fred Luthans (D)None of the above

272. Fish-bone Analysis is used in which of the following :

(A)Collective bargaining (B)Quality circles

(C)Quality of work life (D)Training

273. The doctrine of Quality Circle got popularity in which of the following countries :

(A)U.S.A (B)India

(C)Japan (D)U.K

274. Which of the following aims control through setting productivity measures based on best-industry practices?

(A)Pareto diagram (B) Quality circles

(C)Kaizens (D) Benchmarking

275. Fish bone analysis as a tool of quality circle was advanced by

(A) Edward Deming (B) Joseph Juran

(C) Kouru Ishi Kawa (D) Phillip Crosby

276. Who introduced the concept of quality circles in India ?

(A)P. V. Rao (B)Udai Pareek

(C)Dharani P. Sinha (D)S. R. Udpa

277. In which industry, Quality circles in India were first introduced ?

(A)Bharat Electronics Ltd.

(B)Bharat Heavy Electricals Ltd.

(C)Bharat Heavy Plates and Vessels

(D)Bharat Earth Movers Ltd.

278. In which public sector organization quality circles was first introduced in India.

(A)Hindustan Aeronautics Ltd.

(B)Bharath Earth Movers Ltd.

(C)Bharath Heavy Electricals Ltd.

(D)Hindustan Machine Tools Ltd.

279. A voluntary group of workers, to examine work-related problems that affect quality of output, is called :

(A)Quality of work life (B)Quality team

(C)Quality circle (D)All the above

280. The concept of quality circle is a brain child of :

(A)Ishikawa Japanese engineer

(B)Munchu, H.R.M. Expert

(C)Peter Drucker

(D)Japanese union for scientists and engineers

281. Who is the father of Quality Circles?

(A)Lewin (B)Ishikawa

(C)Udpa (D)Robert Owen

282. Arrange the following processes of quality circle in the order in which they occur.

(i)Pareto Analysis

(ii)Fish Bone Analysis

(iii)Pie Chart

(iv)Brain Storming Exercise

Code:

(A)	(i)	(iv)	(ii)	(iii)
(B)	(iv)	(ii)	(i)	(iii)
(C)	(iii)	(i)	(iv)	(ii)
(D)	(iv)	(i)	(ii)	(iii)

283. Match the following development dimensions of HRD function :

List-I

(a)Job enrichment

(b)Career development

(c)Key performance areas

(d)Succession Planning

List-II

(i)Analyzing the job

(ii)Matching the role and the person

(iii)Developing the person in the role

(iv)Developing the role for the person

	(a)	(b)	(c)	(d)
(A)	(iv)	(iii)	(ii)	(i)
(B)	(i)	(iv)	(iii)	(ii)
(C)	(iv)	(iii)	(i)	(ii)
(D)	(i)	(iii)	(ii)	(iv)

284. Who coined the term 'informal sector'?

(A)Keith Davis (B)Amartya Sen

(C)Mahabub Ul Haq (D)Keith Hart

285. Power distance, uncertainty avoidance, individualism and masculinity as dimensions of cross–cultural comparative model is given by

(A)Kluckhohn & Strodthbeck

(B)Geert Hofstede

(C)Andres Lauvent

(D)Hall and Trompenaar

286. Job - analysis includes :

(A)Job description (B)Job specification

(C)Both (A) and (B) (D)Job evaluation

287. Which of the following is ***not*** a method of Job Analysis?

(A)Critical Incident Approach

(B)Job Elements Approach

(C)Position Analysis Questionnaire

(D)Application Blank

288. Which of the following case of methods of Job analysis information?

(A)The interview (B)Questionnaire

(C)Observation and Diary (D)All the above

289. By-product of Job Analysis are :

(A)Job Enrichment and Job Evaluation

(B)Job Description and Job Specification

(C) Job Rotation and Job Transfer

(D)Job Satisfaction and Job Specification

290. Job analysis includes :

(A) Job description and job enlargement

(B) Job enlargement and job enrichment

(C) Job description and job specification

(D) All of the above

291. Job analysis involves

(A)Job description and job specification

(B)Job order and job description

(C)Job specification and job order

(D)Job satisfaction and job description

292. Monitoring employees through a preplanned series of position is called :

(A)Promotion (B)Succession planning

(C)Job reporting (D)Job rotation

293. Approaches to job design includes :

(A)Engineering approach

(B)Human approach

(C)The job characteristic approach

(D)All the above

294. Which of the following is a strategy of job design that increases job depth by meeting employee's needs for psychological growth?

(A)Job rotation

(B)Job enrichment

(C)Job enlargement

(D)Job enrichment and job enlargement

295. Job design does ***not*** involve which one of the following considerations :

(A)How much autonomy should be given to individual employees?

(B)What tasks should be allocated?

(C)Who should be involved / consulted?

(D)Ignoring where the job is located

296. When a worker has a say in the work methods that he/she wishes to utilise in his/her job is characterized by :

(A)Skill variety (B) Job identity

(C)Job significance (D) Autonomy

297. The job design would be LEAST formal in a

(A)matrix structure

(B)professional bureaucracy

(C)divisionalized structure

(D)machine bureaucracy

298. Restructuring of job content and division of responsibility between jobs to increase the amount of responsibility is called :

(A)Job Enlargement (B)Job Enrichment

(C)Job Analysis (D)Job evaluation

299. The provision of training and practice in increased range of skills is known as____ :

(A)Job enlargement (B)Job enrichment

(C)Job Analysis (D)Job Evaluation

300. The internal wage differentials and relative worth of the job for the organization are determined by

(A)Job Analysis (B)Job Design

(C)Job Enrichment (D)Job Evaluation

301. While formulating a wage structure, a Wage Board should consider:-

(A)Requirements of social justice

(B)Capacity of the industry to pay

(C)Possibility of reduction in work force

(D)Periodicity for review of wage structure

302. The purpose of job enrichment is to

(A)expand the number of tasks an individual can do

(B)increase job efficiency

(C)increase job effectiveness

(D)increase job satisfaction of middle management

303. Which one is ***not*** a non-quantitative job evaluation method?

(A)Ranking method

(B)Grading method

(C)Point rating method

(D)Job-classification method

304. Thesystematic process of making job evaluation determinations about a job based upon its content and the way is which it actually functions within the organization is called:

(A)Job Determination (B) Job Analysis

(C)Job Evaluation (D) Job Grading

305. Match the following with List-A to List-B

List-A

(a)Job Rotation
(b)Job Instruction
(c)Vestible training
(d)Programmed Instruction

List-B

(i)The trainer appraises the performance of the trainee, provides feedback information and corrects the trainee

(ii)The movement of the trainee from one job to another

(iii)Simulation of actual work conditions in a class room

(iv)The subject matter to be learned is presented in a service of carefully planned sequential units.

	(a)	(b)	(c)	(d)
(A)	(iv)	(iii)	(ii)	(i)
(B)	(ii)	(i)	(iii)	(iv)
(C)	(iii)	(iv)	(ii)	(i)
(D)	(i)	(ii)	(iii)	(iv)

306. The method by which relative worth of Jobs in an organization is determined is called as :

(A)Job Specification (B)Job Description

(C)Job Analysis (D)Job Evaluation

307. Which of the following is the most analytical method of evaluation?

(A)Ranking Method

(B)Grading Method

(C)Factor-Comparision Method

(D)Point Method

308. Under job Evaluation techniques ranking method includes :

(A)Simple ranking (B)Ranking the key jobs

(C)Paired comparison (D)All the above

309. An organized factual statement of the duties and responsibilities of a specific job is known as :

(A)Job description (B)Job specification

(C)Job evaluation (D)Job enrichment

310. Match the following :

Personal management function

(a)Job enrichment

(b)Job description

(c)Job specification

(d)Job evaluation

Deals with

(i) determining relative worth of various jobs

(ii)restructuring job content to include more responsibility

(iii)qualification of job performers

(iv)functions required to be performed on the job

	(a)	(b)	(c)	(d)
(A)	(i)	(iii)	(iv)	(ii)
(B)	(ii)	(iv)	(iii)	(i)
(C)	(i)	(iv)	(iii)	(ii)
(D)	(i)	(iii)	(iv)	(ii)

311. Match the following:

Group A

(a) Point ranking method

(b) Paid holidays

(c) Provident fund

(d) Job grading method

Group B

(i)Non-Analytical method of job-evaluation

(ii)Fringe benefits

(iii)Analytical method of job-evaluation

(iv)Perquisites

	(a)	(b)	(c)	(d)
(A)	(iii)	(iv)	(ii)	(i)
(B)	(iii)	(ii)	(i)	(iv)
(C)	(ii)	(i)	(iii)	(iv)
(D)	(i)	(iv)	(ii)	(iii)

312. Arrange the following steps of job evaluation process in the correct sequence :

(i)Job description / Specification

(ii) Employee Classification

(iii) Job Evaluation Programme

(iv) Job Analysis

(A) (i) (ii) (iii) (iv)

(B) (iv) (i) (iii) (ii)

(C) (iv) (iii) (ii) (i)

(D) (ii) (i) (iii) (iv)

313. Organize the following steps in job evaluation in the sequence of their occurrence :

(i)Preparing key or benchmarking job

(ii)Selecting comparable and compensable factors

(iii) Job analysis data

(iv) Administration of Position Analysis Questionnaire

(A) (iii), (i), (ii), (iv)

(B) (i), (iii), (iv), (ii)

(C) (i), (iii), (ii), (iv)

(D) (ii), (iii), (i), (iv)

314. Match the following :

List- I

(a) Job specification

(b) Career

(c) Job analysis

(d) Job description

List- II

(i)Procedure for determining duties and skills for a job and the kind of person required to perform

(ii)List of Job's duties, responsibilities, reporting, relations, working conditions

(iii)List of job's human requirements in terms of education, skills, personality etc.

(iv)The occupational positions a person has had over many years

Codes:

	(a)	(b)	(c)	(d)
(A)	(i)	(ii)	(iii)	(iv)

(B)	(i)	(iii)	(ii)	(iv)
(C)	(iii)	(iv)	(i)	(ii)
(D)	(iv)	(iii)	(ii)	(i)

315. A broad statement of the purpose, duties and responsibilities of a job or position, may be referred to as :

(A) Job Analysis (B)Task Analysis

(C) Job Description (D)Job Specification

316. Match List – I with List – II. Select the correct answer from the codes given below

List – I

(a) Theory – X

(b) Theory – Y

(c) Job Enrichment

(d) Job Enlargement

List – II

(i) Integration of behaviour is the key process in Management.

(ii) Calls for vertical job loading.

(iii)Based on the traditional conception of control and command.

(iv)To provide more control over one's activities and greater participation in decisions.

Codes:

	(a)	(b)	(c)	(d)
(A)	(i)	(ii)	(iii)	(iv)
(B)	(iii)	(i)	(ii)	(iv)
(C)	(iii)	(i)	(iv)	(ii)
(D)	(i)	(iv)	(ii)	(iii)

317. What is broad-banding?

(A)Clubbing manpower structure

(B)Integrating information system

(C)Flexible pay-banding allowing grade mobility performance

(D)None of the above

318. Job description provides information about characteristics required to perform activities.

(A)Forming supportive objectives

(B)Delegating the authority

(C)Establishing enterprise objectives

(D) Identifying and classifying activities.

319. The provision of training and practice in an increased range of skills is known as :

(A) Job enrichment (B)Job enlargement

(C)Job evaluation (D)Job analysis

320. The process of establishing the value of jobs in a Job hierarchy, is known as :

(A)Job Analysis

(B)Job Evaluation

(C)Job Requirement

(D)Performance Evaluation

321. A list of Jobs duties, Responsibilities, reporting relationships and working conditions is called :

(A)Job enhancement (B)Job specification

(C)Job description (D)Job enlargement

322. The process of studying and collecting information relating to a specific job is known as :

(A)Job Analysis (B)Job Specification

(C)Job Description (D)Motion Study

323. The horizontal expansion of jobs is termed as :

(A)Job enrichment (B)Job enlargement

(C)Job sharing (D)Job involvement

324. A written statement of the human qualification, education and experience needed to perform a job is referred to as:

(A) Job enrichment (B) Job specification

(C) Job design (D) Job description

325. Job evaluation is the evaluation of _____.

(A)Work (B)Worker

(C)Working Conditions (D)All the above

326. A systematic comparison done in order to determine the value of Job is called :

(A)Job upgradation (B)Job enrichment

(C)Job Evaluation (D)Job analysis

327. When monotony in work is reduced by giving a wider variety of duties to employees, this is known as :

(A)Job rotation (B)Job redesign

(C)Job enlargement (D)Job enrichment

328. Modifying methods of performing a job to reduce the levels of skill or skills demanded is known as :

(A) Multi – tasking (B) De - skilling

(C) Multi – skilling (D) None of these

329. the value of jobs in a job hierarchy is known as

(i)Job analysis

(ii)Job requirement

(iii)Job evaluation

(iv)Performance evaluation

Find the correct combination according to the Code.

(A) (i)and (ii) (B) (ii)and (iii)

(C) (iii)and (iv) (D) (i)and (iv)

330. The distinction between 'job enrichment' and 'job enlargement' is

(A)semantics

(B)'job enrichment' is vertical loading while 'job enlargement' is horizontal loading

(C)'job enrichment' is the outgrowth of Hertzberg's theory while 'job enlargement' is of Maslow's orientation.

(D)'job enrichment' is more for the individual and the other is more of organisation making

331. Job Evaluation criterion comes from:

(A) Job manual (B) Job description

(C) Job specification (D) Job duration

332. The process of determining the tasks that make-up a job and the skills, abilities and responsibilities needed to perform the job is called

(A) Job Analysis (B) Job Description

(C) Job Enrichment (D) All of the above

333. One of the following is ***not*** included in job descriptions :

(A) Job title (B) Location

(C) Penal actions (D) Duties

334. Match the following :

List – A

(i) Job Analysis

(ii) Job Description

(iii) Job Specification

(iv) Job Classification

List – B

(a) Grading jobs according to scale of pay

(b) A statement of human qualities to fill the job

(c) A process of obtaining job facts

(d)A statement of duties and responsibilities of a job

Codes:

	(i)	(ii)	(iii)	(iv)
(A)	(c)	(d)	(b)	(a)
(B)	(c)	(d)	(a)	(b)
(C)	(a)	(b)	(c)	(d)
(D)	(b)	(c)	(d)	(a)

335. Minimum wages are fixed by :

(A)Trade unions (B)Employees

(C)State Governments(D)Court of law

336. Which of the following is ***not*** a determinant of wages?

(A)Prevailing wages

(B)Bargaining strength of Unions

(C)Job Evaluation

(D)Performance Appraisal

337. Wage Boards set right

(A)Inter-regional differentials

(B)Inter-sectoral differentials

(C)Intra-industry differentials

(D)Inter-industry differentials

338. Wage Boards evolve wage structure for :

(A)Single Firm (B)Different Industries

(C)One Industry (D)Nation as a whole

339. Wage survey method is used for getting information regarding :

(A)Prevailing Wages (B)Variable Pay

(C)Dearness Allowance (D)All the above

340. Who among the following are ***not*** included as members of Wage Board?

(A)Employers' Representatives

(B)Workers' Representatives

(C)Consumers' Representatives

(D)Economists, Wage Experts and Members of Parliament

341. Which of the following is a method of state regulation of wages?

(A)Wage Boards

(B)Enactment of Minimum Wage Legislation

(C)Labour Courts and Tribunals

(D)All of the above

342. Which of the following is ***not*** a method of State Regulation of Wages?

(A)Minimum Wage Legislation

(B)Ordinances

(C)Wage Boards

(D)Industrial Tribunals

343. Which of the following is ***not*** a method for fixation of minimum wages in India under the Minimum Wage Act, 1948?

(A)Notification Method

(B)Committee Method

(C)Wage Boards

(D)None of the above

344. Who among the following was the chairman of the Second National Commission on Labour :

(A)Dr. P.B. Gajendragadkar

(B)Dr. Ravindra Verma

(C)Dr. Satya Narayan Jatia

(D)Justice P.N. Bhagwati

345. Which of the following is ***not*** a wage incentive plan?

(A)Halsey Plan (B)Rowan Plan

(C)Barth System (D)Beveridge Plan

346. Which of the following is ***not*** a type of wage differential?

(A)Occupational wage differential

(B)Geographical wage differential

(C)Wage Differentials on the basis of sex

(D)Personal wage differential

347. Which of the following statements about characteristics of labour is ***not*** true?

(A)Labour is a perishable commodity.

(B)Labour cannot be separated from the person.

(C)Workers have no reserve price.

(D)Labour is as flexible and mobile as capital.

348. Which of the following statements about labour market is ***not*** true?

(A)Labour market like commodity market is analyzed by supply, demand and price equilibrium.

(B)Labour Market is relatively more local than commodity market.

(C)Unlike a commodity market, the relationship between a buyer and seller in a labour market is not temporary.

(D)Monopoly in the labour market is high.

349. Money Wage is otherwise called as

(A)Real wage (B)Living wage

(C)Nominal wage (D)Fair wage

350. Which of the following requirements of a Perfect Market are ***not*** found in the Labour Market :

(A)Large number of buyers and sellers

(B)Same price

(C)Same quality

(D)None of the above

351. If money wages are fixed or constant, which of the following situation will be applicable :

(A)Real wages may also be constant

(B)Real wages may fall

(C)Real wages may rise

(D)All the above

352. Voluntary Retirement Scheme (VRS) is introduced to get rid off :

(A)Inefficient employees

(B)Surplus employees

(C)Problematic employees

(D)None of the above

353. Labour Market is :

(A)Perfect Market

(B)Imperfect Market

(C)Monopolistic Market

(D)None of the above

354. Who among the following are ***not*** included in the labour force of a country?

(A)Employees (B)Employers

(C)Domestic Servants (D)Housewives

355. Which of the following is ***not*** a characteristics of Indian Labour Market?

(A)Migratory character

(B)Low level of literacy

(C)High Degree of Unionization

(D)High rates of Absenteeism and Labour Turnover

356. Who among the following propounded the marginal productivity theory of wages?

(A)Davidson (B)Webbs

(C)Maurice Dobb (D)J.B. Clark

357. Under which of the following theories of wages, trade unions play a vital role in wage determination :

(A)Marginal Productivity theory of Wages

(B)Wage Fund Theory

(C)Residual Claimant Theory

(D)Collective Bargaining Theory

358. After all other factors of production are paid, wages are paid to labour from the left-out fund: is the theme of :

(A)Subsistence theory

(B)Marginal Productivity theory

(C)Wage fund theory

(D)Residual claimant theory

359. Match the following :

Theory of Wages

(a)Exploitation theory

(b)Subsistence theory

(c)Marginal Productivity theory

(d)Wage fund theory

Propounders

(i)J.S. Mill

(ii)J.B. Clark

(iii)Karl Marx

(iv)David Ricardo

	(a)	(b)	(c)	(d)
(A)	(iii)	(iv)	(ii)	(i)
(B)	(iii)	(ii)	(iv)	(i)
(C)	(ii)	(iii)	(iv)	(i)
(D)	(iii)	(i)	(ii)	(iv)

360. Match the following :

Theory of wage

(a)Bargaining theory

(b)Demand and Supply theory

(c)Purchasing Power theory

(d)Equity theory

Contributor

(i)J.Stacy Adams

(ii)A.C.Pigou

(iii)John Davidson

(iv)Alfred Marshall

	(a)	(b)	(c)	(d)
(A)	(iii)	(iv)	(ii)	(i)
(B)	(iv)	(ii)	(i)	(iii)
(C)	(ii)	(i)	(iii)	(iv)
(D)	(iii)	(ii)	(iv)	(i)

361. The Residual Claimant Theory of Wages was propounded by :

(A)Karl Marx (B)David Ricardo

(C)David John (D)Francis A. Walker

362. Karl Marx is said to be the proponent of which of the following theories of wages?

(A) Subsistence Theory of Wage

(B) Wage Fund Theory

(C) Surplus Value Theory of Wage

(D) Marginal Value Theory of Wage

363. Match the following :

Contributors

(a)David Ricardo

(b)James Stuart Mill

(c)F.W. Walker

(d)J.B. Clark

Wage Theories

(i)Marginal Productivity Theory

(ii)Residual Claimant Theory

(iii)Wage Fund Theory

(iv)Subsistence Theory

Codes:

	(a)	(b)	(c)	(d)
(A)	(iv)	(ii)	(i)	(iii)
(B)	(iii)	(ii)	(iv)	(i)
(C)	(iv)	(iii)	(ii)	(i)
(D)	(ii)	(iv)	(iii)	(i)

364. Match the following :

Theories of Wages

(a)Subsistence Theory

(b)Wage Fund Theory

(c)Residual Claimant Theory

(d)Surplus Value Theory

Propounders

(i)Karl Marx

(ii)Francis Walker

(iii)J.S. Mill

(iv)David Ricardo

	(a)	(b)	(c)	(d)
(A)	(iii)	(iv)	(i)	(ii)
(B)	(iv)	(iii)	(ii)	(i)

(C) (ii) (i) (iii) (iv)

(D) (i) (iii) (iv) (ii)

365. Out of the following theories of wages which one is also called as Iron Law of Wages?

(A)Wage Fund Theory

(B)Subsistence Theory

(C)Marginal Productivity Theory

(D) Collective Bargaining Theory

366. Give the correct sequence of the following

(i)LivingWage (ii)Minimum Wage

(iii)Fair Wage (iv)Subsistence Wage

Codes:

(A) (iv) (i) (iii) (ii)

(B) (iv) (ii) (iii) (i)

(C) (ii) (iv) (iii) (i)

(D) (ii) (iv) (i) (iii)

367. Match the following :

Theory of wages

(a) Wage Fund Theory

(b) Marginal Productivity Theory

(c) Bargaining Theory

(d). Investment Theory

Propagators

(i)John Bates Clark

(ii)John Davidson

(iii) John Stuart Mill

(iv)Gilelman

Codes:

	(a)	(b)	(c)	(d)
(A)	(ii)	(iv)	(i)	(iii)
(B)	(iii)	(i)	(ii)	(iv)
(C)	(iv)	(ii)	(iii)	(i)
(D)	(i)	(iii)	(ii)	(iv)

368. The "Marginal Discounted Product of Labour" as a modified version of Marginal Productivity Theory was advanced by

(A) Taussig (B) Kalecki

(C) Ricardo (D) Adam Smith

369. Wages paid on the basis of units produced are called :

(A)Time Rated (B)Money Wages

(C)Piece Rated (D)Real Wages

370. Which of the following is ***not*** a component of wages?

(A)Basic Wage (B)Dearness Allowance

(C)Fringe Benefits (D)Incentives

371. Which of the following theory of migration explains the pressures of the places of origin and attraction of the places of destination?

(A)Affluence driven skill scarcity theory

(B)Population ecology theory

(C)Push and pull theory

(D)None of the above

372. Which of the following is concerned with intra-industry wage differentials?

(A)Wage Survey (B)Job Evaluation

(C)Wage Board (D)None of the above

373. Formula for Labour Turnover rate is :

(A)$\text{Labour Turnover} = \frac{\text{Temporary total loss}}{\text{Temporary partial loss}} \times 100$

(B)$\text{Labour Turnover} = \frac{\text{Permanent total loss}}{\text{Permanent partial loss}} \times 100$

(C)Labour Turnover=(No. of Employees left during specific period÷ Average No. of employees during the same period)x100

(D)$\text{Labour Turnover} = \frac{\text{Number of Employees present}}{\text{Number of Employees left}} \times 100$

374. Wages expressed in terms of money are called :

(A)Nominal wages (B)Real wages
(C)Wage scales (D)Fringe Benefits

375. If a wage rate is determined by job evaluation, it is called :

(A)Real wage (B)Standard wage rate
(C)Piece - rate (D)Time - rate

376. The committee on Fair Wages was appointed in India in the year______.

(A) 1946 (B) 1947
(C) 1948 (D) 1949

377. Minimum wage is :

(A)The wage paid or received in monetary terms.
(B)The total amount of remuneration received by an employee during a given period.
(C)The amount of wage arrived after discounting nominal wage from the living cost.
(D)The amount of remuneration which could meet the nominal needs of the average employee.

378. In an inflationary economy like ours to–day, which of the following components of wages becomes more important :

(A)Overtime (B) Incentive
(C)Bonus (D) Dearness Allowance

379. Which of the following is ***not*** an incentive plan that relates wages with productivity?

(A)Taylor's differential piece-rate system
(B)The Beveridge Plan
(C)The Scanlon Plan
(D)The Halsey Premium Plan

380. Which of the following is ***not*** an objective of wage incentive programmes?

(A)Developing ownership interest
(B)Improving employee retention
(C)Reducing labour cost
(D)Facilitating the separation of employees

381. When the same rate of incentives is paid to the employees for each unit of goods produced by them, it is called

(A)Straight piece rate
(B)Differential piece rate
(C)Task and time bonuses
(D)None of the above

382. When more than one piece rate is offered to the individuals for goods produced by them, it is called:

(A)Straight piece rate
(B)Differential piece rate
(C)Priestman bonus plan
(D)None of the above

383. Which of the following methods discourages too much speed in the production by the employees?

(A)Straight piece rate
(B)Differential piece rate
(C)Task and time bonuses
(D)None of the above

384. Evaluating the relative worth of the employees in the organization and then deciding the awards for them is called:

(A)Merit rating
(B)Differential piece rate
(C)Task and time bonuses
(D)Straight piece rate

385. Which of following incentive systems recommends a two-piece rate for wage determination?

(A)Merrick multiple piece rate plan
(B)Taylor's differential piece rate plan
(C)Emerson efficiency plan
(D)Gnatt task and bonus system

386. In which of the following methods is the standard time stated as minutes and points?

(A)Bedeaux system

(B)Barth variable incentive plan

(C)Task and time bonus

(D)None of the above

387. Which of the following incentive plans has the following equation for computing the earnings of employees? (Actual hours worked × Time rate) + (Actual time worked / Standard time) × Time saved × Time rate:

(A)Emerson efficiency plan

(B)Rowan incentive plan

(C)Halsey incentive plan

(D)Barth variable incentive plan

388. Which of the following is ***not*** usually a group incentive plan?

(A)Halsey incentive plan

(B)Priestman bonus plan

(C)Rucker incentive plan

(D)Towne's incentive plan

389. Achieving cost saving ***not*** only on labour cost but also on overheads is the crux of

(A)Towne's incentive plan

(B)Priestman bonus plan

(C)Rucker incentive plan

(D)Halsey incentive plan

390. In which method is the standard time expressed in terms of man-minutes called "MANT"?

(A)Hayne's incentive plan

(B)Rowan incentive plan

(C)Barth variable incentive plan

(D)Bedeaux system

391. Which of the following is an example of fringe benefits?

(A)Health and accident insurance

(B)Contribution to superannuation funds

(C)Leave facilities

(D)All of the above

392. The machinery of wage board in India is primarily used in connection with

(A)Settlement of Industrial Disputes

(B)State Regulation of Wages.

(C)Determination of Wages

(D)Promoting Equal Wages for Equal Work.

393. After the report of the Royal Commission on Labour, which of the following legislations was first enacted ?

(A)Minimum Wages Act

(B)Equal Remuneration Act

(C)Payment of Wages Act

(D)Payment of Gratuity Act

394. Most of the social security benefits to workers in India are calculated on the basis of

(A)Basic wage

(B)Basic wage and Dearness Allowance

(C)Basic wage, D.A. and Medical allowance

(D)Basic wage, D.A., Medical and House rent allowance

395. Which of the following is true of Indian Labour Market ?

(A)It is a Perfect Market

(B)Monopolistic Market

(C)Imperfect Market

(D)None of the above

396. Which of the following statements is false?

(A)Good wage structure shall address to internal equity and external parity.

(B)Pay related decisions need not base on employer's capacity to pay.

(C)Wage survey is the method for knowing the 'prevailing wages'.

(D)Low wages and high productivity is exploitation.

397. Which of the following is given to workers in the unorganized sector or sweated industries?

(A)Living Wages

(B)Fair Wages

(C)Statutory Minimum Wages

(D)None of the above

398. Arrange the following according to their comparative position from lowest to the highest:

(i)Statutory Minimum Wage

(ii)Subsistence Wage

(iii)Living Wage

(iv) Fair Wage

(A)	(i)	(iii)	(ii)	(iv)
(B)	(ii)	(iv)	(i)	(iii)
(C)	(ii)	(i)	(iv)	(iii)
(D)	(i)	(iii)	(iv)	(ii)

399. Which of the following statements appear to be correct?

(A)Wage differential is desirable for the growth and development of the society.

(B)There should be no wage differential in the country.

(C)The state through regulation of wages can eliminate wage differentials.

(D)None of the above

400. Which of the following is ***not*** a characteristic of labour market?

(A)Same wage rate

(B)More sellers than buyers

(C)Heterogeneity in labour services

(D)Limited mobility of labour

401. Which of the following factors affect supply of labour?

(A)Population and Labour Force Participation Rate

(B)Skill, Experience and Job Qualification

(C)Mobility of Labour and Organization of Buyers and Sellers

(D)All the above

402. Which of the following ***cannot*** be said to be a type of wage differential?

(A)Occupational Wage Differential

(B)Geographical Wage Differential

(C)Inter-industry Wage Differential

(D)National Wage Differential

403. Fixing lower retirement age for workers will result in:

(A)increased supply of labour

(B)reduced supply of labour

(C)will have no effect on supply of labour

(D)None of the above

404. Which of the following industries lead to seasonal unemployment?

(A)Sugar industry

(B)Construction industry

(C)Ice-cream industry

(D)All the above

405. Who among the following is ***not*** included in the labour force?

(A)Workers / employees

(B)Self-employed people

(C)Domestic servants

(D)House-wives

406. Which of the following types of unemployment is also known as Disguised Unemployment?

(A)Frictional unemployment

(B)Technological unemployment

(C)Seasonal unemployment

(D)Under employment

407. Outsourcing, when it is done internationally, affects which of the following in the country which out–sources :

(A)Supply of labour

(B)Demand for labour

(C)Both supply and demand

(D) None of the above

408. Which of the following can be said to be a correct concept of wages?

(A) Wage is a reward

(B) Wage is a compensation

(C) Wage is the price of labour

(D) Wage is an incentive to work more

409. Tripartite Wage Boards in India followed which of the following principles while making their recommendations?

(A) Minimum Wage Principle

(B) Fair Wage Principle

(C) Living Wage Principle

(D) None of the above

410. The amount sufficient to enable a worker to live in reasonable comfort, having regard to all obligations to which an average worker would ordinarily be subject to:

(A)Minimum Wage (B)Fair Wage

(C)Living Wage (D)Nominal Wage

411. A test which measures, what it is intended to measure is

(A) Reliable test (B) Standardised test

(C) Objective test (D) Valid test

412. The wage which has to be paid by an employer to his workers, irrespective of his ability, is known as :

(A) Living wage (B)Fair wage

(C) Minimum wage (D)None of the above

413. Fair wage is defined as :

(A)Monthly wage paid with Dearness Allowance

(B)Wage that is lower than living wage but more than minimum wage

(C)Wages paid with incentive

(D)Fair wage includes all allowances

414. Labour Turnover is :

(A)The rate of change in the working staff of a concern during a definite period

(B)Number of Employees joining the organization

(C)Number of Employees promoted during a year

(D)Number of Employees transferred to other departments

415. The Gregory Committee recommended that:

(A)The amount of dearness allowance should be fixed in terms of rupees and not as a percentage of actual income

(B)Either to equate the absolute amount of dearness allowance to full compensation for the weighted average of the earnings of all wage groups below the ceiling wage of Rs.200/-

(C)To equate the same to full compensation for the weighted average earnings of all wage groups below the weighted average as calculated

(D) All of the above

416. During the second World War, a Board of Conciliation under the chairmanship of Sir S. S. Ranganekar was setup. He was a retired _____ judge.

(A)High Court (B)Supreme Court

(C)Industrial Court (D)None of the above

417. The minimum remuneration for a class four employee on entry as recommended by the Third pay commission was:

(A)Rs.285/- per month(B)Rs.165/- per month

(C)Rs.185/- per month(D)Rs.175/- per month

418. The NCL has attempted to assess the General Wage Policy of the Government since independence. For this purpose, it chose the following indicators. They are:

(A)The state of industrial harmony

(B)Changes in workers level of living

(C)Changes in productivity

(D) All of the above

419. The plans having skill-based structures in which employees are paid for the jobs they perform are grouped into two types. These are as follows:

(A)Knowledge plans which link pay differentials to the depth of knowledge related to one occupation

(B)Multi-skill plans which link pay differentials to the number of different sets of tasks an employee is supposed to perform

(C)Semi-skill plans

(D)(A) and (B)both

420. The following are the major component of compensation system:

(A)Salary (B) Basic salary

(C)Advanced salary (D) Consolidated salary

421. Flexible benefits plan will help:-

(A)Control costs

(B)Enhance employee satisfaction

(C)Increase efficiency

(D)(A) and (B) both.

422. Which are the administrative problems caused due to individual incentives

(A)The difficulty in setting production standards that are accepted by both management and workers

(B)The cost of tracking output in the multiple jobs and calculating payments

(C)The cost of time study to set and keep current production standards for multiple jobs

(D)All of the above

423. One of the salient features of The Payment of Wages (Amendment) Bill, 2002 is to substitute the expressions a 'Central Government' or a 'State Government' by the expression '_____', in conformity with the other labour laws.

(A)Union Government

(B)Appropriate Government

(C)Home ministry

(D)Finance Ministry

424. A corporate wide pay plan that uses a structured formula to allocate a portion of annual company profits to employees is known as :

(A) Gain sharing (B) Profit sharing

(C) ESOPS sharing (D) All of the above

425. Standing Labour Conference (SLC) was constituted in line with the recommendations of Royal Commission on Labour in the year :

(A) 1942 (B) 1944

(C) 1946 (D) 1948

426. An incentive plan, where improvements in group productivity determines the total amount of money that is allocated, is described as :

(A)Profit sharing (B)Gain sharing

(C)Bonus sharing (D)None of these

427. The Employee Stock Ownership Plan (ESOP) was developed by :

(A)Michael Porter (B)Kaplan

(C)P. F. Drucker (D)Louis Kelso

428. Wage determination is mostly done through tools which are

(A) Objective (B) Subjective

(C) Both of (A) & (B) (D) None of these

429. Voluntary Retirement is operated as a part of:

(A)Transfer and promotion policy

(B)Exit policy

(C)Deployment

(D) Lockout

430. Referal system in HRM relates to:

(A)Refering a supplier by another supplier

(B) Refering a consultant for organizational developement

(C) Refering a candidate for job by existing employee

(D)Refering a leader to lead employees

431. The process of deciding what positions the firm will have to fill is called:

(A)Recruitment (B)Selection

(C)Personnel Planning (D)Interviewing

432. Training evaluation criteria include all but:

(A)Reactions (B)Results

(C)Relevance (D)Behaviour

433. The component of an effective performance management process that explains each employees role in terms of his or her day-to-day work is called:

(A)Role clarification

(B)Goal alignment

(C)Developmental goal setting

(D)Direction sharing

434. Balance Score Card emphasizes on:

(A)only the strategy

(B)the importance of measuring business performance

(C)critical incident method

(D)intellectual capital

435. Inputs to the selection process include all but:

(A)Job applicants

(B)Human resource planning

(C)Supervision

(D)Job analysis

436. Choose the correct option: Performance Review System, that makes managers rate people on normal distribution curve:

(A)Is ethically correct

(B)Values the full development of peoples potential

(C)Creates misalignment between values and practices

(D)Increases productivity of employees

437. Which of the following techniques is least susceptible to personal biases?

(A)Rating scales (B) Check lists

(C)Forced choices (D) BARS

438. Which of the following is ***not*** an environmental challenge facing human resources?

(A)Competition for scarce inputs

(B)Governmental rules and regulations

(C)Global competition

(D)Enivornmental activities

439. Which of the following is ***not*** a stakeholder of a company?

(A)Employee (B)Customer

(C)Competitiors (D)Shareholder

440. Sabbatical means:

(A)Extra pay for not taking sick leave

(B)An extended leave of absence

(C)Benefits for time not worked

(D)Membership-based,non-financial rewards offered to attract and retain employees

441. Match the following:

Types of organization Structure

(i)Functional

(ii)Network

(iii)Matrix

(iv)Territorial

Characteristics

(a)Maximum use of limited functional resources

(b)Adopts to local conditions

(c) Simple communication

(d)More Agile and flexible

(i)(ii)(iii)(iv)

(A)(a)(c)(b)(d)

(B)(c)(d)(a)(b)

(C)(b)(a)(c)(d)

(D)(d)(b)(a)(c)

442. Which type of unemployement takes place in the economy when there is a business downward?

(A)Fricitional unemployment

(B)Structural unemployment

(C)Cyclical unemployment

(D)Unstructured unemployment

443. Match the correct options: Suspension:

(A)Actual posting of an employee to a specific job

(B)Termination of the services of an employee

(C)Downward movement of an employee in the organizational hierarchy

(D)Prohibiting an employee from attending work and performing normal duties to him/her

444. Choose the correct option:

Industrial Policy(1956)declared by the Government of India aimed at establishing:

(A)Capitalistic economy

(B)Socialistic pattern of society

(C)Mixed economy

(D)Democratic economy

445. An adult worker under the Factories Act,1948 is eligible for leave with wages @1 day for every ………..days worked during the preceding year.

(A) 50 (B) 20

(C) 15 (D) 240

446. Changes in the population characteristics such as age, gender, marital status, income and education are the examples of

(A) Demographic characteristics

(B) Cultural characteristics

(C) Geographic characteristics

(D) None of the above

447. Which of the following is ***not*** an aptitude Test?

(A) Intelligence Test (B) Psychomotor test

(C) Skill Test (D) Job Knowledge Test

448. Match the following :

List – I

(i)Content of a job's duties and responsibilities

(ii) Movement of an employee from one job to the another

(iii) Adding duties and responsibilities that will provide for skill variety task identity and autonomy

(iv) Adding more and different tasks to a specialized job to provide greater variety

List – II

(a) Job enlargement

(b) Job enrichment

(c) Job rotation

(d) Job design

	(i)	(ii)	(iii)	(iv)
(A)	(a)	(b)	(c)	(d)
(B)	(b)	(c)	(d)	(a)
(C)	(d)	(c)	(b)	(a)
(D)	(c)	(b)	(d)	(a)

449. 'Hyrogliphs' essentially is:

(A)Picture language (B)Script

(C)Notations (D)Gestures

450. Match the correct options: Graphic Rating Scale is:

(A)Evaluation based on key incidents

(B)Rating in behavioural terms

(C)A scale that lists a number of traits and a range of performance for each

(D)Evaluation by ratee

---000---

UNIT-III

HUMAN RESOURCE MANAGEMENT (HRM)

1. (C)Efficiency

2. (A)Man

Explanation: Human Resources (HR)

- The company department charged with finding, screening, recruiting and training job applicants, as well as administering employee-benefit programs.
- As companies reorganize to gain competitive edge, human resources plays a key role in helping companies deal with a fast-changing competitive environment and the greater demand for quality employees.
- Research conducted by The Conference Board has found six key people-related activities that human resources completes to add value to a company:

1. Effectively managing and utilizing people.

2.Trying performance appraisal and compensation to competencies.

3.Developing competencies that enhance individual and organizational performance.

4. Increasing the innovation, creativity and flexibility necessary to enhance competitiveness.

5. Applying new approaches to work process design, succession planning, career development and inter-organizational mobility.

6.Managing the implementation and integration of technology through improved staffing, training and communication with employees.

3.(D) All the above

Explanation: Objectives of Human Resource Management:

1. Societal: HRM may contribute ethically and socially regarding the needs and challenges emerging in the society.

2. Organizational: The main objective of HRM is to achieve organizational goals by bringing organizations effectiveness. HRM is not an end but it is a means to assist the organization in order to attain its objectives

3. Functional: Functional objective of HRM deals with contributions of each department regarding their need and effectiveness in order to attain organization goal.

4. Personal: HRM also deals with personal objectives of the individuals so that personal and organizational objectives can be met or order to achieve maximum production and attain competitive advantage. These personal objectives are important in order to maintain, retain and to motivate employees. If this not done employees dissatisfaction and poor performance will result in attrition or low productivity.

4.(B)Dimension of People

Explanation:

- Human resource management (HRM) is the management of an organization's workforce, or human resources.
- It is responsible for the recruitment (attraction), selection, training, assessment, and rewarding of employees.
- The function of HRM was initially dominated by transactional work such as payroll and benefits administration, but due to globalization, technological advancement, and further research.
- HRM now focuses on strategic initiatives like mergers and acquisitions, talent management, succession planning, industrial and labor relations, and diversity and inclusion.

5. (B)Human Resource Management

6. (B) Flow of activities

7. (D) Accounting

8. (B) Human Resource Management

9. (D) All of the above

10.(D) Maintaining

Explanation: Operative Functions of HRM

1. Procurement function: The first operative function of personnel management is procurement. It is concerned with procuring and employing people who possess necessary skill, knowledge and aptitude. Under its purview job analysis, manpower planning, recruitment, selection, placement, induction and internal mobility, etc. included.

2. Development: It is the process of improving, molding, changing and developing the skills, knowledge, creative ability, aptitude, attitude, values and commitment based on present and future requirements both at the individual's and organization's level.

3. Motivation and compensation: It is a process which inspires people to give their best to the organization through the use of intrinsic (achievement, recognition, responsibility) and extrinsic (job design, work scheduling, appraisal based incentives) rewards.

4. Maintenance: It aims at protecting and preserving the physical and psychological health of employees through various welfare measures.

5. Integration function: This tries to integrate the goals of an organization with employee aspirations through various employee-oriented programmes, like redressing grievances promptly, instituting proper disciplinary measures, empowering people to decide things independently, encouraging a participative culture, offering constructive help to trade unions etc.

6. Emerging issues: Effective management of human resources depends on refining HRM practices to changing conditions. Hence the need to look at other important issues that can motivate people to give their best in a dynamic and ever-changing environment.

11.(A)Downsizing

Explanation: Downsize:

- Reducing the size of a company by eliminating workers and/or divisions within the company.
- It is sometimes referred to as "trimming the fat".
- When a company downsizes, it is attempting to find ways to improve efficiency and increase profitability.
- In a business enterprise, downsizing is reducing the number of employees on the operating payroll.
- Downsizing is different from a ***layoff***, with downsizing intended to be a permanent downscaling and a layoff intended to be a temporary downscaling in which employees may later be rehired.
- Businesses use several techniques in downsizing, including providing incentives to take early retirement and transfer to subsidiary companies, but the most common technique is to simply terminate the employment of a certain number of people.
- ***Rightsizing*** is downsizing in the belief that an enterprise really should operate with fewer people.
- ***Dumb sizing*** is downsizing that, in retrospect, failed to achieve the desired effect.

12.(B) Retrenchment

Explanation:

- Retrenchment is something akin to downsizing.
- When a company or government goes through retrenchment, it reduces outgoing money or expenditures or redirects focus in an attempt to become more financially solvent.
- Many companies that are being pressured by stockholders or have had flagging profit reports may resort to retrenchment to shore up their operations and make them more profitable.
- Although retrenchment is most often used in countries throughout the world to refer to layoffs, it can also label the more general tactic of cutting back and downsizing.

13.(D) All the above

14.(B)Personnel Department

15.(D)Dave Ulrich

16.(D)Right sizing

Explanation: Rightsizing:

- The process of a corporation reorganizing or restructuring their business by cost-cutting, reduction of workforce, or reorganizing upper-level management.
- The goal is to get the company molded properly to achieve the maximum profit.
- The term rightsizing is often used by companies instead of downsizing because it sounds less drastic.
- "The company felt that rightsizing was necessary after four quarters of losses."

17.(D)Dearness Allowance

18.(C)Innovative and challenging, making the corporate dynamic

19.(C) (A) and (B) above

20.(C)Retiring people and rehabilitating them

Explanation: Exit policy is a directive by the administration on wrapping up industry operations. It helps an enterprise to draw out from its business (for any reason) while securing the interests of engaged parties.

21.(B) Human resources management.

22.(D)Work with others

23.(B) Motorola

Explanation: Six Sigma:

- Six Sigma is a set of tools and techniques/strategies for process improvement originally developed by Motorola in 1985.
- Six Sigma became well known after Jack Welch made it a central focus of his business strategy at General Electric in 1995.
- Six Sigma seeks to improve the quality of process outputs by identifying and removing the causes of defects (errors) and minimizing variability in manufacturing and business processes.
- It uses a set of quality management methods, including statistical methods, and creates a special infrastructure of people within the organization ("Champions", "Black Belts", "Green Belts", "Yellow Belts", etc.) who are experts in the methods.
- Each Six Sigma project carried out within an organization follows a defined sequence of steps and has quantified value targets, for example; process cycle time reduction, customer satisfaction, reduction in pollution, cost reduction and/or profit increase.
- The term Six Sigma originated from terminology associated with manufacturing, specifically terms associated with statistical modeling of manufacturing processes.

24.(A)Japan

Explanation: Kaizen:

- The Japanese word Kaizen is uded for "improvement", or "change for the better" refers to philosophy or practices that focus upon continuous improvement of processes in manufacturing, engineering, and business management.
- When used in the business sense and applied to the workplace, kaizen refers to activities that continually improve all functions, and involves all employees from the CEO to the assembly line workers.
- It also applies to processes, such as purchasing and logistics that cross organizational boundaries into the supply chain.
- By improving standardized activities and processes, kaizen aims to eliminate waste.
- Kaizen was first implemented in several Japanese businesses after the Second World War.

25.(D) increasing material handling

Explanation: Kanban

- Kanban (literally signboard or billboard) is a scheduling system for lean and just-in-time (JIT) production.

- Kanban is a system to control the logistical chain from a production point of view, and is not an inventory control system.
- Kanban was developed by ***Taiichi Ohno***, at Toyota, to find a system to improve and maintain a high level of production.
- Kanban is one method through which JIT is achieved.
- Kanban became an effective tool in support of running a production system as a whole, and it proved to be an excellent way for promoting improvement.
- Problem areas were highlighted by reducing the number of kanban in circulation.

26.(C) card

27.(A)A means of effective dialogue

28.(C) Strategy

Explanation: Total quality management (TQM)

- Total quality management (TQM) describes a management approach to long–term success through customer satisfaction.
- In a TQM effort, all members of an organization participate in improving processes, products, services, and the culture in which they work.
- The methods for implementing this approach come from the teachings of such quality leaders as Philip B. Crosby, W. Edwards Deming, Armand V. Feigenbaum, Kaoru Ishikawa, and Joseph M. Juran.

The Primary Elements of TQM

- Total quality management can be summarized as a management system for a customer-focused organization that involves all employees in continual improvement.
- It uses strategy, data, and effective communications to integrate the quality discipline into the culture and activities of the organization.
- Customer-focused
- Total employee involvement
- Process-centered
- Integrated system
- Strategic and systematic approach
- Continual improvement
- Fact-based decision making
- Communications

29.(D) (iii) (iv)(i)(ii)

30.(B) Total Quality Management

31.(D)Kaizan

32.(D) Identifying needs of employees

Explanation: Steps in planning

1. Setting Goals and Objectives
2. Data Gathering
3. Analysis and Solutions
4. Recommendations
5. Implementation
6. Follow-up and Periodic Reviews

33.(B) Policy

34.(B) Looking back

35.(C) Human Resource Planning

Explanation: Human Resource Planning (HRP)

- The ongoing process of systematic planning to achieve optimum use of an organization's most valuable asset - its human resources.
- The objective of human resource (HR) planning is to ensure the best fit between employees and jobs, while avoiding manpower shortages or surpluses.
- The three key elements of the HR planning process are forecasting labor demand, analyzing present labor supply, and balancing projected labor demand and supply.

36.(D)All the above

37.(A) Primary

38.(A) (c) (b) (d) (a) (f) (e) (g)

39.(D)It is the process by which an organisation ensures that it has the right number and kind of people at the right place, at the right time.

40.(C) (iv), (iii), (ii), (i)

41.(A)Ratio-Trend Analysis

42.(D) Demand and supply forecasting of manpower

43.(B) It is an integrated approach to performing the personnel function required to meet organizational and individual objectives.

44.(C)Management games

45.(C)Procurement, Development, Compensation, Integration and Maintenance

Explanation: The functions of personnel management

(A) Management Functions

(i) Planning: Planning is a fundamental function of personnel management. It involves deciding in advance what is to be done, where, how and by whom it is to be done.

(ii) Organization: It is used in the sense of an enterprise or a business unit. As a matter of fact, it is referred to as the social system encompassing all formal relations and yet another useful way of looking at organization is to consider it as an essential function of personnel management. In operational sense, organization may be considered as consisting of division of work among people and co-ordination of their activities towards some objectives.

(iii) Directing: It is the managerial function consisting of all those activities which are concerned directly with guiding, influencing and supervising the subordinates in their jobs. It is thus performance oriented. Some elements of the directing function of personnel management are:

- Supervising the work of subordinates to ensure that their performance conforms to plan.
- Maintaining discipline and rewarding effective performance.
- Issuing orders and instructions.
- Motivating the subordinates to direct their behavior in a desired pattern.

(iv)Controlling: Controlling as a function of management means the measurement and correction of performance of activities of subordinates in order to make sure that enterprise objectives and plans devised to attain them are accomplished. Control thus consists in knowing the extent to which actions are in conformity with plans adopted and instructions issued so that errors and deviations are reported and appropriate corrective actions taken. Remedial action may result in alteration of plans, change in the organization structure and modification in the staffing process.

(B) Operative Functions

(i) Procurement: It is concerned with the obtaining of the proper kind and number of personnel necessary to accomplish necessary organization goals. The function is related to subjects like the determination of manpower requirements and their recruitment, selection and placement.

The manpower requirements are calculated in terms and numbers of personnel needed and their quality. Selection and placement cover different activities designed to screen and hire personnel, such as, application forms, psychological tests, interviews and induction.

(ii) Development: After the personnel have been obtained, it is necessary to develop them. Development implies the increase of skill, through training, that is necessary for proper job performance.

This aspect of personnel function has acquired great importance even in our country during the last quarter of a century or so due to greater use of technology in every department of a business enterprise. Development function will be influenced by numerous factors, like induction of new machines, promotions and transfers.

(iii) Compensation: This function can be defined as the adequate and equitable remuneration of personnel for their contributions to organization objectives. In developed countries, compensation cannot be described as a great motivating force as strong as it is in less developed countries.

Compensating remains one of the basic functions of personnel management. A proper wage system takes into consideration a number of factors and subjects like job evaluation, wage policies, wage systems and wage incentive schemes.

(iv) Integration: It can be defined as an attempt to effect a reasonable reconciliation of individual and organisational interests. Integration must follow the above three functions of procurement, development and compensation. The function of integration relates to problems of communication, informal organisation and trade unions.

(v) Maintenance: Maintenance refers to sustaining and improving the conditions that have been established.

In order to accomplish this objective, it would be desirable that research must continue in every direction so that the function of maintenance is performed properly.

46.(B) Developing a pool of job candidates

Explanation: Recruitment:

- Recruitment refers to the process of attracting, screening, selecting, and on boarding a qualified person for a job.
- The stages of the recruitment process include:
- job analysis and developing a person specification; the sourcing of candidates by networking, advertising, or other search methods; matching candidates to job requirements and screening individuals using testing (skills or personality assessment); assessment of candidates' motivations and their fit with organizational requirements by interviewing and other assessment techniques.
- The recruitment process also includes the making and finalizing of job offers and the induction and on boarding of new employees.

47.(D) None of the above

Explanation:Internal Sources of Recruitment

- **Promotions:** Promotion means to give a higher position, status, salary and responsibility to the employee. So, the vacancy can be filled by promoting a suitable candidate from the same organisation.
- **Transfers:** Transfer means a change in the place of employment without any change in the position, status, salary and responsibility of the employee. So, the vacancy can be filled by transferring a suitable candidate from the same organisation.
- **Internal Advertisements:** Here, the vacancy is advertised within the organisation. The existing employees are asked to apply for the vacancy. So, recruitment is done from within the organisation.
- **Retired Managers:** Sometimes, retired managers may be recalled for a short period. This is done when the organisation cannot find a suitable candidate.
- **Recall from Long Leave:** The organisation may recall a manager who has gone on a long leave. This is done when the organisation faces a problem which can only be solved by that particular manager. After he solves the problem, his leave is extended

48.(A) Recruitment

49.(D)All the above

50.(D)Selecting candidates

51.(B)Manpower planning, Job analysis, Recruitment

52.(B) Poaching

53.(A)Process of searching for prospective employee

54.(D) Application Blank

55.(D) All the above

Explanation: The external sources of recruitment:

- **Management Consultants:** Management consultants are used for selecting higher-level staff.
- **Public Advertisements:** The Personnel department of a company advertises the vacancy in newspapers, the internet, etc. This

advertisement gives information about the company, the job and the required qualities of the candidate. It invites applications from suitable candidates.

- **Campus Recruitment:** The organisation conducts interviews in the campuses of Management institutes and Engineering Colleges. Suitable candidates are selected by the organization based on their academic record, communication skills, intelligence, etc. This source is used for recruiting qualified, trained but inexperienced candidates.
- **Recommendations:** The organization may also recruit candidates based on the recommendations received from existing managers or from sister companies.
- **Deputation Personnel:** The organization may also recruit candidates who are sent on deputation by the Government or Financial institutions or by holding or subsidiary companies.

56.(B)Advertisement

57.(D) All the above

58.(B)Acquiring new skills and talent

Explanation: The advantages of using external sources of recruitment:

- It encourages young blood with new ideas to enter the organization.
- It offers wide scope for selection. This is because a large number of suitable candidates will come for the selection process.
- There are less chances of bias or partiality.
- Here there is no need to maintain confidential records.

59.(B) Statement (2)

60.(A)Advertisement

61.(C) (iv) (iii) (ii) (i)

62.(D) Predictor Criterion Model

63.(A)Aptitude Test

Explanation: Aptitude test:

- Employee selection test (such as an IQ test) in which the candidate's innate abilities and potential for achievement (and not his or her knowledge) is ascertained.

64.(D) Statistical Test

65.(A)Proficiency Test

Explanation:

- An achievement test is a test of developed skill or knowledge. The most common type of achievement test is a standardized test developed to measure skills and knowledge learned in a given grade level, usually through planned instruction, such as training or classroom instruction.
- Achievement tests are often contrasted with tests that measure aptitude, a more general and stable cognitive trait.
- High achievement scores usually indicate a mastery of grade-level material, and the readiness for advanced instruction.
- Low achievement scores can indicate the need for remediation or repeating a course grade.

66.(B) Physical Test

Explanation:

- Psychological testing is a field characterized by the use of samples of behavior in order to assess psychological construct(s), such as cognitive and emotional functioning, about a given individual.
- The technical term for the science behind psychological testing is psychometrics.
- By samples of behavior, one means observations of an individual performing tasks that have usually been prescribed beforehand, which often means scores on a test.
- These responses are often compiled into statistical tables that allow the evaluator to compare the behavior of the individual being tested to the responses of a norm group.

67.(B) Intelligence Test

68.(A) (b), (e), (d), (c), (f), (a), (g)

Explanation: Steps in selection process

- **Preliminary Interview:** The purpose of preliminary interviews is basically to eliminate unqualified applications based on information supplied in application forms. The basic objective is to reject misfits. On the other hands preliminary interviews is often called a courtesy interview and is a good public relations exercise.
- **Selection Tests:** Jobseekers who past the preliminary interviews are called for tests. There are various types of tests conducted depending upon the jobs and the company. These tests can be Aptitude Tests, Personality Tests, and Ability Tests and are conducted to judge how well an individual can perform tasks related to the job. Besides this there are some other tests also like Interest Tests (activity preferences), Graphology Test (Handwriting), Medical Tests, Psychometric Tests etc.
- **Employment Interview:** The next step in selection is employment interview. Here interview is a formal and in-depth conversation between applicant's acceptability. It is considered to be an excellent selection device. Interviews can be One-to-One, Panel Interview, or Sequential Interviews. Besides there can be Structured and Unstructured interviews, Behavioral Interviews, Stress Interviews.
- **Reference & Background Checks:** Reference checks and background checks are conducted to verify the information provided by the candidates. Reference checks can be through formal letters, telephone conversations. However it is merely a formality and selections decisions are seldom affected by it.
- **Selection Decision:** After obtaining all the information, the most critical step is the selection decision is to be made. The final decision has to be made out of applicants who have passed preliminary interviews, tests, final interviews and reference checks. The views of line managers are considered generally because it is the line manager who is responsible for the performance of the new employee.
- **Physical Examination:** After the selection decision is made, the candidate is required to undergo a physical fitness test. A job offer is often contingent upon the candidate passing the physical examination.
- **Job Offer:** The next step in selection process is job offer to those applicants who have crossed all the previous hurdles. It is made by way of letter of appointment.
- **Final Selection:** After completion of above all steps candidate finally selected by the organization.

69.(A)Graphology

Explanation: Graphology is the pseudoscientific study and analysis of handwriting, especially in relation to human psychology.

70. (D) It affects the self-improvement efforts of personnel.

71.(B) Physiognomy

Explanation:

- Physiognomy is the assessment of a person's character or personality from his outer appearance, especially the ***face***.
- The term physiognomy can also refer to the general appearance of a person, object or terrain, without reference to its implied characteristics, as in the physiognomy of a plant community.

72.(B) Open Ended

Explanation:

- A job interview is a process in which a potential employee is evaluated by an employer for prospective employment in their company, organization, or firm.
- During this process, the employer hopes to determine whether or not the applicant is suitable for the role.

73.(B) Selection

74.(A)Exit Interview

Explanation:

- An exit interview is a survey conducted with an individual who is separating from an organization or relationship.
- Most commonly, this occurs between an employee and an organization, a student and an educational institution, or a member and an association.
- An organization can use the information gained from an exit interview to assess what should be improved, changed, or remain intact.
- More so, an organization can use the results from exit interviews to reduce employee, student, or member turnover and increase productivity and engagement, thus reducing the high costs associated with turnover.
- Some examples of the value of conducting exit interviews include shortening the recruiting and hiring process, reducing absenteeism, improving innovation, sustaining performance, and reducing possible litigation if issues mentioned in the exit interview are addressed.
- It is important for each organization to customize its own exit interview in order to maintain the highest levels of survey validity and reliability.
- The exit interview fits into the separation stage of the employee life cycle (ELC).
- This stage, the last one of the ELC, spans from the moment an employee becomes disengaged until his or her departure from the organization.
- This is the key time that an exit interview should be administered because the employee's feelings regarding his or her departure are fresh in mind.
- An off-boarding process allows both the employer and employee to properly close the existing relationship so that company materials are collected, administrative forms are completed, knowledge base and projects are transferred or documented, feedback and insights are gathered through exit interviews, and any loose ends are resolved.

75.(A) Dale Yoder

Explanation:

- Selection is the process of picking up individuals (out of the pool of job applicants) with requisite qualifications and competence to fill jobs in the organization.
- "Selection is the process of differentiating between applicants in order to identify and hire those with a greater likelihood of success in a job."

76.(D)Structured interview

Explanation: Structured interview:

- Fixed format interview in which all questions are prepared beforehand and are put in the same order to each interviewee.
- Although this style lacks the free flow of a friendly conversation (as in an unstructured Interview) it provides the precision and reliability required in certain situations.

77.(D) Management games

78.(A)A place

Explanation:

- An assessment centre is a place at which a person, such as a member of staff, is assessed to determine their suitability for particular roles, especially management or military command.
- The candidates' personality and aptitudes are determined by a variety of techniques including interviews, examinations and psychometric testing.

79.(B)Expertise, innovation and rationality

80.(D) Only (A) and (B)

81.(A)(i), (ii), (iii)

82.(B)Introducing the new employee who is designated as a probationer to the job

Explanation: Induction training:

- Training provided to new employees by the employer in order to assist in adjustment to their new job tasks and to help them become familiar with their new work environment and the people working around them.
- This type of training will also outline the basic overview of the business and its

services as well as the new employee's role in the environment.

83.(D) Induction

84.(D) induction

85.(D) Both A and C

86.(C)Induction

87.(C)Introducing employees to the organization culture and situation.

88.(A) (i) (ii) (iii) (iv) (v) (vi)

89.(C)Training, education and development

Explanation:

- Human Resources Development (HRD) as a theory is a framework for the expansion of human capital within an organization through the development of both the organization and the individual to achieve performance improvement.
- Adam Smith states, "The capacities of individuals depended on their access to education".
- The same statement applies to organizations themselves, but it requires a much broader field to cover both areas.
- Human Resource Development is the integrated use of training, organization, and career development efforts to improve individual, group and organizational effectiveness.
- HRD develops the key competencies that enable individuals in organizations to perform current and future jobs through planned learning activities.
- Groups within organizations use HRD to initiate and manage change. Also, HRD ensures a match between individual and organizational needs.

90.(C) Both (A) and (B)

91.(D)All the above

Explanation: HRD systems

- HRD functions are carried out through its systems and sub systems.
- HRD has five major systems and each of the systems has sub systems as elaborated below: the first three systems viz., Career system, Work system and Development system, are individual and team oriented while the fourth and the fifth systems viz. Self renewal system and Culture Systems are organization based.

1. Career system: As an HRD system, career system ensures attraction and retention of human resources through the following sub-systems.

- Manpower planning
- Recruitment
- Career planning
- Succession planning
- Retention

2. Work system: Work-planning system ensures that the attracted and retained human resources are utilized in the best possible way to obtain organizational objectives. Following are the sub systems of the work planning system.

- Role analysis
- Role efficacy
- Performance plan
- Performance feedback and guidance
- Performance appraisal
- Promotion
- Job rotation
- Reward

3. Development system: The environmental situation and the business scenario is fast changing. The human resources within the organization have to raise upto the occasion and change accordingly if the organization wants to be in business. The development system ensures that the retained (career system) and utilized (work system) human resources are also continuously developed so that they are in a position to meet the emerging needs of the hour. Following are some of the developmental sub - systems of HRD that make sure that human resources in the organization are continuously developed.

- Induction
- Training
- Job enrichment
- Self-learning mechanisms
- Potential appraisal
- Succession Development
- Counseling
- Mentor system

4. Self-renewal system: It is not enough to develop individuals and teams in the organizations but occasionally there is a need to renew and re-juvenate the organization itself. Following are some of the sub systems that can be utilized to renew the organization.

- Survey
- Action research
- OD Interventions
- Organizational Retreats

5. Culture system: Building a desired culture is of paramount importance in today's changed business scenario. It is the culture that will give a sense of direction, purpose, togetherness, and teamwork. It is to be noted that whether an organization wants it or not along with the time common ways of doing things (culture) will emerge. If not planned carefully and built systematically such common traits may not help the business but may become a stumbling block. Hence it is very important to have cultural practices that facilitate business. Some of the culture building subsystems are given below:

- Vision, Mission and Goal
- Values
- Communication
- Get-togethers and celebrations
- Task forces
- Small Groups

92.(D) None of the above

93.(D) (iii) (iv) (i) (ii)

94.(B)T.W. Schultz

95. (C)Both (A) and (B)

96. (C)T.V. Rao

97. (B)Manmohan Singh

98. (D)All the above

99. (C) T.V. Rao

Explanation: HR scorecard measures the HR function's effectiveness and efficiency in producing employee behaviors needed to achieve the company's strategic goals.

There are seven steps required to develop HR score card, so that the result are statistically measure

1. define business strategy
2. outline company value chain
3. identify business required organizational outcomes strategy
4. identify required workforce
5. identify relevant HR system
6. design of HR score card for measurement purpose
7. a periodic revaluation based on measurement system from score card.

100. (A)to be clearly related to the organization's objectives

101. (D)Udai Pareek

Explanation:

- The most important aspect of organizational culture are the values it practices.
- Eight values may be examined to develop the profile of an organizational culture that is called OCTAPACE (Openness, Confrontation, Trust, Authenticity, Proactively, Autonomy, Collaboration, and Experimenting).
- **Openness:** The comparative openness in the system should influence the design of HRS. Organizations can be classified in continuum from completely open to completely close. No organization may be on the two extremes of the continuum. However, they will tend to be towards one or the other end. The degree of openness of the organization will be an imp factor in determining the nature of the various dimensions of HRD being designed, as well as the way in which these dimensions should be introduced. organization which are

fairly open may start with several confronting designs of HRS .

- **Confrontation:** This term is used in relation to problem putting the front rather than the back to escaping the problems. A better term would be confrontation exploration that implies facing a problem and working jointly with other concerned to find its solution. If an organization encourages people to recognize a problem, bring it to people concerned, explore with them to under it and search possible ways of dealing with it.
- **Trust:** Which introducing the HRD in an organization trust in another factor which should be considered along with openness. If the level of trust is low, the various dimensions of HRS are likely to be seen with suspicion and therefore the credibility of the system may go down. in such a case the system if introduced may become a vital and cease to perform the main functions for which it meant.
- **Authenticity** is the value underlying trust. It is the willingness of a person to acknowledge the feelings he /she has, and accept himself / herself as well as other who relate to him/her as persons. Authenticity is reflected in the narrowest gap between the stated vales and the actual behavior. This value is important for the development of a culture of mutuality.
- **Proactive:** Can be contrasted with the term react. It in the later action is in response to an act from some source, while in the former the action is taken independently of act form the other source. proaction means anticipating issues in advancing to take advantage of this undertaking conflict or responding to needs of the future in fact creating the future.
- **Autonomy:** It is nothing but willingness to use power without fear and helping other to do same. It multiplies power in system and the basis is collaboration.
- **Collaboration:** involves working together during one another strengths for a common cause. Individuals instead of solving their problems by themselves share their concerns with one another and prepare strategies working out plan of actions and implement them together.
- **Experimenting:** as a value emphasizes the importance given to innovating and trying out new ways of dealing with problems in the organization.

102. (D)Openness, Trust, and Pro-action

103. (D)Openness-Confrontation-Trust-Authenticity-Proaction-Autonomy-Collaboration-Experimentation

104. (B)without having to get approval from anyone else

Explanation: Empowerment refers to increasing the spiritual, political, social, educational, gender, or economic strength of individuals and communities.

105. (C) C.K. Prahlad

106. (A) Standards

107. (D) All the above

108. (C)Standards

Explanation:

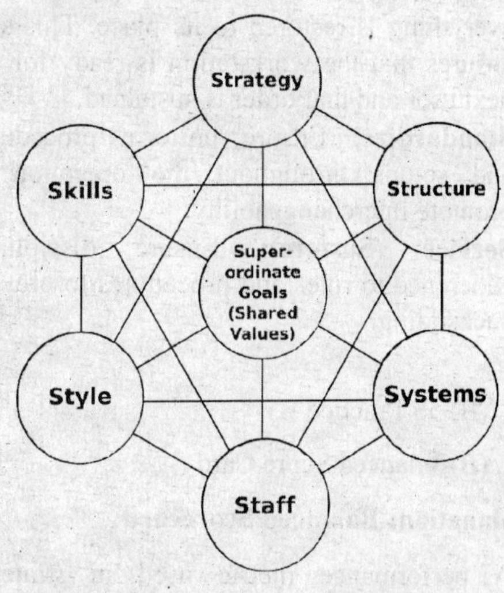

109. (C)Specialize

Explanation:

- **Sorting:** Eliminate all unnecessary tools, parts. Go through all tools, materials, and so forth in the plant and work area. Keep only essential items and eliminate what is not required, prioritizing things per requirements and keeping them in easily-accessible places. Everything else is stored or discarded.

- **Straightening or Setting in Order to Flow:** Arrange the work, workers, equipment, parts, and instructions in such a way that the work flows free of waste through the value added tasks with a division of labour necessary to meet demand. This is by far the most misunderstood and incorrectly applied S and has been responsible for many lean transformations failing to produce the benefits expected. When applied correctly with flow established this step eliminates the majority of the non-value-added time and allows the rest of the zero defect philosophy to be enabled. Put simply until you have an orderly flow you cannot have an orderly flow of problems to solve and the notion of zero defects is impossible.
- **Systematic Cleaning (Shine):** Standardized cleaning-point at a 5S organized plant Clean the workspace and all equipment, and keep it clean, tidy and organized. At the end of each shift, clean the work area and be sure everything is restored to its place. This step ensures that the workstation is ready for the next user and that order is sustained.
- **Standardize:** Ensure uniform procedures and setups throughout the operation to promote interchangeability.
- **Service (Sustain):** Ensure disciplined adherence to rules and procedures to prevent backsliding.

110. (B) 5S Practice

111. (B)Balanced Score Card

Explanation: Balanced Scorecard:

- A performance metric used in strategic management to identify and improve various internal functions and their resulting external outcomes.
- The balanced scorecard attempts to measure and provide feedback to organizations in order to assist in implementing strategies and objectives.

112. (A)Robert S. Kaplan and David P.Norton

113. (B)W.Edwards Deming

Explanation: Deming's PDCA Cycle

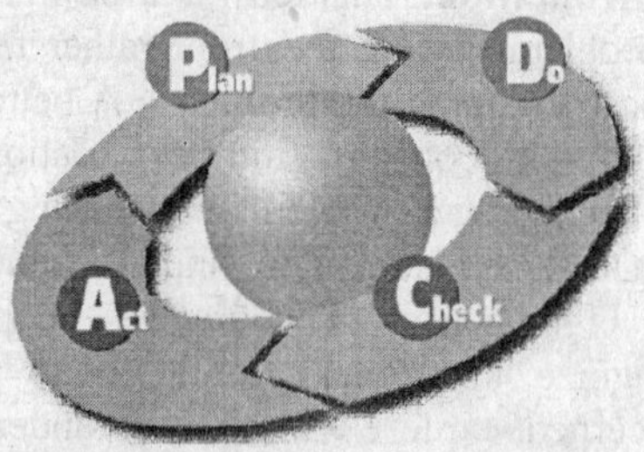

114. (A)Purposes, structure, rewards, mechanisms, relationships and leadership

Explanation: The six-box model is comprised of the following components (boxes):

- **Purposes:** What 'businesses' are we in?
- **Structure:** How do we divide up the work?
- **Relationships:** How do we manage conflict (coordinate) among people? With our technologies?
- **Rewards:** Is there an incentive for doing all that needs doing?
- **Leadership:** Is someone keeping the boxes in balance?
- **Helpful mechanisms:** Have we adequate coordinating technologies?

115. (A)Benchmarking

Explanation: Benchmarking:

- Benchmarking is the process of comparing one's business processes and performance metrics to industry bests or best practices from other industries.
- Dimensions typically measured are quality, time and cost. In the process of best practice benchmarking, management identifies the best firms in their industry, or in another industry where similar processes exist, and compares the results and processes of those studied (the "targets") to one's own results and processes. In this way, they learn how well the targets perform and, more importantly, the business processes that explain why these firms are successful.
- Benchmarking is used to measure performance using a specific indicator (cost

per unit of measure, productivity per unit of measure, cycle time of x per unit of measure or defects per unit of measure) resulting in a metric of performance that is then compared to others.

116. (C)T. V. Rao

Explanation: HRD Matrix:

- HRD Matrix identifies the interrelationships between HRD instruments, processes, outcomes and organisational effectiveness.
- HRD instruments include performance appraisal, counselling, role analysis, potential development, training, reward system, job enrichment, etc.
- These mechanisms may vary depending upon the size of the organisation, the commitment of the top management, the environment, the culture and climate, the perception of the people, technology used, methods employed by the competitors, etc.
- It is in the interest of the organisation that the top management should give due weightage to these factors to keep the workforce motivated all the time providing challenging jobs and designing career planning and suitable compensation packages so that trained employees may not leave the organisation.
- These instruments lead to generation of HRD processes like role clarity, development planning, development climate, risk-taking and dynamism in employees.
- Such HRD processes should result in more competent, satisfied and dynamic people is likely to do better than which does not believe in HRD concept and committed people who, by their contributions, would make the organisation grow. Such HRD outcomes influence organisational effectiveness in the long-run.
- It may be noted that organisational effectiveness also depends on a number of other variable like environment, technology, competitors, etc.
- However, other things being the same, an organisation that has competence.

117. (D)All of the above

118. (D)All the above

119. (D) All the above

120. (A)Working simultaneously in two organizations

Explanation:

- Moon lightning is an act of employee of doing more than one job, in the process of moonlighting employee might separate his/her interest from the main job.

121. (D)All of the above

Explanation: Training: Organized activity aimed at imparting information and/or instructions to improve the recipient's performance or to help him or her attain a required level of knowledge or skill.

122. (A)Reaction, learning, behaviour and results

Explanation:

- The process of examining a training program is called training evaluation.
- Training evaluation checks whether training has had the desired effect.
- Training evaluation ensures that whether candidates are able to implement their learning in their respective workplaces, or to the regular work routines.

Purposes of Training Evaluation

- **Feedback:** It helps in giving feedback to the candidates by defining the objectives and linking it to learning outcomes.
- **Research:** It helps in ascertaining the relationship between acquired knowledge, transfer of knowledge at the work place, and training.
- **Control:** It helps in controlling the training program because if the training is not effective, then it can be dealt with accordingly.
- **Power games:** At times, the top management (higher authoritative employee) uses the evaluative data to manipulate it for their own benefits.

- **Intervention:** It helps in determining that whether the actual outcomes are aligned with the expected outcomes.

Benefits of Training Evaluation

- Evaluation ensures accountability.
- Check the Cost.
- Feedback to the Trainer / Training.

123. (A)Donald Kirkpatrick

124. (B) Need analysis, instructional design, validation, implementation and evaluation

Explanation:

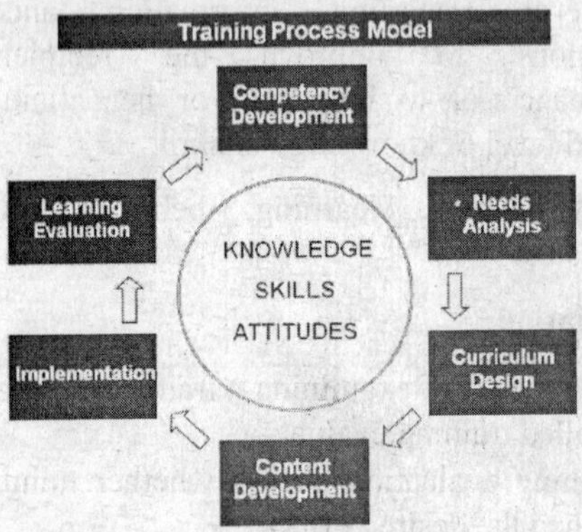

125. (A)T - group training

Explanation: Sensitivity training:

- Training designed to make people more aware of group dynamics and their own behavior, interpersonal traits, and role within a group. Based on the work of ***Kurt Levin*** and ***Ronald Lippit***, it also forms a part of the 'human potential development' movement.
- Sensitivity training involves such groupings as --T groups (T for training), encounter groups, laboratory training groups, and human awareness groups are all names usually associated with what is known as sensitivity training.
- Sensitivity training is about making people understand about themselves and others reasonably, which is done by developing in them social sensitivity and behavioral flexibility.

126. (C)Sensitivity Training

127. (D) All of the above

128. (C)Do not exploit opportunity

129. (D)Potentialities for the next level job

Explanation: Objectives of Sensitivity Training

- Increased understanding, insight, and self awareness about one's own behavior and its impact on others, including the ways in which others interpret one's behavior.
- Increased understanding and sensitivity about the behavior of others, including better interpretation of both verbal and nonverbal clues, which increases awareness and understanding of what the other person is thinking and feeling.
- Better understanding and awareness of group and intergroup processes, both those that facilitate and those that inhibit group functioning.
- Increased diagnostic skills in interpersonal and intergroup situations. For the authors, the accomplishments of the first three objectives provide the basic tools for accomplishing the fourth objective.
- Increased ability to transform learning into action, so that real life interventions will be more successful in increasing member effectiveness, satisfaction, output, or effectiveness.
- Improvement in individuals' ability to analyze their own interpersonal behavior, as well as to learn how to help themselves and others with whom they come in contact to achieve more satisfying, rewarding, and effective interpersonal relationships.
- Different sensitivity programs may emphasize one or more of these goals or may neglect some. However, they are goals that are common to most T groups.

130. (C)Coaching

Explanation: Off the job training:

- Employee training at a site away from the actual work environment.

- It often utilizes ***lectures, case studies, role playing, simulation, audio-visual techniques, business games*** etc.
- In this training management provide enjoyable way of learning skills such as management and bonding for employees that enhances their productivity.

131. (B)(ii) (i) (iv) (iii) (v) (vi)

132. (B)Vestibule Training

Explanation: Training Methods for Operatives:

- Under these methods the new employee is assigned to a specific job at a machine or workshop or laboratory.
- He is instructed by an experienced employee or by a special supervisor who explains to him the method of handling tools, operating the machines etc.

Vestibule Training:

- This method involves the creation of a separate training centre within the plant itself for the purpose of providing training to the new employees.
- An experienced instructor is put in-charge of this training. Machines and tools are also managed in the training centre, so as to create working conditions similar to those in the workshop.
- **Advantage:** No interference with regular production.
- **Disadvantage**: Costly, adds nothing to productions during training period.

Apprenticeship Training:

- This method of training is meant to give the trainee sufficient knowledge and skill in those trades and crafts in which a long period of training is required for gaining complete proficiency.
- Generally, the trainees work as apprentices under the direct supervision of experts for long periods of say, two to seven years.
- This programme consists of providing actual work experience in the actual job as well as imparting theoretical knowledge through class room lectures which may be arranged either in the plant or in the institution attached to the concern.
- This method of training enables the trainees to become all-round craftsmen. But this method is very expensive and also there is no guarantee that a trained worker will continue to work in the same concern after the training is completed.

Internship Training:

- This method of training is generally provided to the skilled and technical personnel.
- The object of this type of training is to bring about a balance between theoretical and practical knowledge, under this method, students from a technical institution possessing only theoretical knowledge are sent to some business enterprise to gain practical work experience.
- Simultaneously, the employees of business enterprises are sent to technical institutions to gain the latest theoretical knowledge on a subject.

133. (B) (ii) (iii) (i) (iv)

134. (D)All the above

135. (C) (c) (a) (b) (d)

136. (A)Find out the training needs

137. (A)(iii) (ii) (i) (iv) (v)

138. (B) Job rotation

139. (B) Simulation

140. (A) e-learning

141. (D) job instruction on a one to one basis

142. (A) Sensitization of an employee for organization

Explanation:

- Sensitivity Training is a form of training that claims to make people more aware of their own prejudices, and more sensitive to others.
- Sensitivity training involves such groupings as T groups (T for training), encounter groups, laboratory training groups, and human awareness groups are all names

usually associated with what is known as sensitivity training.

143. (C)Management games

144. (D)Sharing ideas and experiences and getting to know one's strengths and weaknesses.

145. (A) Structured Interview

146. (A) (b) (c) (d) (a)

147. (C) Vestibule training method

Explanation: Vestibule training:

- A method of job education where educational facilities approximate real working conditions and are equipped with actual production machinery.
- In a typical vestibule training situation used by a manufacturing business, less than ten trainees would be supervised by one skilled trainer, and the training provided simulates on the job training without compromising production speed or quality.
- This training method attempt to duplicate on-the-job-situation in a company classroom.
- It is a classroom training that is often imported with the help of the equipment and machines, which are identical with those in use in the place of work.
- This technique enables the trainees to concentrate on learning new skill rather than on performing on actual job.
- This type of training is efficient to train semi-skilled personnel, particularly when many employees have to be trained for the same kind of work at the same time.
- Often used to train – bank tellers, inspectors, machine operators, typists etc. In this, training is generally given in the form of lectures, conferences, case studies, role-play etc.
- Examples of vestibule training include airlines that use simulators to train pilots and cabin attendants, astronauts who train in mock-up space capsules.

148. (C)Sensitivity training

Explanation: Management development:

- Aspect of organizational development that covers recruitment and assessment of executive level employees and training them in leadership to equip them for higher positions.
- This process generally includes development of cognitive (thinking, idea generation, and decision making), behavioral (choosing appropriate attitudes and values), and environmental (suiting management style to the situation) skills.

149. (B)Arrogance and anger

150. (D)All the above

151. (C)To increase morale

152. (D) T-Group

153. (B)(iv) (iii) (i) (ii)

154. (D)(v), (iv), (i), (ii), (iii)

155. (C)T – group

156. (B) employees

157. (D)Sensitivity training

158. (D) Career Plateau

Explanation: Career progression refers to the upward movement or advancement made by people in a particular job.

159. (D)(iii) (v) (i) (ii) (iv)

Explanation: Stages of career development

The main stages in a career cycle include: development stage, exploration stage, establishment stage, ageing stage and declination stage.

1. Development stage: This stage begins from birth and normally lasts until 14 years old. This is the period in which children want to affirm themselves and have been affected very much by the relationship with family, school and society.

In the beginning of this stage, Games play an important role in developing children's recognition.

In the end of this stage, children have developed ideas about their own hobbies and abilities, maybe with some practical ideas about their future careers.

2. Exploration stage: This stage often lasts from 15 years old to 24 years old. In this period, people have many different career choices and they often tend to choose job careers they have been counseled, tutored or the jobs they think will fit their abilities and wishes. The most important in this stage is that people need to develop a broad knowledge and a variety of job skills.

3. Establishment stage: This stage is from the age of 25 to 44. This is the main stage in the career of a person.

In the beginning of the stage, some people have found their suitable jobs and these helped them have long and settled standings in their career lines. As usual, people pursue their original career choices, but there are still many people considering that this stage is only a trial period to continually test their skills and incentives for advancement in career.

Establishment stage includes 3 periods:

3.1. Trial period: From the age of 25 to about 30, in this period, people work primarily to find out whether the career choice they made is suitable or not.

3.2. Stable period: Normally from the age of 30 to 40, in this period, people often have identified their own career goals and have specific plans to decide what should continually be done to reach those goals. There are two tendencies, continuing the path chosen or turning to another job career.

3.3. Mid – Career crisis period: This period lasts from mid thirties to mid forties. During this period, people often compare what they have tried to pursue, the difficulties in career they have, what they have to sacrifice, the loss they have endured to follow their career path as well as their career ambitions with the achievements they have got in career such as position, salary and so on.

4. Ageing stage: This period continues from the age of 45 to 60. There are many people who jump directly from stable period to this stage without having experienced all the difficulties and failures in mid – career crisis period.

5. Declination stage: Declination stage is the final stage when people are old, less healthy and clairvoyant. In this period, the sense of responsibilities toward the job has decreased and they must accept the new role of the young generation.

160. (B)protean career planning

161. (D)All the above

Explanation:

- Career anchor is what really drives you at work.
- It is a mixture of your motives, values and how you see your own personal competence.
- An American academic called ***Edgar Schein*** developed the concept.
- Differences in Career Anchors help to explain why some people with similar background, education and professional training make such different career choices.
- For example, some engineers are intrinsically interested in their profession, enjoying the challenge of resolving complex technical problems; others see their profession as a step towards senior management, happy to leave the technical problems to others.
- Others quickly set up their own business, anxious to create their own enterprise and to make their distinctive mark on the world.
- The difference is due to their career anchor: The underlying drive or combination of drives that motivates each person to make one choice rather than another.
- A career anchor is the one thing that a person would not give up if forced to make a choice.

162. (A) career anchors

163. (B)(b) (a) (c) (d)

164. (C) Objectives

165. (C)Personal competence

166. (B)Ability to remain with same competencies refining suitably for organizations

167. (B)Succession planning

Explanation: Succession planning

- Succession planning is a process for identifying and developing internal people with the potential to fill key business leadership positions in the company.
- Succession planning increases the availability of experienced and capable employees that are prepared to assume these roles as they become available.

168. (B) Succession planning

169. (A)Performance Phase

170. (D)All of the above

Explanation: Performance Appraisal:

- Performance Appraisal is the systematic evaluation of the performance of employees and to understand the abilities of a person for further growth and development.
- Performance appraisal is generally done in systematic ways which are as follows:
- The supervisors measure the pay of employees and compare it with targets and plans.
- The supervisor analyses the factors behind work performances of employees.
- The employers are in position to guide the employees for a better performance.

Objectives of Performance Appraisal

Performance Appraisal can be done with following objectives in mind:

- To maintain records in order to determine compensation packages, wage structure, salaries raises, etc.
- To identify the strengths and weaknesses of employees to place right men on right job.
- To maintain and assess the potential present in a person for further growth and development.
- To provide a feedback to employees regarding their performance and related status.
- To provide a feedback to employees regarding their performance and related status.
- It serves as a basis for influencing working habits of the employees.
- To review and retain the promotional and other training programmes.

Advantages of Performance Appraisal

- **Promotion:** Performance Appraisal helps the supervisors to chalk out the promotion programmes for efficient employees. In this regards, inefficient workers can be dismissed or demoted in case.
- **Compensation:** Performance Appraisal helps in chalking out compensation packages for employees. Merit rating is possible through performance appraisal. Performance Appraisal tries to give worth to a performance. Compensation packages which includes bonus, high salary rates, extra benefits, allowances and pre-requisites are dependent on performance appraisal. The criteria should be merit rather than seniority.
- **Employees Development:** The systematic procedure of performance appraisal helps the supervisors to frame training policies and programmes. It helps to analyse strengths and weaknesses of employees so that new jobs can be designed for efficient employees. It also helps in framing future development programmes.
- **Selection Validation:** Performance Appraisal helps the supervisors to understand the validity and importance of the selection procedure. The supervisors come to know the validity and thereby the strengths and weaknesses of selection procedure. Future changes in selection methods can be made in this regard.
- **Communication:** For an organization, effective communication between employees and employers is very important. Through performance appraisal, communication can be sought for in the following ways:

- Through performance appraisal, the employers can understand and accept skills of subordinates.
- The subordinates can also understand and create a trust and confidence in superiors.
- It also helps in maintaining cordial and congenial labour management relationship.
- It develops the spirit of work and boosts the morale of employees.
- All the above factors ensure effective communication.
- **Motivation:** Performance appraisal serves as a motivation tool. Through evaluating performance of employees, a person's efficiency can be determined if the targets are achieved. This very well motivates a person for better job and helps him to improve his performance in the future.
- **Performance Appraisal Biases**
- Managers commit mistakes while evaluating employees and their performance. Biases and judgment errors of various kinds may spoil the performance appraisal process. Bias here refers to inaccurate distortion of a measurement. These are:
- **First Impression (primacy effect):** Raters form an overall impression about the ratee on the basis of some particluar characteristics of the ratee identified by them. The identified qualities and features may not provide adequate base for appraisal.
- **Halo Effect:** The individual's performance is completely appraised on the basis of a perceived positive quality, feature or trait. In other words this is the tendency to rate a man uniformly high or low in other traits if he is extra-ordinarily high or low in one particular trait. If a worker has few absences, his supervisor might give him a high rating in all other areas of work.
- **Horn Effect:** The individual's performance is completely appraised on the basis of a negative quality or feature perceived. This results in an overall lower rating than may be warranted. "He is not formally dressed up in the office. He may be casual at work too!".
- **Excessive Stiffness or Lenience:** Depending upon the raters own standards, values and physical and mental makeup at the time of appraisal, ratees may be rated very strictly or leniently. Some of the managers are likely to take the line of least resistance and rate people high, whereas others, by nature, believe in the tyranny of exact assessment, considering more particularly the drawbacks of the individual and thus making the assessment excessively severe. The leniency error can render a system ineffective. If everyone is to be rated high, the system has not done anything to differentiate among the employees.
- **Central Tendency:** Appraisers rate all employees as average performers. That is, it is an attitude to rate people as neither high nor low and follow the middle path. For example, a professor, with a view to play it safe, might give a class grade near the equal to B, regardless of the differences in individual performances.
- **Personal Biases:** The way a supervisor feels about each of the individuals working under him - whether he likes or dislikes them - as a tremendous effect on the rating of their performances. Personal Bias can stem from various sources as a result of information obtained from colleagues, considerations of faith and thinking, social and family background and so on.
- **Spillover Effect:** The present performance is evaluated much on the basis of past performance. "The person who was a good performer in distant past is assured to be okay at present also".
- **Recency Effect:** Rating is influenced by the most recent behaviour ignoring the commonly demonstrated behaviours during the entire appraisal period.
- Therefore while appraising performances, all the above biases should be avoid.

171. (C)Performance appraisal

172. (D)All the above

173. (A)Halo error

Explanation:

Central Tendency Error: Some supervisors tend to rank all employees at about average, regardless of an employee's performance. A supervisor who believes in never rating an employee as excellent is demonstrating central tendency error.

Contrast Error: Supervisors who rate subordinates as they compare against each other rather than how they compare against the performance standards commit contrast error. This error can cause an employee who is performing average against performance standards to rate high because his peers are under performing.

False Attribution: False attribution is the tendency to attribute bad performance to internal causes and good performance to external causes. In other words, if an employee performs well, it's because the employee had help, such as a good leader; and if the employee performs badly, it's because the employee did something wrong, such as procrastinate.

Halo Effect: The halo effect is when a supervisor forms a positive impression of an employee's skill in one area and then gives her high ratings across all rating criteria. Humans tend to view some traits as more important than other traits. When a supervisor rates employees with the traits that he deems more important higher in all rating areas than employees who do not possess those traits, the supervisor is committing the halo effect error.

Leniency Error: Leniency error is the tendency of a supervisor to rate an employee higher than what his performance warrants. Reasons that a supervisor might do this could include avoiding confrontations, or feeling that by giving the employee a high rating, he will work harder to live up to the rating.

Perceived Meaning: Perceived meaning becomes an issue when appraisers do not agree on the meaning of the rating criteria. For example, one supervisor may perceive an employee's constant reporting of problems as initiative, while another supervisor may feel this behavior demonstrates dependence on supervisory assistance instead of initiative.

Recency Error: Recency error happens when a supervisor uses recent events to rate the employee. This usually occurs due to a lack of documentation of the employee's performance over the course of the entire performance appraisal period. An employee who performed highly over the course of the appraisal period may be rated low if the most recent events where negative.

Severity Error: Severity error is the opposite of leniency error. In severity error, a supervisor tends to rate an employee lower than what her performance warrants. A potential cause of the error could be the use of unrealistic standards of comparison, such as the supervisor rating a new employee against himself. In this scenario, the supervisor forgets that it took time to reach the level of performance he operates at, and a new employee would not have had enough time to develop to that level.

Stereotyping: Stereotyping is the tendency to apply the same generalizations to all members of specific social groups. One of the more common types of stereotyping that occur in the workplace is gender stereotyping. Research conducted by Madeline Heilman, a professor of psychology at NYU, suggests that women are often evaluated more negatively than men, even when both are trained to do a job the same way.

174. (C) Strictness/Leniency error

175. (A)Halo effect

176. (D) All the above

177. (C)Assessment centers

Explanation: Methods of performance appraisals

(A)Past Oriented Methods

1. **Rating Scales:** Rating scales consists of several numerical scales representing job related performance criterions such as dependability, initiative, output, attendance, attitude etc. Each scales ranges from excellent to poor. The total numerical scores are computed and final conclusions are derived. Advantages – Adaptability, easy to use, low cost, every type of job can be

evaluated, large number of employees covered, no formal training required. Disadvantages – Rater's biases

2. **Checklist:** Under this method, checklist of statements of traits of employee in the form of Yes or No based questions is prepared. Here the rater only does the reporting or checking and HR department does the actual evaluation. Advantages – economy, ease of administration, limited training required, standardization. Disadvantages – Raters biases, use of improper weighs by HR, does not allow rater to give relative ratings

3. **Forced Choice Method:** The series of statements arranged in the blocks of two or more are given and the rater indicates which statement is true or false. The rater is forced to make a choice. HR department does actual assessment. Advantages – Absence of personal biases because of forced choice. Disadvantages – Statements may be wrongly framed.

4. **Forced Distribution Method:** here employees are clustered around a high point on a rating scale. Rater is compelled to distribute the employees on all points on the scale. It is assumed that the performance is conformed to normal distribution. Advantages – Eliminates Disadvantages – Assumption of normal distribution, unrealistic, errors of central tendency.

5. **Critical Incidents Method:** The approach is focused on certain critical behaviors of employee that makes all the difference in the performance. Supervisors as and when they occur record such incidents. Advantages – Evaluations are based on actual job behaviors, ratings are supported by descriptions, feedback is easy, reduces recency biases, chances of subordinate improvement are high. Disadvantages – Negative incidents can be prioritized, forgetting incidents, overly close supervision; feedback may be too much and may appear to be punishment.

6. **Behaviorally Anchored Rating Scales:** statements of effective and ineffective behaviors determine the points. They are said to be behaviorally anchored. The rater is supposed to say, which behavior describes the employee performance. Advantages – helps overcome rating errors. Disadvantages – Suffers from distortions inherent in most rating techniques.

7. **Field Review Method:** This is an appraisal done by someone outside employees' own department usually from corporate or HR department. Advantages – Useful for managerial level promotions, when comparable information is needed, Disadvantages – Outsider is generally not familiar with employees work environment, Observation of actual behaviors not possible.

8. **Performance Tests & Observations:** This is based on the test of knowledge or skills. The tests may be written or an actual presentation of skills. Tests must be reliable and validated to be useful. Advantage – Tests may be apt to measure potential more than actual performance. Disadvantages – Tests may suffer if costs of test development or administration are high.

9. **Confidential Records:** Mostly used by government departments, however its application in industry is not ruled out. Here the report is given in the form of Annual Confidentiality Report (ACR) and may record ratings with respect to following items; attendance, self expression, team work, leadership, initiative, technical ability, reasoning ability, originality and resourcefulness etc. The system is highly secretive and confidential. Feedback to the assessee is given only in case of an adverse entry. Disadvantage is that it is highly subjective and ratings can be manipulated because the evaluations are linked to HR actions like promotions etc.

10. Essay Method: In this method the rater writes down the employee description in detail within a number of broad categories like, overall impression of performance, promoteability of employee, existing capabilities and qualifications of performing jobs, strengths and weaknesses and training needs of the employee. Advantage – It is extremely useful in filing information gaps about the employees that often occur in a better-structured checklist. Disadvantages – It its highly dependent upon the writing skills of rater and most of them are not good writers. They may get confused success depends on the memory power of raters.

11. Cost Accounting Method: Here performance is evaluated from the monetary returns yields to his or her organization. Cost to keep employee, and benefit the organization derives is ascertained. Hence it is more dependent upon cost and benefit analysis.

12. Comparative Evaluation Method (Ranking & Paired Comparisons):

- These are collection of different methods that compare performance with that of other co-workers.
- The usual techniques used may be ranking methods and paired comparison method.

13. Ranking Methods:
Superior ranks his worker based on merit, from best to worst. However how best and why best are not elaborated in this method. It is easy to administer and explanation.

14. Paired Comparison Methods: In this method each employee is rated with another employee in the form of pairs.

(B) Future Oriented Methods

1. Management by Objectives:

- It means management by objectives and the performance is rated against the achievement of objectives stated by the management. MBO process goes as under:
    - Establish goals and desired outcomes for each subordinate
    - Setting performance standards
    - Comparison of actual goals with goals attained by the employee
    - Establish new goals and new strategies for goals not achieved in previous year.

Advantage: It is more useful for managerial positions.

Disadvantages: Not applicable to all jobs, allocation of merit pay may result in setting short-term goals rather than important and long-term goals etc.

2. Psychological Appraisals:

- These appraisals are more directed to assess employees potential for future performance rather than the past one.
- It is done in the form of in-depth interviews, psychological tests, and discussion with supervisors and review of other evaluations.
- It is more focused on employees emotional, intellectual, and motivational and other personal characteristics affecting his performance.
- This approach is slow and costly and may be useful for bright young members who may have considerable potential.
- However quality of these appraisals largely depend upon the skills of psychologists who perform the evaluation.

3. Assessment Centers:

- This technique was first developed in USA and UK in 1943.
- An assessment center is a central location where managers may come together to have their participation in job related exercises evaluated by trained observers.
- It is more focused on observation of behaviors across a series of select exercises or work samples.
- Assessees are requested to participate in in-basket exercises, work groups, computer simulations, role playing and other similar

activities which require same attributes for successful performance in actual job.

- The characteristics assessed in assessment center can be assertiveness, persuasive ability, communicating ability, planning and organizational ability, self confidence, resistance to stress, energy level, decision making, sensitivity to feelings, administrative ability, creativity and mental alertness etc.

Disadvantages:

- Costs of employees traveling and lodging, psychologists, ratings strongly influenced by assessee's inter-personal skills.
- Solid performers may feel suffocated in simulated situations.
- Those who are not selected for this also may get affected.

Advantages:

- Well-conducted assessment center can achieve better forecasts of future performance and progress than other methods of appraisals.
- Also reliability, content validity and predictive ability are said to be high in assessment centers.
- The tests also make sure that the wrong people are not hired or promoted.
- Finally it clearly defines the criteria for selection and promotion.

4.360-Degree Feedback:

- It is a technique which is systematic collection of performance data on an individual group, derived from a number of stakeholders like immediate supervisors, team members, customers, peers and self.
- In fact anyone who has useful information on how an employee does a job may be one of the appraisers.
- This technique is highly useful in terms of broader perspective, greater self-development and multi-source feedback is useful. 360-degree appraisals are useful to measure inter-personal skills, customer satisfaction and team building skills.
- However on the negative side, receiving feedback from multiple sources can be intimidating, threatening etc.
- Multiple raters may be less adept at providing balanced and objective feedback.

178. (C)Behaviourally Anchored Rating Scales

Explanation: Behaviorally Anchored Rating Scales (BARS)

This is a new appraisal technique which has recently been developed. Its supports claim that it provides better, more equitable appraisals as compared to other techniques. The procedure for BARS is usually five stepped.

1. Generate Critical Incidents: Persons with knowledge of the job to be appraised (job holders/ supervisors) are asked to describe specific illustrations (critical incidents) of effective and ineffective performance.

2. Develop Performance Dimensions: These people cluster the incidents into a smaller set of performance dimensions. Each cluster is then defined.

3. Reallocate Incidents: Any group of people who also know the job then reallocate the original critical incidents. They are given the cluster's definitions, and critical accidents, and asked to redesign each incident to the dimension it best describes. Typically a critical incident is retained if some percentage (usually 50 lo 80%) of this group assigns it lo the same cluster as the previous group did.

4. Scale of Incidents: This second group is generally asked to rate (7 or 9 point scales are typical) the behaviour described in the incident as to how effectively or ineffectively it represents performance on the appropriate dimension. ,,

5. Develop Final Instrument: A subset of incidents (usually 6 or 7 per cluster) are used as "behaviour anchors" for the performance dimensions.

Though BARS technique is more time-consuming and expensive than other appraisal tools, yet it has got certain advantages, such as:

1. A more accurate gauge, since BARS is done by persons expert in the technique, the results are sufficiently accurate.

2. Clear Standards: The critical incidents along the scale help to clarify what is meant by "extremely good" performance, "average" performance and so forth.

3. Feedback: The use of critical incidents may be more useful in providing feedback to the people being appraised.

4. Independent dimensions: Systematically clustering the critical incidents into 5 or 6 performance dimensions, helps in making the dimensions more independent of one another.

5. Rater: Independence. The technique is not biased by the experience and evaluation of the rater.

179. (C)Superiors Subordinates, Customers and Peers

Explanation: 360 Degree Appraisal:

- An appraisal made by top management, immediate superior, peers, subordinates, self and customers is called 360 Degree Appraisal.
- Here, the performance of the employee or manager is evaluated by six parties, including himself. So, he gets a feedback of his performance from everyone around him.
- This method is very reliable because evaluation is done by many different parties.
- These parties are in the best position to evaluate the employee or manager because they are continuously interacting and working with him. This method is mostly used to evaluate the performance of the employees.
- However, it is also used to evaluate other qualities such as talents, behaviour, values, ethical standards, tempers, loyalty, etc.
- 360 degree appraisal was first developed by ***General Electric (GE)***, USA in 1992. Today it is used by all major organisations. In India, it is used by Crompton Greaves, Wipro, Infosys, Reliance Industries, etc.

The six parties involved in 360 degree appraisal are:

1. Top Management: The top management normally evaluates the middle level managers. However, in a small organisation, they also evaluate the performance of the lower level managers and senior employees.

2.Immediate Superior: The immediate superior is in a very good position to evaluate the performance of his subordinates. This is because they have direct and accurate information about the work performance of their subordinates.

3. Peers / Co-workers: Peer or colleagues also evaluate each other's performance. They work continuously with each other, and they know each other's performance. Peer evaluation is used mostly in cases where team work is important.

4. Subordinates: The Subordinates can also evaluate the performance of his superior. Now-a-days students are asked to evaluate the performance of their teachers.

5. Self Appraisal: In the self-appraisal, a person evaluates his own performance. He should be honest while evaluating himself. This results in self-development.

6. Customers: Customers can also evaluate the performance of the employees who interacts with them. This evaluation is best because it is objective. It is also given a lot of importance because the customer is the most important person for the business. Organisations use customer appraisals to improve the strengths and remove the weaknesses of their employees.

360 Degree Appraisal is becoming more popular because many parties are available for evaluation. Therefore, there is no "bias" or "halo effect". Hence the evaluation will become more realistic.

180. (C)Assertion is right and it will control reason

181. (C)(iv) (v) (vi) (iii) (ii) (i)

182. (D)(ii) (iii) (i)

183. (C) (iv), (ii), (v), (i), (iii)

184. (A)(ii) (i) (iii) (iv)

185. (A)(i) (ii) (iii) (iv)

186. (B)Critical Incidence Method

187. (D)Attributes and traits are of no importance in Performance Appraisal.

188. (B) Performance Appraisal

189. (A)Identification, measurement, management

190. (A)E.A. Locke & Gary Lutham

Explanation: Goal Setting Theory:

- Locke's research showed that there was a relationship between how difficult and specific a goal was and people's performance of a task. He found that specific and difficult goals led to better task performance than vague or easy goals.
- Telling someone to "Try hard" or "Do your best" is less effective than "Try to get more than 80% correct" or "Concentrate on beating your best time." Likewise, having a goal that's too easy is not a motivating force. Hard goals are more motivating than easy goals, because it's much more of an accomplishment to achieve something that you have to work for.
- A few years after Locke published his article, another researcher, Dr Gary Latham, studied the effect of goal setting in the workplace. His results supported exactly what Locke had found, and the inseparable link between goal setting and workplace performance was formed.
- In 1990, Locke and Latham published their seminal work, "A Theory of Goal Setting and Task Performance." In this book, they reinforced the need to set specific and difficult goals, and they outlined three other characteristics of successful goal setting.

Five Principles of Goal Setting:

To motivate, goals must have:

- Clarity.
- Challenge.
- Commitment.
- Feedback.
- Task complexity.

191. (D) All the above

192. (D)Behaviourally Anchored Rating Scales

193. (B)performance management

194. (D)all of the above

195. (A)Weekly

196. (D)yearly

197. (D)direction sharing

198. (A)role clarification

199. (D)assign consequences for performance

200. The(A)Specific

Explanation:

201. (A) participatively set goals are more difficult

202. (D) all of the above

203. (A)the employee's direct supervisor

204. (C)Appraising of employees

205. (D)what to measure and how to measure

206. (C) graphic rating scale

207. (C) graphic rating scale

Explanation: A Graphic rating scale refers to any rating scale that consists of points on a continuum and it is a label that is given to a wide category of rating formats. This is a scale which people use to indicate ratings of a particular attribute.

208. (D)all of the above

209. (A)generic dimensions of performance

210. (A)alternation ranking

Explanation: Alternation Ranking: A rating method used in job evaluation and performance evaluation whereby the rater is asked to select the best and worst employees from a listing of all employees and then rank them accordingly.

211. (D)involves listing all the subordinates to be rated, crossing out the names of any not known well enough to rank, indicating the employee who is the highest on each characteristic being measured and who is the lowest, and then alternating between the next highest and lowest until all employees have been ranked.

212. (C)alternation ranking

213. (D)paired comparison

214. (D)involves listing all the subordinates to be rated, crossing out the names of any not known well enough to rank, indicating the employee who is the highest on each characteristic being measured and who is the lowest, and then alternating between the next highest and lowest until all employees have been ranked.

Explanation: Forced distribution:

- A rating system used by companies to evaluate their employees.
- The system requires the managers to evaluate each individual, and rank them typically into one of three categories (excellent, good, poor).
- The system is thought to be relatively widely-used, but remains somewhat controversial due to the competition it creates, and also the reality that not all employees will fit neatly into one of the categories and might end up in a category that does not reflect their true performance.
- One of the first companies to use this system was ***General Electric***, in the 1980s.

215. (D)forced distribution

216. (C) forced distribution

217. (B)forced distribution

218. (D) critical incident

Explanation: Critical incident method

- Critical incidents are a special category of employee behaviors that focus on two distinct areas: particularly outstanding behaviors and particularly questionable behaviors.
- The critical incidents method of performance appraisal is based on managers' spending time during the year observing and gathering behavioral data on their employees, while looking extra carefully for those critical incidents.
- The critical incidents for performance appraisal is a method in which the manager writes down positive and negative performance behavior of employees throughout the performance period.
- Each employee will be evaluated as such and one's performance appraisal will be based on the logs that are put in the evaluation form.
- The manager maintains logs on each employee, whereby he periodically records critical incidents of the workers behavior.
- At the end of the rating period, these recorded critical incidents are used in the evaluation of the workers' performance.
- The critical incidents file of performance appraisal is a form of documentation that reflect all data about employee performances.

219. (C)requires that the supervisor keep a log of positive and negative examples of a subordinate's work-related behavior.

220. (B)it does not include a numerical rating

221. (A)behaviorally anchored rating scale

222. (B)combines the benefits of narratives, critical incidents, and quantified scales by assigning scale points with specific examples of good or poor performance

223. (B)generate critical incidents

224. (B)Second

225. (C)Third

226. (C) are time consuming

227. (A)is based on progress made toward the accomplishment of measurable goals

228. (D)all of the above

229. (C)complexity

230. (A)unclear standards

231. (B)Halo effect

232. (D) halo effects

233. (C)central tendency

Explanation:

Central tendency error: In performance appraisals or recruitment interviews, tendency of managers and interviewers to rate all or most of the employees or interviewees as average.

234. (A)rank employees

235. (B)leniency

Explanation: Leniency error:

- Performance appraisal or interview bias which occurs when a manager or interviewer rate an employee or the interviewee too positively.
- It is opposite of strictness error.

236. (C) strictness

237. (C)conscientiousness

238. (A)Agreeableness

239. (D)impose a distribution for performance

240. (A)Bias

241. (B)base appraisals on subjective supervisory observations

242. (D)immediate supervisor

243. (D)all of the above

244. (B)4-5

245. (C)logrolling

246. (A)reduction of social loafing in the team

247. (D)ratings are higher than when rated by supervisors or peers

248. (B)upward feedback

249. (C) upward feedback

250. (D)more inflated ratings

251. (B)multi source assessment

252. (D)additional professional development

253. (B)satisfactory-promotable

254. (D)compare the person's performance to that of other employees

255. (C)Relief

256. (B)provide examples of critical incidents

257. (A)feel threatened during the interview

258. (A)identify the standards by which the employee is judged

259. (C) employee competency

260. (D)Performance Appraisal System

261. (D) Performance Appraisal

262. (C) Objectives

263. (C)Confidential reports

264. (B)Halo effect

265. (C)Uniformity of standards

266. (C)Peter Drucker

267. (A)Peter F. Drucker

268. (A)P.F. Drucker

269. (B)It becomes difficult to assign responsibilities in a changing situation

270. (D)Interview method

271. (A)Evic Tryst

272. (B)Quality circles

Explanation: Quality circles:

- Started in Japan in the early 1960s, QCs have spread all over the world.
- Quality Circles became extremely popular in the 1980s, particularly in the aerospace, automobile, steel and consumer goods industries.
- The primary topics of discussion in most QCs are related to quality, but they also consider others such as cost, safety and efficiency.
- QC members identify a problem, study it and present their recommendations for change and improvement to a committee.
- A quality circle (QC) is a group of employees that meet regularly to solve problems affecting its work area. The ideal size of the group is six to eight members.
- A quality circle generally recommends solutions for quality which may be implemented by management.
- The main features of a quality circle are as follows:

o A quality circle is a voluntary group.

o Members meet at periodic intervals to discuss quality-related activities.

o A quality circle has its own terms of reference and offers recommendations to management for implementation.

o Members of a quality circle vary between six to eight members and generally they come from a particular work area.

o The ultimate purpose of a quality circle is to improve organizational functioning.

Advantage of Quality Circles

- Generation of Creative Ideas.
- Improvement in Productivity.
- Better Teamwork.
- Higher Motivation.
- Development of Problem Solving Skills.

Conditions Necessary for Making Quality Circles Effective

- Top management support.
- Education and training of managers and workers.
- Timely implementation of ideas generated by quality circles.
- Sharing gains in productivity with workers.
- Facilities for meetings and discussions.
- Regular monitoring of working of quality circles.

273. (C)Japan

274. (B) Quality circles

275. (C) Kouru Ishi Kawa

276. (D)S. R. Udpa

277. (B)Bharat Heavy Electricals Ltd.

278. (C)Bharath Heavy Electricals Ltd.

279. (C)Quality circle

280. (A)Ishikawa Japanese engineer

281. (B)Ishikawa

282. (B) (iv) (ii) (i) (iii)

283. (D) (i) (iii) (ii) (iv)

284. (D)Keith Hart

285. (B)Geert Hofstede

286. (C)Both (A) and (B)

Explanation: Job analysis

- It is primary tool in personnel management. In this method, a personnel manager tries to gather, synthesize and implement the information available regarding the workforce in the concern.
- Job analysis is the process by means of which a description is developed of the present methods and procedures of doing a job, physical conditions in which the job is done, relation of the job to other jobs and other conditions of employment.

- Job analysis is useful in:
  - o Recruitment and selection
  - o Establishing a base for compensation of employees
  - o Can be used for employee development, performance appraisal and training.
  - o A personnel manager has to undertake job analysis so as to put right man on right job.

Methods of Job Analysis

- Job description
- Job specification

287. (D)Application Blank

288. (D)All the above

289. (B)Job Description and Job Specification

290. (C) Job description and job specification

291. (A)Job description and job specification

292. (B)Succession planning

Explanation: Succession planning

- Identification and development of potential successors for key positions in an organization, through a systematic evaluation process and training.
- Unlike replacement planning (which grades an individual solely on the basis of his or her past performance) succession planning is largely predictive in judging an individual for a position he or she might never have been in.

293. (D)All the above

Explanation: Job Design

- The first operative function of HRM is job design and job analysis.
- ***Job design follows job analysis i.e. it is the next step after job analysis.***
- Job design means to decide the contents of a job. It fixes the duties and responsibilities of the job, the methods of doing the job and the relationships between the job holder (manager) and his superiors, subordinates and colleagues.
- It aims at outlining and organizing tasks, duties and responsibilities into a single unit of work for the achievement of certain objectives.
- It also outlines the methods and relationships that are essential for the success of a certain job. In simpler terms it refers to the what, how much, how many and the order of the tasks for a job/s.
- Job design essentially involves integrating job responsibilities or content and certain qualifications that are required to perform the same. It outlines the job responsibilities very clearly and also helps in attracting the right candidates to the right job. Further it also makes the job look interesting and specialized.
- Job design is a continuous and ever evolving process that is aimed at helping employees make adjustments with the changes in the workplace. The end goal is reducing dissatisfaction, enhancing motivation and employee engagement at the workplace.
- **Integration of work, rewards and qualification:** "Job Design integrates work content (tasks, functions, relationships), the rewards and qualifications required including skills, knowledge and abilities for each job in a way that meets the needs of employees and the organization."
- The whole process of job design is aimed to address various problems within the organizational setup, those that pertain to ones description of a job and the associated relationships.
- More specifically the following areas are fine tuned:
  - Checking the work overload.
  - Checking upon the work under load.
  - Ensuring tasks are not repetitive in nature.
  - Ensuring that employees don not remain isolated.
  - Defining working hours clearly.
  - Defining the work processes clearly.

294. (B)Job enrichment

295. (A)How much autonomy should be given to individual employees?

296. (A)Skill variety

297. (B)professional bureaucracy

298. (B)Job Enrichment

Explanation:

- Job Enrichment loads the job ***vertically***.
- Job Enrichment means adding duties and responsibilities that will provide for skill variety, task identity, task significance, autonomy and feedback on job performance.
- The employee does more planning and controlling with less supervision but more self-evaluation.
- In other words, transferring some of the supervisor's tasks to the employee and making his job enriched.

299. (B)Job enrichment

300. (D)Job Evaluation

Explanation:

- Job evaluation is an effort to determine the relative value of every job in a plant and what the fair basic wage for such a job should be. Helps in removing inequalities.
- **Kimball and Kimball**: " Job evaluation represents an effort to determine the relative value of every job in a plant and to determine what the fair basic wage for such a job should be."
- **Wendell French:** "Job Evaluation is a process of determining the relative worth of the various jobs within the organization so that differential wages may be paid to jobs of different worth. "
- It is a process which is helpful even for framing compensation plans by the personnel manager.
- Job evaluation is the process of analyzing and assessing the various jobs systematically to ascertain their relative worth in an organization.
- To be objective, job evaluation should "rate the job not the man." Should be clear, easily understood, and sold to employees. Should not result in salary decrease/demotions for existing employees.
- Job evaluation is the process that establishes every position's internal relative worth to a company by measuring a position's potential fulfillment of duties against the amount of value being given by the present employee.
- Job evaluation measures job worth in an internal sense, as well as in an economic one.

301. (D)Periodicity for review of wage structure

302. (C)increase job effectiveness

Explanation:

- Job Enrichment loads the job ***vertically***.
- Job Enrichment means adding duties and responsibilities that will provide for skill variety, task identity, task significance, autonomy and feedback on job performance.
- The employee does more planning and controlling with less supervision but more self-evaluation.
- In other words, transferring some of the supervisor's tasks to the employee and making his job enriched.

303. (C)Point rating method

Explanation:

- Job evaluation is an effort to determine the relative value of every job in a plant and what the fair basic wage for such a job should be. Helps in removing inequalities.
- **Kimball and Kimball**: " Job evaluation represents an effort to determine the relative value of every job in a plant and to determine what the fair basic wage for such a job should be."
- **Wendell French:** "Job Evaluation is a process of determining the relative worth of the various jobs within the organization so that differential wages may be paid to jobs of different worth. "
- It is a process which is helpful even for framing compensation plans by the personnel manager.
- Job evaluation is the process of analyzing and assessing the various jobs systematically to ascertain their relative worth in an organization.

- To be objective, job evaluation should "rate the job not the man." Should be clear, easily understood, and sold to employees. Should not result in salary decrease/demotions for existing employees.
- Job evaluation is the process that establishes every position's internal relative worth to a company by measuring a position's potential fulfillment of duties against the amount of value being given by the present employee.
- Job evaluation measures job worth in an internal sense, as well as in an economic one.

Job Evaluation Methods

A. Non-Analytical Methods

1. **Job Ranking:** Ranking system is a very simple method of job evaluation. Under this system the job raters simply rank one job against various others without assigning point value.
2. **Job Classification and Grading Method:** Numbers of predetermined grades or classifications are first established and then various jobs are assigned within each grade or class.

B. Analytical Methods

1.Point Rating System: Assumes it is possible to assign points to the different job factors as well as to each degree of each factor involved in jobs and the sum total of these points gives an index of relative value of jobs.

2. Factor Comparison System: A mixture of point & simple ranking .After locating major common factors, each job is ranked for each compensable factor and then ratings are combined for each job in an overall numerical rating for the job. It is easy now to assign money value to jobs in direct proportion to points assigned.

304. (C)Job Evaluation

305. (B) (ii) (i) (iii) (iv)

306. (D)Job Evaluation

307. (C)Factor-Comparision Method

308. (D)All the above

309. (A)Job description

Explanation:

- Job description is an organized factual statement of job contents in the form of duties and responsibilities of a specific job.
- The preparation of job description is very important before a vacancy is advertised.
- It tells in brief the nature and type of job.
- ***"Job Description implies objective listing of the job title, tasks, and responsibilities involved in a job."***
- Job description is a word picture in writing of the duties, responsibilities and organizational relationships that constitutes a given job or position.
- It defines continuing work assignment and a scope of responsibility that are sufficiently different from those of the other jobs to warrant a specific title.
- Job description is a broad statement of purpose, scope, duties and responsibilities of a particular job.

310. (B)(ii) (iv) (iii) (i)

311. (D)(i) (iv) (ii) (iii)

312. (B)(iv) (i) (iii) (ii)

313. (A)(iii) (i) (ii) (iv)

314. (C)(iii) (iv) (i) (ii)

315. (C)Job Description

Explanation: Job Description:

- A broad, general, and written statement of a specific job, based on the findings of a job analysis.
- It generally includes duties, purpose, responsibilities, scope, and working conditions of a job along with the job's title, and the name or designation of the person to whom the employee reports.
- Job description usually forms the basis of job specification.

316. (B) (iii) (i) (ii) (iv)

317. (C)Flexible pay-banding allowing grade mobility performance

Explanation:

- Broadbanding is a job grading structure that falls between using spot salaries vs. many job grades to determine what to pay particular positions and incumbents within those positions.
- While broadbanding gives the organization using it some broad job classifications, it does not have as many distinct job grades as traditional salary structures do.
- Broadbanding reduces the emphasis on 'status' or hierarchy and places more of an emphasis on lateral job movement within the company.
- In a broadbanding structure an employee can be more easily rewarded for lateral movement or skills development, whereas in traditional multiple grade salary structures pay progression happens primarily via job promotion.
- Broadbanding is a more flexible pay system. This flexibility, however, can lead to internal pay relativity problems as there isn't as much control over salary progression as there would be within a traditional multi-level grading structure.
- Broadbanding eliminates the present hierarchical grading structure and narrow salary ranges.
- In broadbanding, jobs with similar responsibilities and skill requirements are grouped in "bands" or job families.
- Employees can receive salary increases when they improve job knowledge, skills and abilities without having to be reclassified.
- Enhances organizational effectiveness by producing flatter organizational structures and reduces the perceived need to create additional levels of classification and/or supervision to justify higher pay.
- Broad Banding is a type of salary program that replaces multiple grades and ranges with a limited number of wide ranges. Employees move through salary ranges without traditional promotions or job delineation, based on individual skill attainment, and expansion of duties, rather than on any prescribed time pattern.

318. (A)Forming supportive objectives

Explanation:

- Job description is an organized factual statement of job contents in the form of duties and responsibilities of a specific job.
- The preparation of job description is very important before a vacancy is advertised.
- It tells in brief the nature and type of job.
- ***"Job Description implies objective listing of the job title, tasks, and responsibilities involved in a job."***
- Job description is a word picture in writing of the duties, responsibilities and organizational relationships that constitutes a given job or position.
- It defines continuing work assignment and a scope of responsibility that are sufficiently different from those of the other jobs to warrant a specific title.
- Job description is a broad statement of purpose, scope, duties and responsibilities of a particular job.

Contents of Job Description

- Job Identification
- Job Summary
- Job Duties and Responsibilities
- Supervision specification
- Machines, tools and materials
- Work conditions
- Work hazards
- Definition of unusual terms

319. (A)Job enrichment

Explanation: Job enrichment:

- A job design technique that is a variation on the concept of job enlargement. Job enrichment adds new sources of job satisfaction by increasing the level of responsibility of the employee.
- While job enlargement is considered a horizontal restructuring method, job

enrichment is a vertical restructuring method by virtue of giving the employee additional authority, autonomy, and control over the way the job is accomplished. Also called job enhancement or vertical job expansion.

- According to **Robert N.Ford**, Job enrichment means to make jobs which:

1. Have a greater variety.
2. Requires higher level of knowledge and skills.
3. Give workers more autonomy.
4. Give workers more responsibility.
5. Give workers opportunities for personal growth, and
6. A meaningful work experience.

- The meaning of Job enrichment is depicted in the following image or picture.
- **Job enrichment** means a vertical expansion of a job. It is different from job enlargement.
- **Job enlargement** means a horizontal expansion of a job.
- Job enrichment makes the job more meaningful, enjoyable and satisfying. It gives the workers more autonomy for planning and controlling the job. It also gives the workers more responsibility. Job enrichment gives the workers opportunities for achievement, recognition, advancement and growth. So, the workers are motivated to work harder.
- Therefore, Job enrichment makes the job a source of motivation.

320. (B)Job Evaluation

Explanation: Kimball and Kimball: " Job evaluation represents an effort to determine the relative value of every job in a plant and to determine what the fair basic wage for such a job should be."

321. (C)Job description

Explanation: Job description is a broad statement of purpose, scope, duties and responsibilities of a particular job.

322. (A)Job Analysis

Explanation: Job analysis is primary tool in personnel management. In this method, a personnel manager tries to gather, synthesize and implement the information available regarding the workforce in the concern.

323. (B)Job enlargement

Explanation: Job enlargement:

- A job design technique in which the number of tasks associated with a job is increased (and appropriate training provided) to add greater variety to activities, thus reducing monotony.
- Job enlargement is considered a horizontal restructuring method in that the job is enlarged by adding related tasks.
- Job enlargement may also result in greater workforce flexibility.

324. (C) Job design

Explanation: Job design:

- Work arrangement (or rearrangement) aimed at reducing or overcoming job dissatisfaction and employee alienation arising from repetitive and mechanistic tasks.
- Through job design, organizations try to raise productivity levels by offering non-monetary rewards such as greater satisfaction from a sense of personal achievement in meeting the

increased challenge and responsibility of one's work.

- Job enlargement, job enrichment, job rotation, and job simplification are the various techniques used in a job design exercise.

325. (D)All the above

Explanation: Job evaluation is the process of analyzing and assessing the various jobs systematically to ascertain their relative worth in an organization.

326. (C)Job Evaluation

327. (A)Job rotation

Explanation: Job rotation:

- A job design technique in which employees are moved between two or more jobs in a planned manner.
- The objective is to expose the employees to different experiences and wider variety of skills to enhance job satisfaction and to cross-train them.

328. (B)De - skilling

Explanation: De-skilling: Decrease in the quality and range of the practical knowledge of individuals, organizations, or societies due to attrition, automation, computerization, downsizing, lack of learning opportunities, or neglect.

329. (C) (iii)and (iv)

330. (B)'job enrichment' is vertical loading while 'job enlargement' is horizontal loading

331. (C) Job specification

332. (A) Job Analysis

333. (C) Penal actions

334. (A) (c) (d) (b) (a)

335. (C)State Governments

336. (D)Performance Appraisal

337. (C)Intra-industry differentials

338. (D)Nation as a whole

339. (D)All the above

340. (C)Consumers' Representatives

341. (D)All of the above

342. (D)Industrial Tribunals

343. (C)Wage Boards

344. (B)Dr. Ravindra Verma

345. (C)Barth System

Explanation:

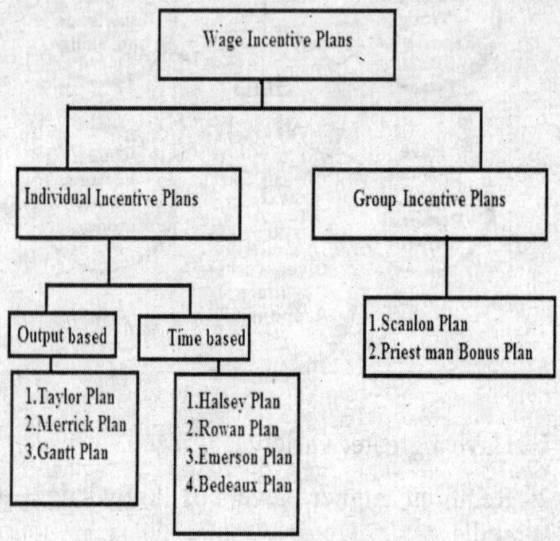

346. (D)Personal wage differential

347. (D)Labour is as flexible and mobile as capital.

348. (D)Monopoly in the labour market is high.

349. (C)Nominal wage

350. (C)Same quality

351. (B)Real wages may fall

352. (A)Inefficient employees

353. (B)Imperfect Market

354. (D)Housewives

355. (C)High Degree of Unionization

356. (D)J.B. Clark

Explanation:

Marginal productivity theory of wages

- This theory proposed by ***J.B. Clark.***
- "Marginal productivity means the net addition or net subtraction caused in the total production by employing or withdrawing one unit of production."
- A producer always compares the marginal product value with the price of a marginal input unit.
- This theory states that price of each factor of production tends to be equal to its marginal productivity.

357. (D)Collective Bargaining Theory

Collective Bargaining Theory

- The bargaining theory of wages holds that wages, hours, and working conditions are determined by the relative bargaining strength of the parties to the agreement.
- This idea of bargaining was developed to a considerable extent by ***John Davidson***, who proposed in *The Bargain Theory of Wages* (1898) that the determination of wages is an extremely complicated process involving numerous influences that interact to establish the relative bargaining strength of the parties.
- In the **bargaining theory of wages**, there is no single economic principle or force governing wages. Instead, wages and other working conditions are determined by workers, employers, and unions, who determine these conditions by negotiation.

358. (D)Residual claimant theory

359. (A) (iii) (iv) (ii) (i)

360. (A) (iii) (iv) (ii) (i)

361. (D)Francis A. Walker

Explanation:

Residual Claimant Theory of Wages:

- This theory is offered by American economist ***Francis A. Walker***. He says, "Wages equal the whole product minus rent interest and profit."
- *According to this theory labour receives what remains after the payment of rent, profits, taxes and interest out of the national income.*
- **Jevon** says, "The wages of working man are ultimately coincident with what he produces, after the deduction of rent, taxes and the interest on capital."

362. (C) Surplus Value Theory of Wage

Explanation:

Surplus Value Theory of Wage

- Surplus value is a specific expression of the capitalist form of exploitation, in which the surplus product takes the form of surplus value.
- The production and appropriation of surplus value constitute the essence of the fundamental economic law of capitalism. ***Karl Marx*** pointed out that "production of surplus value is the absolute law" of the capitalist mode of production.

363. (C)(iv) (iii) (ii) (i)

364. (B)(iv) (iii) (ii) (i)

365. (B)Subsistence Theory

Explanation:

Subsistence Theory of wages:

- This theory advanced by ***David Ricardo*** and other classical economist, was based on the population theory of Thomas Malthus.
- The market price of labour would always tend towards the minimum required for subsistence.
- According to this theory, the wage in the long run tends to be equal to the level of subsistence. By minimum level of subsistence means the amount which is just sufficient to meet the basic necessities of life of the workers and their family.
- It is argued that if wages exceed the subsistence level the labour will marry and will produce children. The supply of labour will increase then the demand and money wages will fall to the level of subsistence.

- If wages remain below the subsistence level, the labour will not be able to maintain their families. The death rate will increase due to hunger and supply of labour will fall than its demand. Again wages will rise to the subsistence level.

366. (B)(iv) (ii) (iii) (i)

367. (B) (iii) (i) (ii) (iv)

368. (A) Taussig

369. (C)Piece Rated

370. (C)Fringe Benefits

371. (C)Push and pull theory

372. (B)Job Evaluation

373. (C)Labour Turnover=(No. of Employees left during specific period÷ Average No. of employees during the same period)x100

374. (B)Real wages

Explanation: Real wages: Income of an individual, organization, or country, after taking into consideration the effects of inflation on purchasing power.

375. (B)Standard wage rate

376. (C)1948

377. (A)The wage paid or received in monetary terms.

378. (D) Dearness Allowance

379. (D)The Halsey Premium Plan

380. (D)Facilitating the separation of employees

381. (A)Straight piece rate

382. (B)Differential piece rate

383. (C)Task and time bonuses

384. (A)Merit rating

385. (B)Taylor's differential piece rate plan

386. (A)Bedeaux system

387. (B)Rowan incentive plan

388. (A)Halsey incentive plan

389. (C)Rucker incentive plan

390. (A)Hayne's incentive plan

391. (D)All of the above

392. (D)Promoting Equal Wages for Equal Work.

393. (C)Payment of Wages Act

394. (A)Basic wage

395. (C)Imperfect Market

396. (A)Good wage structure shall address to internal equity and external parity.

397. (C)Statutory Minimum Wages

398. (C) (ii) (i) (iv) (iii)

399. (C)The state through regulation of wages can eliminate wage differentials.

400. (A)Same wage rate

401. (D)All the above

402. (D)National Wage Differential

403. (C)will have no effect on supply of labour

404. (C)Ice-cream industry

405. (D)House-wives

406. (D)Under employment

407. (C)Both supply and demand

408. (C) Wage is the price of labour

409. (A) Minimum Wage Principle

410. (A)Minimum Wage

Explanation: Minimum Wage: Minimum wage is the wage that is able to provide not only for bare physical needs but also for preservation of efficiency of worker plus some measure of education, health and other things.

411. (D) Valid test

412. (A)Living wage

Explanation: Living Wage: Living wage is that which workers can maintain the health and decency, a measure of comfort and some insurance against the more important misfortune of lie.

413. (B)Wage that is lower than living wage but more than minimum wage

Explanation:

- A fair wage lies between the minimum wage and the living wage which is the goal.
- Wages must be paid on an industry wise and region basis having due regard to the financial capacity of the unit.

414. (A)The rate of change in the working staff of a concern during a definite period

415. (D) All of the above

416. (A)High Court

417. (C)Rs.185/- per month

418. (D) All of the above

419. (D)(A) and (B)both

420. (C)Advanced salary

421. (D)(A) and (B) both.

422. (D)All of the above

423. (B)Appropriate Government

424. (B) Profit sharing

Explanation: A Profit Sharing system pays out if the company beats the goals set to trigger the Profit Sharing payout, but it doesn't tell people what they need to do to make the profits happen.

425. (A) 1942

426. (B)Gain sharing

Explanation:

- A Gain sharing system is very specific in telling people what needs to happen, both overall and in their specific area, if we are going to hit the targeted performance level. This intensive planning and feedback system is key to Gain sharing's enduring power to drive employee and company performance.
- Gains haring is a system that includes:

(1) a financial measurement and feedback system to monitor company performance and distribute gains in the form of bonuses when appropriate, and

(2) a focused involvement system to eliminate barriers to improved company performance.

- Gain sharing systems vary widely in terms of their design and the degree to which they are integrated into the regular operating systems of the company.
- Of course, the more they are integrated into the day-to-day operational systems, the more commitment there is to the Gain sharing system. And, the more commitment there is to achieving overall business goals (including the Gain sharing goals) the better the resulting performance is.

427. (D)Louis Kelso

Explanation: An employee stock ownership plan (ESOP):

- It is an employee-owner scheme that provides a company's workforce with an ownership interest in the company.
- In an ESOP, companies provide their employees with stock ownership, often at no cost to the employees.
- Shares are given to employees and may be held in an ESOP trust until the employee retires or leaves the company.
- The shares are then sold. In 1956, ***Louis Kelso***, invented the first ESOP, which allowed the employees of Peninsula Newspapers to buy out the company founders.

428. (C) Both of (A) & (B)

Explanation: Determination of minimum wages or fringe benefits:

- The concept of "Minimum Wage" stands for different standard of different countries.
- The fair wage committee in India has observed that in India the level of the national income is so low at present that it is generally accepted that the country cannot afford to prescribe by law a minimum wage

must provide not merely for the bare sustenance of life but for the preservation of the efficiency of the worker.

- Thus, a minimum wage is one, which may be sufficient to enable worker to live in reasonable comfort having regard to all obligations.

Principles of Wage Determination

The following principles have always been the bases of the wage determination process.

All are economically valid. At different stages they have collectively, and singularly, been used to determine wage increases.

1. Preserving real income: This is the argument used by employees and Unions viewing wages as an income. Following this principle usually results in wages being indexed to inflation. In periods of rising inflation, indexation becomes a problem of an institutionalised wage-price spiral. Underlying aspects that have also impacted on real wage preservation arguments have been a "basic" minimum wage, and comparative wage justice.

2. Labour productivity: A valid economic theory connects wages to labour productivity. Conflict arises over the measurement of productivity. Rewarding labour with a wage increase when technology, and/or capital investment, increases labour efficiency, may not be justified.

3. The capacity of business to afford wage increases: This emphasises wages as a cost of production, and the threat of wage increases to squeeze profits. This "capacity" argument is that followed by business owners.

4. The capacity of the Economy to absorb wage increases: This "capacity" argument views the macro impact of wage increases on inflation, competitiveness, and other aspects of internal and external balance; as well as the affect on business profits and investment from 3. This is the main argument of the Federal Government recognising the macro policy potential of an Incomes Policy to address external and internal balance goals to supplement demand management policies, and the effects on income distribution.

The Methods of Wage Determination

- Generally wage determination can be through a centralised, regulated, institutionalised system, or a decentralised system.
- Collective bargaining is when workers with similar employment conditions and skills unite, usually through a union, to present their wage demands to their employer(s).
- Enterprise bargaining is when workers at the same plant bargain with the employer.
- An award is an agreement that sets out both wages and working conditions.
- Our reliance on a centralised system, often based on indexation, has dominated wage determination over the last century.

429. (B)Exit policy

430. (C)Refering a candidate for job by existing employee

431. (C)Personnel Planning

432. (A)Reactions

433. (A)Role clarification

434. (B)the importance of measuring business performance

435. (C)Supervision

436. (C)Creates misalignment between values and practices

437. (D) BARS

438. (A)Competition for scarce inputs

439. (C)Competitiors

440. (B)An extended leave of absence

441. (B)(c)(d)(a)(b)

442. (C)Cyclical unemployment

443. (D)Prohibiting an employee from attending work and performing normal duties to him/her

444. (B)Socialistic pattern of society

445. (B) 20

446. (A) Demographic characteristics

447. (D) Job Knowledge Test

448. (C) (d) (c) (b) (a)

449. (A)Picture language

450. (C)A scale that lists a number of traits and a range of performance for each

---000---

UNIT-IV

INDUSTRIAL RELATION & SOCIAL SECURITY

1. Who are the three major actors of Industrial Relations?

(A)Workers (B) Employers

(C)Government (D) All the above

2. Who defined Industrial Relation as a "Rule Making Process"?

(A) Robert Hoxie (B) Selig Perlman

(C) John T. Dunlop (D) Mc Kersie

3. Which of the following factors is helpful in promoting peaceful industrial relations?

(A)Mutual understanding

(B)Freedom of expression

(C)Freedom of Association and collective Bargaining

(D)All the above

4. Which of the following is ***not*** true in regard to the approaches to industrial Relations?

(A)Giri Approach (B) Dunlop Approach

(C)Nehru Approach (D) Gandhi Approach

5. "Formulation of rules and their implementation are the bread and butter of industrial relations" is commented by:

(A)John T. Dunlop (B)Alvin W. Gouldner

(C)Allan Flanders (D)Kochan

6. Who said, there are three actors of industrial relations?

(A)Lester (B) Dale yoder

(C)Dunlop (D)Krikardy

7. Good industrial relations refer to :

(A)Absence of industrial disputes

(B)Greater use of Collective Bargaining

(C)Friendly attitude of Employer and Trade Unions

(D)All the above

8. Find out the approach which does ***not*** include industrial relations

(A)Psychological approach

(B)Sociological approach

(C)Human relations approach

(D)Physiological approach

9. Joint Consultative Board (J.C.B.) of industry and labour was set up in 1951 with the initiative of :

(A)V.V. Giri (B) G.L. Nanda

(C)Morarji Desai (D)Jagjivan Ram

10. Three tier framework of industrial relations was proposed by :

(A)Kochan, T.A., et. al (B)Richardson J.H.

(C)Clark Kerr (D)John T. Dunlop

11. A system of industrial relations where social and labour issues are discussed between trade unions and management at enterprise level is

(A)Bipartism (B)Tripartism

(C)Social dialogue (D)None of the above

12. The relations between government and transnational corporations are divided into liberal, neo-mercantilist and neo-imperialist categories by :

(A)Richardson, J.H. (B)Clark Kerr

(C)Kochan, T.A., et.al (D)John T. Dunlop

13. Who proposed that industrial relations activities take place among three principal social partners at three levels?

(A)John T. Dunlop (B) Richardson, J.H.

(C)Kochan, T.A. et.al (D)Clark Kerr

14. Characteristics of Industrial Relations do ***not*** include :

(A)Industrial Relations are outcome of employment relationship in an industrial enterprise.

(B)Industrial Relations promote the skills and methods of adjustment and co-operation with each other.

(C)Industrial Relations create complex rules and regulations to maintain cordial relations.

(D)Industrial Relations system creates an environment of distrust and conflict.

15. Who are ***not*** the Actors of Industrial Relations?

(A)Workers and their organizations

(B)Employers and their organizations

(C)Community and cultural associations

(D)Government and the role of the State

16. Which of the following ***cannot*** be said to be a body in the field of industrial relations?

(A) Joint Management Council

(B) Works Committee

(C) Shop Level Council

(D) Canteen Committee

17. Which one of the following is ***not*** a necessary condition for establishing and maintaining good industrial relations?

(A)Keep the employees informed about decision which affect their interests

(B)Payment of fair wages and adequate wage structure

(C)Maintain good relations with nearby industries

(D)Establishment of an atmosphere of participation

18. The scope of industrial relations does ***not*** include

(A)Employer and Employee relations

(B)Employer and Trade Union relations.

(C)Employer, Employee and Trade Union relations.

(D)Employer and Customer relations.

19. Who are ***not*** the actors according to Dunlop's framework of industrial relations system?

(A)Managers and their representatives

(B)Workers and their organizations

(C)Specialized government agencies

(D)Communities and their associations

20. Identify the correct definition of industrial relations:

(A)Relations between or among human beings

(B)Relations between employer and employees as individuals

(C)Relations between parties in an employment context

(D)Collective relationship between management and trade unions

21. Which of the following is ***not*** included under the concept of industrial relations?

(A)Employer - Union Relations

(B)Employer - State Relations

(C)Employer - Customer Relations

(D)Employer - Union State Relations

22. Who has propounded the system concept of industrial relations? Find out from the following :

(A)L. N. Allen Flander (B)L. N. Flax

(C)John T. Dunlop (D)Neil N. Chamberlein

23. The concept of industrial relations is :

(A)Static

(B)Dynamic

(C)Both Static and Dynamic

(D)None of the above

24. Who among the following gave a model for industrial relations?

(A)Harold J. Laski (B)Adam Smith

(C)John T. Dunlop (D)Heneman

25. Match the following :

List - I

(a)Trusteeship Theory

(b)Revolutionary Theory

(c)Placating Theory

(d)Human Relations Theory

List - II

(i)Elton Mayo

(ii)Labour welfare

(iii)Karl Marx

(iv)Gandhi

Code:

	(a)	(b)	(c)	(d)
(A)	(iv)	(iii)	(ii)	(i)
(B)	(iii)	(iv)	(i)	(ii)
(C)	(iv)	(i)	(ii)	(iii)
(D)	(i)	(iii)	(ii)	(iv)

26. Who observed that the respect for rules depends on the manner of their formulation?

(A)Web, S. and Web, B. (B)Flanders, A.

(C)Durkheim, E. (D)Gouldner, A.

27. The Origin, growth and development of employment's organizations in India can be identified as :

(A)Before 1933 (B) After 1933

(C)Before 1947 (D) After 1947

28. The concept/theory of industrial capitalism/dialectical materialism was developed by :

(A)Karl Marx (B)Mahatma Gandhi

(C)Dunlop J. T. (D)Thakur C. P.

29. The International Organization of Employer's(I.O.E) with headquarters in Genevas was formulated in:

(A)1910 (B)1920

(C)1930 (D)1940

30. Benefits (India) of globalization like sustained economic growth, free markets, economic globalization, privatization etc., were summarized by:

(A)First National Commission on Labour

(B)Second National Commission on Labour

(C)National Labour Board

(D)International Labour Organisation

31. Who said "Industrial Societies necessarily create industrial relations defined as complex of interrelations among workers, managers and governments" :

(A)John T. Dunlop (B)P.H. Casselman

(C)I.L.O. (D)None of the above

32. Fill up the blanks from one of the suitable words given in the bracket "Select the correct combination":

(i) Award, (ii) Bi - partite Body,

(iii) Tripartite Body, (iv) Check off,

(v)Deduction, (vi)International Federation,

(vii) Settlement, (viii)Consultative body

(a)The decision of Labour Court is called __

(b)Canteen Committee is a ________

(c)Deduction of union membership fee is called____

(d)I.L.O. is a ________

(A)(ii), (v), (vi), (viii)

(B)(viii), (iv), (ii), (i)

(C)(i), (ii), (iv), (iii)

(D)(iii), (v), (vii), (i)

33. Match the following

List-I

(a)ILO

(b)Karl Marx

(c)Award

(d)Settlement

List-II

(i)USSR

(ii)Geneva

(iii)Conciliation

(iv)Arbitration

Code:

	(a)	(b)	(c)	(d)
(A)	(i)	(iii)	(iv)	(ii)
(B)	(iv)	(ii)	(iii)	(i)
(C)	(ii)	(i)	(iv)	(iii)
(D)	(iii)	(iv)	(ii)	(i)

34. Arrange the following in proper sequence :

(i)Establishment of the Indian Labour Conference

(ii)First Bombay Factory Commission

(iii)Submission of the Report of the Royal Commission on Labour

(iv)Establishment of the ILO

(A) (ii) (iv) (iii) (i)

(B) (iv) (ii) (iii) (i)

(C) (iii) (ii) (iv) (i)

(D) (i) (ii) (iii) (iv)

35. Arrange the following in a proper sequence according to the year in which they came into existence :

(a) Indian Labour Conference

(b) Defence of India Rules

(c) Industrial Disputes Act

(d)Scheme of Labour Management Co-operation (Joint Management Councils)

(e)First National Commission on Labour

(f)Workers' participation in management in Industries

(g)Second National Commission on Labour

(A) (a), (c), (d), (e), (f), (g), (b)

(B) (b), (a), (c), (d), (e), (f), (g)

(C) (c), (d), (e), (f), (g), (a), (b)

(D) (d), (e), (f), (g), (a), (b), (c)

36. First time the May Day was celebrated in India in :

(A) 1923 (B) 1927

(C) 1935 (D) 1947

37. The provisions regarding equal pay for equal work to men and women are provided under which of the following :

(A)Fundamental Rights

(B)Directive Principles of State Policy

(C)Preamble

(D)In all the above

38. There is only one source of authority – management. They own and, therefore, they control – is the argument of

(A)Pluralists (B)Radicalists

(C)Trusteeship (D)Unitarists

39. Match List – I with List – II :

List – I

(a) Joint Management Council consisting of representatives of workers and management was considered by the Indian Labour Conference (ILC) in its 15th Session in the year

(b) Works Committees were set-up under the Industrial Disputes Act in the year

(c) ILO established in the year

(d)First National Commission on Labour submitted its report in the year

List – II

(i) 1958

(ii) 1947

(iii) 1919

(iv) 1969

Codes:

	(a)	(b)	(c)	(d)
(A)	(i)	(ii)	(iii)	(iv)
(B)	(iv)	(i)	(iii)	(ii)
(C)	(iii)	(i)	(ii)	(iv)
(D)	(ii)	(iv)	(i)	(iii)

40. Which of the following trends in the employment relations in the new economic era is ***not*** correct?

(A) Declining stability and security

(B) Declining labour intensity

(C) No shift from contract of service to contract of service

(D) Declining mutual commitment

41. Match the following :

List – I

(a) Human Capital Approach

(b) Socio-Psychological Approach

(c) Poverty Alleviation Approach

(d) World Human Development Approach

List – II

(i) David Mcclelland

(ii) UNDP

(iii)T.W. Scultz

(iv) World Bank

Codes:

	(a)	(b)	(c)	(d)
(A)	(ii)	(iv)	(i)	(iii)
(B)	(iii)	(iv)	(ii)	(i)
(C)	(iii)	(i)	(iv)	(ii)
(D)	(iv)	(ii)	(i)	(iii)

42. A willful disobedience of authority is called :

(A)Insubordination (B) Indiscipline

(C)Willful disobedience (D) Misconduct

43. Which of the following is ***not*** within the scope of "Adjudication"?

(A)Conciliation (B) Labour Court

(C)Industrial Tribunal (D) National Tribunal

44. Outplacement services are provided to employees who have been :

(A)Dismissed(B) Rendered surplus

(C)Retired (D) Given voluntary retirement

45. What notice period is required for going on strike/lockout in public utility services?

(A)One week (B) Three weeks

(C)Six weeks (D) Nine weeks

46. A situation where management is unable to provide employment due to non-availability of work is called:

(i)Lock out (ii)Lay off

(iii)Termination (iv)Closure

Find the correct combination according to the code.

(A) (i) and (ii) (B) (ii) and (iii)

(C) (i) and (iii) (D) (ii) and (iv)

47. Which one of the settlement methods is ***not*** relevant here for disputes?

(A)Collective Bargaining

(B)Compulsory Adjudication

(C)Voluntary Arbitration

(D)Reference to Civil Court

48. Lock out means

(A)An antithesis of strike

(B)Refusal to employ any person in employment

(C)The temporary closing of a place of employment

(D)Illegal strike

49. The problem of industrial discipline was debated by the Indian Labour Conference (ILC) held in India in

(A) 1948 (B) 1952

(C) 1957 (D) 1960

50. The outside third party who is brought into settle a dispute, and he or she has the authority to make a decision is called

(A) Government (B) An Arbitrator

(C) Union (D) Legal Expert

51. 'Rege Committee' is related to:

(A)Working conditions in Indian Industry

(B)Social security in Indian Industry

(C)Individual differences in Indian Industry

(D)None of the above

52. The first stage of conflict resolution is to :

(A)Analyze the problem

(B)Choose a solution

(C)Think through possible solution

(D)Define the problem

53. Which is the correct order of settlement of industrial disputes?

(i)Industrial Tribunal (ii)National Tribunal

(iii)Conciliation (iv)Labour Court

(A) (iii) (i) (iv) (ii)

(B) (iii) (iv) (i) (ii)

(C) (i) (iv) (iii) (ii)

(D) (iii) (ii) (iv) (i)

54. An enquiry that is conducted afresh because of the objections raised by alleged employee is called:

(A) Domestic enquiry (B) De-novo enquiry

(C) Ex-parte enquiry (D) None of the above

55. Which of the following is machinery for settlement of industrial disputes?

(A) Indian Labour Conference

(B) Joint Management Council

(C) Industrial Tribunal

(D) Standing Labour Committees

56. Which of the following is ***not*** machinery for settlement of industrial disputes in India?

(A)Indian Labour Conference and Standing Labour Committee

(B)Conciliation officers

(C)Labour Court

(D)National Tribunal

57. Which of the following is/are the methods of settlement of Industrial Disputes?

(A)Negotiation (B) Conciliation

(C)Both (A) and (B) (D) None of the above

58. Arrange the following dispute settlement methods in order of their applications :

(i)Conciliation / Mediation

(ii)Adjudication

(iii)Voluntary Arbitration

(iv)Collective Bargaining

(A) (iv) (i) (iii) (ii)

(B) (iv) (iii) (ii) (i)

(C) (i) (iv) (iii) (ii)

(D) (i) (iii) (iv) (ii)

59. Which one of the following methods is regarded as the most ideal for settlement of Industrial Dispute?

(A)Adjudication

(B)Mediation / Conciliation

(C)Collective Bargaining

(D)Voluntary Arbitration

60. Which of the following is ***not*** machinery for settlement of industrial disputes in India?

(A)Board of Conciliation

(B)Labour Court

(C)Collective Bargaining

(D)Industrial Tribunal

61. Match the following :

List-I

(a)Conciliation Machinery

(b)Consultation Machinery

(c)Adjudication Machinery

(d)Arbitration Machinery

List-II

(i)Indian Labour Conference

(ii)Industrial Tribunal

(iii)Arbitration

(iv)Board of Conciliation

	(a)	(b)	(c)	(d)
(A)	(iii)	(ii)	(i)	(iv)
(B)	(ii)	(iii)	(iv)	(i)
(C)	(iv)	(i)	(ii)	(iii)
(D)	(i)	(iv)	(iii)	(ii)

62. Match the following :

(Method)

(a)Conciliation

(b)Collective Bargaining

(c)Investigation

(d)Adjudication

(Product)

(i)Report

(ii)Award

(iii)Settlement

(iv)Agreement

Code:

	(a)	(b)	(c)	(d)
(A)	(iii)	(i)	(ii)	(iv)
(B)	(iii)	(iv)	(i)	(ii)
(C)	(ii)	(i)	(iii)	(iv)
(D)	(iv)	(iii)	(i)	(ii)

63. Match List-I with List-II.

List-I

(a)Strike

(b)Lockout

(c)Lay-off

(d)Closure

List-II

(i)The action of employer is temporarily closing down his undertaking.

(ii)Refusal of the employer to employ the workers because of coal, power and raw material.

(iii)Temporary cessation of work by a group of employees in order to express their grievances.

(iv)Permanently closing down of the establishment by the employer.

Codes:

	(a)	(b)	(c)	(d)
(A)	(iii)	(i)	(ii)	(iv)
(B)	(iii)	(ii)	(iv)	(i)
(C)	(ii)	(iii)	(i)	(iv)
(D)	(i)	(iii)	(iv)	(ii)

64. Which of the following is ***not*** adjudication machinery under the Industrial Disputes Act?

(A)Labour Court (B) Court of Enquiry

(C)Industrial Tribunal (D) National Tribunal

65. Find the machinery which is ***not*** method of settlement of industrial dispute :

(A) consultation (B) works committee

(C) conciliation (D) Adjudication

66. Who considered collective bargaining as the most important concept for determining the terms and conditions of employment

(A) Sidney and Beatrice Webb

(B)Robert Hoxie

(C) John T.Dunlop

(D) Samuel Gompers

67. Find out the characteristics of collective bargaining which is ***not*** applicable;

(A)It is a collective process.

(B)It is a flexible process.

(C)It is not a bipartile process.

(D)It is interdisciplinary system.

68. Who has started that "Collective bargaining is essentially a process in which employees act as a group in seeking to shape conditions and relationships in their employment.

(A)R. F. Hoxie (B)L. G. Reynolds

(C)Dale Yoder (D)J. F. Richardson

69. Who among the following advocated the use of collective bargaining as the best method for promoting healthy labour management relations in India?

(A)Mahatma Gandhi (B)Guljarilal Nanda

(C)Khandubhai Desai (D)V.V. Giri

70. Which part of the wages is governed by the escalatory clause in a collective bargaining agreement?

(A)Basic Wage (B) Dearness Allowance

(C)Wage Incentives (D) None of the above

71. Which of the following countries is said to be the home of collective bargaining?

(A)United Kingdom (B) Sweden

(C) United States of America (D)France

72. Match the following :

List – I

(a) Collective Bargaining

(b) Wage Boards

(c) Wage

(d) Salary

List – II

(i) Institutions set up by the Government for fixation and revision of wages.

(ii)It is a procedure in which compromise is reached through balancing of opposed strengths.

(iii)Remuneration paid to the clerical and managerial personnel on monthly or annual basis.

(iv)Remuneration paid by the employer for the services of hourly, daily, weekly and fortnightly employees.

	(a)	(b)	(c)	(d)
(A)	(i)	(ii)	(iii)	(iv)
(B)	(iv)	(ii)	(i)	(iii)
(C)	(ii)	(iv)	(i)	(iii)
(D)	(ii)	(i)	(iv)	(iii)

73. The first to introduce the term collective bargaining :

(A)Sidney and Beatrice webb

(B)Samuel Gompers

(C)Clark Kerr

(D)Robert Hoxie

74. Grievance is:

(A)A feeling of dissatisfaction

(B)A dispute raised by a trade union

(C)Refusal of the management of a demand

(D)An act of indiscipline

75. Which is ***not*** the characteristics of grievances?

(A)Factual (B)Fabricated

(C)Disguised (D)Imaginary

76. The grievance arising out of legitimate needs of employees remaining unfulfilled may be termed as :

(A) Disguised Grievance

(B) Imaginary Grievance

(C) Factual Grievance

(D) Work-Group Grievance

77. Who said 'as discipline is a control of management on employee, grievance is a control of employee on management'

(A)Michael J. Jucius (B)Richard P. Calhoon

(C)Windell French (D)Dale Yoder

78. Which of the following has ***not*** been provided under the provisions of the code of discipline?

(A)Trade union recognition

(B)Unfair Labour practices

(C)Grievance handling

(D)Worker's participation in management

79. Consider the following punishments :

(i)Warning or censure

(ii)Demotion

(iii)Fine and withholding of increments

(iv)Discharge and dismissal

Which of the above fall under the minor punishments?

(A) (i) and (ii)

(B) (i), (ii) and (iii)

(C) (i) and (iii)

(D) (i), (ii) and (iv)

80. Which of the following is/are the essence of model grievance procedure?

(A)Settlement at the lower level

(B)Settlement as expeditiously as possible

(C)Settlement to the satisfaction of the aggrieved

(D)All the above

81. The Code of Discipline makes provisions for which of the following :

(A)Unfair Labour practices

(B)Grievance redressal

(C)Recognition of Trade Union

(D)All the above

82. If a employees have given letters, memos and documents to study the organization policy is called:

(A)Business games (B)Role play

(C) In tray activity (D)Case studies

83. An enquiry that is conducted afresh because of the objections raised by alleged employee, is called :

(A)ex-parte enquiry (B)domestic enquiry

(C)de-novo enquiry (D)none of the above

84. Arrange the sequence followed in a disciplinary procedure.

(i)Charge sheet

(ii)Reporting the misconduct

(iii)Awarding the punishment

(iv)Domestic enquiry

(A) (i) (ii) (iv) (iii)

(B) (i) (iii) (ii) (iv)

(C) (ii) (i) (iv) (iii)

(D) (ii) (iv) (i) (iii)

85. Assertion (A): Grievance and Discipline are mutually complementary control mechanisms.

Reason (R): Discipline is a control of the management on employee and Grievance is a control of the employee on the management.

(A) (A) is right but (R) is wrong

(B) Both (A) and (R) are wrong

(C) (A) is wrong and (R) is right

(D) Both (A) and (R) are right

86. The headquarters of Central Board for Workers' Education is located at______.

(A)New Delhi (B)Mumbai

(C)Chennai (D)Nagpur

87. Which of the following statements about workers' participation in Management in India is ***not*** true?

(A)It is a part of the 20 point Economic programme.

(B)It is provided in the Directive Principles of State Policy.

(C)It is made a Constitutional provision under the 42nd Amendment Act.

(D)It is a justiceable right of the workers.

88. The Scheme of Workers' Participation in Management as provided under the 20 point programme, 1975 did ***not*** provide for :

(A)Shop Councils (B)Unit Councils

(C)Joint Councils (D)None of the above

89. The coverage of workers' participation under a comprehensive labour relations legislation was recommended by

(A)The First National Commission on Labour, 1969

(B)The Second National Commission on Labour,2002

(C)Participation of Workers' in Management Bill, 1990

(D)Scheme of Employees Participation in Public Sector Undertakings (1983)

90. Which part of the Indian Constitution bears provisions relating to workers' participation in management?

(A)The Preamble

(B)The Directive Principles of State Policy

(C)Fundamental Rights

(D)None of the above

91. Which one of the following is called the World Parliament of Labour ?

(A)Governing body of ILO

(B)International Labour Conference

(C)United Nations

(D)UNICEF

92. The scheme of workers participation in Management was introduced by Government of India in:

(A)1965 (B)1975

(C)1985 (D)1995

93. To which of the following the two voluntary schemes of workers' participation in management introduced in the year 1975 and 1977 do ***not*** apply :

(A)Manufacturing

(B)Mining Industries

(C)Commercial and Service Organisations

(D)Central Public Sector Undertakings

94. The scheme of workers' participation in management in industry in India was introduced Through:

(A) Code of Discipline in industry

(B) 20-point Economic Programme

(C)Industrial Employment (Standing Orders) Act

(D)None of the above

95. The main objective of workers' participation in management is ______.

(A)To promote increased productivity for the

advantage of organisation, workers and society at large

(B)To develop, enhance and utilise resources effectively

(C)To improve various skills of workers in organisation

(D)To respond to the members' demands both formally and informally

96. Which one of the following does ***not*** come under the schemes of workers' participation in management, 1975 & 1977?

(A)Joint Management Council

(B)Shop Councils

(C)Joint Councils

(D)Unit Councils

97. Which of the following is ***not*** a tripartite body?

(A)Works Committee (B) Wage Boards

(C)Indian Labour Conference (D) I. L. O

98. The first commission to recommend tripartism consultation in India was

(A)The First National Commission on Labour

(B)The Second National Commission on Labour

(C)The Royal Commission on Labour

(D)The Indian Labour Conference

99. Which of the following is ***not*** a tripartite body?

(A)Indian Labour Conference

(B)Joint Management Councils

(C)Standing Labour Committee

(D)Wage Boards

100. Which of the following is ***not*** a voluntary tripartite body?

(A)Indian Labour Conference

(B)Standing Labour Committee

(C)Central Advisory Board

(D)None of the above

101. Which of the following is ***not*** a tripartite body as created in 1942 :

(A)Indian Labour Conference

(B)Standing Labour Committee

(C)Tripartite Implementation and Evaluation Committee

(D)None of the above

102. Which one of the following is a tripartite body?

(A)Works Committee

(B)Canteen Management Committee

(C)Wage Board

(D)Joint Management Council

103. Revolutionary theory of trade union is proposed by :

(A)Webbs (B)Hoxie

(C)Karl Marx (D)Gandhi

104. Theories on Trade Unionism were proposed by :

(A)Elton Mayo, Marx and Gandhi

(B)Marx, Weber and Gandhi

(C)Pearlman, Weber and Webbs

(D)Pearlman, Webbs and Marx

105. Which of the following is ***not*** a characteristics of Trade Union ?

(A)Is an association of employers or the employees or of the independent workers?

(B)Is relatively a permanent combination but not temporary or casual.

(C)Is an association of workers who are engaged in not securing economic benefits for their members?

(D)Is influenced by a member of ideologies.

106. Who among the following defined trade unions as a continuous association of wage earners:

(A)S. D. Punekar (B)Dankert

(C)Webbs (D)V.V. Giri

107. Trade union means any combination formed primarily for the purpose of regulating the relations between

(A)Workmen and employers permanently

(B)Workmen and workmen permanently

(C)Workmen and employers, workmen and workmen, employers and employers temporary or permanent

(D)Workmen and employers, workmen and workmen, employers and employers permanently

108. Which of the following is ***not*** a Trade Union method as described by Webb's?

(A)Mutual Insurance (B)Legal enactment

(C)Collective Bargaining (D) Strike

109. Which of the following systems of wage payment a trade union will advocate which may even be useful for the inefficient members?

(A)Piece-rated wages

(B)Time-rated wages

(C)Performance-oriented wages

(D)Wages based on productivity

110. Match the following Theories of trade unionism with the contributors who propagated them :

Theory of Trade Unionism

(a)Industrial Democracy Theory

(b)Scarcity - consciousness Theory

(c)Socio - Psychological Theory

(d)Class collaboration and harmony Theory

Contribution

(i)M. K. Gandhi

(ii)Robert F. Hoxie

(iii)Sydney and Beatvice webbs

(iv)Selig Pearlman

	(a)	(b)	(c)	(d)
(A)	(iv)	(ii)	(iii)	(i)
(B)	(iii)	(iv)	(ii)	(i)
(C)	(i)	(iii)	(iv)	(ii)
(D)	(ii)	(i)	(iii)	(iv)

111. Who had propagated social engineering in industrial jurisprudence :

(A)Roscoe pound (B)Ehilrich

(C)Both A and B (D)None of the above

112. Who among the following was ***not*** a labour leader in India?

(A)B. P. Wadia (B)N. M. Lokhande

(C)Raja Ram Mohan Roy (D)V. V. Giri

113. Which one of the following is correct so for as the definition of trade union is concerned?

(A)Trade union is a temporary organisation

(B)Trade union is a continuous organisation

(C)Trade union is an economic organisation

(D)Trade union is a political organisation

114. Which among the following is ***not*** a short-term objective of trade unions?

(A)Wage increase

(B)Enhancement of dearness allowance

(C)Social Security

(D)Establishment of a Socialist Society

115. Which of the following is ***not*** a type of trade union?

(A)Craft Union (B) Stable Union

(C)Company Union (D) Industrial Union

116. Trade Union movement in India emerged between:

(A) 1920-1930 (B) 1850-1870

(C) 1870-1880 (D) 1930-1947

117. The first trade union in India was organized in :

(A) 1884 (B) 189

(C) 1918 (D)1920

118. Recognition of trade union is made by the provision of

(A)Trade Unions Act of 1926

(B)Industrial Dispute Act 1947

(C)Code of Discipline

(D)Factories Act of 1948

119. A Trade Union should be registered as per the law must have

(A) 20% of the workers

(B) 150 workmen

(C)Minimum 17 persons

(D)None of the above

120. Which is ***not*** a structure of Trade Union of Industrial Organization?

(A)Craft union (B) General union

(C)Industrial union (D) Consumers' union

121. Which one of the following is ***not*** an industrial relations legislation :

(A)I D Act, 1947

(B)Minimum Wages Act, 1948

(C)Trade Union Act, 1926

(D)Industrial Employment (Standing Orders) Act, 1946

122. The most important year in the history of Indian Trade Union Movement has been :

(A) 1920 (B) 1922

(C) 1940 (D) 1947

123. The founder of Ahmadabad Textile Labour Association was :

(A)V. V. Giri (B)M. K. Gandhi

(C)B. P. Wadia (D)N. M. Lokhande

124. The first union led by Maniben Kara and Kamala Sinha (two women) in India was :

(A)HMS -1948 (B)INTUC -1948

(C)AITUC -1920 (D)BMS -1954

125. The Bombay Mill Hands Association under the Presidentship of N.M. Lokhande which is often referred to as the starting point of the Indian Labour Movement, was established in :

(A) 1878 (B) 1879

(C) 1890 (D) 1891

126. Match the following :

Trade Union

(a) INTUC

(b) AITUC

(c) BMS

(d) CITU

Year of establishment

(i) 1970

(ii) 1955

(iii) 1947

(iv) 1920

	(a)	(b)	(c)	(d)
(A)	(iii)	(ii)	(i)	(iv)
(B)	(iii)	(iv)	(ii)	(i)
(C)	(iii)	(iv)	(i)	(ii)
(D)	(iv)	(iii)	(i)	(ii)

127. The First Indian Trade Union led by women was

(A)A.I.T.U.C. (B)I.N.T.U.C.

(C)H.M.S. (D)C.I.T.U.

128. Match the following trade unions according to the year of formation :

List – I	**List – II**
(a) AITUC	(i) 1947

(b) CITU	(ii) 1948
(c) INTUC	(iii) 1920
(d) HMS	(iv) 1970

Codes:

	(a)	(b)	(c)	(d)
(A)	(iii)	(iv)	(i)	(ii)
(B)	(ii)	(iii)	(iv)	(i)
(C)	(iii)	(i)	(ii)	(iv)
(D)	(i)	(ii)	(iii)	(iv)

129. Which one of the following Federations was organized in 1920 :

(A)INTUC (B)AITUC

(C)CITU (D)HMS

130. Which of the following was the first National Labour Federation organised in India?

(A) INTUC (B) AITUC

(C) CITU (D) HMS

131. Among the following trade unions which one is called the first modern trade union of India?

(A)Bombay Millhands Association

(B)Kamgar Hitwardhak Sabha

(C)Madras Labour Union

(D)All India Trade Union Congress

132. Which of the following federations is ***not*** affiliated to any political party?

(A)INTUC (B) NFITU

(C)AITUC (D) HMS

133. Arrange the events in Indian Trade Unionism in the order in which they have occurred from earliest to the latest :

(a)Formation of CITU

(b)Formation of UTUC

(c)Formation of AITUC

(d)Formation of INTUC

(A)	(c)	(d)	(b)	(a)
(B)	(d)	(b)	(a)	(c)
(C)	(a)	(c)	(d)	(b)
(D)	(b)	(a)	(c)	(d)

134. Match the trade union leaders associated with the trade unions :

Trade unions

(a)Madras Labour Union

(b)Ahmedabad Textile Labour Association

(c)All India Railwaymen's Federation

(d)Indian National Trade Union Congress

Trade union leaders

(i)V.V. Giri

(ii)A.R. Ramanujam

(iii)Mahatma Gandhi

(i)B.P. Wadia

	(a)	(b)	(c)	(d)
(A)	(iii)	(iv)	(ii)	(i)
(B)	(ii)	(i)	(iii)	(iv)
(C)	(i)	(ii)	(iv)	(iii)
(D)	(iv)	(iii)	(i)	(ii)

135. UTUC was formed in the year :

(A) 1949 (B) 1984

(C) 1920 (D) 1947

136. Who is the President of INTUC?

(A)Sanjeeva Reddy (B)Dutta Samanth

(C)Sitaram Etchuri (D)S. R. Kulkarni

137. BMS is affiliated to one of the following political parties :

(A)Indian National Congress

(B)Bharteeya Janata Party

(C)Communist Party of India (Marxists)

(D)Bahujan Samaj Party

138. The founder of Textile Labour Association

was:

(A)V. V. Giri (B)Gulzarilal Nanda

(C)M.K. Gandhi (D)Jaya Prakash Narayan

139. The oldest trade union in the country is:

(A)INTUC (B) AITUC

(C)CITU (D)HMS

140. Match the following :

List-II

(a)Madras Labour Union

(b)Ahmedabad Textile Labour Association

(c)Bombay Mill Hands Association

(d)Kamgar Hitwardhan Sabha

List-II

(i) 1890

(ii) 1909

(iii) 1917

(iv) 1920

Codes:

	(a)	(b)	(c)	(d)
(A)	(iv)	(iii)	(ii)	(i)
(B)	(iii)	(iv)	(i)	(ii)
(C)	(ii)	(i)	(iii)	(iv)
(D)	(i)	(ii)	(iv)	(iii)

141. INTUC, AITUC, HMS and UTUC adopted the code of conduct for Trade Union Rivalry in the year:

(A) 1948 (B) 1958

(C) 1968 (D) 1978

142. Who among the following was the First Trade Union Leader in India ?

(A)N.M. Lokhande (B)B.P. Wadia

(C)G.L. Nanda (D)M.K. Gandhi

143. Match the following :

Trade Union Federation	**Year of Formation**
(a)AITUC	(i)1947
(b)CITU	(ii)1948
(c)INTUC	(iii)1920
(d)HMS	(iv)1970

Codes:

	(a)	(b)	(c)	(d)
(A)	(iv)	(iii)	(i)	(ii)
(B)	(iii)	(i)	(iv)	(ii)
(C)	(iii)	(iv)	(i)	(ii)
(D)	(ii)	(iii)	(iv)	(i)

144. Which of the following provides for recognition of trade unions in India?

(A)Inter-Union Code of Conduct

(B)Code of Discipline in Industry

(C)Code of Efficiency and Welfare

(D)Code of Ethics

145. According to the Trade Unions Act, 1926 a minor member of the union :

(A)Can be elected as Office-bearer

(B)Can be elected as Office-bearer for one term

(C)Cannot be a member of the registered union

(D)Cannot be elected as Office-bearer of the registered trade union

146. Which of the following ***cannot*** be regarded as a union security measure?

(A)Closed-shop agreement

(B)Union-shop agreement

(C)Check-off

(D)Open-shop agreement

147. Intra-Union rivalry means :

(A)Rivalry between unions

(B)Rivalry within the same union

(C)Rivalry between unions and management

(D)Rivalry between unions and government

148. The code of discipline implemented by the central Government was :

(A)Voluntary in nature

(B)Compulsory in nature

(C)Partly voluntary and partly compulsory

(D)None of the above

149. The primary source of income for the union is :

(A)Membership subscription

(B)Donations

(C)Sale of periodicals

(D)Other sources

150. Who among the following will ***not*** be regarded as an outsider in trade union?

(A)Political leader

(B)Persons working in other industry

(C)Lawyers

(D)Ex – employees

151. The provision regarding political fund under the trade union Act, 1926 is :

(A)Creation of political fund is compulsory

(B)It is optional

(C)It is partly compulsory and partly voluntary

(D)None of the above

152. Which of the following is ***not*** a part of the structure of Trade Union in India ?

(A)Craft Union (B) Industrial Union

(C)Company Union (D) Federations

153. The basic function of trade union is

(A)To protect and promote the interest of the workers.

(B)Acquiring the control of industry by workers.

(C)Imbibing sincerity and discipline in workers.

(D)To provide cultural and recreational facilities.

154. Which of the following aims to check inter and intra union rivalry in India?

(A)The Trade Union Act

(B)The Code of Discipline in Industry

(C)The Inter Union Code of Conduct.

(D)All the above

155. Which of the following is ***not*** a type of labour legislation?

(A)Protective (B) Regulative

(C)Social Security (D) Social Legislation

156. A list of Unfair Labour Practices on the part of Trade Unions and Employers was inserted in

(A)Trade Union Act, 1926

(B)The Factories' Act, 1948

(C)The Industrial Disputes Act, 1947

(D)None of the above

157. Which of the following contributes in promoting healthy industrial relations in an organization?

(A)Compulsory Arbitration

(B)Adjudication

(C)Collective Bargaining

(D)Voluntary Arbitration

158. In which of the following an Individual Dispute ***cannot*** take the form of Industrial Dispute without the help of the Trade Union?

(A)Termination (B) Dismissal / Discharge

(C)Retrenchment (D) Promotion

159. Which of the following directly aims to control inter and intra–union rivalry in India?

(A)The Industrial Dispute Act, 1947

(B)Code of Discipline in Industry

(C)Inter-Union Code of Conduct

(D)Trade Unions Act, 1926

160. Which of the following is ***not*** regarded as Trade Union Weapon?

(A)Strike (B) Check-off

(C)Picketing (D) Boycott

161. Which of the following is ***not*** long term objective of Trade Union?

(A)Establishment of Socialist Society

(B)Nationalisation of Industries

(C)Parliament of Proletariate

(D)Higher Wages and Short hours of work

162. Which of the following can be said to be the first Trade Union in India?

(A) Amalgamated Society of Railway Servants of India and Burma

(B) Kamgar Hitvardhak Sabha

(C) Madras Labour Union

(D) Bombay Millhand's Association

163. Which of the following ***cannot*** be said to be the short-term objective of trade unions?

(A) Higher wages

(B) Shorter Hours of work

(C) Establishment of Socialist society

(D) Better conditions of Employment

164. Arrange the following in the order of their coverage from lower to higher :

(i) Regional Union (ii) Craft Union

(iii) Industrial Union (iv) Confederation

(v) Federation

(A) (i) (ii) (iii) (iv) (v) (B) (ii) (iii) (i) (v) (iv)

(C) (iii) (ii) (i) (iv) (v) (D) (iv) (i) (ii) (iii) (v)

165. A Trade Union means "An association of workers in one or more professions carried on mainly for the purpose of protecting and advancing the members' economic interest in connection with their daily work". Identify the author :

(A) Sidney and Beatrice Webb

(B) J. Cunnison

(C) G.D.H. Cole

(D) Clyde E. Dankert

166. A union may claim recognition for an industry in a local area, if it has membership of

(A) 10% of the workers in that industry.

(B) 15% of the workers in that area.

(C) 25% of the workers of that industry in that area.

(D) 30% of the workers in similar industry.

167. Who among the following advocated the Trusteeship Theory of Trade Union?

(A) N.M. Lokhande (B) B.P. Wadia

(C) G.L. Nanda (D) M.K. Gandhi

168. Inter and intra-union rivalry in Trade Unions is reduced by

(A) The provisions of the Industrial Disputes Act 1947

(B) By voluntary tripartite code of inter-union rivalry – 1957

(C)By bipartite mutual agreement at the industry level

(D) Above all

169. 'Employment Injury' means personal injury to an employee caused by accident or occupational disease arising out of and in the course of employment being an insurable employment if the accident occurs or occupational disease is contracted only within territorial limits of India and not outside India. This statement is:

(A) correct.

(B) incorrect.

(C) true only in case of occupational injury.

(D) true only in case of accident.

170. Sequence the following as per the chronological order :

(i)Formation of ILO (ii) Moore Report

(iii)AITUC (iv) INTUC

(v)First World War

(A) (ii), (v), (i), (iii), (iv)

(B) (v), (iv), (i), (ii), (iii)

(C) (iii), (ii), (iv), (v), (i)

(D) (iv), (iii), (ii), (i), (v)

171. Which of the following is method of Union recognition?

(A)Secret Ballot

(B)Membership Verification

(C)Check-off System

(D)All the above

172. Workers do join Trade Unions : Find out the incorrect reason out of the following :

(A)To attain economic security

(B)To improve bargaining power

(C)To ventilate their grievancies

(D)To satisfy their family needs

173. Match the following :

List – I(Unions)

(a)Craft Union

(b)General Union

(c)Industrial Union

(d)Federation

List – II (Functions)

(i) Associations of workers or different categories

(ii) Based on craft non-managerial personnel

(iii)Either unionization of the same industry or different industry

(iv)Unionization of workers any region or any job occupation

Codes:

	(a)	(b)	(c)	(d)
(A)	(ii)	(iv)	(i)	(iii)
(B)	(ii)	(i)	(iii)	(iv)
(C)	(iv)	(i)	(ii)	(iii)
(D)	(i)	(ii)	(iii)	(iv)

174. Who identified the types of unions as business, predatory, dependent and friendly?

(A)Roberts, B.C. (B)Robert F. Hoxie

(C)Kirkaldy, H.S. (D)Perlman Selig

175. Trade Union ***cannot*** represent legally if it is :

(A)not registered

(B)not recognized

(C)led by political leader

(D)working for multiple industries

176. Match the following :

List – I

(a)Check-off system

(b)Report

(c)Award

(d)Political fund

List – II

(i)Registered trade union

(ii)Arbitration

(iii)Union subscription

(iv)Conciliation

	(a)	(b)	(c)	(d)
(A)	(iv)	(iii)	(iv)	(i)

(B)	(iii)	(iv)	(i)	(ii)
(C)	(iii)	(iv)	(ii)	(i)
(D)	(ii)	(iii)	(iv)	(i)

177. As per the rights of the registered trade unions, account books can be inspected :

(A)Only by the trade union members of the concerned union

(B)Only by the office bearers of the concerned unions

(C)Members and office bearers of the trade union at such time as provided in the rules

(D)Members of any trade union

178. Which of the following codes aims to check the problem of trade union rivalries in India?

(A)Code of discipline in industry

(B)Inter-union code of conduct

(C)Code of efficiency and welfare

(D)None of the above

179. As a result of the New Economic Policy which of the following has been badly affected?

(A)Trade Unions (B) Collective Bargaining

(C)Strikes (D) All the above

180. Where the recruitment happens through the compulsory intervention of trade unions, the system is called

(A) Closed shop (B) Union shop

(C) Open shop (D) None of the above

181. Match the following :

Trade Union	**Political Affiliation**
(a)INTUC	(i) Congress (I)
(b)AITUC	(ii)CPI (M)
(c)CITU	(iii)CPI
(d)BMS	(iv)BJP

Code:

	(a)	(b)	(c)	(d)
(A)	(iv)	(iii)	(ii)	(i)
(B)	(i)	(ii)	(iii)	(iv)
(C)	(i)	(iii)	(ii)	(iv)
(D)	(i)	(iv)	(iii)	(ii)

182. Which of the following are ***not*** significant causal factors for grievances?

(A)Wages, working conditions and supervision

(B)Management policies, practices and maladjustment of employees

(C)Both (A) and (B) above

(D)None of the above

183. The Central Trade Union AITUC is associated with :

(A)Bharatiya Janta Party

(B)Congress Party of India

(C)Communist Party of India (Marxist)

(D)Communist Party of India

184. Match the following :

Trade Union	**Year of Estb.**
(a)INTUC	(i)1920
(b)AITUC	(ii)1970
(c)CITU	(iii)1947
(d)BMS	(iv)1954

Code:

	(a)	(b)	(c)	(d)
(A)	(iv)	(iii)	(ii)	(i)
(B)	(i)	(ii)	(iii)	(iv)
(C)	(iv)	(i)	(iii)	(ii)
(D)	(iii)	(i)	(ii)	(iv)

185. The Central Trade Union CITU is associated with :

(A) Congress Party of India

(B) Communist party of India Marxist

(C) Communist Party of India

(D) Shiv Sena

186. "Hind Mazdoor Sabha" established in which year?

(A) 1940 (B) 1942

(C) 1948 (D) 1952

187. Negotiation of labour contract by Union and Management is referred to as

(A) Industrial Relations

(B) Trade Union

(C) Collective Bargaining

(D) Consumerism

188. Which among the following is odd one?

(A)BMS (B) FICCI

(C)AITUC (D) INTUC

189. Match the following :

List – A

(i) Indian Trade Union Act

(ii)Industrial Dispute Act

(iii)The Workmen's Compensation Act

(iv)The Employees' State Insurance Act

List – B

(a) 1923

(b) 1926

(c) 1948

(d) 1947

Codes:

(i) (ii) (iii) (iv)

(A) (b) (d) (a) (c)

(B) (b) (c) (d) (a)

(C) (b) (d) (c) (a)

(D) (a) (c) (b) (d)

190. Which of the following statements is ***not*** true in explaining the concept and scope of labour welfare?

(A)Labour welfare has no roots in social work.

(B)Long Arm of the job and social invasion of workplace' concepts, explain the mutuality between intramural and extra-mural labour welfare

(C)Labour welfare is a social concept.

(D)Corporate social responsibility is an extended concept of welfare.

191. Who is the champion of the 'Welfare movement' propagated in mid 19th century?

(A)Frederick Winslow Taylor

(B)Andrew Ure

(C)Sheebhom Rownlvee

(D)Robert Owners

192. Welfare is considered as

(A)Total Concept (B) Social Concept

(C) Relative Concept (D) All the above

193. Which of the following experiments is associated with the welfare movement?

(A)Hawthorne Experiment

(B)New Lanark Experiment

(C)Ahmadabad Experiment

(D)None of the above

194. The seven approaches to philosophy or theory of labour welfare were first identified by

(A)K.N. Vaid (B) M.V. Moorthy

(C)A.M. Sharma (D) I.D. Punekar

195. Who considered 'want', 'ignorance', 'squalor', 'idleness' and 'disease' as five giants on the road to social security ?

(A)V.V. Giri (B) M.V. Moorthy

(C)Lord Beveridge (D)Pal Chu

196. The success of welfare work depends on six basic principles was advocated by

(A)S.D. Punekar (B) D. Paul Choudhury

(C)A. M. Sharma (D) M.V. Moorthy

197. The father of the Employees State Insurance Scheme in India is :

(A)B.P. Wadia (B)B.P. Adarkar

(C)V.V. Giri (D)N.M. Lokhande

198. Robert Owen, the founder of 'Welfare Movement' conducted which of the following experiments?

(A)New Lanark Experiment

(B)Hawthorne Experiment

(C)Experiment on Illumination

(D)None of the above

199. Trusteeship theory of labour welfare was propounded by

(A)G. L. Nanda (B) Mahatma Gandhi

(C)Indira Gandhi (D) None of the above

200. Minimum conditions of welfare is explained by

(A) Dr. Aykroid's formula

(B) Subsistence Theory

(C) Both (A) and (B)

(D) None of the above

201. Which of the following is ***not*** a principle of Labour Welfare?

(A) The Principle of Uniformity

(B)The Principle of Co-ordination and Integration

(C) The principle of Association

(D) The Principle of Timeliness

202. Match the following :

List – I(Theme)

(a)The labour welfare philosophy is meant for guarding the interests of labour against the exploitation of employers.

(b)The labour welfare philosophy exposes the cause of empathic considerations by the employer of employee well being

(c) The employer has to set out a portion of the profits for the benefit of the employees

(d)Labour Welfare is provided for pacifying the agitating working class

List – II(Theory)

(i) Trusteeship Theory

(ii) Placating Theory

(iii) Policing Theory

(iv) Philanthropic Theory

Codes:

	(a)	(b)	(c)	(d)
(A)	(ii)	(iv)	(iii)	(i)
(B)	(iii)	(iv)	(i)	(ii)
(C)	(iii)	(i)	(ii)	(iv)
(D)	(iv)	(ii)	(iii)	(i)

203. Which of the following are ***not*** the theories of Labour Welfare?

(A)Policing Theory and Placating Theory

(B)Religious Theory and Trusteeship Theory

(C)Functional Theory and Public Relations Theory

(D)Subsistence Theory and Residual Claimant Theory

204. "Welfare work is a means of securing, preserving and increasing the efficiency of labour" is the theme of

(A)Paternalistic Theory(B)Religious Theory

(C)Functional Theory (D)Placating Theory

205. The central theme of paternalistic theory of labour welfare is :

(A)Welfare enhances workers' efficiency

(B)Employees are treated as the guardians of the industrial property

(C)Workers are treated as members of the industrial family

(D)Welfare is a kind of investment

206. Who is called as the father of Labour Welfare Movement?

(A)Frederick Herzberg (B)Robert Owen

(C)F.W. Taylor (D)Charles Babbage

207. The welfare is a state of living of an individual or a group in desirable relation to the total environment , animate and inanimate , according to :

(A)K. N. Vaid (B)A. M. Sharma

(C)M. V. Moorthy (D)S.D. Punekar

208. 'Trusteeship theory' of labour welfare was proposed by :

(A)M. K. Gandhi (B) V. V. Giri

(C)BalGangadharTilak (D) Jawaharlal Nehru

209. The concept of the stewardship of one's possessions to increase wealth, using one's talent and displaying the surplus in public causes was emphasized by :

(A) Conflict Theory of Karl Marx

(B)Trusteeship Theory of M.K.Gandhi

(C)Rational Theory of Robert Hoxie

(D)Behavioural Theory of Max Weber

210. Welfare programmes undertaken outside the organisation are called :

(A)Statutory welfare programme

(B)Intra mural welfare programmes

(C)Extra mural welfare programmes

(D)Non statutory welfare programmes

211. Match the following

List-I

(a) Policing theory

(b)Religious theory

(c)Functional theory

(d) Placating theory

List-II

(i) Labour welfare work is taken up in a spirit of atonement

(ii)Passing the laws and strictly implementing them to ascertain that welfare measures are provided

(iii)Welfare work is a means of securing,preserving and increasing efficiency means of securing their cooperation

(iv)Workers are becoming conscious of their rights and welfare work is the best means of securing their cooperation

	(a)	(b)	(c)	(d)
(A)	(ii)	(i)	(iv)	(iii)
(B)	(ii)	(i)	(iii)	(iv)
(C)	(i)	(iii)	(iv)	(ii)
(D)	(iii)	(iv)	(ii)	(i)

212. Which of the following is ***not*** a principle of labour welfare?

(A)Policing Theory of Labour Welfare

(B)Religious Theory of Labour Welfare

(C)The Philanthropic Theory of Labour Welfare

(D)Productivity Theory of Labour Welfare

213. Sequence the following developments by their period of occurrence from earliest to the latest :

(i)The Labour Investigation Committee

(ii)The Whitley Commission

(iii)The Enactment of Factories Act

(iv)The 1st National Commission on Labour

(A)	(ii)	(i)	(iii)	(iv)
(B)	(ii)	(iii)	(iv)	(i)
(C)	(i)	(ii)	(iv)	(iii)
(D)	(iv)	(ii)	(iii)	(i)

214. Which of the following statements relating to Welfare Officer is not true

(A)The provision of Welfare Officer is given in both the Factories Act, 1948 and the Mines Act, 1952.

(B)Welfare Officer's duties and responsibilities are defined and prescribed in the legislation.

(C)Welfare Officer's appointment is tagged to the provision of minimum workforce employed in an organisation

(D)The Welfare Officer's role was designed as a 'Third force'.

215. Match the following List-I with list-II:

List-I

(a)Royal Commission on

(b)Bombay Textile Labour

(c)Second Labour

(d)Labour Investigation

(e)Second National

List-II

(i) 1937 Labour

(ii) 1946 Enquiry committee

(iii) 1929 Ministers' Conference

(iv) 2002 Committee

(v) 1941 Commission on Labour

	(a)	(b)	(c)	(d)	(e)
(A)	(ii)	(i)	(iii)	(iv)	(v)
(B)	(iii)	(ii)	(i)	(v)	(iv)
(C)	(iii)	(v)	(iv)	(i)	(ii)
(D)	(iii)	(i)	(v)	(ii)	(iv)

216. Assertion (A): Intra-mural and extra-mural welfare are mutually complimentary.

Reason (R): The work-life balances need to be ensured in order to get the best output from an employee.

(A)Assertion is wrong but Reason is logical.

(B)Both Assertion and Reason are wrong.

(C)Assertion and Reason are right.

(D)The Assertion is right but Reason is wrong.

217. Which of the following is ***not*** included under intra-mural labour welfare facilities :

(A)Latrines and Urinals

(B)Washing Facilities

(C)Creches

(D)Housing Facilities

218. Classification of labour welfare facilities under (a) Extra-mural and (b) Intra-mural was done by :

(A)I.L.O.

(B)The Study Group constituted by the Govt. of India in 1959

(C)Indian Labour Conference

(D)National Commission on Labour, 1969

219. Which of the following ***cannot*** be regarded as an organisation in the field of Labour Welfare :

(A)Central Board of Workers' Education

(B)Consumer Courts

(C)Workmen's compensation commissioner

(D)Employees' State Insurance Corporation

220. Choose the appropriate answer from the option given below : In India, Labour Welfare work of trade unions is ______

(A)Not developed at all

(B)Developed to some extent

(C)Fully developed

(D)Highly developed

221. Which of the following ***cannot*** be said to be an extra-mural welfare facility?

(A)Hospital (B) Transport facility

(C)Sports (D) Canteens and First Aid Boxes

222. Which of the following is ***not*** an agency of providing labour welfare?

(A) State (B) Employer

(C) Trade Unions (D) Customers

223. Which of the following is ***not*** a statutory welfare facility under the Factories Act, 1948?

(A) Canteen (B) Sports facility

(C) Creche (D) First-Aid Appliances

224. Under which part of the Indian Constitution necessity of more labour welfare is emphasized :

(A) Fundamental Rights

(B) Directive Principles of State Policy

(C) Both under Fundamental Rights and Directive Principles of State Policy

(D) None of the above

225. Match the following :

Contributors

(a) Robert Owen

(b) Mahatma Gandhi

(c) Beveridge

(d) Adarkar

Contribution

(i) Social Security

(ii) Employee State Insurance

(iii) Welfare Movement

(iv) Trusteeship Theory

Code:

	(a)	(b)	(c)	(d)
(A)	(iii)	(i)	(ii)	(iv)
(B)	(iii)	(iv)	(i)	(ii)
(C)	(ii)	(iii)	(i)	(iv)
(D)	(iii)	(ii)	(iv)	(i)

226. Sequence the following from the earliest to the latest :

(i) Gajendragadkar Commission

(ii) First Factory Commission

(iii) Whitely Commission

(iv) Rege Committee

Codes:

(A)	(ii)	(iii)	(iv)	(i)
(B)	(iii)	(ii)	(i)	(iv)
(C)	(ii)	(iv)	(iii)	(i)
(D)	(iii)	(i)	(ii)	(iv)

227. Match the following :

Commission/Committee

(a) First Factory Commission

(b) Royal Commission on Labour

(c) Labour Investigation Committee

(d) First National Labour Commission

Year

(i) 1946

(ii) 1969

(iii) 1931

(iv) 1875

	(a)	(b)	(c)	(d)
(A)	(i)	(iii)	(iv)	(ii)
(B)	(iv)	(ii)	(iii)	(i)
(C)	(iv)	(iii)	(i)	(ii)
(D)	(ii)	(i)	(iii)	(iv)

228. Sequence the following offices from latest to earliest in their emergence.

(a) Labour Officer

(b) Safety Officer

(c) Personnel Officer

(d) Welfare Officer

(A) (b) (c) (d) (a)

(B) (a) (c) (d) (b)

(C) (c) (b) (a) (d)

(D) (a) (d) (c) (b)

229. Which of the following is a non-statutory welfare facility?

(A)Welfare Officer (B)Creche

(C)Transport facility (D) Canteen

230. Who opined that the "Labour Welfare officer should ***not*** merely remain looking after the interests of the management , but also consider they are custodians of the rights and privileges of the workers ?

(A)G. L. Nanda (B)V. V. Giri

(C)Morarji Desai (D)M. K. Gandhi

231. Match the following :

Welfare funds

(a)Coal Mines Welfare Fund Act

(b)The Mica Mines Welfare Fund Act

(c)The Iron Ore Mines Labour Welfare Fund Act

(d)The Lime Stone And Dolomite Mines Labour Welfare Fund Act

Years

(i) 1973

(ii) 1961

(iii) 1946

(iv) 1947

	(a)	(b)	(c)	(d)
(A)	(ii)	(iii)	(i)	(iv)
(B)	(iv)	(ii)	(iii)	(i)
(C)	(ii)	(iv)	(i)	(iii)
(D)	(iv)	(iii)	(ii)	(i)

232. Which of the following recommended to the Government of India to consider making social security as a fundamental human right ?

(A)The Labour Investigation Committee

(B)The Royal Commission on Labour

(C)The First National Commission on Labour

(D)The second National Commission on Labour

233. Which of the following ***cannot*** be regarded as a statutory welfare facility for factory workers?

(A)Canteen (B) Housing

(C)Shelter and Rest rooms (D) First Aid Box

234. Who among the following is ***not*** included in labour force?

(A)Persons below 15 years of age

(B)Housewives and pensioners

(C)Mentally Disabled

(D)All the Above

235. The scope of state regulation of wages in the present scenario in India particularly , in the organized sector is :

(A)Increasing (B) Decreasing

(C)Irrelevant (D) None of the above

236. The ongoing industrialization in the country is contributing to which type of unemployment?

(A)Cyclical Unemployment

(B)Frictional Unemployment

(C)Seasonal Unemployment

(D)Technological Unemployment

237. The programmes generally providing benefits for meeting the minimum needs of persons of small means are called

(A)Social Insurance (B) Social Assistance

(C)Mutual Aid (D) None of the above

238. Which of the following ***cannot*** be regarded as extra mural labour welfare facility?

(A)Canteen (B) Housing

(C)Hospital (D) Playground

239. Who among the following is ***not*** regarded as welfare agency for factory workers?

(A)Employer

(B) Trade Unions

(C)N.G.Os

(D) State and Central Government

240. There shall be delegation of authority in the welfare fields, either by election to committees, or by proper nomination, according to

(A)Principle of Timeliness

(B)Principle of Accountability

(C)Principle of Evaluation and Assessment

(D)Principle of Responsibility

241. The need for imparting necessary education to workers in India had been emphasized first by :

(A)The Royal Commission on Labour

(B)The Indian Industrial Commission

(C)The Labour Investigation Committee

(D)None of the above

242. Which of the following is an agency for providing labour welfare facilities in Factories?

(A)Management (B) Trade Union

(C)Government (D) NGO

243. Which of the following is ***not*** included under intra-mural labour welfare facilities?

(A)Canteen (B) Crèche

(C)Hospitals (D)Shelter, Rest rooms

244. One first aid box must be provided for every

(A) 150 workers (B) 200 workers

(C) 250 workers (D) 300 workers

245. The author of the book 'Principles of Labour Welfare' is :

(A)K. N. Vaid (B)M. V. Murthy

(C)S. C. Pant (D)T. N. Bhagoliwal

246. Which of the following is ***not*** a labour welfare agency?

(A) Bharat Sewak Samaj

(B) Harijan Sewak Sangh

(C) Central Social Welfare Board

(D) Standing Labour Committee

247. Which of the following does ***not*** affect the supply of labour?

(A) Population(B) Labour force participation

(C) Strike (D) Mobility of labour

248. "A desirable state of existence comprehending physical, mental, moral and emotional health or well being" is the theme of which concept of Labour Welfare?

(A) Social Concept (B) Total Concept

(C) Relative Concept (D) Positive Concept

249. **Assertion (A):** Labour Welfare is relative to time and space.

Reason (R): It shall be universal and perpetual.

(A) Assertion and Reason are right.

(B)Assertion is wrong and Reason is right.

(C)Both Assertion and Reason are wrong.

(D)Assertion is right but its explanation given in Reason is wrong.

250. "Labour is ***not*** a commodity" – is the assertion made by

(A)the Declaration of Philadelphia adopted by 26th session of ILO

(B)the Magna Carta

(C)the Constitution of India

(D)the International Labour Conference

251. Match the following :

Concept

(a) Industrial Democracy

(b) Industrial Citizenship

(c) Class Conflict

(d) Welfare Movement

Propagators

(i) Karl Marx

(ii)Robert Owen

(iii) Peter F. Drucker

(iv) Sydney & Beatrize Webbs

Codes:

	(a)	(b)	(c)	(d)
(A)	(iii)	(i)	(ii)	(iv)
(B)	(iv)	(iii)	(i)	(ii)
(C)	(ii)	(i)	(iv)	(iii)
(D)	(ii)	(iv)	(i)	(iii)

252. **Assertion (A):** Industrial Labour in India has been migratory.

Reason (R): Driving force in migration comes almost entirely from one end of the channel that is the village end.

(A) Both (A) and (R) are wrong.

(B) (A) is wrong and (R) is right.

(C) (A) is right and (R) also is right.

(D) (A) is right and (R) is wrong.

253. Which of the following is ***not*** a method of social security?

(A)Social Assistance (B)Social Action

(C)Social Insurance (D)Mutual Assistance

254. Who has given the concept of 'Core competence'?

(A)Sumantra Ghosal & C.A. Bartlett

(B)T. Deal and A. Kennedy

(C)C.K. Prahalad and G. Hamel

(D)C.A. Forehand and B. Von Gilnev

255. The Central Social Welfare Board was established by :

(A) Parliamentary enactment

(B) Resolution of Cabinet

(C)Registration under company Act, 1956

(D) The order of the President

256. The interaction between Government and NGOs in India mostly relates to

(i)Policies and legislation related to disadvantaged sections.

(ii) Economic policies

(iii)Operational collaboration forprogrammes with or without Government funding

(iv)Peaceful protest movement of people in which NGOs are involved.

Select the correct answer from the codes given below:

Codes:

(A) (i) and (ii) (B) (i), (ii) and (iv)

(C) (i), (iii) and (iv) (D) (iii) and (iv)

257. The term 'Social Justice' is originally based on the teachings of

(A) St. Thomas Aquinas (B) Karl Marx

(C) John Rawls (D) B.R. Ambedkar

258. "Creating jobs, guaranteeing rights at work, extending social protection and promoting social dialogue" are contents of which of the following programmes of ILO ?

(A)Human Rights

(B)Decent Work

(C)International Programme on the Elimination of Child Labour

(D)INDUS Child Labour Project

259. ILO was formed in the year

(A) 1919 (B) 1947

(C) 1951 (D) 1926

260. The constitution of India upholds the principle 'Freedom of Association' as a fundamental right enunciated by I. L. O. convention in:

(A)Article 20(C) (B) Article 19(C)

(C)Article 24(C) (D) Article 18(C)

261. Which ILO convention is concerned with equal remuneration for equal work'?

(A)Convention No. 98

(B)Convention No. 99

(C)Convention No. 100

(D)Convention No. 101

262. The international labour code consists of :

(A)The conventions and Recommendations of I. L. O

(B)The proposals submitted by the member countries

(C)The opinions of the U. N. O

(D)All the above

263. The number of bipartite committees as provided under the factories Act, 1948 :

(A) 1 (B) 2

(C) 3 (D) 4

264. Which of the following statements relating to I.L.O. is ***not*** true ?

(A)I.L.O. is a tripartite body.

(B)I.L.O. has a standing labour committee.

(C)I.L.O. Believes not only in people at work but also their development.

(D)I.L.O. Recommendations are compulsorily binding in nature.

265. The primary function of I.L.O. is to formulate the international labour standards in the shape of

(A)Conventions only

(B)Recommendations only

(C)Both (A) and (B)

(D) None of the above

266. Which of the following statements about I.L.O. is ***not*** true?

(A)I.L.O is a tripartite body.

(B)I.L.O was established in 1919.

(C)I.L.O passes only recommendations.

(D)I.L.O conventions are mandatory for those countries which ratify them.

267. India ratified I.L.O. Convention No. 144 on tripartite consultation among government, employer's and worker's representatives in :

(A)1968 (B)1958

(C)1978 (D)1988

268. The code of discipline was ratified by the Indian Labour Conference to ensure discipline in industry. Identify the year of ratification out of the following :

(A) 1957 (B) 1958

(C) 1942 (D) 1962

269. In which year the formation of the National Renewal Fund to protect the interest of the workers was announced :

(A) 1956 (B) 1991

(C) 1969 (D)1992

270. Arrange the following in the order they appeared. Use the codes given below :

(A)First Labour Legislation

(B)I. L. O.

(C)Indian Constitution

(D)E. S. I. Corporation

(A) (iv) (ii) (iii) (i)

(B) (i) (ii) (iii) (iv)

(C) (ii) (i) (iv) (iii)

(D) (i) (ii) (iv) (iii)

271. Ravindra Verma was the Chairman of

(A)Royal Commission on Labour

(B)First National Commission on Labour

(C)Second National Commission on Labour

(D)Labour Investigation Committee

272. The Tripartite Declaration of Principles concerning MNEs and social policy enunciated by ILO was in

(A) 1976 (B) 1977

(C) 1978 (D) 1979

273. The Chairman of the Second National Commission on Labour was

(A) Gajendra Gadkar (B) Ravindra Verma

(C) George Fernandes (D) Vallabh Bhai Patel

274. Find out the origin of the statement in a socialist democracy labour is a partner in the common task of development, should participate in it with enthusiasm.

(A)Constitution of India

(B)Directive principles of State Policy

(C)Industrial Policy Resolution 1956

(D)Royal Commission on Labour

275. The goal of I LO is

(A) creation of jobs for men and women

(B)not just creation of jobs but the creation of jobs of acceptable quality

(C)not overcoming under employment

(D)not to provide freedom of choice in employment

276. The basic postulates on which the ILO standards lie are

(A) Labour is not a commodity

(B) Freedom of expression and of association are essential to sustained progress

(C) Poverty anywhere constitutes danger to prosperity everywhere

(D) All the above

277. The establishment of Indian Labour Conference and Standing Labour Committee in India was on the pattern of

(A) ILO

(B) Report of Royal Commission on Labour

(C) Both (A) and (B)

(D) None of the above

278. Plenary labour conference was initial name of which of the following organization?

(A)ILO

(B)Standing labour committee

(C)Indian labour conference

(D)International labour conference

279. Which of the following has done considerable work in the field of labour welfare?

(A)CARE (B) WHO

(C) ILO (D) UNICEF

280. What is the full form of RMMS?

(A)Retired Mill Mazdoor Seva

(B)Rashtriya Mill Mazdoor Seva

(C)Rashtriya Mill Mazdoor Sangh

(D)Retired Mill Mazdoor Sangh

281. Employee stock option plan (ESOP)aims at

(A)Only as an incentive to employee

(B)Only for employee retention

(C)Both (A) and (B)

(D)None of the above

282. ILO stands for:

(A)International Labour Office

(B)International Labour Order

(C)International Labour Organization

(D)International Labour Audit

283. The leading social insurance program is:

(A) Unemployment insurance

(B) Social security for retirees

(C)Medicare

(D)Public assistance programs such as food stamps.

284. Most social welfare programs are:

(A) Uniform throughout the states.

(B) Widely supported by Americans.

(C)Run jointly by federal and state governments.

(D)Managed entirely by the federal government.

285. Which of the following is ***not*** an element of physical evidence?

(A) Employee dress (B) Employee Training

(C) Equipment (D) Facility design

286. Principle of Natural Justice in Domestic Enquiry ensures:

(A)Justice in time

(B)Justice through Advocate

(C)Opportunity given to the delique employee being heard

(D)Payment of subsistence allowance

287. Collective Bargaining is handled between:

(A)Employees and Employees

(B) Employees and Trade union

(C) Trade union and Advocate

(D) Employer and Employees

288. Which of the following describes the process by which individuals come to agreement?

(A)Negotiation (B)Avoidance

(C)Accomodation (D)Fighting actively

289. _________absolves the employer's liability under the Maternity Benefit Act and Workmens Compensation Act.

(A)Employees Provident Fund Act, 1952

(B)Industrial Employment (Standing Order)Act,1946

(C)Employee State Insurance Act, 1948

(D)Industrial Dispute Act, 1947

290. Globalization is ruthless, rootless, jobless, fruitless was stated by :

(A)U. N. O (B)U. N. D. P

(C)I. L. O (D)W. H. O

---000---

UNIT-IV

INDUSTRIAL RELATION & SOCIAL SECURITY

1. (D) All the above

Explanation: Industrial relations:

- Employer-employee relationships that are covered specifically under collective bargaining and industrial relation laws.
- In broader sense industrial relations means all such relationships that a business enterprise maintains with various sections of society including employee, state (Government), customers and public in industries contact.
- It refers to all types of relationships between employer and employee, trade union and management, workers and union and between employee and employee.
- The parties involved in industrial relations i.e. employees and the employers have a common purpose of production.
- They willingly bind themselves to work together. Economic interest brings employees for wages and employers hire their services as a factor of production.
- It highlights interpersonal relations but ignores conflicts of interest.

2. (C) John T. Dunlop
3. (D)All the above
4. (C)Nehru Approach

Explanation: Approaches to industrial Relations

- Psychological approach
- Sociological approach
- Human relations approach
- Theoretical perspectives
    - Unitary Perspective
    - Pluralistic-Perspective
- Marxist Perspective
- The System Approach: The system approach was developed by J. P. Dunlop of Harvard University in 1958.

5. (A)John T. Dunlop
6. (C)Dunlop
7. (D)All the above
8. (D)Physiological approach
9. (B) G.L. Nanda
10. (A)Kochan, T.A., et. al
11. (A)Bipartism
12. (C)Kochan, T.A., et.al
13. (C)Kochan, T.A. et.al
14. (D)Industrial Relations system creates an environment of distrust and conflict.

Explanation: Characteristics of Industrial Relations:

- The important actors in industrial relations are the employers, the employees and their unions, and the government.
- It involves the deliberate selection of strategies and the framing of rules and procedures by the management that would improve the industrial relations of an organization.
- Industrial relations emphasize the development and execution of activities that accomplish the joint objectives of both the employers and the unions, resulting in improved industrial relations.
- The protection of the interests and the fulfilment of the needs of both the employers and the employees are the fundamental characteristics of industrial relations.

15. (C)Community and cultural associations
16. (D) Canteen Committee
17. (A)Keep the employees informed about decision which affect their interests
18. (D)Employer and Customer relations.
19. (D)Communities and their associations
20. (D)Collective relationship between management and trade unions
21. (C)Employer - Customer Relations

22.(C)John T. Dunlop

23.(C)Both Static and Dynamic

24.(C)John T. Dunlop

Explanation: Dunlop's Contribution to Industrial Relations

- According to Dunlop industrial relations system consists of three agents – management organizations, workers and formal/informal ways they are organized and government agencies.
- He proposed that three parties—employers, labor unions, and government-- are the key actors in a modern industrial relations system.
- He also argued that none of these institutions could act in an autonomous or independent fashion. Instead they were shaped, at least to some extent, by their market, technological and political contexts.
- Dunlop's model identifies three key factors to be considered in conducting an analysis of the management-labor relationship: Environmental or external economic, technological, political, legal and social forces that impact employment relationships.
- Characteristics and interaction of the key actors in the employment relationship: labor, management, and government. Rules that are derived from these interactions that govern the employment relationship.
- The Dunlop's model gives great significance to external or environmental forces. In other words, management, labor, and the government possess a shared ideology that defines their roles within the relationship and provides stability to the system.

25. (A)(iv) (iii) (ii) (i)

26. (C)Durkheim, E.

27. (A)Before 1933

28. (A)Karl Marx

29. (B)1920

Explanation:

- The International Organisation of Employers was created in 1920, and it is the only international organisation that represents the interests of business in labour and social policy.
- It has 150 national employer organizations members in 143 countries. CEA is an active member of the IOE since 1994.
- The IOE is involved in the activities of the International Labour Organization (ILO), acting as Secretariat to the Employers' group, during the International Labour Conference, as well as during the Governing Body Sessions.
- The IOE supports strengthening national business organisations in the world, with special emphasis during last years to the employers' organisations in the area of South-East Europe.
- The Organisation is guiding corporate members in matters of international labour standards, business and human rights, CSR, occupational health and safety, and international industrial relations.
- The International Organisation of Employers represents "the largest network of the private sector in the world" for sharing information and experiences, representing business in international forums, including the G20 intergovernmental process, on labour and social policy.

30.(B)Second National Commission on Labour

31.(A)John T. Dunlop

32.(C)(i), (ii), (iv), (iii)

33. (C) (ii)(i)(iv)(iii)

34.(A) (ii) (iv) (iii) (i)

35.(B) (b), (a), (c), (d), (e), (f), (g)

36.(A) 1923

Explanation:

- The first May Day celebration in India was organised in Madras by the Labour Kisan Party of Hindustan on 1 May 1923.
- This was also the first time the red flag was used in India.The party leader Singaravelu

Chettiar made arrangements to celebrate May Day in two places in 1923.

37.(B)Directive Principles of State Policy

38.(D)Unitarists

39.(A) (i) (ii) (iii) (iv)

40.(C) No shift from contract of service to contract of service

41. (C) (iii) (i) (iv) (ii)

42. (A)Insubordination

Explanation:

- Insubordination is defined as an employee's willful disregard for a manager's direct orders. Inappropriate language can also constitute insubordination in certain cases.
- In today's white-collar world, despite several generations of performance and learning development tools formally embedded in work cultures, insubordination remains a managerial challenge.

43.(A)Conciliation

Explanation:

- Adjudication is the legal process by which an arbiter or judge reviews evidence and argumentation including legal reasoning set forth by opposing parties or litigants to come to a decision which determines rights and obligations between the parties involved.
- Three types of disputes are resolved through adjudication:
    - Disputes between private parties, such as individuals or corporations.
    - Disputes between private parties and public officials.
    - Disputes between public officials or public bodies.

44.(A)Dismissed

45.(C)Six weeks

46.(D) (ii) and (iv)

Explanation: Strikes

- A strike is a very powerful weapon used by trade unions and other labor associations to get their demands accepted.
- It generally involves quitting of work by a group of workers for the purpose of bringing the pressure on their employer so that their demands get accepted.
- When workers collectively cease to work in a particular industry, they are said to be on strike.
- According to Industrial Disputes Act 1947, a strike is "a cessation of work by a body of persons employed in an industry acting in combination; or a concerted refusal of any number of persons who are or have been so employed to continue to work or to accept employment; or a refusal under a common understanding of any number of such persons to continue to work or to accept employment".

Picketing:

- Picketing involves walking up and down outside the work place indicating a strike is in process.
- When workers are dissuaded from work by stationing certain men at the factory gates, such a step is known as picketing.
- Pickets are workers who are on strike that stand at the entrance to their workplace.
- It is basically a method of drawing public attention towards the fact that there is a dispute between the management and employees.

Gherao:

- Gherao in Hindi means to surround.
- It denotes a collective action initiated by a group of workers under which members of the management are prohibited from leaving the industrial establishment premises by workers who block the exit gates by forming human barricades.
- The workers may gherao the members of the management by blocking their exits and forcing them to stay inside their cabins.
- The main object of gherao is to inflict physical and mental torture to the person

being gheraoed and hence this weapon disturbs the industrial peace to a great extent.

47. (D)Reference to Civil Court

48. (C)The temporary closing of a place of employment

Explanation: Lockouts:

- A lockout is a work stoppage in which an employer prevents employees from working. It is declared by employers to put pressure on their workers.
- This is different from a strike, in which employees refuse to work.
- Thus, a lockout is employers' weapon while a strike is raised on part of employees.

49.(C) 1957

50.(B) An Arbitrator

51.(A)Working conditions in Indian Industry

Explanation:

- The Rege Committee, reporting in 1946, concluded that the majority of factory workers had little stake in agriculture.
- They were pushed rather than pulled to the cities. Their occasional visits to the village homes were more for rest than for attending to cultivation.
- The Rege Committee differed with the Whiteley Commission on the need for an industrial worker to retain a nexus with his village. Since most of the industrial workers were landless, there was no necessity of going back to the village frequently.
- There is nothing to suggest that conditions of employment, wages and housing are any better in the village than in the town. It seems desirable that the conditions of living in industrial areas should be improved and the causes which compel the workers to go back to the villages should be removed.
- The Commission pointed out the evil associated with this method of recruitment and recommended direct recruitment instead, either by the manager of the unit or by an officer specially appointed by him for the purpose.
- The Rege Committee agreed with the Royal Commission on the evils of the system and urged that steps should be taken to regularise the system of recruitment for industries or put some method into it.

52.(D)Define the problem

53.(B) (iii) (iv) (i) (ii)

54.(C) Ex-parte enquiry

55.(C) Industrial Tribunal

56.(A)Indian Labour Conference and Standing Labour Committee

57.(B) Conciliation

Explanation:

Conciliation

- Conciliation is an alternative out-of-court dispute resolution instrument.
- Like mediation, conciliation is a voluntary, flexible, confidential, and interest based process. The parties seek to reach an amicable dispute settlement with the assistance of the conciliator, who acts as a neutral third party.
- The main difference between conciliation and mediation proceedings is that, at some point during the conciliation, the conciliator will be asked by the parties to provide them with a non-binding settlement proposal. A mediator, by contrast, will in most cases and as a matter of principle, refrain from making such a proposal.

Benefits of Conciliation

- Conciliation ensures party autonomy.
- The parties can choose the timing, language, place, structure and content of the conciliation proceedings.
- Conciliation ensures the expertise of the decision maker.
- The parties are free to select their conciliator. A conciliator does not have to have a specific professional background.
- The parties may base their selection on criteria such as; experience, professional and

/ or personal expertise, availability, language and cultural skills.

- A conciliator should be impartial and independent.
- Conciliation is time and cost efficient.
- Due to the informal and flexible nature of conciliation proceedings, they can be conducted in a time and cost-efficient manner.
- Conciliation ensures confidentiality.
- The parties usually agree on confidentiality.
- Thus, disputes can be settled discretely and business secrets will remain confidential.

58.(B) (iv) (iii) (ii) (i)

59.(C)Collective Bargaining

Explanation: Collective Bargaining:

- The process of negotiating the terms of employment between an employer and a group of workers.
- The terms of employment are likely to include items such as conditions of employment, working conditions and other workplace rules, base pay, overtime pay, work hours, shift length, work holidays, sick leave, vacation time, retirement benefits and health care benefits.

60.(A)Board of Conciliation

Explanation:

Boards of Conciliation (The Industrial Disputes Act, 1947- Section 5)

(1)The appropriate Government may as occasion arises by notification in the Official Gazette constitute a Board of Conciliation for promoting the settlement of an industrial dispute.

(2)A Board shall consist of a chairman and two or four other members, as the appropriate Government thinks fit.

(3)The chairman shall be an independent person and the other members shall be persons appointed in equal numbers to represent the parties to the dispute and any person appointed to represent a party shall be appointed on the recommendation of that party: Provided that, if any party fails to make a recommendation as aforesaid within the prescribed time, the appropriate Government shall appoint such persons as it thinks fit to represent that party.

(4)A Board, having the prescribed quorum, may act notwithstanding the absence of the chairman or any of its members or any vacancy in its number: Provided that if the appropriate Government notifies the Board that the services of the chairman or of any other member have ceased to be available, the Board shall not act until a new chairman or member, as the case may be, has been appointed.

61.(C) (iv) (i) (ii) (iii)

62.(D) (iv) (iii) (i) (ii)

63.(A) (iii) (i) (ii) (iv)

64.(B) Court of Enquiry

Explanation: Authorities under Industrial Disputes Act 1947

1. Works Committee:

(1) in the case of any industrial establishment in which one hundred or more workmen are employed or have been employed on any day in the preceding twelve months, the appropriate Government may by general or special order require the employer to constitute in the prescribed manner a Work Committee consisting of representative of employer and workmen engaged in the establishment, so however that the number of representatives of workmen on the Committee shall not be less than the number of representatives of the employer. The representatives of the workmen engaged in the establishment and in consultation with their trade union if any, registered under the Indian Trade Unions Act, 1927 (16 of 1927).

(2) It Shall be the duty of the Works Committee to promote measure, for securing and preserving amenity and good relations between the employer and workmen and, to that end, to comment upon matters of their common interest or concern and, endeavour to compose any material difference of opinion in respect of such matters.

2. Conciliation Officers:

(1)The appropriate Government may, by notification in the Official Gazette, appoint such number of persons as it think fit, to be Conciliation Officers, charged with the duty of mediating in and promoting the settlement of industrial disputes.

(2)A Conciliation Officer may be appointed for a specified area or for specified industries in a specified area or for one or more specified industries and either permanently or for a limited period.

3. Board o Conciliations

(1)The appropriate Government may as occasion arises, by notification in the Official Gazette, constitute a Board of Conciliation for promoting the settlement of any industrial dispute.

(2) A Board shall consist of a Chairman and two or four other members, as the appropriate Government thinks fit.

(3) The Chairman shall be an independent person and the other members shall be persons appointed in equal numbers to represent the parties to the dispute and any person appointed to represent a party shall be appointed on the recommendation of the party :

Provided that if the appropriate Government notifies the Board that the services of the Chairman or of any other member have ceased to be available, the Board shall not act until a new Chairman or member, as the case may be, has been appointed.

4. Court of inquiry

(1) The appropriate Government may as occasion arises by notification in the Official Gazette, constitute a Court of inquiry for inquiring into any matter appearing to be connected with or relevant to an industrial dispute.

(2) A Court may consist of one independent person or of such number of independent persons as the appropriate Government may think fit and where a Court consist of two or more members, one of them shall be appointed as the Chairman.

(3) A Court, having the prescribed quorum, may act, notwithstanding the absence of the chairman or any of its members of any vacancy in its number :

Provided that, if the appropriate Government notifies the Court that the service of the Chairman has ceased to be available, the Court shall not act until a new Chairman has been appointed.

5. Labour Courts

(1) The appropriate Government may, by notification in the Official Gazette, constitute one or more Labour Courts for the adjudication of industrial disputes relating to any matters specified in the Second Schedule and for performing such other functions as the case may be assigned to them under this Act.

(2) A labour Court shall consist of one person only to be appointed by the appropriate Government.

(3) A person shall not be qualified for appointment as the Presiding Officer of a Labour Court, unless -

(a) he is, or has been, a Judge of a High Court : or

(b) he has, for a period of not less than three years, been a District Judge or an Additional District Judge ; or

(c) [omitted by Act 46 of 1982 S. 3]

(d) he has held any judicial office in India for not less than seven years; or

(e) he has been the Presiding Officer of a labour Court constituted under any Provincial Act or State Act for not less than five years.

6. Tribunals

(1) The appropriate Government may, by notification in the Official Gazette, constitute one or more Industrial Tribunals for the adjudication of industrial disputes relating to any matter, whether specified in the Second Schedule or the Third Schedule 1[and for

performing such other functions as may be specified to them under this Act.]

(2) A Tribunal shall consist of one person only to be appointed by the appropriate Government.

(3) A person shall not be less qualified for appointment as the presiding Officer of a Tribunal unless -

(a) he is, or has been, Judge of a High Court ; or

(aa) he has, for a period of not less than three years, been a District Judge or an Additional District Judge; 2[* *].

(b) [omitted by Act 46 of 1982 S. 4].

(4) The appropriate Government may, if it so thinks fit, appoint two persons at assessors, to advise the Tribunal in proceeding before it.

7. National Tribunals

(1)The Central Government may, by notification in the Official Gazette, constitute one or more National Industrial Tribunals for the adjudication of industrial disputes which, in the opinion of the Central Government, involve questions of national importance or are of such a nature that industrial establishments situated in more than one State are likely to be interested in, or affected by such disputes.

(2)A National Tribunal shall consist of one person only to be appointed by the Central Government.

(3)A person shall not be qualified for appointment as the presiding Officer of a National Tribunals unless 3[he is or has been a Judge of a High Court.].

(4)The Central Government may, if it so thinks fit, appoint two persons as assessors to advise the National Tribunals in the proceeding before it.

65.(A) consultation

66.(D) Samuel Gompers

67.(C)It is not a bipartile process.

68.(C)Dale Yoder

69.(D)V.V. Giri

70.(C)Wage Incentives

71.(A)United Kingdom

72. (D) (ii) (i) (iv) (iii)

73. (A)Sidney and Beatrice webb

74. (A)A feeling of dissatisfaction

Explanation: Grievance

- Grievance procedure is a formal communication between an employee and the management designed for the settlement of a grievance. The grievance procedures differ from organization to organization.

Grievance procedure in Indian industry

- The 15th session of Indian Labor Conference held in 1957 emphasized the need of an established grievance procedure for the country which would be acceptable to unions as well as to management.
- In the 16th session of Indian Labor Conference, a model for grievance procedure was drawn up. This model helps in creation of grievance machinery.
- According to it, workers' representatives are to be elected for a department or their union is to nominate them.
- Management has to specify the persons in each department who are to be approached first and the departmental heads who are supposed to be approached in the second step.
- The Model Grievance Procedure specifies the details of all the steps that are to be followed while redressing grievances. These steps are:
- **STEP 1:** In the first step the grievance is to be submitted to departmental representative, who is a representative of management. He has to give his answer within 48 hours.
- **STEP 2:** If the departmental representative fails to provide a solution, the aggrieved employee can take his grievance to head of the department, who has to give his decision within 3 days.
- **STEP 3:** If the aggrieved employee is not satisfied with the decision of departmental head, he can take the grievance to Grievance

Committee. The Grievance Committee makes its recommendations to the manager within 7 days in the form of a report. The final decision of the management on the report of Grievance Committee must be communicated to the aggrieved employee within three days of the receipt of report. An appeal for revision of final decision can be made by the worker if he is not satisfied with it. The management must communicate its decision to the worker within 7 days.

- **STEP 4:** If the grievance still remains unsettled, the case may be referred to voluntary arbitration.

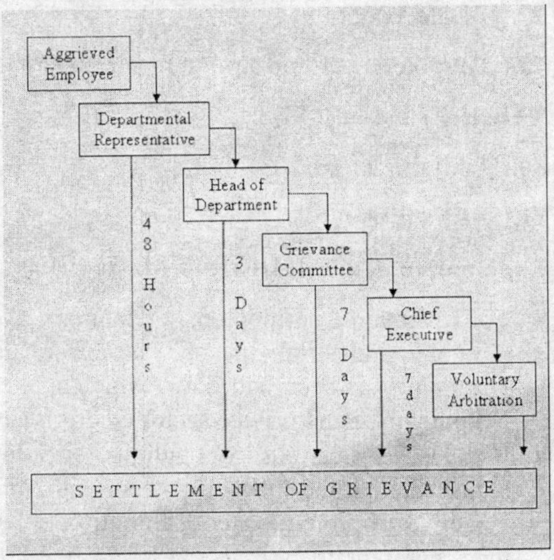

75.(B)Fabricated

Explanation: Greivance

- Dissatisfaction is any state or feeling of discontent.
- Dissatisfaction orally made known by one employee to another is a complaint.
- A complaint becomes a grievance when brought to the notice of the management.
- Grievances generally give rise to unhappiness, frustration, indifference, discontent, poor morale, and poor efficiency that is change in attitude, perception and behavior.
- According to Fillipo, "The term would include any discontent and dissatisfaction that affects organizational performance. It can either stated or unvoiced, written or oral, legitimate or ridiculous.

(a) A complaint is a discontent that has not assumed importance.

(b) A complaint becomes grievance when the employee feels that injustice has been committed.

Characteristics of grievances

(i) It may be unvoiced or expressly stated.

(ii) It may be written or oral

(iii) It may be valid, legitimate or untrue or false.

(iv) It may relate to the organizational work.

(v) An employee may feel an injustice has been done.

(vi) It may affect the performance or work.

Types of grievances

(a) Visible grievances

(b) Hidden grievances

- An employee may feel that there has been an infringement of his rights.
- Grievances exist in the minds of individuals.
- Grievances may be concerning employment, working conditions, change of service conditions, biased approach, non-application of principle of natural justice, work loads and work norms.

Need for grievance procedure

(i) Identification and analysis of grievances, nature nod causes.

(ii) Helps at formulating and implementing the policies and programmes.

(iii)It is problem solving, dispute-settling mechanism.

(iv)Strengthen good industrial relationship.

(v)It detects the flaws in working conditions and helps to take corrective measures.

(vi)Build good morale, maintains code of discipline.

(vii)Brings uniformity in handling grievances.

(viii)It develops faith of employees.

(ix) Reduces personality conflicts.

(x) It acts as a pressure valve.

(xi)Provides judicial protection to the employees.

(xii) Provides avenues to present the problems.

Grievance redressal system

- Enables the parties to resolve differences in peaceful, orderly and expeditious manner.
- Enables the parties to investigate and discuss the problem

(i) Open-door policy

(ii) Step ladder type

(iii) Grievance handling committee

Basic element of grievance procedure

1. Existence of sound channel.

2. The procedure should be simple, definite and prompt.

3. It should be clearly defined.

4. Helpful attitude of management.

5. Fact-oriented system.

6. Respect for decisions.

7. Adequate publicity.

8. Periodic Review.

Steps in handling grievances

1. Receive and define the nature of dissatisfaction.

(a) Manner and attitude when complaint is received

(b) Assessment must be made that the complaint is presented fairly.

(c) Statement and issues must not be pre-judged.

(d) Proper time and attention is given.

2. Get the facts

(a) Facts be separated from impressions and opinions.

(b) Consult the policies.

(c) Consult the records.

3. Analyze and decide.

4. Apply the answer.

5. Follow-up

76.(C) Factual Grievance

77.(D)Dale Yoder

78.(D)Worker's participation in management

79.(C) (i) and (iii)

80.(D)All the above

81.(D)All the above

Explanation: Code of Discipline in Industry

- To maintain harmonious relations and promote industrial peace, a Code of Discipline has been laid down which applies to both public and private sector enterprises.
- It specifies various obligations for the management and the workers with the objective of promoting cooperation between their representatives.

The basic objectives of Code of Discipline:

- Maintain peace and order in industry.
- Promote constructive criticism at all levels of management and employment.
- Avoid work stoppage in industry
- Secure the settlement of disputes and grievances by a mutually agreed procedure

82.(C) In tray activity

Explanation: In-tray and case study exercises are designed to simulate a real work situation. They are a very common exercise at assessment centres.

83.(B)domestic enquiry

Explanation:

- Domestic enquiry is a disciplinary procedure to be followed by all the establishments whenever they are willing to take strong action against employee.
- This enquiry is based on the principle of natural justice and has to be conducted unbiased manner.

84.(D) (ii) (iv) (i) (iii)

85.(B) Both (A) and (R) are wrong

86.(D)Nagpur

87. (D)It is a justiceable right of the workers.

88. (B)Unit Councils

Explanation: Workers participation in Management

- A process by which subordinate employees, either individually or collectively, become involved in one or more aspects of organizational decision making within the enterprises in which they work.
- Workers' participation in management is an essential ingredient of Industrial democracy.
- The concept of workers' participation in management is based on Human Relations approach to Management which brought about a new set of values to labour and management.
- Traditionally the concept of Workers' Participation in Management (WPM) refers to participation of non-managerial employees in the decision-making process of the organization. Workers' participation is also known as 'labour participation' or 'employee participation' in management.
- ***In Germany it is known as co-determination while in Yugoslavia it is known as self-management.***
- The International Labour Organization has been encouraging member nations to promote the scheme of Workers' Participation in Management.
- Workers' participation in management implies mental and emotional involvement of workers in the management of Enterprise.
- It is considered as a mechanism where workers have a say in the decision-
- **International Institute of Labour Studies:** WPM is the participation resulting from the practices which increase the scope for employees' share of influence in decision-making at different tiers of organizational hierarchy with concomitant (related) assumption of responsibility.
- **ILO:** Workers' participation, may broadly be taken to cover all terms of association of workers and their representatives with the decision-making process, ranging from exchange of information, consultations, decisions and negotiations, to more institutionalized forms such as the presence of workers' member on management or supervisory boards or even management by workers themselves (as practiced in Yugoslavia).
- According to Keith Davis, Participation refers to the mental and emotional involvement of a person in a group situation which encourages him to contribute to group goals and share the responsibility of achievement.
- According to Walpole, Participation in Management gives the worker a sense of importance, pride and accomplishment; it gives him the freedom of opportunity for self-expression; a feeling of belongingness with the place of work and a sense of workmanship and creativity.
- Clegg says, "It implies a situation where workers representatives are, to some extent, involved in the process of management decision making, but where the ultimate power is in the hands of the management".
- According to Dr. Davis, "it is a mental and emotional involvement of a person in a group situation which encourages him to contribute to goals and share responsibilities in them".

Objectives of Workers Participation in Management:

- To raise level of motivation of workers by closer involvement.
- To provide opportunity for expression and to provide a sense of importance to workers.
- To develop ties of understanding leading to better effort and harmony.

- To act on a device to counter-balance powers of managers.
- To act on a panacea for solving industrial relation problems.

Specific of Purpose of Workers' Participation

1.It helps in managing resistance to change which is inevitable. For the growth and development of industry, changes have to be welcomed, otherwise the organization will stagnate and be left behind. If the need for change is jointly felt by all partners of production its acceptance can be high. Workers' participation in change strategy can facilitate acceptable solutions with a view to secure effective and smooth implementations of decisions.

2.Workers' participation can encourage communication at all levels. Since both partners of production are involved in the decision-making there will be fewer changes of distortion and/ or failure in communicating the decision.

3. Joint decision- making ensures the there will be minimum industrial conflict an economic growth can be free form distracting strife.

4. Workers' participation at the plant level can be seen as the first step to establishing democratic values in society at large.

Forms of Participation

Collective Bargaining: Collective bargaining results in collective agreements which lay down certain rules and conditions of service in an establishment. Such agreements are normally binding on the parties. Theoretically, collective bargaining is based on the principle of balance of power, but, in actual practice, each party tries to outbid the other and get maximum advantage by using, if necessary, threats and counterthreats like; strikes, lockouts and other direct actions. Joint consultation, on the other hand, is a particular technique which is intended to achieve a greater degree of harmony and cooperation by emphasising matters of common interest. Workers prefer to use the instrument of collective bargaining rather than ask for a share in management. Workers' participation in the U.S.A has been ensured almost exclusively by means of collective agreements and their application and interpretation rather than by way of labour representation in management.

Works Councils: These are exclusive bodies of employees, assigned with different functions in the management of an enterprise. In West Germany, the works councils have various decision-making functions. In some countries, their role is limited only to receiving information about the enterprise. In Yugoslavia, these councils have wider decision-making powers in an enterprise like; appointment, promotion, salary fixation and also major investment decisions.

Joint Management Councils and Committees: Mainly these bodies are consultative and advisory, with decision-making being left to the top management. This system of participation is prevalent in many countries, including Britain and India. As they are consultative and advisory, neither the managements nor the workers take them seriously.

Board Representation: The role of a worker representative in the board of directors is essentially one of negotiating the worker's interest with the other members of the board. At times, this may result in tension and friction inside the board room. The effectiveness of workers' representative at the board depend upon his ability to participate in decision-making, his knowledge of the company affairs, his educational background, his level of understanding and also on the number of worker representatives in the Board.

Workers Ownership of Enterprise: Social self-management in Yugoslavia is an example of complete control of management by workers through an elected board and workers council. Even in such a system, there exist two distinct managerial and operative functions with different sets of persons to perform them. Though workers have the option to influence all the decisions taken at the top level, in actual practice, the board and the top management team assume a fairly independent role in taking major policy decisions for the enterprises, especially in economic matters.

89.(A)The First National Commission on Labour, 1969

90.(B)The Directive Principles of State Policy

91.(A)Governing body of ILO

92.(B)1975

93.(C)Commercial and Service Organisations

94.(B) 20-point Economic Programme

Explanation:

- Government of India on 30th October, 1975 announced a scheme of workers participation in management which consisted of establishment of Joint Councils and Shop council as part of its 20 point economic programs.
- The scheme envisages for the establishment of joint councils and shop councils in manufacturing and mining industries employing 500 or more employees in public, private and co-operative sectors.
- The scheme contemplated participation of workers in the decision-making process in the matters relating to production, productivity ,absenteeism, safety measures, general discipline, working conditions and welfare, and overall efficiency of the shop/department.

95.(A)To promote increased productivity for the advantage of organisation, workers and society at large

96.(D)Unit Councils

97.(A)Works Committee

98.(C)The Royal Commission on Labour

99.(C)Standing Labour Committee

100. (C)Central Advisory Board

101. (A)Indian Labour Conference

102. (C)Wage Board

103. (B)Hoxie

Explanation: Trade union

- An organization whose membership consists of workers and union leaders, united to protect and promote their common interests.
- The principal purposes of a labor union are to
(1) negotiate wages and working condition terms,
(2) regulate relations between workers (its members) and the employer,
(3) take collective action to enforce the terms of collective bargaining,
(4) raise new demands on behalf of its members, and
(5) help settle their grievances.

A trade union may be:

(a) A company union that represents interests of only one company and may not have any connection with other unions. Also called house union, a company union is often a bogus one and generally illegal.

(b) A general union that represents workers from several companies in the same industry. Also called industrial union.

(c) A craft union that represents skilled workers in a particular field such as carpentry or welding.

104. (B)Marx, Weber and Gandhi

Explanation: Theories of Trade Unionism

1. Political Revolutionary Theory of Labour Movement of Marx and Engels: This theory is based on Adam Smiths theory of labour value. Its short run purpose is to eliminate competition among labour, and the ultimate purpose is to overthrow capitalist businessman. Trade union is pure simple a class struggle, and proletarians have nothing to lose but their chains and they a world to win.

2. Webbs Theory of Industrial Democracy: Webb's book 'Industrial democracy' is the Bible of trade unionism. According to Webb, trade unionism is an extension of democracy from political sphere to industrial sphere. Webb agreed with Marx that trade unionism is a class struggle and modern capitalist state is a transitional phase which will lead to democratic socialism. He considered collective bargaining as the process which strengthens labour.

3. Cole's Theory of Union Control of Industry: Cole's views are given in his book "World of Labour" 1913. His views are somewhere in between Webb and Marx. He agrees that unionism is class struggle and the ultimate is the control of industry by labour and not revolution as predicted by Marx.

4. Common's Environment Theory: He was skeptical of generalisations and believed only that which could be proved by evidence. He agreed that collective bargaining was an instrument of class struggle, but he summarised that ultimately there will be partnership between employers and employees.

5. Mitchell's Economic Protection Theory of Trade Unionism: Mitchell, a labour leader, completely rejected individual bargaining. According to him unions afford economic protection to.

6. Simons Theory of Monopolistic, anti-Democratic Trade Unionism: He denounced trade unionism as monopoly founded on violence. And he claimed monopoly power has no use save abuse.

7. Perlman's Theory of the "Scarcity Consciousness" of Manual Workers: He rejected the idea of class consciousness as an explanation for the origin of the trade union movement but substituted it with what he called job consciousness.

According to him, 'working people in reality felt an urge towards collective control of their employment opportunities, but hardly towards similar control of industry.' Perlman observed that three dominant factors emerged from the rich historical data:

the capacity or incapacity of the capitalist system to survive as a ruling group in the face of revolutionary attacks (e.g., failure in Russia).

the source of the anti-capitalist influences being primarily from among the intellectuals in any society.

the most vital factor in the labour situation was the trade union movement. Trade unionism, which is essentially pragmatic, struggles constantly not only against the employers for an enlarged opportunity measure in income, security and liberty in the shop and industry, but struggles also, whether consciously or unconsciously, actively or passively, against the intellectual who would frame its programmes and shape its policies.

But Perlman also felt that a theory of the labour movement should include a theory of the psychology of the labouring man. For instance, there was a historical continuity between the guilds and trade unions, through their common fundamental psychology; the psychology of seeking a livelihood in the face of limited economic opportunity. It was when manual workers became aware of a scarcity of opportunity, that they banded together into unions for the purpose of protecting their jobs and distributing employment opportunities among themselves equitably, and to subordinate the interests of the individual to the whole labour organism. Unionism was ruled thus by this fundamental scarcity consciousness (Perlman, 1970).

7. Hoxies Functional Classification of Unionism: He classified Unionism on the basis of their functions. His classification were Business Unionism for protecting the interest of various craftmen, "Uplift unionism" for the purpose of contributing better life such as association of sales engineers etc. "Revolutionary Unionism" which is eager to replace existing social order, "Predatory Unionism" which rests on these support of others.

8. Tannenbaum's Theory of Man Vs. Machine: According to him Union is formed in reaction to alienation and loss of community in an individualistic and unfeeling society. In his words, the union returns to the workers his society, which he left behind him when he migrated from a rural background to the anonymity of an urban industrial location. The union gives the worker a fellowship and a value system that he shares with others like him.

Institutionally, the trade union movement is an unconscious effort to harness the drift of our time and reorganise it around the cohesive identity that men working together always achieve.

105. (C)Is an association of workers who are engaged in not securing economic benefits for their members?

106. (C)Webbs

107. (C)Workmen and employers, workmen and workmen, employers and employers temporary or permanent

108. (A)Mutual Insurance

109. (B)Time-rated wages

110. (B)(iii) (iv) (ii) (i)

111. (A)Roscoe pound

112. (C)Raja Ram Mohan Roy

113. (B)Trade union is a continuous organisation

114. (C)Social Security

115. (B) Stable Union

116. (A) 1920-1930

117. (C) 1918

118. (C)Code of Discipline

119. (D)None of the above

120. (D) Consumers' union

121. (B)Minimum Wages Act, 1948

122. (A) 1920

123. (B)M. K. Gandhi

124. (A)HMS -1948

125. (C) 1890

126. (B) (iii) (iv) (ii) (i)

127. (C)H.M.S.

128. (A)(iii) (iv) (i) (ii)

129. (B)AITUC

130. (B)AITUC

131. (D)All India Trade Union Congress

132. (B) NFITU

133. (A) (c) (d) (b) (a)

134. (D) (iv) (iii) (i) (ii)

135. (A) 1949

136. (A)Sanjeeva Reddy

137. (B)Bharteeya Janata Party

138. (C)M.K. Gandhi

139. (B) AITUC

140. (B)(iii) (iv) (i) (ii)

141. (B) 1958

142. (B)B.P. Wadia

143. (C)(iii) (iv) (i) (ii)

144. (B)Code of Discipline in Industry

145. (D)Cannot be elected as Office-bearer of the registered trade union

146. (C)Check-off

147. (A)Rivalry between unions

148. (C)Partly voluntary and partly compulsory

149. (A)Membership subscription

150. (B)Persons working in other industry

151. (B)It is optional

Explanation: A registered Trade Union may constitute a separate fund, from contributions separately levied for or made to that fund, from which payments may be made, for the promotion of the civic and political interests of its members, in furtherance of any of the objects specified in sub-section (2).

152. (A)Craft Union

Explanation: Industrial unionism contrasts with craft unionism, which organizes workers along lines of their specific trades, i.e., workers using the same kind of tools, or doing the same kind of work with approximately the same level of skill, even if this leads to multiple union locals (with different contracts, and different expiration dates) in the same workplace.

153. (B)Acquiring the control of industry by workers.

154. (C)The Inter Union Code of Conduct.

155. (D) Social Legislation

156. (A)Trade Union Act, 1926

157. (C)Collective Bargaining

158. (D) Promotion

159. (C)Inter-Union Code of Conduct

160. (B) Check-off

Explanation: Check off: Practice in unionized (organized) establishments under which an employer regularly deducts union dues from the employees' wages and passes them on to the union. Check off may require a written authorization from the employee for the deduction.

161. (D)Higher Wages and Short hours of work

162. (D) Bombay Millhand's Association

Explanation:

- Bombay Millhand's Association formed in 1890.
- The Amalgamated Society of railway servants of India and Burma formed in 1897
- The Kamgar Hitwardhak Sabha Bombay formed in 1910.
- Madras Labour Union-1918: Along with V. Kalyanasundaram Mudaliar, Wadia founded the Madras Labour Union, one of India's first organised labour unions.

163. (C) Establishment of Socialist society

164. (B) (ii) (iii) (i) (v) (iv)

165. (A) Sidney and Beatrice Webb

166. (C) 25% of the workers of that industry in that area.

167. (D) M.K. Gandhi

168. (B) By voluntary tripartite code of inter-union rivalry – 1957

169. (B) incorrect.

170. (A)(ii), (v), (i), (iii), (iv)

171. (D)All the above

172. (D)To satisfy their family needs

173. (A)(ii) (iv) (i) (iii)

174. (B)Robert F. Hoxie

175. (A)not registered

176. (C)(iii) (iv) (ii) (i)

177. (C)Members and office bearers of the trade union at such time as provided in the rules

178. (A)Code of discipline in industry

179. (A)Trade Unions

180. (A) Closed shop

181. (C)(i)(iii) (ii) (iv)

182. (D)None of the above

183. (D)Communist Party of India

184. (D)(iii) (i) (ii) (iv)

185. (B)Communist party of India Marxist

186. (C) 1948

187. (C) Collective Bargaining

Explanation: Collective Bargaining:

- The process of negotiating the terms of employment between an employer and a group of workers.
- The terms of employment are likely to include items such as conditions of employment, working conditions and other workplace rules, base pay, overtime pay, work hours, shift length, work holidays, sick leave, vacation time, retirement benefits and health care benefits.
- The collective bargaining process may involve antagonistic labor strikes or employee lockouts if the two sides are having trouble reaching an agreement.

188. (B) FICCI

Explanation:

- The Federation of Indian Chambers of Commerce and Industry (FICCI) is an association of business organizations in India.

- Established in 1927, on the advice of Mahatma Gandhi by GD Birla and Purushottam Das Thakurdas, it is the largest, oldest and the apex business organisation in India.
- It is a non-government, not-for-profit organisation. FICCI draws its membership from the corporate sector, both private and public, including SMEs and MNCs.
- It is involved in sector specific business policy consensus building, and business promotion and networking.
- The headquarter of FICCI at New Delhi and has presence in 11 states in India and 8 countries across the world.

189. (A) (b) (d) (a) (c)

190. (A)Labour welfare has no roots in social work.

191. (D)Robert Owners

192. (D) All the above

193. (B)New Lanark Experiment

194. (B) M.V. Moorthy

195. (C)Lord Beveridge

196. (D) M.V. Moorthy

197. (B)B.P. Adarkar

198. (A)New Lanark Experiment

199. (B) Mahatma Gandhi

200. (C) Both (A) and (B)

201. (A) The Principle of Uniformity

202. (B) (iii) (iv) (i) (ii)

203. (D)Subsistence Theory and Residual Claimant Theory

204. (C)Functional Theory

205. (B)Employees are treated as the guardians of the industrial property

206. (B)Robert Owen

207. (C)M. V. Moorthy

208. (A)M. K. Gandhi

209. (B)Trusteeship Theory of M.K.Gandhi

210. (C)Extra mural welfare programmes

211. (A)(ii) (i) (iv) (iii)

212. (D)Productivity Theory of Labour Welfare

213. (A)(ii) (i) (iii) (iv)

214. (B)Welfare Officer's duties and responsibilities are defined and prescribed in the legislation.

215. (D)(iii) (i) (v) (ii) (iv)

216. (C)Assertion and Reason are right.

217. (D)Housing Facilities

218. (A)I.L.O.

219. (B)Consumer Courts

220. (B)Developed to some extent

221. (D) Canteens and First Aid Boxes

222. (D) Customers

223. (B) Sports facility

224. (B)Directive Principles of State Policy

225. (B)(iii) (iv) (i) (ii)

226. (A)(ii) (iii) (iv) (i)

227. (C)(iv) (iii) (i) (ii)

228. (D)(a) (d) (c) (b)

229. (C)Transport facility

230. (B)V. V. Giri

231. (D)(iv) (iii) (ii) (i)

232. (D)The second National Commission on Labour

233. (B) Housing

234. (D)All the Above

235. (B) Decreasing

236. (D)Technological Unemployment

237. (B) Social Assistance

238. (B) Housing

239. (C)N.G.Os

240. (D)Principle of Responsibility

241. (A)The Royal Commission on Labour

242. (A)Management

243. (C)Hospitals

244. (A) 150 workers

245. (B)M. V. Murthy

246. (D) Standing Labour Committee

247. (B) Labour force participation

248. (B) Total Concept

249. (D)Assertion is right but its explanation given in Reason is wrong.

250. (A)the Declaration of Philadelphia adopted by 26th session of ILO

251. (B) (iv) (iii) (i) (ii)

252. (C) (A) is right and (R) also is right.

253. (B)Social Action

254. (C)C.K. Prahalad and G. Hamel

255. (C)Registration under company Act, 1956

256. (C) (i), (iii) and (iv)

257. (A) St. Thomas Aquinas

258. (B)Decent Work

259. (A) 1919

260. (B) Article 19(C)

261. (C)Convention No. 100

262. (A)The conventions and Recommendations of I. L. O

263. (A) 1

264. (D)I.L.O. Recommendations are compulsorily binding in nature.

265. (C)Both (A) and (B)

266. (C)I.L.O passes only recommendations.

267. (C)1978

268. (B) 1958

269. (B) 1991

270. (B)(i)(ii)(iii)(iv)

271. (C)Second National Commission on Labour

272. (B) 1977

273. (B) Ravindra Verma

274. (C)Industrial Policy Resolution 1956

275. (B)not just creation of jobs but the creation of jobs of acceptable quality

276. (D) All the above

277. (C) Both (A) and (B)

278. (A)ILO

279. (C) ILO

280. (C)Rashtriya Mill Mazdoor Sangh

281. (C)Both (A) and (B)

282. (C)International Labour Organization

283. (B) Social security for retirees

284. (C)Run jointly by federal and state governments.

285. (B) Employee Training

286. (C)Opportunity given to the delique employee being heard

287. (D) Employer and Employees

288. (A)Negotiation

289. (C)Employee State Insurance Act, 1948

290. (B)U. N. D. P

---000---

UNIT-V

FINANCIAL MANAGEMENT

1. Which of the following is ***not*** one of the important objectives of Financial Management?

   (A) Profit maximization

   (B) Wealth maximisation

   (C) Value maximisation

   (D) Social responsibility

2. The basic goal of financial management is :

   (A)Maximising the profit

   (B)Maximising shareholders' wealth in the long run

   (C)Maximising the rate of dividend

   (D)Minimising the business risk

3. The Basic objective of Financial Management is

   (A) Maximization of Profit

   (B)Maximization of Shareholders Wealth

   (C)Ensuring financial discipline in the organization

   (D)None of the above

4. The goal of financial management is to:

   (A)Maximise the wealth of Preference Shareholders

   (B)Maximise the wealth of Debenture holders

   (C)Maximise the wealth of Equity shareholders

   (D) All of the above

5. One of the goals of financial management is :

   (A)Wealth maximization

   (B) Hostile take-over

   (C) To raise funds from outsiders

   (D) None of the above

6. Which objective of financial management considers the risk and time value of money?

   (A) Profit Maximization objective

   (B) Wealth Maximization objective

   (C) Turnover Maximization objective

   (D) Growth Maximization objective

7. Which is the task of a finance manager?

   (A) Investment decision

   (B) Dividend decision

   (C) Management of income

   (D) All of the above

8. The term financial engineering is related to

   (A) Cost of production

   (B) Financial restructuring

   (C) Product planning

   (D) Capital issue

9. The Tax shield would result in:

   (i) increase in tax liability

   (ii) increase in EPS

   (iii) decrease in EPS

   (iv) decrease in tax liability

   Codes:

   (A) (ii) and (iv) (B) (i) and (iii)

   (C) (i) and (iv) (D) (iii) and (iv)

10. Among the following financial derivatives, which involves the least risk for the holder?

    (A) Forward (B) Option

    (C) Futures (D) Swap

11. Which of the following is ***not*** one of the benefits of E-Commerce?

    (A)E-Commerce offers greater flexibility in meeting consumer needs.

(B)E-Commerce can help to reduce cost.

(C)E-Commerce increases potential market share.

(D)E-Commerce increases the net cost per contact.

12. Which one of the following facilitates E-Commerce?

(A)Public relations (B) Direct marketing

(C) Personal selling (D) Product quality

13. Financial risk arises from

(A) R & D and operations stages of value chain

(B)GNP growth rate and competitive environment

(C)Volatility of interest rates, currency rates, commodities prices and stock prices

(D)Changes in laws and regulations

14. The first stock exchange was set up in India in:

(A) Calcutta (B) Bombay

(C) Delhi (D) Madras

15. The main objective of Stock Exchange is to:

(A)Provide facilities for speculation

(B)Safeguard the interest of investors

(C)Help in the capital formation in the country

(D)Provide a ready market for securities

16. Contango charge is paid by a:

(A)Bull speculator to bear speculator

(B)Bear speculator to bull speculator

(C)Lame duck to bull speculator

(D)Bull to lane duck speculator

17. Which of the following would increase company's debt ratio?

(i)An increase in cost incurred while filing for bankruptcy

(ii)An increase in corporate tax rate

(iii)An increase in personal tax rate

(iv)A decrease in firm's business risk

Choose the right combination

(A) (i),(ii)and (iii) (B) (ii), (iii)and (iv)

(C) (ii) and (iv) (D) (iii)and (iv)

18. The double entry system of record of all economic transactions between the residents of a country and the rest of the world carried out in a specific period of time is referred to as:

(A) Balance of Trade

(B) Balance of Payments

(C) Current Account

(D) Capital Account

19. Increase in net RBI credit for central government represents:

(A)Budgetary Deficit (B) Revenue Deficit

(C)Fiscal Deficit (D) Monetized Deficit

20. Pre-emptive right of equity shareholders means that they :

(A)Can vote to protect their rights

(B)Can maintain their proportional ownership by purchasing additional equity shares issued by firm

(C)Can be elected as directors

(D)None of the above

21. Who is a Merchant Middleman?

(A) Stock Broker

(B) Commission Agent

(C) Retailer

(D) Selling Agent of a Company

22. A Bond can be issued at a premium, if

(A) Coupon rate is greater than required return

(B) Coupon rate is less than required return

(C) Coupon rate is equal to required return

(D) None of the above

23. Match the following :

List – 1

(a) Number of years required to

(b) A method which uses

(c) Theoretically correct

(d) A technique which ascertains

List – 2

(i)NPV recover the initial outlay is determined by

(ii)Pay Back period accounting information for evaluating proposed capital expenditure is

(iii)IRR technique for selection of Investment project is

(iv) ARR a discount rate that equates the aggregate present values of net cash inflows with that of the aggregate present values of net cash outflows is

	(a)	(b)	(c)	(d)
(A)	(i)	(iii)	(iv)	(ii)
(B)	(ii)	(iv)	(i)	(iii)
(C)	(i)	(ii)	(iv)	(iii)
(D)	(iii)	(iv)	(ii)	(i)

24. In terms of relative risk, which of the following is true?

(A)Debt is risky for investors, while equity is risky for firm

(B)Both debt and equity are risky for investors

(C)Both debt and equity are risky for firm

(D)Debt is risky for the firm, while equity is risky for investors

25. SDR is the currency of IMF which is in the form of:

(A) Paper currency

(B) Gold

(C) Silver and gold both

(D) Book-keeping entry only

26. Gresham's law is related to:

(A) Consumption and Demand

(B) Supply and Demand

(C) Circulation of Money

(D) Deficit Financing

27. If the intrinsic value of the share is greater than market value, such shares are :

(A) Under valued (B) Over valued

(C) Neutral (D) None of the above

28. Which of the following is ***not*** a market oriented pricing technique?

(A)Penetration pricing

(B) Going rate pricing

(C) Perceived value pricing

(D)Early-cash recovery pricing

29. Trade credit is a:

(A)Negotiated source of finance

(B) Hybrid source of finance

(C) Spontaneous source of finance

(D) Source of credit from the owners of the business

30. Mutually exclusive investment proposals are these:

(A) Wherein the acceptance of one proposal leads to rejection of all other proposals

(B)That requires special sources of financing

(C)That has unique features

(D)The reduce the total risk complexion of the firm

31. Match the following :

List-I

(i)Net present value method

(ii)Average rate of return

(iii)Internal rate of return

(iv)Pay back method

List-II

(a)Inflow after interest and tax

(b)Discounted cash flow

(c)Traditional method

(d)Decision based on cut-off rate

Codes:

	(i)	(ii)	(iii)	(iv)
(A)	(d)	(a)	(b)	(c)
(B)	(d)	(c)	(b)	(a)
(C)	(b)	(a)	(d)	(c)
(D)	(a)	(c)	(d)	(b)

32. Balance of Payment is

(A) Balance of trade + Net earnings on invisibles

(B) Foreign exchange inflow – Foreign exchange outflow

(C) Balance of current account + Balance of capital account +Statistical discrepancy

(D) Export of goods – Import of goods

33. Additional revenue generated by selling an additional unit is:

(A) Incremental revenue

(B) Marginal revenue

(C) Total revenue

(D) Average revenue

34. Internal rate of return method applied for capital budgeting decision

(A)Allows to take different discount factors.

(B)Uses cost of capital as discount factor.

(C)May give more than one IRR

(D)Distinguishes between the IRR for lending and borrowing decision

35. The factors affecting to P/E multiple are:

(A) Dividend pay-out ratio and required return

(B) Required return and expected growth rate

(C) Dividend pay-out ratio and expected growth rate

(D) Dividend pay-out ratio, required return and expected growth rate

36. Short term financing instruments may contain

(i)Commercial Paper (ii) Public Deposits

(iii)Term Loans (iv)Trade Credit

Find the correct combination according to the code.

(A) (i) ,(ii) and (iii) are correct

(B) (ii), (iii)and (iv) are correct

(C) (iii)and (iv) are correct.

(D) (i), (ii)and (iv) are correct.

37. NPV is the sum of :

(A)Present values of all the cash flows expected to occur over the life of a project

(B)Present values of the positive cash flows expected to occur over the life of a project

(C)Cumulative values of the positive cash flows expected to occur over the life of a project.

(D)Total value of the positive and negative cash flows expected to occur over the life of a project.

38. Which of the following formula is used to calculate Pay Back Period when cash inflows are constant?

(A) Fixed Assets/Current Assets

(B) Fixed Assets/Current Liabilities

(C)Initial Investment cost/Annual cash inflows

(D) None of the above

39. The Internal Rate of Return (IRR) is determined where

(A) The Net Present Value is positive

(B) The Net Present Value is negative

(C)The Net Present Value is zero

(D)None of the above

40. In investment decision, β is associated with

(A) Return (B) Risk

(C) Return and Risk (D) None of the above

41. The exchange rate between the currencies of two countries will be equal to the ratio of the price indices in these countries is explained by:

(A) Inflation adjustment

(B) Purchase power parity

(C) Interest rate parity

(D) Transaction exposure

42. The nature of amalgamation as uniting of interests or acquisition is described in which Accounting standard issued by ICAI.

(A)AS - 13 (B)AS - 14

(C)AS - 15 (D)AS - 16

43. In capital lease depreciation is claimed by :

(A)Lesser (B) Lessee

(C)Both (D) None of the above

44. Corporate control is maintained intact by issuing shares through :

(A)Public offer (B)Rights issue

(C)Book building (D)None of the above

45. Convertible bond is :

(A)Debt+Warrant (B)Debt+Cash

(C)Debt+Share (D)None of the above

46. Corporate-Governance deals with value creation for :

(A)Corporate (B)Shareholders

(C)Stakeholders (D)None of the above

47. The principal value of a bond is called :

(A)Coupon rate (B)Par value

(C)Maturity value (D)Market value

48. Trade credit is a:

(A)Negotiated source of finance

(B)Hybrid source of finance

(C)Spontaneous source of finance

(D)Source of credit from the owners of the business

49. IRR is the rate of interest :

(A) equal to the cost of capital of the proposal

(B) prevailing rate of interest in the market

(C) paid on the bonds by the firm

(D) that makes the NPV of capital proposal almost zero

50. Mutually exclusive investment proposals are those :

(A)Wherein the acceptance of one proposal leads to rejection of all other proposals

(B)That require special sources of financing

(C)That have unique features

(D)That reduce the total risk complexion of the firm

51. Theoretically, with the issue of rights share the value of existing shares

(A) will increase (B) will not change

(C)will reduce (D) may increase or decrease

52. When the cash flow outcomes of succeeding period depends on what has happened before, the probabilities of succeeding period are known as

(A)joint probabilities

(B)conditional probabilities

(C)simple probabilities

(D)decision tree

53. A high risk, high-yield often unsecured bond rated below investment grade is known as:

(A)Income-bond (B)Subordinated debentures

(C) Junk bond (D) Serial bond

54. Which one of the following represents number of years required to recover the initial investment?

(A) Accounting rate of return

(B) Payback period

(C) Internal rate of return

(D) Net present value

55. Other things being equal, stocks which are highly liquid command

(A) Higher dividend payout ratio

(B) Lower dividend payout ratio

(C) Higher P/E multiples

(D) Lower P/E multiples

56. Which statement is true about deep discount bonds?

(A) These are in the form of low interest bonds

(B) These bonds are sold at a discounted value and on maturity face value of the bond is paid to the investors

(C) There is no interest payout during lock-in period

(D) None of the above

57. Financial leverage is:

(A)EBIT Sales × 100

(B)EBITEBT

(C)Sales Fixed Assets

(D)Profit Sales × Capital

58. The value of the firm is maximized when the:

(A) Market price of equity share is maximum

(B) Market price of equity share is minimum

(C) Market value of debt is maximum

(D) None of the above

59. Match the following:

List – I (Form of Dividend)	**List- II (Feature)**
(i) Cash Dividend	(a) Securities
(ii) Stock Dividend	(b) Promissory notes
(iii) Bond Dividend	(c) Liquidity
(iv) Property Dividend	(d) Bonus shares

	(i)	(ii)	(iii)	(iv)
(A)	(d)	(b)	(c)	(a)
(B)	(a)	(c)	(d)	(b)
(C)	(c)	(d)	(b)	(a)
(D)	(b)	(a)	(d)	(c)

60. Match the following:

List – I

(i) The price at which

(ii) A contract that gives

(iii) An agreement to buy or

(iv) The possibility of

List – II

(a) Option instrument is traded.

(b) Forward Contract the holder the right but not the obligation.

(c) Spot price sell a security on a specified date for a specified price.

(d) Counter party default by any one risk party to the transaction

	(i)	(ii)	(iii)	(iv)
(A)	(a)	(c)	(d)	(b)
(B)	(b)	(a)	(c)	(d)
(C)	(c)	(a)	(b)	(d)
(D)	(d)	(c)	(a)	(b)

61. Match the following

List – I

(i) The price of one currency

(ii) The difference between the

(iii) The rate of exchange of two

(iv) Rate of exchange of the

List – II

(a) Spread expressed in terms of the currency of another country

(b) Spot rate Ask price and Bid price

(c) Cross currencies on the basis of rate exchange quotes of other pairs of currencies

(d) Exchange day on which the transaction rate has taken place and of the day the transaction is executed

Code:

	(i)	(ii)	(iii)	(iv)
(A)	(a)	(c)	(d)	(b)
(B)	(d)	(a)	(c)	(b)
(C)	(b)	(c)	(a)	(d)
(D)	(c)	(b)	(d)	(a)

62. Choose customer order processing in sequential order from the following

(A) Invoice raised, establish credit status, check credit limit, goods deliver, issue delivery note

(B) Issue delivery note, establish credit status, check credit limit, invoice raised, goods deliver

(C) Establish credit status, check credit limit, issue delivery note, goods deliver, invoice raised

(D) Check credit limit, invoice raised, establish credit status, issue delivery note, goods deliver

63. The stock of ABB Ltd. (Face Value Rs 10.00) quotes Rs 520.00 on NSE and the 3 months future price quotes at Rs 532. The borrowing rate is given as 15% p.a. What would be the theoretical price of 3 month ABB future if the expected annual dividend yield is 25% p.a. payable before expiry?

(A) Rs 540.00 (B) Rs 539.00

(C) Rs 537.00 (D) Insufficient data

64. Ms. Patil can earn a return of 20% by investing in equity shares on her own. Now she is considering a recently announced Equity based mutual fund scheme in which initial expenses and annual recurring expenses are 5 per cent and 1.5 per cent respectively. How much should the mutual fund earn to provide Mrs. Patil, a return of 20%?

(A) 18.43% (B) 22.55%

(C) 21.50% (D) Insufficient data.

65. The Beta co-efficient of equity stock of Loyalty Ltd. is 1.6. The risk free rate of return is 12% and the required rate of return is 18% on the market portfolio. If the dividend expected during the coming year is Rs 2.50 and the growth rate of dividend and earnings is 8%, at what price the stock of Loyalty Ltd. can be sold (based on CAPM)?

(A) Rs 18.38 (B) Rs 15.60

(C) Rs 12.50 (D) None of the above.

66. Match List-I (Activity) with List-Il (Associated organization) and select the correct answer by using the codes given below the lists:

List-I (Activity)

(a) Mutual fund

(b)Public issue of capital

(c) Forward trading

(d)Option pricing

List-II (Associated organization)

(i)Stock exchange

(ii)Assets Management Company

(iii)Merchant banking

(iv) Forex market

Codes:

	(a)	(b)	(c)	(d)
(A)	(iii)	(ii)	(iv)	(i)
(B)	(iii)	(ii)	(i)	(iv)
(C)	(ii)	(iii)	(i)	(iv)
(D)	(ii)	(iii)	(iv)	(i)

67. Which of the following are the methods of market new issues of securities?

(i)Listing of securities

(ii)Jobbers and brokers

(iii)Private placement of securities

(iv)Privileged subscriptions

Select the correct answer using the codes given below.

Codes:

(A) (i) and (ii) (B) (ii) and (iii)

(C) (iii)and(iv) (D) (i), (ii) ,(iii) and(iv)

68. Match the following

List–I (items /method)

(a) Rate of return method

(b)Purchase consideration

(c)Diminishing Balance Method

(d)Fifo Method

List – II (used/ Application)

(i)Capital budgeting

(ii) Merger

(iii)Depreciation

(iv)Stock valuation

Code:

	(a)	(b)	(c)	(d)
(A)	(i)	(iii)	(ii)	(iv)
(B)	(iii)	(ii)	(iv)	(i)
(C)	(i)	(ii)	(iii)	(iv)
(D)	(i)	(iv)	(iii)	(ii)

69. The Capital Asset Pricing Model (CAPM) establishes the relationship between:

(A) Risk and EPS

(B) Risk and value of the firm

(C) Risk and the required rate of return

(D) None of the above

70. The amount by which the face value of a bond exceeds its current price is known as :

(A)Bond premium(B) Intrinsic value of bond

(C)Bond discount (D) Future value of bond

71. Beta in the context of security analysis indicates:

(A) Systematic risk (B) Unsystematic risk

(C) Total risk (D) All of the above

72. Which method of capital budgeting focuses on liquidity of a project?

(A) Net present value (B) Profitability index

(C)Payback period(D) Internal rate of returns

73. Capital budgeting is concerned with budgeting for :

(A)Capital income (B) Capital expenditure

(C)Capital gains (D) Investment Appraisal

74. Assertion (A): Walter's and Gordon's models are applicable to firms in which all financing is done through retained earnings and with zero leverage.

Reason (R): The market price of the share, according to Gordon model is favourably effected with the increasing payment of dividends.

(A) Both A and R are correct

(B) Both A and R are wrong

(C) A is correct but R is wrong

(D) A is wrong but R is correct

75. Arrange the components of current assets in the order of liquidity

(i)Sundry Debtors (ii)Bills Receivables

(iii)Inventories (iv) Cash and Bank

(A) (iv) (iii) (ii) (i) (B) (iv) (ii) (i) (iii)

(C) (i) (iv) (ii) (iii) (D) (iii) (ii) (iv) (i)

76. The term Opportunity Cost refers to:

(A)Variable Cost

(B) Short-run cost

(C)The cost forgone in favour of production of another product

(D)Cost related to an optimum level of production

77. Opportunity costs are also known as:

(A) Spill-over costs (B) Money costs

(C) Alternative costs (D) Sunk costs

78. **Assertion (A):** Optimal Capital Structure is the Capital structure at the level of debt, equity proportion, where the market value per share is maximum and cost of capital is minimum

Reason (R): Earning per share multiplied by price-earning ratio gives market price per share.

(A) A is correct but R is wrong

(B) Both A and R are wrong

(C) Both A and R are correct

(D) A is wrong but R is correct

79. **Assertion (A):** Venture capital is the capital to raise to invest in high risk projects.

Reason (R): ICICI was established to finance only venture capital projects.

(A) Both A and R are correct

(B) A is correct but R is wrong

(C) Both A and R are wrong

(D) A is wrong but R is correct

80. Free cash flow means:

(A)Cash available for financing incremental working capital

(B)Cash available for financing additional investment in plant and machinery

(C)Cash available for meeting financial flows like debt servicing, dividend payments etc.

(D) None of the above

81. Which of the following is foreign investment?

(A) Equity (B) Debenture

(C) FDI (D) Government Bonds

82. A portfolio consisting of two risky securities can be made riskless i.e.θp=0, if

(A) the securities are perfectly positively correlated

(B) the securities are perfectly negatively correlated

(C) if the correlation ranges between 0 and 1

(D) none of the above

83. **Assertion (A):** High capital gearing leads to greater speculation. .

Reason (R): Proportion of equity share capital in relation to the total capital comprising the other securities is small leading to capitalization being highly geared.

Codes:

(A) Both A and R are true and R is the correct explanation of A.

(B) Both A and R are true but R is not a correct explanation of A.

(C) A is true but R is false.

(D) A is false but R is true.

84. For calculating weighted average cost of capital, cost of each source of capital is multiplied by proportion applicable to it. The proportions may be based on

(A) Book values only

(B) Target capital structure only

(C) Market values only

(D) All of the above

85. The cost of equity can be measured as

(A) Rate of interest (1 – t).

(B) Rate of dividend (1– t).

(C) Rate of dividend× (Face value – Issue Price)/n

(D) $\frac{D_1}{P_0} + g$

86. With reference to Working Capital Management, the term 'float' relates to:

(A) Inventory Management

(B) Receivables Management

(C) Cash Management

(D) Marketable Securities

87. A Ltd. has beta (β) of 1.25. The risk free rate of return is 0.08 and Rm=0.15. Share price is Rs. 30. The expected return is:

(A) 10% (B) 8%

(C) 15% (D) 16.75%

88. As per CAPM cost of equity (R_j) is equal to :

(A) $R_f + \left(\bar{R}_M - R_f\right) B_j$

(B) $\bar{R}_M + \left(R_f - \bar{R}_M\right) B_j$

(C) $R_j + \left(R_f - \bar{R}_M\right) B_j$

(D) $B_j + (\bar{R}_M - R_f) R_j$

89. Voltas Ltd. has a beta of 0.865. If the expected market return is 17.50 and the risk free rate of return is 8.50%, what is the appropriate required rate of return of the co.? (use the CAPM)

(A) 16.825% (B) 16.582%

(C) 16.285% (D) 16.258%

90. Weighted Average Cost of Capital may contain

(i) Cost of Equity

(ii) Cost of Debt

(iii) Cost of goods purchased

(iv)Cost of initial investment

Find the correct combination according to the code:

(A) (i), (ii), &(iii) are correct

(B) (ii), (iii), &(iv) are correct.

(C) (iii), &(iv)are correct.

(D) (i) &(ii)are correct

91. NSU Co. Ltd., is operating in an industry in which the average rate of return on market portfolio is 10%. The beta coefficient of the company is computed as 1.75 and return on Government Security (risk free) is 6%. What will be the required rate of return on a stock of the company?

(A) 12.5 % (B) 13.0 %

(C) 12.9 % (D) 12.0 %

92. The capital structure theories which argue that capital structure is relevant to the value of firm contain

(i)Net Income Approach

(ii)Net Operating Income Approach

(iii)Traditional Approach

(iv)Modigliani and Miller Approach

Find the correct combination according to the code:

(A) (i) &(ii)are correct.

(B) (i) &(iii)are correct.

(C) (iii) &(iv)are correct.

(D) (ii) &(iv) are correct.

93. Working capital refers to the capital mobilised for meeting

(A) Long-term financial needs of the company

(B) To meet day-to-day financial obligations of the company

(C) To meet the future financial requirements of the company

(D) None of the above

94. Assertion (A): The investors in the capital market have been showing a decisive shift in favour of fixed income instruments.

Reason (R): The debt instruments have active secondary market.

Codes:

(A) Both A and R are true and R is the correct explanation of A.

(B)Both A and R are true but R is not a correct explanation of A.

(C)A is true but R is false.

(D)A is false but R is true.

95. You require capital for purchase of fixed assets. What is this capital called :

(A) Floating capital (B) Reserve capital

(C) Circulating capital(D) Fixed capital

96. Which of the following is a main method of issue of stocks?

(A) Vendor placing

(B) Public issue through Prospectus

(C) Private placements

(D) None of the above

97. Interest is paid on a deep discount bond :

(A)Monthly

(B)Half yearly

(C)Annually

(D)At the end of life of bond (maturity)

98. Liberal credit policy may enhance the sales but will lead to :

(A)faster collection (B)higher turnover

(C)increase in bad debts(D)none of the above

99. The P/E ratio approach to stock valuation is also known as:

(A)Earnings multiplier approach

(B) Dividend discounting approach

(C) Required rate of return

(D) None of the above

100. According to 'dividend discount model' the value of an equity share is equal to :

(A)Present value of dividends expected from equity ownership

(B)Present value of dividends expected from equity ownership plus present value of sale price expected when equity share is sold

(C)Present value of dividends and bonus expected from equity ownership

(D)None of the above

101. Annual cash dividends divided by annual earnings or alternatively dividend per share divided by earnings per share is known as :

(A)cost of equity (B)cash profit

(C)dividend - payout ratio(D)retention ratio

102. Assuming constant rate of growth of dividend, value of share will be equal to

(A) P0 = D0r – g (B) P0 =D1r – g

(C) P1 =D0r + g (D) P1 =D0r+ g

103. Dividend is paid only out of :

(A) Cash (B)Current or Accumulated profit

(C)Reserves (D) Capital profit

104. The Irrelevance Theory of dividend is also known as :

(A)Guthman Theory (B)W. B. Theory

(C)M. M. Theory (D)Vanhorne Theory

105. Which of the following is the main assumption of Waltar Valuation Model?

(A)All financing is done through Retained earnings and external sources of funds.

(B)With additional investment the firms business risk will change.

(C)There is a change in the key variables such as EPS and DPS

(D) None of the above

106. Which of the following is an important money market instrument?

(A)Debentures (B) Commercial Paper

(C) Public Deposits (D) None of the above

107. The amount of dividend that can be legally distributed is governed by :

(A)Company law

(B) Judicial pronouncement in leading cases

(C)Contractual restrictions

(D)All above

108. Match the following :

List-I

(a) Harry Markowitz

(b) David Durand

(c) Dow structure

(d) M.J. Gordon

List-II

(i)Dividend Theory

(ii)CAPM

(iii)Capital

(iv)Technical Analysis

Code:

	(a)	(b)	(c)	(d)
(A)	(iv)	(iii)	(ii)	(i)
(B)	(ii)	(iii)	(iv)	(i)
(C)	(ii)	(i)	(iii)	(iv)
(D)	(iii)	(ii)	(iv)	(i)

109. In financial evaluation of a acquisition, the value of merger focuses on :

(A)corporate value (B)stakeholder value

(C)shareholder value (D)none of the above

110. The division of a company into two separate independent companies is known as :

(A)Spin off (B)Dissolution

(C)Liquidation (D) Split up

111. In a merger bargain, the exchange ratio is determined on the basis of :

(A)Potential of merging company

(B)Issued capital of the two companies

(C)Market share

(D)Future value of company to the acquirer

112. When merger is in the nature of consolidation, the accounting approach will be :

(A)Purchase method

(B)Pooling of interest method

(C)Combination

(D)None of the above

113. Long term sources of finance may contain

(i)Retained earnings

(ii)Inter corporate deposits

(iii)Debentures

(iv)Preference share capital

Find the correct combination according to the code:

(A) (i) (iii) & (iv) are correct

(B) (ii) (iii) &(iv)are correct

(C) (ii) &(iii) are correct

(D) (ii) &(iv) are correct

114. When a firm proposes to acquire another firm, the merger proposal may be viewed as a

(A)Working capital management proposal

(B) Capital budgeting proposal

(C) Financing decision

(D) Dividend decision

115. In an endeavour to maximize corporate value, a finance manager has to factor in the following

(A) Optimization Principle

(B) Risk-return Principle

(C) Marginal Principle

(D) All the above

116. Value of the merged firm shall be

(A) Less than the acquired firm

(B) More than the acquirer

(C)Greater than the target and the acquirer

(D) None of the above

117. Which global company has been recently acquired by Tata Steel?

(A)VSL (B) NUMUS

(C)CORUS (D) BSL

118. The method of payment in Mergers and Acquisitions may include:

(i) Cash

(ii)Loan stock

(iii) Ordinary shares

(iv) Convertible loan stock

(A) (i) & (iii) only (B) (i) & (ii) only

(C) (i), (ii), (iii) & (iv)(D) (ii) & (iv) only

119. The term 'Exchange Ratio' is used in

(A) Profitability Assessment

(B) Capital Structure

(C) Mergers and Acquisitions

(D) Leverages

120. A transaction, where financial securities are issued against the cash flow generated from a pool of assets is called:

(A) Securitization

(B) Credit Default swaps

(C) Credit Linked Notes

(D) Total return swaps

121. To get book value per share, what numerator is divided by what denominator?

(i)Networth as numerator

(ii)Number of outstanding equity shares as denominator

(iii)Value of outstanding equity shares as numerator

(iv)Total assets as denominator

Choose the right combination

(A) (i) and (iii) (B) (i) and (ii)

(C) (ii) and (iv) (D) (iii) and(iv)

122. Which of the following are considered as capital components for the purpose of computing weighted average cost of capital?

(i)Common stock & Preferred stock

(ii)Short term loans from Banks

(iii)Commercial Papers

(iv)Long term Debt

Choose the right combination

(A) (i) & (ii) (B) (ii), (iii)& (iv)

(C) (i) & (iv) (D) (i), (ii) (iii) & (iv)

123. SEBI was established in:

(A)1993 (B)1992

(C)1988 (D) 1990

124. MRTP Act came into force in:

(A) 1969 (B) 1970

(C) 1971 (D) 1980

125. Managerial accounting information is generally prepared for

(A) Shareholders (B) Creditors

(C) Managers (D) Regulatory agencies

126. Managerial accounting information

(A) Relates to the entity as a whole and is highly aggregated

(B) Relates to sub-units of the entity and may be very detailed

(C) Is prepared only once a year

(D) is constrained by the requirements of generally accepted accounting principles

127. Which of the following is ***not*** an internal user of management information?

(A) Creditor (B) Department manager

(C) Controller (D) Treasurer

128. Managerial accounting does ***not*** encompass

(A) Calculating product cost

(B) Calculating earnings per share

(C) Determining cost behavior

(D) Profit planning

129. Management accounting is applicable to

(A) Service entities

(B) Manufacturing entities

(C) Not-for-profit entities

(D) All of these

130. Financial statements for external users can be described as

(A) User-specific (B) General-purpose

(C) Special-purpose (D) Management reports

131. Management accounting reports can be described as

(A) General-purpose

(B) Macro-reports

(C) Special-purpose

(D) Classified financial statements

132. The reporting standard for external financial reports is

(A) Industry-specific

(B) Company-specific

(C)Generally accepted accounting principles

(D) Department-specific

133. Internal reports are generally

(A) Aggregated (B) Detailed

(C) Regulated (D) Unreliable

134. The document of an organization that depicts authority relationships within the company is the

(A) Chart of accounts (B) Ledger

(C) Organization chart (D) Constitution

135. Which one of the following costs would ***not*** be included in inventory?

(A) Period costs (B) Prime costs

(C) Conversion costs(D) Indirect labour costs

136. Product costs consist of:

(A)Conversion costs and unexpired expenses

(B) Prime costs and manufacturing overhead

(C) Selling and administrative expenses

(D) Period costs

137. Product costs are also called:

(A) Direct cost (B) Prime cost

(C) Inventoriable cost (D) Capitalisable cost

138. Share capital of a company may be reduced by :

(A)A special resolution

(B)An ordinary resolution

(C)By the Company Law board's permission

(D)By the board of Director

139. Buffer Stock is built to cater to :

(A) Machine Breakdown

(B) Import Substitution

(C) Fluctuating load

(D) Diversification

140. The root cause of the current European Crisis is:

(A)Currency crisis

(B)Unsuitable Sovereign Debt

(C)Stagflation

(D)Overheatedness

141. Altman proposed a model of predicting:

(A)financial distress

(B)market failure

(C)high performance of firm

(D)insolvency of the firm

142. As per Pecking-Order theory, the first financing choice in order of preference is:

(A)Retained earnings

(B)Non-convertible debt

(C)Preference shares

(D)Equity

143. Which of the following approaches to dividend valuation assumes a constant non-growing dividend stream?

(A)Constant growth model

(B)Variable growth model

(C)Zero growth model

(D) Gordon model

144. Which is the correct sequence, if we arrange various sources of finance from costliest to cheapest in terms of their cost of capital?

(A)Equity, Retained earnings, Debt, Preference

(B) Retained earnings, Equity, Preference, Debt,

(C) Debt, Equity, Preference ,Retained earnings,

(D) Preference , Debt, Equity, Retained earnings

145. Which of the following is a non-DCF technique?

(A)PI (B) IRR

(C)NPV (D) ARR

146. Which is the correct equation that calculates P(Profit before tax) Assume seliing price per unit=Rs.S, variable cost per unit=Rs.V Number of units sold=U units and Total fixed costs=Rs. F.

(A)P=SV-F (B)P=U(S-V)-F

(C)P=FS-V (D)P=S(V-F)

147. When there is an official incease in exchange rate of the Indian rupee,then it is called:

(A)Appreciation (B)Deflation

(C)Depreciation (D)Revaluation

148. In case the company goes into liquidation,which of the following is repayable first?

(A)Equity capital

(B)Redeemable Preference Capital

(C)Cumulative preference capital

(D)Debentures

149. The basic objective of financial management is:

(A)Maximisation of profits

(B)Maximisation of shareholder's wealth

(C)Ensuring financial discipline in the organisation

(D)Ensuring returns to debenture-holders

150. Assume the following facts:

−Risk free return,rf=7.75%

−Beta,β=2

−Expected return of investors,r=16%

What will be the expected returns as per CAPM model?

(A) 4.125% (B) 16.00%

(C) 11.875% (D) 7.75%

151. The discount rate that makes NPV equal to zero is known as

(A) Benefit–Cost ratio

(B) Internal Rate of Return

(C) Discounted Pay-back period

(D) Profitability Index

152. Profit after tax is equal to

(A) PBIT– Interest and Dividend

(B) PBIT – Interest – Tax – Depreciation

(C) PBIT – Interest – Tax

(D) PBIT+ Interest

153. Match the following :

List – I	**List – II**
(i) Mercantilism	(a) France
(ii) Cameralism	(b) Spain
(iii) Physiocrats	(c) England
	(d) Germany

Code:

	(i)	(ii)	(iii)
(A)	(a)	(b)	(c)
(B)	(b)	(c)	(d)
(C)	(c)	(d)	(a)
(D)	(a)	(c)	(b)

154. Match the following :

Group – I:

(a) Debt Service Ratio

(b) Preference Dividend Coverage Ratio

(c) Cash to Debt Service Ratio

(d) Gross Profit Ratio

Group – II:

(i)Net income before charging interest and income tax Fixed Interest charges.

(ii)Net income after interest and Income Tax

Preference Dividend

(iii)Gross Profit x 100 Net Sales

(iv)Annual cash flow before interest and taxes Sinking Fund

	(a)	(b)	(c)	(d)
(A)	(i)	(ii)	(iv)	(iii)
(B)	(i)	(iv)	(iii)	(ii)
(C)	(ii)	(iii)	(iv)	(i)
(D)	(ii)	(iv)	(i)	(iii)

155. If you do ***not*** know the discount rate for a project, the right investment criterion to be used will be

(A) IRR (B) NPV

(C) ARR (D) All the above

156. The root cause of the current European Crisis is:

(A)Currency crisis

(B)Unsuitable Sovereign Debt

(C)Stagflation

(D)Overheatedness

157. As per Pecking-Order theory, the first financing choice in order of preference is:

(A)Retained earnings

(B)Non-convertible debt

(C)Preference shares

(D)Equity

158. Which of the following approaches to dividend valuation assumes a constant non-growing dividend stream?

(A)Constant growth model

(B)Variable growth model

(C)Zero growth model

(D) Gordon model

159. Which is the correct sequence, if we arrange various sources of finance from costliest to cheapest in terms of their cost of capital?

(A)Equity, Retained earnings, Debt, Preference

(B) Retained earnings, Equity, Preference, Debt,

(C) Debt, Equity, Preference ,Retained earnings,

(D) Preference, Debt, Equity, Retained earnings

160. Which of the following is a non-DCF technique?

(A)PI (B)IRR

(C)NPV (D)ARR

161. Which is the correct equation that calculates P(Profit before tax) Assume seliing price per unit=Rs.S, variable cost per unit=Rs.V Number of units sold=U units and Total fixed costs=Rs. F.

(A)P=SV-F (B)P=U(S-V)-F

(C)P=FS-V (D)P=S(V-F)

162. When there is an official incease in exchange rate of the Indian rupee,then it is called:

(A)Appreciation (B)Deflation

(C)Depreciation (D)Revaluation

163. In case the company goes into liquidation, which of the following is repayable first?

(A)Equity capital

(B)Redeemable Preference Capital

(C)Cumulative preference capital

(D)Debentures

164. The basic objective of financial management is:

(A)Maximisation of profits

(B)Maximisation of shareholder's wealth

(C)Ensuring financial discipline in the organisation

(D)Ensuring returns to debenture-holders

165. Assume the following facts:

−Risk free return,rf=7.75%

−Beta,β=2

−Expected return of investors,r=16%

What will be the expected returns as per CAPM model?

(A)4.125% (B)16.00%

(C)11.875% (D)7.75%

166. Consider the following statements

(i) Operational loss is a source of funds

(ii) Decrease in working capital is source of funds

(iii) Additions to fixed assets are application of funds

(iv)Introduction of fresh capital is an application of funds

Which of the above statements are applicable while preparing the funds flow statement?

(A) (i) and (ii) (B) (i) and (iii)

(C) (ii) and (iii) (D) (i), (iii) and (iv)

167. The improvement in the value of the objective function per unit increase in a right-hand side is the

(A) Sensitivity value (B) shadow price.

(C) Slack value. (D) Constraint coefficient

168. If coupon rate=required rate, the value of the bond would be equal to its:

(A)par value (B)redemption value

(C)issued value (D)YTM

169. Cash-reserve-ratio refers to

(A)A ratio between the liquid cash to be maintained by a commercial bank with that of total deposits of the bank.

(B) A ratio between the total deposits with that of liquid cash maintained by a bank.

(C) The % of total deposits to the % of cash that must be invested by a bank as per instructions of the central bank of the country.

(D) The % of liquid cash to be maintained by a bank with that of its investment.

170. Income and Expenditure Account of non-profit organization is a

(A) Real Account

(B) Nominal Account

(C) Personal Account

(D) Representative Personal Account

171. The pay - back period refers to :

(A)The number of years a project takes to recover its investment (original) cost.

(B)The number of instalments to make payment.

(C) The time - lag between investment and commissioning of the Project.

(D) The time required to attain break – even point.

172. Capital budgeting decisions are generally :

(A) Irreversible (B) Reversible

(C) Irrevocable (D) Revocable

173. "The optimal pay-out ratio for growth firm is nil and declining firm is 100%" is established by

(A) Gordon model (B) Walter model

(C) Both (A) and (B) (D) None of the above

174. Cash-reserve-ratio refers to

(A)A ratio between the liquid cash to be maintained by a commercial bank with that of total deposits of the bank

(B)A ratio between the total deposits with that of liquid cash maintained by a bank

(C)The % of total deposits to the % of cash that must be invested by a bank as per instructions of the central bank of the country

(D)The % of liquid cash to be maintained by a bank with that of its investment

175. The pay - back period refers to :

(A)The number of years a project takes to recover its investment (original) cost

(B)The number of instalments to make payment

(C)The time - lag between investment and commissioning of the Project

(D)The time required to attain break - even point

176. Capital budgeting decisions are generally:

(A) Irreversible (B) Reversible

(C) Irrevocable (D) Revocable

177. "The optimal pay-out ratio for growth firm is nil and declining firm is 100%" is established by:

(A)Gordon model (B) Walter model

(C)Both (A) and (B) (D) None of the above

178. The payment of an account payable would:

(A)Increase owner's equity

(B)Increase net assets

(C)Have no effect on net assets

(D)Have no effect on total assets

179. The balance in the capital account after all closing entries have been posted is:

(A)Equal to net income or loss for the period

(B)The same as the balance of the account on the work sheet

(C)The balance that will appear on the balance sheet

(D)Always more than the balance of the account on the work sheet

180. Under which of the following method the time value of money is ***not*** considered?

(A) Net present value method

(B) Internal rate of return method

(C) Payback period method

(D) All of the above

181. If r<k, the payout of dividend should be 100% according to:

(A)Modigliani-Miller (B)Walter

(C)Du-Pont (D)Ezra Solomen

182. Present value of annuity is calculated by discounting it by:

(A)Cost of Capital (B)IRR

(C)Zero coupon rate (D)YTM

183. Match the pair for the following and indicate the correct option:

List-I

(a) Constant growth

(b) Profitability index

(c) Modigliani-Miller approach

(d) Leveraged buyout

List-II

(i) Capital Budgeting Technique

(ii) Capital Structure Theory

(iii)Corporate Restructuring

(iv)Share valuation model

	(a)	(b)	(c)	(d)
(A)	(i)	(ii)	(iii)	(iv)
(B)	(ii)	(iii)	(iv)	(i)
(C)	(iii)	(ii)	(i)	(iv)
(D)	(iv)	(i)	(ii)	(iii)

184. Penetration pricing of a product of a firm implies:

(A)low initial price followed by a high price

(B)high initial price followed by a low price

(C)moderate price of a product

(D)fluctuating price of a product

185. In determining the adjusted present value, tax shields on financing effects are discounted at:

(A) Opportunity cost of equity

(B) Marginal cost of debt

(C) Weighted average cost of debt

(D) Average of A and B above

---000---

UNIT-V

FINANCIAL MANAGEMENT

1. (D) Social responsibility

Explanation: Functions of Financial Management

1. Estimation of capital requirements: A finance manager has to make estimation with regards to capital requirements of the company. This will depend upon expected costs and profits and future programmes and policies of a concern. Estimations have to be made in an adequate manner which increases earning capacity of enterprise.

2. Determination of capital composition: Once the estimation have been made, the capital structure have to be decided. This involves short- term and long- term debt equity analysis. This will depend upon the proportion of equity capital a company is possessing and additional funds which have to be raised from outside parties.

3. Choice of sources of funds: For additional funds to be procured, a company has many choices like:

- Issue of shares and debentures
- Loans to be taken from banks and financial institutions
- Public deposits to be drawn like in form of bonds.
- Choice of factor will depend on relative merits and demerits of each source and period of financing.

4. Investment of funds: The finance manager has to decide to allocate funds into profitable ventures so that there is safety on investment and regular returns is possible.

5. Disposal of surplus: The net profits decision have to be made by the finance manager.

6. Dividend declaration: It includes identifying the rate of dividends and other benefits like bonus.

7. Retained profits: The volume has to be decided which will depend upon expansional, innovational, diversification plans of the company.

8. Management of cash: Finance manager has to make decisions with regards to cash management. Cash is required for many purposes like payment of wages and salaries, payment of electricity and water bills, payment to creditors, meeting current liabilities, maintenance of enough stock, purchase of raw materials, etc.

9. Financial controls: The finance manager has not only to plan, procure and utilize the funds but he also has to exercise control over finances. This can be done through many techniques like ratio analysis, financial forecasting, cost and profit control, etc.

2. (A)Maximizing the profit

Explanation: Financial management:

- Financial Management means planning, organizing, directing and controlling the financial activities such as procurement and utilization of funds of the enterprise.
- The financial management is generally concerned with procurement, allocation and control of financial resources of a concern.
- The financial management means to collect finance for the company at a low cost and to use this collected finance for earning maximum profits.
- Thus, financial management means to plan and control the finance of the company. It is done to achieve the objectives of the company.

3. (B)Maximization of Shareholders Wealth

Explanation: Objectives of Financial Management:

- To ensure regular and adequate supply of funds to the concern.
- ***To ensure adequate returns to the shareholders:*** which will depend upon the

earning capacity, market price of the share, expectations of the shareholders.

- ***To ensure optimum funds utilization:*** Once the funds are procured, they should be utilized in maximum possible way at least cost.
- ***To ensure safety on investment***, i.e, funds should be invested in safe ventures so that adequate rate of return can be achieved.
- ***To plan a sound capital structure:***-There should be sound and fair composition of capital so that a balance is maintained between debt and equity capital.

4. (C)Maximise the wealth of Equity shareholders

Explanation:

- The goal of financial management is to maximize the current value per share of the existing stock.
- Maximize the market value of the existing owners' equity.

5. (A)Wealth maximization

6. (B) Wealth Maximization objective

Explanation:

- **Dr. S. N. Maheshwari:** "Financial management is concerned with raising financial resources and their effective utilisation towards achieving the organisational goals."
- **Richard A. Brealey:** "Financial management is the process of putting the available funds to the best advantage from the long term point of view of business objectives."

7. (D) All of the above

8. (A) Cost of production

Explanation: Financial Engineering:

- The use of mathematical techniques to solve financial problems.
- Financial engineering uses tools and knowledge from the fields of computer science, statistics, economics and applied mathematics to address current financial issues as well as to devise new and innovative financial products.
- Financial engineering is sometimes referred to as quantitative analysis and is used by regular commercial banks, investment banks, insurance agencies and hedge funds.
- Financial engineering is a multidisciplinary field involving financial theory, the methods of engineering, the tools of mathematics and the practice of programming.

9. (A) (ii) and (iv)

Explanation: Tax shield:

- A reduction in taxable income for an individual or corporation achieved through claiming allowable deductions such as mortgage interest, medical expenses, charitable donations, amortization and depreciation. These deductions reduce taxpayers' taxable income for a given year or defer income taxes into future years.
- Tax shields vary from country to country, and their benefits will depend on the taxpayer's overall tax rate and cash flows for the given tax year.
- A taxes shield is the reduction in income taxes that results from taking an allowable deduction from taxable income.
- For example, because interest on debt is a tax-deductible expense, taking on debt creates a tax shield.
- Since a tax shield is a way to save cash flows, it increases the value of the business, and it is an important aspect of business valuation.

10.(B) Option

Explanation:

- Financial derivatives are financial instruments that are linked to a specific financial instrument or indicator or commodity, and through which specific financial risks can be traded in financial markets in their own right.
- Transactions in financial derivatives should be treated as separate transactions rather than as

integral parts of the value of underlying transactions to which they may be linked.

- The value of a financial derivative derives from the price of an underlying item, such as an asset or index. Unlike debt instruments, no principal amount is advanced to be repaid and no investment income accrues.
- Financial derivatives are used for a number of purposes including risk management, hedging, arbitrage between markets, and speculation.
- A security whose price is dependent upon or derived from one or more underlying assets.
- The derivative itself is merely a contract between two or more parties.
- Its value is determined by fluctuations in the underlying asset.
- ***The most common underlying assets include stocks, bonds, commodities, currencies, interest rates and market indexes.***
- Most derivatives are characterized by high leverage.

11. (D)E-Commerce increases the net cost per contact.

Explanation: E-Commerce

- E-Commerce is business transactions on the Web.
- **Benefits of E-Commerce:**
    - Overcome Geographical Limitations
    - Gain New Customers With Search Engine Visibility
    - Lower Costs
    - Locate the Product Quicker
    - Eliminate Travel Time and Cost
    - Provide Comparison Shopping
    - Enable Deals, Bargains, Coupons, and Group Buying
    - Provide Abundant Information
    - Create Targeted Communication
    - Remain Open All the Time
    - Create Markets for Niche Products.

12.(B) Direct marketing

13.(C)Volatility of interest rates, currency rates, commodities prices and stock prices

Explanation: Financial risk

- The probability of loss inherent in financing methods which may impair the ability to provide adequate return.
- The possibility that shareholders will lose money when they invest in a company that has debt, if the company's cash flow proves inadequate to meet its financial obligations. When a company uses debt financing, its creditors will be repaid before its shareholders if the company becomes insolvent.
- Financial risk also refers to the possibility of a corporation or government defaulting on its bonds, which would cause those bondholders to lose money.

14. (B) Bombay

15. (B)Safeguard the interest of investors

Explanation:

Objective of Stock Exchange:

- Stock Exchange in any country serve one basic objective That is Funding to companies listed on that stock exchange.
- Companies float their IPOs on exchange and in return give buyers right of ownership and annual dividends(sometimes twice a year).
- Companies sell their right of ownership to traders/investors/FIIs etc and in return generates capital for their companies.
- Stock Exchanges also attract lots of FIIs which is good for country economy.

16.(A)Bull speculator to bear speculator

Explanation:

- **Contango:** A situation where the futures price of a commodity is above the expected future spot price.
- Contango refers to a situation where the future spot price is below the current price, and people are willing to pay more for a commodity at some point in the future than the actual expected price of the commodity.
- This may be due to people's desire to pay a premium to have the commodity in the future

rather than paying the costs of storage and carry costs of buying the commodity today.

17.(C) (ii) and (iv)

18.(B) Balance of Payments

Explanation: Balance Of Trade (BOT):

- The difference between a country's imports and its exports. Balance of trade is the largest component of a country's balance of payments.
- Debit items include imports, foreign aid, domestic spending abroad and domestic investments abroad.
- Credit items include exports, foreign spending in the domestic economy and foreign investments in the domestic economy.
- A country has a trade deficit if it imports more than it exports; the opposite scenario is a trade surplus.
- It is also referred to as "trade balance" or "international trade balance."

The balance of payments (BOP):

- It is the method countries use to monitor all international monetary transactions at a specific period of time.
- Usually, the BOP is calculated every quarter and every calendar year. All trades conducted by both the private and public sectors are accounted for in the BOP in order to determine how much money is going in and out of a country.
- If a country has received money, this is known as a credit, and if a country has paid or given money, the transaction is counted as a debit.
- Theoretically, the BOP should be zero, meaning that assets (credits) and liabilities (debits) should balance, but in practice this is rarely the case.
- Thus, the BOP can tell the observer if a country has a deficit or a surplus and from which part of the economy the discrepancies are stemming.

Current Account:

- The difference between a nation's total exports of goods, services and transfers, and its total imports of them.
- Current account balance calculations exclude transactions in financial assets and liabilities.

Capital Account:

- A national account that shows the net change in asset ownership for a nation.
- The capital account is the net result of public and private international investments flowing in and out of a country.
- It may also refer to an account showing the net worth of a business at a specific point in time.

19.(D) Monetized Deficit

Explanation: Budget Deficit:

- A financial situation that occurs when an entity has more money going out than coming in.
- The term "budget deficit" is most commonly used to refer to government spending rather than business or individual spending.
- When it refers to federal government spending, a budget deficit is also known as the "national debt."
- The opposite of a budget deficit is a budget surplus, and when inflows are equal to outflows, the budget is said to be balanced.

Revenue Deficit:

- When the net amount received (revenues less expenditures) falls short of the projected net amount to be received.
- This occurs when the actual amount of revenue received and/or the actual amount of expenditures do not correspond with predicted revenue and expenditure figures.
- This is the opposite of a revenue surplus, which occurs when the actual amount exceeds the projected amount.

Fiscal Deficit:

- When a government's total expenditures exceed the revenue that it generates (excluding money from borrowings).

- Deficit differs from debt, which is an accumulation of yearly deficits.

Monetized Deficit:

- Monetized deficit is when the government prints money to pay down the deficit.

20.(B)Can maintain their proportional ownership by purchasing additional equity shares issued by firm

Explanation:

- The right of current shareholders to maintain their fractional ownership of a company by buying a proportional number of shares of any future issue of common stock.
- Most states consider preemptive rights valid only if made explicit in a corporation's charter.
- It is also called subscription privilege or subscription right.

Preemptive Right:

- A privilege extended to select shareholders of a corporation that will give them the right to purchase additional shares in the company before the general public has the opportunity in the event there is a seasoned offering.
- A preemptive right is written in the contract between the purchaser and the company, but does not function like a put option.
- It is also known as "preemption rights".

21.(C) Retailer

Explanation: Merchant Middleman:

- Merchant middleman buys and sells goods at a profit. They undertake ownership and possession of goods and deal in their own names. They work for profit and bear the risks of trade.
- Merchant middlemen include wholesalers and retailers. In other words, the home trade of a country consists of wholesale trade and retail trade.

22.(A) Coupon rate is greater than required return

Explanation: Bond:

- A debt investment in which an investor loans money to an entity (corporate or governmental) that borrows the funds for a defined period of time at a fixed interest rate.
- Bonds are used by companies, municipalities, states and U.S. and foreign governments to finance a variety of projects and activities.
- Bonds are commonly referred to as fixed-income securities and are one of the three main asset classes, along with stocks and cash equivalents.

23. (B) (ii) (iv) (i) (iii)

24.(D)Debt is risky for the firm, while equity is risky for investors

25. (D) Book-keeping entry only

Explanation: Special Drawing Rights (SDR):

- An international type of monetary reserve currency, created by the International Monetary Fund (IMF) in 1969, which operates as a supplement to the existing reserves of member countries.
- Created in response to concerns about the limitations of gold and dollars as the sole means of settling international accounts, SDRs are designed to augment international liquidity by supplementing the standard reserve currencies.
- Also called paper gold, an SDR is neither paper nor gold but an accounting entry.
- It is not backed by any currency or precious metal, and is used only among governments and IMF for balance Of payments settlements.

26.(C) Circulation of Money

Explanation: Gresham's Law:

- A monetary principle stating that "bad money drives out good."
- In currency valuation, Gresham's Law states that if a new coin ("bad money") is assigned the same face value as an older coin

containing a higher amount of precious metal ("good money"), then the new coin will be used in circulation while the old coin will be hoarded and will disappear from circulation.

27.(A) Under valued

Explanation: Intrinsic Value:

- The actual value of a security, as opposed to its market price or book value.
- The intrinsic value includes other variables such as brand name, trademarks, and copyrights that are often dificult to calculate and sometimes not accurately reflected in the market price.
- One way to look at it is that the market capitalization is the price (i.e. what investors are willing to pay for the company) and intrinsic value is the value (i.e. what the company is really worth).
- Different investors use different techniques to calculate intrinsic value.
- The amount by which a call option is in the money, calculated by taking the difference between the strike price and the market price of the underlier.
- The amount by which a put option is in the money, calculated by taking the difference between the strike price and the market price of the underlier.

28.(D)Early-cash recovery pricing

Explanation:

Penetration Pricing:

- A marketing strategy used by firms to attract customers to a new product or service.
- Penetration pricing is the practice of offering a low price for a new product or service during its initial offering in order to attract customers away from competitors.
- The reasoning behind this marketing strategy is that customers will buy and become aware of the new product due to its lower price in the marketplace relative to rivals.

Going-rate-pricing:

- Setting a price for a product or service using the prevailing market price as a basis.
- Going rate pricing is a common practice with homogeneous products with very little variation from one producer to another, such as aluminum or steel.
- All firms do have the power to fix a price, but instead of doing so, in a competitive market situation firms fix a price which is equal to the average price charged by all firms in an industry, ie,it collects all the prices firms with same product and compute the average.

Perceived-value-pricing:

- The valuation of good or service according to how much consumers are willing to pay for it, rather than upon its production and delivery costs.
- Using a perceived value pricing technique might be somewhat arbitrary, but it can greatly assist in the effective marketing of a product since it sets product pricing in line with its perceived value by potential buyers.

Early cash recovery:

- Frequently, especially for the small firm, long-term sales and profits must give way to the more immediate problem of economic survival.
- When this occurs, you can establish a lower price on one or more of the firm's products that will result in rapid recovery of cash.

29.(A)Negotiated source of finance

Explanation: Trade Credit:

- An agreement where a customer can purchase goods on account (without paying cash), paying the supplier at a later date.
- Usually when the goods are delivered, a trade credit is given for a specific amount of days - 30, 60 or 90.
- Jewelry businesses sometimes extend credit to 180 days or longer.
- Basically, this is a credit a company gives to another for the purchase of goods and services.

30.(A) Wherein the acceptance of one proposal leads to rejection of all other proposals

Explanation: Mutually exclusive investment proposals

- If a firm is evaluating two mutually exclusive investment proposals whose lives are both unequal and shorter than the firm's production horizon, the firm should:
  - extend the investment's lives to equal the production horizon
  - evaluate the investment's cash flows only over the life of the shorter lived investment
  - Evaluate the investment's cash flows over the life of the longer-lived investment.

31.(C) (b) (a) (d) (c)

32.(C) Balance of current account + Balance of capital account +Statistical discrepancy

Explanation: Balance Of Payments (BOP):

- A record of all transactions made between one particular country and all other countries during a specified period of time.
- BOP compares the dollar difference of the amount of exports and imports, including all financial exports and imports.
- A negative balance of payments means that more money is flowing out of the country than coming in, and vice versa.

33. (B) Marginal revenue

Explanation:

Incremental Revenue :

- It is the increase of revenue between new revenue and previous revenue.

Incremental Revenue = New Revenue - Previous Revenue

- The additional revenues from an additional quantity.
- It is similar to marginal revenue, except that marginal revenue refers to the revenue from the next unit.
- Incremental revenue might be the additional revenues from the next 200 units.

Marginal Revenue (MR):

- The increase in revenue that results from the sale of one additional unit of output.
- Marginal revenue is calculated by dividing the change in total revenue by the change in output quantity.
- While marginal revenue can remain constant over a certain level of output, it follows the law of diminishing returns and will eventually slow down, as the output level increases.
- Perfectly competitive firms continue producing output until marginal revenue equals marginal cost.

Total revenue:

- The overall measure of all sources of a company's income, including its sales, for a given period of time.
- This number is not the same as the profits or the earnings of the company.
- Total revenue is calculated by multiplying the price of the product sold by the quantity sold. PQ = R.
- Total profit is total revenue minus costs incurred. R-C = P

Average Revenue Per Unit (ARPU):

- A measure of the revenue generated per user or unit.
- Average revenue per unit allows for the analysis of a company's revenue generation and growth at the per-unit level, which can help investors to identify which products are high or low revenue-generators.

34.(B)Uses cost of capital as discount factor.

35. (D) Dividend pay-out ratio, required return and expected growth rate

36. (D) (i), (ii)and (iv) are correct.

37. (A)Present values of all the cash flows expected to occur over the life of a project

Explanation:

- The difference between the present value of cash inflows and the present value of cash outflows. NPV is used in capital budgeting to analyze the profitability of an investment or project.
- NPV analysis is sensitive to the reliability of future cash inflows that an investment or project will yield.
- Formula:

$$NPV = \sum_{t=1}^{T} \frac{C_t}{(1+r)^t} - C_0$$

- In finance, the net present value (NPV) or net present worth (NPW) of a time series of cash flows, both incoming and outgoing, is defined as the sum of the present values (PVs) of the individual cash flows of the same entity.
- In the case when all future cash flows are incoming (such as coupons and principal of a bond) and the only outflow of cash is the purchase price, the NPV is simply the PV of future cash flows minus the purchase price (which is its own PV).
- NPV is a central tool in discounted cash flow (DCF) analysis and is a standard method for using the time value of money to appraise long-term projects.
- Used for capital budgeting and widely used throughout economics, finance, and accounting, it measures the excess or shortfall of cash flows, in present value terms, above the cost of funds.
- NPV can be described as the "difference amount" between the sums of discounted: cash inflows and cash outflows.
- It compares the present value of money today to the present value of money in the future, taking inflation and returns into account.
- The NPV of a sequence of cash flows takes as input the cash flows and a discount rate or discount curve and outputs a price; the converse process in DCF analysis — taking a sequence of cash flows and a price as input and inferring as output a discount rate (the discount rate which would yield the given price as NPV) — is called the yield and is more widely used in bond trading.

38. (C)Initial Investment cost/Annual cash inflows

Explanation: Payback period:

- It is the time in which the initial cash outflow of an investment is expected to be recovered from the cash inflows generated by the investment.
- It is one of the simplest investment appraisal techniques.
- The formula to calculate payback period of a project depends on whether the cash flow per period from the project is even or uneven.
- In case they are even, the formula to calculate payback period is:

Payback Period =
Initial Investment/Cash Inflow per Period

- When cash inflows are uneven, we need to calculate the cumulative net cash flow for each period and then use the following formula for payback period:

- Payback Period = A +B/C

  In the above formula,

  A is the last period with a negative cumulative cash flow;

  B is the absolute value of cumulative cash flow at the end of the period A;

  C is the total cash flow during the period after A

- **Decision Rule:** Accept the project only if its payback period is LESS than the target payback period.

39.(C)The Net Present Value is zero

Explanation: Internal rate of return (IRR):

- It is the rate of growth that a project or investment is expected to create, expressed as a percentage, over a specified term.
- IRR is, in essence, the theoretical interest rate earned by the project, which makes it handy when comparing one investment opportunity to another.
- The higher the IRR the greater the value of the project.
- Technically, IRR is the discount rate that generates a net present value of ***zero*** for a series of future cash flows.
- One of the disadvantages of the IRR calculation is that it presumes that all cash flows will be reinvested in the projection at the same rate.
- Internal rate of return (IRR) is the interest rate at which the net present value of all the cash flows (both positive and negative) from a project or investment equal zero.
- Internal rate of return is used to evaluate the attractiveness of a project or investment. If the IRR of a new project exceeds a company's required rate of return, that project is desirable. If IRR falls below the required rate of return, the project should be rejected.
- The internal rate of return (IRR) or economic rate of return (ERR) is a rate of return used in capital budgeting to measure and compare the profitability of investments.
- It is also called the discounted cash flow rate of return (DCFROR) or the rate of return (ROR).
- In the context of savings and loans the IRR is also called the effective interest rate. The term internal refers to the fact that its calculation does not incorporate environmental factors (e.g., the interest rate or inflation).

40.(B) Risk

Explanation:

- ***Beta*** is a historical measure of volatility. Beta measures how an asset (i.e. a stock, an ETF, or portfolio) moves versus a benchmark (i.e. an index).
- ***Alpha*** is a historical measure of an asset's return on investment compared to the risk adjusted expected return.
- A beta of 1.0 implies a positive correlation (correlation measures direction, not volatility) where the asset moves in the same direction and the same percentage as the benchmark.
- A beta of -1 implies a negative correlation where the asset moves in the opposite direction but equal in volatility to the benchmark.
- A beta of zero implies no correlation between the assets.
- Any beta above zero would imply a positive correlation with volatility expressed by how much over zero the number is.
- Any beta below zero would imply a negative correlation with volatility expressed by how much under zero the number is.
- For example a beta of 2.0 or -2.0 would imply volatility twice the benchmark. A beta of 0.5 or -0.5 implies volatility one-half the benchmark.

41.(B) Purchase power parity

Explanation: Inflation adjustment or deflation:

- Inflation adjustment or deflation is accomplished by dividing a monetary time series by a price index, such as the Consumer Price Index (CPI).
- The deflated series is then said to be measured in "constant dollars," whereas the original series was measured in "nominal dollars" or "current dollars."
- Inflation-adjustment is not always necessary when dealing with monetary variables--sometimes it is simpler to forecast the data in nominal terms or to use a logarithm transformation for stabilizing the variance--but it is an important tool in the toolkit for analyzing economic data.

Purchasing power parity (PPP):

- It is an economic theory and a technique used to determine the relative value of currencies, estimating the amount of adjustment needed on the exchange rate between countries in order for the exchange to be equivalent to (or on par with) each currency's purchasing power.

Interest rate parity:

- A theory in which the interest rate differential between two countries is equal to the differential between the forward exchange rate and the spot exchange rate.
- Interest rate parity plays an essential role in foreign exchange markets, connecting interest rates, spot exchange rates and foreign exchange rates.
- Interest rate parity is a no-arbitrage condition representing an equilibrium state under which investors will be indifferent to interest rates available on bank deposits in two countries.

Transaction Exposure:

- The risk, faced by companies involved in international trade, that currency exchange rate will change after the companies have already entered into financial obligations.
- Such exposure to fluctuating exchange rates can lead to major losses for firms.

42.(B)AS - 14

43. (B) Lessee

Explanation:

- A lease considered to have the economic characteristics of asset ownership.
- A capital lease would be considered a purchased asset for accounting purposes.
- An operating lease, on the other hand, would be handled as a true lease, or rental, for accounting purposes.
- The choice of lease classification will have important results on a firm's financial statements. A lease falls into this category if any of the following requirements are met:

1. The life of the lease is 75% or greater of the assets useful life.

2. The lease contains a purchase agreement for less than market value.

3. The lessee gains ownership at the end of the lease period.

4. The present value of lease payments is greater than 90% of the asset's market value.

- A finance lease or capital lease is a type of lease. It is a commercial arrangement where:
  1. the lessee (customer or borrower) will select an asset (equipment, vehicle, software);
  2. the lessor (finance company) will purchase that asset;
  3. the lessee will have use of that asset during the lease;
  4. the lessee will pay a series of rentals or installments for the use of that asset;
  5. the lessor will recover a large part or all of the cost of the asset plus earn interest from the rentals paid by the lessee;
  6. the lessee has the option to acquire ownership of the asset (e.g. paying the last rental, or bargain option purchase price);
- The finance company is the legal owner of the asset during duration of the lease.

44.(B)Rights issue

Explanation:

Public offer:

- The sale of equity shares or other financial instruments by an organization to the public in order to raise funds for business expansion and investment.
- Public offerings of corporate securities in the U.S. must be registered with and approved by the SEC and are normally conducted by an investment underwriter.

Rights Offering (Issue):

- An issue of rights to a company's existing shareholders that entitles them to buy additional shares directly from the company in proportion to their existing holdings, within a fixed time period.

- In a rights offering, the subscription price at which each share may be purchased in generally at a discount to the current market price. Rights are often transferable, allowing the holder to sell them on the open market.

Book building:

- The process by which an underwriter attempts to determine at what price to offer an IPO based on demand from institutional investors.

45. (C)Debt+Share

Explanation:

- A bond that can be converted into a predetermined amount of the company's equity at certain times during its life, usually at the discretion of the bondholder.
- Issuing convertible bonds is one way for a company to minimize negative investor interpretation of its corporate actions.
- For example, if an already public company chooses to issue stock, the market usually interprets this as a sign that the company's share price is somewhat overvalued. To avoid this negative impression, the company may choose to issue convertible bonds, which bondholders will likely convert to equity anyway should the company continue to do well.
- Convertible bonds are most often issued by companies with a low credit rating and high growth potential.

46.(C)Stakeholders

Explanation:

- The system of rules, practices and processes by which a company is directed and controlled.
- Corporate governance essentially involves balancing the interests of the many stakeholders in a company - these include its shareholders, management, customers, suppliers, financiers, government and the community. Since corporate governance also provides the framework for attaining a company's objectives, it encompasses practically every sphere of management, from action plans and internal controls to performance measurement and corporate disclosure.
- Corporate governance refers to the system by which corporations are directed and controlled.
- The governance structure specifies the distribution of rights and responsibilities among different participants in the corporation (such as the board of directors, managers, shareholders, creditors, auditors, regulators, and other stakeholders) and specifies the rules and procedures for making decisions in corporate affairs.
- Governance provides the structure through which corporations set and pursue their objectives, while reflecting the context of the social, regulatory and market environment.
- Governance is a mechanism for monitoring the actions, policies and decisions of corporations.
- Governance involves the alignment of interests among the stakeholders.

47.(B)Par value

Explanation:

Coupon rate:

- The yield paid by a fixed income security.
- A fixed income security's coupon rate is simply just the annual coupon payments paid by the issuer relative to the bond's face or par value.
- The coupon rate is the yield the bond paid on its issue date.
- This yield, however, will change as the value of the bond changes, thus giving the bond's yield to maturity.

Par value:

- Par value is the face value of a bond.
- A dollar amount that is assigned to a security when representing the value contributed for each share in cash or goods.

Maturity value:

- The amount that will be received at the time a security is redeemed at its maturity.
- For most securities, maturity value equals par value.

Market value:

- It is the price at which an asset would trade in a competitive auction setting.
- Market value is often used interchangeably with open market value, fair value or fair market value, although these terms have distinct definitions in different standards, and may differ in some circumstances.
- The current quoted price at which investors buy or sell a share of common stock or a bond at a given time. Also known as "market price."
- The market capitalization plus the market value of debt. Sometimes referred to as "total market value."

48.(A)Negotiated source of finance

Explanation: Trade credit:

- Trade credit is an agreement where a customer can purchase goods on account (without paying cash), paying the supplier at a later date.
- Usually when the goods are delivered, a trade credit is given for a specific amount of days - 30, 60 or 90.

49.(D) that makes the NPV of capital proposal almost zero

Explanation:

- The discount rate often used in capital budgeting that makes the net present value of all cash flows from a particular project equal to zero.
- The higher a project's internal rate of return, the more desirable it is to undertake the project.
- As such, IRR can be used to rank several prospective projects a firm is considering. Assuming all other factors are equal among the various projects, the project with the highest IRR would probably be considered the best and undertaken first.
- IRR is sometimes referred to as "economic rate of return (ERR)."

50.(A)Wherein the acceptance of one proposal leads to rejection of all other proposals

Explanation: Mutually exclusive investment proposals:

- If a firm is evaluating two mutually exclusive investment proposals whose lives are both unequal and shorter than the firm's production horizon, the firm should:
  1. extend the investment's lives to equal the production horizon.
  2. evaluate the investment's cash flows only over the life of the shorter lived investment.
  3. evaluate the investment's cash flows over the life of the longer-lived investment.

51.(C)will reduce

52.(B)conditional probabilities

53. (C) Junk bond

Explanation:

Income Bond:

- A type of debt security in which only the face value of the bond is promised to be paid to the investor, with any coupon payments being paid only if the issuing company has enough earnings to pay for the coupon payment.

Subordinated debentures:

- A loan (or security) that ranks below other loans (or securities) with regard to claims on assets or earnings.
- It is also known as a "junior security" or "subordinated loan." Subordinated debenture (also known as subordinated loan, subordinated bond, subordinated debt or junior debt) is debt which ranks after other debts should a company fall into receivership or be closed.

- Such debt is referred to as subordinate, because the debt providers (the lenders) have subordinate status in relationship to the normal debt.
- Subordinated debenture has a lower priority than other bonds of the issuer in case of liquidation during bankruptcy, below the liquidator, government tax authorities and senior debt holders in the hierarchy of creditors. Because subordinated debenture is repayable after other debts have been paid, they are more risky for the lender of the money.

Junk bond:

- A colloquial term for a high-yield or non-investment grade bond. Junk bonds are fixed-income instruments that carry a rating of 'BB' or lower by Standard & Poor's, or 'Ba' or below by Moody's. Junk bonds are so called because of their higher default risk in relation to investment-grade bonds.

Serial bond:

- A bond issue in which a portion of the outstanding bonds matures at regular intervals until eventually all of the bonds have matured.
- As they mature gradually over a period of years, these bonds are used to finance a project providing regular, level or predictable income streams.
- Serial bonds are also used to finance projects with regular, level debt payments such as residential developments.

54.(B) Payback period

Explanation: Accounting Rate of Return (ARR):

- The amount of profit, or return, that an individual can expect based on an investment made.
- Accounting rate of return divides the average profit by the initial investment in order to get the ratio or return that can be expected.
- This allows an investor or business owner to easily compare the profit potential for projects, products and investments.
- The length of time required to recover the cost of an investment.

The payback period:

- The payback period of a given investment or project is an important determinant of whether to undertake the position or project, as longer payback periods are typically not desirable for investment positions. Calculated as:

Payback Period = Cost of Project ÷ Annual Cash Inflows.

Internal rate of return:

- The discount rate often used in capital budgeting that makes the net present value of all cash flows from a particular project equal to zero.
- Generally speaking, the higher a project's internal rate of return, the more desirable it is to undertake the project.
- As such, IRR can be used to rank several prospective projects a firm is considering. Assuming all other factors are equal among the various projects, the project with the highest IRR would probably be considered the best and undertaken first.
- IRR is sometimes referred to as "economic rate of return (ERR)."

Net present value:

- The difference between the present value of cash inflows and the present value of cash outflows.
- NPV is used in capital budgeting to analyze the profitability of an investment or project.
- NPV analysis is sensitive to the reliability of future cash inflows that an investment or project will yield.

55.(C) Higher P/E multiples

Explanation: Price-Earnings Ratio(P/E Ratio):

- A valuation ratio of a company's current share price compared to its per-share earnings.
- Calculated as:

$$\text{P/E Ratio} = \frac{\text{Market Value per Share}}{\text{Earnings per Share (EPS)}}$$

- EPS is usually from the last four quarters (trailing P/E), but sometimes it can be taken from the estimates of earnings expected in the next four quarters (projected or forward P/E).

56.(B) These bonds are sold at a discounted value and on maturity face value of the bond is paid to the investors

Explanation: Deep-Discount Bond:

- A bond that sells at a significant discount from par value.
- A bond that is selling at a discount from par value and has a coupon rate significantly less than the prevailing rates of fixed-income securities with a similar risk profile.

57.(B)EBITEBT

Explanation:

- Financial leverage can be defined as the degree to which a company uses fixed-income securities, such as debt and preferred equity.
- With a high degree of financial leverage come high interest payments.
- As a result, the bottom-line earnings per share is negatively affected by interest payments.
- As interest payments increase as a result of increased financial leverage, EPS is driven lower.
- As mentioned previously, financial risk is the risk to the stockholders that is caused by an increase in debt and preferred equities in a company's capital structure.
- As a company increases debt and preferred equities, interest payments increase, reducing EPS.
- As a result, risk to stockholder return is increased.
- A company should keep its optimal capital structure in mind when making financing decisions to ensure any increases in debt and preferred equity increase the value of the company.

Degree of Financial Leverage:

- This measures the percentage change in earnings per share over the percentage change in EBIT. This is known as "degree of financial leverage" (DFL).
- It is the measure of the sensitivity of EPS to changes in EBIT as a result of changes in debt.
- **Formula:**

DFL= % Change in EPS or
EBIT÷%Change in EBIT-Interest

- A shortcut to keep in mind with DFL is that, if interest is 0, then the DLF will be equal to 1.

58.(A) Market price of equity share is maximum

59.(C) (c) (d) (b) (a)

60. (C) (c) (a) (b) (d)

61. (B) (d) (a) (c) (b)

62. (C) Establish credit status, check credit limit, issue delivery note, goods deliver, invoice raised

63. (C) Rs 537.00

Explanation:

Theoritical price of 3 month ABB Ltd. Future is;

Spot + Cost of Carry – Dividend

= 520 + 520 × 0.15 × 0.25 – 2.50 (25% of FV Rs. 10)

= 520 + 19.50 – 2.50

= Rs 537.

64.(B) 22.55%

Explanation:

R2 = [1/1 – Initial Expenses (%) R1] + Recurring Expenses (%)

Where R2 = Mutual Fund earnings

R1 = Personal earnings of Ms. Rathore

= [(1 / 1-0.05) × 20%] + 1.5%

= 0.2150 + 0.015

= 22.55%.

65.(A) Rs 18.38

Explanation: Expected rate of return: (By applying CAPM)

Re = Rf + ßi (Rm – Rf)

= 12% + 1.6 (18% –12%)

= 12% + 9.6%

= 21.6%

Price of Stock; (with the use of dividend growth model formulae)

Re = D1 /P0 = g

0.216 = 2.50 / P0 + 0.08

So, P0 = 2.50 / (0.216 – 0.08)

= 2.50 / 0.136

= Rs 18.38.

66.(D) (ii) (iii) (iv) (i)

67. (C) (iii)and(iv)

68.(C) (i) (ii) (iii) (iv)

69. (C) Risk and the required rate of return

Explanation:

- In finance, the capital asset pricing model (CAPM) is used to determine a theoretically appropriate required rate of return of an asset, if that asset is to be added to an already well-diversified portfolio, given that asset's non-diversifiable risk.
- The model takes into account the asset's sensitivity to non-diversifiable risk (also known as systematic risk or market risk), often represented by the quantity beta (β) in the financial industry, as well as the expected return of the market and the expected return of a theoretical risk-free asset.
- CAPM "suggests that an investor's cost of equity capital is determined by beta."
- An extension to the CAPM is the dual-beta model, which differentiates downside beta from upside beta.
- The CAPM was introduced by Jack Treynor (1961, 1962),William Sharpe (1964), John Lintner (1965) and Jan Mossin (1966) independently, building on the earlier work of Harry Markowitz(1952) on diversification and modern portfolio theory.
- The capital asset pricing model (CAPM) describes the relationship between risk and expected return, and it serves as a model for the pricing of risky securities.
- CAPM says that the expected return of a security or a portfolio equals the rate on a risk-free security plus a risk premium. If this expected return does not meet or beat our required return, the investment should not be undertaken.
- The commonly used formula to describe the CAPM relationship is as follows:
- Required (or expected) Return = RF Rate + (Market Return - RF Rate)x Beta

70.(A)Bond premium

Explanation:

Premium Bond:

- A bond that is trading above its par value.
- A bond will trade at a premium when it offers a coupon rate that is higher than prevailing interest rates.
- This is because investors want a higher yield, and will pay more for it.

Bond discount:

- The amount by which the market price of a bond is lower than its principal amount due at maturity.
- This amount, called its par value, is often $1,000. As bond prices are quoted as a percent of face value, a price of 98.00 means that the bond is selling for 98% of its face

value of $1,000.00 and the bond discount is 2%.

Intrinsic Value:

- The actual value of a company or an asset based on an underlying perception of its true value including all aspects of the business, in terms of both tangible and intangible factors.
- This value may or may not be the same as the current market value.

71.(A) Systematic risk

Explanation:

- Security analysis is the analysis of tradeable financial instruments called securities.
- These can be classified into debt securities, equities, or some hybrid of the two.
- More broadly, futures contracts and tradeable credit derivatives are sometimes included.
- Security analysis is typically divided into fundamental analysis, which relies upon the examination of fundamental business factors such as financial statements, and technical analysis, which focuses upon price trends and momentum.
- Quantitative analysis may use indicators from both areas.
- **Definition of Beta:** A measure of the volatility, or ***systematic risk***, of a security or a portfolio in comparison to the market as a whole. Beta is used in the capital asset pricing model (CAPM), a model that calculates the expected return of an asset based on its beta and expected market returns.
- It is also known as "beta coefficient."

72.(C)Payback period

Explanation: Profitability index:

An index that attempts to identify the relationship between the costs and benefits of a proposed project through the use of a ratio calculated as:

Profitability index=PV of future cash flow÷ Initial investment

73.(D) Investment Appraisal

Explanation: Capital Budgeting:

- The process in which a business determines whether projects such as building a new plant or investing in a long-term venture are worth pursuing.
- Often times, a prospective project's lifetime cash inflows and outflows are assessed in order to determine whether the returns generated meet a sufficient target benchmark.
- It is also known as "investment appraisal."
- It is the process of allocating resources for major capital, or investment, expenditures. One of the primary goals of capital budgeting investments is to increase the value of the firm to the shareholders.
- Popular methods of capital budgeting include net present value (NPV), internal rate of return (IRR), discounted cash flow (DCF) and payback period.

74.(A) Both A and R are correct

75.(B) (iv) (ii) (i) (iii)

Explanation:

Sundry Debtors:

- Sundry can mean various, miscellaneous, or diverse.
- Sundry debtors might refer to a company's customers who rarely make purchases on credit and the amounts they purchase are not significant.
- Sundry debtor is an entity from who amounts are due for goods sold or services rendered or in respect of contractual obligations.
- Also termed: debtor, trade debtor, and account receivable.
- **Sundry creditors**: Refers to companies or individuals to which money is owed.
- **Sundry:** Miscellaneous small or infrequent customers that are not assigned individual ledger accounts but are classified as a group.

Bills receivables:

- Debtors are those people to whom we have made sales and now amount need to be received but sometime debtors issue bills to use them until received money from them which is called bills receivables.

Inventory:

- The raw materials, work-in-process goods and completely finished goods that are considered to be the portion of a business's assets that are ready or will be ready for sale.
- Inventory represents one of the most important assets that most businesses possess, because the turnover of inventory represents one of the primary sources of revenue generation and subsequent earnings for the company's shareholders/owners.

Cash and Bank Accounts:

- Where there is only a journal being maintained for the purpose of recording transactions in an organisation, Cash
- Account and Bank Account are nothing but ledger accounts.
- Every transaction is recorded in the journal and posted there from into the ledger.
- Therefore with regard to cash and bank transactions (or for that matter any transactions) we see recording and posting taking place.

76.(C)The cost forgone in favour of production of another product

77. (A) Spill-over costs

78. (C) Both A and R are correct

79. (B) A is correct but R is wrong

80. (C)Cash available for meeting financial flows like debt servicing, dividend payments etc.

Explanation: Free Cash Flow (FCF):

- A measure of financial performance calculated as operating cash flow minus capital expenditures.
- Free cash flow (FCF) represents the cash that a company is able to generate after laying out the money required to maintain or expand its asset base.
- Free cash flow is important because it allows a company to pursue opportunities that enhance shareholder value.
- Without cash, it's tough to develop new products, make acquisitions, pay dividends and reduce debt.
- It can also be calculated by taking operating cash flow and subtracting capital expenditures.

81. (C) FDI

82.(B) the securities are perfectly negatively correlated

83.(D) A is false but R is true.

84.(D) All of the above

85. (D) $\frac{D_1}{P_0} + g$

Explanation:

- In financial theory, the return that stockholders require for a company.
- The traditional formula for cost of equity (COE) is the dividend capitalization model:

> ***COE=[Dividend per share(for next year)÷ Current Market value of stock]+Growth rate of dividends***

- A firm's cost of equity represents the compensation that the market demands in exchange for owning the asset and bearing the risk of ownership.

86. (C) Cash Management

Explanation:

- Working capital management involves the relationship between a firm's short-term assets and its short-term liabilities.
- The goal of working capital management is to ensure that a firm is able to continue its

operations and that it has sufficient ability to satisfy both maturing short-term debt and upcoming operational expenses.

- The management of working capital involves managing inventories, accounts receivable and payable, and cash.
- A managerial accounting strategy focusing on maintaining efficient levels of both components of working capital, current assets and current liabilities, in respect to each other.
- Working capital management ensures a company has sufficient cash flow in order to meet its short-term debt obligations and operating expenses.

87.(A) 10%

88.

(A) $R_f + \left(\bar{R}_M - R_f\right) B_j$

89.(C) 16.285%

Explanation:

Required rate of return:

= 8.50% + (17.5% – 8.5%) × 0.865

= 8.50% + 9.0% × 0.865

= 8.50% + 7.785%

= 16.285%.

90.(D) (i) &(ii)are correct

Explanation: Weighted Average Cost of Capital (WACC):

- A calculation of a firm's cost of capital in which each category of capital is proportionately weighted.
- All capital sources - common stock, preferred stock, bonds and any other long-term debt - are included in a WACC calculation.
- All else equal, the WACC of a firm increases as the beta and rate of return on equity increases, as an increase in WACC notes a decrease in valuation and a higher risk.
- The WACC equation is the cost of each capital component multiplied by its proportional weight and then summing:

$$WACC = \frac{E}{V} * Re + \frac{D}{V} * Rd * (1 - Tc)$$

Where:

Re = cost of equity

Rd = cost of debt

E = market value of the firm's equity

D = market value of the firm's debt

V = E + D

E/V = percentage of financing that is equity

D/V = percentage of financing that is debt

Tc = corporate tax rate

Businesses often discount cash flows at WACC to determine the Net Present Value (NPV) of a project, using the formula:

NPV = Present Value (PV) of the Cash Flows discounted at WACC.

91.(B) 13.0 %

92. (B) (i) &(iii)are correct.

93.(B) To meet day-to-day financial obligations of the company

Explanation: Working Capital:

- A measure of both a company's efficiency and its short-term financial health.
- The working capital ratio is calculated as:

Working Capital=Current Assets-Current Liabilities

- This ratio indicates whether a company has enough short term assets to cover its short term debt. Anything below 1 indicates negative W/C (working capital).

- While anything over 2 means that the company is not investing excess assets. Most believe that a ratio between 1.2 and 2.0 is sufficient.
- It is also known as "net working capital", or the "working capital ratio".

94.(C)A is true but R is false.

95. (A) Floating capital

96. (B) Public issue through Prospectus

Explanation: Types of issue of shares in Indian capital market:

- Under the Securities and Exchange Board of India (SEBI) Guidelines, the securities can be offered for sale in the primary market in different ways.
- Each method of issue has got its procedure and mechanism.
- The methods of issues of securities are:

1. Public Issue through Prospectus
2. Offer for Sale
3. Issue through Private Placement of Securities
4. Offer through Book-building Process
5. Public Offer through Stock Exchange On-line System
6. Vendor Placing
7. Private Placement.

97. (D)At the end of life of bond (maturity)

Explanation:

- A zero-coupon bond or discount bond or deep discount bond is a bond bought at a price lower than its face value, with the face value repaid at the time of maturity.
- ***It does not make periodic interest payments, or have so-called "coupons", hence the term zero-coupon bond.***
- When the bond reaches maturity, its investor receives its par (or face) value.

98. (C)increase in bad debts

Explanation: A liberal credit policy:

- A liberal credit policy means your company extends favorable terms to buyers who make purchases on accounts or through short-term financing. Offering discounts for early payments or allowing lengthy repayment periods with no penalty are examples of liberal credit terms.
- **Attract Customers:** Liberal credit policies make it easier for customers to buy from you, which increase your customer base and revenue. The lower the rates, and the longer you give your credit buyers to repay the debt, the more advantageous it is for them to purchase from you as opposed to competitors.
- **More Sales:** Buyers are also more likely to purchase larger quantities more often when you have favorable credit. It makes more sense for your consumers or business buyers to stock up on products if they like your current prices and credit terms, and believe prices will go higher. Plus, if your terms are much more favorable than those offered by competitors, you may capture business in other product or service categories over time as buyers shift away from previous providers.
- **Poor Cash Flow:** A potential disadvantage is that liberal credit policies often lead to lower turnover ratios on your accounts receivable. This means that the typical time frame between a purchase and payment is longer than with more aggressive credit practices. Delays in cash collection from account holders reduce your near-term cash flow. This limits your ability to invest money in new equipment and inventory, or to pay off debt and expenses. In fact, when you sell products or supplies on account, you send inventory out of your business without increasing cash.
- **Bad Debt:** The worst-case scenario with liberal credit is bad debt. In addition to not collecting the cash, you also have lost the inventory or work time performing service, and you lower your revenue at the time you write off the bad debt.

99. (A)Earnings multiplier approach

Explanation:

Earnings Multiplier:

- An adjustment made to a company's P/E ratio that takes into account current interest rates.
- The earnings multiplier is used to discount future earnings, and allows investors to compare expected growth to an amount of money invested over the same period at current rates.

Dividend Discount Model (DDM):

- A procedure for valuing the price of a stock by using predicted dividends and discounting them back to present value.
- The idea is that if the value obtained from the DDM is higher than what the shares are currently trading at, then the stock is undervalued.

Value of stock=[Dividend per share÷(Discount rate-Dividend growth rate)

Required Rate of Return (RRR):

- The minimum annual percentage earned by an investment that will induce individuals or companies to put money into a particular security or project.
- The required rate of return (RRR) is used in both equity valuation and in corporate finance.
- Investors use the RRR to decide where to put their money.
- They compare the return of an investment to all other available options, taking the risk-free rate of return, inflation and liquidity into consideration in their calculation.
- For investors using the dividend discount model to pick stocks, the RRR affects the maximum price they are willing to pay for a stock.

100. (B)Present value of dividends expected from equity ownership plus present value of sale price expected when equity share is sold

101. (C)dividend - payout ratio

Explanation:

Dividend - payout ratio:

- The percentage of earnings paid to shareholders in dividends.
- It is calculated as:

Dividend - payout ratio= Yearly Dividend per share ÷ Earning per share =Dividends÷ Net Income

- A reduction in dividends paid is looked poorly upon by investors, and the stock price usually depreciates as investors seek other dividend-paying stocks.
- A stable dividend payout ratio indicates a solid dividend policy by the company's board of directors.

Retention ratio:

- The percent of earnings credited to retained earnings.
- In other words, the proportion of net income that is not paid out as dividends.
- It is calculated as:

Retention ratio=(Net Income-Dividends)÷Net Income

102. (A) P0 = D0r – g

103. (B)Current or Accumulated profit

Explanation:

- Dividends only of Profits.
- (a) Dividends can only be declared or paid out of :
  (i) the current profits of the company,
  (ii) the past accumulated profits and
  (iii) moneys provided by the government for the payment of dividends in pursuance of a guarantee given by that government.
- No dividend can be paid out of capital(Sec. 205 (i)).

- (b) companies are not entitled to pay any dividend unless present or arrears of depreciation have been provided for out of the profits and an amount of 10 % or reports has been transferred to reserve. However, central government may allow any company to declare or pay dividends out of profits before providing for any depreciation.
- (c) Capital Profits may also be utilised for the declarations of dividend provided:
  (i) there is nothing in the Article prohibiting the distribution of dividend out of capital profits;
  (ii) they have been reallied in cash: and
  (iii) they ave been realised in cash and
  (iii) they remain as profits after revaluation of all assets and liabilities.
  (d) Dividend cannot be paid out of accumulated profits unless current losses are made good.

104. (C)M. M. Theory

Explanation: Dividend irrelevance comes from Modigliani-Miller's capital irrelevance model

105. (D) None of the above

Explanation: Walter's Valuation model:

- ***James E Walter*** contradicted that in the long run the share prices reflect only the present value of the expected dividends.
- He believed that dividends are one the most important factors that determine the market valuation.
- Retained earnings influence stock prices only through their effect on further dividends.
- He developed a very simple principle to show the way the dividend can be used to maximize the wealth position of the share holders.
- According to the Walter Model:

$$P = [D + (E - D) \times ROI / Kc] / Kc$$

Where,

P= Market price per share E= Earnings per share

D = Dividend per share Kc= Cost of Capital (Capitalisation rate)

ROI = Return on Investment (also called return on internal retention)

Assumptions:

- The return on investment always remains even.
- The company has an infinite life and is going to be concerned.
- The key variables like EPS and DPS do not change.
- The earnings being made are either distributed as dividends or invested internally instantly.

106. (B) Commercial Paper

Explanation:

Debentures:

- A type of debt instrument that is not secured by physical assets or collateral.
- Debentures are backed only by the general creditworthiness and reputation of the issuer.
- Both corporations and governments frequently issue this type of bond in order to secure capital.
- Like other types of bonds, debentures are documented in an indenture.

Commercial Paper:

- An unsecured, short-term debt instrument issued by a corporation, typically for the financing of accounts receivable, inventories and meeting short-term liabilities.
- Maturities on commercial paper rarely range any longer than 270 days. The debt is usually issued at a discount, reflecting prevailing market interest rates.

Public Deposits:

- The public deposits refer to the deposits that are attained by the numerous large and small firms from the public.
- The public deposits are generally solicited by the firms in order to finance the working capital requirements of the firm.

- The companies offer interest to the investors over public deposits.
- The rate of interest, however, varies with the time period of the public deposits.
- The companies generally offer 8 to 9 percent interest rate on the deposits made for one year.
- The companies offer 9 to 10 percent interest rate over public deposits for two years while 10 to 11 percent interest rate is offered for the three year deposits.
- There are rules regulating the fixed deposits.

Public deposits:

- Public deposits are an important source of financing the medium-term and long-term requirements of a company.
- The term 'public deposit' implies any money received by a company through the deposits or loans collected from the public.
- The public includes the general public, employees and shareholders of the company but excludes the money received in the form of shares and debentures.
- In India, this method of raising finance has gained a lot of importance because of the several advantages relating to public deposits:
- It is an easier method of mobilising funds, especially during periods of credit squeeze.
- It also enables the company to create contact with a large number of investors.
- It ensures the availability of funds for a longer duration and provides flexibility to the financial structure of the company. There is no risk of over-capitalisation and the deposits can be repaid when they are not required.
- There is no dilution of shareholders' control as the depositors have no voting rights and cannot interfere with the internal management of the company.

107. (A)Company law

108. (B) (ii) (iii) (iv) (i)

109. (C)shareholder value

Explanation: Mergers and Acquisitions (M&A): Valuation Matters

- Investors in a company that are aiming to take over another one must determine whether the purchase will be beneficial to them. In order to do so, they must ask themselves how much the company being acquired is really worth.
- Naturally, both sides of an M&A deal will have different ideas about the worth of a target company: its seller will tend to value the company at as high of a price as possible, while the buyer will try to get the lowest price that he can.
- There are, however, many legitimate ways to value companies. The most common method is to look at comparable companies in an industry, but deal makers employ a variety of other methods and tools when assessing a target company. Here are just a few of them:
- **Comparative Ratios:** The following are two examples of the many comparative metrics on which acquiring companies may base their offers:

1. **Price-Earnings Ratio (P/E Ratio):** With the use of this ratio, an acquiring company makes an offer that is a multiple of the earnings of the target company. Looking at the P/E for all the stocks within the same industry group will give the acquiring company good guidance for what the target's P/E multiple should be.
2. **Enterprise-Value-to-Sales Ratio (EV/Sales):** With this ratio, the acquiring company makes an offer as a multiple of the revenues, again, while being aware of the price-to-sales ratio of other companies in the industry.

- **Replacement Cost:** In a few cases, acquisitions are based on the cost of replacing the target company. For simplicity's sake, suppose the value of a company is simply the sum of all its equipment and staffing costs. The acquiring company can literally order the target to sell at that price, or it will create a competitor for the same cost. Naturally, it takes a long time to assemble good management, acquire property and get the right equipment. This method of establishing a price certainly wouldn't make much sense in a service industry where the key assets - people and ideas - are hard to value and develop.

- **Discounted Cash Flow (DCF):** A key valuation tool in M&A, discounted cash flow analysis determines a company's current value according to its estimated future cash flows. Forecasted free cash flows (net income + depreciation/amortization - capital expenditures - change in working capital) are discounted to a present value using the company's weighted average costs of capital (WACC). Admittedly, DCF is tricky to get right, but few tools can rival this valuation method.
- **Corporate values:** The operating philosophies or principles that guide an organization's internal conduct as well as its relationship with its customers, partners, and shareholders. Core values are usually summarized in the mission statement or in the company's statement of core values.
- **Stakeholder value:** The value delivered to shareholders because of management's ability to grow earnings, dividends and share price. In other words, shareholder value is the sum of all strategic decisions that affect the firm's ability to efficiently increase the amount of free cash flow over time.
- **Shareholder value:** The value delivered to shareholders because of management's ability to grow earnings, dividends and share price. In other words, shareholder value is the sum of all strategic decisions that affect the firm's ability to efficiently increase the amount of free cash flow over time.

110. (D) Split up

Explanation:

Spin off:

- The creation of an independent company through the sale or distribution of new shares of an existing business/division of a parent company.
- A spinoff is a type of divestiture.

Dissolution:

- Dissolution means to end a legal entity or agreement such as a marriage, adoption, or corporation, or unions.

Liquidation:

- When a business or firm is terminated or bankrupt, its assets are sold and the proceeds pay creditors.
- Any leftovers are distributed to shareholders.
- Any transaction that offsets or closes out a long or short position.
- In law, liquidation is the process by which a company (or part of a company) is brought to an end, and the assets and property of the company redistributed.
- Liquidation is also sometimes referred to as winding-up or dissolution, although dissolution technically refers to the last stage of liquidation.

Split up:

- A corporate action in which a single company splits into two or more separately run companies.
- Shares of the original company are exchanged for shares in the new companies, with the exact distribution of shares depending on each situation.
- This is an effective way to break up a company into several independent companies. After a split-up, the original company ceases to exist.

111. (B)Issued capital of the two companies

112. (B)Pooling of interest method

Explanation:

Purchase method:

- An accounting method specifically related to mergers and acquisitions.
- Under the purchase method, the acquiring company and its fair value are listed.
- Any difference between the price paid for an acquisition and the fair value is treated as goodwill.
- The method prevents a company from creating a provision for the restructuring of

the acquisition that will create future losses, since those losses should be treated as part of the cost of the acquisition.

Purchase Acquisition:

- An accounting method used in mergers and acquisitions with which the purchasing company treats the target firm as an investment, adding the target's assets to its own fair market value.

Pooling of Interests:

- A method of accounting that allows the balance sheets of two companies to be added together during an acquisition or merger.
- Pooling of interests is one of the accounting methods that companies can choose to employ when combining assets.
- The alternative would be the purchase method in which the purchasing company adds the absorbed company's assets to its fair market value.

113. (A) (i) (iii) & (iv) are correct

114. (B) Capital budgeting proposal

115. (D) All the above

116. (B) More than the acquirer

117. (C)CORUS

118. (C) (i), (ii), (iii) & (iv)

119. (C) Mergers and Acquisitions

Explanation:

Exchange Ratio:

- The relative number of new shares that will be given to existing shareholders of a company that has been acquired or merged with another.
- After their old company shares have been delivered, the exchange ratio is used to give shareholders the same relative value in new shares of the merged entity.

120. (A) Securitization

121. (B) (i) and (ii)

122. (C) (i) & (iv)

123. (C)1988

Explanation: SEBI:

- The Securities and Exchange Board of India (frequently abbreviated SEBI) is the regulator for the securities market in India.
- It was established in the year 1988 and given statutory powers on 12 April 1992 through the SEBI Act, 1992.

124. (B) 1970

Explanation: Monopolies and restrictive trade practices act, 1969.(MRTP ACT)

- The Monopolies and Restrictive Trade Practices Act, 1969, aims to prevent concentration of economic power to the common detriment, provide for control of monopolies and probation of monopolistic, restrictive and unfair trade practice, and protect consumer interest.
- Monopolistic trade practice is that which represents abuse of market power in the production and marketing of goods and services by eliminating potential competitors from market and taking advantage of the control over the market by charging unreasonably high prices, preventing or reducing competition, limiting technical development, deteriorating product quality or by adopting unfair or deceptive trade practices.
- ***The act came into force from 1 st June, 1970, and has been amended in 1991.***

125. (C) Managers

Explanation: Management accounting focuses mainly on the preparation of reports for the internal users of financial information, i.e. managers are all levels of the entity.

126. (B) Relates to sub-units of the entity and may be very detailed

Explanation: Management accounting pertains to subunits of the entity and may be very detailed.

127. (A) Creditor

Explanation: Creditors are external to the entity.

128. (B) Calculating earnings per share

Explanation: Calculating earnings per share is a function for external users of financial information.

129. (D) All of these

Explanation: Management accounting applies to any business entity.

130. (B) General-purpose

Explanation: Financial statements prepared for external users are general purpose financial reports.

131. (C) Special-purpose

Explanation: Management accounting reports provides special purpose information for a particular user for a specific reason.

132. (C)Generally accepted accounting principles

Explanation: The reporting standard for external financial reports is generally accepted accounting principles.

133. (B) Detailed

Explanation: Internal reports are generally very detailed.

134. (C) Organization chart

Explanation: An organizational chart depicts authority relationships within a company.

135. (A) Period costs

Explanation: Period costs are costs that are identified with a specific time period rather than with a saleable product and therefore do not become part of inventory.

136. (B) Prime costs and manufacturing overhead

Explanation: Product costs include direct materials, direct labour (collectively known as prime costs) and manufacturing overhead.

137. (C) Inventoriable cost

Explanation: Product costs are also called inventoriable costs because they will eventually become part of finished goods inventory.

138. (A)A special resolution

139. (C) Fluctuating load

Explanation: Buffer stock: A supply of inputs held as a reserve to safeguard against unforeseen shortages or demands.

140. (B)Unsuitable Sovereign Debt

141. (A)financial distress

142. (A)Retained earnings

143. (C)Zero growth model

144. (B) Retained earnings, Equity, Preference, Debt,

145. (D) ARR

146. (B)P=U(S-V)-F

147. (A)Appreciation

148. (D)Debentures

149. (B)Maximisation of shareholder's wealth

150. (C) 11.875%

151. (B) Internal Rate of Return

152. (C) PBIT – Interest – Tax

153. (C) (c) (d) (a)

154. (A)(i) (ii) (iv) (iii)

155. (A) IRR

156. (B)Unsuitable Sovereign Debt

157. (A)Retained earnings

158. (C)Zero growth model

159. (B) Retained earnings, Equity, Preference, Debt,

160. (D)ARR

161. (B)P=U(S-V)-F

162. (A)Appreciation

163. (D)Debentures

164. (B)Maximisation of shareholder's wealth

165. (C)11.875%

166. (C) (ii) and (iii)

167. (B) shadow price.

Explanation: Shadow price

- Opportunity cost of an activity or project to a society, computed where the actual price is not known or, if known, does not reflect the real sacrifice made.
- The actual market value of one share of a money market fund. In this case, shadow pricing refers to securities that are accounted for based on amortized costs rather than a market valuation assignment.
- The assignment of dollar values to non-marketed goods such as production costs and intangible assets. Shadow pricing is usually subject to various assumptions and is fairly subjective within certain guidelines.

168. (A)par value

169. (C) The % of total deposits to the % of cash that must be invested by a bank as per instructions of the central bank of the country.

170. (B) Nominal Account

171. (A)The number of years a project takes to recover its investment (original) cost.

Explanation: Payback Period:

- The length of time required to recover the cost of an investment.
- The payback period of a given investment or project is an important determinant of whether to undertake the position or project, as longer payback periods are typically not desirable for investment positions.
- It is calculated as:

Payback period=Cost of Project÷ Annual cash inflows

- All other things being equal, the better investment is the one with the shorter payback period.
- There are two main problems with the payback period method:
  - o It ignores any benefits that occur after the payback period and, therefore, does not measure profitability.
  - o It ignores the time value of money. Because of these reasons, other methods of capital budgeting, like net present value, internal rate of return or discounted cash flow, are generally preferred.

172. (A)Irreversible

Explanation:

- Capital budgeting (or investment appraisal) is the planning process used to determine whether an organization's long term investments such as new machinery, replacement machinery, new plants, new products, and research development projects are worth the funding of cash through the firm's capitalization structure (debt, equity or retained earnings).
- It is the process of allocating resources for major capital, or investment, expenditures. One of the primary goals of capital budgeting investments is to increase the value of the firm to the shareholders.
- Many formal methods are used in capital budgeting, including the techniques such as:
  - Accounting rate of return
  - Payback period
  - Net present value
  - Profitability index
  - Internal rate of return
  - Modified internal rate of return
  - Equivalent annuity
  - Real options valuation
- These methods use the incremental cash flows from each potential investment, or project.
- Techniques based on accounting earnings and accounting rules are sometimes used - though economists consider this to be

improper - such as the accounting rate of return, and "return on investment."

- Simplified and hybrid methods are used as well, such as payback period and discounted payback period.

173. (B) Walter model

174. (C)The % of total deposits to the % of cash that must be invested by a bank as per instructions of the central bank of the country

175. (A)The number of years a project takes to recover its investment (original) cost

176. (A)Irreversible

177. (B)Walter model

178. (D)Have no effect on total assets

179. (C)The balance that will appear on the balance sheet

180. (C) Payback period method

181. (B)Walter

182. (A)Cost of Capital

183. (D) (iv)(i)(ii)(iii)

184. (A)low initial price followed by a high price

185. (B) Marginal cost of debt

---000---

UNIT-VI

MARKETING MANAGEMENT

1. The term marketing may be described as the performance of business activities that:

(A) Gives profit to the organisation

(B) Directs flow of goods from producer to consumer

(C) Directs selling

(D) Aims at satisfying the consumers

2. Which of the following statement is true?

(A)The essence of marketing is a transaction of an exchange.

(B)Marketing–orientation is philosophy, which has to pervade the organization structure

(C)Marketing is also a managerial function involving analysis, planning and control marketing activities in an organization.

(D)All of the above

3. Who coined the term "Marketing Myopia"?

(A)Peter Drucker (B) Stanton

(C)Philip Kotler (D) Theodore Levitt

4. Who defines advertising as "any paid form of non-personal presentation and promotion of ideas, goods and services by an identified sponsor?

(A) Philip Kotler

(B) C.K. Prahlad

(C) Chartered Institute of Marketing

(D) American Marketing Association

5. Who is associated with the statement that marketing is the process of creation and delivery of standard of Living?

(A)Mc Nair (B) Mazur

(C)Kotler (D) Peter Drucker

6. According to Kotler....is the easiest marketing mix element to adjust.

(A)Price (B) Channel

(C)Product features (D) Promotion

7. The first concept of marketing is:

(A)Selling Concept

(B)Relationship Marketing Concept

(C)Product concept

(D)Societal Marketong Concept

8. 'Marketing is a human activity directed at satisfying needs and wants through Exchange process'; is the statement of

(A) Cundiff ad Still (B) Kenneth Andrews

(C) Philip Kotler (D) Kishwar S. Kan

9. Demarketing is done if one of the demand state is existing

(A) Negative demand (B) Latent demand

(C) Overfull demand (D) Irregular demand

10. Market is defined as:

(A) A place where buyers and sellers meet

(B) A place where goods are sold

(C) A place where goods are bought

(D) A set of actual and potential buyers of a product

11. In "Marketing Myopia" the tendency of firms is to take a :

(A)broad view of the market

(B)narrow view of the market

(C)narrow view of MIS

(D)broad view of MIS

12. "Marketing mayopia" is based upon :

(A)current product offerings

(B)forecasting the future product offering

(C)dropping a product

(D)adding a product

13. Green marketing principles relates to :

(A)Agriculture marketing

(B)Preservation of environment

(C)Social marketing environment

(D)Organic product marketing

14. Marketing concept emphasizes on :

(A)Customer - oriented products

(B)Value creation

(C)Sales orientation

(D)Production orientation

15. State which one is ***not*** a function of marketing:

(A)Identification of customers needs and wants

(B)Product planning and development

(C)Guiding the funding agencies

(D)Communicating

16. Consumers are aware of damages caused by packaging, product process, so they prefer :

(A)Social marketing concept

(B)Green marketing concept

(C)Direct marketing concept

(D)Organic marketing concept

17. Under which concept of marketing customer remains focused?

(A)Marketing (B)Production

(C)Product (D)Selling

18. Who authored the book "positioning - the battle for the mind" ?

(A)Philip Kotler and Gary Arm Strong

(B)Theodore Levitt

(C)Peter F. Drucker

(D)AlRice and Jack Trout

19. How do you distinguish marketing and selling?

(A) They are one and the same

(B) Marketing is a part of selling

(C) Selling is a part of marketing

(D) No relationship between selling and marketing

20. In the buying decision process, what is the term used for a person who first suggests buying the product?

(A) Consumer (B) Decider

(C) Initiator (D) Influencer

21. Which of the following indicates the distinction between Advertising and Publicity?

(A) Advertising is expensive, publicity is less expensive.

(B) Advertising is through T.V., publicity is through print media.

(C) Advertising is a paid form of communication, Publicity is not a paid form of communication.

(D) Advertising is through film stars, Publicity is through cricketers.

22. What is the basis for segmenting vitamin market?

(A)Age (B) Place of distribution

(C)Gender (D) Income status

23. Which concept of marketing maintains that the company aggressively promotes and pushes its products?

(A)Marketing (B) Product

(C)Production (D) Selling

24. Macro Marketing environment refers to :

(A)Internal to the company

(B)Employees and shareholders of a company

(C)External to the company

(D)Stake holders

25. Environment scanning involves :

(A)Weather Forecasting

(B)Studying depression in a sea

(C)Identifying threats and opportunities

(D)Identifying strengths and weaknesses

26. Which of the following is ***not*** included in 7 Ps of services marketing?

(A)People (B) Products

(C)Physical Evidence (D) Public Relations

27. Which of the following factors does ***not*** influence the pricing strategy of a firm?

(A)Market (B) Competition

(C)Cost (D)R & D

28. In the diffusion of innovation who are the people ***not*** willing to try out the product :

(A)Innovators (B)Progressive people

(C)Early adopters (D)Early majority

29. Who authored book "Policy and Management"?

(A) Gladden (B) Weber

(C) Dimock (D) Appleby

30. Match the following

List -1 (Authors)

(a) William J.Stanton

(b) Cundiff and Still

(c) Mc Carthy

(d) Philip Kotler

List -2 (Books)

(i)Principles of Marketing

(ii) Basic Marketing

(iii)Sales Management

(iv)Fundamentals of Marketing

	(a)	(b)	(c)	(d)
(A)	(i)	(ii)	(iii)	(iv)
(B)	(iv)	(iii)	(ii)	(i)
(C)	(ii)	(iii)	(i)	(iv)
(D)	(iii)	(ii)	(iv)	(i)

31. Match the following

List-I (Companies)

(a) Xerox

(b) Columbia Pictures

(c) Carrier

(d) Missouri Pacific Railroad

List-II (Market definition)

(i)We provide climate control in the home

(ii) We are a people and goods mover

(iii)We help improve office productivity

(iv)We market entertainment

	(a)	(b)	(c)	(d)
(A)	(iii)	(iv)	(ii)	(i)
(B)	(iii)	(ii)	(i)	(iv)
(C)	(iii)	(iv)	(i)	(ii)
(D)	(iii)	(ii)	(iv)	(i)

32. In marketing, needs are defined as:

(A) primary needs

(B) physiological needs

(C) psychological needs

(D) any felt deprivations

33. Select name of the country having maximum percent of GDP attributed to services:

(A) United States (B) China

(C) Germany (D) India

34. Marketing research does ***not*** normally

(A)Gather environmental information

(B)Provide a continuous source of information

(C)Relate to all aspects of marketing operations

(D)Describe the current situation

35. A marketing plan is composed of three basic components, namely

1. Objectives	2. Policies
3. Program	4. Procedure
5. Hints	6. Decision
7. Command	8. Periodic
9. Diversity	

(A) 1, 2 and 3 only (B) 6, 7 and 8 only

(C) 5, 7 and 9 only (D) 2, 3 and 9 only

36. Marketers can do on-line marketing by creating an electronic presence on :

(A)the internet, placing ads on-line

(B)participating in forums, newsgroups, web communities

(C)using webcasting and e-mail

(D)all of the above

37. Marketing information system is the system of information that flows to assist :

(A)Promotional programmes

(B)Sales personnels development

(C)Marketing planning and decision making

(D)Marketing-mix

38. It is a set of procedures and sources used by managers to obtain everyday information about developments in the marketing environment. It is known as

(A) Internal Records System

(B) Marketing Intelligence System

(C) Marketing Research System

(D) Marketing Decision Support System

39. Marketing information system gathers information from internal sources like marketing intelligence and marketing research to help the manager in

(A) Assessing the information needs.

(B) Developing the needed information.

(C) Distributing the information.

(D) All of the above.

40. The following is used for identifying the total resources required for meeting customers' requirements

(A)Capacity Planning

(B) Process Planning

(C)Inventory Management

(D) Master Production Schedule

41. Marketing Research involves the following three steps. Arrange them in a sequence to make it meaningful

(i)Data collection

(ii)Systematic design

(iii)Analysis of data

(A)(i), (ii), (iii)

(B) (i), (iii) ,(ii)

(C) (ii), (i), (iii)

(D) (iii), (i), (ii)

42. The practice of selling two or more separate products together for a single price is :

(A) Bundling (B) Dumping

(C) Both (A) and (B) (D) None of the above

43. Selling the products only through a single wholesaler or retailer is called

(A) Extensive distribution strategy

(B) Selective distribution strategy

(C) Exclusive distribution strategy

(D) Mass merchandise strategy

44. Company's ability to provide individually differentiated product for each consumer is called as:

(A) Digitalization (B) Disintermediation

(C) Customerization (D) Connectivity

45. The scientific system of collecting and analysis of data pertaining to market is known as:

(A) Production Research

(B) Advertising Research

(C) Marketing Research

(D) None of the above

46. In channels of distribution of Industrial products which level is popular?

(A)Zero level and one level

(B)One level and two levels

(C)Two level only

(D)Multi level

47. Which of the following is the sole vehicle for creating and delivering customer value?

(A)Marketing channel

(B)Marketing communication

(C)Marketing mix

(D)Marketing research

48. Marketing research data is gathered by:

(A) Observation

(B) In-depth interviews

(C) Controlled experiment

(D) All of the above

49. Conditions for existence of exchange potential

1. Existence of two parties

2. Something of value to offer to other party

3. Capability of communication and delivery on both parties

4. Liberty to accept or reject the exchange offer

(A) 1 and 2 should exist

(B) 2 and 3 should exist

(C) 3 and 4 should exist

(D) All the above should exist

50. On the basis of the statement given below, answer the following question:
Puffery in advertisement is:

(1)An exaggerated claim in an advertisement that is considered as illegal

(2) An exaggerated claim in an advertisement that is considered as legal

(3)Usage of claims like 'best', 'greatest', 'finest', for a product or service

(4)Based on the concept of 'Placebo Effect'

(A)Options (1) and (3) are correct

(B) Options (1) and (2) are correct

(C) Options (1) ,(3)and (4) are correct

(D) Options (2),(3) and (4) are correct

51. Because personal selling is taking on a more prominent role in the corporate marketing mix, selling today:

(A)requires fewer and less intensive communication skills than previously

(B) has become a less attractive career for college graduates

(C)Involves more use of communications and computer technologies

(D)Places greater focus on short-term persuasion, with less emphasis on consultation and problem solving

52. Market risk is also known as

(A)Systematic risk or diversifiable risk

(B)Unsystematic risk or diversifiable risk

(C)Systematic risk or non diversifiable risk

(D)Unsystematic risk or non diversifiable risk

53. In the buying decision process, what is the term used for a person who first suggests buying the product or service?

(A) Influencer (B) Initiator

(C) Decider (D) Buyer

54. Impulse buying implies :

(A)Purchasing with little or no advance planning

(B)Purchasing involving all family members

(C)Purchasing involving all relatives

(D)None of the above

55. Given below are two statements, one labelled as Assertion (A), and the other labelled as Reason (R). State the correct answer from code given below.

Assertion (A): Pure-click companies can be search engines, Internet service providers, commerce sites, transaction sites, content sites and enabler sites.

Reason (R): Pure-click companies are those companies that have launched a website without any previous existence as a firm.

Code:

(A) (A) is correct, but (R) is wrong.

(B) Both (A) and (R) are correct.

(C) (A) is wrong, but (R) is correct.

(D) Both (A) and (R) are wrong.

56. Match List-I and List-II.

List – I (Characteristics of Services)

(i) Intangibility

(ii)Inseparability

(iii)Variability

(iv)Perishability

List–II (Marketing Strategy applied considering a characteristic of service)

(a) Preparing a service blue print showing each service and process in a flow chart.

(b) Tangiblize the intangible

(c) To train more service providers and build up client confidence.

(d) Use differential pricing

Code:

	(i)	(ii)	(iii)	(iv)
(A)	(b)	(a)	(c)	(d)
(B)	(b)	(c)	(a)	(d)
(C)	(a)	(c)	(b)	(d)
(D)	(b)	(a)	(d)	(c)

57. The first commandment in marketing is :

(A)know thy customer

(B)know thy product

(C)know thy markets

(D)know thy price

58. Which of the following is ***not*** included in 7 P's of services marketing ?

(A) Physical evidence (B) People

(C) Marketing plan (D) Process

59. Which of the following is ***not*** included in 7 P's of services marketing?

(A) Process (B) People

(C) Pricing (D) Public relations

60. Before a company decides to target a particular market segment, which important factors are to be examined against organization's objectives and resources?

(A) Market size

(B) Growth rate

(C) Structural attractiveness

(D) All of the above

61. Who coined the term 4 Ps?

(A) Philip Kotler (B) Stanton

(C) Peter Drucker (D) Mc Carthy

62. What is the term used if a market is divided into distinct groups of buyers who might require separate products or marketing mixes?

(A) Market Targetting

(B) Market Positioning

(C) Market Segmentation

(D) Market Co-ordination

63. Segmentation of consumers based on factors like climatic conditions and regions are known as :

(A)Demographic segmentation

(B)Cultural segmentation

(C)Geographic segmentation

(D)Administrative segmentation

64. Which of the demographic variables is ***not*** used by marketers for demographic segmentation?

(A) Gender (B) Age

(C) Occupation (D) Poverty

65. It has been described as a cluster of complementary goods and services that are closely related in the minds of consumers but are spread across a diverse set of industries. It is known as

(A) Market Place (B) Market Space

(C) Meta-Market (D) Marketing Mix

66. Product mix refers to :

(A)The ingredients used for making a product

(B)Features of a product

(C)Marketing mix elements

(D)A group of products

67. A Marketing database is built as an aid to

(A) Market research

(B) Product-mix expansion

(C) Reducing cost of production

(D) Price hike

68. Which of the following is ***not*** a variable for segmenting the market?

(A)Sex (B) Age

(C)Income (D) Sales

69. Arrange the following steps of a five-stage model of the consumer buying process :

(i)Evaluation of Alternatives

(ii)Need Arousal

(iii)Information search

(iv) Purchase Decision

(v)Post Purchase behaviour

Code:

(A) (iv)	(ii)	(iii)	(i)	(v)
(B) (iii)	(ii)	(i)	(iv)	(v)
(C) (i)	(ii)	(iv)	(iii)	(v)
(D) (ii)	(iii)	(i)	(iv)	(v)

70. It refers to the total number of items in the Product Mix. It is known as following.

(A) The width of product mix

(B) The length of product mix

(C) The depth of product mix

(D) The consistency of product mix

71. A zero level channel refers to

(A) Personal selling (B) Direct Marketing

(C) Buying from a retailer (D) Advertising

72. Based on the customer value hierarchy, there are five product levels. Arrange them in lower value to higher value to the customer

(i) Expected product (ii) Basic product

(iii) Core product (iv) Potential product

(v) Augmented product

(A) (i) (ii) (iii) (iv) (v)(B) (iii) (ii) (i) (v) (iv)

(C) (iii) (iv) (v) (ii) (i)(D) (i) (v) (iv) (iii) (ii)

73. Arrange the following marketing concepts in an order, so that the last concept should mean "everything matters in marketing".

(i) The selling concept

(ii)The marketing concept

(iii) The holistic marketing concept

(iv) The product concept

(v) The production concept

(A) (i) (ii) (iii) (v) (iv)(B) (v) (iv) (iii) (ii) (i)

(C) (v) (iv) (i) (ii) (iii)(D) (i) (ii) (v) (iv) (iii)

74. The study of human populations in terms of size, density, location, age, gender, race, occupation, and other statistics is called:

(A)Geothermy (B) Demography

(C) Hemos-popography (D) Ethnography

75. In case of Product/Market, the cell showing New Product and Existing Market is referred as :

(A)Market Penetration

(B)Product Development

(C)Market Development

(D)Diversification

76. Which of the Marketing - Mix order is correct?

(A)price, product, place, promotion

(B)product, price, promotion, place

(C)product, price, place, promotion

(D)product, place, price, promotion

77. Which of the following is ***not*** the stage of product life cycle?

(A) Introduction (B) Growth

(C) Market segmentation (D) Decline

78. Which of the following PLC stages is in correct order?

(A) introduction, adolescence, growth, decline

(B)introduction, growth, maturity, decline

(C)introduction, maturity, growth, decline

(D)introduction, growth, saturation, maturity

79. The process of turning marketing strategies into specific day-to-day,month-to-month actions is called:

(A)Analysis (B)Implementation

(C)Planning (D)Control

80. Skimming price for a new product is:

(A)Low initial price (B)Average price

(C)High initial price (D)Moderate price

81. Match the List – I with List – II :

List – I

(Stage of the product life cycle)

(a) Introduction Stage

(b) Growth Stage

(c) Maturity Stage

(d)Decline Stage

List – II

(Marketing strategy applied in the stage of the product life cycle)

(i) Market Modification

(ii) Rapid Skimming Strategy

(iii) Enter New Market Segments

(iv)Continuation Strategy

Codes:

	(a)	(b)	(c)	(d)
(A)	(iii)	(ii)	(iv)	(i)
(B)	(ii)	(iii)	(i)	(iv)
(C)	(ii)	(iii)	(iv)	(i)
(D)	(iv)	(ii)	(i)	(iii)

82. From the following, the 4 Ps of marketing coined originally are

1. Product 2. Price

3. Packaging 4. People

5. Promotion 6. Place

(A) 1, 2, 3 and 4 (B) 1,2, 5 and 6

(C) 3,4,6 and 5 (D) 1, 2, 5 and 4

83. Match the following :

List – 1	**List – 2**
(Marketing Variables)	**(Qualities)**
(a) Product	(i) Shape

(b) Price (ii)Advertising

(c) Promotion (iii) Discounts

(d) Place (iv)Layout of store

	(a)	(b)	(c)	(d)
(A)	(i)	(ii)	(iii)	(iv)
(B)	(iii)	(iv)	(i)	(ii)
(C)	(iv)	(iii)	(ii)	(i)
(D)	(i)	(iii)	(ii)	(iv)

84. Match the following

List – I

(a) Need

(b) Want

(c) Demand

List – II

(i)want supported by purchasing power

(ii) felt deprivation

(iiii)expression for specific good

	(a)	(b)	(c)
(A)	(ii)	(iii)	(i)
(B)	(i)	(ii)	(iii)
(C)	(iii)	(ii)	(i)
(D)	(i)	(iii)	(ii)

85. Match the following

List – I (Four Ps)	**List – II (Four Cs)**
(a) Product	(i) Convenience
(b) Price	(ii) Communication
(c) Place	(iii) Customer Solution
(d) Promotion	(iv) Customer Cost

	(a)	(b)	(c)	(d)
(A)	(iii)	(i)	(iv)	(ii)
(B)	(iii)	(iv)	(i)	(ii)
(C)	(i)	(ii)	(iii)	(iv)
(D)	(iv)	(iii)	(ii)	(i)

86. Standardized and customized flow of activities, simple and complex number of steps and customer involvement by which a service is delivered is called:

(A) Place Mix (B) Physical Evidence Mix

(C) Process Mix(D) People Mix

87. Which of the following order about product life cycle is correct?

(A) Introduction, Maturity, growth and decline.

(B) Introduction, growth, maturity and decline.

(C) Introduction, decline, maturity and growth.

(D) Growth, maturity, decline and introduction.

88. One-level channel of distribution consists of

(A) Producer – consumer

(B) Producer – dealer – consumer

(C) Producer–dealer–retailer-consumer

(D)Producer–dealer–wholesaler–retailer–consumer

89. At which stage of the new product development, the launching of new product will take place

(A) Business Analysis

(B) Test Marketing

(C) Commercialization

(D) Marketing strategy development

90. Which of the following is ***not*** a stage in the new product development?

(A)generation of ideas

(B)screening

(C)market segmentation

(D)commercialization

91. Which of the following is ***not*** the stage of new product development?

(A) Idea Generation (B) Business Analysis

(C) Test Marketing(D) Market Segmentation

92. In which stage of new product development process, the product and marketing programs are tested in realistic market settings?

(A) Concept Development and Testing

(B) Idea Screening

(C) Test Marketing

(D) Commercialization

93. Developing new products for new markets, is called

(A) Market Penetration

(B) Diversification

(C) Product Development

(D) Market Development

94. A brand is a means of :

(A)Naming the products

(B)Packaging of the products

(C)Contents of the products

(D)Identifying and differentiating the company's products

95. If a company uses its company name for its entire range of products offered, then it is called

(A) Private branding

(B) Corporate branding

(C) Product-line branding

(D) Specific product branding

96. The Branding strategy which uses a different brand name for each product is known as:

(A) Overall Family Branding

(B) Line Family Branding

(C) Individual Branding

(D) Brand Extension

97. The Psycho graphical factors in Market Segmentation will include :

(A)Income and occupation

(B)Sex and Age

(C)Hobbies and activities

(D)Living standard and Income

98. Consumers' Risk is :

(A)the lowest allowable probability of accepting a bad lot

(B) the largest allowable probability of rejecting a good lot

(C) the largest allowable probability of accepting a bad lot

(D) none of the above

99. Pricing a product will have certain objectives and they are

1. Attracting employees

2. Profit maximisation

3. Sales maximisation

(A) 1 and 2 are true (B) 1 and 3 are true

(C) 2 and 3 are true (D) 1, 2 and 3 are true

100. When companies make marketing decisions by considering consumers' wants and the long-run interests of the company, consumer, and the general population, they are practicing which of the following principles?

(A)Innovative marketing

(B)Consumer-oriented marketing

(C)Value marketing

(D)Societal marketing

101. If Honda uses its company name to cover such different products as its automobiles, lawn mowers, and motorcycles, it is practicing which of the following strategies?

(A)new brand strategy

(B)line extension strategy

(C) multibrand strategy

(D)brand extension strategy

102. The process that turns marketing strategies and plans into marketing actions in order to accomplish strategic marketing objectives is called:

(A)Marketing strategy.

(B)Marketing control.

(C)Marketing analysis.

(D)Marketing implementation.

103. Making profit by taking advantage of different prices prevailing in different markets is referred as

(A) Hedging (B) Speculation

(C) Arbitrage (D) Gambling

104. Which of the following is ***not*** the element of promotion-mix?

(A) Advertising (B) Place

(C) Personal selling (D) Publicity

105. Promotion mix includes:

(A)Advertising, publicity, personal selling and sales promotion

(B) Physical attributes, brand, package and product life cycle

(C)Brand name, product benefits, delivery and credit

(D)Transportation, material handling, packaging and customer service

106. Which of the following is ***not*** element of Promotion - Mix?

(A)Advertising (B)Sales promotion

(C)Personal selling (D)Direct marketing

107. Distribution channel aims at moving products from producer to :

(A)Ultimate Consumer (B)Retailors

(C)Stockists (D)Brokers

108. Which of the following is ***not*** constituent of promotion-mix :

(A)Advertising (B) Sales promotion

(C)Direct marketing (D) Publicity

109. Sequence of steps to be taken in a Selling System include

(i) Receipt of Order

(ii) Processing Order

(iii) Shipment of merchandise

(iv) Accounting for sale

The correct chronological order for these

(A) (i) (iv) (iii) (ii) (B) (i) (iv) (ii) (iii)

(C) (i) (ii) (iv) (iii) (D) (i) (ii) (iii) (iv)

110. Which one of the following is ***not*** coming under principles of personal selling :

(A) Prospecting

(B) Presentation and demonstration

(C) Promoting

(D) Follow-up and maintenance

111. Skimming pricing implies :

(A)Experimental pricing (B)Low pricing

(C)High pricing (D)None of the above

112. When a consumer derives more satisfaction from a product/service than his expectation, it is known as :

(A)Consumer satisfaction

(B)Consumer delight

(C)Consumer dazzling

(D)Consumer dissatisfaction

113. Which city is more favourable for selling electric blankets?

(A)Mumbai (B)Chennai

(C)Shillong (D)Pune

114. AIDA model of advertising objectives includes

(A) Action, Interest, Demand, Attention

(B) Attention, Innovation, Desire, Action

(C) Awareness, Interest, Desire, Action

(D) Attention, Interest, Desire, Action

115. Selection of specific media in which advertisements will be run and when they will be run to reach the target market is called

(A) Advertising (B) Public Relations

(C) Media Planning (D) Publicity

116. Which of the following is ***not*** a function of distribution agency?

(A) Transportation (B) Servicing

(C) Inventorying (D) Manufacturing

117. In business situations, personal selling is :

(A)Inside Selling (B)Outside Selling

(C)Both of the above (D)None of the above

118. Mass communication tools available to marketers include :

(A)Advertising (B)Sales promotion

(C)Public relations (D)All the above

119. The financial results of marketing endeavours should be analysed in terms of

(A)Sales volume (B) Market share

(C)Marketing costs (D)All the above

120. The Green Marketing concept refers to :

(A)Agricultural marketing

(B)Environment friendly

(C)Agro - based industrial marketing

(D)Euro - Agricultural marketing

121. Which of the following activates a consumer to accomplish his goal?

(A)Motivation (B)Perception

(C)Attitude (D)Behaviour

122. A diverse collection of incentive tools designed to stimulate quicker buying of a particular product or service by consumers or the trade is known as

(A) Advertising (B) Personal selling

(C) Publicity (D) Sales promotion

123. When a consumer derives more satisfaction from a product/service than his expectation, it is known as:

(A) Consumer satisfaction

(B) Consumer delight

(C) Consumer dazzling

(D) Consumer dissatisfaction

124. What is consumer market?

(A) Buyer's (B) Seller's

(C) Distributors (D) None of the above

125. When a company introduced a new Product, to its surprise, an article appeared in a news paper about the good qualities of the product. This is referred to as:

(A) Advertising (B) Sales Promotion

(C) Publicity (D) Personal selling

126. Which one of the following is the function of Foreign Exchange Market?

(A) Transfer of purchasing power

(B) Minimising exchange rate risks

(C) Credit for international business

(D) All the above

127. Which of the following are consumer promotion tools?

1. Premium

2. Coupons

3. Samples

(A) 1 and 2 are true (B) 1 and 3 are true

(C) 2 and 3 are true (D) 1, 2 and 3 are true

128. Which of the following is ***not*** a tangible dominant?

(A) Detergents

(B) Automobiles

(C) Investment Management

(D) Soft drinks

129. _______is the difference between customer expectations and perceptions.

(A) Customer Delight

(B) Customer Satisfaction

(C)Customer Gap

(D) The supplier Gap

130. Which of the following information forms available to the marketing manager can usually be accessed more quickly and cheaply than other information sources?

(A)Marketing intelligence

(B)Marketing research

(C)Customer profiles

(D)Internal databases

131. Mass communication tools available to marketers include:

(A) Advertising (B) Sales promotion

(C) Public relations (D) All the above

132. If the agreement is silent, an arbitration reference is to appoint:

(A) Sole arbitrator

(B) Two or more arbitrators

(C) Both (a) and (b)

(D) None of the above

133. Specifying the order in which individual jobs are to be executed :

(A) Planning (B) Loading

(C) Sequencing (D) Routing

134. Market Model was proposed by:

(A)Harry Markowitz (B)P.Samuelson

(C)Philip Kotler (D)William Sharpe

135. Which of the following is an example of impulse buying?

(A)Buying mutual funds

(B)Buying ice-creams

(C)Buying a car

(D)Buying a house

136. When a manager focuses on making whatever products are easy to produce, and then trying to sell them, that manager has a-----------orientation.

(A)Marketing (B) Production

(C)Sales (D) Profit

137. **Assertion(A):**Dividing a segment into sub-segments with a distinctive set of traits seeking a special combination of benefits

Reasoning(R): Godrej company introduced Ezee to target the consumers who wanted mild washing detergent foe woolen clothes.

(A)Both (A) and (R) are correct and (R) is correct explaination of (A)

(B) Both (A) and (R) are correct but (R) is not the correct explaination of (A)

(C)(A) is correct but (R) is incorrect

(D) (A) is incorrect but (R) is incorrect

138. The gap between what customers expect and what they receive when dealing with a firm is:

(A)Related to the price they paid for something,not its quality

(B)Always positive because the higher of the two values is counted first

(C)One measure of their satisfaction with a firm and its products

(D)Impossible to measure because it is subjective, not objective

139. ....describes changes in an individual consumer behaviour arising from experience

(A)Modeling (B)Perception

(C)Learning (D)Motivation

140. ....is defined as the difference between the benefits a customer sees from a market offering and the costs of obtaining those benefits.

(A)Profit margin (B)Surplus

(C)Customer value (D)Consumer surplus

141. FOB Pricing is

(A) Price skimming

(B) Penetration pricing

(C) Psychological pricing

(D) Pricing in international trade

142. Skimming Pricing is useful for :

(A)Luxury goods (B) Consumption goods

(C)Necessities. (D)Industrial goods

143. A firm that serves small market segments not being served by bigger firms is known as a ___.

(A) Market challenger(B) Market leader

(C) Market follower (D) Market nicher

144. Companies that attack other firms including market leader in an attempt to build market share are called:

(A) Market followers

(B) Market challengers

(C) Market penetrators

(D) Market Nichers

145. Which of the following is not a form of direct marketing?

(A) Personal selling.

(B)Advertising.

(C)Telephone marketing.

(D)Direct-mail marketing.

146. A firm that is willing to maintain its market share and not rock the boat is known as a ________.

(A)market challenger (B)market leader

(C)market follower (D)market nicher

147. When the total market expands, the ________ usually gains the most.

(A)market challenger (B)market leader

(C)market follower (D)market nicher

148. The marketing communications mix consists of six major modes of communications. Which of the following is ***not*** one of these modes?

(A) Personal selling.

(B) Direct marketing.

(C) Sales promotions.

(D) Packaging.

149. AIDA Model is used mainly for:

(A)Promotion Decision

(B)Product Decision

(C)Pricing Decision

(D)Redressal of Grievances

150. Marketing is a process of converting the potential customers into ....

(A) Actual customers

(B) Prospective customers

(C) Marketers

(D) None of these

---000---

UNIT-VI

MARKETING MANAGEMENT

1. (B) Directs flow of goods from producer to consumer

Explanation: Definition of Marketing

- **Committee of the American Marketing Association:** "Marketing is the performance of business activities that direct the flow of goods and services from producer to consumer or user".
- **American Marketing Association:** "Marketing is that part of economics which deals with the creation of time, place and possession utilities"
- **W. J. Stanton:** "Marketing is a total system of interacting business activities designed to plan, promote and distribute want satisfying products and services to present and potential consumers"
- **Harry L. Harsen:** "Marketing is the process of discovering and translating consumer wants into product and service specifications and then in turn helping to make it possible for more and more consumers to enjoy more and more of these products and services".
- **Kotler and Armstrong:** "Marketing is the business function that identifies customers' needs and wants, determines which target markets the organisation can serve best, and designs appropriate products, services, and programmes to serve these markets"

2. (D)All of the above.
3. (D) Theodore Levitt
4. (D) American Marketing Association
5. (B) Mazur
6. (A)Price
7. (C)Product concept
8. (C) Philip Kotler
9. (C) Overfull demand

Explanation: Demarketing:

- Efforts aimed at discouraging (not destroying) the demand for a product which:
  (1) a firm cannot supply in large-enough quantities, or
  (2) does not want to supply in a certain region where the high costs of distribution or promotion allow only a too little profit margin.
- ***Common demarketing strategies include higher prices, scaled-down advertising, and product redesign.***
- Demarketing is a ***strategy of reverse marketing*** in which a company discourages product demand in areas where they cannot realize a desired profit.
- Strategies for this include increased prices and reduced advertising in that area.

10. (A) A place where buyers and sellers meet

Explanation: Market:

- A medium that allows buyers and sellers of a specific good or service to interact in order to facilitate an exchange.
- The price that individuals pay during the transaction may be determined by a number of factors, but price is often determined by the forces of supply and demand.
- The general market where securities are traded.
- People with the desire and ability to buy a specific product/service.

11. (B)narrow view of the market

Explanation: Marketing myopia:

- A short-sighted and inward looking approach to marketing that focuses on the needs of the company instead of defining the company and its products in terms of the customers' needs and wants. It results in the failure to see and adjust to the rapid changes in their markets.
- Marketing Myopia suggests *that businesses will do better in the end if they concentrate*

on meeting customers' needs rather than on selling products.

- Marketing myopia is an advertising strategy that does not focus on the needs and wants of consumers, but the desires of a company to sell specific goods or services in the economic market.

12.(A)current product offerings

13. (B)Preservation of environment

Explanation: Green marketing

- Green marketing is the marketing of products that are presumed to be environmentally safe.
- Thus green marketing incorporates a broad range of activities, including product modification, changes to the production process, packaging changes, as well as modifying advertising.

14.(A)Customer - oriented products

Explanation: The Marketing Concept

- The marketing concept is the philosophy that firms should analyze the needs of their customers and then make decisions to satisfy those needs, better than the competition.
- In 1776 in The Wealth of Nations, ***Adam Smith*** wrote that the needs of producers should be considered only with regard to meeting the needs of consumers. While this philosophy is consistent with the marketing concept, it would not be adopted widely until nearly 200 years later.
- Management philosophy according to which a firm's goals can be best achieved through identification and satisfaction of the customers' stated and unstated needs and wants.

15.(C)Guiding the funding agencies

Explanation: Marketing function:

- A role that helps a company to identify and source potentially successful products for the marketplace and then promote them by differentiating them from similar products.
- **Functions of marketing:**

  (1)Research function

  (2)Buying function

  (3)Product development and management

  (4)Production function

  (5)Promotion function

  (6)Standardization and grading

  (7)Pricing function

  (8)Distribution function

  (9)Risk bearing function

  (10)Financing function

  (11) After sales-service

16.(D)Organic marketing concept

17.(A)Marketing

18.(D)AlRice and Jack Trout

19. (C)Selling is a part of marketing

Explanation: Marketing and selling

- Marketing and selling are related but differ greatly.
- Marketing plays a major role in creating new channels/clients and maintaining the existing channels and this contributes to more sales.
- Selling involves making more sales so as to increase the company's revenues.
- Despite the difference, the two functions are dependent on each other and therefore a firm should form a system where the two functions are carried out together.
- Marketing is the planning, pricing, promotion, packaging, advertising and selling of any product or service.
- Selling is therefore only a sliver of the overall marketing of any product or service and therein lies the difference.

20.(D) Influencer

Explanation:

- **Consumer:** A consumer is a person or group of people, such as a household, who are the final users of products or services.
- **Initiator:** An initiator can refer to a person that takes an initiative in making something happen.
- **Influencer:** Influencer marketing, is a form of marketing that has emerged from a variety of recent practices and studies, in which focus is placed on specific key individuals (or types of individual) rather than the target market as a whole.
- It identifies the individuals that have influence over potential buyers, and orients marketing activities around these influencers.
- Influencers may be potential buyers themselves, or they may be third parties. These third parties exist either in the supply chain (retailers, manufacturers, etc.) or may be so-called value-added influencers (such as journalists, academics, industry analysts, professional advisers, and so on).

21.(C)Advertising is a paid form of communication, Publicity is not a paid form of communication.

22. (A)Age

Explanation:

By sex: vitamins for men and for women. Women need more iron and calcium than men.

By age: older people have different needs than children. You might need several different products: for babies, growing children, teens, adults, and senior citizens

23.(D) Selling

24. (C)External to the company

Explanation:

- The market environment is a marketing term and refers to factors and forces that affect a firm's ability to build and maintain successful relationships with customers.
- Three levels of the environmment are:
- **Micro (internal) environment:** Small forces within the company that affect its ability to serve its customers.
- **Meso environment:** The industry in which a company operates and the industry's market(s).
- **Macro (national) environment:**
- Larger societal forces that affect the microenvironment.
- The major external and uncontrollable factors that influence an organization's decision making, and affect its performance and strategies.
- These factors include the economic factors; demographics; legal, political, and social conditions; technological changes; and natural forces.
- Specific examples of macro environment influences include competitors, changes in interest rates, changes in cultural tastes, disastrous weather, or government regulations.
- Macromarketing addresses big/important issues at the nexus of marketing and society.

25.(C)Identifying threats and opportunities

Explanation: Environmental scanning:

- Careful monitoring of an organization's internal and external environments for detecting early signs of opportunities and threats that may influence its current and future plans.
- In comparison, surveillance is confined to a specific objective or a narrow sector.

26.(D) Public Relations

The 7 P's of Services Marketing

1. Product: In case of services, the 'product' is intangible, heterogeneous and perishable. Moreover, its production and consumption are inseparable. Hence, there is scope for customizing the offering as per customer requirements and the actual customer encounter therefore assumes particular significance.

2. Pricing: Pricing of services is tougher than pricing of goods. While the latter can be priced easily by taking into account the raw material costs, in case of services attendant costs - such as labor and overhead costs - also need to be factored in.

3. Place: Since service delivery is concurrent with its production and cannot be stored or transported, the location of the service product assumes importance. Service providers have to give special thought to where the service would be provided.

4. Promotion: Since a service offering can be easily replicated promotion becomes crucial in differentiating a service offering in the mind of the consumer. Thus, service providers offering identical services such as airlines or banks and insurance companies invest heavily in advertising their services. This is crucial in attracting customers in a segment where the services providers have nearly identical offerings.

5. People: People are a defining factor in a service delivery process, since a service is inseparable from the person providing it.

6. Process: The process of service delivery is crucial since it ensures that the same standard of service is repeatedly delivered to the customers. Therefore, most companies have a service blue print which provides the details of the service delivery process, often going down to even defining the service script and the greeting phrases to be used by the service staff.

7. Physical Evidence: Since services are intangible in nature most service providers strive to incorporate certain tangible elements into their offering to enhance customer experience.

27.(D)R & D

Explanation:

1. The level of Competition
2. Perceived value of your product
3. Product development cost
4. Economic trend
5. Level of market demand
6. Demographics
7. Class of targeted customers

28.(B)Progressive people

Explanation: Diffusion of Innovations Theory:

- A hypothesis outlining how new technological and other advancements spread throughout societies and cultures, from introduction to wider-adoption. The diffusion of innovations theory seeks to explain how and why new ideas and practices are adopted, with timelines potentially spread out over long periods.
- The way in which innovations are communicated to different parts of society and the subjective opinions associated with the innovations are important factors in how quickly diffusion - or spreading - occurs.
- Factors that affect the rate of innovation diffusion include the mix of rural to urban population within a society, the society's level of education and the extent of industrialization and development.

29.(D) Appleby

30.(B)(iv) (iii) (ii) (i)

31.(C) (iii) (iv) (i) (ii)

32. (D) any felt deprivations

33. (A) United States

34. (B)Provide a continuous source of information

Explanation: Definition of Marketing Research

- **American Marketing Association (AMA):** "Marketing Research is the systematic gathering, recording and analysing of data about problems relating to the marketing of goods and services."
- **Philip Kotler:** "Marketing research is a systematic problem analysis, model building and fact finding for the purpose of improved decision-making and control in the marketing of goods and services."
- **Paul Green and Donald Tull:** "Marketing research is the systematic and objective

search for, and analysis of, information relevant to the identification and solution of any problem in the field of marketing."

- **David Luck, Donald Taylor and Hugh Wales:** "Marketing Research is the application of scientific methods in the solution of marketing problems."
- **The Marketing Research Process:** Once the need for marketing research has been established, most marketing research projects involve these steps:
  - Define the problem
  - Determine research design
  - Identify data types and sources
  - Design data collection forms and questionnaires
  - Determine sample plan and size
  - Collect the data
  - Analyze and interpret the data
  - Prepare the research report

35.(A) 1, 2 and 3 only

Explanation: Marketing plan

- A marketing plan may be part of an overall business plan. Solid marketing strategy is the foundation of a well-written marketing plan. While a marketing plan contains a list of actions, a marketing plan without a sound strategic foundation is of little use.
- A marketing plan is a comprehensive blueprint which outlines an organization's overall marketing efforts. A marketing process can be realized by the marketing mix, which is outlined in step 4. The last step in the process is the marketing controlling.
- The marketing plan can function from two points: strategy and tactics (P. Kotler, K.L. Keller). In most organizations, "strategic planning" is an annual process, typically covering just the year ahead. Occasionally, a few organizations may look at a practical plan which stretches three or more years ahead.

36.(D)all of the above

37.(C)Marketing planning and decision making

Explanation: Marketing information system:

- A system that analyzes and assesses marketing information, gathered continuously from sources inside and outside an organization.
- Timely marketing information provides basis for decisions such as product development or improvement, pricing, packaging, distribution, media selection, and promotion.
- **Donald Cox and Robert Good:** "An MIS may be defined as a set of procedures and methods for the regular, planned collection, analysis, and presentation of information for use in making marketing decisions. This of course is a step beyond logistics systems, which handle inventory control, orders, and so forth."
- **Prof. Mudit Katyani:** MIS is a planned tactic to do analysis of mainly three system requirements viz., people, information, and technology. It is required at all levels of management in executing operational, managerial, and strategic decisions. Its intention is to design the procedures which give a comprehensive report in a timely manner."

38. (C) Marketing Research System

39.(D) All of the above.

40.(A)Capacity Planning

41.(C) (ii), (i), (iii)

42. (A) Bundling

Explanation:

Bundling:

- A marketing strategy that joins products or services together in order to sell them as a single combined unit.
- Bundling allows the convenient purchase of several products and/or services from one company.
- The products and services are usually related, but they can also consist of dissimilar products which appeal to one group of customers.

Dumping:

- In international trade, the export by a country or company of a product at a price that is lower in the foreign market than the price charged in the domestic market.
- As dumping usually involves substantial export volumes of the product, it often has the effect of endangering the financial viability of manufacturers or producers of the product in the importing nation.
- Dumping is also a colloquial term that refers to the act of offloading a stock with little regard for its price.
- In economics, "dumping" is a kind of predatory pricing, especially in the context of international trade. It occurs when manufacturers export a product to another country at a price either below the price charged in its home market or below its cost of production.

43.(C) Exclusive distribution strategy

Explanation:

Extensive distribution strategy:

- A distribution strategy that utilizes multiple delivery channels and a high distribution volume to reach as many potential customers as possible.
- An extensive distribution strategy is often used in an attempt to achieve market penetration by making information about a product or product line, as well as the product themselves, available to a large number of individuals.
- It is opposite of selective distribution.

Selective distribution strategy:

- Type of product distribution that lies between intensive distribution and exclusive distribution, and in which only a few retail outlets cover a specific geographical area.
- Considered more suitable for high-end items such as 'designer' or prestige goods.
- Selective distribution is a retail strategy that involves making a product or group of products available only in certain markets.
- This is the opposite of open distribution, where a product line is distributed to as many markets as possible.
- There are several reasons for employing this approach, including the potential for limiting competition and minimizing distribution costs so that net profits are higher.
- **Selective distribution:** distribution of products only to those wholesalers or retailers who (a) agree to sell the product for no less than a certain price, (b) patronize the distributor on a regular basis or for at least a certain dollar amount annually, or (c) meet specific requirements established by the distributor as outlined by the manufacturer. Selective distribution is used primarily for hard goods , such as appliances, stereo equipment, or furniture. It allows manufacturers to maintain more control over the way their products are sold and minimizes price competition among sellers of the products.
- **Exclusive distribution:** retail selling strategy typically used by manufacturers of high-priced, generally upscale merchandise, such as cars or jewelry, whereby manufacturers grant certain dealers exclusive territorial rights to sell the product. The retailer benefits from the lack of competition, and the manufacturer benefits from a greater sales commitment on the part of the retailer. Additionally, exclusive distribution gives the manufacturer greater control over the way the product is merchandised.
- **Mass merchandiser:** Huge retail store offering a very wide range of product categories such as accessories, appliances, clothing, furniture, office equipment and stationery, and shoes.

44.(C) Customerization

Explanation:

Digitalization: Integration of digital technologies into everyday life by the digitization of everything that can be digitized.

Disintermediation:

- Disintermediation is a process that provides a user or end consumer with direct access to a product, service or information that would otherwise require a mediator such as a wholesaler, lawyer or salesperson.
- The World Wide Web has often eliminated the need for a mediator.
- End consumers merely have to research the product, service or information for themselves, thus changing the relationship they have with the manufacturer or service provider.

Customerization:

- The process that occurs when a business customizes products or services by using feedback obtained from its clients.
- A company uses a more advanced form of customerization when it can tailor its products, services and communication on an individualized basis according to specific customer preferences.

45.(C) Marketing Research

Explanation: Marketing Research:

- "Marketing Research is a systematic method of collecting, recording and analyzing of data, which is used to solve marketing problems."
- Marketing research is a systematic process. It first collects data (information) about the marketing problem. Secondly, it records this data. Then it analysis (studies) this data and draws conclusions about it. After that, it gives suggestions (advice) for solving the marketing-problem.

Features of Marketing Research

- Wide and comprehensive scope
- Systematic and scientific
- Science and art
- Collects and analyzes data
- Continuous and dynamic process
- Tool for decision-making
- Benefits company and consumers
- Similar to military intelligence
- Applied research
- Connected with MIS
- Reduces gap between producers and consumers
- Uses different methods.

Limitations:

- It does not give accurate results.
- It provides suggestions and not solutions.
- It is also a costly and time-consuming process.
- Accurate data collection and critical analysis:

46.(A)Zero level and one level
47.(C)Marketing mix

Explanation: Marketing Mix:

- It is the set of marketing tools that the firm uses to pursue its marketing objectives in the target market.
- It is the sole vehicle for creating and delivering customer value.

48.(D) All of the above

49.(D) All the above should exist

50. (D) Options (2),(3) and (4) are correct

51. (C)Involves more use of communications and computer technologies

52. (C)Systematic risk or non diversifiable risk

Explanation: Market Risk:

- The possibility for an investor to experience losses due to factors that affect the overall performance of the financial markets.
- Market risk, also called "systematic risk," cannot be eliminated through diversification, though it can be hedged against.
- The risk that a major natural disaster will cause a decline in the market as a whole is an example of market risk.
- Other sources of market risk include recessions, political turmoil, changes in interest rates and terrorist attacks.

53.(B) Initiator

54. (A)Purchasing with little or no advance planning

Explanation: Impulse buying:

- Spur of the moment, unplanned decision to buy, made just before a purchase.
- Research findings suggest that emotions and feelings play a decisive role in purchasing, triggered by seeing the product or upon exposure to a well crafted promotional message.
- Such purchases ranges from small (chocolate, clothing, magazines) to substantially large (jewelry, vehicle, work of art) and usually (about 80 percent of the time) lead to problems such as financial difficulties, family disapproval, or feeling of guilt or disappointment.

55.(B) Both (A) and (R) are correct.

56. (B) (b) (c) (a) (d)

57. (A)know thy customer

Explanation: The Ten Commandments in marketing:

1. Know Your Customer
2. Keep an Eye on the Competition
3. Don't Be All Things to All People
4. Repeat Business is the Most Profitable
5. Encourage Word-of-Mouth Marketing
6. Use a Variety of Marketing Methods
7. Focus on a Few Key Themes
8. Maintain High Ethical Standards
9. Measure Customer Satisfaction
10. Adapt to Market Changes

58.(C) Marketing plan

Explanation: The 7 P's of Services Marketing:

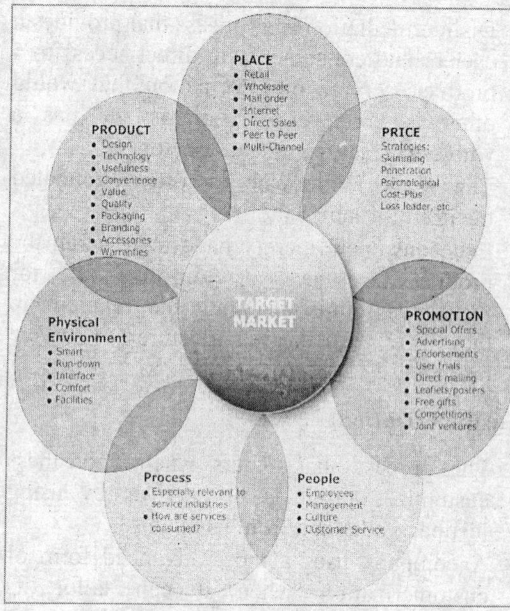

59.(D) Public relations

60.(D) All of the above

61. (D) Mc Carthy

62. (C) Market Segmentation

Explanation: Market targeting:

- It is the second step in the product promotion process, market targeting refers to picking a specific group or small set of groups to which a business will advertise.
- It is based on the idea that, because it's not really possible to make or do something that will please everyone, a business has to specialize.
- Companies select an advertising group to strengthen their brands, as well as to get an idea of potential sales for production or financing purposes.
- ***They can use three main approaches for this: universal, selective or concentrated.***
- It is common for an organization to reevaluate its target groups and related campaigns over time because markets are always somewhat flexible.
- Market targeting differs from target marketing in that a product is already

established and decisions must be made as to which market is most appropriate for it.

- In target marketing, a company finds a market it wants to serve and then develops a product appropriate for that market.

Market positioning:

- An effort to influence consumer perception of a brand or product relative to the perception of competing brands or products.
- Its objective is to occupy a clear, unique, and advantageous position in the consumer's mind.
- Market positioning is the manipulation of a brand or family of brands to create a positive perception in the eyes of the public.
- If a product is well positioned, it will have strong sales, and it may become the go-to brand for people who need that particular product.
- Poor positioning, on the other hand, can lead to bad sales and a dubious reputation.
- A number of things are involved in market positioning, with entire firms specializing in this activity and working with clients to position their products effectively.

Market Segmentation:

- The process of defining and subdividing a large homogenous market into clearly identifiable segments having similar needs, wants, or demand characteristics.
- Its objective is to design a marketing mix that precisely matches the expectations of customers in the targeted segment.
- Four basic factors that affect market segmentation are:
  (1) clear identification of the segment,
  (2) measurability of its effective size,
  (3) its accessibility through promotional efforts, and
  (4) its appropriateness to the policies and resources of the company.
- The four basic market segmentation-strategies are based on (a) behavioral (b) demographic, (c) psychographic, and (d) geographical differences.
- Generally three criteria can be used to identify different market segments:
  - Homogeneity (common needs within segment)
  - Distinction (unique from other groups)
  - Reaction (similar response to market).

Market Co-ordination:

- Ongoing and spontaneous coordination of separate economic activities of individuals (engaged in a division of labor) by the price signals generated by the interaction of demand and supply in a market.
- Interaction of demand and supply in the market generates the price signals that cause an ongoing and spontaneous coordination of separate economic activities of individuals engaged in a division of labor.

63.(C)Geographic segmentation

Explanation: Demographic segmentation:

- Demographic segmentation consists of dividing the market into groups based on variables such as age, gender family size, income, occupation, education, religion, race and nationality.
- Demographic segmentation is one of the most commonly used forms of segmentation as it is clearly identifiable. The variables used for Demographic segmentation help divide a large population into specific customer groups.
- Each and every individual has an age, gender, income etc. Thus for mass marketing, this becomes one of the best ways to diversify individuals. This also helps in analyzing lots of data in shorter time for market research as well as for promotions.
- The main demographic segmentation variables are summarised below:
  - Age
  - Life-cycle stage
  - Gender:
  - Income:
  - Social class:
  - Lifestyle:

- Within business studies we focus on the most commonly used bases for segmentation:
  - Geographical bases (region, urban/non-urban environment...)
  - Demographic bases (age, gender, life cycle phase...)
  - Psychographic bases (lifestyle, values, personality...)
  - Behaviour bases (seeking profits, degree of use, and degree of loyalty...)

64.(D) Poverty

65.(C) Meta-Market

Explanation:

Marketplace:

- A marketplace is the space, actual, virtual or metaphorical, in which a market operates.
- The term is also used in a trademark law context to denote the actual consumer environment, i.e. the 'real world' in which products and services are provided and consumed.

Market space:

- Virtual realm in the commercial world in which trading activity occurs.
- All commercial activity over the internet and other online media occurs in marketspace.

Meta-market:

- Two or more distinct markets those are associated in some way to a product or service.
- For example, the meta-market for house cleaning products includes homeowners and domestic cleaning service companies.
- Meta Market is a web-based market centered around an event or an industry, rather than a single product.
- These are markets of complementary products that are closely related in the minds of consumers, but spread across different industries.

Marketing mix:

- A planned mix of the controllable elements of a product's marketing plan commonly termed as 4Ps: product, price, place, and promotion.
- These four elements are adjusted until the right combination is found that serves the needs of the product's customers, while generating optimum income. Sometimes the first P (Product) is substituted by presentation.

66.(D)A group of products

Explanation: Product mix:

- It is also known as ***product assortment***, refers to the total number of product lines that a company offers to its customers.
- For example, a small company may sell multiple lines of products. Sometimes, these product lines are fairly similar, such as dish washing liquid and bar soap, which are used for cleaning and use similar technologies.
- Other times, the product lines are vastly different, such as diapers and razors. The four dimensions to a company's product mix include width, length, depth and consistency.

67.(A) Market research

68.(D) Sales

69. (D) (ii) (iii) (i) (iv) (v)

Explanation:

1.Need/Problem Recognition or Identification:

- This is the initial stage where an individual comes to the realization that she has a problem (or opportunity).
- It is only once an individual recognizes a problem that she can start looking for a solution.
- This stage cannot be skipped, and is always the first stage of the process.

2. Information Gathering/Determination of Alternatives:

- This is the second stage of the purchase process where an individual now begins to look for solutions to their problems or to the opportunities that they've identified.

- There are often more ways than one to achieve the given objective.

3. Assessment of Alternatives/Alleviation of Risk:

- The third phase of the process is the Assessment of Alternatives with an eye to reduce risk, and maximize the probability the objective set forth is satisfied.
- The more complex and costly the possible solutions, the more questions that have to be asked and answered.
- Each alternative is assessed in turn.

4. Purchase:

- The fourth phase of the buying process is in making the actual purchase.
- Now that the individual has decided what alternative they will go with because it offers the best perceived combination of goal achievement and minimization of risk ... they purchase.

5. Post Purchase Evaluation:

- This is the last phase of the Buying Cycle and once again it involves the individual asking themselves a series of questions, but this time the questions are designed to help the individual learn from his/her mistakes.

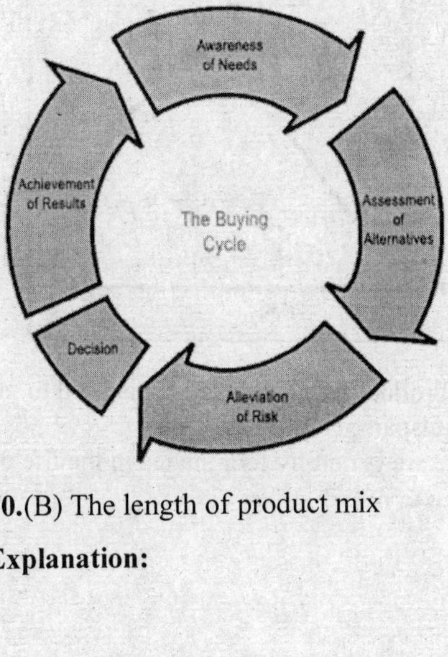

70.(B) The length of product mix

Explanation:

Width of product mix:

- The width of a company's product mix pertains to the number of product lines that a company sells.
- The product mix width of an organisation is the total number of products offered by the company.

Length of product mix:

- Product mix length pertains to the number of total products or items in a company's product mix.

Depth of product mix:

- Depth of a product mix pertains to the total number of variations for each product.
- Variations can include size, flavor and any other distinguishing characteristic.

Consistency of product mix:

- Product mix consistency pertains to how closely related product lines are to one another--in terms of use, production and distribution.
- A company's product mix may be consistent in distribution but vastly different in use.

Product Market Mix Strategy:

- Small companies usually start out with a product mix limited in width, depth and length; and have a high level of consistency.
- However, over time, the company may want to differentiate products or acquire new ones to enter new markets.
- A company can also sell the existing products to new markets by coming up with new uses for their product.

71.(B) Direct Marketing

Explanation:

Zero Level channel or Direct Marketing Channel:

- It consists of a manufacturer directly selling to the end consumer.
- This might mean door to door sales, direct mails or telemarketing.

- There will be no intermediaries in this type of chennel, like wholesalers.

One Level channel:

- As the name suggests, the one level channel has an intermediary in between the producer and the consumer.
- An example of this can be insurance in which there is an insurance agent between the insurance company and the customer.

Two level Channel:

- A widely used marketing channel especially in the FMCG and the consumer durables industry which consists of a wholesaler and a retailer.

Three level channel:

- It is observed in both the FMCG and the consumer durables industry, the three level channel can combine the roles of a distributor on top of a dealer and a retailer.
- The distributor stocks the most and spreads it to dealers who in turn give it to retailers.

72.(B) (iii) (ii) (i) (v) (iv)

73. (C) (v) (iv) (i) (ii) (iii)

74. (B) Demography

75.(B)Product Development

Explanation:

- A product development strategy may be appropriate if the firm's strengths are related to its specific customers rather than to the specific product itself.
- In this situation, it can leverage its strengths by developing a new product targeted to its existing customers.
- Similar to the case of new market development, new product development carries more risk than simply attempting to increase market share.

76.(C)product, price, place, promotion

Explanation: Marketing mix:

- A planned mix of the controllable elements of a product's marketing plan commonly termed as ***4Ps: product, price, place, and promotion.***
- These four elements are adjusted until the right combination is found that serves the needs of the product's customers, while generating optimum income. Sometimes the first P (Product) is substituted by presentation.
- Usually referring to ***E. Jerome McCarthy's 4 P classification*** for developing an effective marketing strategy, which encompasses: product, price, placement (distribution) and promotion.
- When it's a consumer-centric marketing mix, it has been extended to include three more Ps: people, process and physical evidence, and three Cs: cost, consumer and competitor.
- Depending on the industry and the target of the marketing plan, marketing managers will take various approaches to each of the four Ps.

77. (C) Market segmentation

78.(B)introduction, growth, maturity, decline

Explanation:

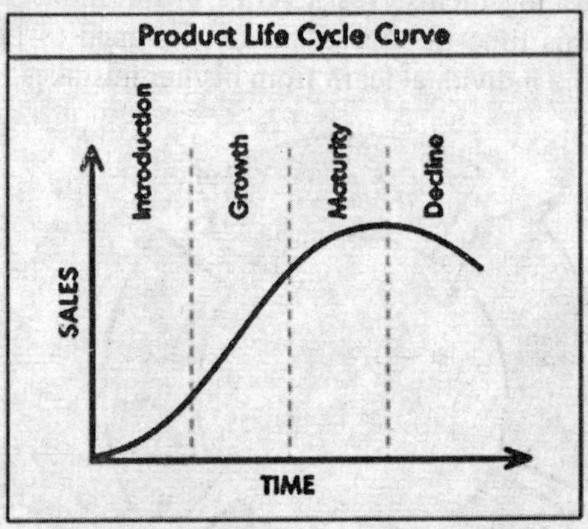

- The Product Life Cycle (PLC) is used to map the lifespan of a product.
- There are generally four stages in the life of a product.

- These four stages are the Introduction stage, the Growth stage, the Maturity stage and the Decline stage. T
- he above graph illustrates the four stages of the PLC.

79.(B)Implementation

80.(C)High initial price

Explanation: Price Skimming:

- A product pricing strategy by which a firm charges the highest initial price that customers will pay.
- As the demand of the first customers is satisfied, the firm lowers the price to attract another, more price-sensitive segment.

81.(C) (ii) (iii) (iv) (i)

82. (B) 1,2, 5 and 6

83. (D) (i) (iii) (ii) (iv)

84.(A) (ii) (iii) (i)

85. (B) (iii) (iv) (i) (ii)

86. (C) Process Mix

87. (B) Introduction, growth, maturity and decline.

Explanation: Product Life Cycle Stages:

- **Introduction Stage**: This stage of the cycle could be the most expensive for a company launching a new product. The size of the market for the product is small, which means sales are low, although they will be increasing.
- **Growth Stage**: The growth stage is typically characterized by a strong growth in sales and profits, and because the company can start to benefit from economies of scale in production, the profit margins, as well as the overall amount of profit, will increase.
- **Maturity Stage**: During the maturity stage, the product is established and the aim for the manufacturer is now to maintain the market share they have built up. They also need to consider any product modifications or improvements to the production process which might give them a competitive advantage.
- **Decline Stage**: Eventually, the market for a product will start to shrink, and this is what's known as the decline stage.

88. (A) Producer – consumer

89.(C) Commercialization

Explanation: Commercialization the process of launching a new product; it may involve heavy promotion and filling the distribution networks with the product.

90.(C)market segmentation

91. (D) Market Segmentation

Explanation:

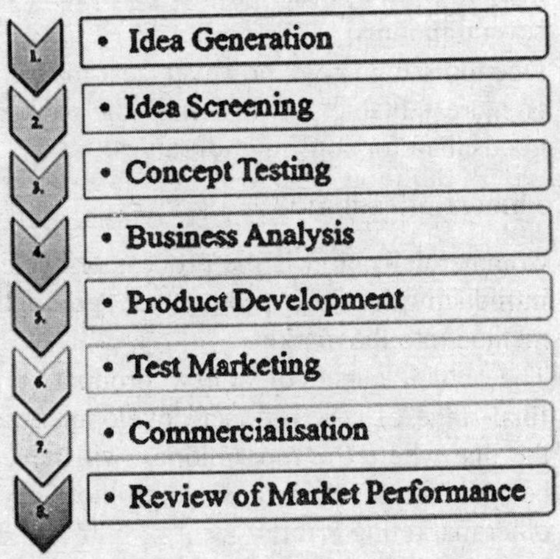

92.(C) Test Marketing

Explanation:

Idea screening:

- A process used to evaluate innovative product ideas, strategies and marketing trends.
- Idea screening criteria are used to determine compatibility with overall business objectives and whether the idea would offer a viable return on investment.

- Whatever does not meet these criteria is typically discarded.

Test marketing:

- Product development stage where the product and its marketing plan are exposed to a carefully chosen sample of the population for deciding if to reject it before its full scale launch.
- Test marketing is an experiment conducted in a field laboratory (the test market) comprising of actual stores and real-life buying situations, without the buyers knowing they are participating in an evaluation exercise.
- It simulates the eventual market-mix to ascertain consumer reaction.
- Depending on the quality and quantity of sales data required for the final decision, test marketing may last from few weeks to several months.
- Due to its high cost, however, test marketing is more suitable for fast moving packaged goods than for consumer durables.

Commercialization:

- Commercialization is the process or cycle of introducing a new product or production method into the market.
- The actual launch of a new product is the final stage of new product development and the one where the most money will have to be spent for advertising, sales promotion, and other marketing efforts.
- The Commercialization process has three key aspects:

  1. The funnel: It is essential to look at many ideas to get one or two products or businesses that can be sustained long-term.

  2. It is a stagewise process, and each stage has its own key goals and milestones.

  3. It is vital to involve key stakeholders early, including customers.

93.(B) Diversification

94.(D)Identifying and differentiating the company's products

Explanation:

- **Brand:** Brand is the "name, term, design, symbol, or any other feature that identifies one seller's product distinct from those of other sellers"
- **Branding:** The process involved in creating a unique name and image for a product in the consumers' mind, mainly through advertising campaigns with a consistent theme. Branding aims to establish a significant and differentiated presence in the market that attracts and retains loyal customers.

95.(B) Corporate branding

Explanation:

Private branding:

- A brand placed on products that a large manufacturer has created for a smaller retailer.
- The smaller retailer places their own private brand label on the final good which was created by a third party manufacturer.
- Private branding is a cost effective way to gain access to producing a product without requiring a large manufacturing or design team.
- It is also known as ***private label***.

Corporate branding:

- Corporate branding refers to a company applying its name to a product.
- The product and the company name become the brand name.
- The company can advertise several of its products under a single brand name in a practice referred to as family branding or umbrella branding.
- To consumers, corporate branding represents a level of quality that they have come to expect from the company.
- They will expect every product with the same brand name to have the same level of quality that they are familiar with.

Product-line branding:

- A group of related products manufactured by a single company.

96.(C) Individual Branding

Explanation:

Family branding:

- Family branding is a type of marketing tactic.
- It involves using one brand name to market multiple products.
- For example, a company may use one brand to market soap, lotion, hair shampoo, and nail polish.
- This differs from branding individual products, which involves giving each product its own name and image.
- For example, a company may sell lipstick and nail polish, giving each product line a separate marketing identity.

Individual branding:

- Marketing policy under which each product has its own brand, different from every other product in the same product family or from the same firm.

Brand Extension:

- A common method of launching a new product by using an existing brand name on a new product in a different category.
- A company using brand extension hopes to leverage its existing customer base and brand loyalty to increase its profits with a new product offering.
- For brand extension to be successful, there usually must be some logical association between the original product and the new one.
- A weak or nonexistent association can result in brand dilution. Also, if a brand extension is unsuccessful, it can harm the parent brand.

97.(C)Hobbies and activities

Explanation: Some categories of *psychographic factors* used in *market segmentation include*: activity, interest, opinion (AIOs); attitudes; values; behavior.

98.(C) the largest allowable probability of accepting a bad lot

Explanation:

Consumer's risk:

- Probability of loss from accepting a batch from the producer which, in fact, should have been rejected.
- Consumer risk is a potential risk found in all consumer-oriented products, that a product not meeting quality standards will pass undetected though the manufacturer's quality control system and enter the consumer marketplace.

99. (C) 2 and 3 are true

100. (D)Societal marketing

Explanation: Innovative marketing:

- It is a process where a product is marketed and communicated to the target group by the help of ideas and process which were not used earlier.
- It can be done through changes in the product design, launching the product in unique place, promoting through unconventional method, uniquely pricing the product etc.

Consumer-oriented marketing:

- A service offered by companies that focuses on the internal and external needs of a business's customers.
- Consumer orientation establishes and monitors standards of customer satisfaction and strives to meet the clientele's needs and expectations related to the product or service sold by the business.
- As today the market is characterised by a number of products, a variety of diverse customers and stiff competition. In such a scenario, marketing with consumer in mind has become a necessity.
- Marketing managers are shifting their focus from selling a product to creating something that is needed.
- Starting from product creation to selling and servicing, consumer focus is given the

utmost priority.

- The focus group discussions, Surveys and feedbacks done by companies to understand consumers are some examples to show how much importance is given to consumers.

Value marketing:

- Values-Based Marketing is a business term describing companies whose core values are tightly aligned with their business strategy.
- Common examples include Ben & Jerry's Ice Cream and The Body Shop. Consumers buy based as much on an emotional connection with protecting the Earth and animal rights, as their satisfaction with the ice cream and the cosmetics.

Societal marketing:

- A promotional process whereby a business first assesses the interests of targeted consumers and then aims to deliver products more effectively and efficiently than its competition so that it benefits their customer's and society's overall welfare.
- The societal marketing approach tends to balance the pursuit of business profits with consumer desires and society's best interests.

101. (D)brand extension strategy

102. (D)Marketing implementation.

103. (C) Arbitrage

Explanation:

Hedging:

- Making an investment to reduce the risk of adverse price movements in an asset. Normally, a hedge consists of taking an offsetting position in a related security, such as a futures contract.
- Investors use this strategy when they are unsure of what the market will do.
- A perfect hedge reduces your risk to nothing (except for the cost of the hedge).

Speculation:

- The act of trading in an asset, or conducting a financial transaction, that has a significant risk of losing most or all of the initial outlay, in expectation of a substantial gain.
- With speculation, the risk of loss is more than offset by the possibility of a huge gain; otherwise, there would be very little motivation to speculate.

Arbitrage:

- The simultaneous purchase and sale of an asset in order to profit from a difference in the price.
- It is a trade that profits by exploiting price differences of identical or similar financial instruments, on different markets or in different forms.
- Arbitrage exists as a result of market inefficiencies; it provides a mechanism to ensure prices do not deviate substantially from fair value for long periods of time.

Gambling Income:

- Any income that is the result of games of chance or wagers on events with uncertain outcomes (gambling).
- This income is subject to taxation.
- Gambling income includes any money earned playing slot machines, bingo or the lottery.
- It also includes money derived from betting on horse races, boxing, sumo wrestlers and almost anything else.

Gambling Loss:

- A loss resulting from games of chance or wagers on events with uncertain outcomes (gambling).
- These losses can only be claimed against gambling income.
- Gambling losses include the cash lost at the slot machines or when a "sure bet" comes up lame in the race.
- Total gambling losses claimed cannot exceed gambling income.

104. (B) Place

105. (A)Advertising, publicity, personal selling and sales promotion

106. (D)Direct marketing

Explanation: Promotion mix:

- A specific combination of promotional methods used for one product or a family of products.
- Elements of a promotion mix may include print or broadcast advertising, direct marketing, personal selling, point of sale displays, and/or merchandising.
- There are five main aspects of a promotional mix as under:

  1. Advertising: Presentation and promotion of ideas, goods, or services by an identified sponsor. Examples: Print ads, radio, television, billboard, direct mail, brochures and catalogs, signs, in-store displays, posters, motion pictures, Web pages, banner ads, and emails.

  2. Personal selling: A process of helping and persuading one or more prospects to purchase a good or service or to act on any idea through the use of an oral presentation. Examples: Sales presentations, sales meetings, sales training and incentive programs for intermediary salespeople, samples, and telemarketing. Can be face-to-face selling or via telephone.

  3. Sales promotion: Media and non-media marketing communication are employed for a pre-determined, limited time to increase consumer demand, stimulate market demand or improve product availability. Examples: Coupons, sweepstakes, contests, product samples, rebates, tie-ins, self-liquidating premiums, trade shows, trade-ins, and exhibitions.

  4. Public relations: Paid intimate stimulation of supply for a product, service, or business unit by planting significant news about it or a favorable presentation of it in the media. Examples: Newspaper and magazine articles/reports, TVs and radio presentations, charitable contributions, speeches, issue advertising, and seminars.

  5. Direct Marketing is a channel-agnostic form of advertising that allows businesses and nonprofits to communicate straight to the customer, with advertising techniques such as mobile messaging, email, interactive consumer websites, online display ads, fliers, catalog distribution, promotional letters, and outdoor advertising.

  6. Corporate image: Corporate image may also be considered as the sixth aspect of promotion mix. The image of an organization is a crucial point in marketing. If the reputation of a company is bad, consumers are less willing to buy a product from this company as they would have been, if the company had a good image.

  7. Sponsorship is sometimes added as an seventh aspect.

107. (A)Ultimate Consumer

Explanation: Channels of distribution

Producer-Customer:

- This is the simplest and shortest channel in which no middlemen is involved and producers directly sell their products to the consumers.
- It is fast and economical channel of distribution.
- Under this channel the producer or entrepreneur performs all the marketing activities himself and has full control over distribution.
- A producer may sell directly to consumers through door-to-door salesmen, direct mail or through his own retail stores.
- Big firms adopt this channel to cut distribution costs and to sell industrial products of high value. Small producers and producers of perishable commodities also sell directly to local consumers.

Producer-Retailer-Customer:

- This channel of distribution involves only one middlemen called 'retailer'.
- Under this channel, the producer sells his product to big retailers (or retailers who buy goods in large quantities) who in turn sell to the ultimate consumers.

- This channel relieves the manufacturer from burden of selling the goods himself and at the same time gives him control over the process of distribution.
- This is often suited for distribution of consumer durables and products of high value.

Producer-Wholesaler-Retailer-Customer:

- This is the most common and traditional channel of distribution.
- Under this channel, two middlemen i.e. wholesalers and retailers are involved.
- Here, the producer sells his product to wholesalers, who in turn sell it to retailers and retailers finally sell the product to the ultimate consumers.
- This channel is suitable for the producers having limited finance, narrow product line and who needed expert services and promotional support of wholesalers.
- This is mostly used for the products with widely scattered market.

Producer-Agent-Wholesaler-Retailer-Customer:

- This is the longest channel of distribution in which three middlemen are involved.
- This is used when the producer wants to be fully relieved of the problem of distribution and thus hands over his entire output to the selling agents.
- The agents distribute the product among a few wholesalers.
- Each wholesaler distribute the product among a number of retailers who finally sell it to the ultimate consumers.
- This channel is suitable for wider distribution of various industrial products.

108. (D) Publicity

Explanation: Constituent of promotion-mix:

1. Advertising: Presentation and promotion of ideas, goods, or services by an identified sponsor. Examples: Print ads, radio, television, billboard, direct mail, brochures and catalogs, signs, in-store displays, posters, motion pictures, Web pages, banner ads, and emails.

2. Personal selling: A process of helping and persuading one or more prospects to purchase a good or service or to act on any idea through the use of an oral presentation. Examples: Sales presentations, sales meetings, sales training and incentive programs for intermediary salespeople, samples, and telemarketing. Can be face-to-face selling or via telephone.

3. Sales promotion: Media and non-media marketing communication are employed for a pre-determined, limited time to increase consumer demand, stimulate market demand or improve product availability. Examples: Coupons, sweepstakes, contests, product samples, rebates, tie-ins, self-liquidating premiums, trade shows, trade-ins, and exhibitions.

4. Public relations: Paid intimate stimulation of supply for a product, service, or business unit by planting significant news about it or a favorable presentation of it in the media. Examples: Newspaper and magazine articles/reports, TVs and radio presentations, charitable contributions, speeches, issue advertising, and seminars.

5. Direct Marketing: It is a channel-agnostic form of advertising that allows businesses and nonprofits to communicate straight to the customer, with advertising techniques such as mobile messaging, email, interactive consumer websites, online display ads, fliers, catalog distribution, promotional letters, and outdoor advertising.

6. Corporate image: Corporate image may also be considered as the sixth aspect of promotion mix. The Image of an organization is a crucial point in marketing. If the reputation of a company is bad, consumers are less willing to buy a product from this company as they would have been, if the company had a good image.

7. Sponsorship: It is sometimes added as an seventh aspect.

109. (D) (i) (ii) (iii) (iv)

110. (C)Promoting

Explanation: The Main Principles of Personal selling are.

- Professionalism
- Negotiation
- Relationship marketing

111. (C)High pricing

Explanation:

- **Market skimming pricing:** An approach under which a producer sets a high price for a new high-end product (such as an expensive perfume) or a uniquely differentiated technical product (such as one-of-a-kind software or a very advanced computer). Its objective is to obtain maximum revenue from the market before substitutes products appear.
- **Price Skimming:**A product pricing strategy by which a firm charges the highest initial price that customers will pay. As the demand of the first customers is satisfied, the firm lowers the price to attract another, more price-sensitive segment.

112. (A)Consumer satisfaction

Explanation:

Consumer satisfaction:

- Customer satisfaction, a term frequently used in marketing, is a measure of how products and services supplied by a company meet or surpass customer expectation.
- Customer satisfaction is defined as "the number of customers, or percentage of total customers, whose reported experience with a firm, its products, or its services (ratings) exceeds specified satisfaction goals."

Consumer delight:

- The very favorable experience of the client of a business when they have received a good or service that significantly surpasses what they had initially anticipated.
- A marketing department can use instances of customer delight to a company's advantage by requesting referrals and obtaining testimonials from delighted customers that can help attract new customers.

113. (C)Shillong

114. (D) Attention, Interest, Desire, Action

Explanation:

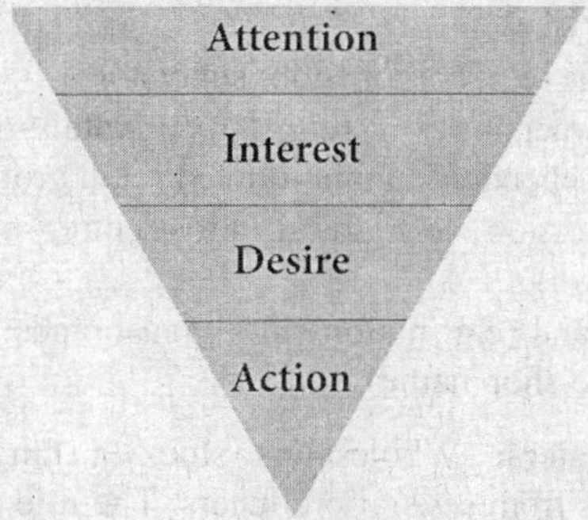

- AIDA is an acronym used in marketing and advertising that describes a common list of events that may occur when a consumer engages with an advertisement. The base of brand promotion also.
- **Attention (Awareness):** attract the attention of the customer.
- **Interest:** raise customer interest by focusing on and demonstrating advantages and benefits (instead of focusing on features, as in traditional advertising).
- **Desire:** convince customers that they want and desire the product or service and that it will satisfy their needs.
- **Action:** lead customers towards taking action and/or purchasing.
- Using a system like this gives one a general understanding of how to target a market effectively.
- Moving from step to step, one loses some percent of prospects.
- AIDA is a historical model, rather than representing current thinking in the methods of advertising effectiveness.

115. (C) Media Planning

116. (D) Manufacturing

Distribution - Role of Intermediaries

Retailers:

- Retailers operate outlets that trade directly with household customers. Retailers can be classified in several ways:
  - Type of goods being sold (e.g. clothes, grocery, furniture)
  - Type of service (e.g. self-service, counter-service)
  - Size (e.g. corner shop; superstore)
  - Ownership (e.g. privately-owned independent; public-quoted retail group
  - Location (e.g. rural, city-centre, out-of-town)
  - Brand (e.g. nationwide retail brands; local one-shop name).

Wholesalers: Wholesalers stock a range of products from several producers. The role of the wholesaler is to sell onto retailers. Wholesalers usually specialize in particular products.

Distributors and dealers: Distributors or dealers have a similar role to wholesalers – that of taking products from producers and selling them on. However, they often sell onto the end customer rather than a retailer. They also usually have a much narrower product range. Distributors and dealers are often involved in providing after-sales service.

Franchises: Franchises are independent businesses that operate a branded product (usually a service) in exchange for a licence fee and a share of sales.

Agents: Agents sell the products and services of producers in return for a commission (a percentage of the sales revenues)

117. (B)Outside Selling

Explanation:

- In the sales and marketing, "personal selling" singles out those situations in which a real human being is trying to sell something to another face-to-face.
- Personal selling is the interpersonal arm of the promotion mix. The sales force acts as a critical link between a company and its customers.
- Salespeople represent the company to the customer and the customer to the company to produce customer satisfaction and company profit.

118. (D)All the above

119. (D)All the above

120. (B)Environment friendly

121. (A)Motivation

122. (D) Sales promotion

Explanation: Sales promotion: Stimulation of sales achieved through contests, demonstrations, discounts, exhibitions or trade shows, games, giveaways, point-of-sale displays and merchandising, special offers, and similar activities.

123. (B) Consumer delight

Explanation:

Customer satisfaction:

- A term frequently used in marketing, is a measure of how products and services supplied by a company meet or surpass customer expectation.
- Customer satisfaction is defined as "the number of customers, or percentage of total customers, whose reported experience with a firm, its products, or its services (ratings) exceeds specified satisfaction goals."

Customer delight:

- The very favorable experience of the client of a business when they have received a good or service that significantly surpasses what they had initially anticipated.
- A marketing department can use instances of customer delight to a company's advantage by requesting referrals and obtaining testimonials from delighted customers that can help attract new customers.

124. (A) Buyer's

Explanation: Consumer markets:

- Markets dominated by products and services designed for the general consumer.
- Consumer markets are typically split into four primary categories: consumer products, food and beverage products, retail products, and transportation products.
- Industries in the consumer markets often have to deal with shifting brand loyalties and uncertainty about the future popularity of products and services.

125. (C) Publicity

126. (D) All the above

Explanation:

- Foreign exchange market is a market where currencies are traded internationally every day, making forex larger than all bond markets put together.
- Currency markets are in form of spot, forward, futures and options markets.
- **Functions of the Foreign Exchange Market:**

  (i)To effect transfer of purchasing power between countries- transfer function;

  (ii)To provide credit for foreign trade - credit function; and

  (iii)To furnish facilities for hedging foreign exchange risks - hedging function.

127. (D) 1, 2 and 3 are true

128. (C) Investment Management

129. (C)Customer Gap

130. (D)Internal databases

131. (D)All the above

132. (A) Sole arbitrator

133. (C) Sequencing

134. (D)William Sharpe

135. (B)Buying ice-creams

136. (B) Production

137. (A)Both (A) and (R) are correct and (R) is correct explaination of (A)

138. (C)One measure of their satisfaction with a firm and its products

139. (C)Learning

140. (C)Customer value

141. (D) Pricing in international trade

Explanation: Free On Board (FOB):

- A trade term requiring the seller to deliver goods on board a vessel designated by the buyer.
- The seller fulfills its obligations to deliver when the goods have passed over the ship's rail.
- When used in trade terms, the word "free" means the seller has an obligation to deliver goods to a named place for transfer to a carrier.

142. (A)Luxury goods

Explanation:

- Price skimming is a pricing strategy in which a marketer sets a relatively high price for a product or service at first, then lowers the price over time.
- High price aimed at higher income groups for luxury or status goods, or at extracting maximum returns from a market for a new technology product before competitors emerge.

143. (D) Market nicher

144. (B) Market challengers

Explanation: Market Penetration:

- It is a measure of brand or category popularity.
- It is defined as the number of people who buy a specific brand or a category of goods at least once in a given period, divided by the size of the relevant market population.

Market follower:

- A company that allows other more dominant firms to lead the way within the marketplace that it does business in.
- For example, a smaller business that is a market follower might keep close tabs on the activities at major market leader firms and seek to copy or improve upon the leader's product releases and marketing efforts.

Market niche:

- A small but profitable segment of a market suitable for focused attention by a marketer.
- Market niches do not exist by themselves, but are created by identifying needs or wants that are not being addressed by competitors, and by offering products that satisfy them.

Market Challenger:

- A firm that has a market share below that of the market leader, but enough of a market presence that it can exert upward pressure in its effort to gain more control.
- Market challengers are able to jockey for industry leadership several ways: challenging the market leader on price (direct approach), increasing product differentiation or improving customer service (indirect approach), or launching an entirely new product or service in order to change the field (radical approach).

145. (B)Advertising.

146. (C)market follower

147. (B)market leader

148. (D) Packaging.

149. (A)Promotion Decision

150. (A) Actual customers

---000---

UNIT-VII

PRODUCTION MANAGEMENT AND OPERATION RESEARCH

1. " production" may be defined as an act of:
   (A)Creating utility (B) Earning profit
   (C)Destroying utility (D) Providing services
2. Production system which enables for maximizing the scale advantage is:
   (A)Flow type (B) Intermittent type
   (C)Batch type (D) None of the above
3. Addition of value to raw materials through application of technology is :
   (A) Product (B) Production
   (C) Advancement (D) Transformation
4. The real aim of production is:
   (A) To create material goods
   (B) To eliminate poverty
   (C) To satisfy people's wants
   (D) To provide basic necessities
5. Acceptance sampling is used in
   (A) Job production (B) Batch production
   (C) Mass production (D) All of these
6. Match the following:

   Types of Production System

   (a)Job type
   (b)Mass type
   (c)Batch type
   (d)Project type

   Characteristics

   (i)Stationery layout and Unique
   (ii)Functional Departments and Complicated Material management
   (iii)Huge Volume and Standard Design
   (iv) Large Variety and Less Investment

   Choose the correct option:

	(a)	(b)	(c)	(d)
(A)	(iv)	(iii)	(ii)	(i)
(B)	(i)	(ii)	(iii)	(iv)
(C)	(iii)	(iv)	(ii)	(i)
(D)	(ii)	(i)	(iv)	(iii)

7. Qualities required for production concept
   (i)Products are widely available and inexpensive
   (ii)Managers concentrate on high production efficiency and low cost
   (iii)Mass distribution
   (iv)All the above
   (A) (i) and (ii) are true
   (B) (ii) and (iii) are true
   (C) (i) and (iii) are true
   (D) All the above are true
8. The primary role of a production manager is
   (A) To meet the production target and delivery schedule
   (B) To produce goods/services of right quality
   (C)To produce goods/services by right quantity at the predetermined time
   (D) All of the above
9. Addition of value to raw materials through application of technology is :
   (A) Product (B) Production
   (C) Advancement (D) Transformation
10. Production cost refers to prime cost plus
    (A)Factory overheads
    (B)Factory and administration overheads

(C)Factory, administration and sales overheads

(D)Factory, administration, sales overheads and profit

11. Which one of the following is not the function of Production Management?

(A)Production, Planning and Control

(B)Procurement of Raw Materials

(C)Market Intelligence and Survey

(D)Plant Location and Layout

12. The responsibility of production manager is to take decisions relating to :

(A) System Design (B) System operation

(C) Inventory control (D) Quality control

13. Organize the following activities in production planning process in the correct order:

(i)Master Production Schedule

(ii)Raw Material Purchase Orders

(iii)Aggregate Production Planning

(iv) Material Requirements Planning

Choose the right option:

(A)	(iii)	(i)	(ii)	(iv)
(B)	(iii)	(i)	(iv)	(ii)
(C)	(iv)	(iii)	(ii)	(i)
(D)	(i)	(ii)	(iii)	(iv)

14. In inventory control theory, the economic order quantity is:

(A)average level of inventory

(B)optimum lot size

(C)capacity of a warehouse

(D)lot size corresponding to break-even analysis

15. Goods used by an organization in producing other goods is called:

(A) Consumer goods (B) Industrial goods

(C) Speciality goods (D) None of the above

16. Which of the following is not an element of production management?

(A) Plant (B) Profit

(C) Process (D) People

17. Gantt chart is used for:

(A) Inventory control

(B) Material handling

(C) Production schedule

(D) Machine repair schedules

18. Which one of the following chart gives simultaneously information about the progress of work and machine loading?

(A)Process chart

(B)Machine load chart

(C)Man-machine chart

(D)Gantt chart

19. Bar chart is suitable for

(A) Large project (B) Major work

(C) Minor work (D) All of these

20. Which of the following charts are used for plant layout design?

(A)Operation process chart (B) Travel chart

(C) Man machine chart (D) All of these

21. Economic lot size is known as:

(A)The lot size for which the total cost per time period is minimum.

(B)The ordering cost and carrying cost are minimum.

(C)The lot size that strikes a balance between ordering cost and carrying cost.

(D)The quantity to be ordered each time is fixed.

22. Decision on plant layout and location are concerned with :

(A)System design (B) System operations

(C)System control (D) None of the above

23. The main object of scientific layout is

(A) to produce better quality of product

(B) to utilise maximum floor area

(C) to minimise production delays

(D) all of these

24. According to Muther, the basic principle of best layout is:

(A) Principle of over-all integration

(B) Principle of flow

(C) Principle of flexibility

(D) All of these

25. Which factor needs not to be considered in the location of a plant?

(A)Management Institution

(B)Availability of power

(C)Infrastructure facilities

(D)Marketing facilities

26. In order to avoid excessive multiplication of facilities, the layout preferred is

(A) Product layout (B) Process layout

(C) Group layout (D)static layout

27. The product layout

(A) lowers overall manufacturing time

(B) requires less space for placing machines

(C) utilizes machine and labour better

(D) all of these

28. Product layout is also known as

(A) Analytical layout (B) synthetic layout

(C) Static product layout (D) none of these

29. Product layout is used for

(A) Job production (B) Batch production

(C) Mass production (D) Any one of these

30. Product layout is best suited where

(A) One type of product is produced

(B) Product is standardized

(C) Product is manufactured in large quantities

(D) all of the above

31. In product layout

(A)Specialized and strict supervision is required

(B)Machines cannot be used to their maximum capacity

(C)Manufacturing cost rises with a fall in the volume of production

(D) All of the above

32. The type of layout used for manufacturing steam turbines, is

(A) Product layout (B) process layout

(C) Fixed position layout (D) None of these

33. Which of the following type of layout is suitable for automobile manufacturing concern?

(A) Product layout (B) Fixed position layout

(C) Process layout (D) Combination layout

34. In process layout:

(A) Handling and back-tracking of materials is too much

(B) Production control is more difficult and costly

(C) Routing and scheduling is more difficult

(D) All of the above

35. Process layout is also known as

(A)Analytical layout (B) Synthetic layout

(C) Static product layout(D) None of these

36. Process layout is employed:

(A)Where low volume of production is required

(B)Where similar jobs are manufactured on similar machines

(C)Where machines are arranged on functional basis

(D)All of the above

37. Which of the following is not to be considered for plant location decision?

(A) Availability of labour

(B) Availability of power

(C) Availability of raw material

(D) Brand image

38. Which of the following departments is not directly affected by the facilities location decision?

(A) Production (B) Marketing

(C) Personnel (D) Finance

39. Which among the following will suit the best as location for a chemical plant?

(A) Desert Area (B) Coastal Area

(C) Plains (D) Hill Area

40. Decision on plant layout and location are concerned with:

(A) System design (B) System operations

(C) System control (D) None of the above

41. Fixed Position Layout is used when

(A)the operation requires heavy tools and equipments.

(B)the operation requires only hand tools and simple equipments.

(C)the continuity of production process is to be maintained.

(D)none of the above

42. When work stations are arranged according to the progressive steps by which the product is produced, it is called a:

(A) Functional layout (B) Process layout

(C) Job shop layout (D) Product layout

43. CRAFT considers exchanges of locations for those departments which

(A) have the same area

(B) have a common border

(C) either (A) or (B)

(D) have same costs per unit of distance

44. Fixed position layout is also known as

(A) Analytical layout (B) Synthetic layout

(C) Static product layout (D) None of these

45. In fixed position layout

(A)Total production cost is less

(B) Material movement is less

(C) Capital investment is minimum

(D) All of these

46. Which one of the following is ***not*** the Type of Plant Layout?

(A)Process Layout (B) Product Layout

(C)Fixed Layout (D) Selection Layout

47. Ship building and construction of dams and bridges are typical examples of:

(A) Fixed position layout

(B) Functional layout

(C) Product layout

(D) Project type layout

48. When making purchase decisions the main consideration involved in organizational buying is

(A) Product quality (B) Price

(C) Service (D) All the above

49. A Floor plan for determination and arranging the desired machinery and equipment of a Plant is referred to as:

(A) Plant Location (B) Plant Lay-Out

(C) Product Design (D) Process Planning

50. Batch production is appropriately applicable to:

(A) Medicine production

(B) Sugar production

(C) Petroleum products

(D) Agriculture produce

51. Strategic production planning decisions include :

(A) Quality development

(B) Make or Buy decision

(C) Manpower planning

(D) Layout planning

52. Production control is concerned with :

(A) Establishment of Quality Standard norms

(B) Execution of production plan

(C) Expediting the production process

(D) Product Quality control

53. In which stage of product life cycle, the company takes decision whether to maintain, harvest or drop the product?

(A) Introduction (B) Growth

(C) Maturity (D) Decline

54. Production Management Tactical Planning decisions include:

(A) Establishing parameters for measuring operational efficiency and productivity.

(B) Establishing quality specifications and test details.

(C) Determining starting and finishing time of each job in the work stations.

(D None of the above

55. The aggregate production plan spans:

(A) Short time horizon

(B) Intermediate time horizon

(C) Long time horizon

(D) None of the above

56. The time that elapses between the purchase of raw materials and the collection of cash for sales is referred as:

(A) Production cycle (B) Operating cycle

(C) Cash cycle (D) Organization cycle

57. Tempering is a process of :

(A) Joining (B) Heat Treatment

(C) Surface Treatment (D) Forming

58. Moving average forecasting is used to

(A) establish the trend of the past

(B) forecast the current demand

(C) forecast market competition

(D) forecast Quasi demand

59. Vogel's Approximation method is used to :

(A) Study the Time and motion problem

(B) Solve the transportation problem

(C) Study the production scheduling problem

(D) Forecast demand

60. Product Mix includes :

(A) Product line (B) Product Depth

(C) Product Breadth (D) All the above

61. Product mix is done on a single assembly line for the purpose of:

(A) reducing WIP inventory

(B) meeting varied choice of customers

(C) leveling workload and reducing idle time

(D) reduce cost per unit

62. The number of product lines a company carries is called

(A) Product range (B) Product mix depth

(C) Product mix width (D) Product line length

63. MRP stands for :

(A) Material Requirement Planning

(B) Material Reordering Planning

(C) Material Requisition Planning

(D) Material Recording Planning

64. Which one of the following is the objective of production scheduling?

(A)Where to start the operation

(B)When to start the operation

(C)How to start the operation

(D)When to start as well as stop the operation

65. The factors to be considered for production scheduling are:

(A) Component design (B) Route sheet

(C) Time standards (D) all of these

66. The production scheduling is simpler and high volume of output and high labour efficiency are achieved in the case of:

(A) Product layout

(B) Process layout

(C) Fixed position layout

(D)Combination of line and process layout

67. Which of the following is the objective of production scheduling?

(A) Where to start the operation

(B) When to start the operation

(C) How to start the operation

(D)When to start as well as stop the operation

68. At which stage of new product development process, the launching of New Product will take place?

(A) Business Analysis

(B) Commercialization

(C) Test Marketing

(D) Marketing Strategy Development

69. In production control, scheduling includes:

(A)Deciding about the time when the production will reach various departments.

(B)Estimating the time to be consumed in these departments.

(C)How much time will be taken in transferring production from one department to another?

(D)All of the above.

70. In production management, dispatching includes :

(A) Giving work to machines and places.

(B) Providing materials, tools, etc. to works.

(C) Issuing appropriate orders for production process.

(D) All of the above.

71. Dispatching:

(A) Prescribes the sequence of operations to be followed

(B)Determines the programme for the operations

(C)Is concerned with the starting of processes

(D)Regulates the progress of job through various processes

72. In manufacturing management, the term 'Dispatching' is used to describe

(A) Dispatch of sales order

(B) Dispatch of factory mail

(C) Dispatch of finished product of the user

(D)Dispatch of work orders through shop floor

73. Scheduling:

(A) Prescribes the sequence of operations to be followed

(B) Determines the programme for the operations

(C) Is concerned with starting of processes

(D) Regulates the progress of job through various processes

74. Production scheduling is done to achieve :

(A) Maximum utilization of the plant and machinery

(B) Maximum utilization of the work force

(C) Minimize inventories of raw materials and work in progress

(D) All of the above

75. The objective of Operations Management is to enhance the performance of an organization in terms of its:

(A) Productivity (B) Product quality

(C)Competitiveness (D) Overall performance

76. Read the following statements and select correct answer

Statement-1: Operations Research is useful for optimization of resources.

Statement-2: Operations Research does not determine the optimum replacement policies.

(A) Statements 1 and 2 are true

(B)Statement 1 is true but statement 2 is not true

(C)Statement 1 is not true but statement 2 is true

(D) Both statements 1 and 2 are not true

77. Quantitative techniques used to solve business problems are called:

(A) Operations management

(B) Operation science

(C) Operation research

(D) Management operation

78. Read the following statements and select the correct combination given there under:

Statement-1: Linear Programming is a mathematical function.

Statement-2: Transportation model is one of the parts of Linear Programming.

(A) Statement 1 is true but 2 is not true

(B) Statements 1 and 2, both are true

(C) Statement 1 is not true but 2 is true

(D) Both the statements 1 and 2 are not true

79. Linear programming can be applied successfully to:

(A) Chemical industry(B) Oil industry

(C) Banks (D) All of these

80. A feasible solution to the linear programming problem should:

(A) Satisfy the problem constraints

(B) Optimize the objective function

(C) Satisfy the problem constraints and non-negativity restrictions

(D)Satisfy the non-negativity restrictions

81. Work study involves:

(A) Only method study

(B) Only work measurement

(C) Method study and work measurement

(D) Only motion study

82. Work study refers to:

(A)Analysis of work into smaller parts followed by re-arrangement of these parts to give the same effectiveness at lesser cost.

(B)Analytical investigation of the methods involved in the work.

(C)Developing new methods to give work effectiveness.

(D) All of the above

83. Work study is mainly aimed at:

(A) Determining the most efficient method of performing a job

(B) Establishing the minimum time of completion of a job

(C) Developing the standard method and standard time of a job

(D) Economizing the motions involved on the part of the worker while performing a job

84. The average time recorded by work study man for an operation is called

(A) Standard time (B) Normal time

(C) Representative time (D) None of these

85. The work study is done by means of

(A) Planning chart (B) Process chart

(C) Stop watch (D) Any one of these

86. Travel charts are used to

(A) Analyze material handling

(B) Determine inventory control difficulties

(C) Plan material handling procedure and routes

(D) all of the above

87. Work measurement is essential for

(A) Labour utilization and efficiency

(B) Determining the delivery dates

(C) Introducing financial incentive schemes

(D) All of the above

88. Work measurement refers to:

(A)The length of time it takes to complete a work task assigned to a specific job

(B) Improving work methods

(C)Arrangement of machines according to sequence of operations

(D) Planning the work and working the plans

89. The main objective of work measurement is to

(A) Plan and schedule of production

(B) Formulate a proper incentive scheme

(C)Estimate the selling prices and delivery dates

(D) All of the above

90. Work sampling is applied for:

(A) Estimation of the percentage utilisation of machine tools

(B) Estimating the percentage of the time consumed by various job activities

(C) Finding out time standards, especially where the job is not repetitive and where time study by stop watch method is not possible

(D)All of the above

91. Infeasibility means that the number of solutions to the linear programming models that satisfies all constraints is

(A) At least 1. (B)Zero.

(C) An infinite number. (D) At least 2.

92. Which of the following conditions are necessary for applying linear programming?

(A)These must be a well defined objective function.

(B)The decision variables should be interrelated and non-negative.

(C)The resources must be in limited supply.

(D)All of the above

93. Sensitivity analysis may be used in

(A) Linear programming

(B) PERT

(C) Transportation programming

(D) CPM

94. Linear Programming is a technique used in :

(A)Plant Layout

(B) Production Programme

(C)Product Mix

(D)Manufacturing Sequence

95. In L.P.P. a basic solution is called Degenerate if :

(A)None of the variables vanish

(B)All basic variables have infinite values

(C)L.P.P. has a finite no. of solution

(D)One or more of the basic variables vanish

96. Surplus variables are introduced for solving :

(A)The transportation problem

(B)The L.P.P. problem with constraints are of less than type

(C)The CPM problems

(D)The L.P.P. problems with constraints are of greater than type

97. A LPP will have an unbounded solution if :

(A)The objective function is non linear

(B)If all the basic solutions vanish

(C)If for atleast one j, for which $y_{ij} \leq 0$, $Z_j - C_j$ is negative

(D)If for all j, for which $y_{ij} \leq 0$, $Z_j - C_j$ is positive

98. Mini Max method of decision making is done when :

(A) The problem is under risk

(B) The problem is under uncertainty

(C) The problem is of deterministic type

(D)The problem is under linear programming problem

99. The Graphical method can be used to solve

(A)A linear programming problem with all integer data base.

(B)A linear programming problem with two decision variables.

(C)Any linear programming problem.

(D)A transportation problem with two origins and two destinations.

100. Linear programming models solve problems dealing with:

(A)Relatives and absolutes

(B) Routes and mixes

(C) Dispersions and similarities

(D) Rupees and percentages

101. Which of the following is a valid objective function for a linear programming problem?

(A)Max 5xy (B)Min $4x + 3y + (2/3)z$

(C)Max $5x^2 + 6y^2$ (D)Min $(x_1 + x_2)/x_3$

102. Slack is:

(A)The difference between the left and right sides of a constraint.

(B)The amount by which the left side of a $<$ constraint is smaller than the right side.

(C)The amount by which the left side of a $>$ constraint is larger than the right side.

(D)Exists for each variable in a linear programming problem.

103. When slack of an activity is positive

(A)It represents a situation where extra resources are available and the completion of project is not delayed

(B)It represents that a programme falls behind schedule and additional resources are required to complete the project in time

(C) The activity is critical and any delay in its performance will delay the completion of whole project

(D) Any one of the above

104. When slack of an activity is negative:

(A)It represents a situation where extra resources are available and the completion of project is not delayed

(B)It represents that a programme falls behind schedule and additional resources are required to complete the project in time

(C) The activity is critical and any delay in its performance will delay the completion of whole project

(D) All of the above

105. Slack represents the difference between the:

(A) Earliest completion time and latest allowable time

(B) Latest allowable time and earliest completion time

(C) Earliest completion time and normal expected time

(D)Latest allowable time and normal allowable time

106. A constraint that does not affect the feasible region is a

(A) Non-negativity constraint.

(B) Redundant constraint.

(C) Standard constraint.

(D) Slack constraint.

107. All of the following statements about a redundant constraint are correct *except:*

(A)A redundant constraint does not affect the optimal solution.

(B)A redundant constraint does not affect the feasible region.

(C)Recognizing a redundant constraint is easy with the graphical solution method.

(D)At the optimal solution, a redundant constraint will have zero slack.

108. All linear programming problems have all of the following properties *except*

(A)Linear objective function that is to be maximized or minimized.

(B)A set of linear constraints.

(C) Alternative optimal solutions.

(D)Variables that is all restricted to nonnegative values.

109. To find the optimal solution to a linear programming problem using the graphical method:

(A)Find the feasible point that is the farthest away from the origin.

(B)Find the feasible point that is at the highest location.

(C)Find the feasible point that is closest to the origin.

(D)None of the alternatives is correct.

110. The maximization or minimization of a quantity is the

(A) Goal of management science.

(B) Decision for decision analysis.

(C) Constraint of operations research.

(D) Objective of linear programming.

111. Time study refers to:

(A)Developing a standard time to do a particular task

(B)Improving work methods

(C)Value analysis

(D)Value engineering

112. Time study is used to:

(A) Determine standard costs

(B) Determine the number of machines a person may run

(C) Provide a basis for setting piece price or incentive wages

(D) All of the above

113. Time study is carried out:

(A)by finding all the significant information's regarding the job, work place and machine tool etc.

(B)by breaking up each operation into small elements which are measurable with the help of the measuring device accurately

(C)by observing and recording the time taken by the operator for an operation

(D) all of the above

114. In time study, the rating factor is applied to determine:

(A) Standard time of a job

(B) Merit rating of the worker

(C) Fixation of incentive rate

(D) Normal time of a worker

115. Time study is carried out to determine the time required to complete job by

(A) a slow worker (B)a fast worker

(C) an average worker (D)an apprentice

116. Probabilistic time for completion of any activity can be found out from

(A) Optimistic time (B) Pessimistic time

(C) Most likely time (D) all of these

117. The Pessimistic Time Estimate is :

(A)Maximum possible time it could take to accomplish the job

(B)Minimum possible time it could take to accomplish the job

(C)The total time estimate of the critical path

(D)None of the above

118. The probabilistic time is given by (where to = Optimistic time, tp = Pessimistic time, and tn = Most likely time)

(A) $\frac{t_0 + t_p + t_n}{3}$

(B) $\frac{t_0 + 2t_p + t_n}{4}$

(C) $\frac{t_0 + 4t_p + t_n}{5}$

(D) $\frac{t_0 + t_p + 4t_n}{6}$

119. The pessimistic time estimate is :

(A)the maximum time to be taken in the accomplishment of goal ;

(B)the minimum time to be taken in the accomplishment of goal ;

(C)the total time estimate of the critical path

(D)none of the above

120. Relaxation Allowances are considered in :

(A) Time Study (B) Method Study

(C)Ergonomic Study(D)Feasibility Study

121. SQC requires determination of :

(A)Quality tolerance limit

(B)Quantity measurement

(C)Production lead time

(D)Inventory carrying cost

122. Which of the following is a common cause of Machine Break down?

(A) Inadequate preventive maintenance

(B) Dirt, Oil and Chemicals accumulation

(C) Incorrect machine set-up

(D) All the above

123. In North -West corner rule for solving a transportation problem :

(A) the first assignment is made in the cell occupying the lower left - hand corner of the transportation table

(B)the last assignment is made in the cell occupying the upper left hand corner of the transportation table

(C)the last assignment is made in the cell occupying the lower right hand corner of the transportation table

(D)the first assignment is made in the cell occupying the upper left - hand corner of the transportation table

124. The necessary and sufficient condition for the existence of a feasible solution to the transportation problem is :

(A)number of rows should be equal to the number of columns

(B)the total destination requirement equals the total origin capacity, $\sum_{i=1}^{m} a_i = \sum_{j=1}^{n} b_j$

(C)the total destination requirement is not equal to the total origin capacity, $\sum_{i=1}^{m} a_i \neq \sum_{j=1}^{n} b_j$

(D)the total destination requirement is more than the total origin capacity, $\sum_{i=1}^{m} a_i \succ \sum_{j=1}^{n} b_j$

125. A transportation problem will be said to be

balanced if :

(A)No. of rows is equal to the no. of columns

(B)No. of warehouses is equal to the no. of factories

(C)Total supply is equal to the Total Demand

(D)Total Demand is equal to the Estimated Demand

126. In a transportation problem involving 10 origins and 5 destinations, the number of constraints representing origin capacity and destination requirements is equal to:

(A) 50 (B) 49
(C) 15 (D) 14

127. A-B-C analysis is used in:

(A)CPM (B) Inventory control

(C) PERT (D) All of these

128. The ABC analysis in inventory management is carried out on the basis of :

(A)60/30/10 rule (B)80/20 rule

(C)50/30/20 rule (D)None of the above

129. In A-B-C analysis, which classes of items are generally large in number?

(A)A (B) B
(C)C (D) none of these

130. A-B-C analysis

(A) is a basic technique of materials management

(B) is meant for relative inventory control

(C) does not depend upon the unit cost of the item but on its annual consumption

(D) all of the above

131. ABC Analysis is normally used in :

(A)SQC (B)Production Control

(C)Value Analysis (D)Inventory Control

132. Just-in-time inventory system implies :

(A)EOQ in purchase orders

(B)Production lots in manufacturing process

(C)Time lag in new material procurement

(D)Production quantities ideally equal to delivery quantities

133. The objective of inventory control is :

(A)to produce required quality of produce

(B)to produce required quantity of produce

(C) to minimize the cost

(D) all the above

134. Queuing theory is associated with

(A) Inventory (B) Sales

(C) Waiting time (D) Production time

135. Service time in queuing theory is usually assumed to follow:

(A) Normal distribution

(B)Poissons distribution

(C)Erlang distribution

(D)exponential law

136. Queuing theory is used for

(A) Job-shop scheduling

(B) Inventory problems

(C) Traffic congestion studies

(D) All of these

137. In Queuing theory M/M/1/∞/FIFO stands for :

(A)Multiple channel, Multiple criteria, single line, infinite population, first in first out

(B)Multiple arrivals, Multiple channels, single distribution infinite population , first in first out

(C)Multiple single channel, Poisson arrivals, exponential service, infinite queue length, first in first out

(D)Poisson arrivals, exponential service, single channel, infinite queue length, first in first out

138. In quencing theory the symbol M/M/1/FIFO/: stands for :

(A)Exponential arrival rate, poisson service rate, single channel, first in first out and infinite queue length

(B)Poisson arrival, exponential service rate, single channel, first in first out and infinite queue length

(C)Poisson arrival, poisson service rate, single server, first in first out and finite queue length

(D)None of the above

139. Acceptance Quality level is:

(A) Maximum number of defectives that the consumers will accept

(B) Fraction defective(s) that the consumer considers acceptable

(C) Fraction defective(s) that the producer considers acceptable

(D) Maximum number of defectives that the producer will allow

140. Which of the following is not an usual assumption of the single - channel queueing model with Poisson Arrivals and exponential service times?

(A)The queue discipline is last come, first served

(B)the mean arrival rate is less than the mean service rate

(C)The calling population is infinite

(D)All of the above

141. The decision making under risk is the process when :

(A)the probability distribution of the variable is known

(B)the objective function is not known

(C)how to take the decision is not known

(D)none of the above

142. The main advantage of the Delphi technique over other judgemental forecasting technique is :

(A)The opinion of others are not allowed to influence individual experts

(B)It requires that a consensus be reached

(C)It is based on the majority decision

(D)For this less information is required

143. The project whose acceptance precludes the acceptance of one or more alternative projects is known as :

(A)Independent project

(B)Dependent project

(C)Mutually exclusive project

(D)Contingent project

144. Tactical production planning decision includes

(A) Layout planning (B) Machine loading

(C) Production process (D) Plant location

145. Decision variables:

(A)tell how much or how many of something to produce, invest, purchase, hire, etc.

(B)represent the values of the constraints.

(C)measure the objective function.

(D)must exist for each constraint.

146. PERT requires:

(A) single time estimate

(B) double time estimate

(C) triple time estimate

(D) none of these

147. PERT stands for :

(A)Project Evaluation and Renew Technique

(B)Project Evaluation and Review

Technique

(C)Perfect Evaluation and Review Tactics

(D)Preferred Evaluation and Research Team

148. PERT:

(A)provides an approach for keeping planning up-to-date

(B)provides a way for management to require that planning be done on a uniform and logical basis

(C)permits management to foresee quickly the impact of variations from the plan

(D)all of the above

149. PERT analysis is based upon

(A)optimistic time (B)pessimistic time

(C)most likely time (D)all of these

150. The Critical Path of a network is :

(A)For which earliest start time and latest start time are same

(B)The shortest time path through a network

(C)For which earliest finish time and latest finish time are same

(D)The longest time path through a network

151. Which of the following are the guidelines for the construction of a network diagram?

(A)Each activity is represented by one and only one arrow in the network.

(B)Dangling must be avoided in a network diagram.

(C)Dummy activity consumes no time or resource.

(D)all of the above

152. Critical path method:

(A) Helps in ascertaining time schedules

(B)Makes better and detailed planning possible

(C)provides a standard method for communicating project plans schedules and to time and cost performance

(D)all of the above

153. Critical Path Method (CPM) is concerned with estimation of:

(A) Optimistic time

(B) Production lead time

(C) Pessimistic time

(D) None of the above

154. In a network shown in the below figure, the critical path is along:

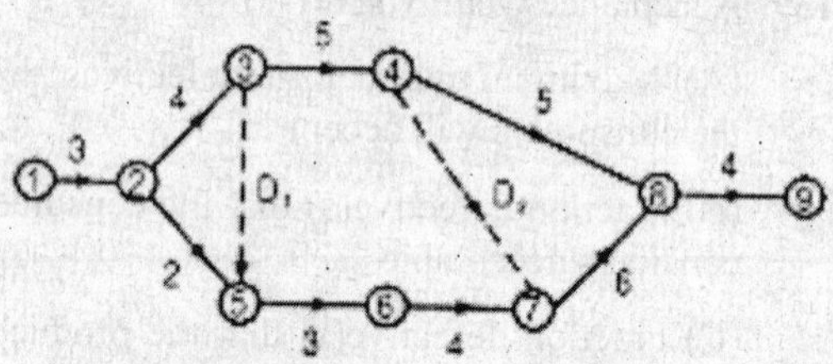

(A)1-2-3-4-8-9

(B)1-2-3-5-6-7-8-9

(C)1-2-3-4-7-8-9

(D)1-2-5-6-7-8-9

155. A critical activity has:

(A) Maximum slack (B) Minimum slack

(C) Zero slack (D) Average slack

156. PERT/CPM network analysis can be used for:

(A) Project appraisal

(B) Project implementation

(C) Project monitoring and control

(D) All of the above

157. PERT is applied for:

(A) Marketing programmes and advertising programmes

(B) Installation of machinery

(C) Research and development of products

(D) All of these

158. A diagram showing the path followed by men and materials while performing a task is known as:

(A) String diagram (B) Flow process chart

(C) Travel chart (D) Flow diagram

159. A company spends considerable amount on publicity to promote sales. This expenditure in break even chart is shown below the:

(A)Fixed cost line (B) Variable cost line

(C)Total cost line (D) Sales revenue line

160. Critical Path Method network analyses is done with the objective of :

(A) Determining the completion time for the project

(B) Determining the product quality

(C) Determining the production cost

(D) Determining the pay-back period

161. In CPM, the cost slope is determined by:

(A) $\dfrac{Crash\ \cos t}{Normal\ \cos t}$

(B) $\dfrac{Crash\ \cos t - Normal\ \cos t}{Normal\ \text{time} - Crash\ \ time}$

(C) $\dfrac{Normal\ \cos t}{Crash\ \cos t}$

(D) $\dfrac{Normal\ \cos t - Crash\ \cos t}{Normal\ time - Crash\ time}$

162. PERT is:

(A) Event oriented technique.

(B) Activity oriented technique.

(C) Both a & b

(D) None of the above.

163. A dummy activity in a net work diagram

(A)is represented by a dotted line

(B)is an artificial activity

(C)does not consume time or resources

(D)all of these

164. In managing a project, a network is better suited than Gantt chart because

(A) It can be updated more easily

(B) It clearly brings out the interdependencies between the different activities

(C) Both (A) and (B)

(D) None of the above

165. Which among the following is not concerned with the PERT evolution?

(A) Polaris Project

(B) Lock head Aircraft Corporation

(C) Both (A) and (B)

(D) None of the above

166. Which of the following statement is correct about the network diagram?

(A)The events are represented graphically by circles or nodes at the beginning and the end of activity by arrows.

(B)The tail end of the arrow represents the start of an activity.

(C)The head of the arrow represents the end of an activity.

(D)all of the above

167. The mathematical technique for finding the best use of limited resources of a company in the maximum manner is known as:

(A) Value analysis

(B) Network analysis

(C)Linear programming

(D)Quening theory

168. SQC requires determination of:

(A) Quality tolerance limit

(B) Quantity measurement

(C) Production load time

(D) Inventory carrying cost

169. Jigs are used in machine tool for holding :

(A) tools (B) work piece

(C) head stock (D) tail stock

170. Specifying the order in which individual jobs are to be executed :

(A) Planning (B) Loading

(C) Sequencing (D) Routing

171. Ergonomics is another name of :

(A) Chemical Engineering

(B) Human Engineering

(C) Mechanical Engineering

(D) Electrical Engineering

172. Cost Reduction can be achieved through :

(A) Work Sampling

(B) Value Analysis

(C) Quality Assurance

(D) Supply Chain management

173. The chart which gives an estimate about the amount of materials handling between various work stations is known as

(A)flow chart (B)process chart

(C)travel chart (D)operation chart

174. X Chart is used for :

(A) Cost control (B) Quality control

(C) Programme control (D) Job control

175. Which of the following is not an application of Markov Analysis?

(A)Brand switching analysis

(B)Accounts receivables problem

(C)Optimal maintenance policy

(D)Product mix decisions

176. Under the traditional distribution structure in International Marketing, which of the following controls a fixed supply of goods that are sold as high prices to a small group of customers?

(A)Exporter (B) Cartel

(C)Importer (D) Manufacturer

177. The correct sequence of phases in value engineering is:

(A)Creative phase, information phase, investigation phase, evaluation phase

(B)Information phase, creative phase, investigation phase, evaluation phase

(C)Investigation phase, information phase, creative phase, evaluation phase

(D)Creative phase, investigation phase, evaluation phase, information phase

178. In value engineering, the term value refers to:

(A) Manufacturing cost of the product

(B) Selling price of the product

(C) Total cost of the product

(D) Utility of the product

179. In value engineering, important consideration is given to

(A) Customer satisfaction

(B) Function concept

(C) Profit maximization

(D) Cost reduction

180. The aim of value engineering is to

(A)find the depreciation value of a machine

(B) determine the selling price of a product

(C)minimize the cost without change in quality of the product

(D)all of the above

181. Valve analysis is particularly of interest when:

(A)jobbing work economics are involved

(B)production is on large scale

(C)only few components are involved

(D)costly equipment is used

182. The value engineering technique in which experts of the same rank assemble for product development is called

(A)Delphi

(B) Morphological analysis

(C) Brainstorming

(D) Direct expert comparison

183. Simplex method is the method used for

(A) Value analysis

(B) Network analysis

(C)Linear programming

(D)Quening theory

184. The routing function in a production system design is concerned with:

(A) Manpower utilization

(B) Quality assurance of the product

(C) Machine utilization

(D)Optimizing material flow through the plant

185. Routing:

(A)prescribes the sequence of operations to be followed

(B)determines the programme for the operations

(C)is concerned with starting of processes

(D)regulates the progress of job through various processes

186. Direct expenses include

(A)factory expenses

(B)selling expenses

(C)administrative expenses

(D)none of these

187. String diagram is used

(A)for checking the relative values of various layouts

(B)when a group of workers are working at a place

(C)where processes require the operator to be moved from one work place to another

(D)all of the above

188. Which of the following statement is correct?

(A)A-B-C analysis is based on Pareto's principle.

(B)Simulation can be used for inventory control.

(C)Economic order quantity formula ignores variations in demand pattern

(D)all of the above

189. The most important function of inventory control is

(A)stock control system

(B)to run the stores effectively

(C)technical responsibility for the state of materials

(D)all of the above

190. In break even analysis, total cost consists of:

(A)fixed cost + sales revenue

(B)variable cost + sales revenue

(C)fixed cost + variable cost

(D)fixed cost + variable cost + profit

191. At the breakeven point:

(A)total cost is more than the sales revenue

(B)total cost is less than the sales revenue

(C)total cost is equal to sales revenue

(D)fixed cost is equal to variable cost

192. Break even analysis is a:

(A)short term analysis

(B)long term analysis

(C)average of short and long term analysis

(D)any one of these

193. Break even analysis consists of:

(A)fixed expenses (B)variable cost

(C)sales revenue (D)all of these

194. Breakeven point is the point where

(A)fixed and variable cost lines intersect

(B)fixed and total cost lines intersect

(C)variable and total cost lines intersect

(D)sales revenue and total expensive lines intersect

195. M.T.M. is used to:

(A)improve existing methods

(B)establish time standards

(C)develop effective methods in advance of the beginning of production

(D)all of the above

196. Which of the following are the principles of material handling?

(A)keep all the handling to the minimum

(B)select only efficient handling equipment

(C)move the heaviest weight to the least distance

(D)all of the above

197. Which of the following statement is correct?

(A)When slack of an activity is zero, it falls only on critical path.

(B)CPM technique is useful to minimise the direct and indirect expenses.

(C)Critical path of a net work represents the minimum time required for completion of project.

(D)all of the above

198. Dummy activities are used to

(A)determine the critical path

(B)determine the project completion time

(C)maintain the required net work

(D)none of these

199. In jobbing production

(A)highly skilled workers are needed

(B)unit costs are high

(C)operations are labour-intensive

(D)all of these

200. The start or completion of task is called

(A)an event (B)an activity

(C)a duration (D)none of these

201. The process capability of a machine is defined as the capability of the machine to:

(A)produce a definite volume of work per minute

(B)perform definite number of operations

(C)produce job at a definite spectrum of speed

(D)hold a definite spectrum of tolerance and surface finish

202. The production cost per unit can be reduced by

(A)producing more with increased inputs

(B)producing more with the same inputs

(C)eliminating idle time

(C)minimising resource waste

203. Operations management is applicable

(A)mostly to the service sector

(B)to services exclusively

(C)mostly to the manufacturing sector

(D)to manufacturing and service sectors

204. Productivity can be improved by:

(A)increasing inputs while holding outputs steady

(B)decreasing outputs while holding inputs steady

(C)increasing inputs and outputs in the same proportion

(D)decreasing inputs while holding outputs steady

(E)none of the above

205. AQL (Acceptable Quality Level) is :

(A)Quality level acceptable in the society

(B)Fraction defective (f) that the user considers acceptable

(C)Fraction defective (f) that the producer considers acceptable

(D)Quality level acceptable in the industry

206. Decision tree analysis is a useful tool for analysing :

(A)sequential decisions in the face of cost

(B)isolated decisions in the face of risk

(C)sequential decisions in the face of risk

(D)quick decisions in the face of returns

207. Techniques of managerial control are useful in:

(A) Selection of plant location

(B) Identifying appropriate strategy

(C) Profit planning

(D) Conducting shareholder's meetings

208. Product mix consist:

(A) 2 P (B) 6 P

(C) 4 P (D) None of these

209. The technique used for classifying inventory according to the value of usage is called :

(A)XYZ Analysis (B)DCF Analysis

(C)ABC Analysis (D)DEF Analysis

210. Objective of Value Engineering is

(A) Reduce cost without reducing the quality.

(B) Increase value without increasing the cost.

(C) Reduce cost by reducing the quality.

(D) None of the above

211. Cost Reduction can be achieved through :

(A) Work Sampling

(B) Value Analysis

(C) Quality Assurance

(D) Supply Chain management

212. Negative inventory means:

(A)excess stock of materials

(B)material in transit

(C)no. of units we owe to customers

(D)no. of defectives

213. Product Management do not cover one of the following aspects :

(A)Product - line

(B)Product - Mix

(C)Product - coordination

(D)Product life cycle

214. Operations Management will never be successful if they ignore:

(A)Govt. Rules (B) Latest Technology

(C)Demand Pattern (D) Quality of Goods

215. Decision on plant layout and location are concerned with:

(A)System design (B) System operations

(C)System control (D) None of the above

216. PERT stands for:

(A)Production Estimation & Research Technique

(B)Project Evaluation and Review Technique

(C)Project Estimation & Research Technique

(D)None of the above

217. The process of environmental analysis consists of the following sequential steps:

(A) Monitoring, Scanning, Forecasting and Assessment

(B) Scanning, Monitoring, Forecasting and Assessment

(C) Monitoring, Forecasting, Scanning and Assessment

(D) Assessment, Monitoring, Forecasting and Scanning

218. Match the right clusters with industries:

Group – I (Industries)	**Group – II (Clusters)**
(a) Jewellery and Gems	(i) Vapi (Gujarat)
(b) Auto parts	(ii) Surat (Gujarat)
(c) Chemicals	(iii)Tiruppur(TN)
(d) Textiles	(iv) Vijayawada (A.P)

Codes:

	(a)	(b)	(c)	(d)
(A)	(i)	(iii)	(iv)	(ii)
(B)	(iii)	(iv)	(i)	(ii)
(C)	(ii)	(iv)	(i)	(iii)
(D)	(iv)	(ii)	(iii)	(i)

219. Arrange the following levels of a product in an ascending order (sequence) in which they add customer value

(A) Potential product-Core benefit-Basic product-Augmented product –Expected product

(B)Augmented product-Core benefit-Expected product-Potential product- Basic product

(C)Core benefit-Basic product-Augmented product-Expected product-Potential product

(D) Core benefit-Basic product-Expected product-Augmented product-Potential product

220. Basis for production, planning and control is:

(A)Accurate demand estimate

(B)Capacity installed

(C)Need to beat competition

(D)Finance available

221. Which one of the following would not be classified as manufacturing overhead?

(A) Indirect labour

(B) Direct materials

(C) Insurance on factory building

(D) Indirect materials

222. In manufacturing a product, prime costs are

(A)Raw materials and manufacturing overhead

(B)Indirect materials and manufacturing overhead

(C)Indirect labour and manufacturing overhead

(D) Direct materials and direct labour

223. A manufacturing process requires small amounts of glue. The glue used in the process is classified as

(A) A prime cost

(B) An indirect material

(C) A direct material

(D) Miscellaneous expense

224. The wages of a maintenance worker in a manufacturing plant would be classified as

(A) A prime cost (B) Direct labour

(C) Indirect labour (D) Compliance costs

225. Which of the following is not a manufacturing cost category?

(A) Cost of goods sold

(B) Direct materials

(C) Direct labour

(D) Manufacturing overhead

226. Lubricants, used irregularly in a production process, are classified as:

(A) Miscellaneous expense

(B) Direct materials

(C) Indirect materials

(D)Immaterial items

227. Which of the following is not another name for the term manufacturing overhead?

(A) Factory overhead

(B) Pervasive costs

(C) Burden

(D) Indirect manufacturing costs

228. Because of automation, which component of product cost is declining?

(A) Direct labour

(B) Direct materials

(C) Manufacturing overhead

(D) Advertising

229. The product cost that is most difficult to associate with a product is

(A) Direct materials

(B) Direct labour

(C) Manufacturing overhead

(D) Raw materials

230. TQM's major emphasis is on:

(A) Product quality

(B)Company profitability

(C)Customer delight

(D)Employee training

231. The work of factory employees that can be physically associated with converting raw material into finished goods is classified as

(A) Manufacturing overhead

(B) Indirect materials

(C) Indirect labour

(D) Direct labour

232. Both direct materials and indirect materials are classified as

(A) Raw materials

(B) Manufacturing overhead

(C) Merchandise inventory

(D) Non-Current assets

233. Planning is a function that involves

(A)Hiring the right people for a particular job

(B)Coordinating the accounting information system

(C) Setting goals and objectives for an entity

(D) Analyzing financial statements

234. Which of the following is not a management function?

(A) Demotivating (B) Planning

(C) Controlling (D) Directing

235. The model that applies to Economic Order Quantity for Inventory Management, was proposed to be applied to Cash Management by:

(A)Miller and Orr (B) William J. Baumol

(C)William Sharpe (D) David Durand

236. The main advantage of the Delphi technique over other judgmental forecasting technique is :

(A)The opinion of others are ***not*** allowed to influence individual experts

(B)It requires that a consensus be reached

(C) It is based on the majority decision

(D) For this less information is required

237. Decision theory helps management in:

(A)Analyzing a problem

(B)Deciding sequence of activities

(C)Selecting the most cost effective alternative

(D)Postpone administrative action

238. Which is the most inaccurate method of forecasting?

(A)Delphi method (B) Market research

(C)Exponential smoothing (D) Time series

239. Delphi technique is used in:

(A)Organizing (B) Operating

(C)Staffing (D) Forecasting

240. Henry Ford is noted for his contributions to

(A) standardization of parts

(B) statistical quality control

(C)assembly line operations

(D)scientific management

---000---

UNIT-VII

PRODUCTION MANAGEMENT AND OPERATION RESEARCH

1. (A)Creating utility

Explanation:

- The processes and methods used to transform tangible inputs (raw materials, semi-finished goods, subassemblies) and intangible inputs (ideas, information, knowledge) into goods or services.
- Resources are used in this process to create an output that is suitable for use or has exchange value.

2. (A)Flow type

Explanation:

Methods of production:

- Production is at the heart of all industry and is the process of using the resources of a firm to convert 'inputs' into 'outputs', which are products or services desired by customers.

Job production:

- Job production is used to create one-off orders or 'jobs' especially made for the purpose.
- Job production helps to ensure that the product or service matches the customer's exact needs, as closely as the firm is able, because it is literally 'custom-made'.
- In many cases, skilled or specialised staff make products of very high quality, or which have individual character that might have less appeal if they were mass-produced.
- Job production is a relatively expensive process because it requires specialized and skilled staff who concentrates on the individual job or project.
- Small businesses that are built on the skills of the owner, such as a window cleaner or a hairdresser, use job production techniques.

Batch production:

- Products are produced in small or large batches.
- This process is useful to a firm that makes a number of different variations of basically similar products.
- Examples would include; a bakery, a car exhaust pipe factory or a toothpaste manufacturer.
- A toothpaste manufacturer will set its weekly batches of production of each product according to the orders from the supermarkets and wholesalers. It is crucial th
- at the machinery can be quickly cleaned and re-configured for each new batch to minimize unproductive time.

Flow production:

- This is a production line method, where product is continuously produced, flowing from one stage of production to the next.
- Workers and, increasingly robots, carry out individual repetitive tasks aiming to work as quickly as possible without loss of quality.
- This is the method pioneered by ***Henry Ford for his Model T car***, and the efficiencies he gained enabled him to produce large numbers of cars at low cost.
- Any product made in high volumes will almost certainly be made on a flow production line.
- This approach to production has close links with FW Taylor and his 'Scientific school of management' – Taylor's motivational theories were all about creating the workplace and forms of reward to maximise efficiency.
- Flow production systems are typically capital intensive and it is important to keep them running smoothly with high levels of capacity utilisation, so that these high overhead costs are spread over as many units as possible.

- Once set up properly, flow production lines can in some cases produce millions of consistently high quality products.

Cell production

- This is a form of flow production in which the line is separated into a number of sections, each looked after by a group of workers called a 'cell'.
- Cells take responsibility for work in their area, such as quality, job rotation, training and so on.

Intermittent type production

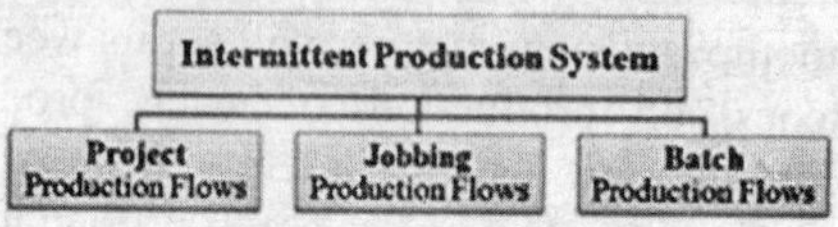

3. (B) Production

Explanation: Product:

- A good, idea, method, information, object or service created as a result of a process and serves a need or satisfies a want. It has a combination of tangible and intangible attributes (benefits, features, functions, uses) that a seller offers a buyer for purchase. For example a seller of a toothbrush not only offers the physical product but also the idea that the consumer will be improving the health of their teeth.
- A commercially distributed good that is (1) tangible personal property, (2) output or result of a fabrication, manufacturing, or production process, and (3) passes through a distribution channel before being consumed or used.
- A good or service that most closely meets the requirements of a particular market and yields enough profit to justify its continued existence. As long as cars are manufactured, companies such as Michelin that produce tires fill the market need and continue to be profitable.

4. (C) To satisfy people's wants

Explanation: The main aim of production is profit as the manufacturing companies just aims for profit.

5. (C) Mass production

6. (A) (iv) (iii) (ii) (i)

7. (D) All the above are true

Explanation: Aspects of quality in a business context:

- **Producing:** Providing something.
- **Checking:** Confirming that something has been done correctly.
- **Quality Control**: Controlling a process to ensure that the outcomes are predictable.
- **Quality Management**: Directing an organization so that it optimizes its performance through analysis and improvement.
- **Quality Assurance**:Obtaining confidence that a product or service will be satisfactory. (Normally performed by a purchaser).

8. (D) All of the above

Explanation:

- A production manager is involved with the planning, coordination and control of manufacturing processes. They ensure that goods and services are produced efficiently and that the correct amount is produced at the right cost and level of quality.
- A production manager is involved in the pre-production (planning) stage as well as the production (control and supervision) stage.
- A large part of production management involves dealing with people, particularly those who work in your team.
- Production managers are also involved with product design and purchasing.

9. (B) Production

10.(A)Factory overheads

11.(C)Market Intelligence and Survey

Explanation:

Functions of Production Management:

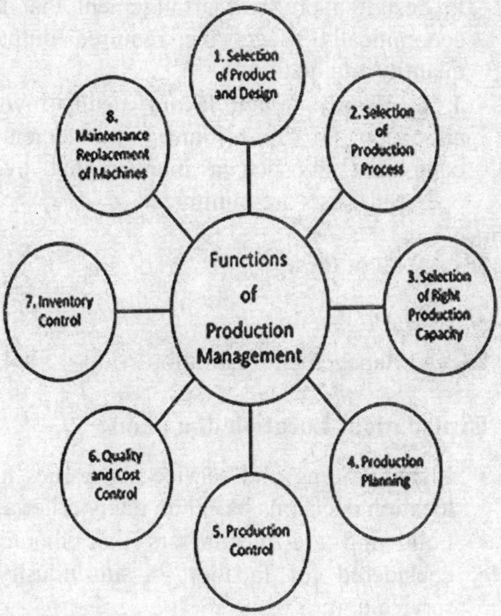

12.(A)System Design

Explanation: The responsibility of production manager:

- Forecasting the requirements of the production in order to achieve the production target.
- Making most efficient utilization of the available sources for production.
- Minimizing 'throughput time' and 'work in process inventory'. This can be achieved by systematic production planning and also by very efficient execution of the plans.
- One of the most important responsibility of a production manager deals with reducing material handling cost, which generally is achieved by the use of efficient material handling system and also by using plant layouts which must be developed in a proper or correct way.
- Reducing the quality cost with the help of analysis of non conformances on periodic basis and also by following suitable actions (both corrective and preventive).
- Building team spirit among the workmen and also motivating by means of personal involvement. This task of motivation can also be achieved by designing and implementing suitable financial incentive schemes.
- To device accurate methodology involving method study of manufacturing, along with the other engineering economic principles.
- Improving the productivity level of the workers on continuous basis by workmen's training and by bringing into use the standards of the performance derived from work measurement studies etc.

13. (B) (iii) (i) (iv) (ii)

14. (B)optimum lot size

15. (B) Industrial goods

Explanation:

- **Consumer goods:** Products that are purchased for consumption by the average consumer. Alternatively called final goods, consumer goods are the end result of production and manufacturing and are what a consumer will see on the store shelf. Clothing, food, automobiles and jewelry are all examples of consumer goods. Basic materials such as copper are not considered consumer goods because they must be transformed into usable products.
- **Industrial goods:** Machinery, manufacturing plants, materials, and other goods or component parts for use or consumption by other industries or firms. Demand for industrial goods is usually based on the demand for consumer goods they help produce (called derived demand). They are classified as (1) Production goods, that enter the production of a final product, such as the raw materials and component parts, or (2) Support goods, that assist in the production process, such as fixed equipment and machinery, instruments, jigs, tools, etc.
- **Specialty goods:** Item that is extraordinary or unique enough to motivate people to make an unusual effort to get it. Examples are designer clothes, exotic perfumes, limited-edition cars, stunning designs, works of famous painters.

16.(D) People

Explanation: The job of coordinating and controlling the activities required to make a product, typically involving effective control of scheduling, cost, performance, quality, and waste requirements.

17.(C) Production schedule

Explanation:

- A Gantt chart is a visual representation of a project schedule.
- A type of bar chart, a Gantt charts show the start and finish dates of the different required elements of a project.
- Henry Laurence Gantt, an American mechanical engineer, is recognized for developing the Gantt chart.

18.(C)Man-machine chart

19.(C) Minor work

20.(D) All of these

21.(B)The ordering cost and carrying cost are minimum.

Explanation: Economic lot size:

- Quantity of material or units of a manufactured good that can be produced or purchased within the lowest unit cost range.
- It is determined by reconciling the decreasing unit cost of larger quantities with the associated increasing unit cost of handling, storage, insurance, interest, etc.

22.(C)System control

Explanation: A plant layout:

- Plant layout refers to the arrangement of physical facilities such as machinery, equipment, furniture etc. within the factory building in such a manner so as to have quickest flow of material at the lowest cost and with the least amount of handling in processing the product from the receipt of material to the shipment of the finished product.
- **Riggs**: "the overall objective of plant layout is to design a physical arrangement that most economically meets the required output – quantity and quality."
- **J. L. Zundi**: "Plant layout ideally involves allocation of space and arrangement of equipment in such a manner that overall operating costs are minimized.

23. (D) all of these

24. (D) All of these

25. (A)Management Institution

Explanation: Location of a plant:

- Manufacturing and service companies make location decisions based on many criteria.
- Following are the factors that should be considered for location of an industry or service unit:

(1) Primary Factors:

- Nearness to customers
- Near raw materials
- Supply of capital
- Logistic facilities and infrastructure
- Skilled labour availability
- Power supply
- Business climate

(2) Secondary Factors:

- Host community and political factors
- Natural factors
- Historical factors
- Initial start and living conditions
- Personal factors
- Government policies
- Environmental considerations
- International factors

26.(B) Process layout

27.(D) all of these

28.(B) synthetic layout

29.(C) Mass production

30. (D) all of the above

31. (D) All of the above

32. (C) Fixed position layout

33. (A) Product layout

34. (D) All of the above

35. (A)Analytical layout

36. (D)All of the above

37. (D) Brand image

Explanation: Brand image

- Brand image is the current view of the customers about a brand. It can be defined as a unique bundle of associations within the minds of target customers. It signifies what the brand presently stands for. It is a set of beliefs held about a specific brand.
- In short, it is nothing but the consumers' perception about the product. It is the manner in which a specific brand is positioned in the market.
- Brand image conveys emotional value and not just a mental image. Brand image is nothing but an organization's character. It is an accumulation of contact and observation by people external to an organization.

38. (D) Finance

39. (B) Coastal Area

40. (C) System control

Explanation: Main factors which affect a plant location:

- Law and order situation,
- Availability of infrastructure facilities,
- Good industrial relations,
- Availability of skilled workforce,
- Social infrastructure,
- Investor friendly attitude,
- Nearness to market,
- Nearness to raw-materials' source,
- Nearness to supportive industries and services, and
- Must meet safety requirements.

41.(A)the operation requires heavy tools and equipments.

Explanation:

- A production technique used to assemble products that are too large, bulky, or fragile to safely or effectively move to a location for completion.
- In a fixed position layout, personnel, supplies, and equipment are brought to the site where the product will be assembled, rather than the product being moved through an assembly line or set of assembly stations.

42.(D) Product layout

Explanation: Product Layout: It is also called as flow-shop layout; equipment or work processes are arranged according to the progressive steps by which the product is made.

43.(C) either (A) or (B)

Explanation: CRAFT consider exchange of locations for those departments, which either are the same area or have a common border.

44.(C) Static product layout

45. (D) All of these

46. (D) Selection Layout

Explanation:

- **Process layout:** It is also called functional layout. All machines performing similar type of operations are grouped at one location in the process layout e.g. all lathes, milling machines, cutting machines etc in the engineering shop will be clustered in their like groups. Thus all forging will be done in one area and all the lathes will be placed in another area. In this layout, several products may share a machine to make its full use.

- **Product layout:** In this type of layout, the machines are arranged in the sequence as required by the particular product. All machines as required to balance the particular product the product line layout. In this layout, one product goes through all the machines lined up, in the order required by its manufacture. The best known example of this type of layout is seen in motor car production. To make this layout successful, the work load on the various machines must be balanced. The process of getting even loading at each stage of production is called line balancing.

- **Fixed Position Layout**: A production technique used to assemble products that are too large, bulky, or fragile to safely or effectively move to a location for completion. In a fixed position layout, personnel, supplies, and equipment are brought to the site where the product will be assembled, rather than the product being moved through an assembly line or set of assembly stations.

- Single large, high cost components or products.
- Product is static.
- Labour, tools and equipment come to the work rather than vice versa.

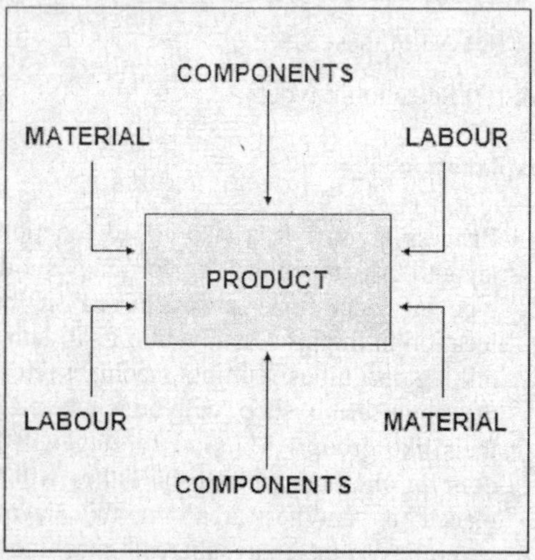

47.(A) Fixed position layout

Explanation:

- **Functional Layout:** This is also called process-oriented layout. A factory that has a functional layout is one in which manufacturing operations are grouped together on the basis of the function, technology or equipment used. A factory that uses this approach would install all equipment of a particular type in one area with separate areas assigned each type of equipment. Thus, a manufacturer using lathes would put all of them in one area. One alternative to a functional layout is a product-oriented layout, in which the equipment are placed in the exact sequence the operations will be carried out. Functional layouts are common for two reasons. First, functional layouts reflect traditional factory organization and as workshops.
- **Product layout:** Part of the manufacturing process which allows for the repetitive assembly of highly standardized products. When a manufacturing operation utilized product layout, production work can be layout in a straight line with labor and equipment subdivided in a smooth line.
- **Project layout:** It is also called fixed position layout. In this type of layout product to be produced remain at fixed position and machine, material and man are brought at the assembly position. Examples: Aeroplane, ships and heavy machines.
- **Cellular Layouts:** Primarily this type of layout is an attempt to reduce the complexity of process layouts. It divides transforming resource up into small clusters which can be used to act upon different products or product groups. Within each cell layout can be almost identical to product layout.

48. (D) All the above

49. (B) Plant Lay-Out

50. (A) Medicine production

Explanation: Batch production:

- A manufacturing process in which components or goods are produced in groups (batches) and not in a continuous stream.

- Batch production is a technique used in manufacturing, in which the object in question is created stage by stage over a series of workstations. With job production and flow production it is one of the three main production methods.
- Batch production is most common in bakeries and in the manufacture of sports shoes, pharmaceutical ingredients, purifying water (APIs), inks, paints and adhesives. In the manufacture of inks and paints, a technique called a colour-run is used.
- A colour-run is where one manufactures the lightest colour first, such as light yellow followed by the next increasingly darker colour such as orange, then red and so on until reaching black and then starts over again.

51.(B)Make or Buy decision

Explanation: Strategic Planning for Production:

- "Strategic planning for production implies focusing on the alignment of production management within an organization with its corporate and business strategies to gain a strategic advantage."
- Strategic planning gives only a broad view whereas production planning gives overall essential details of production.
- Strategic planning for production is done after considering the latest objectives of the organization and the current environmental conditions.
- It is a guide for tomorrow's decisions and results. All other production plans are based on this plan. Strategic planning for production coordinates (brings together) the production plan with the overall (main) plans and strategies of the organization.
- It also coordinates the production plan with the other department plans like the finance plan, purchasing plan, marketing plan, etc.
- So, strategic planning for producing is a broad over view of production. It tells us, how the organization will achieve its production objectives.
- The strategic planning for production is useful for:
  - Planning the production design.
  - Finding out the number of skilled, semi-skilled and unskilled workers required for production.
  - Preparing the departmental plans.
- Strategic production planning is done to achieve the main objectives of the organization.
- The prime objective of most organizations is to increase sales and earn a high profit. Both these objectives can be achieved if the consumers are satisfied.
- So, the planners must try to satisfy the consumers. They must find out and satisfy the needs and expectations of the consumers.
- They must design and make the products to fulfill the demands of the consumers.
- They must also consider the engineering and cost aspects of production. That is, they must try to produce better a quality product at the lowest possible cost.
- If the strategic planning for production is successful, all consumers will satisfy, and this will increase the sales and profit of the organization

52.(D)Product Quality control

Explanation:

- A production (or manufacturing) planning and control (MPC) system is concerned with planning and controlling all aspects of manufacturing, including materials, scheduling machines and people, and coordinating suppliers and customers. An effective MPC system is critical to the success of any company.
- An MPC system's design is not a one-off undertaking; it should be adaptive to respond to changes in the competitive

arena, customer requirements, strategy, supply chain and other possible problems.

53.(D) Decline

54.(A)Establishing parameters for measuring operational efficiency and productivity.

Explanation:

- Tactical planning is such an important part of a company's strategic planning process that management consulting companies are often hired to assist companies in preparing tactical plans.
- A company usually begins with its objectives and then develops strategies for how to carry out their objectives.
- Tactical plans are the specific action steps necessary to get results.

55.(B) Intermediate time horizon

Explanation:

Aggregate plan:

- It is also called the production plan; it details the aggregate production rate decisions, work force decisions, and inventory scheduling decisions over an intermediate planning horizon.
- The aggregate plan is an intermediate range plan that typically spans one full year so that it can react to all the seasonal swings in the demand.

Aggregate plan units:

- At this level of planning, there is not a lot of detail. Individual end product identity is typically not present.
- Instead, planning is performed for a composite or average unit of product in a particular family of similar products.
- Decisions are typically aggregated into monthly time periods. Weekly or daily detail is not needed at this level of decision making.
- Eventually that finer detail will surface after the aggregate plan is further broken down (disaggregated).

56. (B) Operating cycle

Explanation: Operating cycle

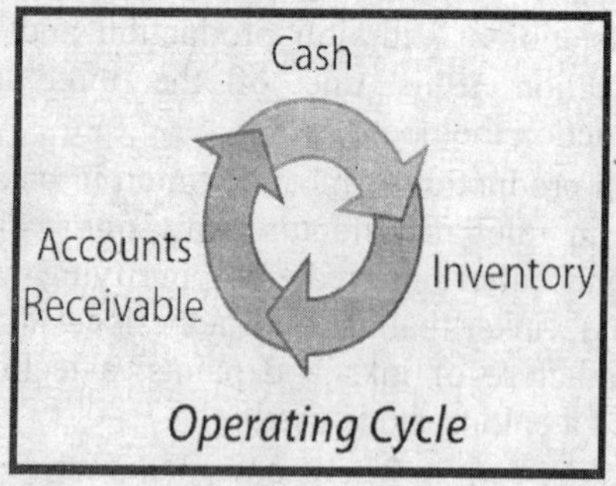

57.(B) Heat Treatment

Explanation: Tempering may refer to a heat treatment technique for metals and alloys

58.(B)forecast the current demand

Explanation:

- The moving average forecast is based on the assumption of a constant model.
- Since the model assumes a constant underlying mean, the forecast for any number of periods in the future is the same as the estimate of the parameter:
- In practice the moving average will provide a good estimate of the mean of the time series if the mean is constant or slowly changing.

59. (B)Solve the transportation problem

Explanation:

- Vogel's approximation method is a mathematical technique to solve logistics related problems.
- Vogel's method can be used to find out an optimal solution to cost of transportation.
- The method is iterative in nature. It means that we make some initial assumption and determine "Initial solution". Then we go on making refinements and repeat the calculations, till we achieve 'optimal solution'.

60.(D)All the above

Explanation: Product mix:

- It is also known as product assortment, refers to the total number of product lines that a company offers to its customers.
- For example, a small company may sell multiple lines of products. Sometimes, these product lines are fairly similar, such as dish washing liquid and bar soap, which are used for cleaning and use similar technologies. Other times, the product lines are vastly different, such as diapers and razors.
- The four dimensions to a company's product mix include width, length, depth and consistency.
- **Width:** The width of a company's product mix pertains to the number of product lines that a company sells.
- **Length:** Product mix length pertains to the number of total products or items in a company's product mix.
- **Depth:** Depth of a product mix pertains to the total number of variations for each product. Variations can include size, flavor and any other distinguishing characteristic.
- **Consistency:** Product mix consistency pertains to how closely related product lines are to one another--in terms of use, production and distribution. A company's product mix may be consistent in distribution but vastly different in use.
- **Product Market Mix Strategy:** Small companies usually start out with a product mix limited in width, depth and length; and have a high level of consistency. However, over time, the company may want to differentiate products or acquire new ones to enter new markets. A company can also sell the existing products to new markets by coming up with new uses for their product.

61.(C)leveling workload and reducing idle time

62.(C)Product mix width

63.(A) Material Requirement Planning

Explanation: Materials Requirement Planning (MRP):

- One of the first software based integrated information systems designed to improve productivity for businesses.
- A materials requirement planning (MRP) information system is a sales forecast-based system used to schedule raw material deliveries and quantities, given assumptions of machine and labor units required to fulfill a sales forecast.

64.(D)When to start as well as stop the operation

Explanation:

- Scheduling is the last of the planning functions. It determines when an operation is to be performed, or when work is to be completed; the difference lies in the detail of the scheduling procedure.
- In a centralized control situation - where all process planning, loading, and scheduling for the plant are done in a central office- the details of the schedule may specify the starting and finishing time for an operation.
- On the other hand, the central schedule may simply give a completion time for the work in a given department.

65. (D) all of these

66. (A) Product layout

67. (D)When to start as well as stop the operation

68. (B) Commercialization

Explanation:

Commercialization

- Launch the product
- Produce and place advertisements and other promotions
- Fill the distribution pipeline with product
- Critical path analysis is most useful at this stage

Stages of new product development process:

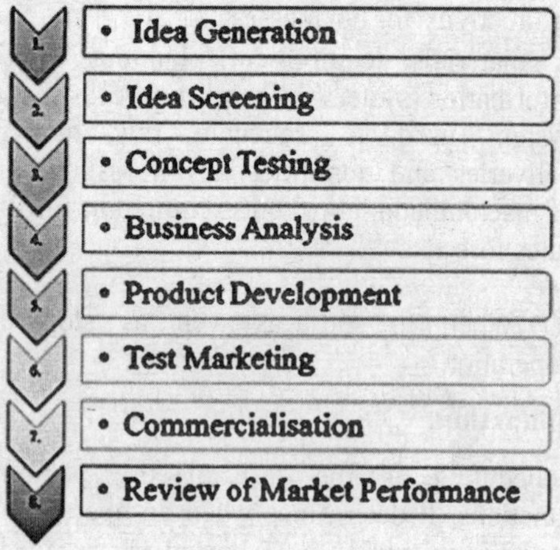

69. (D)All of the above.

Explanation:

- Scheduling is an important tool for manufacturing and engineering, where it can have a major impact on the productivity of a process.
- In manufacturing, the purpose of scheduling is to minimize the production time and costs, by telling a production facility when to make, with which staff, and on which equipment. Production scheduling aims to maximize the efficiency of the operation and reduce costs.
- Production scheduling tools greatly outperform older manual scheduling methods.
- These provide the production scheduler with powerful graphical interfaces which can be used to visually optimize real-time work loads in various stages of production, and pattern recognition allows the software to automatically create scheduling opportunities which might not be apparent without this view into the data.
- Companies use backward and forward scheduling to allocate plant and machinery resources, plan human resources, plan production processes and purchase materials.
- Forward scheduling is planning the tasks from the date resources become available to determine the shipping date or the due date.
- Backward scheduling is planning the tasks from the due date or required-by date to determine the start date and/or any changes in capacity required.
- The benefits of production scheduling include:
    - Process change-over reduction
    - Inventory reduction, leveling
    - Reduced scheduling effort
    - Increased production efficiency
    - Labor load leveling
    - Accurate delivery date quotes
    - Real time information

70.(D) All of the above.

Explanation: Dispatching:

- Dispatching is a function of Production controlling.
- It ensures the timely movement of semi finished items from one machines to another machine.
- Ultimately the target set at the stage of production planning are achieved with the help of this dispatching function, because it deals with the movement of semi finished items from one machine to another within a specified time frame.
- We have to follow this time constraints if we want to achieve efficiency in our plant.
- Thus in a nut shell dispatching is just like a steering of a BUS so that it can reach at its destination at scheduled time and safely.

71.(C)Is concerned with the starting of processes

72.(D)Dispatch of work orders through shop floor

73. (B) Determines the programme for the operations

74. (D) All of the above

Explanation: Production scheduling involves allocation of facilities, materials requirement planning and employee scheduling based on available resources and subject to constraints.

75. (D) Overall performance

Explanation: Objective of Operations Management:

- Production involves the things which are essential for the manufacture of products.
- The objective of the production management is 'to produce goods services of right quality and quantity at the right time and right manufacturing cost'.

1. Right quality: The quality of product is established based upon the customers needs. The right quality is not necessarily best quality. It is determined by the cost of the product and the technical characteristics as suited to the specific requirements.

2. Right quantity: The manufacturing organization should produce the products in right number. If they are produced in excess of demand the capital will block up in the form of inventory and if the quantity is produced in short of demand, leads to shortage of products.

3. Right time: Timeliness of delivery is one of the important parameter to judge the effectiveness of production department. So, the production department has to make the optimal utilization of input resources to achieve its objective.

4. Right manufacturing cost: Manufacturing costs are established before the product is actually manufactured. Hence, all attempts should be made to produce the products at pre-established cost, so as to reduce the variation between actual and the standard (pre-established) cost.

76. (B) Statement 1 is true but statement 2 is not true

77. (C) Operation research

78. (B) Statements 1 and 2, both are true

79. (D) All of these

80. (C) Satisfy the problem constraints and non-negativity restrictions

81. (C) Method study and work measurement

82. (D) All of the above

Explanation: Work Study:

- It is the systematic examination of the methods of carrying out activities such as to improve the effective use of resources and to set up standards of performance for the activities carried out.
- A generic term for those techniques, particularly method study and work measurement, which are used in the examination of human work in all its contexts, and which lead systematically to to the investigation of all the factors which affect the efficiency and economy of the situation being reviewed, in order to effect improvement.
- Components of Work Study:

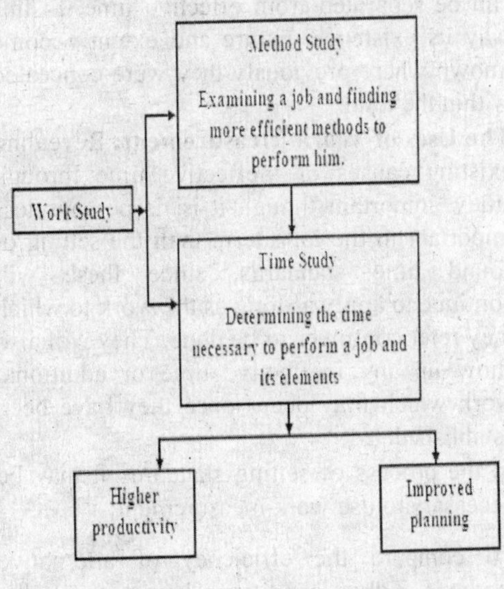

83.(A) Determining the most efficient method of performing a job

84.(C) Representative time

85.(C) Stop watch

86.(D) all of the above

87.(D) All of the above

Explanation:

- Work measurement is the application of techniques designed to establish the time for a qualified worker to carry out a specified job at a defined level of performance.
- **Purpose of Work Measurement:** Method study is the principal technique for reducing the work involved, primarily by eliminating unnecessary movement on the part of material or operatives and by substituting good methods for poor ones. Work measurement is concerned with investigating, reducing and subsequently eliminating ineffective time, that is time during which no effective work is being performed, whatever the cause.
- Work measurement, as the name suggests, provides management with a means of measuring the time taken in the performance of an operation or series of operations in such a way that ineffective time is shown up and can be separated from effective time. In this way its existence, nature and extent become known where previously they were concealed within the total.
- **The Uses of Work Measurement:** Revealing existing causes of ineffective time through study, important though it is, is perhaps less important in the long term than the setting of sound time standards, since these will continue to apply as long as the work to which they refer continues to be done. They will also show up any ineffective time or additional work which may occur once they have been established.
- In the process of setting standards it may be necessary to use work measurement:
- To compare the efficiency of alternative methods. Other conditions being equal, the method which takes the least time will be the best method.
- To balance the work of members of teams, in association with multiple activity charts, so that, as nearly as possible, each member has a task taking an equal time to perform.
- To determine, in association with man and machine multiple activity charts, the number of machines an operative can run.

88.(A)The length of time it takes to complete a work task assigned to a specific job

Explanation: Work measurement:

- Application of time and motion study and activity sampling techniques to determine the time for a qualified worker to complete a specific job at a defined level of performance.
- Work measurement is used in budgeting, manpower planning, scheduling, standard costing, and in designing worker incentive schemes.

89. (D) All of the above

90. (D)All of the above

91. (B)Zero.

92. (D)All of the above

93. (A) Linear programming

Explanation: Sensitivity analysis:

- A technique used to determine how different values of an independent variable will impact a particular dependent variable under a given set of assumptions.
- This technique is used within specific boundaries that will depend on one or more input variables, such as the effect that changes in interest rates will have on a bond's price.
- Sensitivity analysis is a way to predict the outcome of a decision if a situation turns out to be different compared to the key prediction(s).

94.(C)Product Mix

95.(D)One or more of the basic variables vanish

Explanation: A basic feasible solution is called degenerate if one of its RHS coefficients. (Excluding the objective value) is 0. This basic feasible solution is degenerate.

96.(B) The L.P.P. problem with constraints are of less than type

Explanation: Surplus variable:

- In Linear programming a surplus variable is a variable which is subtracted from a constraint to turn the inequality into an equation.
- This is required to turn an inequality into an equality where a linear combination of variables is greater than or equal to a given constant in the former.
- As with the other variables in the augmented constraints, the surplus variable cannot take on negative values, as the Simplex algorithm requires them to be positive or zero.

97.(D) If for all j, for which yij≤0, Zj−Cj is positive.

98.(D)The problem is under linear programming problem.

Explanation:

- Minimax is a decision rule used in decision theory, game theory, statistics and philosophy for minimizing the possible loss for a worst case (maximum loss) scenario.
- Alternatively, it can be thought of as maximizing the minimum gain (maximin).
- Originally formulated for two-player zero-sum game theory, covering both the cases where players take alternate moves and those where they make simultaneous moves, it has also been extended to more complex games and to general decision making in the presence of uncertainty.

99. (B)A linear programming problem with two decision variables.

100. (B) Routes and mixes

101. (B)Min $4x + 3y + (2/3)z$

102. (B)The amount by which the left side of a < constraint is smaller than the right side.

Explanation:

- In an optimization problem, a slack variable is a variable that is added to an inequality constraint to transform it to an equality.
- Introducing a slack variable replaces an inequality constraint with an equality constraint and a nonnegativity constraint
- In linear programming, this is required to turn an inequality into an equality where a linear combination of variables is less than or equal to a given constant in the former. As with the other variables in the augmented constraints, the slack variable cannot take on negative values, as the Simplex algorithm requires them to be positive or zero.
- If a slack variable associated with a constraint is zero in a given state, the constraint is binding, as the constraint restricts the possible changes of the point.
- If a slack variable is positive in a given state, the constraint is non-binding, as the constraint does not restrict the possible changes of the point.
- If a slack variable is negative in a given state, the point is infeasible, and not allowed, as it does not satisfy the constraint.

103. (D) Any one of the above

104. (B)It represents that a programme falls behind schedule and additional resources are required to complete the project in time

105. (A) Earliest completion time and latest allowable time

106. (B) Redundant constraint.

Explanation:

- **Non-Negativity Constraints:** The linear inequalities x>=0 and y>=0. These are included because x and y are usually the number of items produced and you cannot produce a negative number of items, the smallest number of items you could produce is zero. These are not (usually) stated, they are implied.

- **Redundant constraint:** Any constraint which does not affect the solution space of a linear programming problem is redundant constraint. A constraint is redundant if its removal would not alter the feasible solution space. And when a problem has a redundant constraint, at least one of the other constraints in the problem is more restrictive than the redundant constraint. e.g. $2x1+x2\leq20$ and $x2\leq25$, here $x2\leq25$ is a redundant constraint.
- **Slack variable**: In an optimization problem, a slack variable is a variable that is added to an inequality constraint to transform it to an equality. Introducing a slack variable replaces an inequality constraint with an equality constraint and a non negativity constraint.

107. (D)At the optimal solution, a redundant constraint will have zero slack.

108. (C) Alternative optimal solutions.

109. (D)None of the alternatives is correct.

Explanation: Feasible Region :

- The **feasible region** determined by a collection of linear inequalities is the collection of points that satisfy all of the inequalities.
- To sketch the feasible region determined by a collection of linear inequalities in two variables: Sketch the regions represented by each inequality on the same graph, remembering to shade the parts of the plane that you do not want. What is unshaded when you are done is the feasible region.

Graphical Method

- The **graphical method** for solving linear programming problems in two unknowns is as follows.
- Graph the feasible region.
- Compute the coordinates of the corner points.
- Substitute the coordinates of the corner points into the objective function to see which gives the optimal value. This point gives the solution to the linear programming problem.
- If the feasible region is not bounded, this method can be misleading: optimal solutions always exist when the feasible region is bounded, but may or may not exist when the feasible region is unbounded.
- If the feasible region is unbounded, we are ***minimizing*** the objective function, and its coefficients are non-negative, then a solution exists, so this method yields the solution.

110. (D) Objective of linear programming.

111. (A)Developing a standard time to do a particular task.

Explanation:

- Time study is a direct and continuous observation of a task, using a timekeeping device (e.g., decimal minute stopwatch, computer-assisted electronic stopwatch, and videotape camera) to record the time taken to accomplish a task and it is often used when:
    - there are repetitive work cycles of short to long duration,
    - wide variety of dissimilar work is performed, or
    - process control elements constitute a part of the cycle.
    - Time study as "a work measurement technique consisting of careful time measurement of the task with a time measuring instrument, adjusted for any observed variance from normal effort or pace and to allow adequate time for such items as foreign elements, unavoidable or machine delays, rest to overcome fatigue, and personal needs.

112. (D) All of the above

113. (D) all of the above

114. (C) Fixation of incentive rate

115. (C) an average worker

116. (D) all of these

117. (A)Maximum possible time it could take to accomplish the job

Explanation: Estimation times involved in PERT:

1. Optimistic Time Estimate (TOPT): This is the fastest time an activity can be completed. For this, the assumption is made that all the necessary resources are available and all predecessor activities are completed as planned.

2. Most Likely Time Estimate (TLIKELY): Most of the times, project managers are asked only to submit one estimate. In that case, this is the estimate that goes to the upper management.

3. Pessimistic Time Estimate (TPESS): This is the maximum time required to complete an activity. In this case, it is assumed that many things go wrong related to the activity. A lot of rework and resource unavailability are assumed when this estimation is derived.

118. (D) $\frac{t_0 + t_p + 4t_n}{6}$

119. (A)the maximum time to be taken in the accomplishment of goal

120. (A) Time Study

Explanation: Relaxation allowances are an important part of determining standard times for any task. Traditional methods of calculating relaxation allowances are reviewed and their application to construction operations.

121. (A)Quality tolerance limit

Explanation:

- Statistical quality control (SQC) is the term used to describe the set of statistical tools used by quality professionals. Statistical quality control can be divided into three broad categories:
- **Descriptive statistics** are used to describe quality characteristics and relation-ships. Included are statistics such as the mean, standard deviation, the range, and a measure of the distribution of data.
- **Statistical process control (SPC):** Involves inspecting a random sample of the output from a process and deciding whether the process is producing products with characteristics that fall within a predetermined range.

122. (D) All the above

Explanation: Common causes of Machine Break down:

- Not reading the operator's manual
- Improper maintenance
- Poor electrical connections.
- Overrunning machine's capability
- Not replacing worn parts when needed
- Tightener misalignment
- Improper storage.
- Improper weather-related use
- Ignoring warning signals.
- Asking untrained personnel to operate equipment.

123. (B)the last assignment is made in the cell occupying the upper left hand corner of the transportation table

124. (B)the total destination requirement equals the total origin capacity, $\sum_{i=1}^{m} a_i = \sum_{j=1}^{n} b_j$

Explanation:

- In a transportation table, an ordered set of four or more cells is said to form a loop if:
- Any two adjacent cells in the ordered set lie in the same row or in the same column.
- Any three or more adjacent cells in the ordered set do not lie in the same row or in the same column.
- A feasible solution to a transportation problem is basic if and only if the corresponding cells in the transportation

table do not contain a loop. To find an initial basic feasible solution we apply:

(1) The North-West corner rule

(2) Vogel`s Approximation method.

125. (C)Total supply is equal to the Total Demand

Explanation:

- The "transportation problem" refers to a special class of linear programming problems dealing with the distribution of single commodity from various sources of supply to various points of demand in such a manner that the total transportation costs are minimized.
- It was first studied by F. L. Hitchcock in 1941, then separately by T. C. Koopmans in 1947, and finally placed in the framework of linear programming and solved by simplex method by G. B. Dantzig in 1951.
- It is now accepted as one of the important analytical and planning tool in business and industry.

126. (C) 15

127. (B) Inventory control

128. (B)80/20 rule

Explanation:

- The ABC analysis is a business term used to define an inventory categorization technique often used in materials management.
- It is also known as Selective Inventory Control. Policies based on ABC analysis:
- A ITEMS: very tight control and accurate records
- B ITEMS: less tightly controlled and good records
- C ITEMS: simplest controls possible and minimal records
- The ABC analysis provides a mechanism for identifying items that will have a significant impact on overall inventory cost, while also providing a mechanism for identifying different categories of stock that will require different management and controls.
- The ABC analysis suggests that inventories of an organization are not of equal value. Thus, the inventory is grouped into three categories (A, B, and C) in order of their estimated importance.
- 'A' items are very important for an organization. Because of the high value of these 'A' items, frequent value analysis is required. In addition to that, an organization needs to choose an appropriate order pattern (e.g. 'Just- in- time') to avoid excess capacity.
- 'B' items are important, but of course less important, than 'A' items and more important than 'C' items. Therefore 'B' items are intergroup items.
- 'C' items are marginally important.

129. (C)C

130. (D) all of the above

131. (D)Inventory Control

132. (D)Production quantities ideally equal to delivery quantities

Explanation: Just In Time (JIT):

- An inventory strategy companies employ to increase efficiency and decrease waste by receiving goods only as they are needed in the production process, thereby reducing inventory costs.
- This method requires that producers are able to accurately forecast demand.

133. (D) all the above

Explanation: The objectives of inventory management are to keep track of items that are on hand. It should also track new items added to inventory while also tracking items used or removed.

134. (C) Waiting time

135. (D)exponential law

136. (D) All of these

137. (D)Poisson arrivals, exponential service, single channel, infinite queue length, first in first out

Explanation: The first M in the notation stands for Poisson input, second M for Poisson output, 1 for the number of servers and N for capacity of the system.

138. (C)Poisson arrival, poisson service rate, single server, first in first out and finite queue length

Explanation:

- Examples of queueing systems that can be defined with this convention are:
- **M/M/1:** This is the simplest queueing system to analyze. Here the arrival and service time are negative exponentially distributed (poisson process). The system consists of only one server. This queueing system can be applied to a wide variety of problems as any system with a very large number of independent customers can be approximated as a Poisson process. Using a Poisson process for service time however is not applicable in many applications and is only a crude approximation.
- **M/D/n:** Here the arrival process is Poisson and the service time distribution is deterministic. The system has n servers. (e.g. a ticket booking counter with n cashiers.) Here the service time can be assumed to be same for all customers)
- **G/G/n:** This is the most general queueing system where the arrival and service time processes are both arbitrary. The system has n servers. No analytical solution is known for this queueing system.

139. (B) Fraction defective(s) that the consumer considers acceptable

Explanation:

- The **acceptable quality limit (AQL)** is the worst tolerable process *average* (*mean*) in percentage or ratio that is still considered acceptable; that is, it is at an **acceptable quality level**.
- Closely related terms are the rejectable quality limit and level (RQL). In a quality control procedure, a process is said to be at an acceptable quality level if the appropriate statistic used to construct a control chart does not fall outside the bounds of the acceptable quality limits. Otherwise, the process is said to be at a rejectable control level.
- An acceptable quality level is a test and/or inspection standard that prescribes the range of the number of defective components that is considered acceptable when random sampling those components during an inspection

140. (C)The calling population is infinite

Explanation: Assumptions of the Basic Single-Server Model:

- Poisson arrival rate
- Exponential service times
- First-come, first-served queue discipline
- Infinite queue length
- Infinite calling population

141. (A)the probability distribution of the variable is known

Explanation:

- When the outcome of a decision is not known with certainty, a manager faces a decision-making problem under either conditions of risk or conditions of uncertainty.
- A decision is made under risk when a manager can make a list of all possible outcomes associated with a decision and assign a probability of occurrence to each one of the outcomes.
- The process of assigning probabilities to outcomes sometimes involves rather sophisticated analysis based on the manager's extensive experience in similar situations or on other data.
- Probabilities assigned in this way are objective probabilities.
- In other circumstances, in which the manager has little experience with a particular decision situation and little or no relevant

historical data, the probabilities assigned to the outcomes are derived in a subjective way and are called subjective probabilities.

- Subjective probabilities are based upon hunches, "gut feelings," or personal experiences rather than on scientific data.

142. (B)It requires that a consensus be reached

Explanation: The Delphi method is based on structural surveys and makes use of information from the experience and knowledge of the participants, who are mainly experts in the relevant field(s).

143. (A)Independent project

Explanation:

- **Independent project:** A project whose acceptance or rejection does not prevent the acceptance of other projects under consideration
- **Mutually exclusive projects** means that the acceptance of one project eliminates the others from consideration. Projects are said to be mutually exclusive when they cannot be undertaken simultaneously.
- **Contingent project:** A project that can be accepted only if one or more other projects is accepted first. See: independent project, mutually exclusive project.

144. (B) Machine loading

(C) Production process (D) Plant location

Explanation:

Tactical Level Decisions: These decisions are mainly for medium to short term, which is one year to 3 months. Some of these decisions are:

(a)Production Control: This is related to a scheduling of operations, machines' allocation and monitoring of actual against planned production. The focus is to meet performance objectives in terms of operating costs, timely production, flexibility, agility, set-up time reduction, etc.

(b)Stock Control (Material): This pertains to planning decisions related to stocks of raw material sub-assemblies or finished products. The decisions related to these came under inventory control. This involves decision regarding replenishment quantity and replenishment timing of the stock.

(c)Method: This area is related to decision regarding how to perform a work in the best possible way so that human effort and fatigue are minimum. Measurement and standardization of these methods are treated in the specialized domain of work-study or time and motion study. Work-measurement and ergonomics are other two related areas.

(d)Machine: This involves planning related to acquisition of machine, make or buy decision related to the product, arrangement for developing the capacity of the plant in terms of machine capacity, maintenance planning as a long-term planning, etc.

145. (A)tell how much or how many of something to produce, invest, purchase, hire, etc.

Explanation:

- The variables in a linear program are a set of quantities that need to be determined in order to solve the problem; i.e., the problem is solved when the best values of the variables have been identified.
- The variables are sometimes called decision variables because the problem is to decide what value each variable should take.
- Typically, the variables represent the amount of a resource to use or the level of some activity.
- Frequently, defining the variables of the problem is one of the hardest and/or most crucial steps in formulating a problem as a linear program.
- Sometimes creative variable definition can be used to dramatically reduce the size of the problem or make an otherwise non-linear problem linear.

146. (C) triple time estimate

147. (B)Project Evaluation and Review Technique

148. (D)all of the above

149. (D)all of these

150. (D)The longest time path through a network

Explanation:

- The essential technique for using CPM is to construct a model of the project that includes the following:
- A list of all activities required to complete the project (typically categorized within a work breakdown structure),
- The time (duration) that each activity will take to completion, and
- The dependencies between the activities.
- Using these values, CPM calculates the longest path of planned activities to the end of the project, and the earliest and latest that each activity can start and finish without making the project longer.
- This process determines which activities are "critical" (i.e., on the longest path) and which have "total float" (i.e., can be delayed without making the project longer). In project management, a critical path is the sequence of project network activities which add up to the longest overall duration.
- This determines the shortest time possible to complete the project.
- Any delay of an activity on the critical path directly impacts the planned project completion date (i.e. there is no float on the critical path).

151. (D)all of the above

152. (D)all of the above

153. (D) None of the above

Explanation: Benefits of CPM:

- Provides a graphical view of the project.
- Predicts the time required to complete the project.
- Shows which activities are critical to maintaining the schedule and which are not.
- CPM models the activities and events of a project as a network.
- Activities are depicted as nodes on the network and events that signify the beginning or ending of activities are depicted as arcs or lines between the nodes.
- The following is an example of a CPM network diagram:
- **CPM Diagram**

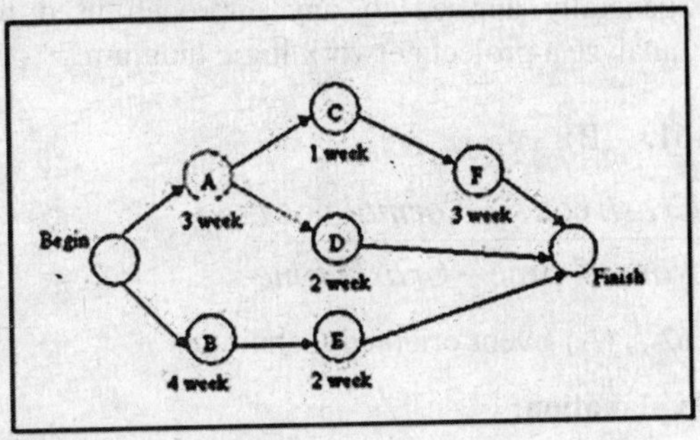

154. (A)1-2-3-4-8-9

155. (C) Zero slack

156. (D) All of the above

157. (D) All of these

158. (D) Flow diagram

159. (B) Variable cost line

160. (A) Determining the completion time for the project

Explanation:

- The critical path method (CPM) is a project modeling technique developed in the late 1950s by Morgan R. Walker of DuPont and James E. Kelley, Jr. of Remington Rand.
- Kelley attributed the term "critical path" to the developers of the Program Evaluation and Review Technique which was developed at about the same time by Booz Allen Hamilton and the U.S. Navy.

- The precursors of what came to be known as Critical Path were developed and put into practice by DuPont between 1940 and 1943 and contributed to the success of the Manhattan Project.
- CPM is commonly used with all forms of projects, including construction, aerospace and defense, software development, research projects, product development, engineering, and plant maintenance, among others. Any project with interdependent activities can apply this method of mathematical analysis. Although the original CPM program and approach is no longer used, the term is generally applied to any approach used to analyze a project network logic diagram.

161. (B)

$$\frac{Crash\ cost - Normal\ cost}{Normal\ time - Crash\ time}$$

162. (A) Event oriented technique.

Explanation:

- **PERT Event**: a point that marks the start or completion of one or more activities. It consumes no time and uses no resources. When it marks the completion of one or more tasks, it is not "reached" (does not occur) until *all* of the activities leading to that event have been completed.
- **Predecessor event:** an event that immediately precedes some other event without any other events intervening. An event can have multiple predecessor events and can be the predecessor of multiple events.
- **Successor event:** an event that immediately follows some other event without any other intervening events. An event can have multiple successor events and can be the successor of multiple events.
- **PERT activity:** the actual performance of a task which consumes time and requires resources (such as labor, materials, space, machinery). It can be understood as representing the time, effort, and resources required to move from one event to another. A PERT activity cannot be performed until the predecessor event has occurred.
- **Optimistic time (O):** the minimum possible time required to accomplish a task, assuming everything proceeds better than is normally expected
- **Pessimistic time (P):** the maximum possible time required to accomplish a task, assuming everything goes wrong (but excluding major catastrophes).
- **Most likely time (M)**: the best estimate of the time required to accomplish a task, assuming everything proceeds as normal.
- **Expected time (T_E):** the best estimate of the time required to accomplish a task, accounting for the fact that things don't always proceed as normal (the implication being that the expected time is the average time the task would require if the task were repeated on a number of occasions over an extended period of time).

$$\mathbf{T_E = (O + 4M + P) \div 6}$$

163. (D)all of these

164. (C) Both (A) and (B)

165. (C) Both (A) and (B)

166. (D)all of the above

167. (C)Linear programming

168. (A) Quality tolerance limit

169. (A) tools

170. (C) Sequencing

171. (B) Human Engineering

Explanation: Ergonomics (or human factors) is the scientific discipline concerned with the understanding of the interactions among humans and other elements of a system, and the profession that applies theoretical principles, data and methods to design in order to optimize human well being and overall system performance.

172. (B) Value Analysis

173. (C)travel chart

174. (B) Quality control

Explanation:

- In statistical quality control, the X and R chart is a type of control chart used to monitor a variable's data when samples are collected at regular intervals from a business or industrial process.
- X-Bar and R Charts: This set of two charts is the most commonly used statistical process control procedure. Used to monitor process behavior and outcome overtime.
- An X-bar and R (range) chart is a pair of control charts used with processes that have a subgroup size of two or more.
- X-Bar and R charts draw a control chart for subgroup means and a control chart for subgroup ranges in one graphic.
- Interpreting both charts together allows you to track both process center and process variation and detect the presence of special causes.
- Generally, a user focuses on the range portion of the chart first, confirming that the process is in control.

175. (D)Product mix decisions

176. (B) Cartel

Explanation: Cartel:

- A formal or informal agreement among firms in an oligopolistic industry.
- Cartel members may agree on such issues as prices, total industry output, market shares, and the division of profits.

177. (A)Creative phase, information phase, investigation phase, evaluation phase

178. (D) Utility of the product

179. (D) Cost reduction

180. (C)minimize the cost without change in quality of the product

181. (B)production is on large scale

182. (C) Brainstorming

183. (C)Linear programming

184. (C) Machine utilization

185. (A)prescribes the sequence of operations to be followed

186. (D)none of these

187. (D)all of the above

188. (A)A-B-C analysis is based on Pareto's principle.

189. (D)all of the above

190. (C)fixed cost + variable cost

191. (C)total cost is equal to sales revenue

192. (A)short term analysis

193. (D)all of these

194. (D)sales revenue and total expensive lines intersect

195. (D)all of the above

196. (D)all of the above

197. (D)all of the above

198. (C)maintain the required net work

199. (D)all of these

200. (A)an event

201. (A)produce a definite volume of work per minute

202. (B)producing more with the same inputs

203. (D)to manufacturing and service sectors

204. (D)decreasing inputs while holding outputs steady

205. (B)Fraction defective (f) that the user considers acceptable

Explanation:

- The standard definition of Acceptable Quality Level (AQL) is "the maximum defective percent (or the maximum number of defects per hundred units) that, for purpose of sampling inspection, can be considered satisfactory as a process average".

- Basically, we will randomly select a sampling size quantity (based on the AQL tables) to be inspected, and after inspection, according to the number of defects found (critical, major, minor defects), we will advice you to accept or to reject your shipment

206. (C)sequential decisions in the face of risk

Explanation:

- Decision trees are graphical representations of alternative choices that can be made by a business, which enable the decision maker to identify the most suitable option in a particular circumstance.
- For example, they will be used when oil and gas exploration companies have to decide whether to invest in a particular gas field, or in choosing to allocate resources to exploiting one gas field rather than another.
- Decision trees are a helpful visual tool when it is possible to measure the probability of an event occurring and the likely financial outcomes of making a particular decision.
- A schematic tree-shaped diagram used to determine a course of action or show a statistical probability.
- Each branch of the decision tree represents a possible decision or occurrence.
- The tree structure shows how one choice leads to the next, and the use of branches indicates that each option is mutually exclusive.
- Decision Trees are excellent tools for helping you to choose between several courses of action.
- They provide a highly effective structure within which you can lay out options and investigate the possible outcomes of choosing those options.
- They also help you to form a balanced picture of the risks and rewards associated with each possible course of action.
- A decision tree is a decision support tool that uses a tree-like graph or model of decisions and their possible consequences, including chance event outcomes, resource costs, and utility.
- It is one way to display an algorithm.
- Decision trees are commonly used in operations research, specifically in decision analysis, to help identify a strategy most likely to reach a goal.

207. (C) Profit planning

208. (C) 4 P

209. (A)XYZ Analysis

Explanation:

XYZ Analysis:

- XYZ analysis is more used in ralation of the customer demad for finished goods . X is high demand, Y medium demand, Z very low or exporadic demand.
- ABC/XYZ Analysis is usede to generate the strategic for the supply and inventory control and production strategy High runners are built to JIT Medium runners are produced to stock or to order and low runners are built to order BR.
- XYZ analysis is one of the basic supply chain techniques, often used to determine the inventory valuation inside stores.
- It's also strategic as it intends to enable the Inventory manager in exercising maximum control over the highest stocked item, in terms of stock value.
- A system of categorization, with similarities to Pareto analysis, the method usually categorizes inventory into three bands with each band having a different management control associated.
- Although different criteria may be applied to each category the typical method of "scoring" an inventory item is that of annual stock value of said item (qty in stock X cost of item) with

the result then ranked and then scored (X, Y or Z).

- Not all stock is equally valuable and therefore doesn't require the same management focus.
- The results of the XYZ analysis provide information that helps evaluate how each inventory part should be monitored and controlled. These controls are typically:
- X class items which are critically important and require close monitoring and tight control – while this may account for large value these will typically comprise a small percentage of the overall inventory count.
- Y class are of lower criticality requiring standard controls and periodic reviews of usage.
- Z class require the least controls, are sometimes issues as "free stock" or forward holding.
- Classification of inventory in terms of XYZ is also quite strategic as It can form the basis of various activity including leading plans on alternative stocking arrangements (consignment stock), reorder calculations and can help determine at what intervals inventory checks are carried out (for example X class items may be required to be checked more frequently than Z class stores. Based on the ABC and XYZ analysis there is another control mechanism , popularly known as AX control.
- XYZ analysis is more used in ralation of the customer demad for FG (finished goods) X is high demand, Y medium demand, Z very low or exporadic demand

ABC Analysis:

- ABC analysis classifies the raw materials based on their consumption during a particular time period (usually one year). Depending upon the company to company A B & C items can be as under:
- A - Approx 5% to 10% of the Items accounting for 60% to 80% of the consumption value
- B - Approx 10 % to 30% of the Items accounting for 10% to 30% of the consumption value
- C -Approx 60% to 85% of the Items accounting for 5% to 15% of the consumption value
- ABC Analysis ABC analysis classifies the raw materials based on their consumption during a particular time period (usually one year).
- Depending upon the company to company A B & C items can be as under A - Approx 5% to 10% of the Items accounting for 60% to 80% of the consumption value B - Approx 10 % to 30% of the Items accounting for 10% to 30% of the consumption value C -Approx 60% to 85% of the Items accounting for 5% to 15% of the consumption value.
- ABC/XYZ Analysis is usede to generate the strategic for the supply and inventory control and production strategy.
- High runners are built to JIT Medium runners are produced to stock or to order and low runners are built to order.

DCF Analysis:

- It can be hard to understand how stock analysts come up with "fair value" for companies, or why their target price estimates vary so wildly.
- The answer often lies in how they use the valuation method known as discounted cash flow (DCF).
- However, you don't have to rely on the word of analysts.
- With some preparation and the right tools, you can value a company's stock yourself using this method.
- In simple terms, discounted cash flow tries to work out the value of a company today, based on projections of how much money it's going to make in the future.

- DCF analysis says that a company is worth all of the cash that it could make available to investors in the future.
- It is described as"discounted" cash flow because cash in the future is worth less than cash today.
- **DCF:** A valuation method used to estimate the attractiveness of an investment opportunity.
- Discounted cash flow (DCF) analysis uses future free cash flow projections and discounts them (most often using the weighted average cost of capital) to arrive at a present value, which is used to evaluate the potential for investment.
- If the value arrived at through DCF analysis is higher than the current cost of the investment, the opportunity may be a good one.
- It is calculated as:

$$DCF = \frac{CF_1}{(1+r)^1} + \frac{CF_2}{(1+r)^2} + \dots + \frac{CF_n}{(1+r)^n}$$

CF = Cash Flow

r = discount rate (WACC)

- Also known as the Discounted Cash Flows Model.

210. (A) Reduce cost without reducing the quality.

Explanation:

- Value Engineering is a systematic method to improve the "Value" of goods and services by using an examination of function.
- Value, as defined, is the ratio of Function to Cost.
- Value can therefore be increased by either improving the Function or reducing the cost.
- It is a primary tenet of Value Engineering that basic functions be preserved and not be reduced as a consequence of pursuing Value improvements.
- Value engineering is an approach to productivity improvement that attempts to increase the value obtained by a customer of a product by offering the same level of functionality at a lower cost.
- Value engineering is sometimes used to apply to this process of cost reduction prior to manufacture, while "value analysis" applies the process to products currently being manufactured.

211. (B) Value Analysis

212. (C)no. of units we owe to customers

213. (C)Product - coordination

Explanation:

- Product management involves a number of different roles and functions.
- Depending on the size and types of the business organization, the activities may be focused around the product, or to the things and tasks that needed to be accomplished in order to successfully bring a product to the market.
- Hence, product management functions can be categorized into two disciplines: product planning and product marketing.

Product Management Aspects

- **Product planning:** refers to the continuous process of systematically making decisions about all aspects of product development and management. The functions involve in this discipline generally include defining of new product, production differentiation, gathering of market requirements, and planning and scheduling of production activities. The analysis and planning of the product's life cycle, as well as the management of product portfolio, are also done in this phase.
- **Product marketing**, on the other hand, is focused on the marketing tasks for the product. Its main role is to determine and implement strategies on how products will reach and attract customers. The activities that are usually involved in this phase

include production positioning, production promotion, and outbound messaging. The discipline can be functionally divided or done separately with product planning. However, in order for the two disciplines to be effective, a synergy between them is necessary.

214. (B) Latest Technology

215. (C)System control

216. (B)Project Evaluation and Review Technique

217. (B) Scanning, Monitoring, Forecasting and Assessment

218. (C) (ii) (iv) (i) (iii)

219. (D) Core benefit-Basic product-Expected product-Augmented product-Potential product

220. (A)Accurate demand estimate

221. (B) Direct materials

Explanation: Direct materials are classified as direct materials, not manufacturing overhead.

222. (D) Direct materials and direct labour

Explanation: Direct materials and direct labour are often referred to as prime costs because of their direct association with the manufacturing of the finished product.

223. (B) An indirect material

Explanation: The glue would be classified as an indirect material as the physical association with the finished product is too small in terms of cost.

224. (C) Indirect labour

Explanation: These wages would be classified as indirect labour.

225. (A) Cost of goods sold

Explanation: The three manufacturing categories are direct materials, direct labour and manufacturing overhead.

226. (C) Indirect materials

Explanation: Lubricants used in a production process are classified as overhead because they do not physically become part of the finished product.

227. (B) Pervasive costs

Explanation: Terms such as factory overhead, indirect manufacturing costs and burden as sometimes used instead of manufacturing overhead.

228. (A) Direct labour

Explanation: Automation often replaces direct labour in the product cost.

229. (C) Manufacturing overhead

Explanation: Manufacturing overhead is most difficult to associate with a product because the costs are indirectly associated with the manufacture of the finished product.

230. (A) Product quality

231. (D) Direct labour

Explanation: The work of factory employees that can be physically and economically traced to converting raw materials into finished goods is considered direct labour.

232. (A) Raw materials

Explanation: Both direct and indirect materials are included in raw materials.

233. (C) Setting goals and objectives for an entity

Explanation: Planning requires management to look ahead and to establish objectives.

234. (A) Demotivating

Explanation: Management are concerned with directing and motivating, not demotivating.

235. (B)William J. Baumol

236. (B)It requires that a consensus be reached

Explanation: Delphi technique

- A systematic forecasting method that involves structured interaction among a group of experts on a subject.
- The Delphi technique typically includes at least two rounds of experts answering questions and giving justification for their answers, providing the opportunity between rounds for changes and revisions.
- The multiple rounds, which are stopped after a pre-defined criterion is reached, enable the group of experts to arrive at a consensus forecast on the subject being discussed.

237. (C)Selecting the most cost effective alternative

Explanation:

- Decision theory is concerned with identifying the values, uncertainties and other issues relevant in a given decision, its rationality, and the resulting optimal decision.
- It is closely related to the field of game theory as to interactions of agents with at least partially conflicting interests whose decisions affect each other.

238. (C)Exponential smoothing

Explanation:

- Exponential smoothing is a technique that can be applied to time series data, either to produce smoothed data for presentation, or to make forecasts.
- The time series data themselves are a sequence of observations. The observed phenomenon may be an essentially random process, or it may be an orderly, but noisy, process.
- Whereas in the simple moving average the past observations are weighted equally, exponential smoothing assigns exponentially decreasing weights over time.

239. (D) Forecasting
240. (C)assembly line operations

---000---

UNIT-VIII

RESEARCH METHODOLOGYAND INFORMATION TECHNOLOGY

1. If two dice are thrown, the probability that the sum of their points is greater than 10 is:

(A) 1/9 (B) 1/12

(C) 1/3 (D) 1/18

2. A Binomial distribution is characterized as β(16,0.5) i.e. sample size is 16 and the probability of success is 0.5. The mean and variance of this distribution will be respectively:

(A) 8, 4 (B) 8, 8

(C) 4, 8 (D) 4, 4

3. Two variables are said to be perfectly negatively correlated if:

(A) Covariance between them is positive

(B) Coefficient of correlation between them is –1

(C) Covariance between them is negative

(D) None of the above

4. Which type of sampling is appropriate when the population consists of well defined groups such that the elements within each group are homogeneous and between each group they are heterogeneous?

(A) Cluster Sampling

(B) Simple Random Sampling

(C) Stratified Sampling

(D) Judgement Sampling

5. Match the following :

List-I

(a)Poisson distribution

(b)Normal distribution

(c)Chi-Square distribution

(d)Binomial distribution

List-II

(i)Mean is greater than variance

(ii)Mean & Variance are same

(iii)Symmetric

(iv) Positively skewed

Codes:

	(a)	(b)	(c)	(d)
(A)	(ii)	(i)	(iii)	(iv)
(B)	(iv)	(i)	(iii)	(ii)
(C)	(ii)	(iii)	(iv)	(i)
(D)	(iv)	(ii)	(i)	(iii)

6. A critical activity is defined as one whose:

(A) Total float is zero

(B) Free float is zero

(C) Duration is the longest

(D) Duration is the smallest

7. If the regression coefficient of the independent variable in a simple regression equation is negative, then which of the following statement is correct?

(A) The coefficient of correlation between the variables is zero.

(B) The coefficient of correlation between the variables is the positive square root of the coefficient of determination.

(C) The coefficient of correlation between the variables is the negative square root of the coefficient of determination.

(D) None of the above.

8. If a hypothesis is tested at a significant level of 5%, then it means that:

(A)There is 5% probability that the null hypothesis will be rejected though it is true.

(B) There is 5% probability that the null hypothesis will be false.

(C) There is 5% probability that the null hypothesis will be true.

(D) There is 95% probability that the alternative hypothesis will be false.

9. A machine on the average produces 5% defective items. What are the mean and variance in a set of 32 items?

(A) 16, 8 (B) 16, 4

(C) 4, 16 (D) None of the above

10. In a transportation problem involving 10 origins and 5 destinations, the number of constraints representing origin capacity and destination requirements is equal to:

(A) 50 (B) 49

(C) 15 (D) 14

11. The critical path of a network is

(A) for which earliest start time and latest start time are same

(B) the shortest time path through a network

(C) for which earliest finish time and latest finish time are same

(D) the longest time path through a network

12. If a person buys one ticket of a State lottery, then the probability that he wins a price is 0.11. If a person buys one ticket each month for five months, what is the probability that he will win least one price ?

(A) 0.55 (B) 0.50

(C) 0.44 (D) 0.56

13. The standard error of the mean of a random sample of size two or more.

(A)Always exceeds the population standard deviation.

(B)Either exceeds or equals the population standard deviation.

(C)Is always lower than the population standard deviation

(D)Is always equal to the population standard deviation

14. A store manager is trying to explore the relationship between percentage fat content (Y) and price (X) of various dairy products. He finds that the coefficient of determination is 0.4624 and the estimated regression line is Y = 0.5 – 0.02 X. The coefficient of correlation would be:

(A) 0.68 (B) – 0.68

(C) – 0.02 (D) 0.4624

15. Which of the following statement on testing of hypothesis is always true?

(A) When the null hypothesis is rejected at 5%, it is always rejected at 1% level of significance.

(B) When the null hypothesis is rejected at 1%, it is also rejected at 5% level of significance.

(C) When the null hypothesis is not rejected at 1%, it is rejected at 5% level of significance.

(D) No definite assertion can be made.

16. If the regression coefficient B in Y = A + B X is equal to zero, then the regression line will:

(A) pass through the origin

(B) be parallel to the x-axis

(C) be parallel to the y-axis

(D) Neither intersect x-axis nor y-axis

17. Statistical Quality Control requires determination of

(A) Quality tolerance limit

(B) Quantity measurement

(C) Production lead time

(D) Inventory carrying cost

18. If a hypothesis is statistically significant, then it is concluded that:

(A) the observed result is probably not due to chance.

(B) the observed result is probably a chance result.

(C) the observed result cannot possibly be due to chance.

(D) the null hypothesis of no relationship is probably true.

19. The Binomial distribution with parameters n and p approaches Poisson distribution if :

(A) n is large and p is small

(B) n is large and both p and q are not close to zero

(C) n is large and p is large

(D) n is small and p is small

20. The technique used to measure the degree of association between the two variables is known as :

(A) Regression Analysis (B) Dispersion

(C) Correlation Analysis (D) Skewness

21. A and B play a game where each is asked to select a number from 1 to 25. If the two numbers match, both of them win a prize. The probability that they will ***not*** win a prize in a single trial is :

(A) 1/25 (B) 24/25

(C) 2/25 (D) None of the above

22. Analysis of Co-variance is used for :

(A) removing the effect of one or more unwanted factors in an analysis of variance

(B) increasing precision in randomised experiments

(C) studying regression in a multiple classification

(D) all of the above

23. Three numbers are selected at random without replacement from the set of the numbers {1, 2, ..., N}. The conditional probability that the third numbers lies between the first two numbers if the first number is known to be smaller than the second is :

(A) 1/6 (B) 1/3

(C) 1/2 (D) None of the above

24. The two lines of regression are 3x+2y=26 and 6x+y=31 then the mean of X is :

(A) 3 (B) 4

(C) 7 (D) 9

25. A speaks the truth in 70 percent cases and B in 80 percent cases. The probability that they will contradict each other in describing a single event:

(A) 0.36 (B) 0.38

(C) 0.4 (D) 0.42

26. A maximum likelihood estimator is always :

(A) consistent (B) unbiased

(C) efficient (D) none of these

27. If X is normally distributed with mean 30 and s.d. 5, and Φ (x) denotes $\frac{1}{\sqrt{2\pi}}\int_0^{\infty} e^{-\frac{1}{2}t^2}\,dt$ then P (26≤x≤40) and $p(x \geq 45)$ are given by :

(A) Φ (.8)+ Φ (2) and Φ (3)− ½

(B) Φ (2)+ Φ (.8) and 1/2 − Φ (3)

(C) Φ (2)− Φ (.8) and 1/2 + Φ (3)

(D) Φ (2)− Φ (.8) and 1/2 − Φ (3)

28. Half percent of the letters mailed in a city have incorrect address. Out of 200 such letters mailed in a day the probability of finding at most 3 incorrect addresses is :

(A) $3\frac{e}{\delta}$ (B) $\frac{8}{3}e^{1}$

(C) $\frac{1}{6}6^{1}$ (D) $\frac{5}{2}e^{1}$

29. If the independent variables x_i (i=1, 2, ... n) are normally distributed about a common mean, a, with a common variance σ_2, their mean is also normally distributed about a, but with a variance.

(A) $n\sigma^2$ (B) $\sigma^{2/n}$

(C) $(\sigma_2)n$ (D) $\sigma^{n/2}$

30. The two lines of regression are 3x+2y=26 and 6x+y=31 then the mean of x is :

(A) 3 (B) 4

(C) 7 (D) 9

31. Chi-square distribution is :

(A) Continuous (B) Multimodal

(C) Symmetrical (D) None of the above

32. Mode of process in Decision support system is :

(A) Batch (B) Online

(C) Offline (D) Real Time

33. The weighted average of possible returns, with weights being the probabilities of occurrence is known as :

(A) Expected return (B) Variability of returns

(C) Average returns (D) Variance of returns

34. In M/M/1/∞/FIFO the probability that exactly n customers are in the queueing system under steady state is :

(A) $P_n=(1-\rho)^n\rho^n$ (B) $P_n=(1-\rho)\rho^n$

(C) $P_n=(1+\rho)^n\rho^n$ (D) $P_n(1+\rho)\rho^n$

(where ρ is traffic intensity)

35. If a six faced dice is thrown, the probability that the number appearing on the upper most face of the dice is an even number :

(A) 1/6 (B) 1/3

(C) 1/2 (D) 1/4

36. Mean and standard deviation of a Binomial Distribution are 4 and $\sqrt{\frac{8}{3}}$ respectively. Then the values of the parameters n and p are :

(A) 4 and 2/3 (B) 12 and 1/3

(C) 4 and 1/3 (D) 12 and 2/3

37. Let the two regression lines be 5x-6y+90=0 and 15x-8y=130. Then the correlation coefficient between x and y is :

(A) 2/3 (B) 1/3

(C) 8/15 (D) 5/6

38. The level of significance is the probability of committing the :

(A) type-I error (B) type-II error

(C) standard error (D) probable error

39. A company is producing steel rods. Assuming that the length of steel rods follows normal distribution with mean 10 inches & variance equal to 0.04 sq. inches. The standard error of mean, when a random sample of 16 is taken, will be:

(A) 4/10 (B) 2/20

(C) 2/40 (D) None of these

40. Judgement sampling to select the sampling units from population is termed as:

(A) Probability sampling

(B) Non-probability sampling

(C) Systematic sampling

(D) None of these

41. Correlation coefficient between two variables X & Y is calculated as 0.63. If the measurements of X & Y are changed to $U=\frac{X-10}{5}$ & $V=\frac{Y+5}{10}$ the new value of correlation coefficient will be:

(A) 0.063 (B) 0.315

(C) 0.63 (D) None of these

42. A person appears in an interview for a job in the two companies say X and Y. The chances of selection in company X is 0.7 and chances of selection in Y is 0.6. The probability of his selection in either of the two companies will be:

(A) 0.42 (B) 0.88

(C) 0.50 (D) None of these

43. In a normal distribution, mean (m) ± 3σ (3 standard deviation) limits contains approximately:

(A) 99.73% of the observations

(B) 99.27% of the observations

(C) 96% of the observations

(D) 95% of the observations

44. Half percent of the letters mailed in a city have incorrect addresses. Out of 200 such letters mailed in a day, the probability of finding at most 3 incorrect addresses is:

(A) $\frac{3e}{8}$ (B) $\frac{8}{3}e^{-1}$

(C) $\frac{1}{6}e^{-1}$ (D) $\frac{5}{2}e^{-1}$

45. If X is a random variable normally distributed with mean u and variance σ^2, then the mean deviation about mean is given by:

(A) $\frac{1}{\sqrt{2\pi}}$ (B) $\sqrt{\frac{2}{\pi}}$

(C) $\frac{\sigma}{\sqrt{2\pi}}$ (D) $\sqrt{2\sigma}$

46. The level of significance is the probability of committing:

(A) type I error (B) type II error

(C) standard error (D) probable error

47. Which of the following tests is used to test a hypothesis about the mean of a univariate normal distribution with unknown variance?

(A) Normal test (B) Student's test

(C) Paired t-test (D) Chi-square test

48. Mean and variance of Binomial Distribution are:

(A) m and σ^2 (B) m and nq

(C) m and np (D) np and npq

(Where the terms have usual statistical meaning)

49. Different types of Probability Distribution include:

1. Binomial distribution

2. Poisson distribution

3. Normal distribution

4. Exponential distribution

(A) 1 and 2 only (B) 1, 2 and 3 only

(C) 3 and 4 only (D) 1, 2, 3 and 4

50. Hypothesis is tested in the following research design:

(A) Exploratory and Descriptive

(B) Descriptive and Causal

(C) Causal and Exploratory

(D) Experimental and Exploratory

51. The regression lines cut each other at the point of

(A) Average of X and Y

(B) Average of X only

(C) Average of Y only

(D) Median of X and Y

52. Small sample means

(A) Less than 10 (B) Less than 15

(C) Less than 20 (D) Less than 30

53. The qualitative value of an exposure through a given medium is related to:

(A) Reach (B) Frequency

(C) Impact (D) All of the above

54. The two lines of regression are $3x + 2y = 26$ and $6x + y = 31$ then the mean of x is

(A) 3 (B) 4

(C) 6 (D) 7

55. For which distribution(s) Mean and Median are equal?

(i) Binomial Distribution;

(ii) Poisson Distribution;

(iii) Exponential Distribution; or

(iv) Normal Distribution

Codes:

(A) (i) (B) (ii)

(C) (i) & (iii) (D) (ii) & (iv)

56. If the regression coefficient B in Y = A + B X is equal to zero, then the regression line will:

(A) pass through the origin

(B) be parallel to the x-axis

(C) be parallel to the y-axis

(D) Neither intersect x-axis nor y-axis

57. Cars are parked in a very big parking lot. A researcher is required to estimate the proportion of cars that are red or the proportion of cars that are from a Japanese manufacturer. Which of the following statement is ***not*** correct?

(A) A convenience sample of cars parked near the gate may give a biased estimate of the proportion of cars which are from a Japanese Manufacturer.

(B) Different investigators may get different estimates for the proportion of cars that are red.

(C) The sample proportion of cars that are red is an unbiased estimate of the population proportion if the sampling method is simple random.

(D) A sample of 100 cars in a convenience sample is always better than a sample of 20 cars from a proper random sampling method.

58. If a hypothesis is statistically significant, then it is concluded that

(A) the observed result is probably not due to chance.

(B) the observed result is probably a chance result.

(C) the observed result cannot possibly be due to chance.

(D) the null hypothesis of no relationship is probably true.

59. From the following which is more suitable for causal relationship involving 2 or more variables :

(A) Correlation (B) Regression Analysis

(C) Factor Analysis (D) Time series Analysis

60. A measure characterizing a population is called a parameter and a similar measure for a sample is called :

(A) Standard error (B) Non Parameter

(C) Sampling error (D) Statistic

61. In the case of normal distribution about 68% of data lies within :

(A) $\overline{X}$ + quartile deviation

(B) $\overline{X}$ + 2 standard deviation

(C) $\overline{X}$ + mean deviation

(D) $\overline{X}$ + standard deviation

62. In which of the following situations the Classical definition of probability ***cannot*** be used :

(A) The total no. of outcomes is small

(B) The total no. of success is zero

(C) The total no. of outcomes is infinitely large

(D) The total no. of outcomes exceeds the total no. of success

63. Standard error of 'r' is given by :

(A) $\frac{r^2 - n}{100}$ (B) $\frac{1-r^2}{\sqrt{n}}$

(C) $\frac{1-r^2}{n}$ (D) R^2

64. The power of a test of hypothesis is ***not*** related to the probability of committing the :

(A) type I error (B) type II error

(C) standard error (D) probable error

65. If the independent variates x_i (i = 1, 2, …..n) are normally distributed about a common mean, a, with a common variance, σ^2, their mean is also normally distributed about a, but with a variance

(A) $n\,\sigma^2$ (B) σ^2/n

(C) $(\sigma^2)^n$ (D) $\sigma^2/2$

66. The weak law of large numbers is another version of

(A) convergence in probability

(B) random number generation

(C) financial probability law

(D) poisson probability law

67. The basic assumptions underlying the t-test for the difference of two sample means are that the parent populations' are____ and population variances are___.

(A) of any shape; equal and known

(B) normal; equal and known

(C) normal; equal but unknown

(D) normal; unequal but known

68. The probability that a contractor will get a plumbing contract is 2/3 and that he will get an electric contract is 4/9. If the probability of his getting at least one of the two contracts is 4/5 , then the probability that he will get both contracts is:

(A) 10/45 (B) 8/27

(C) 14/45 (D) 26/45

69. If a random variable X follows Poisson distribution such that P(X = 1) = P(X = 2), then the mean of the distribution is

(A) 1 (B) 2

(C) 3 (D) 4

70. The value of R1.23 lies between

(A) –1 and +1 (B) –1 and 0.0

(C) 0.0 and +1 (D) – 0.5 and + 0.5

71. The probability of drawing a 'Spade' from a well shuffled packet of cards is:

(A) 1/52 (B) 4/52

(C) ¼ (D) 2/3

72. If both the regression coefficients are negative, the correlation coefficient would be:

(A) Negative (B) Positive

(C) Zero (D) None of these

73. Chi-square distribution is:

(A) Continuous

(B) Multimodel

(C) Symmetrical referred

(D) Nome of the above

74. There will be only one regression line in case of two variables if:

(A) r = 0 (B) r = ± 1

(C) r = 0.5 (D) None of them

75. A critical activity is defined as one whose:

(A) Total float is zero

(B) Free float is zero

(C) Duration is the longest

(D) None of the above

76. 't' Distribution was discovered by:

(A) Karl Pearson (B) Fisher

(C) Laplace (D) Gosset

77. In order to find independence of two variables which are attributes, the following test is most appropriate test :

(A) '*t*' test (B) 'Z' test

(C) 'F' test (D) 'Chi-square' test

78. In cluster sampling, the clusters are so formed as :

(A) The units in the cluster are as homogeneous as possible

(B) The units in the cluster are as heterogeneous as possible

(C) The clusters are heterogeneous among themselves

(D) Some stratification factor may be chosen

79. Which of the following distribution can be used as an approximation to Binomial probability distribution under certain conditions :

(A) Normal Distribution

(B) Exponential Distribution

(C) Chi-square Distribution

(D) *t*-Distribution

80. Factor analysis is used for :

(A) Data reduction

(B) Data expansion

(C) Data generalisation

(D) Data specification

81. Which one is a parametric test?

(A) Chi-square test (B) *t*-test

(C) Mann-Whitney test (D) Sign test

82. If a person buys one ticket of a State lottery, then the probability that he wins a price is 0.11. If a person buys one ticket each month for five months, what is the probability that he will win least one price?

(A) 0.55 (B) 0.50

(C) 0.44 (D) 0.56

83. The standard error of the mean of a random sample of size two or more.

(A) Always exceeds the population standard deviation.

(B) Either exceeds or equals the population standard deviation.

(C) Is always lower than the population standard deviation

(D) Is always equal to the population standard deviation.

84. A store manager is trying to explore the relationship between percentage fat content (Y) and price (X) of various dairy products. He finds that the coefficient of determination is 0.4624 and the estimated regression line is Y = 0.5 – 0.02 X. The coefficient of correlation would be

(A) 0.68 (B) – 0.68

(C) – 0.02 (D) 0.4624

85. Which of the following statement on testing of hypothesis is always true?

(A) When the null hypothesis is rejected at 5%, it is always rejected at 1% level of significance.

(B) When the null hypothesis is rejected at 1%, it is also rejected at 5% level of significance.

(C) When the null hypothesis is not rejected at 1%, it is rejected at 5% level of significance.

(D) No definite assertion can be made.

86. Line of best fit is another name given to :

(A) Moving average method

(B) Method of Least Squares

(C) Trend Line method

(D) Straight line method

87. Total Float is:

(A) $L_j – E_j – +$ (B) $E_j – E_i – +$

(C) $L_j – E_j$ (D) $E_j – L_i – +$

88. Independent float =

(A) Total float - Head Slack

(B) Earliest Start Time- Earliest Finish Time

(C) Free Float – Total Float

(D) None of the above.

89. Structure variable is synonymous with:

(A) Task (B) Relations

(C) Styles (D) Attitude

90. Sampling distribution will be approximately normal, if sample size is

(A) Large (B) Sufficiently large

(C) Small (D) None of these

91. Match the items from List –I, with the items in List-II

List – I

(a) Chi-Square test

(b) Annual reports

(c) Multi-Variate

(d) Data Processing

List – II

(i) Secondary data

(ii) Information of Companies system

(iii) Hypothesis testing

(iv) Factor Analysis

Code:

	(a)	(b)	(c)	(d)
(A)	(iv)	(ii)	(i)	(iii)
(B)	(iii)	(i)	(iv)	(ii)
(C)	(iii)	(iv)	(i)	(ii)
(D)	(iv)	(i)	(iii)	(ii)

92. Statement :

X – When the data are interval ratio, we can use the mean as a measure of central tendency.

Y – Sum of absolute deviations from median is minimum.

(A) Both X and Y are correct

(B) Both X and Y are incorrect

(C) X is correct, but Y is incorrect

(D) X is incorrect, but Y is correct

93. Which of the following is ***not*** one of the six sectors considered by CSO while computing National Income?

(A)Primary Sector (B)Social Sector

(C)Foreign Sector (D)Secondary Sector

94. Statistical methods of quality control can:

(A)help to decide number of defectives

(B)prevent defects in products

(C)improve customer satisfaction

(D)determine process capability

95. Power of a hypothesis test indicates:

(A)How fast the hypothesis gives answer

(B)How well the hypothesis is stated

(C)Probability of rejecting null hypothesis when it is false

(D)Probability of accepting null hypothesis when it is true

96. While editing the completed questionares the researcher does ***not*** check for:

(A)Consistency (B)Accuracy

(C)Homogenity (D)Brevity

97. Alternate Hypothesis for $H_0:\mu\leq 50$ is:

(A)$H_1:\mu\geq 50$ (B)$H1:\mu=50$

(C)$H1:\mu>50$ (D)$H1:\mu\neq 50$

98. Which of the following is ***not*** a qualititave research technique?

(A)Focus group (B)Survey technique

(C)Deoth interview (D)Word association

99. The standard error of the mean will decrease:

(A)As the sample size increases

(B) As the sample standard deviation increases

(C)To a point and then remains constant

(D) As the sample size decreases

100. For a 't' distribution, increasing the sample size will affect :

(A) degrees of freedom

(B)the 't' ratio

(C)standard error of mean

(D)All of the above

101. Which of the following is ***not*** a hypothesis put forward to explain the rationale for issuing bonus shares and stock splits?

(A)Signalling hypothesis

(B)Trading range hypothesis

(C)Attention hypothesis

(D)Alternate hypothesis

102. A problem can be considered as Linear Programming Problem,if and only if it has:

(1)Objective function

(2)Constraints

(3)Alternative course of action

(4)Latest technology

(A) (1) only (B)(1) and (2)

(C)(1),(2) and (3) (D)(1),(2)and (4)

103. The number of telephone calls received per day to a particular telephone number can be best modeled by using the:

(A)Binomial distribution

(B)Uniform distribution

(C)Possion distribution

(D)Normal distribution

104. Questionnaire is a :

(A) Research method

(B) Measurement Technique

(C) Tool for data collection

(D) All the above

105. Historical data is used in estimating future demand under

(A) Survey method.

(B) Expert opinion method.

(C) Statistical method.

(D)Complete Enumeration method.

106. Which of the following figures represents perfect negative correlation between price and sales of a particular product of a company?

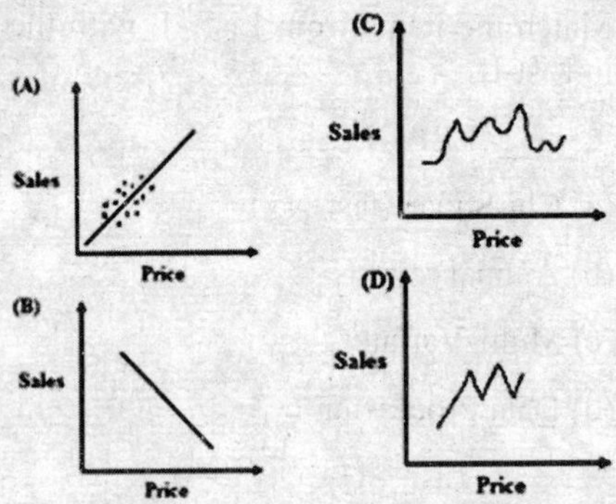

107. The value of R 1.23 lies between :

(A)21 and 11 (B)21 and 0

(C)0 and 1 (D)0 and ∞

108. Chi-square distribution is :

(A)Continuous (B)Multimodel

(C)Symmetrical (D)None of them

109. In case of Binomial distribution, the mean is :

(A)Always greater than variance

(B)Always equal to variance

(C)Always less than variance

(D)None of these

110. Correlation Coefficient is equal to :

(A)Arithmetic mean of both regression coefficients

(B)Geometric mean of both regression coefficients

(C)Difference of two regression coefficients

(D)None of these

111. When Null hypothesis (Ho) is true and test rejects it, it is called :

(A)Type - I error

(B)Type-II error

(C)Level of significance

(D)None of these

112. Historical data is used in estimating future demand under

(A)Survey method.

(B)Expert opinion method.

(C)Statistical method.

(D)Complete Enumeration method.

INFORMATION TECHNOLOGY

113. Which of the following is ***not*** a type of internet connection?

(A) ISDN (B) Dial-up

(C) Leased-Line (D) ISP

114. E B C I D C is an :

(A)64-bit code (B)32-bit code

(C)16-bit code (D)8-bit code

115. Which of the following devices would be considered a typical sequential access medium?

(A) Magnetic Hard Disk

(B) Magnetic Floppy Disk

(C) Magnetic Tape

(D) CD ROM

116. Gegabyte refers to

(A) 1024 Bytes (B) 1024 Kilobytes

(C) 1024 Megabytes (D) 102400 Bytes

117. Growing popularity of DBMS is due to :

(A)User friendliness

(B)Report writing

(C)Better response time

(D)Query processing

118. Wide area network is

(A)Network of computers spread over a small geographical area.

(B) Network of computers spread over a large geographical area.

(C) Network of computers in a room.

(D) None of these

119. The type of transmission channel which can transmit data in one direction only is known as:

(A) Simplex (B) Half Duplex

(C) Full Duplex (D) Half Simplex

120. Gegabyte refers to:

(A) 1024 Bytes (B) 1024 Kilobytes

(C) 1024 Megabytes(D)102400 Bytes

121. LAN stands for

(A) Large Area Network

(B) Local Area Network

(C) Long Accurate Network

(D) Lay Access Network

122. Processing data in groups collected over periods of time is known as

(A) Time - sharing

(B) Batch processing

(C) Real – time processing

(D) Multi – processing

123. A source programme is

(A) a programme written in machine language

(B) a programme to be translated into machine language

(C) the machine language translation of a programme written in high-level language

(D) none of the above

124. A network topology where all computers are connected to a central hub is called :

(A) Ring (B) Bus

(C) Star (D) Token

125. Which of the following is ***not*** an operating system?

(A) OS/2 (B) Win XP

(C) Oracle (D) UNIX

126. A common coding language for the www is :

(A) HTML (B) Front page

(C) Netscape (D) Listserver.

127. Transistor Technology was used in which generation of Computers?

(A) First (B) Second

(C) Third (D) Fourth

128. 'Firmware' is associated with :

(A) Application software for firms.

(B) Special purpose hardware device.

(C) Benchmark software.

(D) Software in ROM.

129. The concept of 'cylinder' is used in respect of the device :

(A) Tape Drive

(B) Disk Pack

(C) Compact Disk

(D)Daisy Wheel Printer.

130. Point-of- Sale or POS pertains to :

(A) Sales points plotted in computer graphics

(B) Sales between two locations

(C) A value that identifies the location of sales data in storage.

(D) An input-output device updating sales and inventory.

131. Packet switching on the Internet refers to :

(A) Type of circuitry

(B) Switching components

(C) Method of data movement.

(D) Packet of hard copy of documents.

132. One KB stands for :

(A) 100 bytes (B) 10000 bytes

(C) 999 bytes (D) 1024 bytes

133. Which of the following devices would be considered a typical sequential access medium?

(A) Magnetic Hard Disk

(B) Magnetic Floppy Disk

(C) Magnetic Tape

(D) CD ROM

134. Which of the following is known as 'Information Superhighway'?

(A)Intra-net (B)Extra-net

(C)i-pad II (D)Internet

135. Organise the following in the correct sequence:

(1) Knowledge
(2) Business Intelligence
(3) Data
(4) Information

Choose the right option:

(A)(1),(2), (3),(4)

(B) (1),(4), (2),(3)

(C) (3),(4), (1),(2)

(D) (3),(4), (2),(1)

136. A source programme is :

(A)a programme written in machine

language

(B)a programme to be translated into machine language

(C)the machine language translation of a programme written in high - level language

(D)none of the above

137. Management Information System usually:

(I)Provides managers with a generalized computing and telecommunication strategy fot problem solving

(II)Serves managers interested in weekly,monthly and yearly results on various performance parameters

(III)Performs and records daily routine transactions necessary for conducting business

(A)(I)only (B)(II) only

(C)(III) only (D)(I)and (II)

138. The growing popularity of relational DBMS is due to :

(A)report writing

(B)its menu drivenness

(C)better response time

(D)query processing

139. Which of the following ***cannot*** be done by e - mail?

(A)Forward a received message to several people

(B)Send a message to many recipients

(C)Place a message on a corporate bulletin board

(D)Correspond with people worldwide

140. Growing popularity of relational DBMS due to :

(A)User friendliness

(B)Report Writing

(C)Better Response time

(D)Query Processing

141. A number system with a base of 8 is known as :

(A) Binary (B) Decimal

(C) Octal (D) Hexadecimal

142. A digital computer is based on the principle of:

(A) measurement (B) logic

(C) multiplication (D) counting

143. How many types of storage loops exist in magnetic bubble memory

(A) 8 (B) 4

(C) 16 (D) 2

144. The linking of computers with a communication system is called

(A) networking (B) pairing

(C) interlocking (D) assembling

145. Standardization means

(A) connecting two computer systems

(B) compatibility between different computer systems from different suppliers.

(C) always using a standard parallel interface

(D) joining a computer user group

146. Which memory is nonvolatile and may be written only once?

(A) RAM (B) EP-ROM

(C) SRAM (D) PROM

147. For creating and editing legal documents which application package would be most useful:

(A) spreadsheet (B) word-processing

(C) graphic (D) communication

148. Word-processing is used for

(A) presentation of data in graphical form

(B) what-if analysis

(C) entry, verifying, updating, retrieving etc. of records

(D) creation, storage, editing etc. of text.

149. Which of the 'following statements is wrong?

(A) An EPROM can be programmed, erased and reprogrammed by the user with an EPROM programming instrument

(B) magnetic tape is non volatile

(C) magnetic core and semiconductor memories are used as mass memory medium

(D) RAM is a type of volatile memory

150. Which of the following program is useful for merging names and address with repetitive letters for mass mailing

(A)word-processing and database integrated program

(B) database management and spreadsheet program

(C) graphics program

(D) communication program

151. The data bus in 8080A/8085 micro-processor is a group of

(A)eight bi-directional lines that are used to transfer 8 bits between the micro-processor and its I/O and memory

(B) sixteen bi-directional lines that are used for data transfer between the micro-processor and memory

(C) eight undirectional lines that are used for I/O devices

(D) eight lines used to transfer data among the registers

152. The operation of a digital computer is based on .....principle.

(A) counting (B) measuring

(C) electronic (D) logical

153. DBMS stand for:

(A) database marketing system

(B) database management studies

(C) database management system

(D) database marketing strategies

154. An integrated circuit is

(A) a complicated circuit

(B) an integrating device

(C) much costlier than a single transistor

(D) fabricated on a tiny silicon chip

155. A dumb terminal with a keyboard and CRT and connected to a computer is

(A) an off-line device

(B) an on-line device

(C) neither on-line nor off-line device

(D) both (A) and (B)

156. When a bank teller uses a computer terminal to know the balance in a customer's accounts it is an example of ?

(A) on-line updating

(B) off-line processing

(C) on-line query

(D) on-line processing

157. Most important advantage of an IC is its

(A) easy replacement in case of circuit failure

(B) extremely high reliability

(C) reduced cost

(D) low power consumption

(E) None of the above.

158. The concept that many users can share a computer is called:

(A) time-sharing

(B) distributed processing

(C) parallel processing

(D) interpersonal relationship

159. Which one of the following words has computer meaning and a computer meaning

(A) node (B) bus

(C) quick (D) plotter

160. Which of the following is a computer program

(A) utility software

(B) application package

(C) operating system

(D) all of the above computer programs

161. The computer stores its program and data in its:

(A) ALU (B) control unit

(C) memory (D) cache memory

162. What is the number of read-write heads in the drive for a 9-track magnetic tape?

(A) 9 (B) 16

(C) 18 (D) 27

163. An operating system

(A) is not required on large computers

(B) is always supplies with computer

(C) is always written in BASIC

(D)consists of programs that help in the operation of computer

164. The number of tracks on a 1/2 inch wide magnetic tape is

(A) 7 (B) 9

(C) 18 (D) 16

165. Which type of computers have really brought the advantages of computers to homes and small business

(A) minicomputers (B) microcomputers

(C)super computers (D) mainframes

166. The tangible part of a computer system is called:

(A) input data (B) output data

(C) software (D) hardware

167. Large computers which can process huge data at high speeds are known as:

(A) networks (B) minicomputers

(C) microcomputers(D) mainframes

168. What is the most common speed in rpm at which the hard disk usually rotate

(A) 2400 (B) 3600

(C) 4700 (D) 1600

169. Computerized railway reservation system is an example of:

(A) on-line application

(B) off-line application

(C) both (A) and (B)

(D) None of the above.

170. Managers who have no technical knowledge about a computer can be easily trained to operate a/an

(A) minicomputer (B) personal computer

(C) super computer (D) microcomputer

171. Present day computers are based on

(A) analog technology

(B) hybrid technology

(C) digital technology

(D) None of the above.

172. Electronic telecommunications system joining millions of computers together.

(A) E-mail (B) Internet

(C) US Mail (D) UPS

173. Following is ***not*** a social bookmarking site:

(A) Digg (B) Delicious

(C) Sqidoo (D) Facebook

174. Following is ***not*** a network protocol:

(A) HTTP (B) SMTP

(C) TCP/IP (D) Z39.50

175. Identify the odd one from the following:

(A) Koha (B) VTLS

(C) SLIM++ (D) SOUL

176. The concept of Artificial Intelligence (AI) belongs to___:

(A) Second Generation Computers

(B) Third Generation Computers

(C) Fourth Generation Computers

(D) Fifth Generation Computers

177. Computer memory is measured in _

(A) Bytes (B) Kilobytes

(C) Megabytes (D) All of the above

178. What are three types of basic languages used in computer programming?

(A) Zero, low and high levels

(B) COBOL, BASIC and PROLOG

(C) FOTRAN, PL/I and SNOWBOL

(D) Machine, Assembly and high level languages

179. When CD-ROM was prepared and made?

(A) 1985 (B) 1982

(C) 1980 (D) 1977

180. Which of the following software is useful for word processing?

(A) DBASE (B) LIBSYS

(C) WordStar (D) CDS/ISIS

181. What is a bug?

(A) Computer Virus

(B) Error in Computer Configuration

(C) Error in a Programme

(D) None of these

182. Which is ***not*** a programming language?

(A) FORTRAN (B) BASIC

(C) COBOL (D) ASCII

183. Raw, unevaluated, unprocessed and unorganized facts is known as:

(A) Data (B) Information

(C) Knowledge (D) Wisdom

184. Information retrieval is fastest from

(A) Floppy Disk (B) Magnetic Tape

(C) Hard Disk (D) None of the above

185. Match the following commands with their purposes in MS Excel

List – I

(i) To see only the record that you need command

(ii) To create cross tabulated data

(iii) The read-only documents to create or restyle your documents

(iv) The assistance that use templates to create documents and to make design decisions on their own

List – II

(a) Filter

(b) Pivot Table

(c) Templates

(d) Wizards

	(i)	(ii)	(iii)	(iv)
(A)	(a)	(b)	(c)	(d)
(B)	(b)	(c)	(d)	(a)
(C)	(c)	(d)	(b)	(a)
(D)	(d)	(a)	(c)	(b)

---000---

UNIT-VIII

RESEARCH METHODOLOGYAND INFORMATION TECHNOLOGY

1. (B) 1/12

Explanation: Probability:

- Probability (or likelihood) is a measure or estimation of how likely it is that something will happen or that a statement is true.
- Probabilities are given a value between 0 (0% chance or will not happen) and 1 (100% chance or will happen).
- The higher the degree of probability, the more likely the event is to happen, or, in a longer series of samples, the greater the number of times such event is expected to happen.

2. (A) 8, 4

Explanation: Binomial Distribution:

- A probability distribution that summarizes the likelihood that a value will take one of two independent values under a given set of parameters or assumptions.
- The underlying assumptions of the binomial distribution are that there is only one outcome for each trial, that each trial has the same probability of success and that each trial is mutually exclusive.

3. (B) Coefficient of correlation between them is −1
4. (C) Stratified Sampling
5. (C) (ii) (iii) (iv) (i)
6. (B) Free float is zero
7. (C) The coefficient of correlation between the variables is the negative square root of the coefficient of determination.
8. (A)There is 5% probability that the null hypothesis will be rejected though it is true.
9. (D) None of the above
10. (C) 15
11. (B) the shortest time path through a network
12. (C) 0.44
13. (C)Is always lower than the population standard deviation
14. (B) − 0.68
15. (B) When the null hypothesis is rejected at 1%, it is also rejected at 5% level of significance.
16. (B) be parallel to the x-axis
17. (A) Quality tolerance limit
18. (A) the observed result is probably not due to chance.
19. (A)n is large and p is small
20. (C)Correlation Analysis
21. (B)24/25
22. (D)all of the above
23. (B)1/3
24. (B) 4
25. (B)0.38
26. (D)none of these
27. (C) $\Phi(2) - \Phi(.8)$ and $1/2 + \Phi(3)$
28. (B) $\frac{8}{3}e^{1}$
29. (B) $\sigma^{2/n}$
30. (B) 4
31. (A)Continuous
32. (D) Real Time
33. (A)Expected return

34.(B) $P_n=(1-\rho)\rho^n$

35.(C) 1/2

36.(B)12 and 1/3

37.(A) 2/3

38.(A) type-I error

39.(C) 2/40

40.(B) Non-probability sampling

41.(C) 0.63

42.(A) 0.42

43.(A) 99.73% of the observations

44.(B) $\frac{8}{3}e^{-1}$

45.(A) $\frac{1}{\sqrt{2\pi}}$

46.(A) type I error

47.(B) Student's test

48.(D) np and npq

49.(D) 1, 2, 3 and 4

50.(D) Experimental and Exploratory

51.(A) Average of X and Y

52.(D) Less than 30

53.(C) Impact

54.(B) 4

55.(D) (ii) & (iv)

56.(B) be parallel to the x-axis

57.(D) A sample of 100 cars in a convenience sample is always better than a sample of 20 cars from a proper random sampling method.

58.(A) the observed result is probably not due to chance.

59.(A)Correlation

60.(D) Statistic

61.(D) $\overline{X}$ + standard deviation

Explanation:

- If you add percentages, you will see that approximately:
  - o 68% of the distribution lies within one standard deviation of the mean.
  - o 95% of the distribution lies within two standard deviations of the mean.
  - o 99.7% of the distribution lies within three standard deviations of the mean.
- These percentages are known as the "empirical rule".

62.(C)The total no. of outcomes is infinitely large

Explanation:

- **Classical probability** is the frequency of an event occurs divided by total number of possible outcomes. This can only be used when all events are equally likely.
- The classical or theoretical definition of probability assumes that there are a finite number of outcomes in a situation and all the outcomes are equally likely.
- **Empirical probability** of event A is the limit as n goes to infinity of (m/n) where m is the number of times that A is satisfied in the experiment and n is the number of times you run the experiment. Basically, it is the probability you will observe the event given that you run an infinite number of experiments like tossing a die an infinite number of times and seeing how often you get a "6".
- **Subjective probability** is your belief of what the probability is. If someone believes that the probability of getting heads is 0.6 then this is a subjective probability.

63.(B) $\frac{1-r^2}{\sqrt{n}}$

Explanation:

- The standard error is the estimated standard deviation or measure of variability in the sampling distribution of a statistic.

- A low standard error means there is relatively less spread in the sampling distribution.
- The standard error indicates the likely accuracy of the sample mean as compared with the population mean. T
- he standard error decreases as the sample size increases and approaches the size of the population.
- Sigma (σ) denotes the standard error; a subscript indicates the statistic.
- For example, the standard error of the mean is represented by σM. To find the standard error of the mean, divide the standard deviation by the square root of the sample size:

$$\sigma_M = \frac{\sigma}{\sqrt{N}}$$

Where σ is the standard deviation of the original sampling distribution and N is the sample size.

64.(B)type II error

65.(B) σ^2/n

66.(A) convergence in probability

67.(C) normal; equal but unknown

68.(C) 14/45

69.(B) 2

70.(C) 0.0 and +1

71.(B) 4/52

72.(A) Negative

73.(A) Continuous

74.(B) r = ± 1

75.(A) Total float is zero

76.(D) Gosset

77.(A) '*t*' test

Explanation:

t-test:

- A t-test is any statistical hypothesis test in which the test statistic follows a Student's t distribution if the null hypothesis is supported.
- It can be used to determine if two sets of data are significantly different from each other, and is most commonly applied when the test statistic would follow a normal distribution if the value of a scaling term in the test statistic were known.
- For example, a t-test could be used to compare the average floor routine score of the U.S. women's Olympic gymnastic team to the average floor routine score of China's women's team.

'Z-Test':

- A statistical test used to determine whether two population means are different when the variances are known and the sample size is large.
- The test statistic is assumed to have a normal distribution and nuisance parameters such as standard deviation should be known in order for an accurate z-test to be performed.

F-Test:

- The F-test is designed to test if two population variances are equal.
- It does this by comparing the ratio of two variances.
- So, if the variances are equal, the ratio of the variances will be 1.
- An F-test is any statistical test in which the test statistic has an F-distribution under the null hypothesis.
- It is most often used when comparing statistical models that have been fitted to a data set, in order to identify the model that best fits the population from which the data were sampled.
- Exact F-tests mainly arise when the models have been fitted to the data using least squares.
- The name was coined by ***George W. Snedecor, in honour of Sir Ronald A. Fisher.***

chi-square test:

- A chi-squared test, also referred to as chi-square test or χ^2 test, is any statistical hypothesis test in which the sampling distribution of the test statistic is a chi-squared distribution when the null hypothesis is true.
- Also considered a chi-squared test is a test in which this is asymptotically true, meaning that the sampling distribution (if the null hypothesis is true) can be made to approximate a chi-squared distribution as closely as desired by making the sample size large enough.

78.(A)The units in the cluster are as homogeneous as possible

Explanation:

- Cluster sampling is a sampling technique used when "natural" but relatively ***homogeneous groupings*** are evident in a statistical population.
- It is often used in marketing research.
- In this technique, the total population is divided into these groups (or clusters) and a simple random sample of the groups is selected.
- Then the required information is collected from a simple random sample of the elements within each selected group.
- This may be done for every element in these groups or a subsample of elements may be selected within each of these groups.
- A common motivation for cluster sampling is to reduce the total number of interviews and costs given the desired accuracy.
- Assuming a fixed sample size, the technique gives more accurate results when most of the variation in the population is within the groups, not between them.

79.(A) Normal Distribution

80.(A) Data reduction

Explanation: Factor Analysis:

- Factor analysis attempts to identify underlying variables, or factors, that explain the pattern of correlations within a set of observed variables.
- Factor analysis is often used in data reduction to identify a small number of factors that explain most of the variance that is observed in a much larger number of manifest variables.
- Factor analysis can also be used to generate hypotheses regarding causal mechanisms or to screen variables for subsequent analysis.

81.(B) *t*-test

Explanation: Parametric test:

- Parametric tests are more powerful.
- The data in these tests is derived from interval and ratio measurements.
- In parametric test it is assumed that the data follows normal distribution.
- Examples of parametric tests are *t*-test, Z-test and F-test.
- Observations must be independent .i.e. selection of any one item should not affect the chances of selecting any others be included in the sample.

82.(C) 0.44

83.(C) Is always lower than the population standard deviation

84.(B) – 0.68

85.(B) When the null hypothesis is rejected at 1%, it is also rejected at 5% level of significance.

86. (B) Method of Least Squares

Explanation: Line of Best Fit:

- A straight line drawn through the center of a group of data points plotted on a scatter plot. Scatter plots depict the results of gathering data on two variables; the line of best fit shows whether these two variables appear to be correlated.

- A more precise method for determining the line of best fit is a mathematical calculation called the least squares method.
- The line of best fit is used in regression analysis, and is a key input in statistical calculations such as the sum of squares.
- It can also be used as a tool for analyzing investment risk or trading activity.

87.(A) $L_j - E_j -$ +

88.(B) Earliest Start Time- Earliest Finish Time

89.(A) Task

90.(A) Large

91.(B) (iii) (i) (iv) (ii)

92.(A) Both X and Y are correct

93.(B)Social Sector

94.(D)determine process capability

95.(C)Probability of rejecting null hypothesis when it is false

96.(D)Brevity

97.(C)H1:μ>50

98.(B)Survey technique

99.(A)As the sample size increases

100. (D)All of the above

101. (D)Alternate hypothesis

102. (C)(1),(2) and (3)

103. (C)Possion distribution

104. (C) Tool for data collection

105. (C) Statistical method.

106. (B)

(B)

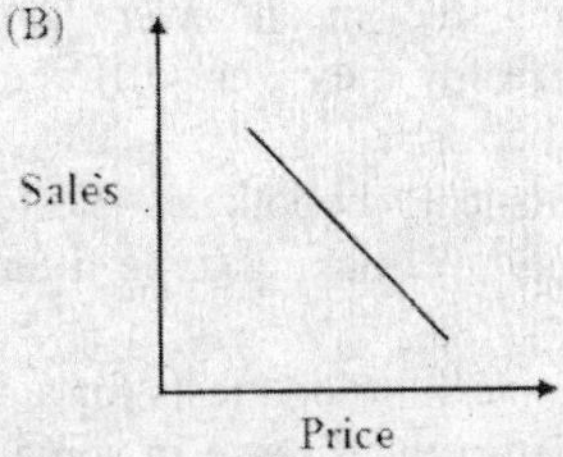

107. (C)0 and 1

108. (A)Continuous

109. (B)Always equal to variance

110. (B)Geometric mean of both regression coefficients

111. (A)Type - I error

Explanation: Type-I and Type-II Error:

- In statistics, a type I error (or error of the first kind) is the ***incorrect rejection of a true null hypothesis***.
- A null hypothesis is a prediction that there will be no significant difference in a specific outcome of individuals or groups that are treated in different ways.
- A type I error is a false positive.
- Usually a type I error leads one to conclude that a supposed effect or relationship exists when in fact it doesn't.
- For example, that a test shows a patient to have a disease they are tested for, when in fact the patient does not have the disease, or that a medical treatment should cure a disease, when in fact it doesn't.
- A type II error (or error of the second kind) is the ***failure to reject a false null hypothesis***.
- A type II error is a false negative.
- Examples of type II errors would be a blood test failing to detect the disease it was designed to detect, in a patient who really has the disease; or a clinical trial of a medical treatment failing to show that the treatment works when really it does.
- When comparing two means, concluding the means were different when in reality they were not different would be a Type I error;

concluding the means were not different when in reality they were different would be a Type II error.

- All statistical hypothesis tests have a probability of making type I and type II errors.
- For example, all blood tests for a disease will falsely detect the disease in some proportion of people who don't have it, and will fail to detect the disease in some proportion of people who do have it.
- A test's probability of making a type I error is denoted by α.
- A test's probability of making a type II error is denoted by β.

112. (C)Statistical method.

INFORMATION TECHNOLOGY

113. (D) ISP

114. (D)8-bit code

Explanation:

- Extended Binary Coded Decimal Interchange Code (EBCDIC) is an 8-bit character encoding used mainly on IBM mainframe and IBM midrange computer operating systems.
- EBCDIC descended from the code used with punched cards and the corresponding six bit binary-coded decimal code used with most of IBM's computer peripherals of the late 1950s and early 1960s.

115. (C) Magnetic Tape

116. (C) 1024 Megabytes

117. (D)Query processing

118. (B) Network of computers spread over a large geographical area.

119. (A) Simplex

Explanation:

- Communication channels can be classified as simplex, half-duplex, or full-duplex
- **Simplex channel:** A communications channel that can transmit data in only one direction.
- **Half-duplex channel:** A communications channel that can transmit data in either direction, but not simultaneously.
- **Full-duplex channel:** A communications channel that permits data transmission in both directions at the same time.

120. (C) 1024 Megabytes

121. (B) Local Area Network

122. (B) Batch processing

123. (C) the machine language translation of a programme written in high-level language

124. (C) Star

125. (C) Oracle

126. (A) HTML

127. (B) Second

128. (D) Software in ROM.

129. (B) Disk Pack

130. (D) An input-output device updating sales and inventory.

131. (C) Method of data movement.

132. (D) 1024 bytes

133. (C) Magnetic Tape

Explanation: Magnetic tape:

- Magnetic tape is a medium for magnetic recording, made of a thin magnetizable coating on a long, narrow strip of plastic film.
- It was developed in ***Germany***, based on magnetic wire recording.
- Devices that record and play back audio and video using magnetic tape are tape recorders and video tape recorders.
- A device that stores computer data on magnetic tape is a tape drive (tape unit, streamer).

- Magnetic tape revolutionized broadcast and recording.
- It is a key technology in early computer development, allowing unparalleled amounts of data to be mechanically created, stored for long periods, and to be rapidly accessed.

134. (D)Internet

135. (C) (3),(4), (1),(2)

136. (C)the machine language translation of a programme written in high - level language

137. (B)(II) only

138. (D)query processing

139. (C)Place a message on a corporate bulletin board

140. (D)Query Processing

141. (C) Octal

142. (D) counting

143. (D) 2

144. (A) networking

145. (B)compatibility between different computer systems from different suppliers.

146. (C) SRAM

147. (B) word-processing

148. (D) creation, storage, editing etc. of text.

149. (C)magnetic core and semiconductor memories are used as mass memory medium

150. (A)word-processing and database integrated program

151. (A)eight bi-directional lines that are used to transfer 8 bits between the micro-processor and its I/O and memory

152. (A) counting

153. (C) database management system

154. (D) fabricated on a tiny silicon chip

155. (B) an on-line device

156. (C) on-line query

157. (B) extremely high reliability

158. (A) time-sharing

159. (A) node

160. (D) all of the above computer programs

161. (C) memory

162. (B) 16

163. (D)consists of programs that help in the operation of computer

164. (B) 9

165. (B) microcomputers

166. (D) hardware

167. (C) microcomputers

168. (B) 3600

169. (A) on-line application

170. (B) personal computer

171. (C) digital technology

172. (B) Internet

173. (C) Sqidoo

174. (D) Z39.50

175. (A) Koha

176. (D) Fifth Generation Computers

177. (D) All of the above

178. (D) Machine, Assembly and high level languages

179. (A) 1985

180. (C) WordStar

181. (C) Error in a Programme

182. (D) ASCII

183. (A) Data

184. (C) Hard Disk

185. (A) (a)(b)(c)(d)

---000---

UNIT-IX

STRATEGIC MANAGEMENT

1. Which one of the following is ***not*** a basic element in the Strategic Management?

   (A) Environmental scanning

   (B) Strategy formulation

   (C) Strategy implementation

   (D) Functional strategy

2. Strategic planning is about

   (A) Strategic thinking

   (B) Strategic programming

   (C) Tactical Planning

   (D) Portfolio Planning

3. A company is said to be multinational, if :

   (A)Production and marketing are done in many countries

   (B)Domestically produced items are sold globally

   (C)Raw materials are procured from many countries

   (D)Workers are hired globally

4. Ansoff's growth vector refers to :

   (A)Generic strategies

   (B)Product - market strategies

   (C)Both of the above

   (D)None of the above

5. According to Ansoff, firms operate on the two dimensions of :

   (A) New Products and New Function

   (B) Vision and Mission

   (C) Backward and Forward Integration

   (D) Vertical and Horizontal Integration

6. Which one is ***not*** part of Ansoff's Growth Matrix?

   (A)Focused Development

   (B)Market Development

   (C)Product Development

   (D)Diversification

7. Which of the following is the best technique to manage the existing products?

   (A) Ansoff matrix

   (B) BCG matrix

   (C) Mc Kinsey 7s Framework

   (D) Five forces of competition

8. Five forces model was developed by :

   (A) Alderfer (B)Maslow

   (C)Porter (D)Elton Mayo

9. Five forces model was developed by :

   (A)Alderfer (B)Maslow

   (C)Porter (D)Elton Mayo

10. Michael Porter's five forces model belongs to:

    (A) Planning School

    (B) Positioning School

    (C) Cognitive School

    (D) Competitive Strategy School

11. Five forces model is used for :

    (A)Competitor analysis

    (B)Organizational analysis

    (C)Industry analysis

    (D)Corporate analysis

12. Which one is ***not*** the part of Porter's five force model?

    (A)Threat of new entrants

    (B)Firm's core competency

    (C)Rivalry among existing players

(D)Threat of substitutes

13. Which of the following is ***not*** a force in the Porters Five Forces Model?

(A)Bargaining Power of Buyers

(B) Bargaining Power of Suppliers

(C)Industry Rivalry

(D) Bargaining Power of Dealers

14. Which of the following is ***not*** included in the five forces of competition?

(A) Bargaining power of suppliers

(B) Bargaining power of consumers

(C) Threat of substitutes

(D) Strategic planning

15. Which one are ***not*** the Michael E. Porter's generic strategies?

(A)Focus (B) Cost leadership

(C)Differentiation (D) Core competence

16. Which of the following is ***not*** an element of the Porter's Generic competitive strategy model?

(A)Cost leadership

(B)Focus

(C)Product Differentiation

(D)Leadership

17. Which is ***not*** a generic strategy, as suggested by Micheal Porter?

(A)Differentiation

(B)Diversification

(C)Focus

(D)Cost Leadership

18. Which of the following is ***not*** a generic strategy as given by Michael Porter?

(A) Overall cost leadership

(B) Focus

(C) Line Pruning

(D) Differentiation

19. Which one is ***not*** the part of Michael Porter's five forces model?

(A) Threat of substitutes

(B) Firm's core competence

(C) Rivalry among existing players

(D) Threat of new entrants

20. Which one is ***not*** Porter's generic strategy?

(A)Growth Strategy

(B)Cost Leadership Strategy

(C)Differentiation Strategy

(D)Focus Strategy

21. Global Depository Receipt is an instrument for :

(A)Foreign Direct Investment

(B)Foreign Institutional Investment

(C)Public Bonds

(D)None of the above

22. TRIP covers the aspects related to :

(A)Patents

(B)Trade in services

(C)Globalization of business

(D)Labour practices

23. Entry barriers for a company to enter an industry can occur due to :

(A)Economics of scale

(B)Product differentiation

(C)Switching costs

(D)All the above

24. Which is ***not*** a support activity in a corporate value chain analysis?

(A)Human Resource Management

(B)Services

(C)Technology development

(D)Procurement

25. In growth share matrix 'cash cow' indicates :

(A)High business growth -High market share

(B)High business growth - Low market share

(C)Low business growth - High market share

(D)Low business growth - Low market share

26. In Growth Share Matrix 'Question Mark' indicates:

(A)High business growth-High market Share

(B)High business growth-Low market Share

(C) Low business growth-High market Share

(D)Low business growth-Low market share

27. In growth - share matrix 'Star' indicates :

(A)High business growth -High market share

(B)High business growth - Low market share

(C)Low business growth - High market share

(D)Low business growth - Low market share

28. Which of the following is the best technique to manage the existing products?

(A) Ansoff Matrix

(B) Balanced score card

(C) BCG Matrix

(D) Product life cycle analysis

29. Which of the following terms is ***not*** a part of the BCG model?

(A)Star (B)Cash cow

(C)Cat (D)Dog

30. As per "BCG" model "HOLD" strategy is used for :

(A)Dogs (B)Stars

(C)Question Marks (D)Cash Cows

31. Business unit which holds a large market share in a mature and slow growing industry is called:

(A) Star (B) Dog

(C) Question Mark (D) Cash cow

32. Which business unit generates substantial cash surplus due to low industry growth rate and high profit share?

(A) Dog (B) Cash cow

(C) Question mark (D) Star

33. Which one of the following represents the best long run opportunity in a firm's business portfolio?

(A)Star (B)Question Mark

(C)Cash COW (D)DOG

34. The dimensions of Group Mapping are :

(A)Price versus Product-line breadth

(B)Price versus Volume of production

(C)Production capacity versus Cost of production

(D)Total demand versus Market share

35. Market entry strategies vary from country to country because of :

(A)Varied political environment

(B)Varied cultural environment

(C)Varied economic conditions

(D)All of the above

36. Policies of WTO are formulated by :

(A)Heads of the member countries

(B)Trading Blocks

(C)Ministerial conference

(D)None of the above

37. Which level of managers translates the corporate strategy into concrete objectives for their individual business?

(A)Corporate level (B)Multi-Business level

(C)Functional level (D)Business level

38. Which of the following books was ***not*** written by Michael E. Porter?

(A)Competitive strategy

(B)Competiting for the future

(C)Competitive advantage

(D)Competitive advantages of nations

39. The concept of 'Core Competence' is advanced by :

(A)Ghoshal and Nohria

(B)Prahallad and Hammel

(C)Evans and Lorange

(D)Friedman and Philips

40. Which of the following helps a manager to identify the opportunities and threats in the competitive industry environment?

(A) Analysis of organizational structure.

(B) Analysis of competitive forces.

(C) Analysis of operations.

(D) Market Research

41. Essence of strategy at strategic Business Unit level is:

(A) How to build core competency

(B) How to gain competitive advantage

(C) How to gain market share

(D) All of the above

42. Which one of the following is a primary activity in a value chain?

(A) Operations

(B) Firm infrastructure

(C)Technology development

(D) Procurement

43. Which strategy requires a company to concentrate its efforts in one or more narrow segments instead of broad based strategy?

(A) Cost leadership (B) Focus

(C) Differentiation (D) None of the above

44. Firms choose a focus strategy to serve the needs of which of the following?

(A) Buyers group

(B) Different-segment of a product line

(C) Different geographical market

(D) All of the above

45. Which of the following is the characteristic of a strategic business unit?

(A) It serves a homogenous set of markets.

(B) It serves a unique set of products.

(C)It owns responsibility for its own profitability.

(D) All of the above.

46. Which one of the following is ***not*** a generic strategy?

(A) Cost Leadership

(B) Product Differentiation

(C) Cost focus

(D) Group focus

47. Which of the following is ***not*** Porter's generic strategy?

(A) Focus (B) Cost Leadership

(C) Differentiation (D)Market segmentation

48. A retrenchment strategy is designed to reduce:

(A) technical losses

(B) financial losses

(C)the scale and scope of the business operation

(D) all of the above

49. Eliminate–reduce–raise–create grid is germane to:

(A) Competitive Strategy

(B) Blue Ocean Strategy

(C) Red Ocean Strategy

(D) None of the above

50. Match the following :

List – I

(a) Ansoff

(b) C.K. Prahlad

(c) Peter F. Drucker

(d) Alfred Chandler

List – II

(i)Case competency

(ii)Management by Objectives

(iii)Cascade Approach

(iv) Structure follows Strategy

Codes:

	(a)	(b)	(c)	(d)
(A)	(i)	(iii)	(ii)	(iv)
(B)	(ii)	(iii)	(i)	(iv)
(C)	(iii)	(i)	(ii)	(iv)
(D)	(iv)	(ii)	(iii)	(i)

51. Growth strategy requires that a firm should

(A) realign its product market environment

(B) acquire new firm

(C) go for new product development

(D) expand the market

52. What describes the market, product and technological areas of business?

(A) BCG Matrix (B) GE Nine Cell Matrix

(C) 7's framework (D) Company's Mission

53. Name the factors taken into consideration in internal Analysis

(A) Firm Resources

(B) Objective, plans and policies of the firm

(C) The type of business involved

(D) All of the above

54. Diversification is to a new business area that has no obvious connection with any of the company's existing areas refer to:

(A) Forward integration

(B) Backward integration

(C) Conglomerate diversification

(D) Concentric diversification

55. Who plays an important role in the success of products and services and in increasing the marketing share of the firm in business?

(A) Functional level Managers

(B) Corporate level Managers

(C) Business level Managers

(D) All of the above

56. Which level of Managers translates the corporate strategy into concrete objectives for their individual business?

(A) Business level

(B) Corporate level

(C) Multi-Business level

(D) Functional level

57. Which one is ***not*** the overseas market entry strategy followed by Multinational Corporations?

(A) Franchise (B) Collaborations

(C) Joint venture (D) Strategic planning

58. Which of the following is ***not*** a primary activity in a value chain?

(A)Human Resource Management

(B)Marketing and Sales

(C)Operations

(D)Outbound logistics

59. Which is ***not*** a Primary activity in a Corporate value chain Analysis?

(A)Services (B) Technology development

(C)Operations (D)Marketing and Sales

60. Product / Market Expansion grid developed by :

(A)Chandler (B)Peter Drucker

(C)Michel E. Porter (D)Igor Ansoff

61. Which 'S' is ***not*** included in the McKinsey's 7 S Frame work?

(A)Style (B)System

(C)Staff (D)Selection

62. Which of the following book is ***not*** written by Michel E. Porter?

(A)Fortune at the bottom of the Pyramid

(B)Competitive strategy

(C)Competitive advantage

(D)Competitive advantages of nations

63. Which one of the following is the corporate Business portfolio analysis Technique?

(A)Product Portfolio Analysis

(B)Ansoff Matrix

(C)Environmental Analysis

(D)BCG Matrix

64. Which of the following terms best explains the partnership between two or more firms to carry out a specific project in a selected area of business?

(A)Joint Venture

(B)Merger and Acquisition

(C)Cartel

(D)None of the above

65. Cost Leadership Strategy is related to :

(A)Corporate Strategy (B)"SBU" Strategy

(C)Functional Strategy (D)Global Strategy

66. Who is associated with the concept that competence is nothing but 'resourcefulness' meaning "identifying resources when there are no resources"?

(A)Gopal C. Pati and Rabi K. Kanungo

(B)M. Maurice and F. Sellier

(C)Evans and Lorange

(D)A. Martin and G. Ross

67. Which element identities the strategic factors that determine the future of a firm?

(A)Environmental Scanning

(B)Strategy Formulation

(C)Strategy Implementation

(D)Strategy Evaluation and Control

68. Which strategy provides a means for achieving a company's annual objectives?

(A)Marketing Strategy

(B)Operating Strategy

(C)Business Strategy

(D)Corporate Strategy

69. Which method of product portfolio analysis helps in deciding which products are to be retained and which are ***not*** to be retained?

(A)Ansoff's Matrix

(B)Environment Matrix

(C)BCG Matrix

(D)All of the above

70. What enables the management to find out whether the strategic management processes are appropriate, compatible and functioning in the desirable direction?

(A) Implementation control

(B) Special alert control

(C) Premise control

(D) Strategic control

71. Which of the following strategy is regarded unfair?

(A) Collusion (B) Strategic alliance

(C) Differentiation (D) Turnaround strategy

72. Which of the following relationship strategies result into forming of a new organization?

(A) Strategic alliance (B) Partnership

(C) Joint venture (D) None of the above

73. A growth strategy is designed to increase

(A) the scale and scope of the Business operations.

(B) the corporate image of the business.

(C) corporate social responsibility of business.

(D) none of the above.

74. Cost leadership strategy is related to

(A) Functional strategy (B) SBU strategy

(C) Corporate strategy (D) Global strategy

75. Countries derive their competitive advantage in international trade through their

(A) Comparative cost advantage

(B) Contribution to the World trade

(C) Natural endowments

(D) All of the above

76. Which analysis helps to understand the strength and weaknesses of a firm?

(A) Environment analysis

(B) Business analysis

(C) SWOT analysis

(D) None of the above

77. "We must forget to learn and learn forgetting" is ascribed to:

(A) Tom Peters (B) Peter F. Drucker

(C) Abraham S. Maslow (D) Garry Hamel

78. In highly competitive environment an organization to achieve sustained success should be:

(A) Better (B) Bigger

(C) Resilient (D) None of the above

79. Corporate governance is about

(A) Crafting the strategy

(B) Compliance with regulatory regime

(C) Satisfying the stakeholders

(D) governing the company in the interest of government in power

80. Match the following :

List – I

(a) Poisson distribution has the property that

(b) Normal distribution is a

(c) Chi-square distribution is

(d) Binomial distribution has the property that

List – II

(i) Its mean is greater than Variance

(ii) Symmetric distribution

(iii) Positively skewed distribution

(iv) Its mean and variance are equal.

Codes:

	(a)	(b)	(c)	(d)
(A)	(iv)	(ii)	(i)	(iii)
(B)	(iv)	(ii)	(iii)	(i)
(C)	(i)	(ii)	(iii)	(iv)
(D)	(ii)	(iv)	(iii)	(i)

81. Globalization involves

(A) Free flow of technology from one country to another

(B) Free flow of investment from one country to the other

(C) Free flow of people from one country to the other

(D) All the above

82. Which is a short-term strategy for a firm?

(A) Corporate strategy

(B) Business strategy

(C) Company mission

(D) Functional strategy

83. Which is ***not*** a global entry strategy?

(A) Exporting

(B) Joint venture

(C) Merger and Acquisition

(D) Blue ocean strategy

84. Strategies formulated to convert a sick Unit to healthy is referred to:

(A) Turnaround (B) Expansion

(C) Diversification (D) Stabilisation

85. Which one is an international credit rating agency?

(A) Mc Kinsey (B) B C G

(C) Standard and poor (D) I M F

86. Which of the following strategies requires a company to concentrate its efforts in one or more narrow segments instead of a broad based strategy?

(A) Cost-Leadership strategy

(B) Differentiation strategy

(C) Focus strategy

(D) None of the above

87. Distribution strategy of a company will be influenced by

(A) Nature of product

(B) Target segment of consumers

(C) Pricing policy

(D) All of the above

88. Which of the following is an example for unsystematic risk?

(A) Interest rate risk (B) Exchange rate risk

(C) International risk (D) Operating risk

89. A positioning strategy should include the following strategies except

(A) Product strategy

(B) Personnel strategy

(C) Promotion strategy

(D) Advertising strategy

90. Mutual cooperation and net working is:

(A) Win-win strategy

(B) Networking strategy

(C) Franchise strategy

(D) Competitive strategy

91. Match the following :

List – A

(a) How do we succeed

(b) What Business should

(c) How does this unit

List – B

(i)Functional Strategy in this business?

(ii)Business Strategy we are in?

(iii)Corporate Strategy contributes?

	(a)	(b)	(c)
(A)	(i)	(ii)	(iii)
(B)	(iii)	(ii)	(i)
(C)	(i)	(iii)	(ii)
(D)	(ii)	(iii)	(i)

92. When we practice......., we arrange for a product to occupy a clear, distinctive and desirable place relative to competing products in the minds of target consumers.

(A) Positioning (B) Target segmenting

(C) Re-positioning (D) Product distribution

93. The mechanism whereby the organization seeks to earn a profit by selling its goods is known as :

(A) Competitive advantage

(B) Distinctive advantage

(C) Business model

(D) Competitive competence

94. Differentiated business firms are vulnerable to :

(A) Diversification by rivals

(B) Regulatory changes

(C) High costs of R&D

(D)Low-cost competitors offering similar products

95. The rivalry among competing sellers in an industry intensifies:

(A) when buyer demand for the product is growing rapidly.

(B) when customers are brand loyal and their costs to switch to competing brands or substitute products are relatively high.

(C) when buyer demand is strong and sellers have little or no excess capacity and only minimal inventories.

(D) as the number of rivals increases and as they become more equal in size and competitive capability.

96. The 'Generic Competitive Strategies' for outperforming other corporate in a particular industry has been proposed by :

(A) Ansoff (B) C.K. Prahlad

(C) David McLelland (D) Michael Porter

97. If two or more companies are merged and only one of them survives while others loose their independent entity, it is referred to as

(A) Merger (B) Absorption

(C) Amalgamation (D) Combination

98. Which of the following is the highest decision-making authority in the WTO?

(A) General Council

(B) Ministerial Conference

(C) DG Secretariat

(D)The Council (Trade in Goods, Trade in Services and IPRs)

99. WTO come into being in the year

(A) 1975 (B) 1985

(C) 1995 (D) 2001

100. World Trade Organisation provides

(A) Rule based multilateral trading system.

(B) Equity and social justice to the people.

(C) Rule based regional trading system

(D) All of the above

101. The theory of business of an organization is embodied in

(A) Vision (B) Mission Statement

(C) Objectives (D) Policies

102. Relying on the typology suggested by Michael Porter, business strategies could be classified into 3 types. Which of the following does ***not*** fit into their classification?

(A)Cost leadership (B) Differentiation

(C)Industry Attractiveness (D) Focus

103. Which of the following data is ***not*** required for competition analysis?

(A)Recorded data (B) Observable data

(C)Opportunistic data (D)In-House data

104. Which of the following is the ***correct*** sequence for strategy formulation?

(A)Mission-Objectives-Strategy-Policy

(B)Strategy-Vision- Mission- Budget

(C)Vision-Mission-Environmental Analysis-Budget

(D)Vision-Mission-Strategy- Budget

105. A survey of nearly 50 corporations in a variety of countries and industries found 3 most highly rated benefits of strategic management .Which of the following is not of those 3 benefits?

(A)Clearer sense of strategic vision for the firm

(B)Internationalism of strategy,vision and mission

(C)Sharper focus ofn what is strategically important

(D)Improved understanding of a rapidly changing enivornment

106. Identify the incorrect pair of "Strategy-Approach":

(A)Market penetration-Increase number of users

(B)Market development-Sell in new location

(C)Product development-Improve technology

(D)Diversification-Convince non-users to use the product

107. Study the following table about various methods of selective inventory control and answer the question at the end of the table:

Inventory Control Methods

(i)ABC Analysis

(ii)XYZ classification

(iii)VED Analysis

(iv)FSN classification

Concepts

(a)Speed of movement of inventory

(b)Combination of unit cost and consumption pattern

(c)Unit cost of inventory

(d)Criticality of inventory item

Which of the following indicates the correct match of the methods and the concepts?

Code:

(i) (ii) (iii) (iv)

(A)(a) (b) (c) (d)

(B)(b) (c) (d) (a)

(C)(c) (a) (b) (d)

(D)(d) (a) (c) (b)

108. Based on the statement below select the correct answer:

Hybrid Systems:

(1)As similar in operations to the multiple channel system

(2)Are systems where channel members perform complementary services

(3)Are more verticle

(4)Improve level of performance

(A)Statements (1) and (3) are correct

(B) Statements (1) and (2) are correct

(C) Statements (2) and (4) are correct

(D) Options (2) and (3) are correct

109. Which of the following sets of activities truly reflects the strategic implementation?

(A)Leadership implementation, Organizational restructuring, Quality monitoring

(B)Resource allocation, Quality monitoring, Management policies, Leadership implementation

(C) Organizational restructuring, Resource allocation, Management policies, Maintainence management

(D) Leadership implementation, Resource allocation, Management policies, Organizational restructuring

110. "Franchising" is an example of:

(A) Imitiation strategy

(B)Innovation strategy

(C)Broadscope strategy

(D)Marketscope strategy

111. In strategic pricing process, there are various steps undertaken as under:

(i)selecting price method

(ii) selecting the final price

(iii)Studying the competitiors price

(iv)Estimating demand

(v)Selecting the pricing objective

(vi)Estimating cost

Select the correct sequence of steps from the following:

(A)(i)-(v)-(iii)-(ii)-(iv)-(vi)

(B) (v)-(iv)-(vi)-(iii)-(i)-(ii)

(C) (iv)-(iii)-(i)-(ii)-(vi)-(v)

(D) (ii)-(iii)-(v)-(vi)-(iv)-(i)

112. When your firm practices developing and maintaining a strategic fit between your organization's goals and capabilities, it is forming a (an) _____.

(A)mission statement (B)values statement

(C)strategic plan (D)operating plan

113. At the corporate level, a company starts the strategic planning process by defining its overall purpose and _____.

(A)mission (B)values

(C)vision (D)strengths

114. The company's mission needs to be turned into detailed supporting objectives for _____.

(A)success

(B)each level of management

(C)corporate needs

(D)stockholder wealth

115. A strategic plan has this item or items following its marketing objectives.

(A)budgetary requirements

(B)target market selection

(C)research plans

(D)marketing strategies

116. The BCG market growth rate provides a measure of _____.

(A)company strength in the market

(B)decline of competitors

(C)market attractiveness

(D)the unit stock value

117. The BCG relative market share serves as a measure of company _____.

(A)strength in the market (B)sales

(C)diversification (D)success

118. Now that your employer has classified his SBUs, the next step to take in using the BCG approach is to determine _____.

(A) what role each will play in the future.

(B) the tactical plan

(C) the three-year budget

(D) none of the above

119. Which of these is ***not*** one of the common options in using the BCG approach?

(A)build (B)hold

(C)harvest (D)diversify

120. One of these represents marketing's main responsibility for a company.

(A)achieving maximum stockholder wealth

(B)increasing sales

(C)achieving profitable growth

(D)developing new products through research

121. A common practice among marketers is to increase sales to current customers without changing their products. What is this practice called?

(A)market skimming (B)market penetration

(C)market development(D)product extension

122. Why is international trade significant among countries?

(A)For promoting the world peace

(B)For decreasing cost of production

(C)For difference in the taste and preference among nations

(D)To earn foreign exchange

123. SWOT analysis is analytical tool for having :

(A)Comperative advantage

(B)Competitive advantage

(C)Comprehension of current overall situation of a firm

(D)None of the above

124. Emerging market economies are :

(A) A part of developed countries

(B) Newly industrializing countries

(C) A part of developing countries

(D) A part of third world countries

125. What describes the market, product and technological area of business?

(A) Company's mission

(B) Company's vision

(C) Strategic plan

(D) None of the above

126. Which one is part of Michael Porter's generic strategies?

(A) Cost leadership strategy

(B) Focus strategy

(C) Differentiation strategy

(D) All the above

127. Which one is ***not*** of Michael Porters five force model of industry analysis

(A)Threat of new entrants

(B)Substitutes

(C)Intensity of rivalry among existing players

(D)Cost leadership

128. Strategic planning is done by the

(A) Top management

(B) Middle level management

(C) Supervisory level management

(D) All the above

129. What can be defined as the art and science of formulating, implementing and evaluating cross-functional decisions that enable an organization to achieve its objectives?

(A)Strategy formulation

(B)Strategy evaluation

(C)Strategy implementation

(D)Strategic management

130. ______ is used to refer to strategic formulation, implementation and evaluation, with ____ referring only to strategic formulation.

(A)Strategic planning; strategic management

(B)Strategic planning; strategic processing

(C)Strategic management; strategic planning

(D)Strategic management; strategic processing

131. Conducting research to determine internal strengths and weaknesses is performed during which stage of strategic management?

(A)Formulation (B)Implementation

(C)Evaluation (D)Feedback

132. Strategy formulation includes all of the following activities *except*

(A)establishing a company mission.

(B)establishing long-term objectives.

(C)analyzing alternative strategies

(D)measuring organizational performance.

133. What are the three stages of the strategic management process?

(A)Conflict, resolution and implementation

(B)Formulation, implementation and evaluation

(C)Formulation, execution and reward

(D)Formulation, implementation and resolution

134. An important activity in __________ is taking corrective action.

(A)strategy evaluation

(B)strategy implementation

(C)strategy formulation

(D)all of the above

135. _______ means mobilizing employees and managers to put strategies into action.

(A)Formulating strategy

(B)Strategy evaluation

(C)Implementing strategy

(D)Strategic advantage

136. _________ skills are especially critical for successful strategy implementation.

(A)Interpersonal (B) Technical

(C)Conceptual (D) Thinking

137. The activity that comes first in strategy evaluation is

(A)measuring organizational performance

(B)reviewing internal and external factors

(C)establishing annual objectives

(D)establishing long-term objectives

138. Which of the following is called the action phase of the strategic management process?

(A)Strategy formulation

(B)Strategy implementation

(C)Strategy evaluation

(D)Allocating resources

139. _____ is ***not*** a strategy-implementation activity.

(A)Taking corrective actions

(B)Establishing annual objectives

(C)Devising policies

(D)Allocating resources

140. What does strategy implementation involve?

(A)Establishing annual objectives

(B)Devising policies

(C)Allocating resources

(D)All of the above

141. Strategy evaluation is necessary because

(A)internal and external factors are constantly changing.

(B)the SEC requires strategy evaluation.

(C)competitors change their strategies.

(D)the IRS requires strategy evaluation.

142. Strategic management is

(A)a pure science.

(B)based mainly on intuition.

(C)needed mainly when organizational performance falls.

(D)based on the use of quantitative and qualitative information.

143. Which statement best describes intuition?

(A)It represents the marginal factor in decision making.

(B)It represents a minor factor in decision making integrated with analysis.

(C)It should be coupled with analysis in decision making.

(D)It is better than analysis in decision making.

144. The strategic-management process

(A)is a system of independent actions.

(B)follows a strict sequence of activities.

(C)requires long periods of time to be effective.

(D)is a system of interrelated functions.

145. ________ and ________ are external changes transforming business and society today.

(A)E-commerce; strategy

(B)E-commerce; globalization

(C)Strategy; globalization

(D)Corporate culture; stakeholders

146. Which Business unit generates substantial cash surpluses due to low industrial growth rate and high market share?

(A) Dog (B) Cash Cow

(C) Question Mark (D) Star

147. A value chain's primary activities include all of the following EXCEPT:

(A) marketing and sales (B) human resources

(C) operations (D) service

148. The "balanced scorecard" supplies top managers with a ____________ view of the business.

(A)long-term financial

(B)detailed and complex

(C)simple and routine

(D)fast but comprehensive

149. The primary focus of strategic management is:

(A) strategic analysis

(B) the total organisation

(C) strategy formulation

(D) strategy implementation

150. Which of the following is ***not*** an advantage of strategic management?

(A)It provides organizations with a clearer sense of direction and purpose

(B)It helps improve the political, economic, social and technological environment of the organization

(C)It helps orientate management decisions to relevant environmental conditions

(D)It helps organizations be proactive rather than reactive

151. Which of the following defines what business or businesses the firm is in or should be in?

(A)Business strategy (B)Corporate strategy

(C)Functional strategy(D)National strategy

152. Which of the following defines how each individual business unit will attempt to achieve its mission?

(A)Business strategy (B)Corporate strategy

(C)Functional strategy(D)National strategy

153. Which one of the following is ***not*** a primary task of strategic managers?

(A)Establishing strategic objectives

(B)Developing the steps to follow in implementing operational level plans

(C)Defining the business and developing a mission

(D)Developing a strategy

154. Which one of the following is at the core of strategic management?

(A)Choosing which organisational objectives to focus on

(B)Being alert for opportunities to change work responsibilities

(C)Adapting the organisation to a changing external environment

(D)Choosing whether to make decisions autocratically or on the basis of participation

155. Which of these is ***not*** a reason why some firms do not have strategic planning?

(A) Laziness

(B) Competitive leadership

(C) Honest difference of opinion

(D) Poor reward structures

156. Developing a vision and mission, identifying an organization's external opportunities and threats, and determining internal strengths and weaknesses are all ____________ activities.

(A) strategy-formulation

(B) strategy-implementation

(C) long-range planning

(D) short-range planning

157. Which one of these is ***not*** a _________ part of Porter's competitive forces in industry analysis.

(A) Potential entry of new competitors

(B) Bargaining power of suppliers

(C) Development of substitute products

(D) Threat of substitute products and services

158. _________ is based on the assumption that the future will be just like the past.

(A) Delphi forecasts

(B) Econometric models

(C)Linear regression

(D)Scenario forecasts

159. Which of the following was responsible for a model of strategy which attempted to create a balance between efficiency and effectiveness?

(A)Sun Tzu

(B)Max Weber

(C)Frederick Winslow Taylor

(D)Carl Von Clausewitz

160. What are the elements that a Mission Statement of an Organization should include?

(A) Self guidelines for Business Operations

(B) Identifies the reasons for existence of a company and its responsibilities to the stake-holders.

(C) Identifies the firms' customers and their needs and matches them to the products and services.

(D) All of the above

---000---

UNIT-IX

STRATEGIC MANAGEMENT

1. (D) Functional strategy

Explanation:

Basic element in the Strategic Management

- **Vision:** The vision or mission statement of business or organization helps to define purpose and your goals.
- **Mission** statements that are too broad or too limiting will limit the company's ability to set effective goals and grow.
- **Identifying Goals:** Using the objectives outlined in your mission statement, the next step is to identify the goals of business. Both long- and short-term goals should be developed with the intention of meeting these objectives. As goals are met, objectives will change to match up with new goals.

Developing and implementing a plan:

- Analyzing a task or set of goals will help the individual and organization to determine the best way to delegate duties and responsibilities to individuals.
- This is the foundation of strategic management plan. Identify individual steps and mini-goals and objectives within the larger goals and objectives, and assign these accordingly, making sure that everyone is aware of the part he plays in the plan.

Evaluating and Tracking Results:

- Once the process of meeting goals and objective begins, track the results through deadlines met (or not met).
- Post-project evaluation is also helpful when planning and strategizing for future projects.

2. (B) Strategic programming

3. (A)Production and marketing are done in many countries

Explanation:

Multinational Corporation (MNC):

- A corporation that has its facilities and other assets in at least one country other than its home country.
- Such companies have offices and/or factories in different countries and usually have a centralized head office where they co-ordinate global management.
- Very large multinationals have budgets that exceed those of many small countries.
- Sometimes referred to as a "transnational corporation".

4. (B)Product - market strategies

Explanation: Ansoff Matrix Growth Strategies:

- Ansoff's matrix provides four different growth strategies:

1. Market Penetration: The firm seeks to achieve growth with existing products in their current market segments, aiming to increase its market share.

2. Market Development: The firm seeks growth by targeting its existing products to new market segments.

3. Product Development: The firms develop new products targeted to its existing market segments.

4. Diversification: The firm grows by diversifying into new businesses by developing new products for new markets.

5. (A) New Products and New Function

Explanation: Ansoff simplified the competitive position of firms by defining two dimensions:

i. the products - what it sold;
ii. the markets - to whom they are sold.

6. (A)Focused Development

7. (A) Ansoff matrix

8. (C)Porter

Explanation: Porter's five forces:

- Existing competitive rivalry between suppliers
- Threat of new market entrants
- Bargaining power of buyers
- Power of suppliers
- Threat of substitute products (including technology change)

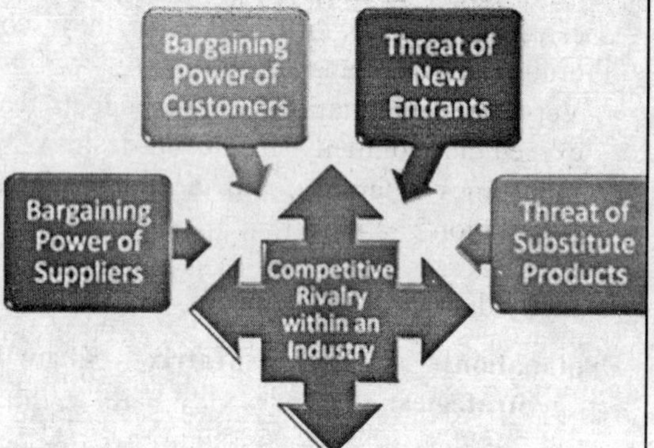

9. (C)Porter

10.(D) Competitive Strategy School

11.(A) Competitor analysis

12.(B)Firm's core competency

Explanation: Porter's "Five Forces":

- Michael E. Porter identifies five forces that influence industry competition:

  1.the threat of new entrants,

  2.the threat of substitute products or services,

  3.the bargaining power of buyers,

  4.the bargaining power of suppliers, and

  5.competitive rivalry.

13.(D) Bargaining Power of Dealers

14.(D) Strategic planning

15.(D) Core competence

16.(D)Leadership

17.(B)Diversification

18.(C) Line Pruning

Explanation: Porter's Generic Strategies:

- If the primary determinant of a firm's profitability is the attractiveness of the industry in which it operates, an important secondary determinant is its position within that industry.
- Even though an industry may have below-average profitability, a firm that is optimally positioned can generate superior returns.
- A firm positions itself by leveraging its strengths. Michael Porter has argued that a firm's strengths ultimately fall into one of two headings: cost advantage and differentiation. By applying these strengths in either a broad or narrow scope, three generic strategies result: cost leadership, differentiation, and focus.
- These strategies are applied at the business unit level. They are called generic strategies because they are not firm or industry dependent.

19.(B) Firm's core competence

20.(A)Growth Strategy

Explanation: Porter's generic strategy

- Cost Leadership Strategy
- Differentiation Strategy
- Focus Strategy

21.(C)Public Bonds

Explanation: Global Depositary Receipt (GDR):

- A bank certificate issued in more than one country for shares in a foreign company. The shares are held by a foreign branch of an international bank. The shares trade as domestic shares, but are offered for sale globally through the various bank branches.
- A financial instrument used by private markets to raise capital denominated in either U.S. dollars or Euros.

22.(A)Patents

23.(D)All the above

Explanation: Barriers to Entry:

- The existence of high start-up costs or other obstacles that prevent new competitors from easily entering an industry or area of business.
- Barriers to entry benefit existing companies already operating in an industry because they protect an established company's revenues and profits from being whittled away by new competitors.

24.(B)Services

25.(C)Low business growth - High market share

26.(B)High business growth-Low market Share

Explanation:

- The BCG Growth-Share Matrix is a portfolio planning model developed by ***Bruce Henderson*** of the Boston Consulting Group in the early 1970's.
- It is based on the observation that a company's business units can be classified into four categories based on combinations of market growth and market share relative to the largest competitor, hence the name "growth-share".
- Market growth serves as a proxy for industry attractiveness, and relative market share serves as a proxy for competitive advantage.
- The growth-share matrix thus maps the business unit positions within these two important determinants of profitability.

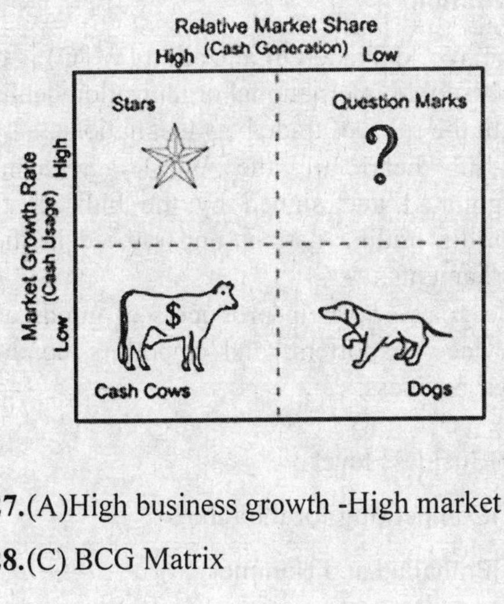

27.(A)High business growth -High market share

28.(C) BCG Matrix

Explanation: Ansoff matrix:

- Strategic marketing planning tool that links a firm's marketing strategy with its general strategic direction and presents four alternative growth strategies as a table (matrix).
- These strategies are seeking growth:
  (1) **Market penetration:** by pushing existing products in their current market segments.
  (2) **Market development:** by developing new markets for the existing products.
  (3) **Product development:** by developing new products for the existing markets.
  (4) **Diversification:** by developing new products for new markets.
- Named after its inventor, the father of strategic management, Igor Ansoff (1941), and first published in 1957 in Harvard business review.

Balanced Scorecard:

- A performance metric used in strategic management to identify and improve various internal functions and their resulting external outcomes.
- The balanced scorecard attempts to measure and provide feedback to organizations in order to assist in implementing strategies and objectives.

BCG Growth-Share Matrix

- Companies that are large enough to be organized into strategic business units face the challenge of allocating resources among those units.
- In the early 1970's the Boston Consulting Group developed a model for managing a portfolio of different business units (or major product lines).
- The BCG growth-share matrix displays the various business units on a graph of the market growth rate vs. market share relative to competitors:
- Resources are allocated to business units according to where they are situated on the grid as follows:

Cash Cow

- A business unit that has a large market share in a mature, slow growing industry.
- Cash cows require little investment and generate cash that can be used to invest in other business units.

Star

- A business unit that has a large market share in a fast growing industry.
- Stars may generate cash, but because the market is growing rapidly they require investment to maintain their lead.
- If successful, a star will become a cash cow when its industry matures.

Question Mark (or Problem Child):

- A business unit that has a small market share in a high growth market.
- These business units require resources to grow market share, but whether they will succeed and become stars is unknown.

Dog:

- a business unit that has a small market share in a mature industry.
- A dog may not require substantial cash, but it ties up capital that could better be deployed elsewhere.
- Unless a dog has some other strategic purpose, it should be liquidated if there is little prospect for it to gain market share.

29.(C)Cat

30.(D)Cash Cows

31.(D) Cash cow

32.(B) Cash cow

33.(A)Star

34.(D)Total demand versus Market share

Explanation: Strategic group mapping:

- A mechanism for understanding the other players that operate in your field
- Strategic group mapping is a technique for looking at your position in your sector, field or market.
- Hunt coined the term 'strategic group' in 1972 when he noticed sub-groups of businesses with similar characteristics in the same market.
- Michael Porter then expanded the concept in the 1980s. There are a number of benefits to strategic group mapping:
- It can help you identify who your direct and indirect competitors (or possible partners) are
- It can illustrate how easy it might be to move from one strategic group to another
- It may help identify future opportunities or strategic problems
- It ensures you take your customers' or beneficiaries' views into account when developing or assessing your strategy

Purpose

- The purpose of strategic group mapping is to make sure you take the needs or wants of your customers/beneficiaries into account.
- It encourages you to ask different questions about your future strategy, relationships with other businesses in your sector and your understanding of the people who ultimately benefit from your products or services.

35.(D)All of the above

36.(C)Ministerial conference

Explanation:

- The World Trade Organization (WTO) is the only global international organization dealing with the rules of trade between nations.
- At its heart are the WTO agreements, negotiated and signed by the bulk of the world's trading nations and ratified in their parliaments.
- The goal is to help producers of goods and services, exporters, and importers conduct their business.

37.(D)Business level

38.(B)Competiting for the future

39.(B)Prahallad and Hammel

40. (D) Market Research

41. (D) All of the above

42. (A) Operations

43. (B) Focus

44. (D) All of the above

Explanation: Focus strategy

- A marketing strategy in which a company concentrates its resources on entering or expanding in a narrow market or industry segment.
- A focus strategy is usually employed where the company knows its segment and has products to competitively satisfy its needs.
- Focus strategy is one of three generic marketing strategies.

45.(D) All of the above.

Explanation:

- Strategic Business Unit (SBU) is a group of products divisions that are operating on the same strategic characteristic within the market.
- It creates it's a profit center that focuses on marketing, or buying and selling segments. An example of a SBU strategy is Unilever.
- The strategic business unit (SBU) is a separate, specialized subsystem in the company, which acts as an independent company.
- For the first time SBU concept has been applied by the U.S. company General Electric. SBUs are small businesses with a high functional and decision-making autonomy.
- Such units may or may not need to work closely with companies, from which they have been separated.
- SBUs can be used to prepare the diversified company's strategy.

The main features of SBU are:

- Location in the structure of the company,
- These are organizational units without legal personality,
- They utilize formula "product-market",
- Type of activity performed by them is of crucial and decisive importance for the whole company,
- Functional and decision-making autonomy include: laboratory testing, production preparation, production, finance, accounting and marketing,
- SBU has divisionalized structure, which is determined by the size of production, technology and research activities, financial and accounting processes and marketing influences.

46.(C) Cost focus

Explanation: Generic strategy

- Basic approaches to strategic planning that can be adopted by any firm in any market or industry to improve its competitive performance.
- The three fundamental marketing strategies (which, though different, are not mutually exclusive) are: differentiation strategy, focus strategy, and low cost strategy.

47. (D)Market segmentation

48.(D) all of the above

Explanation: A retrenchment strategy:

- A strategy used by corporations to reduce the diversity or the overall size of the operations of the company.
- This strategy is often used in order to cut expenses with the goal of becoming a more financial stable business.
- Typically the strategy involves withdrawing from certain markets or the discontinuation of selling certain products or service in order to make a beneficial turnaround.

49.(B) Blue Ocean Strategy

Explanation: Blue Ocean Strategy :

- It is a business strategy book first published in 2005 and written by ***W. Chan Kim and Renée Mauborgne*** of The Blue Ocean Strategy Institute at INSEAD.

- The book illustrates what the authors believe is the best organizational strategy to generate growth and profits.
- Blue Ocean Strategy suggests that an organization should create new demand in an uncontested market space, or a "Blue Ocean", rather than compete head-to-head with other suppliers in an existing industry.

50. (C) (iii) (i) (ii) (iv)

51. (D) expand the market

Answer: D

Explanation: Strategy aimed at winning larger market share, even at the expense of short-term earnings. Four broad growth strategies are diversification, product development, market penetration, and market development.

52.(D) Company's Mission

Explanation: Company's Mission:

- A company's mission statement is a constant reminder to its employees of why the company exists and what the founders envisioned when they put their fame and fortune at risk to breathe life into their dreams.
- Woe to the company that loses sight of its Mission Statement for it has taken the first step on the slippery slope to failure.

53.(D) All of the above

Internal analysis:

- A review of an organization's strengths and weaknesses that focuses on those factors within its domain.
- A detailed internal analysis will typically give a business a good sense of its basic competencies and the desirable improvements that it can make to help meet the requirements of potential customers within its intended market.

54.(C) Conglomerate diversification

Explanation: Diversification:

- A risk management technique that mixes a wide variety of investments within a portfolio.
- The rationale behind this technique contends that a portfolio of different kinds of investments will, on average, yield higher returns and pose a lower risk than any individual investment found within the portfolio.
- Diversification strives to smooth out unsystematic risk events in a portfolio so that the positive performance of some investments will neutralize the negative performance of others.
- Therefore, the benefits of diversification will hold only if the securities in the portfolio are not perfectly correlated.

55.(D) All of the above

56.(A) Business level

57.(D) Strategic planning

58.(A)Human Resource Management

59.(B) Technology development

Explanation:

- Value chain analysis (VCA) is a process where a firm identifies its primary and support activities that add value to its final product and then analyze these activities to reduce costs or increase differentiation."
- ***In the value chain model, the primary activities directly relate to producing the product.***
- "Value chain represents the internal activities a firm engages in when transforming inputs into outputs."
- VCA is a strategy tool used to analyze internal firm activities.
- Its goal is to recognize, which activities are the most valuable (i.e. are the source of cost or differentiation advantage) to the firm and which ones could be improved to provide competitive advantage.
- The firm that competes through differentiation advantage will try to perform its activities better than competitors would

do.

- If it competes through cost advantage, it will try to perform internal activities at lower costs than competitors would do.
- When a company is capable of producing goods at lower costs than the market price or to provide superior products, it earns profits.
- M. Porter introduced the generic value chain model in 1985.
- Value chain represents all the internal activities a firm engages in to produce goods and services.
- VC is formed of primary activities that add value to the final product directly and support activities that add value indirectly. Below you can see the Porter's VC model.

60.(D)Igor Ansoff

Explanation: Ansoff's Product-Market Expansion Grid:

- *Ian Ansoff* has proposed a useful framework called the product/market expansion grid for detecting new intensive growth opportunities.
- There are four strategies, one for each of the quadrants:

Market Penetration Strategy:

- When the product is in the current market, it can still grow.
- There are three major approaches to increasing current product's market share:

1. Encourage current customers to buy more.
2. Attract competitor's customers.
3. Convince non-users to use the product.

Market-Development Strategy:

- When the current product is launched in a new market, there are three approaches to develop the market:

1. Expand distribution channels.
2. Sell in new locations.
3. Identify the potential users.

Product-Development Strategy:

- When a new product is launched in the current market, the intensive growth strategies could be to:

1. Develop new features.
2. Develop different quality levels.
3. Improve the technology.

Diversification:

- When a new product is launched in a new market, diversification makes good sense as better opportunities are found outside the present business.
- The diversification strategies are of three types:

1.Concentric Diversification Strategy: Develop new products with the earlier technology for new segments

2.Conglomerate Diversification Strategy: Develop new products for new markets.

3.Horizontal Diversification Strategy: Develop new products with new technology for old customers.

61.(D)Selection

Explanation: McKinsey's 7 S Frame work

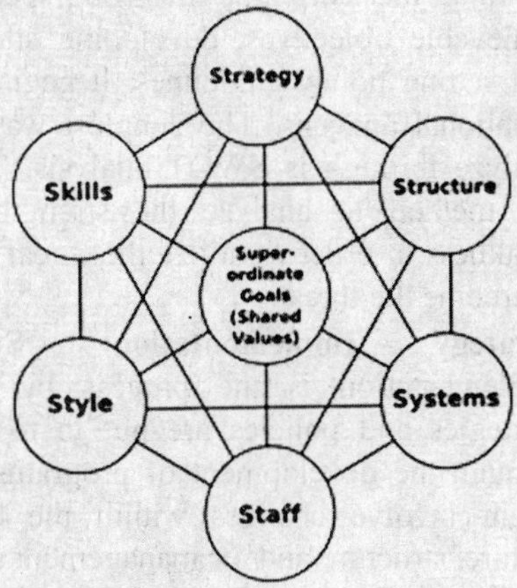

62.(A)Fortune at the bottom of the Pyramid

63.(D)BCG Matrix

64.(A)Joint Venture

65.(B)"SBU" Strategy

Explanation: Cost leadership:

- Strategy used by businesses to create a low cost of operation within their niche.
- The use of this strategy is primarily to gain an advantage over competitors by reducing operation costs below that of others in the same industry.

66.(B)M. Maurice and F. Sellier

67.(A)Environmental Scanning

Explanation:

- **Environmental scanning:** If an organization understands the environment in which it operates, half the problem is solved. This requires an analysis of what is happening outside the organization and an evaluation of current resources (strength and weaknesses) and an assessment of opportunities and threats present in the environment. Environment could be classified as external and internal.
- **Strategy formulation:** Strategy formulation is the development of long range plans for the effective management of environmental opportunities and threats in light of corporate strengths and weaknesses. It includes defining the corporate mission, specifying achievable objectives, developing strategies and setting policy guidelines. It begins with situational analysis. The simplest way is to analyze through is SWOT analysis. This is the method to analyze the strengths and weakness in order to utilize the threat and to overcome the threat.
- **Strategy Implementation:** Strategy implementation is the process by which strategies and policies are put in to action through the development of programs. This might involve changes within the overall culture, structure and/ or management system of the entire organization. Strategies are implemented through a set of programs, budgets and procedures.
- **Strategy Evaluation and control:** Evaluation and control is the process in which corporate activities and performance can be compared with desired performance. Managers at all levels use the clear, prompt, unbiased information from the people below the corporation's hierarchy to take corrective action and resolve problems. It can also pinpoint weaknesses in previously implemented strategic plans and this stimulates the control of performance. The evaluation and the control of performance complete the strategic management model. Based on the performance results, management may need to make adjustments in its strategy formulation or implementation or both.

68.(D)Corporate Strategy

Explanation:

- **Marketing strategy:** An organization's strategy that combines all of its marketing goals into one comprehensive plan. A good marketing strategy should be drawn from market research and focus on the right product mix in order to achieve the maximum profit potential and sustain the business. The marketing strategy is the foundation of a marketing plan.
- **Operating strategy:** The act of a company attempting to close the gap between its business strategy and the actual implementation of that strategy. A very specific plan is devised to include allocation of which resources and how much.
- **Business Strategy:** Business (or Strategic) management is the art, science, and craft of formulating, implementing and evaluating cross-functional decisions that will enable an organization to achieve its long-term objectives. It is the process of specifying the organization's mission, vision and objectives, developing policies and plans, often in terms of projects and programs, which are designed to achieve these objectives, and then allocating resources to implement the policies and plans, projects and programs. Strategic management seeks to coordinate and integrate the activities of the various functional areas of a business in order to achieve long-term organizational objectives. A balanced scorecard is often used to

evaluate the overall performance of the business and its progress towards objectives.

- **Corporate strategy:** The overall scope and direction of a corporation and the way in which its various business operations work together to achieve particular goals.

69.(C)BCG Matrix

Explanation:

Ansoff matrix:

- Strategic marketing planning tool that links a firm's marketing strategy with its general strategic direction and presents four alternative growth strategies as a table (matrix).
- These strategies are seeking growth:
  (1) ***Market penetration:*** by pushing existing products in their current market segments.
  (2) ***Market development:*** by developing new markets for the existing products.
  (3)***Product development:*** by developing new products for the existing markets.
  (4)***Diversification:*** by developing new products for new markets. Named after its inventor, the father of strategic management, Igor Ansoff (1941-), and first published in 1957 in Harvard business review.

The BCG Growth-Share Matrix:

- The BCG Growth-Share Matrix is a portfolio planning model developed by ***Bruce Henderson of the Boston Consulting Group*** in the early 1970's.
- It is based on the observation that a company's business units can be classified into four categories based on combinations of market growth and market share relative to the largest competitor, hence the name "growth-share".
- Market growth serves as a proxy for industry attractiveness, and relative market share serves as a proxy for competitive advantage.
- The growth-share matrix thus maps the business unit positions within these two important determinants of profitability.

70.(C) Premise control

71.(A) Collusion

Explanation:

Collusion:

- A non-competitive agreement between rivals that attempts to disrupt the market's equilibrium.
- By collaborating with each other, rival firms look to alter the price of a good to their advantage.
- The parties may collectively choose to restrict the supply of a good, and/or agree to increase its price in order to maximize profits.
- Groups may also collude by sharing private information, allowing them to benefit from insider knowledge.

Strategic Alliance:

- An arrangement between two companies that have decided to share resources to undertake a specific, mutually beneficial project.
- A strategic alliance is less involved and less permanent than a joint venture, in which two companies typically pool resources to create a separate business entity.
- In a strategic alliance, each company maintains its autonomy while gaining a new opportunity.
- A strategic alliance could help a company develop a more effective process, expand into a new market or develop an advantage over a competitor, among other possibilities.

Differentiation strategy:

- Approach under which a firm aims to develop and market unique products for different customer segments.
- Usually employed where a firm has clear competitive advantages, and can sustain an expensive advertising campaign.
- It is one of three generic marketing strategies; other two are focus strategy and low cost strategy that can be adopted by any firm.

Turnaround strategy:

- "Turnaround strategy is a corporate practice designed and planned to protect (save) a loss-making company and transform it into a profit-making one."
- "Turnaround Strategy is a corporate action that is taken (performed) to deal with issues of a loss-making (sick) company like increasing losses, lower return on capital employed, and continuous decrease in the value of its shares."
- "Turnaround strategy is an analytical approach to solve the root cause failure of a loss-making company to decide the most crucial reasons behind its failure. Here, a long-term strategic plan and restructuring plans are designed and implemented to solve the issues of a sick company."

72.(C) Joint venture

Explanation:

Strategic Alliance:

- An arrangement between two companies that have decided to share resources to undertake a specific, mutually beneficial project.
- A strategic alliance is less involved and less permanent than a joint venture, in which two companies typically pool resources to create a separate business entity.
- In a strategic alliance, each company maintains its autonomy while gaining a new opportunity.
- A strategic alliance could help a company develop a more effective process, expand into a new market or develop an advantage over a competitor, among other possibilities.

Partnership:

- A business organization in which two or more individuals manage and operate the business. Both owners are equally and personally liable for the debts from the business.

Joint Venture:

- A business arrangement in which two or more parties agree to pool their resources for the purpose of accomplishing a specific task.
- This task can be a new project or any other business activity.
- In a joint venture (JV), each of the participants is responsible for profits, losses and costs associated with it. However, the venture is its own entity, separate and apart from the participants' other business interests.

73.(A) the scale and scope of the Business operations.

Explanation: Growth strategy:

- Strategy aimed at winning larger market share, even at the expense of short-term earnings.
- Four broad growth strategies are diversification, product development, market penetration, and market development.

74.(C) Corporate strategy

Explanation:

Cost leadership:

- Strategy used by businesses to create a low cost of operation within their niche.
- The use of this strategy is primarily to gain an advantage over competitors by reducing operation costs below that of others in the same industry.

Functional strategy:

- Organizational plan for human resources, marketing, research and development and other functional areas.
- The functional strategy of a company is customized to a specific industry and is used to back up other corporate and business strategies.

Strategic business unit (SBU):

- An autonomous division or organizational unit, small enough to be flexible and large enough to exercise control over most of the factors affecting its long-term performance.
- Because strategic business units are more agile (and usually have independent missions and objectives), they allow the owning conglomerate to respond quickly to changing economic or market situations.

Corporate strategy:

- The overall scope and direction of a corporation and the way in which its various business operations work together to achieve particular goals.

Global strategy:

- Global strategy as defined in business terms is an organization's strategic guide to globalization.

75.(D) All of the above

76.(C) SWOT analysis

Explanation:

Environmental analysis: Evaluation of the possible or probable effects of external forces and conditions on an organization's survival and growth strategies.

Business analysis:

- Business analysis is a research discipline of identifying business needs and determining solutions to business problems.
- Solutions often include a systems development component, but may also consist of process improvement, organizational change or strategic planning and policy development.

SWOT Analysis:

- A tool that identifies the strengths, weaknesses, opportunities and threats of an organization.
- Specifically, SWOT is a basic, straightforward model that assesses what an organization can and cannot do as well as its potential opportunities and threats.
- The method of SWOT analysis is to take the information from an environmental analysis and separate it into internal (strengths and weaknesses) and external issues (opportunities and threats).
- Once this is completed, SWOT analysis determines what may assist the firm in accomplishing its objectives, and what obstacles must be overcome or minimized to achieve desired results.

77.(A) Tom Peters

78.(C) Resilient

79.(C) Satisfying the stakeholders

Explanation: Corporate Governance:

- The system of rules, practices and processes by which a company is directed and controlled.
- Corporate governance essentially involves balancing the interests of the many stakeholders in a company - these include its shareholders, management, customers, suppliers, financiers, government and the community.
- Since corporate governance also provides the framework for attaining a company's objectives, it encompasses practically every sphere of management, from action plans and internal controls to performance measurement and corporate disclosure.

80.(C) (i) (ii) (iii) (iv)

81.(D) All the above

Explanation: Globalization:

- The tendency of investment funds and businesses to move beyond domestic and national markets to other markets around the globe, thereby increasing the interconnectedness of different markets.
- Globalization has had the effect of markedly increasing not only international trade, but also cultural exchange.

82.(D)Functional strategy

83.(D) Blue ocean strategy

84.(A) Turnaround

Explanation: Turnaround Strategy:

- Turnaround strategy means to convert, change or transform a loss-making company into a profit-making company.
- It means to make the company profitable again.
- The main purpose of implementing a turnaround strategy is to turn the company from a negative point to a positive one.

- If a turnaround strategy is not applied to a sick company, it will close down.
- It is a remedy for curing industrial sickness.
- Turnaround is a restructuring strategy. Here, a loss-bearing company is transformed into a profit-earning company, by making systematic efforts.
- It tries to remove all weaknesses to help a sick company once again become strong, stable and a profit-making institution.
- It tries to reverse the position from loss to profit, from declining sales to increasing sales, from weakness to strength, and from an instability to stability.
- It aids to reduce the brought forward losses of the loss-making company.
- It helps the sick company to stand once again in the market.
- It is a complete U-turn of a planned strategic economic transition.

Business expansion

- A business strategy in which growth is obtained by increasing the number of stores in which customers can buy a company's products and services.
- Unlike relocation, business expansion entails opening up new stores in different physical locations while still maintaining the current business locations.
- The growth of a business' product and service offerings.

Diversification

- Diversification is a strategy that takes a company into new markets with new products or services.
- Companies may choose a diversification strategy for different reasons:
- Companies might wish to create and exploit economies of scope, in which the company tries to utilize its exciting resources and capabilities in other markets.
- Managerial skills found within the company may be successfully used in other markets, where the dominant logic and managerial procedures of management can be successfully transferred to other markets.
- Companies pursuing a diversification strategy may be able to cross-subsidize one product with the surplus of another.
- Companies may also want to use a diversification strategy to spread financial risk over different markets and products, so that the entire success of the company is not reliant on one market or product only.
- The diversification strategy can be split into two different types:
    - Related diversification
    - Unrelated diversification

85.(C) Standard and poor

86.(C) Focus strategy

87.(D) All of the above

88.(D) Operating risk

Explanation: Unsystematic Risk:

- Company or industry specific risk that is inherent in each investment.
- The amount of unsystematic risk can be reduced through appropriate diversification.
- It is also known as "specific risk," "diversifiable risk" or "residual risk."

89.(B) Personnel strategy

Explanation: Positioning Strategy:

- Positioning strategies can be conceived and developed in a variety of ways.
- It can be derived from the object attributes, competition, application, the types of consumers involved, or the characteristics of the product class.
- All these attributes represent a different approach in developing positioning strategies, even though all of them have the common objective of projecting a favorable image in the minds of the consumers or audience.
- There are seven approaches to positioning strategies:

  (1)Using Product characteristics or Customer Benefits as a positioning strategy

  (2) Pricing as a positioning strategy - Quality Approach or Positioning by Price-Quality

(3)Positioning strategy based on Use or Application
(4)Positioning strategy based on Product Process
(5)Positioning strategy based on Product Class
(6)Positioning strategy based on Cultural Symbols
(7)Positioning strategy based on Competitors.

90.(A) Win-win strategy

91.(D) (ii) (iii) (i)

92.(A) Positioning

93.(C) Business model

Explanation: An effective strategy is built on the foundation of the organization's business model, the mechanism whereby the organization seeks to earn a profit by selling its goods.

94.(D)Low-cost competitors offering similar products

95. (D)as the number of rivals increases and as they become more equal in size and competitive capability.

Explanation: Rivalry among existing Firms:

- The intensity of competition, or rivalry, will have a significant impact on the ability to generate adequate margins.
- The intensity of rivalry or competition among firms competing in the same industry varies depending upon a number of factors:
- Industries with one dominant firm tend to be more stable than fragmented industries where one competitor may try to achieve dominance.
- The degree of concentration or the extent to which the industry is monopolistic is an important aspect on how competitors are likely to behave.
- For example, in an oligopolistic situation, such as telecoms networks, price wars should be avoided.
- While avoiding price fixing, competitors can send out pricing signals to move towards a new level of lower or higher prices.
- If an industry stops growing, for any competitor the only way of growing is by taking market share, i.e. competition will intensify until some competitors exit or consolidation takes place.
- In the case of commodity markets, i.e. undifferentiated products such as grain or computer RAM, competition focuses on price, which is particularly damaging to all manufacturers.
- Where there is scope for differentiation, price competition will be lower.
- In markets where products or services are perishable, competition becomes more intense when sales have to be made.
- An example is last minute summer holiday bookings.

96. (D) Michael Porter

97. (A) Merger

98. (A) General Council

99. (C) 1995

100. (A) Rule based multilateral trading system.

101. (A) Vision

Explanation:

- The key components of 'strategic planning' include an understanding of an entity's vision, mission, values and strategies.
- In the commercial world a "Vision Statement" and/or a "Mission Statement" may encapsulate the vision and mission.
- **Vision:** outlines what the organization wants to be, or how it wants the world in which it operates to be (an "idealised" view of the world). It is a long-term view and concentrates on the future.
- **Mission:** Defines the fundamental purpose of an organization or an enterprise, succinctly describing why it exists and what it does to achieve its vision. For example, the charity above might have a mission statement as "providing jobs for the homeless and unemployed".

- **Values:** Beliefs that are shared among the stakeholders of an organization. Values drive an organization's culture and priorities and provide a framework in which decisions are made.
- **Strategy:** Strategy, narrowly defined, means "the art of the general".
- Aa combination of the ends (goals) for which the firm is striving and the means (policies) by which it is seeking to get there.
- A strategy is sometimes called a roadmap - which is the path chosen to plow towards the end vision.

102. (C)Industry Attractiveness

103. (D)In-House data

104. (A)Mission-Objectives-Strategy-Policy

105. (B)Internationalism of strategy,vision and mission

106. (D)Diversification-Convince non-users to use the product

107. (B)(b) (c) (d) (a)

108. (C) Statements (2) and (4) are correct

109. (D) Leadership implementation, Resource allocation, Management policies, Organizational restructuring

Explanation: Strategic implementation:

- The activity performed according to a plan in order to achieve an overall goal.
- For example, strategic implementation within a business context might involve developing and then executing a new marketing plan to help increase sales of the company's products to consumers.
- Strategic implementation put simply is the process that puts plans and strategies into action to reach goals.
- A strategic plan is a written document that lays out the plans of the business to reach goals, but will sit forgotten without strategic implementation.
- The implementation makes the company's plans happen.

110. (A) Imitiation strategy

Explanation: Franchising:

- A continuing relationship in which a franchisor provides a licensed privilege to the franchisee to do business and offers assistance in organizing, training, merchandising, marketing and managing in return for a monetary consideration.
- Franchising is a form of business by which the owner (franchisor) of a product, service or method obtains distribution through affiliated dealers (franchisees).

111. (B) (v)-(iv)-(vi)-(iii)-(i)-(ii)

Explanation:

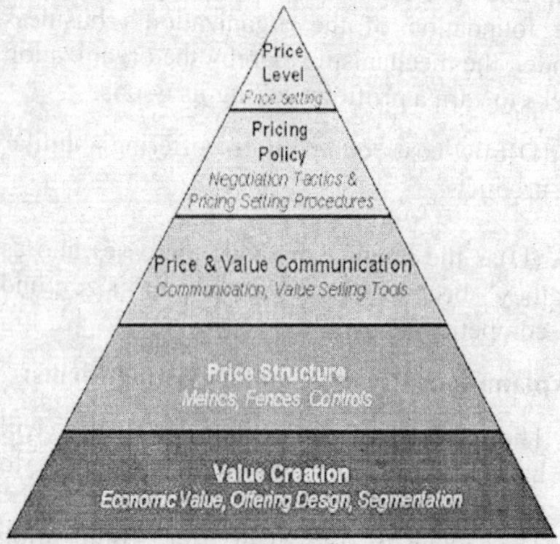

112. (C)strategic plan

113. (A)mission

114. (B)each level of management

115. (D)marketing strategies

116. (C)market attractiveness

117. (A)strength in the market

118. (A) what role each will play in the future.

119. (D)diversify

120. (C)achieving profitable growth

121. (B)market penetration

122. (D)To earn foreign exchange

123. (C)Comprehension of current overall situation of a firm

124. (C) A part of developing countries

125. (A) Company's mission

126. (D) All the above

127. (D)Cost leadership

128. (A) Top management

129. (D)Strategic management

130. (C)Strategic management; strategic planning

131. (A)Formulation

132. (D)measuring organizational performance.

133. (B)Formulation, implementation and evaluation

134. (A)strategy evaluation

135. (C)Implementing strategy

136. (A)Interpersonal

137. (B)reviewing internal and external factors

138. (B)Strategy implementation

139. (A)Taking corrective actions

140. (D)All of the above

141. (A)internal and external factors are constantly changing.

142. (D)based on the use of quantitative and qualitative information.

143. (C)It should be coupled with analysis in decision making.

144. (D)is a system of interrelated functions.

145. (B)E-commerce; globalization

146. (B) Cash Cow

147. (B) human resources

148. (D)fast but comprehensive

149. (B) the total organization

150. (B)It helps improve the political, economic, social and technological environment of the organization

151. (B)Corporate strategy

152. (A)Business strategy

153. (B)Developing the steps to follow in implementing operational level plans

154. (C)Adapting the organisation to a changing external environment

155. (B) Competitive leadership

156. (A) strategy-formulation

157. (C) Development of substitute products

158. (C)Linear regression

159. (D)Carl Von Clausewitz

160. (D)All of the above

Explanation:

- The mission statement should guide the actions of the organization, spell out its overall goal, provide a path, and guide decision-making.
- It provides "the framework or context within which the company's strategies are formulated."

---000---

UNIT-X

ENTERPRENEURSHIP DEVELOPMENT

1. Entrepreneurial failures can be attributed to :

(A) Low quality raw materials

(B) Labour problems

(C) High overhead costs

(D) All of the above

2. Small scale Industry is defined in terms of :

(A)Volume of production

(B)Number of employees

(C)Amount of investment in plant and machinery

(D)Sales turnover

3. If each one of the partners of a firm pulls out of a business and decides to separate, it is called :

(A)Dissolution of partnership

(B)Dissolution of the firm

(C)Lockout of the firm

(D)Bankruptcy of the firm

4. Overdraft is a short-term finance measure to :

(A)Pay taxes

(B)Repay loan

(C)Purchase plant and equipment

(D)meet working capital requirement

5. Rural infrastructure development fund is provided by :

(A)NABARD (B) SIDBI

(C)ICICI (D)Nationalized Banks

6. Which of the following Bank has been entrusted with the responsibility of developing and supporting small business :

(A)NABARD (B) SIDBI

(C)IDBI (D) None of these

7. Technology Development and Modernization Fund is provided by :

(A)SIDBI (B) NABARD

(C)KVIC (D) SIDO

8. Which of the following has been entrusted with the responsibility of developing and supporting small business?

(A) IDBI (B) RBI

(C) NABARD (D) SIDBI

9. Scheduled bank is that bank which is:

(A)Nationalized

(B)Not nationalized

(C)Bared at foreign country

(D)Include in the second schedule of RBI

10. Commercial banks are now permitted to undertake to the business of:

(A) Equipment leasing(B) Mutual funds

(C) Factoring (D) All of these

11. The Government of India established the Small Industries Development Organisation (SIDO) in the year :

(A) 1951 (B) 1972

(C) 1954 (D) 1982

12. Which one of the following agencies has the power to declare any industrial unit as a potentially sick unit?

(A) BIFR (B) SIDBI

(C) IRCI (D) FICCI

13. Policies related to Revival of Sick Units are framed by

(A) IIFT (B) CSIR

(C) SEBI (D) MSME

14. Sick units are referred to :

(A)RBI (B)SIDBI

(C)NIRD (D)BIFR

15. The headquarters of the SIDBI is in

(A) Mumbai (B) Lucknow

(C) New Delhi (D) Hyderabad

16. Which of the following is ***not*** a Trading block?

(A) NAFTA (B) ASEAN

(C) SAARC (D) IMF

17. What BIFR stands for :

(A)Bureau of Industrial Financial Reconstruction

(B)Board of Industrial Financial Reconstruction

(C)Bureau of Industrial Financial Re-engineering

(D)Board of Industrial Financial Re-engineering

18. What is the acronym for SIDBI?

(A)Short Investment Development Bank of India.

(B)Stock Investment Development Bank of India.

(C)Small Investment Development Bank of India.

(D)Small Industries Development Bank of India.

19. Which of the following organizations is meant for promoting small scale industries at district level?

(A) SIDBI (B) DIC

(C) SFCs (D) NABARD

20. Sick enterprise is referred to which of the following bodies for rehabilitation?

(A)Small Industries Development Bank of India (SIDBI)

(B)Small Industries Development Organisation (SIDO)

(C)Board for Industrial and Financial Restructure (BIFR)

(D)National Small Industries Corporation (NSIC)

21. Which of the following is a measure taken for revival of sick SSI :

(A)Margin money scheme

(B)Reservation of items

(C)Export promotion

(D)Tax holiday

22. Principles of entrepreneurship may be applied to :

(A)Government (B) Business

(C)Society (D) All of the above

23. The criteria for small business is :

(A)Capital invested

(B)Number of employees

(C)Number of managers

(D)Type of business

24. Which of the following standardization certificate is related to the protection of environment?

(A)ISO 2000 (B)ISO 9000

(C)ISO 14000 (D) None of these

25. Which is ***not*** a socio-economic rationale for promoting SSI in India?

(A)Employment generation

(B)Export promotion

(C)Offering competition to large-scale industry

(D)Labour intensive

26. Which of the following is ***not*** a part of incentives to SSI?

(A)Subsidy to labour wages

(B)Tax holidays

(C)Lower interest rate

(D)Interest subsidy

27. The interest rate for 'bridge finance' is :

(A)lower than that of short-term loan

(B)equal to that of short-term loan

(C)higher than that of short-term loan

(D)nil

28. Which of the following organizations provide institutional support to SSI?

(A)Indian Institute of Foreign Trade

(B)Tool Design Institute of SIDO

(C)Nationalized Banks

(D)Ministry of Commerce

29. Which of the following contribute to sickness of small enterprises?

(A)Poor financial management

(B)Inadequate quality control

(C)Lack of competitive market strategy

(D)All of the above

30. Which of the following is the cause of sickness of an enterprise?

(A) Lack of adequate capital

(B) Lack of demand for the products

(C) Lack of raw material

(D) All of the above

31. Which of the following is ***not*** a part of the process of business opportunity identification?

(A)Surveying the availability of required raw materials

(B)Identifying the flora and fauna

(C)Market survey

(D)Locating financial resources

32. Which of the following is an example of an external threat?

(A) New trade regulations

(B) Global sales potential

(C) Economies of scale

(D) Decreased competition

33. "Innovation and entrepreneurship" is a book written by:

(A) Philip Kotler (B) C. K. Prahlad

(C) Pradeep Khandwala (D) Peter F. Drucker

34. Strategizing within value frame work is an approach of

(A) Management (B) Administration

(C) Governance (D) Stake holders

35. Which of the following is ***not*** a tool of corporate governance?

(A) Preparation of financial statements

(B) Appointment of independent directors.

(C)Compulsory audit of financial statements.

(D) Time bound promotion of employees.

36. Service Sector is also called

(A) Primary Sector

(B) Secondary Sector

(C) Tertiary Sector

(D) None of the above

37. The definition of Micro, Small and Medium Enterprises (MSMEs) in India is based on:

(A) Total Sales of the Unit

(B) Investment in machines and equipments

(C) Market coverage

(D) Export capacity

38. In MSMED Act, 2006, the investment limit for Micro, Small and Medium Enterprises have been prescribed as:

(A) Rs. 10 lakhs, Rs. 5 crores and Rs. 10 crores

(B) Rs. 5 lakhs, Rs. 1 crore and Rs.10 crores

(C) Rs. 5 lakhs, Rs. 1 crore and Rs. 5 crores

(D) Rs. 10 lakhs, Rs. 10 crores and Rs. 15 crores

39. Entrepreneurship as a theory of business was propounded by:

(A) Douglas McGregor

(B) Thomas A. Coleman

(C) Joseph A. Schumpeter

(D) Adam Smith

40. State Financial Corporation Act encourages in:

(A) Establishing Industrial Estates

(B) Establishing small and medium size industries

(C) Establishing Agricultural Farms

(D) All of the above

41. Micro, Small and Medium Enterprises Development Act, 2006 is related to:

(A) Industrial Policy

(B) Investment Limit

(C) Business Opportunities

(D) None of these

42. An entrepreneurial person employed by a corporation and encouraged to be innovative and creative is referred to as:

(A) Competitor (B) Supplier

(C) Entrepreneur (D) Intrapreneur

43. Environmental issues can be managed by:

(A)Investing in environment friendly process or products.

(B)Managing environmental regulations.

(C)Investing in environmental performance improvement.

(D) All of the above.

44. A formal document of what the entrepreneur intends to do to sell enough of the firm's product or service to make a satisfactory profit is called:

(A) Long range plan (B) Strategic plan

(C) Business plan (D) None of the above

45. Takeover generally involves

(A) the acquisition of part of an undertaking to enable the acquirer to increase the market share of the product concerned.

(B) the acquisition of certain block of equity capital of a company which enables the acquirer to exercise control over the affairs of the company.

(C) taking over the responsibility to have trade agreement for finished product.

(D) taking over certain long-term liabilities of another group company to help it financially.

46. GATT stands for:

(A) General Accord on Tariff and Trade

(B) Generous Agreement on Trade and Tariff

(C) General Agreement on Tariff and Trade

(D)Generalist Agreement on Trade and Tariff

47. GATT was signed in the year:

(A) 1995 (B) 2005

(C) 1947 (D) 1952

48. Today's organizations are working on the principle of:

(A) Production-orientation

(B) Product-orientation

(C) Selling-orientation

(D) consumer-orientation

49. In which year WTO came into being?

(A) 1980 (B) 2000

(C) 2006 (D) 1995

50. Which of the following Act, regulates sick industries specially in India?

(A)ID Act (B) SICA

(C)Companies ACT (D) None of these

51. 'Global Compact' is an initiative of

(A) UN (B) WTO
(C) IMF (D) ILO

52. 'Agenda 21' relates to :

(A)Child Labour

(B)Human Rights

(C)Environment protection

(D)None of these

53. Disclosure of information is a part of :

(A)Global Compact

(B)Human Rights

(C)Social Clause

(D)Corporate Governance

54. Corporate governance revolves around :

(A)Stakeholders (B) Organization
(C)Society (D) All of these

55. Industrial sickness can be caused by :

(A)Lack of market demand

(B)Product obsolescence

(C)Competition from big industries

(D)All the above

56. "SEZ" stands for :

(A)Small Entrepreneurship Zone

(B)Special Entrepreneurship Zone

(C)Sick Economic Zone

(D)Special Economic Zone

57. Which one of the following is ***not*** the purpose of the promotion of small Business?

(A)Generation of employment

(B)Balanced Regional Development

(C)Promotion of Communal Harmony

(D)Reduction in rural poverty

58. Which of the following is ***not*** a phase in Business plan preparation?

(A)Setting business goals

(B)Locating Resources

(C)Tracing Competitions

(D)Developing the Labour Market

59. Arrange the following five steps of small business development in the order in which they shall occur :

(i) Survival

(ii)Success

(iii)Existence

(iv)Resource Maturity

(v)Take-off

(A)	(iii)	(i)	(ii)	(v)	(iv)
(B)	(iii)	(ii)	(i)	(iv)	(v)
(C)	(ii)	(iii)	(iv)	(i)	(v)
(D)	(iii)	(ii)	(i)	(v)	(iv)

60. Which one of the following is ***not*** the reason for sickness of industries?

(A)Inadequate working capital

(B)Huge Market

(C)Out dated Technology

(D)Changing tastes of consumers

61. The MSMED Act, 2006 classified enterprises broadly into:

(A) Two categories

(i) Manufacturing enterprises and

(ii) Service enterprises

(B) Three categories

(i) Micro enterprises

(ii) Small enterprises

(iii) Medium enterprises

(C) Four categories

(i) Micro enterprises

(ii) Small enterprises

(iii) Tiny enterprises

(iv) Medium enterprises

(D) Four categories

(i) Tiny enterprises

(ii) Micro enterprises

(iii) Small business enterprises

(iv)Medium enterprises

62. Which sector is called as Primary Sector in India?

(A) Industrial sector (B) Service sector

(C) External sector (D) Agricultural sector

63. How many times the census of registered Micro, small and medium Enterprises (MSMEs) have been made by Small Industries Development Organization?

(A) 1 (B) 2

(C) 3 (D) 4

64. EDII is situated at

(A) New Delhi (B) Ahmedabad

(C) Patna (D) Kolkata

65. Industrial Policy of which year contained for the very first time a special thrust on measures for promoting and strengthening small tiny and village enterprises:

(A) 1956 (B) 1991

(C) 1948 (D) 1977

66. Which one is not the characteristic feature of entrepreneurship?

(A) Vision (B) Risk Bearing

(C) Initiative and Drive (D) Disloyalty

67. The reason for sickness of small scale industry is:

(A) Lack of capital (B) Lack of market

(C) Severe competition (D) All the above

68. The measure taken by Government to promote small scale industry.

(A) Provision of land

(B) Provision of marketing facilities

(C) Arrangement of credit and raw materials

(D) All the above

69. Small and medium enterprises are

(A) Labour intensive

(B) Capital intensive

(C) Market leader

(D) Industry price determiner

70. Funding through Micro finance to Small and Micro Enterprises is not successful due to

(A) High rate of interest

(B) Out sourcing of method of providing Micro Finance

(C) (A) & (B)

(D) None of the above

71. Match the following:

List-I (Financial Institution)

(a)Industrial Development Bank of India

(b)Small Industries Development Bank of India (SIDBI)

(c)Natural Small Industries Corporation

(d)Industrial Finance Corporation of India

List-II (Year of Establishment)

(i) 1955

(ii) 1964

(iii)1948

(iv) 1989

Codes:

	(a)	(b)	(c)	(d)
(A)	(i)	(iv)	(iii)	(ii)
(B)	(ii)	(iv)	(i)	(iii)
(C)	(iii)	(i)	(ii)	(iv)
(D)	(iii)	(ii)	(i)	(iv)

72. A company using high price and high promotion policy is adopting the following strategy :

(A) Slow skimming (B) Rapid Penetration

(C) Slow Penetration (D) Rapid Skimming

73. What are the economic goals that guide the strategic direction of every viable business organization?

(A) Goal, profit and public image

(B) Public image, growth and profit

(C) Survival, growth and profitability

(D) Growth, profitability and public image

74. Which of the following is the cause of sickness of an enterprise?

(A)Lack of adequate capital

(B) Lack of demand for the products

(C)Lack of competition

(D) All the above

75. The Banking Regulation Act, 1949, does not at all apply to:

(A) State Bank of India and its subsidiaries

(B) Nationalized Banks

(C)Foreign Banks having their offices in India

(D)Primary agricultural credit societies and co-operative and mortgagee banks

76. Which of the following is most likely to cause an immediate increase in the stage of the working population?

(A) A rise in the average size of families

(B) An increase in the birth rate

(C) A fall in the death rate of the over 60 years old

(D) More favourable tax treatment of the earnings, married women

77. You are the manager of a firm. Which of the following activities do you initiate first?

(A) Planning (B) Organizing

(C) Staffing (D) Directing

78. The Industrial Finance Corporation, of India came into existence in

(A) July, 1948 (B) August, 1968

(C) September, 1951 (D) None of these

79. Who is the final authority for deciding the design, form and material of bank notes?

(A) Central Government

(B) Reserve Bank of India

(C) Indian Bank's Association

(D) Note Issuing Authority of India

80. Which of the following is alternatively called Corporate Venturing?

(A) Entrepreneurship

(B) Intrapreneurship

(C) A new product start-up

(D) Venture Capital

81. The following Company is in the news for violation of Corporate Governance through fraudulent practices

(A) Tata Chemicals Ltd.

(B) Reliance Industries Ltd.

(C) Hindustan Unilever Ltd.

(D) Satyam Computers Ltd.

82. Which one of the following is ***not*** the reason for the sickness of Small Enterprise?

(A) Lack of Working Capital

(B) Lack of Market Demand

(C) Lack of Competition

(D) Lack of Raw Material

83. Du Pont analysis was developed:

(i) in 1920

(ii) by F. Donalson Brown

(iii) a mechanical engineer

(iv) in Du Pont corporation

The correct combination is

(A)(i), (iii) and (iv)

(B) (i) and (iv)

(C)(ii), (iii) and (iv)

(D)(i), (ii) and (iv)

84. Which of the following is ***not*** a export document?

(A) Bill of Lading (B) Export license

(C) Carting order (D) Duty drawback

85. Which one of the following is a export promotion measure?

(A) Abolishing export duties

(B) Export subsidies

(C) Marketing incentives

(D) All of the above

86. Which one of the following is international credit rating agency:

(A) IMF (B) World Bank

(C) Standard and Poor(D) WTO

87. Fifth Ministerial Conference of WTO was held in:

(A) Doha (B) Singapore

(C) Mexico (D) Seattle

88. GATT was transformed into WTO in the year:

(A) 2001 (B) 1996

(C) 1995 (D) 2010

89. Give the Acronym of ASEAN

(A) Association of South East Asian Nations

(B) Asian South East African Nations

(C) Association of South East American Nations

(D) Association of South East Ancient Nations

90. The person who introduced the term 'entrepreneur' was :

(A) Peter Drucker (B) J.S. Mill

(C) Richard Cantillon (D) Schumpeter

91. Which is the key factor that an entrepreneur should focus on, in ensuring survival of his enterprises?

(A) Profits (B) Cash flow

(C) Margin (D) Market Share

92. The idea that, 'Extra-ordinary individuals' are the source of entrepreneurial emergence, is putforth by :

(A) McClelland (B) Schumpeter

(C) Weber (D) Drucker

93. In case of SSIs, who said that 'small is beautiful'?

(A) E.F. Schumacher (B) Peter Drucker

(C) Mahatma Gandhi (D) Azim Premji

94. The transformation of an idea into useful application is termed as :

(A) Creativity (B) Invention

(C) Innovation (D) Syndication

95. ..... is a critical attribute of an entrepreneur.

(A) Management Skills

(B) Awarness of Environment

(C) Confidence

(D) Risk-bearing Ability

96. The two broad business categories of small and medium enterprises are :

(A) Manufacturing and Service

(B) Manufacturing and Processing

(C) Manufacturing and Marketing

(D) Processing and Consulting

97. Which of the following is ***not*** the cause of sickness of an enterprise?

(A) Lack of adequate capital

(B) Lack of demand for the products

(C) Lack of raw material

(D) Government Support and Concessions

98. According to Peter Drucker, which of the following is the basic tool for an entrepreneur?

(A) Searching for change

(B) Innovation

(C) Providing something of value

(D) Exploiting opportunities

99. .... is the nodal agency set up by Government of India for the development of small scale sector.

(A) NSIC (B) SIDO

(C) DIC (D) SIDBI

100. The Kumar Mangalam Birla Committee was set up by :

(A) Government of India

(B) Reserve Bank of India

(C) Planning Commission

(D) SEBI

101. The Clause 49 of the Listing Agreement is ***not*** applicable to:

(A) All Listed entities having paid up capital of Rs. 3 Crores and above

(B) Having Net worth of Rs. 25 Crores or more at any time

(C) All Listed entities having paid up capital of Rs. 5 Crores and above and having Net worth of over Rs. 50 Crores

(D) All Listed entities having paid up capital of Rs. 3 Crores and Net worth of Rs. 25 Crores or more any time

102. Which of the following convention of ILO provides for gender equity?

(A)87 (B)98

(C) 100 (D) 105

103. Dynamic process of creating incremental wealth by individuals who assume the risks of equity, time and careers, to infuse resources with value for society is referred as:

(A) Business Plan

(B) Venture Capital

(C) Business Opportunity

(D) Entrepreneurship

104. Marine cargo insurance refers to:

(A) Surface Transport insurance

(B) Aviation insurance

(C) Sea Shipment insurance

(D) None of the above

105. A company has broad choices to enter a foreign market. Arrange the strategies from lower level to higher level involvement:

(i)Licensing

(ii)Direct exporting

(iii)Indirect exporting

(iv)Joint venture

(v) Direct investment

(A) (iii) (ii) (i) (iv) (v)

(B) (i) (ii) (iii) (iv) (v)

(C) (v) (iv) (iii) (ii) (i)

(D) (iv) (v) (i) (ii) (iii)

106. To encourage domestic production or to protect the domestic producer from foreign competitors, government pays to domestic producer by reducing operations cost. Such payments are called:

(A) Bill of Exchange

(B) Foreign Exchange

(C) Bill of Lading

(D) Subsidies

107. Match the following

List-1 (Strategies)

(a) Market penetration

(b) Market development

(c) Product development

(d) Diversification

List- 2 (Market and Products)

(i)New markets-new products.

(ii)New markets current products

(iii)Current markets new products

(iv)Current markets current products

	(a)	(b)	(c)	(d)
(A)	(iv)	(iii)	(ii)	(i)
(B)	(i)	(ii)	(iii)	(iv)
(C)	(iii)	(ii)	(iv)	(i)
(D)	(iv)	(ii)	(iii)	(i)

108. Partnership is a form of business organization in which business debts can be recovered from:

(A) The managing partners

(B) MI the managers and partners

(C) The firm and the managers

(D) The firm and all the partners

109. People who take the risks necessary to organize, manage and receive the financial profits and non-monetary rewards are called:

(A) Suppliers (B) Employees

(C) Competitors (D) Entrepreneurs

110. The exports to countries belonging to erstwhile British empire is called:

(A)ASEAN (B)Commonwealth

(C)SAPTA (D)SAARC

111. In which of the following types of ownership there is no distinction between the business entity and the owner(s):

(A)Company limited by shares

(B)The co-operative organization

(C)Proprietorship

(D)Joint stock company

112. Which is the basic form of Innovation ?

(A) Introduction of novel production process

(B) Improvement and development of existing process

(C) Improvement and development of existing firm

(D) All of the above

113. Which one of the following is not an instrument of trade policy:

(A) Tariffs (B) Subsidies

(C) Import Quotas (D) Letter of credit

114. Fill in the blanks spaces: Ultimately…was replaced by the….on Jan.1,1995.

(A)G.A.T.T, W.T.O.

(B)W.T.O, G.A.T.T

(C)G.A.T.S,W.T.O

(D)I.M.F.,G.A.T.T

115. During whose prime ministership the New Economic Policy was introduced in India?

(A) Indira Gandhi

(B) Rajiv Gandhi

(C) P.V. Narasimha Rao

(D) A.B. Vajpayee

116. In which year was the EXIM Bank established?

(A) 1982 (B) 1983

(C) 1984 (D) 1985

117. Which of the following Policy measures would lead to expansion of Business?

(1) Export Duty

(2) Export subsidy

(3) Liberal Import

(4) Revaluation of Currency

(A) 1, 2 and 4 (B) 1 and 3

(C) 3 and 4 (D) 2 and 4

118. ....is the non-traditional source of finance for entreperenurs.

(A)Bank Loan

(B)Venture Capital

(C)Friends and Relatives

(D)SIDBI

119. Which of the following is ***not*** one of the four elements in innovation process?

(A)New Knowledge Creation

(B)Commercial Application

(C)Organising Resources

(D)Analytical Planning

120. Which of the following is ***not*** a phase in business plan preparation?

(A)Setting business goals

(B)Locating Resources

(C)Analysing Competitions

(D)Developing the labour market

121. The entrepreneurial activity is most prevalent in:

(A)United States

(B)Japan

(C)Germany

(D)Great Britian

122. The elements of good corporate governance in India have been laid down by:

(A)ICSI (B)IOD

(C)ICWAI (D)ICAI

123. Which of the following is not among the thrust areas of policy for SSIs in India?

(A)Resources availability

(B)Rehabilitation of sick SSI units

(C)Timely and adequate credit availability

(D)Quality improvement support

124. What are the areas of primary focus for "Public Entrepreneurship"? Which deals with revitalization of government agencies?

(A)Creation, Innovation

(B)Customer, Creation

(C)Customer, Efficiency

(D)Innovation, Efficiency

125. Which theory considers the possibility of trade between two countries having the same factor endowment and consumer preference?

(A)Comparative advantage theory

(B)Heckscher-ohlin theory

(C)Imitation-gap theory

(D)Absolute advantage theory

126. Which of the following sets of factors should an entrepreneurs considers carefully before selecting a new project?

(A)Investement size,Location technology,Market conditions

(B) Investement size,competition,exper tise,age,gender

(C) Investement size,Market condition,Gestation period,Expertise

(D)Investement size,Repayment capability,Availability of Loans,Profit margins

127. Which of the following methods is the most appropriate measure for cost reduction investement projects with unequal lives?

(A)Equivalent annual cost

(B) Equivalent annual NPV

(C) Equivalent present value index

(D)Capital rationing

128. Activities taken up on part time or casual basis to raise income is :

(A) Self employment

(B) Income generation

(C) Entrepreneurship

(D) None of the above

129. Entrepreneur is a person who :

(A)Initiates Business

(B)Invests Capital

(C)Manages the business

(D)All of the above

130. Activities taken up on part time or casual basis to raise income is :

(A)Self employment

(B)Income generation

(C)Entrepreneurship

(D)None of the above

131. According to Peter Drucker, ______ is the specific tool of entrepreneurs, the means by which they exploit change as an opportunity for a different business or a different service. It is the act that endows resources with a new capacity to create wealth.

(A)innovation (B)wealth

(C)Creativity (D)Efficiency

132. The resistance of employees in an organization against flexibility, growth, and diversification can be overcome by developing:

(A)Entrepreneurship

(B)Intrapreneurship

(C)Managerial domain

(D)Administrative domain

133. For the success of business plan the goals should be

(A)Limitless (B)Generalized

(C)Specific (D)Imaginary

134. Which one of the following is a barrier to new product creation and development?

(A)Trial and error

(B)Opportunity parameter

(C)Opportunity cost

(D)Intrapreneurship culture

135. Which of the following is alternatively called corporate venturing?

(A)Entrepreneurship

(B)Intrapreneurship

(C)Act of stating a new venture

(D)Offering new products by an existing company

136. Developing a new idea through inquiry and testing is called:

(A)Heuristics (B)Forced relationship

(C)Scientific method (D)Value analysis

137. The business plan should be prepared by:

(A)Entrepreneurs (B)Consultants

(C)Engineers (D)All of above options

138. Which of the following is the cause of sickness of an enterprise?

(A)Lack of adequate capital

(B)Lack of demand for the products

(C)Lack of competition

(D)All the above

139. Which of the following shows the process of creating something new?

(A) Business model (B) Modeling

(C)Innovation (D)Creative flexibility

140. Which one of the following gives suggestions for new product and also help to market new products?

(A)Existing products and services

(B) Distribution channels

(C)Federal government

(D) Consumers

141. Which of the following is used by entrepreneurs to acquire experience in an international market before making a major commitment?

(A) Merger (B) Joint venture

(C) Minority interest (D) Majority interest

142. GATT is established in 1947, under:

(A) German leadership (B) French leadership

(C) U.S. leadership (D) U.K. leadership

143. The entrepreneur was distinguished from capital provider in:

(A) Middle ages (B) 18th century

(C)17th century (D) 19th and 20th century

144. A person who managed large project was termed as the entrepreneur in the ______.

(A) Earliest period (B) Middle ages

(C) 17th century (D) 19th and 20th century

145. What is the process by which individuals pursue opportunities without regard to resources they currently control?

(A) Startup management

(B) Entrepreneurship

(C) Financial analysis

(D) Feasibility planning

146. Having less than 50 percent of equity share in an international venture is called:

(A) Minority interest

(B)Joint venture

(C) Majority interest

(D) Exporting

147. Having more than 50% ownership position that provides the entrepreneur with managerial control is called:

(A)Joint venture

(B) Majority interest

(C) Horizontal merger

(D) Diversified activity merger

148. Which one of the following is the process of entrepreneurs developing new products that over time make current products obsolete?

(A) New business model

(B) Anatomization

(C) Creative destruction

(D) None of the given options

149. Which of the following factors is the most important in forcing U.S companies to focus on new product development and increased productivity?

(A)Entrepreneurship

(B) Hyper competition

(C) Governmental laws

(D) Organizational culture

150. Individuals influencing an entrepreneur's career choice and style are known as which of the following?

(A) Role model

(B) Moral-support network

(C) Professional support network

(D) Support system

151. The activity which occurs when the new venture is started is called:

(A) Motivation

(B) Business skills

(C) Departure point

(D) Goal orientation

152. The level at which an individual is viewed by society is called:

(A) Financial status

(B)Qualification

(C)Social status

(D) Achievement

153. Which one of the following is an important source of idea generation due to their familiarity with the needs of market?

(A) Existing products and services

(B) Distribution channels

(C) Federal government

(D) Consumers

154. Members of distribution channels are excellent sources for new ideas because:

(A)They are familiar with the needs of the market

(B)They earn a handsome profit from new business

(C) They do not bother if entrepreneur bears a loss

(D) They have well-developed sales force

155. Which one of the following is the most important characteristic of a successful business website?

(A) Speed (B)Innovation

(C)Graphics (D) Products

156. Which one of the following is the next stage to the Concept Stage of Product Planning and Development Process?

(A) Idea Stage

(B) Product Planning Stage

(C)Product Development Stage

(D) Test Marketing Stage

157. SBA stands for:

(A) Small business accountants

(B)Small business administration

(C)Small business adequacy

(D)Small business advisors

158. Why should an entrepreneur do a feasibility study for starting a new venture?

(A) To see if there are possible barriers to success

(B) To identify possible sources of funds

(C)To estimate the expected sales

(D) To explore potential customers

159. Information regarding all of the following is related to operations, ***except***:

(A)Location (B) Promotion

(C) Raw materials (D) Labor skills

160. Which of the following is ***true*** for Disclosure Document?

(A) It gives recognition that he was the inventor of the idea in past

(B) It gives recognition that he is the first the inventor of the idea

(C)It gives recognition that he will be the invent an idea in future

(D) It gives recognition that he wants to copy the idea

161. In the administrative domain, the commitment of resources is for which of the following?

(A) Periodic intervals

(B)Total amount needed

(C) For certain tasks

(D) For long time

162. Which of the following is a method of selling goods to another country by taking care of transactions?

(A) Indirect exporting

(B) Direct exporting

(C) Importing

(D) Management contract

163. Gazelles are the firms with:

(A) High growth rate

(B)Moderate growth rate

(C) Zero growth rate

(D) Low growth rate

164. Which of the following are the Fast-growth young companies?

(A)Gazelles

(B) Life style

(C) Foundation Company

(D) None of the given options

165. Which of the following factor has allowed small companies to act like they are big ones?

(A)Technology

(B) Customers

(C) Economic development

(D) Competition

---000---

UNIT-X

ENTERPRENEURSHIP DEVELOPMENT

1. (D) All of the above
2. (C)Amount of investment in plant and machinery

Explanation:

- Small Scale Industry is defined as a unit in which investment in original value of plant and machinery should not exceed Rs. 1.5 crore.
- However, to facilitate technology up gradation and enhance competitiveness, the investment limit has been raised to Rs. 5 crore in respect of 71 high tech export oriented items in drugs, pharmaceuticals, hand – tools and knitwear sectors, etc.

3. (B)Dissolution of the firm

Explanation:

Dissolution of partnership:

- The dissolution of a partnership is the process during which the affairs of the partnership are wound up (where the ongoing nature of the partnership relation terminates).
- This should not be confused with the term dissolution when applied to a limited company, which is the event that marks the conclusion of the winding-up.

Dissolution of a firm: The dissolution of partnership between all the partners of a firm is called the "dissolution of the firm".

Lockout of the firm: The withholding of work from employees and closing down of a workplace by an employer during a labor dispute. It is also called shutout.

Bankruptcy of the firm:

- A legal proceeding involving a person or business that is unable to repay outstanding debts.
- The bankruptcy process begins with a petition filed by the debtor (most common) or on behalf of creditors (less common).
- All of the debtor's assets are measured and evaluated, whereupon the assets are used to repay a portion of outstanding debt.
- Upon the successful completion of bankruptcy proceedings, the debtor is relieved of the debt obligations incurred prior to filing for bankruptcy.
- Bankruptcy offers an individual or business a chance to start fresh by forgiving debts that simply can't be paid while offering creditors a chance to obtain some measure of repayment based on what assets are available.
- In theory, the ability to file for bankruptcy can benefit an overall economy by giving persons and businesses another chance and providing creditors with a measure of debt repayment.

4. (D)meet working capital requirement

Explanation:

- Overdraft financing is provided when businesses make payments from their business current account exceeding the available cash balance.
- An overdraft facility enables businesses to obtain short-term funding - although in theory the amount loaned is repayable on demand by the bank.

5. (A)NABARD

Explanation:

NABARD:

- National Bank for Agriculture and Rural Development (NABARD) is an apex development bank in India having headquarters based in Mumbai (Maharashtra).
- The Committee to Review Arrangements for Institutional Credit for Agriculture and Rural Development (CRAFICARD), set up by the Reserve Bank of India (RBI) under the Chairmanship of Shri B. Sivaraman, conceived and recommended the

establishment of the National Bank for Agriculture and Rural Development (NABARD).

- It was established on **12 July 1982** by a special act by the parliament and its main focus was to uplift rural India by increasing the credit flow for elevation of agriculture & rural non farm sector.
- It has been accredited with "matters concerning policy, planning and operations in the field of credit for agriculture and other economic activities in rural areas in India".
- **Mission:** Promoting sustainable and equitable agriculture and rural development through effective credit support, related services, institution building and other innovative initiatives.
- In pursuing this mission, NABARD focuses its activities on :
- **Credit functions**, involving preparation of potential-linked credit plans annually for all districts of the country for identification of credit potential, monitoring the flow of ground level rural credit, issuing policy and operational guidelines to rural financing institutions and providing credit facilities to eligible institutions under various programmes.
- **Development functions**, concerning reinforcement of the credit functions and making credit more productive.
- **Supervisory functions**, ensuring the proper functioning of cooperative banks and regional rural banks.

ICICI

- ICICI Bank was established by the Industrial Credit and Investment Corporation of India, an Indian financial institution, as a wholly owned subsidiary in 1994.
- The parent company was formed in 1955 as a joint-venture of the World Bank, India's public-sector banks and public-sector insurance companies to provide project financing to Indian industry.
- The bank was initially known as the Industrial Credit and Investment Corporation of India Bank, before it changed its name to the abbreviated ICICI Bank.
- The parent company was later merged with the bank.
- ICICI Bank launched internet banking operations in 1998.
- ICICI Bank Limited is a multinational financial services company headquartered in ***Mumbai***, India.
- It is the second largest bank in India by assets and third largest by market capitalisation.
- It offers a wide range of banking products and financial services to corporate and retail customers through a variety of delivery channels and through its specialised subsidiaries in the areas of investment banking, life and non-life insurance, venture capital and asset management.
- The bank has subsidiaries in the United Kingdom, Russia, and Canada; branches in United States, Singapore, Bahrain, Hong Kong, Sri Lanka, Qatar and Dubai International Finance Centre; and representative offices in United Arab Emirates, China, South Africa, Bangladesh, Thailand, Malaysia and Indonesia. The company's UK subsidiary has established branches in Belgium and Germany.
- ICICI Bank is one of the Big Four banks of India, along with State Bank of India, Punjab National Bank and Canara Bank.

Nationalized Banks

- Nationalized banks have always contributed to boost up the economy of India and available in a large number.
- It is also known for offering expeditious service and understands the actual need of its customers.
- In India Nationalized banks have great dominance over private banks as it has fully authority to look after the function and policy of private banks.
- ***Imperial Bank*** was the first banks that was nationalized in 1955 and became famous as ***State Bank of India***.
- After that many banks got the certification of nationalized bank. Some of these are State

Bank of Tranvancore, State Bank of Indore, State Bank of Patiala, State Bank of Saurashtra and more.

- The nationalized banks were established with great purpose to make wide reach of banking function even in the rural area and offers great benefit for those who actually get deprived from such service.
- The nationalized banks are fully committed to offer the best possible service to its rural client and also make them aware about the various benefits, available for them.
- Such banks are fully dedicated to offer quality of service to their clients. In 1969, the total number of nationalized banks was 14 whereas it became 21 in 1980. However State Bank of India became the topmost and the best commercial bank. Besides it also rated top five banks in the world.
- Befor the steps of nationalisation of Indian banks, only State Bank of India (SBI) was nationalised. It took place in July 1955 under the SBI Act of 1955. Nationalisation of Seven State Banks of India (formed subsidiary) took place on 19th July, 1960.
- 1955 : Nationalisation of State Bank of India.
- 1959 : Nationalisation of SBI subsidiaries
- 1969 : Nationalisation of 14 major banks.
- 1980 : Nationalisation of seven banks with deposits over 200 crores.

6. (B) SIDBI

Explanation:

SIDBI

- Small Industries Development Bank of India is an independent financial institution aimed to aid the growth and development of micro, small and medium-scale enterprises (MSME) in India.
- Set up on April 2, 1990 through an act of parliament, it was incorporated initially as a wholly owned subsidiary of Industrial Development Bank of India.
- It is the Principal Financial Institution for the Promotion, Financing and Development of the Micro, Small and Medium Enterprise (MSME) sector and for Co-ordination of the functions of the institutions engaged in similar activities.

IDBI

- ***Industrial Development Bank of India (IDBI)*** Bank Limited is an Indian financial service company headquasrtered Mumbai, India. RBI categorised IDBI as an "other public sector bank". It was established in 1964 by an Act of Parliament to provide credit and other facilities for the development of the fledgling Indian industry.
- Some of the institutions built by IDBI are the Securities and Exchange Board of India (SEBI), National Stock Exchange of India (NSE), the National Securities Depository Limited (NSDL), the Stock Holding Corporation of India Limited (SHCIL), the Credit Analysis & Research Ltd, the Exim Bank (India), the Small Industries Development Bank of India (SIDBI), the Entrepreneurship Development Institute of India, and IDBI Bank, which is owned by the Indian Government.
- IDBI Bank is on a par with nationalized banks and the SBI Group as far as government ownership is concerned. It is one among the 26 commercial banks owned by the Government of India.
- To meet emerging challenges and to keep up with reforms in financial sector, IDBI has taken steps to reshape its role from a development finance institution to a commercial institution.

7. (A) SIDBI

KVIC:

- The Khadi and Village Industries Commission (KVIC) is a statutory body formed by the Government of India, under the Act of Parliament, 'Khadi and Village Industries Commission Act of 1956'.
- It is an apex organization under the Ministry of Micro, Small and Medium Enterprises, with regard to khadi and village industries within India, which seeks to - "plan, promote, facilitate, organise and assist in the establishment and development of khadi and

village industries in the rural areas in coordination with other agencies engaged in rural development wherever necessary.".
- In April 1957, it took over the work of former All India Khadi and Village Industries Board.

8. (D) SIDBI

Explanation: The Reserve Bank of India (RBI)

- India's central banking institution, which formulates the monetary policy with regard to the Indian rupee.
- It was established on 1 April 1935 during the British Raj in accordance with the provisions of the Reserve Bank of India Act, 193
- Following India's independence in 1947, the RBI was nationalised in the year 1949.

9. (D)Include in the second schedule of RBI

Explanation:

- **Scheduled Banks:** Scheduled Banks in India are those banks which have been included in the Second Schedule of Reserve Bank of India (RBI) Act, 1934.
- RBI in turn includes only those banks in this schedule which satisfy the criteria laid down vide section 42 (6) (a) of the Act.
- As on 30 June 1999, there were 300 scheduled banks in India having a total network of 64,918 branches. Scheduled commercial banks in India include State Bank of India and its associates (5), nationalised banks (20), foreign banks (45), private sector banks (32), co-operative banks and regional rural banks.
- "Scheduled banks in India" means the State Bank of India constituted under the State Bank of India Act, 1955 (23 of 1955), a subsidiary bank as defined in the State Bank of India (Subsidiary Banks) Act, 1959 (38 of 1959), a corresponding new bank constituted under section 3 of the Banking Companies (Acquisition and Transfer of Undertakings) Act, 1970 (5 of 1970), or under section 3 of the Banking Companies (Acquisition and Transfer of Undertakings) Act, 1980 (40 of 1980), or any other bank being a bank included in the Second Schedule to the Reserve Bank of India Act, 1934 (2 of 1934), but does not include a co-operative bank".

10.(D) All of these

11.(C) 1954

Explanation:

SIDO:

- Small Industries Development Organisation (SIDO) an apex body at Central level for formulating policy for the development of Small Scale Industries in the country, is headed by the Additional Secretary & Development Commissioner (Small Scale Industries) under Ministry of Small Scale Industries Govt. of India.
- Its head office is based in ***Mumbai***, with its six zonal offices in Delhi, Bhopal, Bangalore, Kolkata, Mumbai and Guwahati.
- SIDO is playing a very constructive role for strengthening this vital sector which has proved to be one of the strong pillars of the economy of the country.
- It is rendering the services in the following areas :
- Advising the Govt. in policy matters concerning small scale sector.
- Providing techno-economic and managerial consultancy, common facilities and extension services.
- Providing facilities for technology up-gradation, modernization quality improvement & infrastructure.
- Human resources development through training and skill up-gradation.
- Providing economic information services.
- Maintaining close liaison and vital linkage with the Central Ministries, Planning Commission, Financial Institutions, State Govts. & similar other developmental organizations/agencies related to the promotion and development of SSI Sector.
- Evolving and coordinating policies for development of ancillaries.
- Monitoring of PMRY Scheme
- Monitoring the working of different Tool Rooms & PPDC's

12.(A) BIFR

13.(D) MSME

14.(D)BIFR

Explanation: a *sick unit* and *referred to* the Board of Industrial and Financial Reconstruction (BIFR)

15.(B) Lucknow

16.(D) IMF

Explanation:

NAFTA:

- The North American Free Trade Agreement (NAFTA) is an agreement signed by Canada, Mexico, and the United States, creating a trilateral trade bloc in North America.
- The agreement came into force on January 1, 1994. It superseded the Canada–United States Free Trade Agreement between the U.S. and Canada.
- NAFTA has two supplements: the North American Agreement on Environmental Cooperation (NAAEC) and the North American Agreement on Labor Cooperation (NAALC).

ASEAN:

- The Association of Southeast Asian Nations is a geo-political and economic organisation of ten countries located in Southeast Asia, which was formed on 8 August 1967 by Indonesia, Malaysia, the Philippines, Singapore and Thailand.
- Since then, membership has expanded to include Brunei, Burma (Myanmar), Cambodia, Laos, and Vietnam.
- Its aims include accelerating economic growth, social progress, cultural development among its members, protection of regional peace and stability, and opportunities for member countries to discuss differences peacefully.
- ASEAN covers a land area of 4.46 million km², which is 3% of the total land area of Earth, and has a population of approximately 600 million people, which is 8.8% of the world's population. The sea area of ASEAN is about three times larger than its land counterpart. In 2011, its combined nominal GDP had grown to more than US$ 2 trillion.
- If ASEAN were a single entity, it would rank as the eighth largest economy in the world.

SAARC:

- The South Asian Association for Regional Cooperation (SAARC) is an organisation of South Asian nations, which was established on 8 December 1985 when the government of Bangladesh, Bhutan, India, Maldives, Nepal, Pakistan, and Sri Lanka formally adopted its charter providing for the promotion of economic and social progress, cultural development within the South Asia region and also for friendship and cooperation with other developing countries.
- It is dedicated to economic, technological, social, and cultural development emphasising collective self-reliance. Its seven founding members are Sri Lanka, Bhutan, India, Maldives, Nepal, Pakistan, and Bangladesh. Afghanistan joined the organisation in 2007.
- Meetings of heads of state are usually scheduled annually; meetings of foreign secretaries, twice annually.
- ***It is headquartered in Kathmandu, Nepal.***

IMF:

- The IMF describes itself as "an organization of 188 countries, working to foster global monetary cooperation, secure financial stability, facilitate international trade, promote high employment and sustainable economic growth, and reduce poverty around the world."
- The organization's stated objectives are to promote international economic cooperation, international trade, employment, and exchange rate stability, including by making financial resources available to member countries to meet balance of payments needs.
- ***Its headquarters are in Washington, D.C., United States.***
- The International Monetary Fund (IMF) is

an international organization that was initiated in 1944 at the Bretton Woods Conference and formally created in 1945 by 29 member countries.

- The IMF's stated goal was to assist in the reconstruction of the world's international payment system post–World War II.
- Countries contribute money to a pool through a quota system from which countries with payment imbalances can borrow funds temporarily.
- Through this activity and others such as surveillance of its members' economies and the demand for self-correcting policies, the IMF works to improve the economies of its member countries.

17.(B)Board of Industrial Financial Reconstruction

BIFR:

- The Board for Industrial and Financial Reconstruction (BIFR) is an agency of the government of India, part of the Department of Financial Services of the Ministry of Finance.
- Its objective is to determine sickness of industrial companies and to assist in reviving those that may be viable and shutting down the others.
- The BIFR was established under the The Sick Industrial Companies (Special Provisions) Act, 1985 (SICA).
- The board was set up in January 1987 and became functional as of 15 May 1987. A new industrial policy was tabled in Parliament on 24 July 1991, aiming to maintain growth in productivity and gainful employment and to encourage the growth of entrepreneurship and upgrades to technology.
- That year the SICA was amended to include public sector enterprises in the board's purview.

CII:

- The Confederation of Indian Industry (CII) is a non-government, not-for-profit, industry-led and industry-managed organisation, seeking to play a proactive role in India's development process.
- The organisation works to create and sustain an environment conducive to the growth of industry in India, partnering industry and government alike through advisory and consultative processes.
- The confederation is headquartered in New Delhi.Adi Godrej was elected as the president for the year 2012-13. Chandrajit Banerjee is the Director General of the confederation.

18.(D)Small Industries Development Bank of India.

19.(B) DIC

20.(C)Board for Industrial and Financial Restructure (BIFR)

21.(D)Tax holiday

Explanation: Tax holiday: A government incentive program that offers a tax reduction or elimination to businesses. Tax holidays are often used to reduce sales taxes by local governments, but they are also commonly used by governments in developing countries to help stimulate foreign investment.

22.(B) Business

23.(A)Capital invested

24.(C)ISO 14000

25.(C)Offering competition to large-scale industry

26.(A)Subsidy to labour wages

27.(C)higher than that of short-term loan

Explanation: Bridge Financing:

- In investment banking terms, it is a method of financing used by companies before their IPO, to obtain necessary cash for the maintenance of operations.
- Bridge financing is designed to cover expenses associated with the IPO and is typically short-term in nature. Once the IPO

is complete, the cash raised from the offering will immediately payoff the loan liability.

- These funds are usually supplied by the investment bank underwriting the new issue. As payment, the company acquiring the bridge financing will give a number of shares to the underwriters, at a discount of the issue price that equally offsets the loan.
- This financing is, in essence, a forwarded payment for the future sales of the new issue.

28.(C)Nationalized Banks

29.(D)All of the above

30.(D) All of the above

31.(B)Identifying the flora and fauna

32.(A) New trade regulations

33.(D) Peter F. Drucker

34.(C) Governance

35.(D) Time bound promotion of employees.

36.(C) Tertiary Sector

Explanation: Service Sector:

- The service sector consists of the "soft" parts of the economy, i.e. activities where people offer their knowledge and time to improve productivity, performance, potential, and sustainability, what is termed affective labor.
- The basic characteristic of this sector is the production of services instead of end products. Services (also known as "intangible goods") include attention, advice, access, experience, and discussion.
- The production of information is generally also regarded as a service, but some economists now attribute it to a fourth sector, the quaternary sector.
- The ***tertiary sector*** of industry involves the provision of services to other businesses as well as final consumers.
- Services may involve the transport, distribution and sale of goods from producer to a consumer, as may happen in wholesaling and retailing, or may involve the provision of a service, such as in pest control or entertainment.
- The goods may be transformed in the process of providing the service, as happens in the restaurant industry. However, the focus is on people interacting with people and serving the customer rather than transforming physical goods.
- For the last 100 years, there has been a substantial shift from the primary and secondary sectors to the tertiary sector in industrialised countries. This shift is called tertiarisation.
- The tertiary sector is now the largest sector of the economy in the Western world, and is also the fastest-growing sector.

37.(B) Investment in machines and equipments

Explanation:

- In accordance with the provision of Micro, Small & Medium Enterprises Development (MSMED) Act, 2006 the Micro, Small and Medium Enterprises (MSME) are classified in two Classes:

  (a)Manufacturing Enterprises: The enterprises engaged in the manufacture or production of goods pertaining to any industry specified in the first schedule to the industries (Development and regulation) Act, 1951). The Manufacturing Enterprise are defined in terms of investment in Plant & Machinery.

  (b)Service Enterprises: The enterprises engaged in providing or rendering of services and are defined in terms of investment in equipment.

38.(A) Rs. 10 lakhs, Rs. 5 crores and Rs. 10 crores

Explanation:

- The Government of India has enacted the Micro, Small and Medium Enterprises Development (MSMED) Act, 2006 in terms of which the definition of micro, small and medium enterprises is as under:

  (a) Enterprises engaged in the manufacture or production, processing or preservation of goods as specified below:

(i) A **micro enterprise** is an enterprise where investment in plant and machinery **does not exceed Rs. 25 lakh;**

(ii) A **small enterprise** is an enterprise where the investment in plant and machinery is **more than Rs. 25 lakh but does not exceed Rs. 5 crore;** and

(iii) A **medium enterprise** is an enterprise where the investment in plant and machinery is **more than Rs.5 crore but does not exceed Rs.10 crore.**

39.(C) Joseph A. Schumpeter

40.(B) Establishing small and medium size industries

41.(B) Investment Limit

42.(D) Intrapreneur

Explanation: Intrapreneur:

- An inside entrepreneur, or an entrepreneur within a large firm, who uses entrepreneurial skills without incurring the risks associated with those activities. Intrapreneurs are usually employees within a company who are assigned a special idea or project, and are instructed to develop the project like an entrepreneur would.
- Intrapreneurs usually have the resources and capabilities of the firm at their disposal.
- The intrapreneur's main job is to turn that special idea or project into a profitable venture for the company.

43.(D) All of the above.

44.(C) Business plan

Explanation:

Business plan: A business plan is a formal statement of a set of business goals, the reasons they are believed attainable, and the plan for reaching those goals. It may also contain background information about the organization or team attempting to reach those goals.

45.(B) the acquisition of certain block of equity capital of a company which enables the acquirer to exercise control over the affairs of the company.

Explanation: Takeover:

- A corporate action where an acquiring company makes a bid for an acquiree.
- If the target company is publicly traded, the acquiring company will make an offer for the outstanding shares.

46.(C) General Agreement on Tariff and Trade

Explanation:

- The General Agreement on Tariffs and Trade (GATT) was a multilateral agreement regulating international trade.
- According to its preamble, its purpose was the "substantial reduction of tariffs and other trade barriers and the elimination of preferences, on a reciprocal and mutually advantageous basis."
- It was negotiated during the United Nations Conference on Trade and Employment and was the outcome of the failure of negotiating governments to create the International Trade Organization (ITO).
- GATT was signed in ***1947*** and lasted until 1994, when it was replaced by the World Trade Organization in 1995.
- The original GATT text (GATT 1948) is still in effect under the WTO framework, subject to the modifications of GATT 1994.

47.(C) 1947

48.(D) consumer-orientation

Explanation:

- A service offered by companies that focuses on the internal and external needs of a business's customers.
- Consumer orientation establishes and monitors standards of customer satisfaction and strives to meet the clientele's needs and expectations related to the product or service sold by the business.

49.(D) 1995

Explanation:

- The World Trade Organization (WTO) is an organization that intends to supervise and liberalize international trade.
- The organization officially commenced on 1 January 1995 under the Marrakech Agreement, replacing the General Agreement on Tariffs and Trade (GATT), which commenced in 1948.The organization deals with regulation of trade between participating countries; it provides a framework for negotiating and formalizing trade agreements, and a dispute resolution process aimed at enforcing participants' adherence to WTO agreements, which are signed by representatives of member governments:fol.9–10 and ratified by their parliaments.
- Most of the issues that the WTO focuses on derive from previous trade negotiations, especially from the Uruguay Round (1986–1994).

50.(B) SICA

51.(A)UN

52.(C)Environment protection

Explanation:

- Agenda 21 is a non-binding, voluntarily implemented action plan of the United Nations with regard to sustainable development.
- It is a product of the UN Conference on Environment and Development (UNCED) held in Rio de Janeiro, Brazil, in 1992.
- It is an action agenda for the UN, other multilateral organizations, and individual governments around the world that can be executed at local, national, and global levels.
- The "21" in Agenda 21 refers to the 21st Century. It has been affirmed and modified at subsequent UN conferences.

53.(D)Corporate Governance

Explanation:

- **Corporate governance** refers to the system by which corporations are directed and controlled.
- The governance structure specifies the distribution of rights and responsibilities among different participants in the corporation (such as the board of directors, managers, shareholders, creditors, auditors, regulators, and other stakeholders) and specifies the rules and procedures for making decisions in corporate affairs.
- Governance provides the structure through which corporations set and pursue their objectives, while reflecting the context of the social, regulatory and market environment.
- Governance is a mechanism for monitoring the actions, policies and decisions of corporations. Governance involves the alignment of interests among the stakeholders.

54.(A)Stakeholders

55.(D)All the above

56.(D)Special Economic Zone

Explanation:

- A Special Economic Zone (SEZ) is a geographical region that has economic laws that are more liberal than a country's typical economic laws.
- The category 'SEZ' covers abroad range of more specific zone types, including Free Trade Zones(FTZ),
- Special Economic Zones have been established in several countries, including India, China, Brazil
- The Special Economic Zones (SEZs) Act 2005 is the culmination of a Government Policy, which was introduced as a vision to impart a globally conducive platform for a competitive structure of Indian exports.

57.(D)Reduction in rural poverty

58. (D)Developing the Labour Market

59. (A) (iii) (i) (ii) (v) (iv)

60. (B)Huge Market

61. (A) Two categories

(i) Manufacturing enterprises and

(ii) Service enterprises

62.(D) Agricultural sector

Explanation:

- The primary sector of the economy is the sector of an economy making direct use of natural resources.
- This includes agriculture, forestry and fishing, mining, and extraction of oil and gas.
- This is contrasted with the secondary sector, producing manufactured and other processed goods, and the tertiary sector, producing services.
- The primary sector is usually most important in less developed countries, and typically less important in industrial countries.
- The manufacturing industries that aggregate, pack, package, purify or process the raw materials close to the primary producers are normally considered part of this sector, especially if the raw material is unsuitable for sale or difficult to transport long distances.
- **Agriculture:** In developed countries primary industry becomes more technologically advanced, for instance the mechanization of farming as opposed to hand picking and planting. In more developed economies additional capital is invested in primary means of production.

63.(D) 4

64.(B) Ahmedabad

Explanation:

- Entrepreneurship Development Institute of India (EDII) is an autonomous and not - for-profit institute set up in 1983
- Registered under the societies registration act 1860 and public trust act 1950.

65.(D) 1977

66.(D) Disloyalty

Explanation:

- Entrepreneurship is the act and art of being an entrepreneur or one who undertakes innovations or introducing new things, finance and business acumen, in an effort to transform innovations into economic goods.
- This may result in new organizations or may be part of revitalizing mature organizations in response to a perceived opportunity.
- The most obvious form of entrepreneurship is that of starting new businesses (referred as startup company); however, in recent years, the term has been extended to include social and political forms of entrepreneurial activity.
- When entrepreneurship is describing activities within a firm or large organization it is referred to as intra-preneurship and may include corporate venturing, when large entities spin-off organizations.

67.(D) All the above

68.(D) All the above

69.(A) Labour intensive

70.(C) (A) & (B)

71.(B) (ii) (iv) (i) (iii)

72.(D) Rapid Skimming

73.(C) Survival, growth and profitability

74.(D) All the above

75.(D)Primary agricultural credit societies and co-operative and mortgagee banks

76.(D) More favourable tax treatment of the earnings, married women

77.(A) Planning

Explanation:

- **Planning**: Planning is the process of thinking about and organizing the activities required to achieve a desired goal.
- Planning involves the creation and maintenance of a plan. As such, planning is a fundamental property of intelligent behavior.

- Planning is also called as ***forethought***.
- This thought process is essential to the creation and refinement of a plan, or integration of it with other plans; that is, it combines forecasting of developments with the preparation of scenarios of how to react to them.
- An important, albeit often ignored aspect of planning, is the relationship it holds with forecasting.
- ***Forecasting*** can be described as predicting what the future will look like, whereas planning predicts what the future should look like.
- The counterpart to planning is spontaneous order.
- **Organizing:** It is the act of rearranging elements following one or more rules.
- Anything is commonly considered organized when it looks like everything has a correct order or placement.
- But it's only ultimately organized if any element has no difference on time taken to find it. In that sense, organizing can also be defined as to place different objects in logical arrangement for better searching.
- **Staffing:** It is the process of acquiring, deploying, and retaining a workforce of sufficient quantity and quality to create positive impacts on the organization's effectiveness
- **Directing:** It is said to be a process in which the managers instruct, guide and oversee the performance of the workers to achieve predetermined goals.
- **Directing**: It is said to be the heart of management process.
- Planning, organizing, staffing have got no importance if direction function does not take place.
- **Directing** initiates action and it is from here actual work starts. Direction is said to be consisting of human factors.

78. (A) July, 1948
79. (C) Indian Bank's Association
80. (B) Intrapreneurship

Explanation:

Corporate venturing: Practice where a large firm takes an equity stake in (or enters into a joint venture arrangement with) a small but innovative or specialist firm, to which it may also provide management and marketing expertise. The objective is to gain a specific competitive advantage.

81.(D) Satyam Computers Ltd.

82.(C) Lack of Competition

83.(D)(i), (ii) and (iv)

Explanation: DuPont Analysis:

- A method of performance measurement that was started by the DuPont Corporation in the 1920s.
- With this method, assets are measured at their gross book value rather than at net book value in order to produce a higher return on equity (ROE).
- It is also known as "DuPont identity".
- DuPont analysis tells us that ROE is affected by three things:
  - Operating efficiency, which is measured by profit margin
  - Asset use efficiency, which is measured by total asset turnover
  - Financial leverage, which is measured by the equity multiplier
- ROE = Profit Margin (Profit/Sales) * Total Asset Turnover (Sales/Assets) * Equity Multiplier (Assets/Equity)

84.(D) Duty drawback

85.(D) All of the above

86.(C) Standard and Poor

87.(C) Mexico

88.(C) 1995

89.(A) Association of South East Asian Nations

90. (C) Richard Cantillon

Explanation:

- The entrepreneur is a factor in microeconomics, and the study of entrepreneurship reaches back to the work of ***Richard Cantillon and Adam Smith.***
- Entrepreneurship is the act and art of being an entrepreneur or one who undertakes innovations or introducing new things, finance and business acumen, in an effort to transform innovations into economic goods. This may result in new organizations or may be part of revitalizing mature organizations in response to a perceived opportunity.
- The most obvious form of entrepreneurship is that of starting new businesses (referred as startup company); however, in recent years, the term has been extended to include social and political forms of entrepreneurial activity.
- When entrepreneurship is describing activities within a firm or large organization it is referred to as intra-preneurship and may include corporate venturing, when large entities spin-off organizations.

91.(B) Cash flow

92.(B) Schumpeter

93.(A) E.F. Schumacher

94.(A) Creativity

95.(D) Risk-bearing Ability

96.(A) Manufacturing and Service

97.(D) Government Support and Concessions

Explanation: Causes of sickness in small scale industry

Internal causes for sickness:

(a) Lack of Finance: This including weak equity base, poor utilization of assets, inefficient working capital management, absence of costing & pricing, absence of planning and budgeting and inappropriate utilization or diversion of funds.

(b) Bad Production Policies : The another very important reason for sickness is wrong selection of site which is related to production, inappropriate plant & machinery, bad maintenance of Plant & Machinery, lack of quality control, lack of standard research & development and so on.

(c) Marketing and Sickness: This is another part which always affects the health of any sector as well as SSI. This including wrong demand forecasting, selection of inappropriate product mix, absence of product planning, wrong market research methods, and bad sales promotions.

(d) Inappropriate Personnel Management: The another internal reason for the sickness of SSIs is inappropriate personnel management policies which includes bad wages and salary administration, bad labour relations, lack of behavioural approach causes dissatisfaction among the employees and workers.

(e) Ineffective Corporate Management: Another reason for the sickness of SSIs is ineffective or bad corporate management which includes improper corporate planning, lack of integrity in top management, lack of coordination and control etc.

External causes for sickness

(a) Personnel Constraint: The first for most important reason for the sickness of small scale industries are non availability of skilled labour or manpower wages disparity in similar industry and general labour invested in the area.

(b) Marketing Constraints: The second cause for the sickness is related to marketing. The sickness arrives due to liberal licensing policies, restrain of purchase by bulk purchasers, changes in global marketing scenario, excessive tax policies by govt. and market recession.

(c) Production Constraints: This is another reason for the sickness which comes under external cause of sickness. This arises due to shortage of raw material, shortage of power, fuel and high prices, import-export restrictions.

(d) Finance Constraints: The another external cause for the sickness of SSIs is lack of finance. This arises due to credit restrains policy, delay in disbursement of loan by govt., unfavorable investments, fear of nationalization.

98. (B) Innovation

99. (B) SIDO

Explanation:

- Small Industries Development Organisat Small Industries Development Organisation (SIDO) an apex body at Central level for formulating policy for the development of Small Scale Industries in the country, is headed by the Additional Secretary & Development Commissioner (Small Scale Industries) under Ministry of Small Scale Industries Govt. of India.
- SIDO is playing a very constructive role for strengthening this vital sector which has proved to be one of the strong pillars of the economy of the country.
- It functions through a network of the field offices namely 30 SISIs, 28 Br. SISIs, 4 RTCs, 7 FTSs, various training and production centers and specialized institutes spread over different parts of the country. Different parts of the country.

100. (D) SEBI

Explanation:

- In early 1999, Securities and Exchange Board of India (SEBI) had set up a committee under Shri Kumar Mangalam Birla, member SEBI Board, to promote and raise the standards of good corporate governance.
- The report submitted by the committee is the first formal and comprehensive attempt to evolve a 'Code of Corporate Governance', in the context of prevailing conditions of governance in Indian companies, as well as the state of capital markets.

101. (C) All Listed entities having paid up capital of Rs. 5 Crores and above and having Net worth of over Rs. 50 Crores

Explanation:

Clause 49 of the Listing Agreement

- SEBI, vide its circular dated February 21, 2000, specified principles of corporate governance and introduced a new clause 49 in the Listing agreement of the Stock Exchanges.
- These principles of corporate governance were made applicable in a phased manner and all the listed companies with the paid up capital of Rs 3 crores and above or net worth of Rs 25 crores or more at any time in the history of the company, were covered as of March 31, 2003.

102. (C)100

103. (D) Entrepreneurship

104. (C) Sea Shipment insurance

105. (A) (iii) (ii) (i) (iv) (v)

106. (D) Subsidies

107. (D) (iv) (ii) (iii) (i)

108. (D) The firm and all the partners

109. (D) Entrepreneurs

110. (B)Commonwealth

111. (C)Proprietorship

112. (D) All of the above

Explanation: Basic form of Innovation

- The '4Ps' model developed by ***John Bessant and Joe Tidd*** provide a powerful tool for such analysis.
- It builds on the hypothesis that successful innovation is essentially about positive change, and puts forward four broad categories where such change can take place:
- **Product innovation:** Changes in the things (products/services) which an organisation offers
- **Process innovation:** Changes in the ways in which products and services are created or delivered
- **Position innovation:** Changes in the context in which the products/services are framed and communicated

- **Paradigm innovation**: Changes in the underlying mental models which shape what the organisation does.

113. (D) Letter of credit

114. (A)G.A.T.T, W.T.O.

115. (C) P.V. Narasimha Rao

116. (A) 1982

117. (D) 2 and 4

118. (B)Venture Capital

Explanation: Venture Capital:

- Money provided by investors to startup firms and small businesses with perceived long-term growth potential.
- This is a very important source of funding for startups that do not have access to capital markets.
- It typically entails high risk for the investor, but it has the potential for above-average returns.

119. (A)New Knowledge Creation

120. (D)Developing the labour market

121. (A)United States

122. (A)ICSI

123. (B)Rehabilitation of sick SSI units

124. (C)Customer, Efficiency

125. (C)Imitation-gap theory

126. (A)Investment size, Location technology, Market conditions

127. (A)Equivalent annual cost

128. (B) Income generation

129. (D)All of the above

Explanation:

Entrepreneur: A person who organizes, operates, and assumes the risk for a business venture.

130. (B) Income generation

131. (A)innovation

132. (B)Intrapreneurship

133. (C)Specific

134. (C)Opportunity cost

135. (B)Intrapreneurship

136. (C)Scientific method

137. (D)All of above options

138. (D)All the above

139. (C)Innovation

Explanation: Innovation is the act of introducing something new.

140. (B) Distribution channels

Explanation:

Consumers:

- Potential entrepreneurs should pay close attention to the final focal point of a new product-the customer.
- This can be an informal or formal survey of consumers expressing their opinions.
- Care should be taken to ensure that the idea represents a large enough market.

Existing Companies:

- Entrepreneurs should establish a formal method for monitoring and evaluating the products and services in the market.
- This may uncover ways to improve on present products, resulting in new product ideas.

Distribution Channels:

- Members of distribution channels are also excellent sources for new ideas because they are familiar with the needs of the market.
- Not only do channel members frequently have suggestions for new product, but they can also help in marketing the entrepreneur's newly developed products.

Federal Government:

- The federal government can be source of new product ideas in two ways.
- First the files of the Patent Office contain numerous new product possibilities.
- Although the patents may not be feasible new product introduction, they can suggest other marketable product ideas.
- Several government agencies and publications are helpful in monitoring patent applications.
- Second new product ideas can come in response to government regulations.
- For example the Occupational Safety and Health Act (OSHA), aimed at eliminating unsafe working condition in industry, mandated that first aid kits be made available in business establishments employing more than three people.
- The kit had to contain specific item that varied according to the company and the industry.
- In response to OSHA, both established and newly formed ventures marketed a wide variety of first aid kits.

141. (C) Minority interest
142. (C) U.S. leadership

Explanation:

- The GATT, as an international agreement, is a treaty. Under United States law it is classified as a congressional-executive agreement.
- Based on the Reciprocal Trade Agreements Act it allowed the executive branch negotiating power over trade agreements with temporary authority from Congress.
- At the time it functioned as a provisional, but promising trade system.

143. (B) 18th century

Explanation:

Middle Ages

- In this age the term ***entrepreneur*** was used to describe both an actor and a person who managed large production projects.
- In such large production projects, this person did not take any risks, managing the project with the resources provided.
- A typical entrepreneur was the cleric who managed architectural projects.

18th Century:

- In the 18th century the person with capital was differentiated from the one who needed capital.
- In other words, entrepreneur was distinguished from the capital provider.

17th Century:

- In the 17th century the entrepreneur was a person who entered into a contract with the government to perform a service Richard Cantillon, a noted economist of the 1700s, developed theories of the entrepreneur and is regarded as the founder of the term.
- He viewed the entrepreneur as a risk taker who "buys at certain price and sells at an uncertain price, therefore operating at a risk."

19th and 20th Centuries:

- In the late 19th and early 20th centuries, entrepreneurs were viewed mostly from an economic perspective.
- The entrepreneur "contributes his own initiative, skill and ingenuity in planning, organizing and administering the enterprise, assuming the chance of loss and gain."

144. (B) Middle ages
145. (B) Entrepreneurship

Explanation:

- Entrepreneurship is a process by which individuals - either on their own or inside organizations - pursue opportunities without regard to the resources they currently control.
- **Stevenson's definition**: The continuous process by which individuals pursue opportunities without regard to resources they currently control, with the intent of increasing value and/or advantage.

146. (A)Minority interest

Explanation: Minority interest: Having less than 50 percent ownership position

147. (B) Majority interest

Explanation: Majority interest: Having more than 50 percent ownership position

148. (C) Creative destruction

Explanation:

- Creative destruction occurs when something new kills something older.
- A great example of this is personal computers.
- The industry, led by Microsoft and Intel, destroyed many mainframe computer companies, but in doing so, entrepreneurs created one of the most important inventions of this century.

149. (B) Hyper competition

Explanation: Hyper competition has forced U.S. companies to focus on new product development and increased productivity.

150. Role model

Explanation:

Role models: Individuals influencing an entrepreneur's career choice and style

Moral-support network: Individuals who give psychological support to an entrepreneur

Professional-support network: Individuals who help the entrepreneur in business activities

151. (C)Departure point

Explanation: Departure points: The activities occurring when the venture is started.

152. (C)Social status

Explanation: Social Status: The level at which an individual in viewed by society.

153. (B) Distribution channels

Explanation:

- Consumer's Potential entrepreneurs should pay close attention to the final focal point of a new product-the customer.
- This can be an informal or formal survey of consumers expressing their opinions.
- Care should be taken to ensure that the idea represents a large enough market.

Distribution Channels:

- Members of distribution channels are also excellent sources for new ideas because they are familiar with the needs of the market.
- Not only do channel members frequently have suggestions for new product, but they can also help in marketing the entrepreneur's newly developed products.

154. (A)They are familiar with the needs of the market

155. (A)Speed

Explanation: A successful website has three characteristics: speed, speed, and speed. Short download time should be the primary concern of website developers.

156. (C)Product Development Stage

Explanation: Product planning and development process

Generally divided into five major stages: idea stage, concept stage, product development stage, test marketing stage, and commercialization stage.

157. (B)Small business administration

158. (A) To see if there are possible barriers to success

Explanation:

- Before preparing a business plan, the entrepreneur should do a quick feasibility study to see if there are possible barriers to success.
- The entrepreneur should clearly define the venture's goals, which provide a framework for the business plan.
- The business plan must reflect reasonable goals.

159. (B) Promotion

Explanation: Operations Information Needs:

The entrepreneur may need information on:

1. Location

2. Manufacturing operations

3. Raw materials 4. Equipment

5. Labor skills

6. Space

7. Overhead

160. (B) It gives recognition that he is the first the inventor of the idea

161. (B)Total amount needed

Explanation: Commitment of Resources:

- An entrepreneur is used to having resources at periodic intervals that are often based on certain tasks or objects being reached.
- These resources, often acquired from others, are usually difficult to obtain, forcing the entrepreneur to maximize any resources used.
- This multistage commitment allows the resource providers (such as venture capitalist or private investors) to have as small an exposure as possible at each stage of business development and to constantly monitor and track record being established.
- *Even though the funding may also be implemented in stages in the administrative domain, the commitment of the recourses is for the total amount needed.*
- Administratively oriented individuals respond to the resources of the rewards offered and receive personal rewards by effectively administering the resources under this control.

162. (B) Direct exporting

Explanation:

- **Direct exporting** through independent distributors or through one's own overseas sales office is another entry method.
- An independent foreign distributor directly contacts foreign customers and takes care of all technicalities.

163. (A) High growth rate

164. (A)Gazelles

Explanation:

- A venture has high growth potential and therefore receives great investor interest.
- The company may start out like a foundation company, but its growth is far more rapid.
- After five to ten years the company could employ around 500 employees.
- These firms are also called gazelles and are most important for the economic development of an area.

165. (A)Technology

Explanation:

- A company needs to use technology to make itself faster and more flexible.
- Technology has allowed small companies to act like they are big ones.
- Large companies can use technology to make them responsive and flexible

---000---

UNIT-XI

ETHICS AND CORPORATE GOVERNANCE

1. Ethical challenges may arise on account of:

(A)Failure of personal character, conflict of personal value & organisational goals and conflict of organisational goals and social values.

(B) Hazardous but popular products

(C) Both (A) and (B)

(D) None of the above

2. The Social Responsibility of a Business is important to:

(A) Owners and Investors (B) Employees

(C) Government (D) All the above

3. 'Ethics' is derived from 'Ethos', a Latin word, which means:

(A) Character (B) Responsibility

(C) Integrity (D) Morality

4. "Work-Diversity" by nature, does not go against Ethics. But an executive assistant while getting transferred from "stores" to "despatch" section created turmoil in the office. He is:

(A) Most ethical in his deal

(B) Fully against work ethics

(C) He is workoholic

(D) A Rigid employer, hard nut to crack

5. Ethical Management is

(A) A Compromise (B) A Compulsion

(C) A Judgement (D) (A) and (B)

6. "Ecology Paradigm" of management refer to :

(A)environmental management

(B)Strategic choice framework

(C)Stockholders' management

(D)none of the above

7. Strategising within value framework is an approach of :

(A)Governance (B)Management

(C)Administration (D)None of the above

8. Economic value added is the measure of:

(A)Shareholders wealth

(B)Strategy evaluation

(C)Stake holders

(D)None of the above

9. Egalitarian behaviour refers to :

(A)natural behaviour

(B)moral behaviour

(C)ethical behaviour wealth

(D)social behaviour

10. Organisation value refers to :

(A)individual belief

(B)Group belief

(C)Corporate believes and ethos

(D)None of the above

11. 'Global Campact' is related to :

(A)Human rights

(B)Social responsibility

(C)Environment protection

(D)Women rights

12. Social responsibility is a responsibility towards :

(A)Employees (B) Government

(C)Society (D) All of these

13. Combination of character and behaviour is known as :

(A)Technological ethics

(B)Ethico - moral ethics

(C)Value based ethics

(D)None of these

14. The most appropriate goal of corporate social responsibility is centred around :

(A)Philanthropic activities

(B)Voluntary activities

(C)Ethical based activities

(D)Legalistic activities

15. Social responsibility is not :

(A)Legal behaviour (B) Legal compliances

(C)Ethical compulsion (D) All of the above

16. Egalitarian behaviour refers to:

(A)natural behaviour (B)moral behaviour

(C)social behaviour (D)ethical behaviour

17. The process through which people are baptized to accept the tradition and maintain the homogeneity of ethos and behaviours is termed as :

(A)Induction (B)Orientation

(C)Acclimatisation (D)Socialization

18. Of the following, who is the most popular woman entrepreneur ?

(A)Sudha Murthy (B)Medha Patkar

(C)Kiran Mazumdar (D)Deepa Mehta

19. Which one of the following is not the Social Responsibility of business?

(A)Adopting villages for development

(B)Setting up educational institutes

(C)Opening research and development department

(D)Construction of temples

20. Which one of the following is not related to Business Ethics?

(A)Environmental Ethics

(B)Social Responsibility of business

(C)Profiteering

(D)Ecological consciousness

21. Ethical values are derived from :

(A)Corporate objectives

(B)Organisational culture

(C)The Bible, the Kuran and the Geeta

(D)Corporate philosophy

22. The pre-conventional, conventional and principled levels of moral development influencing business ethics is given by :

(A)J. Keogh (B)L. Kohlberg

(C)K. Kumar (D)I. Kant

23. In India the first report on Corporate Governance was given by :

(A)Narayana Murty Committee

(B)Cadbury's Committee

(C)Naresh Chandra Committee

(D)Kumarmanglam Birla Committee

24. M. Friedman is associated with which philosophy of Social Responsibility of Business?

(A)Profit Maximisation

(B)Following legal provisions

(C)Adopting ethical practices

(D)None of the above

25. Social responsibility means that a business:

(A) Functions efficiently without harming the society

(B) Abjures the profit motive

(C) Keeps pollution under check

(D) Pays its Taxes to Government

26. Ethical values are derived from

(A) Corporate philosophy

(B) Organisational culture

(C) Corporate objectives

(D) The religious books

27. Which of the following is not related to business ethics?

(A) Social responsibility of business

(B) Environmental ethics

(C) Ecological consciousness

(D) Profiteering

28. Value driven companies are:

(A) sure to be successful in the long run.

(B) sure to be unsuccessful as they are not maximizing profits.

(C) sure to become charitable institutions.

(D) none of the above

29. Which of the following is not the social responsibility of the business?

(A) Promotion of Markets

(B) Promotion of Green Environment

(C) Promotion of Education

(D) Promotion of Public Health

30. The Business Code of Conduct provides guidance to managers and employees

(A) when they encounter an ethical dilemma.

(B) for improving their technical skills.

(C) for pursuing their business goals.

(D) All of the above

31. The study of moral principles or values that determine whether actions are right or wrong and outcomes are good or bad refers to following :

(A) Quality (B) Ethics

(C) Opinions (D) Controls

32. Match List – I with List – II :

List – I (Terms relating to Ethics)

(a)Ethical Climate

(b)Ethical Relativism

(c)Ethical Universalism

(d)Ethical Convergence

List – II (Conceptual description of terms relating to Ethics)

(i)Each society's view of ethics must be considered legitimate and ethical

(ii)There are basic moral principles that transcend cultural and political boundaries

(iii)People pick-up subtle hints and clues that tell them what behaviour is approved and what is forbidden.

(iv)There are growing pressures on international business to follow the same rules in managing ethical behavior and social responsibility

Codes:

	(a)	(b)	(c)	(d)
(A)	(iii)	(i)	(ii)	(iv)
(B)	(i)	(iii)	(ii)	(iv)
(C)	(i)	(iv)	(iii)	(ii)
(D)	(iv)	(i)	(ii)	(iii)

33. An organization's moral obligation toward all of its stakeholders is referred as following:

(A) Value in workplace

(B) Corporate social responsibility

(C) Ethical behaviour

(D) Professionalism

34. ________ is the manager's dilemma when he has to decide on the commercial proposal submitted by his son.

(A)Favouritism (B) Moral Dilemma

(C)Conflict of Interest (D) None of the above

35. "Make use of paper bags instead of plastic bags." It is related to

(A) Environmental Ethics

(B) Green Marketing

(C) Socially Responsible Marketing

(D) Social Marketing

36. Anything dealing with Ethics in Business is:

(A) good, bad or both, to the business gains

(B) not related to religion

(C) not to focus obligation

(D) killing all types of Unfair Trade Practices

37. Ethics provide:

(A) Consumer Autonomy (B) CSR

(C) Justice (D) All of the above

38. Company seeking ethical standard must purport to:

(A) Good Employee Relation

(B) Better Production Portfolio

(C) Economy of Scale

(D) Public Disclosure and Publishing

39. Which of the following is not the act of Corporate Governance?

(A) Protecting the interest of shareholders

(B) Protecting the interest of employees

(C) Fudging of Accounts

(D) Paying Taxes to the Government

40. Corporate Social Responsibility (CSR) is looked as the organized network of making long economic and social relationship of the corporate with the society. But a business of which type, as mentioned below, cannot afford for it, at the first instance?

(A) Large Business (B) Medium Business

(C) Small Business (D)A Business Start-up

41. The evaluation of Business activities and behaviour as right or wrong is called:

(A) Corporate Governance

(B) Business Ethics

(C) Social Responsibility

(D) None of the above

42. Value based organizations are :

(A)Those which are having high market share

(B)Those which are having high share price

(C)Those which declare high dividends

(D)Those which follow ethics and social responsibility

43. Environmental ethics refers to :

(A)Quality of the product

(B)Price of the product

(C)Unfair trade practices

(D)Pollution

44. Corporate governance deals with :

(A)Society (B) Employees

(C)Organization (D) All the above

45. Social Responsibility of business refers to :

(A)Profit maximization of business

(B)Wealth maximization

(C)Concerns towards society and its needs

(D)Concerns towards shareholders' interests

46. Value based organisations are :

(A)Profit - making units

(B)Wealth maximisation units

(C)Organisation that adds value to the products

(D)Organisation practising values

47. Which of the following practice is unethical?

(A)Profitability (B) Profiteering

(C)Customer concerns (D)Sales promotion

48. The three basic approaches to ethical behaviour namely utilitarian approach, individual rights approach and justice approach are given by :

(A)M. Coker (B)S. Berkeley

(C)G. F. Cavanagh (D)J. Warner

49. Who had advanced the Stewardship Theory

of Corporate Governance?

(A)J. H. Davis et. al

(B) D. R. Dalton et. al

(C)D. C. Hambrick et. al

(D)None of the above

50. In the four classification of Social Responsibility of Business proposed by Archie Carroll, which one of the following is not included?

(A)Economic (B)Legal

(C)Ethical (D)Political

51. Environmental Ethics refers to :

(A)Unfair Trade Practices

(B)Pollution

(C)Product price

(D)Quality of the product

52. Corporate governance includes management of :

(A)Employees (B)Organisation

(C)Society (D)All of the above

53. Which one of the following is not the social responsibility of business?

(A) Adopting village for development.

(B) Providing drinking water and medical facilities in remote villages.

(C) Construction of Temples.

(D) Opening in House R & D department.

54. Identify from the options given below, which one is not a source of business ethics?

(A) Religion (B) Legal system

(C) Culture (D) Political system

55. Where law fails,

(A) Ethics also fails

(B) Ethics can succeed

(C) Government can protect

(D) None of the above

56. Which one of the options is not an ethical issue for an organization?

(A) Save water (B) Save energy

(C) Save money (D) Respect woman

57. Which of the following is an example of an external threat?

(A) Economies of scale

(B) Decreased competition

(C) New Trade Regulations

(D) Global sales potential

58. Members of organizations are increasingly finding themselves facing situations in which they are required to define right and wrong conduct. It is most aptly called as following:

(A) Environmental issues of ethics

(B) Social responsibilities of business

(C) Corporate governance & ethics

(D) Ethical Dilemmas of business

59. Situations in which individuals are required to define right and wrong conduct to be complied with are called as following

(A) Ethical climate (B) Ethical dilemmas

(C) Code of Ethics (D) None of the above

60. Arrange the following steps of a simple ethics programme:

(i)Walk the talk

(ii)Size up your company's current ethics

(iii)Train your people

(iv)Solicit feedback from your employees

(v)Create a code of conduct

Code:

(A) (v)	(i)	(iv)	(ii)	(iii)
(B) (ii)	(v)	(iv)	(iii)	(i)
(C) (ii)	(v)	(iii)	(iv)	(i)
(D) (ii)	(iv)	(iii)	(ii)	(i)

61. Who is involved in 'Shoplifting' from the following?

(A) Producer

(B) Seller

(C) Consumer & or a customer

(D) None of the above

62. Match List-I with List-II.

List – I (Ethical Issue)

(a) Unsafe working conditions

(b) Product safety

(c) Environmental Pollution

(d) Following local laws

List – II (Stakeholder affected)

(i) Customers

(ii) Society

(iii) Employees

(iv) Host Country

Code:

	(a)	(b)	(c)	(d)
(A)	(ii)	(iv)	(iii)	(i)
(B)	(iii)	(i)	(ii)	(iv)
(C)	(i)	(iii)	(iv)	(ii)
(D)	(iii)	(ii)	(i)	(iv)

63. Which o of the following is not related to Business Ethics?

(A) Environmental ethics

(B) Social responsibility of business

(C) Profiteering

(D) Ecological consciousness

64. Ethical values are derived from:

(A) Corporate objectives

(B) Organizational culture

(C) The Bible, the Koran and the Geeta

(D) Corporative philosophy

65. Why should business be socially responsible?

(A) To protect customers' requirement

(B) To increase reputation of the company

(C) To protect and serve public interest

(D) To go for organizational development

66. Which of the practice will *not* create an ethical culture in an organization?

(A) Visible role models from an organization

(B) Clearly communicating ethical expectations

(C) Provide ethical training

(D) Punishing whistle blowers

67. In which corporate governance model do financial institutions have major say?

(A) American Model (B) German Model

(C) Japanese Model (D) Indian Model

68. Dependability, predictability and faith are the three elements that constitute :

(A) Values (B) Moral principles

(C) Trust (D) Justice

69. Corporate governance is the key :

(A) To the integrity of corporations

(B) To increase profit

(C) To motivate employees

(D) To implement government policies

70. Abiding by Laws of the land and paying due taxes is part of CSR towards :

(A) Creditors (B) Government

(C) Employees (D) Consumers

71. The view that management's only social responsibility is to maximize profits is referred in :

(A) The classical view

(B) The socioeconomic view

(C) The chapters view

(D) The prudent view

72. A formal statement of an organization's primary values and the ethical rules it expects its employees to follow is called as :

(A) Code of values

(B) Code of ethics

(C) Code of clarity

(D) Code of basics

73. Which one of the following is not the social responsibility of business?

(A)Adopting villages for development

(B)Setting up educational institutes

(C)Opening research and development department

(D)Construction of temples

74. Social responsibility is a responsibility towards :

(A)Employees (B) Government

(C)Society (D)All of these

75. The most appropriate goal of corporate social responsibility is centered around :

(A)Philanthropic activities

(B) Voluntary activities

(C)Ethical based activities

(D)Legalistic activities

76. Social responsibility is not :

(A)Legal behaviour

(B)Legal compliances

(C)Ethical compulsion

(D)All of the above

77. Which one of the following is not the Social Responsibility of business?

(A)Adopting villages for development

(B)Setting up educational institutes

(C)Opening research and development department

(D)Construction of temples

78. Social responsibility means that a business

(A)Functions efficiently without harming the society

(B)Abjures the profit motive

(C)Keeps pollution under check

(D)Pays its Taxes to Government

79. Which o of the following is not related to Business Ethics?

(A)Environmental ethics

(B)Social responsibility of business

(C)Profiteering

(D)Ecological consciousness

80. External environment of business is:

(A)Physical (B) Demographic

(C)Economic (D) All of these

81. Which of the following is not an essential feature of social environment?

(A)Competitiveness

(B)Respect for the individual

(C)Better quality of life

(D)Bailment

82. Which of the following is not a stakeholder in the CSR?

(A)Creditors (B) Environment

(C)Government (D) SEBI

83. Which of the following key force influences a person's ethics?

(A)Nationality

(B)Education

(C)Family influences

(D)Relationship of the firm to the employee

84. A personality measure of the strength of a person's convictions is:

(A)locus of control (B)locus of value

(C)ego strength (D)bench strength

85. Greed is the cornerstone of human values under:

(A)Socialism (B)Capitalism

(C)Mixed economy (D)Racialism

86. Select the correct options:

Sarbanes-Oxley Act,2002 emphasis on:

(A)Enivornmental Protection

(B)Work-life Balance

(C)Total quality Management

(D)Audit function and financial disclosures

87. Which of the following is not a "Public Relations Function"?

(A)Assess the correct reputation

(B)Audit C.S.R

(C)Conduct Positive image building activities

(D)Identify prospective customers

88. Which of the following is not a stakeholder in the CSR?

(A)Creditors (B)Enivornment

(C)Government (D)SEBI

89. Which of the following key force influences a person's ethics?

(A)Nationality

(B)Education

(C)Family influences

(D)Relationship of the firm to the employee

90. A personality measure of the strength of a person's convictions is:

(A)locus of control (B)locus of value

(C)ego strength (D)bench strength

91. Greed is the cornerstone of human values under:

(A)Socialism (B)Capitalism

(C)Mixed economy (D)Racialism

92. The elements of good corporate governance in India have been laid down by:

(A)ICSI (B)IOD

(C)ICWAI (D)ICAI

93. Which of the following is not a stakeholder in the CSR?

(A)Creditors (B)Enivornment

(C)Government (D)SEBI

94. Which of the following key force influences a person's ethics?

(A)Nationality

(B)Education

(C)Family influences

(D)Relationship of the firm to the employee

95. A personality measure of the strength of a person's convictions is:

(A)locus of control (B)locus of value

(C)ego strength (D)bench strength

96. Greed is the cornerstone of human values under:

(A)Socialism (B)Capitalism

(C)Mixed economy (D)Racialism

97. Governance is the system of values, policies and institutions by which a society manages its economic, political and social affairs through interactions within and among the state, civil society and private sector is defined by

(A) World Bank

(B) UNDP

(C) European Commission

(D) None of the above

98. Match the following with regards to environmental ethical issues :

LIST-I

(a) Ozone Depletion

(b) Environmental Health

(c) Logging

(d) Genetic Engineering

LIST-II

(i)Lead poisoning

(ii)Deforestation

(iii)Food controversies

(iv)CFC

Codes:

	(a)	(b)	(c)	(d)
(A)	(iv)	(ii)	(i)	(iii)
(B)	(iv)	(i)	(ii)	(iii)
(C)	(vi)	(iii)	(ii)	(i)
(D)	(iv)	(iii)	(i)	(ii)

99. The principles to be followed for corporate social responsibility are

(A) involvement of stakeholders.

(B) maintaining transparency in reporting.

(C)independent verification of policies and outcome.

(D) All of the above.

100. Match the following :

List – I

(a)Value

(b) Unethical behaviour

(c) Indian ethos

(d) Environmental responsibility

List - II

(i) Aham Brahmasmi

(ii) Recycling Waste

(iii)Bribery

(iv) Trust worthiness

Codes:

(a) (b) (c) (d)

(A) (i) (iii) (ii) (iv)

(B) (iv) (iii) (i) (ii)

(C) (ii) (iii) (iv) (i)

(D) (i) (iii) (iv) (ii)

101. The obligation of an organization behave in a ethical way is known as

(A) Knowledge about ethics

(B) Social responsibility of business

(C) Organisational behaviour

(D) Business without ethics

102. Identify the correct sequence of steps in a value identification process :

(i) Define the role of executive in leading the staff.

(ii) Learn about and discuss the power of shared values.

(iii) Obtain consensus that the leaders are committed to creating value based work place.

(iv)Provide written material the executives can share with their reporting staff.

Codes:

(A) (i), (ii), (iii) and (iv)

(B) (iv), (ii), (iii) and (i)

(C) (ii), (iii), (i) and (iv)

(D) (ii), (iii), (iv) and (i)

103. ______ refers to the study of moral principles or values that determine whether actions are right or wrong and outcomes are good or bad.

(A) Values (B)Multicultural teams

(C) Ethics (D) CSR

104. Corporate social responsibility is most closely related to which of these organizational behavior trends?

(A) Workforce diversity

(B) Employment relationships

(C) Information technology

(D) Workplace values and ethics

105. Which one of the following is not the social responsibility of business?

(A) Adopting villages for development

(B) Setting up educational institutes

(C) Opening research and development department

(D) Construction of temples

---000---

UNIT-XI

ETHICS AND CORPORATE GOVERNANCE

1. (C) Both (A) and (B)

2. (D) All the above

3. (D) Morality

Explanation: Business Ethics:

- The study of proper business policies and practices regarding potentially controversial issues, such as corporate governance, insider trading, bribery, discrimination, corporate social responsibility and fiduciary responsibilities.
- Business ethics are often guided by law, while other times provide a basic framework that businesses may choose to follow in order to gain public acceptance.
- Business ethics are implemented in order to ensure that a certain required level of trust exists between consumers and various forms of market participants with businesses.
- For example, a portfolio manager must give the same consideration to the portfolios of family members and small individual investors. Such practices ensure that the public is treated fairly.

4. (B) Fully against work ethics

5. (C) A Judgement

6. (A)environmental management

Explanation:

- The new ecological paradigm emphasizes the sustainability principle of modern societies in all their dimensions - economic, spatial, demographic, cultural, ecological.
- It is a new strategic global ecological-economic mega-trend of the development of modern society as a sustainable world society.
- The ecological paradigm as a new social regulation of the relationship between modern societies and their natural environment imposes to the economic science and practice the ethical standpoint related to the respect of nature and life in general.
- In this respect, new economy highly appreciates ecological components, principles and standards applied in the sphere of economy: creation of production as a closed economic system, evaluation of ecological costs, implementation of ecological principles and compliance with ecological standards, development of ecological management, formation of "ecological economy", application of new quality indicators of success (Human Development Index and Index of Sustainable Economic Welfare), constitution of a new energy-economy-ecology development tendency.

7. (A) Governance

8. (A)Shareholders wealth

Explanation: Economic Value Added (EVA):

- A measure of a company's financial performance based on the residual wealth calculated by deducting cost of capital from its operating profit (adjusted for taxes on a cash basis).
- Also referred to as "economic profit".
- The formula for calculating EVA is as follows:
  EVA=Net Operating Profit After Taxes (NOPAT) - (Capital * Cost of Capital)
  This measure was devised by Stern Stewart & Co. Economic value added attempts to capture the true economic profit of a company.

9. (D)social behaviour

Explanation:

- Egalitarianism (from French égal, meaning "equal")or, rarely, equalitarianism is a trend of thought that favors equality for particular categories of, or for all, living entities.

- Egalitarian doctrines maintain that all humans are equal in fundamental worth or social status, according to the Stanford Encyclopedia of Philosophy.
- The Cultural theory of risk holds egalitarianism as defined by (1) a negative attitude towards rules and principles, and (2) a positive attitude towards group decision-making, with fatalism termed as its opposite.
- According to the Merriam-Webster Dictionary, the term has two distinct definitions in modern English.
- It is defined either as a political doctrine that all people should be treated as equals and have the same political, economic, social, and civil rights or as a social philosophy advocating the removal of economic inequalities among people or the decentralisation of power. Some sources define egalitarianism as the point of view that equality reflects the natural state of humanity.
- The political doctrine that holds that all people in a society should have equal rights from birth.
- The doctrine of the equality of mankind and the desirability of political and economic and social equality.

10.(C)Corporate believes and ethos

11.(A)Human rights

Explanation:

- The UN Global Compact is a strategic policy initiative for businesses that are committed to aligning their operations and strategies with ten universally accepted principles in the areas of human rights, labour, environment and anti-corruption.
- By doing so, business, as a primary driver of globalization, can help ensure that markets, commerce, technology and finance advance in ways that benefit economies and societies everywhere.

12.(C)Society

13.(B)Ethico - moral ethics

14.(C)Ethical based activities

15.(D) All of the above

16.(C)social behaviour

17.(D)Socialization

18.(C)Kiran Mazumdar

19.(D)Construction of temples

20.(C)Profiteering

21.(D)Corporate philosophy

22.(B)L. Kohlberg

23.(D)Kumarmanglam Birla Committee

24.(A)Profit Maximisation

25.(A)Functions efficiently without harming the society

26.(A) Corporate philosophy

27.(D) Profiteering

28.(D) none of the above

29.(A) Promotion of Markets

30.(D) All of the above

31. (B) Ethics

32.(A) (iii) (i) (ii) (iv)

Explanation:

Ethical Climate:

- Victor and Cullen defined ethical climate as the persistent moral atmosphere of a social system, characterised by mutual perceptions of right and wrong, as well as common assumptions about how moral concerns should be addressed.
- Ethical climate in organisation refers to the way in which an organisation typically handles issues such as responsibility, accountability, communication, regulations, equity, trust, and the welfare of stakeholders.
- An ethical climate is usually about standards of behaviour in the workplace as well as with customers and partners.

Ethical relativism:

- It is the theory that holds that morality is relative to the norms of one's culture.
- That is, whether an action is right or wrong depends on the moral norms of the society in which it is practiced. The same action may be morally right in one society but be morally wrong in another.
- For the ethical relativist, there are no universal moral standards -- standards that can be universally applied to all peoples at all times.
- The only moral standards against which a society's practices can be judged are its own.

Ethical relativism: A tendency to make ethical choices only on the basis of what looks right or reasonable according to one's own belief or value system.

Ethical universalism: It also known as moral universalism or universal morality refers to a system of ethics that applies universally regardless of culture, sex, race, sexuality or nationality. Some of these ethics may be equally correct and yet in conflict with each other.

Ethical convergence: In spite of wide differences in cultures and social institutions, growing pressures for multinationals to follow same rules.

33.(B) Corporate social responsibility

34.(B) Moral Dilemma

35.(A) Environmental Ethics

36.(A) good, bad or both, to the business gains

37.(D) All of the above

38.(D) Public Disclosure and Publishing

39.(C) Fudging of Accounts

40.(D)A Business Start-up

41.(B) Business Ethics

42.(D)Those which follow ethics and social responsibility

43. (A)Quality of the product

Explanation: Environmental Ethics

- Environmental ethics refers to the moral relations between human beings and their natural environment.
- It refers to the value that mankind places on protecting, conserving, and efficiently using resources that the earth provides.
- It is a standard that we use to view issues pertaining to the environment. Some people may have varying degrees of consciousness in this area, but everyone has an environmental ethic that they hold to.
- The key is to balance an awareness and motivation for environmental issues while not neglecting the needs of people.

44.(D) All the above

Explanation:

- Corporate governance refers to the system by which corporations are directed and controlled.
- Corporate governance refers to the set of systems, principles and processes by which a company is governed.
- They provide the guidelines as to how the company can be directed or controlled such that it can fulfil its goals and objectives in a manner that adds to the value of the company and is also beneficial for all stakeholders in the long term.
- Stakeholders in this case would include everyone ranging from the board of directors, management, shareholders to customers, employees and society.
- The management of the company hence assumes the role of a trustee for all the others.

45.(C)Concerns towards society and its needs

46.(D)Organisation practising values

47.(B) Profiteering

Explanation: Profiteering is a pejorative term for the act of making a profit by methods considered unethical.

48.(C)G. F. Cavanagh

49.(C)D. C. Hambrick et. al

50.(D)Political

51.(D) Quality of the product

52.(D)All of the above

53.(D) Opening in House R & D department.

54.(D) Political system

55.(B) Ethics can succeed

56.(C) Save money

57.(C) New Trade Regulations

58.(D) Ethical Dilemmas of business

59.(B) Ethical dilemmas

60.(C) (ii) (v) (iii) (iv) (i)

61.(C) Consumer & or a customer

62.(B) (iii) (i) (ii) (iv)

63.(C) Profiteering

64.(D) Corporative philosophy

65.(C) To protect and serve public interest

66.(D) Punishing whistle blowers

67.(C) Japanese Model

68.(C) Trust

69.(A) To the integrity of corporations

70.(D) Consumers

Explanation:

- Currently, in most companies, CSR activities are a part of other management areas, mainly HR, marketing and corporate communication.
- Some companies undertake activities, including education, environment and housing, with the subtler objective of gaining business by establishing a relationship with communities.
- Others interpret CSR as simply abiding by the law of the land, like paying taxes on time.
- While for some more, CSR is deeply integrated with their businesses and helps social causes.

71.(A) The classical view

72.(B) Code of ethics

73.(D)Construction of temples

74.(D)All of these

75.(B)Voluntary activities

76.(B)Legal compliances

77.(D)Construction of temples

78.(A)Functions efficiently without harming the society

Explanation:

- Social responsibility is a voluntary effort on the part of business to take various steps to satisfy the expectation of the different interest groups.
- The interest groups may be owners, investors, employees, consumers, government, and society or community.
- **Public Image:** The activities of business towards the welfare of the society earn goodwill and reputation for the business. The earnings of business also depend upon the public image of its activities. People prefer to buy products of a company that engages itself in various social welfare programmes. Again, good public image also attracts honest and competent employees to work with such employers.
- **Government Regulation:** To avoid government regulations businessmen should discharge their duties voluntarily. For example, if any burn:-firm pollutes the environment it will naturally come under strict government regulation which may ultimately force the firm to close down its business. Instead, the business firm should engage itself in maintaining a pollution free environment.
- **Survival and Growth:** Every business is a part of the society. So for its survival and growth, support from the society is very much essential. Business utilizes the available resources like power, water, land, roads, etc' of the society- So it should be the

responsibility of every business to spend a part of its profit for the welfare of the society.

- **Employee satisfaction:** Besides getting good salary and working in a healthy atmosphere, employees also expect other facilities like proper accommodation, transportation, education and training. The employers should try to fulfill all the expectations of the employees because employee satisfaction is directly related to productivity and it is also required for the long-term prosperity of the organization. For example, if business spends money on training of the employees, it will have more efficient people to work and thus, earn more profit.
- **Consumer Awareness:** Now-a-days consumers have become very conscious about their rights. They protest against the supply of inferior and harmful products by forming different groups. This has made it obligatory for the business to protect the interest of the consumers by providing quality products at the most competitive price.

79.(C)Profiteering

80.(D) All of these

81.(D)Bailment

82.(D) SEBI

83.(C)Family influences

84.(C)ego strength

85.(B)Capitalism

86.(D)Audit function and financial disclosures

87.(D)Identify prospective customers

88.(D)SEBI

89.(C)Family influences

90. (C)ego strength

91.(B)Capitalism

92. (A)ICSI

93.(D)SEBI

94. (C)Family influences

95.(C)ego strength

96.(B)Capitalism

97.(B) UNDP

98. (B) (iv) (i) (ii) (iii)

99. (D) All of the above.

100. (B) (iv) (iii) (i) (ii)

101. (B) Social responsibility of business

102. (B) (iv), (ii), (iii) and (i)

103. (C) Ethics

104. (D) Workplace values and ethics

105. (D) Construction of temples

---000---

UNIT-XI

UGC-NET/JRF/SET-QUESTION PAPERS & ANSWER KEYS

UGC-NET-MANAGEMENT-PAPER-II-JUNE-12

1. Cardinal measure of utility is required in:

   (A) Utility Theory

   (B) Indifference Curve Analysis

   (C) Revealed Preference

   (D) Inferior Goods

2. A Right-ward shift in Demand Curve indicates:

   (A) A decrease in supply

   (B) An increase in quantity supplied

   (C) An increase in supply over the previous year

   (D) Law of Variable Proportions

3. Which of the following is the condition for equilibrium for Monopolist?

   (A) MR = MC (B) MC = AR

   (C) MR = MC = Price (D) AC = AR

4. Giffen goods are those goods

   (A)for which demand increases as price decreases

   (B)which are in short supply

   (C)which have high elasticity of demand

   (D)which gives rise to a Cob-Web situation.

5. Match List-I with List-II and select the correct answer using the codes given below the lists.

   List – I (Demand Estimation Method)

   (a) Customer Interview Method

   (b) Market Experiment Method

   (c) Regression Method

   (d) Demand Forecasts

   List – II (Steps involved)

   (i)Consumers Interview

   (ii)Time series or Cross Section Data

   (iii)Market Stimulation

   (iv)Market Experiments' Survey

   Codes:

	(a)	(b)	(c)	(d)
(A)	(i)	(iii)	(iv)	(ii)
(B)	(i)	(iii)	(ii)	(iv)
(C)	(ii)	(iv)	(iii)	(i)
(D)	(iv)	(ii)	(i)	(iii)

6. Who divided all activities of the organizations into six groups; Technical, Commercial, Financial, Security, Accounting and Managerial?

   (A) Peter Drucker (B) D. E. Mc Forland

   (C) Henry Fayol (D) George R. Terry

7. What are the elements that a Mission Statement of an Organisation should include?

   (A) Self guidelines for Business Operations

   (B)Identifies the reasons for existence of a company and its responsibilities to the stakeholders.

   (C)Identifies the firms' customers and their needs and matches them to the products and services.

   (D) All of the above (A), (B) and (C).

8. Changes in population characteristics such as age, gender, race, marital status, income and education are examples of change:

   (A) Demographic (B) Cultural

   (C) Geographic (D) Diversity

9. Which of the following is not included as Micro-Environmental Variables?

(A) Prevailing economic and political conditions.

(B) Emerging new technologies

(C) Financial conditions and culture

(D) None of the above

10. During his days at Midvale Steel Company F.W. Taylor saw that employees soldiering – deliberately working at a pace slower than their capabilities. He identified that, worker indulge in soldiering primarily for the following reasons :

(A) Fear of losing jobs if they increase their output.

(B) Faulty wage systems.

(C) Out-dated methods of working

(D) All of the above

11. Among the best known trait approaches to personality measurement – column A gives Traits and column B states the name of authority defining them. Match the correct combination

Traits Author

(A) 20 + needs Murray

(B) 16 traits Eysenck

(C) 3 traits Cattell

(D) 5 traits Costa & Merree

12. "Third Party intervention" as "Conflict Resolution" is:

(A) often required

(B) seldom required

(C)required as a mandate, when conflict remains unresolved

(D) not at all considered as an option

13. The policy of introducing "New Blood" is

(A) Steriotypic

(B) Bureacratic as well as redtapic

(C) Innovative and challenging, making the corporate dynamic

(D)Innovative, challenging, but often resisted

14. An "Assessment Centre" is

(A) A place (B) A technique

(C) Both (A) and (B) (D) None of the above

15. "Organizational learning" and "Learning organization" are:

(A) Same

(B) Different

(C) Reverse to each other

(D) Complementary to each other

16. The value of the firm is maximized when the:

(A) Market price of equity share is maximum

(B) Market price of equity share is minimum

(C) Market value of debt is maximum

(D) None of the above

17. Which of the following is the main assumption of Waltar Valuation Model?

(A)All financing is done through Retained earnings and external sources of funds.

(B) With additional investment the firm's business risk will change.

(C) There is a change in the key variables such as EPS and DPS

(D) None of the above

18. Which of the following is an important money market instrument?

(A) Debentures (B) Commercial Paper

(C) Public Deposits (D) None of the above

19. The method of payment in Mergers and Acquisitions may include:

(i) Cash

(ii) Loan stock

(iii) Ordinary shares

(iv) Convertible loan stock

(A) (i) & (iii) only (B) (i) & (ii) only

(C) (i), (ii), (iii) and (iv)(D) (ii) & (iv) only

20. Working capital refers to the capital mobilised for meeting

(A) Long-term financial needs of the company

(B) To meet day-to-day financial obligations of the company

(C) To meet the future financial requirements of the company

(D) None of the above

21. Which of the following statement is true?

(A) The essence of marketing is a transaction of an exchange.

(B) Marketing–orientation is philosophy, which has to pervade the organization structure

(C) Marketing is also a managerial function involving analysis, planning and control marketing activities in an organisation

(D) All of the above

22. A marketing plan is composed of three basic components, namely:

1. Objectives 2. Policies 3. Program

4. Procedure 5. Hints 6. Decision

7. Command 8. Periodic 9. Diversity

(A) 1, 2 and 3 only (B) 6, 7 and 8 only

(C) 5, 7 and 9 only (D) 2, 3 and 9 only

23. Which of the following is not the stage of new product development?

(A) Idea Generation

(B) Business Analysis

(C) Test Marketing

(D) Market Segmentation

24. Marketing research does not normally:

(A) Gather environmental information

(B) Provide a continuous source of information

(C) Relate to all aspects of marketing operations

(D) Describe the current situation

25. Which of the following is not included in 7 P's of services marketing?

(A) Physical evidence (B) People

(C) Process (D) Marketing plan

26. Which of the following is not the type of Plant Layout?

(A) Product Layout (B) Process Layout

(C) Fixed Position Layout

(D) Residential Layout

27. Which of the following factor is considered in the selection of a plant location?

(A) Source of Raw-materials

(B) Availability of water

(C) Marketing facilities

(D) All the above

28. Work measurement refers to

(A) the length of time it takes to complete a work task assigned to a specific job

(B) improving work methods

(C) arrangement of machines according to sequence of operations

(D) planning the work and working the plans

29. The Graphical method can be used to solve

(A) A linear programming problem with all integer data base.

(B) A linear programming problem with two decision variables.

(C) Any linear programming problem.

(D) A transportation problem with two origins and two destinations.

30. If two dice are thrown, the probability that the sum of their points is greater than 10 is

(A) 1/9 (B) 1/12

(C) 1/3 (D) 1/18

31. A Binomial distribution is characterized as β(16,0.5) i.e. sample size is 16 and the probability of success is 0.5. The mean and variance of this distribution will be respectively:

(A) 8, 4 (B) 8, 8

(C) 4, 8 (D) 4, 4

32. Two variables are said to be perfectly negatively correlated if:

(A) Covariance between them is positive

(B) Coefficient of correlation between them is –1

(C) Covariance between them is negative

(D) None of the above

33. Which type of sampling is appropriate when the population consists of well defined groups such that the elements within each group are homogeneous and between each group they are heterogeneous?

(A) Cluster Sampling

(B) Simple Random Sampling

(C) Stratified Sampling

(D) Judgement Sampling

34. Which of the following is not a type of internet connection?

(A) ISDN (B) Dial-up

(C) Leased-Line (D) ISP

35. Match the following :

List – I

(a)Poisson distribution has the property that

(b)Normal distribution is a

(c)Chi-square distribution is

(d)Binomial distribution has the property that

List – II

(i)Its mean is greater than Variance

(ii)Symmetric distribution

(iii)Positively skewed distribution

(iv)Its mean and variance are equal.

Codes:

(a) (b) (c) (d)

(A) (iv) (ii) (i) (iii)

(B) (iv) (ii) (iii) (i)

(C) (i) (ii) (iii) (iv)

(D) (ii) (iv) (iii) (i)

36. WTO come into being in the year

(A) 1975 (B) 1985

(C) 1995 (D) 2001

37. Which of the following is not Porter's generic strategy?

(A) Focus (B) Cost Leadership

(C) Differentiation (D) Market segmentation

38. Globalization involves:

(A) Free flow of technology from one country to another

(B) Free flow of investment from one country to the other

(C) Free flow of people from one country to the other

(D) All the above

39. Which is a short-term strategy for a firm?

(A)Corporate strategy (B) Business strategy

(C)Company mission (D) Functional strategy

40. Which is not a global entry strategy?

(A) Exporting (B) Joint venture

(C) Merger and Acquisition

(D) Blue ocean strategy

41. Which one is not the characteristic feature of Entrepreneurship?

(A) Vision (B) Risk Bearing

(C) Initiative and Drive (D) Disloyalty

42. Which of the following organizations is meant for promoting small scale industries at district level ?

(A) SIDBI (B) DIC

(C) SFCs (D) NABARD

43. The reason for sickness of small scale industry is:

(A) Lack of capital (B) Lack of market

(C) Severe competition (D) All the above

44. The measure taken by Government to promote small scale industry.

(A) Provision of land

(B) Provision of marketing facilities

(C) Arrangement of credit and raw materials

(D) All the above

45. Small and medium enterprises are:

(A) Labour intensive

(B) Capital intensive

(C) Market leader

(D) Industry price determiner

46. Business propositions are to be selected by making an analysis that, how much the local resources will be depleted in the commencement and the course of Business. This is known as:

(A) Sensitivity Analysis

(B) Common Property Resource use

(C) Environmental Impact Assessment

(D) None of the above

47. Whistle-Blowers are

(A) to be removed from the jobs

(B) to be promoted

(C)to be rewarded for the organisational enrichment

(D)to be protected since they intend to bring out truth.

48. Funding through Micro finance to Small and Micro Enterprises is not successful due to

(A) High rate of interest

(B)Out sourcing of method of providing Micro Finance

(C) (A) & (B) (D) None of the above

49. "Work-Diversity" by nature, does not go against Ethics. But an executive assistant while getting transferred from "stores" to "despatch" section created turmoil in the office. He is:

(A) Most ethical in his deal

(B) Fully against work ethics

(C) He is workoholic

(D) A Rigid employer, hard nut to crack

50. Ethical Management is

(A) A Compromise (B) A Compulsion

(C) A Judgement (D) (A) and (B)

UGC-NET-MANAGEMENT-PAPER-II-J-2012- ANSWER KEYS

Q01 A	Q11 A	Q21 D	Q31 A	Q41 D
Q02 C	Q12 C	Q22 A	Q32 B	Q42 B
Q03 A	Q13 D	Q23 D	Q33 C	Q43 D
Q04 A	Q14 B	Q24 B	Q34 D	Q44 D
Q05 B	Q15 D	Q25 D	Q35 B	Q45 A
Q06 C	Q16 A	Q26 D	Q36 C	Q46 C
Q07 B	Q17 A	Q27 D	Q37 D	Q47 D
Q08 A	Q18 B	Q28 A	Q38 D	Q48 C
Q09 D	Q19 C	Q29 B	Q39 D	Q49 B
Q10 D	Q20 B	Q30 B	Q40 D	Q50 A

---000---

UGC-NET-MANAGEMENT-PAPER-III-JUNE-2012

1. Hawthorne Experiment is related to the

(A) Systems theory

(B) Classical theory

(C) Human relations theory

(D) Scientific management theory

2. Cost incurred in the past and is not affected by a current decision is referred to as :

(A) Sunk cost (B) Marginal cost

(C) Incremental cost (D) Replacement cost

3. The principle of organisation that no employee should report to more than one superior is called:

(A) Scalar principle (B) Span of control

(C) Unity of command (D) Unity of direction

4. 'Rege Committee' is related to:

(A) Working conditions in Indian Industry

(B) Social security in Indian Industry

(C) Individual differences in Indian Industry

(D) None of the above

5. The factors affecting to P/E multiple are

(A)Dividend pay-out ratio and required return

(B) Required return and expected growth rate

(C)Dividend pay-out ratio and expected growth rate

(D)Dividend pay-out ratio, required return and expected growth rate

6. Which of the following is not one of the benefits of E-Commerce?

(A)E-Commerce offers greater flexibility in meeting consumer needs.

(B) E-Commerce can help to reduce cost.

(C)E-Commerce increases potential market share.

(D)E-Commerce increases the net cost per contact.

7. Which among the following is not concerned with the PERT evolution?

(A) Polaris Project

(B) Lockhead Aircraft Corporation

(C) Both (A) and (B)

(D) None of the above

8. Before a company decides to target a particular market segment, which important factors are to be examined against organization's objectives and resources?

(A) Market size

(B) Growth rate

(C) Structural attractiveness

(D) All of the above

9. Balance of Payment is

(A) Balance of trade + Net earnings on invisibles

(B) Foreign exchange inflow – Foreign exchange outflow

(C) Balance of current account + Balance of capital account + Statistical discrepancy

(D) Export of goods – Import of goods

10. Factors contributing to unethical behaviour are:

(A) Poor leadership

(B) Poor internal communication

(C) Lack of management support

(D) All of the above

11. Which of the following is not included in the five forces of competition?

(A) Bargaining power of suppliers

(B) Bargaining power of consumers

(C) Threat of substitutes

(D) Strategic planning

12. Match the following :

List-I(Financial Institution)

(a) Industrial Development Bank of India (IDBI)

(b) Small Industries Development Bank of India (SIDBI)

(c)Natural Small Industries Corporation (NSIC)

(d) Industrial Finance Corporation of India (IFCI)

List-II (Year of Establishment)

(i)1955

(ii)1964

(iii)1948

(iv)1989

Codes:

(a) (b) (c) (d)

(A) (i) (iv) (iii) (ii)   (B) (ii) (iv) (i) (iii)

(C) (iii) (i) (ii) (iv)   (D) (iii) (ii) (i) (iv)

13. The practice of selling two or more separate products together for a single price is :

(A) Bundling   (B) Dumping

(C) Both (A) and (B)   (D) None of the above

14. Which is the oldest and simplest form of organization?

(A) Functional organisation

(B) Committee organisation

(C) Line organisation

(D) Line and staff organisation

15. While considering promotion of an employee, the following is the most important consideration :

(A) Seniority   (B) Competence

(C) Loyalty   (D) Only (A) and (B)

16. Which type of promotion has been described by W. R. Spriegel ?

(i) Departmental Promotion

(ii) Inter-departmental Promotion

(iii) Inter-plant Promotion

(iv) Inter-company Promotion

(A) (i), (ii), (iii)   (B) (ii), (iii), (iv)

(C) (i), (ii), (iv)   (D) (i), (iii), (iv)

17. Market risk is also known as

(A) Systematic risk or diversifiable risk

(B) Unsystematic risk or diversifiable risk

(C)Systematic risk or non diversifiable risk

(D)Unsystematic risk or non diversifiable risk

18. The discount rate that makes NPV equal to zero is known as:

(A) Benefit–Cost ratio

(B) Internal Rate of Return

(C) Discounted Pay-back period

(D) Profitability Index

19. Match the following :

List-I

(i) Poisson distribution

(ii) Normal distribution

(iii) Chi-Square distribution

(iv) Binomial distribution

List-II

I. Mean is greater than variance

II. Mean & Variance are same

III. Symmetric

IV. Positively skewed

Codes:

(i) (ii) (iii) (iv)

(A) II I III IV   (B) IV I III II

(C) II III IV I   (D) IV II I III

20. A critical activity is defined as one whose

(A) Total float is zero.

(B) Free float is zero.

(C) Duration is the longest.

(D) Duration is the smallest.

21. In the buying decision process, what is the term used for a person who first suggests buying the product or service?

(A) Influencer (B) Initiator

(C) Decider (D) Buyer

22. Strategies formulated to convert a sick unit to healthy is referred to :

(A) Turnaround (B) Expansion

(C) Diversification (D) Stabilisation

23. Which one is an international credit rating agency?

(A) Mc Kinsey (B) B C G

(C) Standard and poor (D) I M F

24. Ethical challenges may arise on account of:

(A) Failure of personal character, conflict of personal value & organisational goals and conflict of organisational goals and social values

(B) Hazardous but popular products

(C) Both (A) and (B)

(D) None of the above

25. Supply curve slopes backward towards left, when :

(A) More quantity is supplied at higher prices.

(B) Less quantity is supplied at higher prices.

(C) Same quantity is supplied at higher prices

(D) None of the above

26. Transactional Analysis (TA) is related to:

(A) Learning (B) Attitudes

(C) Perception (D) Personality

27. Which among the following is odd one?

(A) BMS (B) FICCI

(C) AITUC (D) INTUC

28. Which of the following strategies requires a company to concentrate its efforts in one or more narrow segments instead of a broad based strategy?

(A) Cost-Leadership strategy

(B) Differentiation strategy

(C) Focus strategy

(D) None of the above

29. In case where the investment can be made in stages and is dependent on the future outcomes, the capital budgeting technique that can be adopted will be

(A) Simulation technique

(B) Hiller model

(C) Decision-tree analysis

(D) Scenario analysis

30. Statement (i) : In an organization we pay for jobs, we do not pay for men.

Statement (ii): The compensation must be as per the Job assigned.

(A) Statement (i) is correct but (ii) is false.

(B) Statement (ii) is correct but (i) is false.

(C) Both statement (i) and (ii) are correct.

(D) Both statement (i) and (ii) are false.

31. If the regression coefficient of the independent variable in a simple regression equation is negative, then which of the following statement is correct?

(A) The coefficient of correlation between the variables is zero.

(B) The coefficient of correlation between the variables is the positive square root of the coefficient of determination.

(C) The coefficient of correlation between the variables is the negative square root of the coefficient of determination.

(D) None of the above.

32. Selling the products only through a single wholesaler or retailer is called

(A) Extensive distribution strategy

(B) Selective distribution strategy

(C) Exclusive distribution strategy

(D) Mass merchandise strategy

33. Marketing myopia concept was developed by

(A) Philip Kotler (B) Peter Drucker

(C) C. K. Prahlada (D) Theodore Levitt

34. Emerging market economies are :

(A) A part of developed countries

(B) Newly industrializing countries

(C) A part of developing countries

(D) A part of third world countries

35. What describes the market, product and technological area of business?

(A) Company's mission

(B) Company's vision

(C) Strategic plan

(D) None of the above

36. Activities taken up on part time or casual basis to raise income is :

(A) Self employment

(B) Income generation

(C) Entreprencurship

(D) None of the above

37. "The optimal pay-out ratio for growth firm is nil and declining firm is 100%" is established by:

(A) Gordon model (B) Walter model

(C) Both (A) and (B) (D) None of the above

38. Match the following :

List-I

(i) Z – Theory

(ii) Y – Theory

(iii) Hierarchy Needs Theory

(iv) Hygiene Theory

List-II

(a) Hergberg

(b) Maslow

(c) Mc Gregor

(d) Urwick

Codes:

	(a)	(b)	(c)	(d)
(A)	(iv)	(i)	(iii)	(ii)
(B)	(iii)	(ii)	(iv)	(i)
(C)	(iv)	(iii)	(ii)	(i)
(D)	(iii)	(iv)	(i)	(ii)

39. Need-Hierarchy Theory was propounded by:

(A) Peter F. Drucker (B) Abraham Maslow

(C) Mc – Fraland (D) Elton Mayo

40. Additional revenue generated by selling an additional unit is

(A) Incremental revenue

(B) Marginal revenue

(C) Total revenue

(D) Average revenue

41. What is the term used if a market is divided into distinct groups of buyers who might require separate products or marketing mixes?

(A) Market Targetting

(B) Market Positioning

(C) Market Segmentation

(D) Market Co-ordination

42. Bath tub curve is encountered in

(A) Process control

(B) Acceptance sampling

(C) Both (A) and (B)

(D)Maintenance management

43. Cost advantage is referred as

(A) A firm achieving a lower cumulative cost of performing value activities than its competitors

(B) Firm trying to outsource all relative products from one company to gain economies of scale

(C) Firm trying to restrict the cost control measure relative to its nearer competitor

(D) None of the above

44. If a hypothesis is tested at a significant level of 5%, then it means that

(A) There is 5% probability that the null hypothesis will be rejected though it is true.

(B) There is 5% probability that the null hypothesis will be false.

(C) There is 5% probability that the null hypothesis will be true.

(D) There is 95% probability that the alternative hypothesis will be false.

45. The time that elapses between the purchase of raw materials and the collection of cash for sales is referred as

(A) Production cycle

(B) Operating cycle

(C) Cash cycle

(D) Organisation cycle

46. One of the following is not included in job descriptions :

(A) Job title (B) Location

(C) Penal actions (D) Duties

47. In which type of market situation competitors offer same type of products and services for the same price with no differentiation?

(A) Monopolistic competition (B) Monopoly

(C) Oligopoly (D) Perfect competition

48. Sick enterprise is referred to which of the following bodies for rehabilitation?

(A) Small Industries Development Bank of India (SIDBI)

(B)Small Industries Development Organisation (SIDO)

(C)Board for Industrial and Financial Restructure (BIFR)

(D) National Small Industries Corporation (NSIC)

49. Match the following :

List-I

(i) Wealth of Nations

(ii) Income and Substitution effect

(iii) Kinked Demand Curve

(iv) Production function

List-I

I. Robert Giffen

II. Paul M. Sweezy

III. Cobb- Douglas

IV. Adam Smith

Codes:

(i) (ii) (iii) (iv)

(A) IV II I III (B) IV I III II

(C) IV II III I (D) IV I II III

50. The term "Grapevine Communication" is related to

(A) Formal Communication

(B) Informal Communication

(C) Written Communication

(D) Vertical Communication

51. Taylor differential piece rate system is related to:

(A) Time wage system

(B) Piece wage system

(C) Incentive wage system

(D) None of the above

52. Financial risk arises from

(A)R & D and operations stages of value chain

(B)GNP growth rate and competitive environment

(C) Volatility of interest rates, currency rates, commodities prices and stock prices

(D) Changes in laws and regulations

53. A company using high price and high promotion policy is adopting the following strategy :

(A) Slow skimming (B) Rapid Penetration

(C) Slow Penetration (D) Rapid Skimming

54. Which one of the following is the functions of personnel management?

(A) Planning, Organising, Staffing, Directing and Controlling

(B)Planning, Organising, Coordinating, Budgeting and Controlling

(C) Procurement, Development, Compensation, Integration and Maintenance

(D)Perception, Development, Learning, Organisation and Behaviour

55. Match the following :

List-I

(i) Net present value method

(ii) Average rate of return

(iii) Internal rate of return

(iv) Pay back method

List-II

(I) Inflow after interest and tax

(II) Discounted cash flow

(III) Traditional method

(IV) Decision based on cut-off rate

Codes:

(i) (ii) (iii) (iv)

(A) IV I II III (B) IV III II I

(C) II I IV III (D) I III IV II

56. The number of product lines a company carries is called

(A) Product range (B) Product mix depth

(C) Product mix width(D) Product line length

57. Entrepreneurial failures can be attributed to :

(A) Low quality raw materials

(B) Labour problems

(C) High overhead costs

(D) All of the above

58. What are the economic goals that guide the strategic direction of every viable business organization?

(A) Goal, profit and public image

(B) Public image, growth and profit

(C) Survival, growth and profitability

(D) Growth, profitability and public image

59. Match the following :

List-I

(i) Sensitivity training

(ii) Hygiene factors

(iii) Number of subordinates

(iv) Likert's management system

List-II

(a) Leadership

(b) Organisational Development

(c) Motivation

(d) Span of management

Codes:

(i) (ii) (iii) (iv)

(A) (b) (c) (d) (a) (B) (a) (c) (d) (b)

(C) (d) (c) (a) (b) (D) (a) (b) (c) (d)

60. If the intrinsic value of the share is greater than market value, such shares are :

(A) Under valued (B) Over valued

(C) Neutral (D) None of the above

61. Which of the following is not a market oriented pricing technique?

(A) Penetration pricing

(B) going rate pricing

(C) perceived value pricing

(D) Early-cash recovery pricing

62. Which one of the following facilitates E-Commerce?

(A) Public relations (B) Direct marketing

(C) Personal selling (D) Product quality

63. Sensitivity analysis may be used in

(A) Linear programming

(B) Transportation programming

(C) PERT

(D) CPM

64. Sensitivity training method is a part of

(A) On-the-job training method

(B) Off-the-job training method

(C) Vestibule training method

(D) None of the above

65. A machine on the average produces 5% defective items. What are the mean and variance in a set of 32 items?

(A) 16, 8 (B) 16, 4

(C) 4, 16 (D) None of the above

66. Distribution strategy of a company will be influenced by

(A) Nature of product

(B) Target segment of consumers

(C) Pricing policy

(D) All of the above

67. Which of the following is an example for unsystematic risk?

(A) Interest rate risk (B) Exchange rate risk

(C) International risk (D) Operating risk

68. Match the following :

List – A

(i) Job Analysis

(ii) Job Description

(iii) Job Specification

(iv) Job Classification

List – B

(a) Grading jobs according to scale of pay

(b) A statement of human qualities to fill job

(c) A process of obtaining job facts

(d) A statement of duties and responsibilities of a job

Codes:

(i) (ii) (iii) (iv)

(A) (c) (d) (b) (a) (B) (c) (d) (a) (b)

(C) (a) (b) (c) (d) (D) (b) (c) (d) (a)

69. A positioning strategy should include the following strategies except

(A) Product strategy

(B) Personnel strategy

(C) Promotion strategy

(D) Advertising strategy

70. Which among the following will suit the best as location for a chemical plant?

(A) Desert Area (B) Coastal Area

(C) Plains (D) Hill Area

71. When making purchase decisions the main consideration involved in organizational buying is:

(A) Product quality (B) Price

(C) Service (D) All the above

72. Which of the following is to be considered by an investor while exercising the option?

(A) Exercise price

(B) Spot price

(C) Exercise price and spot price

(D) None of the above

73. Match the following :

List – A

(i) Indian Trade Union Act

(ii) Industrial Dispute Act

(iii) The Workmen's Compensation Act

(iv) The Employees' State Insurance Act

List – B

(a) 1923

(b) 1926

(c) 1948

(d) 1947

Codes:

	(i)	(ii)	(iii)	(iv)
(A)	(b)	(d)	(a)	(c)
(B)	(b)	(c)	(d)	(a)
(C)	(b)	(d)	(c)	(a)
(D)	(a)	(c)	(b)	(d)

74. Who creates and implements strategic change in an organization?

(A) Directors (B) Consultants

(C) H. R. Managers (D) Strategist

75. Which of the variables is not used by marketers for demographic segmentation?

(A) Age (B) Income

(C) Gender (D) Poverty

UGC-NET-MANAGEMENT-PAPER-III-J-2012- ANSWER KEYS

Q01 C	Q16 A	Q31 C	Q46 C	Q61 D
Q02 A	Q17 C	Q32 C	Q47 D	Q62 B
Q03 C	Q18 B	Q33 D	Q48 C	Q63 A
Q04 A	Q19 C	Q34 B	Q49 D	Q64 C
Q05 D	Q20 A	Q35 A	Q50 B	Q65 D
Q06 D	Q21 B	Q36 B	Q51 C	Q66 D
Q07 C	Q22 A	Q37 C	Q52 C	Q67 D
Q08 D	Q23 C	Q38 C	Q53 D	Q68 A
Q09 C	Q24 C	Q39 B	Q54 C	Q69 B
Q10 D	Q25 B	Q40 B	Q55 C	Q70 B
Q11 D	Q26 D	Q41 C	Q56 C	Q71 D
Q12 B	Q27 B	Q42 D	Q57 D	Q72 C
Q13 A	Q28 C	Q43 A	Q58 C	Q73 A
Q14 C	Q29 C	Q44 A	Q59 A	Q74 D
Q15 D	Q30 C	Q45 B	Q60 A	Q75 D

---000---

UGC-NET-MANAGEMENT-PAPER-II-DECEMBER-2012

1. The term Opportunity Cost refers to:

(A) Variable Cost

(B) Short-run cost

(C) The cost forgone in favour of production of another product

(D) Cost related to an optimum level of production

2. If two commodities are complementary, then a rise in the price of one commodity will induce:

(A)A rise in the price of the other commodity

(B)An upward shift of demand curve

(C)No shift in demand for the other commodity

(D)A backward shift in demand for the other commodity

3. What is the characteristic of a purely competitive market?

(A) Large number of buyers and sellers

(B) A few sellers

(C) A few buyers

(D) Abnormal profit

4. Willingness to pay minus actual payment is called:

(A) Consumer's surplus

(B) Producer's surplus

(C) Utility cost

(D) Supplier's surplus

5. Match List – I with List – II and select the correct answer using the codes given below the lists :

List – I

(a) Cost Function

(b) Supply Function

(c) Production Function

(d) Oligopoly

List – II

(i) Kinky Demand Curve

(ii) Isoquants

(iii)Engineering Method

(iv) Factor Prices

Codes:

	(a)	(b)	(c)	(d)
(A)	(iii)	(iv)	(ii)	(i)
(B)	(iv)	(iii)	(i)	(ii)
(C)	(iii)	(ii)	(i)	(iv)
(D)	(i)	(ii)	(iii)	(iv)

6. When analysing your business and its environment, it is useful to carefully inspect

(A) Threats

(B) Opportunities

(C) Strengths and weaknesses

(D) All of the above

7. Which of the following is an example of an external threat?

(A) Decreased competition

(B) New Trade Regulations

(C) Global Sales Potential

(D) Economies of Scale

8. Expectancy Theory of Motivation was propounded by

(A) Porter and Lawler (B) McGregor

(C) Vroom (D) J. Stacy Adams

9. Which one of the following is not a step in planning?

(A) Establishing objectives

(B) Developing premises

(C) Determining alternative courses

(D) Identifying needs of employees

10. Planning is looking ahead and control is

(A) Scanning environment

(B) Looking back

(C) Setting targets

(D) Defining objectives

11. Human Resource Management (HRM) is a part of the broad Human Resource Development (HRD) System, as this focus to

(A)Selection, Induction, Training and Development

(B) Operational and Organisational Options

(C) (A) and (B) above

(D) None of the above

12. Performance Appraisal is a double edged tool to:

(A)Create space for the employee to organisationally survive.

(B)Offering challenges for promotion.

(C)Accompanying the course of Demotion.

(D)All of the above.

13. Wage determination is mostly done through tools which are

(A) Objective (B) Subjective

(C) Both of (A) & (B) (D) None of these

14. Job Evaluation criterion comes from

(A) Job manual (B) Job description

(C) Job specification (D) Job duration

15. Exit Policy primarily emphasises in the broad sense, for policy makers as

(A) Removing employees

(B) Down sizing

(C) Retiring people and Rehabilitating them

(D) Bringing new blood to the Corporate

16. The goal of financial management is to

(A)Maximise the wealth of Preference Shareholders

(B)Maximise the wealth of Debenture holders

(C)Maximise the wealth of Equity shareholders

(D) All of the above

17. The Internal Rate of Return (IRR) is determined where

(A) the Net Present Value is positive

(B) the Net Present Value is negative

(C) the Net Present Value is zero

(D) None of the above

18. The Tax shield would result in

(i) increase in tax liability

(ii) increase in EPS

(iii) decrease in EPS

(iv) decrease in tax liability

Codes:

(A) (ii) and (iv)

(B) (i) and (iii)

(C) (i) and (iv)

(D) (iii) and (iv)

19. Which of the following is a main method of issue of stocks?

(A) Vendor placing

(B) Public issue through Prospectus

(C) Private placements

(D) None of the above

20. The Capital Asset Pricing Model (CAPM) establishes the relationship between

(A) Risk and EPS

(B) Risk and value of the firm

(C) Risk and the required rate of return

(D) None of the above

21. 'Marketing is a human activity directed at satisfying needs and wants through Exchange process'; is the statement of

(A) Cundiff ad Still (B) Kenneth Andrews

(C) Philip Kotler (D) Kishwar S. Kan

22. Promotion mix includes

(A) Advertising, publicity, personal selling and sales promotion

(B) Physical attributes, brand, package and product life cycle

(C) Brand name, product benefits, delivery and credit

(D)Transportation, material handling, packaging and customer service

23. Which of the following is not the stage of product life cycle?

(A) Introduction (B) Growth

(C) Market segmentation (D) Decline

24. Which is the basic form of Innovation ?

(A) Introduction of novel production process

(B) Improvement and development of existing process

(C) Improvement and development of existing firm

(D) All of the above

25. The scientific system of collecting and analysis of data pertaining to market is known as

(A) Production Research

(B) Advertising Research

(C) Marketing Research

(D) None of the above

26. Which one of the following is not the function of Production Management?

(A) Production, Planning and Control

(B) Procurement of Raw Materials

(C) Market Intelligence and Survey

(D) Plant Location and Layout

27. Time study refers to:

(A)Developing a standard time to do a particular task

(B) Improving work methods

(C) Value analysis

(D) Value engineering

28. Acceptance Quality level is

(A)Maximum number of defectives that the consumers will accept

(B)Fraction defective(s) that the consumer considers acceptable

(C)Fraction defective(s) that the producer considers acceptable

(D)Maximum number of defectives that the producer will allow

29. In a transportation problem involving 10 origins and 5 destinations, the number of constraints representing origin capacity and destination requirements is equal to:

(A) 50 (B) 49

(C) 15 (D) 14

30. The critical path of a network is

(A) for which earliest start time and latest start time are same

(B) the shortest time path through a network

(C)for which earliest finish time and latest finish time are same

(D)the longest time path through a network

31. If a person buys one ticket of a State lottery, then the probability that he wins a price is 0.11. If a person buys one ticket each month for five months, what is the probability that he will win least one price?

(A) 0.55 (B) 0.50

(C) 0.44 (D) 0.56

32. The standard error of the mean of a random sample of size two or more.

(A) Always exceeds the population standard deviation.

(B) Either exceeds or equals the population standard deviation.

(C) Is always lower than the population standard deviation

(D) Is always equal to the population standard deviation.

33. A store manager is trying to explore the relationship between percentage fat content (Y) and price (X) of various dairy products. He finds that the coefficient of determination is 0.4624 and the estimated regression line is Y = 0.5 – 0.02 X. The coefficient of correlation would be

(A) 0.68 (B) – 0.68

(C) – 0.02 (D) 0.4624

34. Which of the following statement on testing of hypothesis is always true?

(A) When the null hypothesis is rejected at 5%, it is always rejected at 1% level of significance.

(B) When the null hypothesis is rejected at 1%, it is also rejected at 5% level of significance.

(C) When the null hypothesis is not rejected at 1%, it is rejected at 5% level of significance.

(D) No definite assertion can be made.

35. Which of the following devices would be considered a typical sequential access medium?

(A) Magnetic Hard Disk

(B) Magnetic Floppy Disk

(C) Magnetic Tape

(D) CD ROM

36. What describes the market, product and technological areas of business?

(A) BCG Matrix

(B) GE Nine Cell Matrix

(C) 7's framework

(D) Company's Mission

37. Name the factors taken into consideration in Internal Analysis

(A) Firm Resources

(B) Objective, plans and policies of the firm

(C) The type of business involved

(D) All of the above

38. Diversification is to a new business area that has no obvious connection with any of the company's existing areas refer to

(A) Forward integration

(B) Backward integration

(C) Conglomerate diversification

(D) Concentric diversification

39. Which business unit generates substantial cash surplus due to low industry growth rate and high profit share?

(A) Dog (B) Cash cow

(C) Question mark (D) Star

40. Who plays an important role in the success of products and services and in increasing the marketing share of the firm in business?

(A) Functional level Managers

(B) Corporate level Managers

(C) Business level Managers

(D) All of the above

41. Entrepreneurship as a theory of business was propounded by

(A) Douglas McGregor

(B) Thomas A. Coleman

(C) Joseph A. Schumpeter

(D) Adam Smith

42. Policies related to Revival of Sick Units are framed by

(A) IIFT (B) CSIR

(C) SEBI (D) MSME

43. The book 'Innovation and Entrepreneurship' is written by

(A) Harold Koontz (B) Blake and Mouton

(C) Peter F. Drucker (D) None of the above

44. State Financial Corporation Act encourages in:

(A) Establishing Industrial Estates

(B) Establishing small and medium size industries

(C) Establishing Agricultural Farms

(D) All of the above

45. Name the Author of Equity Theory of Motivation.

(A) Blake & Mouton (B) Strube & Garcia

(C) Stancy Adams (D) Albert Bandura

46. Anything dealing with Ethics in Business is

(A) good, bad or both, to the business gains

(B) not related to religion

(C) not to focus obligation

(D) killing all types of Unfair Trade Practices

47. Ethics provide

(A) Consumer Autonomy

(B) CSR

(C) Justice

(D) All of the above

48. Company seeking ethical standard must purport to

(A) Good Employee Relation

(B) Better Production Portfolio

(C) Economy of Scale

(D) Public Disclosure and Publishing

49. Which of the following is not the act of Corporate Governance?

(A) Protecting the interest of shareholders

(B) Protecting the interest of employees

(C) Fudging of Accounts

(D) Paying Taxes to the Government

50. Corporate Social Responsibility (CSR) is looked as the organized network of making long economic and social relationship of the corporate with the society. But a business of which type, as mentioned below, cannot afford for it, at the first instance?

(A) Large Business

(B) Medium Business

(C) Small Business

(D)A Business Start-up

UGC-NET-MANAGEMENT-PAPER-II-D-2012- ANSWER KEYS

Q01 C	Q11 C	Q21 C	Q31 C	Q41 C
Q02 D	Q12 D	Q22 A	Q32 C	Q42 D
Q03 A	Q13 C	Q23 C	Q33 B	Q43 C
Q04 A	Q14 C	Q24 D	Q34 B	Q44 B
Q05 A	Q15 C	Q25 C	Q35 C	Q45 C
Q06 D	Q16 C	Q26 C	Q36 D	Q46 A
Q07 B	Q17 C	Q27 A	Q37 D	Q47 D
Q08 C	Q18 A	Q28 B	Q38 D	Q48 D
Q09 D	Q19 B	Q29 C	Q39 B	Q49 C
Q10 B	Q20 C	Q30 B	Q40 D	Q50 D

---000---

UGC-NET-MANAGEMENT-PAPER-III-DECEMBER-2012

1. Which of the following is not one of the important objectives of Financial Management?

(A) Profit maximisation

(B) Wealth maximisation

(C) Value maximisation

(D) Social responsibility

2. For 'make or buy decision', which cost is to be considered?

(A) Marginal cost (B) Total cost

(C) Fixed cost (D) None of the above

3. Which is the method applied for measuring GNP?

(A) Income method

(B) Expenditure method

(C) Value Added method

(D) All of the above

4. Which of the following project appraisal method is not based on time value of money?

(A) Payback method

(B) Net present value method

(C) Internal rate of return method

(D) Discounted payback method

5. Micro, Small and Medium Enterprises Development Act, 2006 is related to

(A) Industrial Policy

(B) Investment Limit

(C) Business Opportunities

(D) None of these

6. Selection is the process in which candidates for employment are divided into two classes – those who are to be offered employment and those who are not." This is stated by

(A) Dale Yoder (B) Milton M. Mandell

(C) R.D. Agarwal (D) Edwin Flippo

7. Who defines advertising as "any paid form of non-personal presentation and promotion of ideas, goods and services by an identified sponsor?

(A) Philip Kotler (B) C.K. Prahlad

(C) Chartered Institute of Marketing

(D) American Marketing Association

8. The exchange rate between the currencies of two countries will be equal to the ratio of the price indices in these countries is explained by

(A) Inflation adjustment

(B) Purchase power parity

(C) Interest rate parity

(D) Transaction exposure

9. The ultimate mission or purpose is to relate human resources to future enterprise needs, so as to maximize the future return on investment in human resources. It is referred as:

(A) Demand and Supply

(B) Forecasting

(C) Human Resource Planning

(D) Human Resource Development

10. Other things being equal an increase in income leads to a decrease in demand for

(A) Superior Goods (B) Inferior Goods

(C) Both (A) and (B) (D) None of the above

11. "Hind Mazdoor Sabha" established in which year ?

(A) 1940 (B) 1942

(C) 1948 (D) 1952

12. The evaluation of Business activities and behaviour as right or wrong is called

(A) Corporate Governance

(B) Business Ethics

(C) Social Responsibility

(D) None of the above

13. A market structure which consists of one buyer and one seller is referred as

(A) Monopsony (B) Bilateral monopoly

(C) Monopoly (D) Duopoly

14. At which stage of new product development process, the launching of New Product will take place?

(A) Business Analysis

(B) Commercialization

(C) Test Marketing

(D) Marketing Strategy Development

15. The cost of equity can be measured as

(A) Rate of interest (1 – t).

(B) Rate of dividend (1– t).

(C) Rate of dividend× (Face value – Issue Price) n

(D)D1P0+ g

16. If the regression coefficient B in Y = A + B X is equal to zero, then the regression line will

(A) pass through the origin

(B) be parallel to the x-axis

(C) be parallel to the y-axis

(D) Neither intersect x-axis nor y-axis

17. An entrepreneurial person employed by a corporation and encouraged to be innovative and creative is referred to as:

(A) Competitor (B) Supplier

(C) Entrepreneur (D) Intrapreneur

18. Which of the following provides direction, serves as standards for evaluating performance and motivates members of the organization?

(A) Mission (B) Values

(C) Objectives (D) Goals

19. The four systems of Management in terms of Leadership styles are related to

(A) Blake and Mouton (B) Philip Kotler

(C) Peter F. Drucker (D) Rensis Likert

20. In investment decision, β is associated with

(A) Return (B) Risk

(C) Return and Risk (D) None of the above

21. In production control, scheduling includes

(A) Deciding about the time when the production will reach various departments.

(B) Estimating the time to be consumed in these departments.

(C) How much time will be taken in transferring production from one department to another.

(D) All of the above.

22. Making profit by taking advantage of different prices prevailing in different markets is referred as

(A) Hedging (B) Speculation

(C) Arbitrage (D) Gambling

23. Gegabyte refers to

(A) 1024 Bytes (B) 1024 Kilobytes

(C) 1024 Megabytes (D) 102400 Bytes

24. Environmental issues can be managed by

(A) Investing in environment friendly process or products.

(B) Managing environmental regulations.

(C) Investing in environmental performance improvement.

(D) All of the above.

25. A formal document of what the entrepreneur intends to do to sell enough of the firm's product or service to make a satisfactory profit is called

(A) Long range plan (B) Strategic plan

(C) Business plan (D) None of the above

26. Among the following financial derivatives, which involves the least risk for the holder?

(A) Forward (B) Option

(C) Futures (D) Swap

27. Which level of Managers translates the corporate strategy into concrete objectives for their individual business?

(A) Business level (B) Corporate level

(C) Multi-Business level (D) Functional level

28. The number of subordinates a superior can effectively handle is called:

(A) Organising people (B) Span of control

(C) Direction (D) Coordination

29. Selection of specific media in which advertisements will be run and when they will be run to reach the target market is called:

(A) Advertising (B) Public Relations

(C) Media Planning (D) Publicity

30. Statistical Quality Control requires determination of:

(A) Quality tolerance limit

(B) Quantity measurement

(C) Production lead time

(D) Inventory carrying cost

31. With reference to Working Capital Management, the term 'float' relates to

(A) Inventory Management

(B) Receivables Management

(C) Cash Management

(D) Marketable Securities

32. Which communication component is not a paid form of communication?

(A) Advertising (B) Sales promotion

(C) Personal selling (D) Publicity

33. The Government of India established the Small Industries Development Organisation (SIDO) in the year :

(A) 1951 (B) 1972

(C) 1954 (D) 1982

34. Match the following :

List – I

(a) Functional Organisation

(b) Transactional Analysis

(c) ManagerialGrid

(d) Need Theory

List – II

(i) F.W. Taylor

(ii)Mc Clelland

(iii)Eric Berne

(iv) Blake and Mouton

Codes:

	(a)	(b)	(c)	(d)
(A)	(i)	(iii)	(iv)	(ii)
(B)	(i)	(ii)	(iii)	(iv)
(C)	(iv)	(iii)	(ii)	(i)
(D)	(ii)	(i)	(iv)	(iii)

35. Which of the following is not a Trading block?

(A) NAFTA (B) ASEAN

(C) SAARC (D) IMF

36. Takeover generally involves:

(A) the acquisition of part of an undertaking to enable the acquirer to increase the market share of the product concerned.

(B) the acquisition of certain block of equity capital of a company which enables the acquirer to exercise control over the affairs of the company.

(C)taking over the responsibility to have trade agreement for finished product.

(D)taking over certain long-term liabilities of another group company to help it financially.

37. Which of the following is not a function of distribution agency?

(A) Transportation (B) Servicing

(C) Inventorying (D) Manufacturing

38. Cars are parked in a very big parking lot. A researcher is required to estimate the proportion of cars that are red or the proportion of cars that are from a Japanese manufacturer. Which of the following statement is not correct?

(A) A convenience sample of cars parked near the gate may give a biased estimate of the proportion of cars which are from a Japanese Manufacturer.

(B) Different investigators may get different estimates for the proportion of cars that are red.

(C) The sample proportion of cars that are red is an unbiased estimate of the population proportion if the sampling method is simple random.

(D) A sample of 100 cars in a convenience sample is always better than a sample of 20 cars from a proper random sampling method.

39. Who is father of Administrative Management Theory?

(A) Max Weber (B) Frank Gilbraith

(C) Henry Fayol (D) Henry Gantt

40. The process of determining the tasks that make-up a job and the skills, abilities and responsibilities needed to perform the job is called

(A) Job Analysis (B) Job Description

(C) Job Enrichment (D) All of the above

41. GATT stands for

(A) General Accord on Tariff and Trade

(B) Generous Agreement on Trade and Tariff

(C) General Agreement on Tariff and Trade

(D)Generalist Agreement on Trade and Tariff

42. People who take the risks necessary to organize, manage and receive the financial profits and non-monetary rewards are called

(A) Suppliers (B) Employees

(C) Competitors (D) Entrepreneurs

43. A Marketing database is built as an aid to

(A) Market research

(B) Product-mix expansion

(C) Reducing cost of production

(D) Price hike

44. The model that applies to Economic Order Quantity for Inventory Management, was proposed to be applied to Cash Management by:

(A) Miller and Orr (B) William J. Baumol

(C) William Sharpe (D) David Durand

45. If a hypothesis is statistically significant, then it is concluded that

(A) the observed result is probably not due to chance.

(B) the observed result is probably a chance result.

(C) the observed result cannot possibly be due to chance.

(D) the null hypothesis of no relationship is probably true.

46. In which stage of product life cycle, the company takes decision whether to maintain, harvest or drop the product?

(A) Introduction (B) Growth

(C) Maturity (D) Decline

47. Recruitment is concerned with

(A) Selecting the right candidate

(B) Developing a pool of job candidates

(C) Getting applications

(D) None of the above

48. In production management, dispatching includes :

(A) Giving work to machines and places.

(B) Providing materials, tools, etc. to works.

(C) Issuing appropriate orders for production process.

(D) All of the above.

49. Which of the following is the internal source of recruitment?

(A) Advertisement (B) Selection

(C) Both (A) and (B) (D) None of the above

50. Which Business unit generates substantial cash surpluses due to low industrial growth rate and high market share?

(A) Dog (B) Cash Cow

(C) Question Mark (D) Star

51. which stage of New product development process, the product and marketing programs are tested in realistic market settings?

(A) Concept Development and Testing

(B) Idea Screening

(C) Test Marketing

(D) Commercialization

52. The problem of industrial discipline was debated by the Indian Labour Conference (ILC) held in India in

(A) 1948 (B) 1952

(C) 1957 (D) 1960

53. The Branding strategy which uses a different brand name for each product is known as

(A) Overall Family Branding

(B) Line Family Branding

(C) Individual Branding

(D) Brand Extension

54. The two factor theory was propounded by:

(A)Frederick Herzberg (B) A.H. Maslow

(C) Mc Gregor (D) Elton Mayo

55. Match the following

List-I

(a) Percentage change in quantity demanded to percentage change in price.

(b) Percentage change in demand to percentage change in the price of some other commodity.

(c) Homogeneous products

(d)Relationship between quantity of the product demanded and factors that affect the quantity.

List-II

(i)Perfect competition

(ii)Market demand

(iii)Price elasticity

(iv)Cross elasticity

Codes:

	(a)	(b)	(c)	(d)
(A)	(iii)	(iv)	(i)	(ii)
(B)	(iv)	(iii)	(i)	(ii)
(C)	(iii)	(ii)	(i)	(iv)
(D)	(iv)	(ii)	(i)	(iii)

56. F.W. Taylor has done the following studies for improving the production process :

(A)Time Study, Fatigue Study and Fatal Study.

(B)Time Study, Motion Study and Fatal Study.

(C)Time Study, Motion Study and Fatigue Study.

(D)Time Study, Motivation Study and Fatigue Study.

57. Which one is not the overseas market entry strategy followed by Multinational Corporations?

(A) Franchise (B) Collaborations

(C) Joint venture (D) Strategic planning

58. Benefits provided for temporary and permanent disability disfigurement, medical expenses and medical rehabilitation is referred to as

(A) Fringe benefits

(B)Financial incentives

(C) Workers' compensation

(D) None of the above

59. Today's organizations are working on the principle of

(A) Production-orientation

(B) Product-orientation

(C) Selling-orientation

(D) consumer-orientation

60. Identify the correct sequence of control cycle:

(A) Feedback - Evaluation - Adjustment - Action.

(B) Action - Evaluation - Feedback - Adjustment.

(C) Action - Feedback - Evaluation - Adjustment.

(D) Adjustment - Action - Feedback - Evaluation.

61. Negotiation of labour contract by Union and Management is referred to as:

(A) Industrial Relations

(B) Trade Union

(C) Consumerism

(D) Collective Bargaining

62. Goods used by an organization in producing other goods is called

(A) Consumer goods (B) Industrial goods

(C) Speciality goods (D) None of the above

63. The outside third party who is brought into settle a dispute, and he or she has the authority to make a decision is called

(A) Government (B) An Arbitrator

(C) Union (D) Legal Expert

64. Marketing information system gathers information from internal sources like marketing intelligence and marketing research to help the manager in

(A) Assessing the information needs.

(B) Developing the needed information.

(C) Distributing the information.

(D) All of the above.

65. In which year WTO came into being?

(A) 1980 (B) 2000

(C) 2006 (D) 1995

66. One-level channel consists of

(A) Producer-consumer

(B) Producer-dealer-consumer

(C) Producer-dealer-retailer consumer

(D)Producer-dealer-wholesaler-retailer-consumer

67. Batch production is appropriately applicable to:

(A) Medicine production

(B) Sugar production

(C) Petroleum products

(D) Agriculture produce

68. Match the following :

List-I

(a) Harry Markowitz

(b) David Durand

(c) Dow

(d) M.J. Gordon

List-II

(i) Dividend Theory

(ii)CAPM

(iii) Capital structure

(iv)Technical Analysis

Code:

	(a)	(b)	(c)	(d)
(A)	(iv)	(iii)	(ii)	(i)
(B)	(ii)	(iii)	(iv)	(i)
(C)	(ii)	(i)	(iii)	(iv)
(D)	(iii)	(ii)	(iv)	(i)

69. Which one of the following is not a basic element in the Strategic Management?

(A) Environmental scanning

(B) Strategy formulation

(C) Strategy implementation

(D) Functional strategy

70. A written statement of the human qualification, education and experience needed to perform a job is referred to as:

(A) Job enrichment (B) Job specification

(C) Job design (D) Job description

71. Changes in the population characteristics such as age, gender, marital status, income and education are the examples of

(A) Demographic characteristics

(B) Cultural characteristics

(C) Geographic characteristics

(D) None of the above

72. ESI Act applies to

(A) Railways and Mines Industries

(B) Seasonal Factory Workers

(C) Cement Industries

(D) None of the above

73. Porter and Lawler model is related to

(A) Perception (B) Attitudes

(C) Motivation (D) Leadership

74. Which of the following is the best technique to manage the existing products?

(A) Ansoff matrix

(B) BCG matrix

(C) Mc Kinsey 7s Framework

(D) Five forces of competition

75. One of the acceptable methods for obtaining feedback of training is called

(A) Structured Interview

(B) Performance After Training

(C) Improvement After Training

(D) Employee Turnover Rate

UGC-NET-MANAGEMENT-PAPER-III-D-2012- ANSWER KEYS

Q01 D	Q16 B	Q31 C	Q46 D	Q61 D
Q02 A	Q17 D	Q32 D	Q47 B	Q62 B
Q03 D	Q18 C	Q33 C	Q48 D	Q63 B
Q04 A	Q19 D	Q34 A	Q49 D	Q64 D
Q05 B	Q20 B	Q35 D	Q50 B	Q65 D
Q06 A	Q21 D	Q36 B	Q51 C	Q66 B
Q07 D	Q22 C	Q37 D	Q52 C	Q67 A
Q08 B	Q23 C	Q38 D	Q53 C	Q68 B
Q09 C	Q24 D	Q39 C	Q54 A	Q69 D
Q10 B	Q25 C	Q40 A	Q55 A	Q70 C
Q11 C	Q26 B	Q41 C	Q56 C	Q71 A
Q12 B	Q27 A	Q42 D	Q57 D	Q72 B
Q13 B	Q28 B	Q43 A	Q58 C	Q73 C
Q14 B	Q29 C	Q44 B	Q59 D	Q74 A
Q15 D	Q30 A	Q45 A	Q60 C	Q75 A

---000---

UGC-NET-MANAGEMENT-PAPER-II-JUNE-13

1. The hypothesis that 'consumption in one period would be a function of income in that period and the returns on savings of the previous period' is given by:

(A) Irving Fisher (B) Franco Modigliani

(C) Duesenberry (D) Robert Hall

2. From the following identify one which is not a property of Indifference curve?

(A)Indifference curves are downward sloping.

(B)Indifference curves are concave to the origin.

(C)Indifference curves are convex to the origin.

(D) Indifference curves do not intersect each other.

3. Which one of the following statements is true?

(A) Business decisions cannot be taken without a sound knowledge of Macro Economic Theories.

(B) Knowledge of Economic Theory is misleading in making business decisions.

(C) With the help of Economic Theories, it is always possible to predict the future accurately.

(D)Every Economic Theory is based on realistic facts which are common to all societies.

4. Arrange the following in the proper order for decision under capital budgeting.

(i)Estimating the cost and benefits of proposals.

(ii) Deciding the investment objective.

(iii) Selecting the best investment proposal.

(iv)Applying the capital budgeting decision technique.

Codes:

(A) (ii) (iv) (i) (iii) (B) (ii) (iv) (iii) (i)

(C) (ii) (i) (iv) (iii) (D) (ii) (i) (iii) (iv)

5. Match the following items in List – I with the most appropriate options from List – II :

List-I

(a)A lender buys securities to protect himself from a falling interest rate

(b) A borrower buys securities to protect himself

from rising interest rate

(c) A combination of interest rate cap and floor

(d)A combination of two or more interest rate caps

List-II

(i)Interest rate collar

(ii)Interest rate cap

(iii)Interest rate corridor

(iv)Interest rate floor

Codes:

	(a)	(b)	(c)	(d)
(A)	(ii)	(iv)	(iii)	(i)
(B)	(iv)	(ii)	(i)	(iii)
(C)	(iv)	(ii)	(iii)	(i)
(D)	(iii)	(ii)	(i)	(iv)

6. The form of learning in which people acquire new behaviours by systematically observing the rewards and punishments given to others is known as:

(A) Operant conditioning

(B) Positive reinforcement

(C) Modelling

(D) Law of effect

7. Diffusion of routine information takes place through

(A) Downward Communication

(B) Upward Communication

(C) Horizontal Communication

(D) External Communication

8. An integrated group of activities to bring about a change is known as

(A) Organisation development

(B) Interventions

(C) OCTAPACE

(D)Collaborative culture

9. Match the following :

List-I

(a)Motivation is a function of fairness in social exchanges.

(b) People are motivated to behave in ways that produce valued outcomes.

(c) Determining specific levels of performance for workers to attain and then striving to attain them.

(d) When people are frustrated by their inability to meet needs at the next higher level in the hierarchy, they regress to the next lower category of needs and intensify their desire to gratify these needs.

List-II

(i)Expectancy Theory

(ii)Alderfer's ERG Theory

(iii)Equity Theory

(iv)Goal- Setting Theory

Codes:

(a) (b) (c) (d)

(A) (i) (ii) (iii) (iv) (B) (iv) (iii) (ii) (i)

(C) (iii) (i) (iv) (ii) (D) (iii) (iv) (i) (ii)

10. Match the following :

List-I

(a) Self efficacy

(b) Goal setting

(c) Expectancy

(d) Equity Theory

List-II

(i)Determining specific levels of performance for workers to attain them.

(ii)The belief that one's efforts will positively influence one's performance.

(iii)People strive to maintain ratio of their own outcomes to their own inputs that are equal to that of those with whom they compare themselves.

(iv)One's belief about having the capacity to perform a task.

Codes:

(a) (b) (c) (d)

(A) (i) (ii) (iii) (iv) (B) (iv) (i) (ii) (iii)

(C) (iii) (iv) (i) (ii) (D) (ii) (iii) (iv) (i)

11. Human resource planning system includes:

(A) Human resource supply forecast

(B) Human resource inventory

(C) Corporate plan

(D) All of the above

12. Who among the following propounded the concept of collective bargaining?

(A) Beatrice and Gompers

(B) Beatrice and Emerson

(C) Gompers and Emerson

(D) Gautt and Gompers

13. What are the benefits of human resource planning?

(A) Achieve economy in hiring new workers.

(B)Match personnel activities and future organization objectives efficiently.

(C)Improve the utilization of human resources.

(D) All of the above

14. Human Resource Management includes:

1. Employee Grievance

2. Organizational climate

3. Job incentives

4. Recruitment

5. Selection

Select the correct answer from the following:

(A) 1, 2, 3 and 4 (B) 1, 3, 4 and 5

(C) 1 and 5 (D) All of the above

15. Match the following:

List-I

(a) Job Analysis

(b) Job Evaluation

(c) Job Design

(d) Work Flow Analysis

List-II

(i) Determining worth of a job.

(ii)Examining how work adds value to the ongoing process.

(iii)Determining the pertinent facts about the job.

(iv)Organizing work into the tasks required to perform a specific job.

Codes:

(a) (b) (c) (d)

(A) (i) (ii) (iii) (iv) (B) (iv) (iii) (ii) (i)

(C) (iii) (i) (iv) (ii) (D) (ii) (iii) (i) (iv)

16. Which ratio explains that how much portion of earning is distributed in the form of dividend?

(A) Dividend – Debt Ratio

(B) Equity – Debt Ratio

(C) Pay-out Ratio

(D) Earning – Yield Ratio

17. Modern approach to financial management is

(i) The total fund requirement of the firm.

(ii)The asset to be acquired.

(iii) Payment of dividend to shareholders.

(A) (i) only (B) (ii) only

(C) (ii) & (iii) only (D) (i), (ii)& (iii)

18. Participating preference shares are those which participate in the

(A) general meeting of the company

(B) voting

(C) profits over and above their fixed dividend

(D) management of the company

19. Which of the following is one of the critical assumptions of Walters' Model ?

(A) All financing is done through retained earnings; external sources of funds like debt or new equity capital are not used.

(B) The retention ratio, oncedecided upon, is constant.Thus, the growth rate, (g = br) is also constant.

(C) The capital markets are perfect and the investors behave rationally.

(D) All of the above.

20. This consists of two lists of statements or terms and the candidate has to match an item in one list with an item in the other:

List-I (Statement)

(a) Preventing hostile takeover

(b) Leveraged buyout

(c) Accounting for merger

(d) Financing for merger

List-II (Terms)

1. Management buyout

2. Green mail

3. Pooling of interest

4. Cash offer

Codes:

a b c d

(A) 1 2 3 4 (B) 2 1 4 3

(C) 2 1 3 4 (D) 3 4 2 1

21. What kind of pricing strategy a firm should normally follow for marketing electronic goods?

(A) Penetration pricing strategy

(B) Skimming pricing strategy

(C) Cost plus pricing strategy

(D) All of the above

22. Which fact is true about on-line marketing ?

(A) A website which is user friendly.

(B)A website which is user friendly and regularly updated.

(C) A website which is user friendly, regularly updated and make product's graphical image available.

(D) A website which is user friendly, regularly updated, provides product's graphical image and product's price is competitive.

23. Which of the following function involved under marketing management's function?

1. Collection of market information
2. Marketing coordination
3. Marketing controlling
4. All the above

Codes:

(A) 1 & 2 (B) 2 & 3

(C) 3 only (D) 4 only

24. Two statements are given below :

Statement–I:Product concept of marketing holds that consumers would favour those products that are available and highly affordable.

Statement–II : Production concept of marketing holds that consumers would not buy enough of the company's product unless the company undertakes a substantial promotional effort.

Choose the correct option from the four options given below:

(A) Statement I is correct and II is wrong.

(B) Statement II is correct and I is wrong.

(C) Both statements are correct.

(D) Both statements are wrong.

25. Match the following:

List-I

(a)Differentiation

(b) Esteem

(c) Relevance

(d) Knowledge

List-II

1. How familiar and intimate consumers are with the brand.
2. The degree to which a brand is seen as different from others.
3. How well the brand is regarded and respected.
4. The breadth of a brand's appeal.

Codes:

	(a)	(b)	(c)	(d)
(A)	1	2	3	4
(B)	2	3	4	1
(C)	3	4	1	2
(D)	4	3	2	1

26. Work measurement refers to:

(A) the length of time it takes to complete a work task assigned to a specific job.

(B) improving work methods.

(C) arrangement of machines according to operations.

(D) planning the work and working for the plans.

27. Facility planing includes

(A) Determination of production capacity

(B) Determination of production facilities location

(C) Determination of the layout

(D) All the above

28. Match the following :

List-I

(a) For fraction or proportion of defects

(b) For number of defects

(c) For number of defects for unit

(d) For monitoring process variability

List-II

1. R-chart
2. C-chart
3. nP-Chart
4. P-Chart

Codes:

	(a)	(b)	(c)	(d)
(A)	1	2	3	4

(B) 4 3 2 1

(C) 2 1 4 3

(D) 3 4 1 2

29. Statement–I : One of the major causes of the industry for larger capacity is the argument that large facilities facilitate greater economies of scale. But the major concern for building big capacity is that funds will be tied up or scarcity of funds.

Statement–II: A viable alternative to larger capacity production facilities is to develop subcontractor and supplier networks.

(A) Both statements I & II are correct.

(B) Both statements I & II are false.

(C) Statement I is correct and II is false.

(D) Statement II is correct and I is false.

30. In a symmetrical distribution

(A) Mean, Median and Mode values are identical.

(B) Mean, Median and Standard Deviation are equal.

(C) Mean, Median and Correlation are equal.

(D) None of the above

31. From the following, identify the test which can be used both as parametric and non-parametric?

(A) 't' test (B) 'F' test

(C) 'Chi-square' test (D) 'Wil-coxon' test

32. Arrange the following in ascending order in the testing of hypothesis :

(i) Determining the level of significance

(ii) Deciding the Statistical Test and computation

(iii) Setting the hypothesis

(iv) Decision

Codes :

(A) (iii), (ii), (i) and (iv)

(B) (iii), (i), (ii) and (iv)

(C) (i), (iii), (ii) and (iv)

(D) (i), (iii), (iv) and (ii)

33. Y = a + bX refers to:

(A) Y = independent variable, a = slope of the line, b = Y intercept and X = dependent variable

(B) Y = dependent variable, a = slope of the line, b = Y intercept and X = independent variable

(C) Y = independent variable, a = dependent variable, b = Y intercept and X = slope of the line

(D) Y = dependent variable, a = Y intercept, b = slope of the line and X = independent variable

34. Select the most appropriate option from Column B against the items in Column A :

Column A

a. Computer used to operate large corporate systems and databases

b. Data flow diagram

c. Equipment, procedures and end user

Column B

1. Components of information system

2. RAID

3. Structured design

Codes:

	a	b	c
(A)	3	2	1
(B)	2	3	1
(C)	1	2	3
(D)	2	1	3

35. According to Michael Porter, a strategy aims at producing products and services considered unique industry wide and directed at consumers who are relatively price-insensitive is known as

(A) Cost Leadership – Best Value

(B) Differentiation

(C) Focus – Low Cost

(D) Focus – Best Value

36. In context of Industry Analysis which matrix allows strategists to summarise and evaluate economic, social, cultural, demographic, environmental, political, governmental, legal, technological and competitive information ?

(A) EFE Matrix (B) CPM Matrix

(C) BCG Matrix (D) IFE Matrix

37. Which among the following best describes the process of gaining competitive advantage in a firm ?

(A) Strengths → Weaknesses → Distinctive Competencies →Competitive Advantage

(B) Weaknesses → Strengths → Distinctive Advantages → Competitive Advantages

(C) Weaknesses → Strengths →Distinctive Competencies →Competitive Advantages

(D) Distinctive Competencies →Weaknesses → Strengths →Competitive Advantages

38. According to Porter, the nature of competitiveness in a given industry can be viewed as a composite of the following five forces :

1. Rivalry among competing firms.

2. Potential entry of new competitors.

3. Potential development of substitute products.

4. Bargaining power of suppliers.

5. Bargaining power of consumers.

Identify the force which is central (most powerful) to remaining four:

(A)Potential development of substitute products

(B) Potential entry of new competitors.

(C) Bargaining power of consumers.

(D) Rivalry among competing firms.

39. Match the following :

Organizational Structure

a. Functional Structure

b. Divisional Structure

c. Matrix Structure

d. Strategic Business Unit (SBU)

Advantage

1. Clarity of project objectives

2.Smooth delegation of authority and responsibility

3. Simple and unexpensive

4. Ease of fixing accountability

Codes:

a b c d

(A) 1 2 3 4 (B) 3 4 1 2

(C) 3 4 2 1 (D) 4 3 1 2

40. A sound business opportunity is the result of appropriate interaction between :

(A) needs of the society

(B) capabilities of an entrepreneur

(C) resources available in the environment

(D) all of the above

41. "An entrepreneur always searches for change, responds to it and exploit it as an opportunity." Who said it ?

(A) F.W. Taylor (B) Peter F. Drucker

(C) J.R. Tulsian (D) Max Weber

42. An industrial unit, according to RBI, is sick if:

(A) incurred cash loss in the previous year.

(B) likely to incur loss in the following year.

(C) current ratio is less than 1 : 1 with weak debt-equity ratio.

(D) all of the above.

43. Which is not the object of Entrepreneurship Development Programmes?

(A) To create successful entrepreneur

(B)To remove doubts of entrepreneurs and to give solutions to the problems

(C)To create awareness about Government schemes and programmes

(D) None of the above

44. Match the following :

List-I

a. Cėntral Manufacturing Institute

b. Central Pulp and Paper Research Institute

c. Central leather Research Institute

d. Electronic Service and Training Centre

List-II

1. Deals with paper industry

2.Deals with pollution control in Indian Tanneries

3. Deals with Machine Tools

4. Deals with training, technical and consultancy services

Codes:

a b c d

(A) 1 2 3 4 (B) 3 1 2 4

(C) 2 3 4 1 (D) 4 3 1 2

45. The customer joining the queue and leaving it afterwards is defined as

(A) Jockeying (B) Balking

(C) Reneging (D) None of the above

46. Which among the following is not correct with regards to Clause 49 of SEBI Act?

(A) It came into effect from 31st December 2005.

(B) Clause 49 is related to the Listing Agreement to the Indian Stock Exchange.

(C) It desires 50 percent independent Directors.

(D) None of the above

47. Which of the following powers of Directors cannot be exercised without the consent of shareholders in General Meeting?

(A) Power to make calls on shareholders

(B) Power to make loans

(C) Power to buy back its shares

(D) Power to borrow monies exceeding the aggregate of the paid-up capital of the company and its free reserves.

48. The professional having high ranking and trained to uphold the highest standard and effective operations, compliance and administration as corporate governance, is known as

(A) Directors of Company

(B) Chairman of Company

(C) Company Secretary

(D) Shareholders

49. Governance is the system of values, policies and institutions by which a society manages its economic, political and social affairs through interactions within and among the state, civil society and private sector is defined by

(A) World Bank

(B) UNDP

(C) European Commission

(D) None of the above

50. Match the following with regards to environmental ethical issues :

List-I

(a) Ozone Depletion

(b) Environmental Health

(c) Logging

(d) Genetic Engineering

List-II

(i) Lead poisoning

(ii) Deforestation

(iii) Food controversies

(iv) CFC

Codes:

a b c d

(A) (iv) (ii) (i) (iii) (B) (iv) (i) (ii) (iii)

(C) (iv) (iii) (ii) (i) (D) (iv) (iii) (i) (ii)

UGC-NET-MANAGEMENT- PAPER II-JUNE 2013-ANSWER KEYS				
Q01 B	Q11 A	Q21 B	Q31 C	Q41 B
Q02 B	Q12 A	Q22 D	Q32 B	Q42 D
Q03 A	Q13 D	Q23 D	Q33 D	Q43 A
Q04 C	Q14 B	Q24 D	Q34 B	Q44 B
Q05 B	Q15 C	Q25 B	Q35 B	Q45 C
Q06 A	Q16 C	Q26 A	Q36 A	Q46 D
Q07 A	Q17 D	Q27 D	Q37 A	Q47 D
Q08 A	Q18 C	Q28 B	Q38 D	Q48 C
Q09 C	Q19 A	Q29 A	Q39 B	Q49 B
Q10 B	Q20 C	Q30 A	Q40 D	Q50 B

---000---

UGC-NET-MANAGEMENT-PAPER-III-JUNE-13

1. From the following identify one which is not a collusive oligopoly model

(A) Cartels

(B) Edgeworth Model

(C) Price Leadership

(D) Market Share Model

2. The rate at which the consumer can trade one good for another is termed as marginal rate of substitution in

(A) exchange (B) consumption

(C) production (D) the distribution

3. If demand equation is given by D = 1000 – P and the supply equation is given by S = 100 + 4P, price will be

(A) 160 (B) 180

(C) 170 (D) 200

4. Arrange the following steps, involved in the estimation of a demand function using econometric analysis, in the proper order

(i) Collection of data

(ii) Estimating the parameters of the model

(iii)Mathematical specification of the relationship among the variables

(iv)Using the estimates to arrive at the estimates of variables.

(v) Identification of variables

Codes:

(A) (v), (i), (iii), (iv), (ii)

(B) (i), (ii), (iii), (iv), (v)

(C) (i), (ii), (iv), (iii), (v)

(D) (v), (i), (iii), (ii), (iv)

5. Match the items given in Column A with the suitable items given in Column B :

Column A

a. Maximisation of society's welfare even when individuals behave selfishly to further their own economic status.

b. State of balance from which there is no tendency to change.

c. Best possible state within a given set of constraints.

d. A situation wherein a customer always prefer more of goods to less of goods.

Column B

i. Equilibrium

ii. Non-Satiation

iii. The invisible hand

iv. Optimisation

Codes:

a b c d

(A) iv i iii ii (B) ii i iv iii

(C) iii i iv ii (D) iv i ii iii

6. Which one is not the technique of personality measurement?

(A) Projective Technique

(B) Word Association Technique

(C) Raven's Progressive Matrices

(D) Sentence Completion Technique

7. Drive is explained by:

(A) any strong stimulus that impels action.

(B)any object, event exiting in the environment.

(C)anything that increases the repetition of behaviour.

(D) none of the above

8. Consider the following phases of Organisational Development (OD) :

a. Entry into the organisation

b. Development of internal resources

c. Problem identification

d. Specific intervention

e. Building a collaborative culture

Rearrange the above stages in an orderly sequence:

(A) a → c → b → d → e

(B) a → b → c → d → e

(C) c → b → a → e → d

(D) a → c → d → e → b

9. Match the following :

Explanation

a. The beliefs or ideas one has about an object or situation

b. The feelings or emotions one has about an object or situation

c.Psychological discomfort experienced when attitudes and behaviour are inconsistent.

d. How one intends to act or behave toward someone or something.

e.Learned predisposition toward a given object

Term

1. Attitude

2. Cognitive component

3. Affective component

4. Behavioural component

5. Cognitive dissonance

Codes:

a b c d e

(A) 1 2 3 4 5 (B) 2 3 5 4 1

(C) 3 2 4 5 1 (D) 5 3 4 2 1

10. Match the theories given in Column–I with the explanations in Column – II :

Column – I

a. Super ego

b. Closure

c. Immaturity – Maturity Theory

d. Looking glass-self

Column – II

1. Individual moves from a state of passivity as a child to state of activity as an adult.

2. Social values and personal norms that serve as an ethical constraint on behaviour.

3. Perception of a person about how others are perceiving his qualities.

4.People when faced with incomplete information tend to fill gaps themselves.

Codes:

a b c d

(A) 1 2 3 4 (B) 1 2 4 3

(C) 2 1 3 4 (D) 2 4 1 3

11. What is the procedure in which an employer and a group of employees agree to the conditions of work?

(A) Dispute settlement

(B) Collective bargaining

(C) Industrial democracy

(D) None of the above

12. Factor comparison method is used as a technique of

(A) Job Analysis (B) Job Evaluation

(C) Job Design (D) None of the above

13. Succession planning can best be explained by

(A) Activity in which managers make decisions regarding the advancement potential of subordinates.

(B) Activity that focuses on preparing people to fill executive positions.

(C) A chart showing the possible directions and career opportunities available in an organization.

(D) None of the above

14. Employees join union when they

(A)are dissatisfied with certain aspects of their jobs.

(B)feel that they lack influence with management to make the needed change.

(C)feel unionization as a solution to their problems.

(D) all the above

15. Identify the correct sequence of the steps of grievance procedure required to be followed for the grievance handling

1. Departmental Manager

2. Immediate Supervisor

3. Arbitration

4. Trade Union's intervention

(A) 1, 2, 3 & 4 (B) 2, 3, 1 & 4

(C) 2, 1, 4 & 3 (D) 2, 4, 1 & 3

16. Match the following :

List-I

a. Job posting system

b. Career path

c. Skills inventory

d. Career Resource Centre

List-II

1. A company maintained record of employee's abilities, skills, knowledge and education.

2. A chart showing the possible direction and opportunities available to an employee in the organization.

3.A collection of career development materials.

4.A system in which an organization announces job openings.

Codes:

a b c d

(A) 1 2 3 4 (B) 2 3 4 1

(C) 4 2 1 3 (D) 3 4 1 2

17. Match the following :

List-I

(a) Attrition

(b) Down sizing

(c) Involuntary separation

(d) Right sizing

List-I

1. Separation that occurs when an employer decides to terminate its relationship with an employee due to economic necessity.

2. A company's strategy of separation of employees to reduce the scale (size) and scope of its business in order to improve the company's financial performance.

3. The process of reorganizing a company's employees to improve their efficiency.

4. An employment policy designed to reduce the company's workforce by not refilling job vacancies that are created by turnover.

Codes:

a b c d

(A) 1 2 3 4 (B) 4 2 1 3

(C) 3 2 4 1 (D) 2 1 3 4

18. Which one of the following is the advantage of team-based pay for performance plans?

(A) Financial incentives can shape a person's goals.

(B) Can help the firm to attain individual equity.

(C) Fit an individualistic culture.

(D) Aids performance measurement.

19. Which one of the following is not Human Resource requirement estimation method?

(A) Regression Analysis

(B) Ratio Analysis

(C) Top-down Approach

(D) All of the above

20. Which of the following form for improving workers participation in management was included in the recommendations of the Justice Rajinder Sachar Committee report?

(A) Works Committee

(B) Joint Management Council

(C) Workers' representation in the Board of Directors and allotment of equity to workers

(D) Unit Council

21. JK Ltd. has earned 8% return on total assets of Rs. 50,00,000 and has a Net Profit Ratio of 5%. Find out the sales of the firm.

(A)Rs. 4,00,000 (B) Rs. 2,80,000

(C)Rs. 80,00,000 (D) Rs. 83,33,333

22. Net Present Value Method and Internal Rate of Return Method of capital budgeting techniques may give conflicting accept-reject decision due to:

1. Disparity in initial investment

2. Disparity in timing of cash flow

3. Disparity in the life of the project

(A) 1 only

(B) 2 only

(C) 1 and 2 only

(D) 1, 2 and 3

23. Beta B of risk-free investment is

(A) – 1 (B) 0

(C) 1 (D) None of these

24. A firm's inventory planning period is one year. Its inventory requirement for this period is 400 units. Assume that its acquisition costs are Rs. 50 per order. The carrying costs are expected to be Rs. 1 per unit per year for an item. What is EOQ?

(A) 800 units (B) 200 units

(C) 100 units (D) None of the above

25. Margin of Safety ratio can be calculated as

(A) Actual Sales – Breakeven Sales Actual Sales × 100

(B) Actual Sales – Break-even Sales Break even Sales × 100

(C) Break even Sales – Actual Sales Actual Sales × 100

(D) Break even Sales – Actual Sales Break even Sales × 100

26. This cost arises out of the failure of the customers to meet their obligations when payment on credit sales becomes due after the expiry of the credit period.

(A) Default Cost (B) Delinquency Cost

(C) Capital Cost (D) Collection Cost

27. The following data are available from the annual report of a company : Current Assets Rs. 4,80,000; Current Liabilities Rs. 3,00,000; Average total assets Rs. 20,00,000; Operating income Rs. 2,40,000; Average total equity Rs. 8,00,000; Net income Rs. 80,000.

Which of the following statement is correct?

(A) Return on equity exceeds the return on assets.

(B) Working capital is ` 12,00,000.

(C) Current Ratio is 0.625 to 1.

(D) None of the above.

28. The annual credit sales of a firm is Rs.12,80,000 and the debtors amount to Rs. 1,60,000. The debtors turnover and average collection period are_____.

(A) 4 & 90 days (B) 8 & 45 days

(C) 6 & 60 days (D) 8 & 60 days

29. The formula used for valuation of equity shares with assumption of normal growth in dividend is

(A) D0 Ke – g (B)D1Ke – g

(C)E0Ke – g (D)E1Ke – g

30. Match the following :

List – I(Statement)

I. A combination of two puts and one call with the same exercise price and expiration date.

II. A combination of one put and two calls with the same exercise price and expiration date.

III. A portfolio of put and call with the same expiration date but with different exercise price.

IV. A position where the option writer does not hold a share in his portfolio that has a counter balancing effect.

List – II (Term)

1. Strap
2. Strip
3. Strangle
4. Naked option

Codes:

I II III IV

(A) 2 1 3 4 (B) 1 2 3 4

(C) 2 1 4 3 (D) 1 3 2 4

31. "Motivational research is a form of market research that attempts to discover the deeper reasons why people buy." Who said it?

(A) Manson and Rath (B) Stanton

(C) Still and Scweff (D) Philip Kotler

32. In multi level channel arrangement Jobber stands in between ________.

(A) manufacturer and wholesaler

(B) wholesaler and retailer

(C) retailer and consumer

(D) none of these

33. A company following a strategy of advertising the product for a period followed by a period with no advertising is called

(A) Concentration (B) Flighting

(C) Pulsing (D) Continuity

34. Franchise organisation is an example of ______ vertical marketing system.

(A) Corporate (B) Administered

(C) Contractual (D) Co-operative

35. Three statements are given below :

Statement–I: Introducing an existing product in the new market is called market development.

Statement–II: Introducing a new product in the existing market is called diversification.

Statement–III: Introducing an existing product in the existing market is called market penetration.

Choose the correct option about the statements from among the options given below :

(A) Statements I & II are only correct.

(B) Statements I & III are only correct.

(C) Statements II & III are only correct.

(D) Statements I, II & III are correct.

36. Two statements are given below relating to sales promotion :

Statement–I: Sweep Stakes calls for consumers to submit an entry to be examined by a panel of judges who will select the best entry.

Statement–II: A contest asks consumers to submit their names in a drawing.

Choose the most appropriate answer from among the options given relating to the statements:

(A) Statement – I is correct and II is wrong.

(B) Statement – II is correct and I is wrong.

(C) Both statements are wrong.

(D) Both statements are correct.

37. Arrange the following steps in the perceptional process in the sequential order :

1. Interpretation

2. Memory

3. Exposure

4. Attention

(A) 4, 3, 1, 2 (B) 3, 2, 1, 4

(C) 3, 4, 1, 2 (D) 4, 3, 2, 1

38. Match the following :

List – I (Motivational Models)

1. Economic Model

2. Learning Model

3. Psychoanalytic Model

4. Organisational Model

List – II (Elements)

a. Attractive Design

b. Inspiration

c. Sex

d. Cost of Product

Codes:

1 2 3 4

(A) a b c d (B) b c d a

(C) c d a b (D) b d c a

39. Match Item – I with Item – II :

Item – I (Type of Control)

I. Annual Plan Control

II. Profitability Control

III. Efficiency Control

IV. Strategic Control

Item – II (Prime Responsibility)

1. Line and Staff Management or Marketing Controller

2. Top/Middle Management

3. Marketing Controller

4. Top Management/ Marketing Auditor

Codes:

I II III IV

(A) 2 3 1 4 (B) 1 3 2 4

(C) 2 1 4 3 (D) 2 3 4 1

40. Which of the following statement is true?

(A) A brand name is a part of brand which can be vocalised.

(B) A brand is usually composed of a name and mark of a product.

(C) Brand means a name, term and symbol or a mix thereof used to identify the product of a firm and to distinguish.

(D) All of the above

41. The term inventory includes

(A) the stock of raw materials only.

(B) the stock of finished goods only.

(C) the stock of raw materials and goods required for production in a factory or finished goods for sales.

(D) none of the above.

42. Statement – I : Operations research seeks to replace intuitive decision making for large complex problems with an approach that identifies the optimal or best alternative through analysis.

Statement – II : Operations Managers have adopted the approaches and techniques of operations research to improve their decision-making.

(A) Both statements I & II are true.

(B) Both statements I & II are false.

(C)Statement I is true but statement II is false.

(D)Statement II is true but statement I is false.

43. ________ is used for analyzing capacity planning decisions.

(A) Break-even Analysis

(B) Present-value Analysis

(C) Simulation and Waiting Line Analysis

(D) All the above

44. Match the following :

List – I

a. To co-ordinate work centre schedules by

showing the progress of each job

b. The goal of continuous improvement in every

phase of manufacturing

c. Optimal quantity asked to supply that minimises total annual stocking costs

d. End product or service of a conversion system

e. The number of arrivals waiting to be serviced

List – II

i. EOQ

ii. Queue length

iii. Gantt Chart

iv. Kaizen

v. Output

Codes:

a b c d e

(A) iii iv i v ii (B) i ii iii iv v

(C) v iv ii iii i (D) ii iii iv i v

45. Match the following :

List – I

a. Any physically identifiable part of a project

b. The terminal point of an activity

c. The longest chain in the Network

d. Logically and sequentially connected arrows and nodes

List – II

i. Network

ii. Event

iii. Activity

iv. Critical path

Codes:

a b c d

(A) i ii iii iv (B) iii ii iv i

(C) ii iv i iii (D) iv i ii iii

46. For nominal data, the only measure of central tendency, that can be applied is

(A) Arithmetic mean (B) Harmonic mean

(C) Median (D) Mode

47. Tukey Kramer Test is applied when

(A) there is significant difference between means of two groups.

(B) there is significant difference between means of three groups.

(C) there is no significant difference between means of two groups.

(D) there is no significant difference between the means of three groups.

48. The steps taken to solve a problem are given below. Arrange them in the correct order :

(i) Analyse (ii) Test

(iii) Implement (iv) Evaluate

(v) Document (vi) Design

(vii) Develop

Codes:

(A) (i), (vi), (vii), (ii), (v), (iii), (iv)

(B) (i), (ii), (iii), (iv), (v), (vi), (vii)

(C) (i), (vi), (iii), (ii), (iv), (v), (vii)

(D) (i), (vi), (vii), (iii), (ii), (iv), (v)

49. Arrange the steps given below in the proper order in the process of selection of samples :

(i) Determining sample size

(ii) Specifying sampling method

(iii) Selecting samples

(iv) Defining the population

(v) Developing sample frame

Codes:

(A) (iv), (i), (v), (ii), (iii)

(B) (iv), (v), (ii), (i), (iii)

(C) (iv), (v), (i), (ii), (iii)

(D) (iv), (i), (v), (iii), (ii)

50. Match the following :

Column – A

a. Device that connects two dissimilar communication networks.

b. Device that connects two similar networks.

c. Device used to boost the strength of a signal.

d. Device for performing signal transformation between terminal devices and communication circuits.

Column – B

i. Modem

ii. Repeater

iii. Bridge

iv. Gateway

Codes:

	a	b	c	d
(A)	iii	iv	ii	i
(B)	iv	iii	ii	i
(C)	ii	iii	iv	i
(D)	iv	iii	i	ii

51. In reference Part-A and Part-B, which statement is correct?

Part 'A': Strategy is the action plan for achieving organisational objectives.

Part 'B': It is the bridge between the present and desired future.

Statement:

(A) Both Part 'A' and 'B' are correct.

(B) Both Part 'A' and 'B' are incorrect.

(C) Part 'A' is only correct.

(D) Part 'B' is only correct.

52. Match the following :

Table – I

a. Horizontal diversification

b. Vertical diversification

c. Concentric diversification

d. Conglomerate diversification

Table – II

i. New product in new market

ii. New product, current market

iii. Movefirms suppliers or customers business

iv. New product closely related to current product in new market

Codes:

	a b c d		
(A)	i ii iii iv	(B)	iii iv ii i
(C)	ii iii i iv	(D)	ii iii iv i

53. Goals-driven planning is best explained by

(A) planning to overcome critical issues that thwart attempts to be more customer-focused.

(B) hard to come up with good indicators and gather reliable base line data.

(C) carefully managed to focus on solutions.

(D) none of the above.

54. Which organisational structure is considered most complex ?

(A) Functional structure

(B) Divisional structure

(C) Strategic Business Unit (SBU) structure

(D) Matrix structure

55. Statement – I : A nation's competiveness depends on the capacity of its industry to innovate and upgrade.

Statement – II : Companies gain advantage against the world's best competitors because of pressure and challenge.

(A) Both statements I and II are correct.

(B) Both statements I and II are incorrect.

(C) Statement I is correct, but statement II is incorrect.

(D) Statement I is incorrect, but statement II is correct.

56. Brain storming is a group creativity exercise designed to come up with_______.

(A) number of solutions to a single problem

(B) two solutions to a single problem

(C) three solutions to two problems

(D) many solutions to many problems

57. Four core themes of innovation are

(A) recognising the opportunity, finding the resources, developing the venture and creating value.

(B) finding the resources, developing the venture, recognizing the opportunity and creating value.

(C) developing the venture, creating value, recognising the opportunity and finding the resources.

(D) creating the value, recognizing the opportunity, developing the venture and finding the resources.

58. The main activities of SISI (Small Industries Services Institutes) are

(A) Assistance/Consultancy to prospective Entrepreneurs

(B) Assistance/Consultancy to exiting units

(C) (A) and (B)

(D) Assistance/Consultancy and incentives to existing units

59. Five steps of small business development shall occur in the order of

(A) Resource Maturity – Existence – Success – Survival – Takeoff

(B) Success – Existence – Survival – Takeoff – Resource Maturity

(C) Existence – Survival – Success – Takeoff – Resource Maturity

(D) Existence – Success – Survival – Resource Maturity – Takeoff

60. Which is not a socio-economic rationale for promoting SSI in India?

(A) Export Promotion

(B) Employment Generation

(C) Offering competition to large scale industry

(D) Labour intensive

61. A set of processes, customs, policies, laws and institutions, that affects the way in which a corporation is directed, administered or controlled in order to facilitate the interest of stake-holders is known as

(A) Corporate Social Responsibility

(B) Corporate Governance

(C) Corporate Sustainability

(D) Environmental Ethics

62. "We must maintain in good order the property, we are privileged to use, protecting the environment and natural resources" is known as

(A) Protecting business environment

(B) Social responsibility of business

(C) Maintaining good property

(D) Protect natural resources

63. Assertion (A) : The Securities and Exchange Board of India has made Listing Agreement tough to ensure good corporate governance among the companies listed on Indian Stock Exchange.

Reasoning (R) : In the absence of Clause 49, the listed companies may ignore the interest of stakeholders.

(A) (A) and (R) both are correct and (R) is right explanation of (A).

(B) (A) is correct, but (R) is not the correct explanation of (A).

(C) (R) is correct, but (A) is not the right assertion.

(D) Both (A) and (R) are incorrect.

64. A system of control is implemented to assist in aligning the incentives of managers with those of shareholder is known as

(A) Corporate Governance

(B) Government Control

(C) Director of Company

(D) Shareholders

65. Which of the following combination is suitably attributed to the statement that stakeholders should expect fair return on their investment?

(i) Optimization of Profit

(ii) Social Responsibility of Business

(iii) Competition Theory of Business

(iv) Walter's Theory

(A) (i), (ii) and (iii) (B) (ii), (iii) and (iv)

(C) Only (i) and (ii) (D) Only (iii) and (iv)

66. The member countries of WTO have moved to "Product Patent Regime" under

(A) TRIMs (B) TRIPs

(C) SAPTA (D) BOP

67. Which of the following is not an element of logistics system?

(A) Nature of product

(B) Availability of infrastructure

(C) Quality of product

(D) Government policies

68. €/$ exchange rate goes from € 1 = $0.93 to €1 = $0.99. This indicates

(A) Dollar appreciation of 6.45%

(B) Dollar depreciation of 6.45%

(C) Dollar appreciation of 6.06%

(D) Dollar depreciation of 6.06%

69. Statement I: Fixed exchange rate system is disadvantageous.

Statement II : The government can alter the exchange rates.

(A) Statement I is correct, but statement II is incorrect.

(B) Statement I is incorrect, but statement II is correct.

(C) Statement I and statement II both are correct.

(D) Statement I and statement II both are incorrect.

70. Which of these is not a form of preshipment finance?

(A) Advance against export bills sent on collection.

(B) Advances against incentives receivable from Government.

(C) Packing credit.

(D) Pre-shipment credit in foreign currency.

71. Under which of the following exchange rate systems, exchange rates are either held constant or allowed to fluctuate only within very narrow boundaries ?

(A) Fixed exchange rate system.

(B) Freely floating exchange rate system.

(C) Managed float exchange rate system.

(D) Pegged exchange rate system.

72. The degree to which, a firm's present value of future cash flows can be influenced by exchange rate fluctuations is referred to as

(A) Economic exposure

(B) Transaction exposure

(C) Translation exposure

(D) Accounting exposure

73. Bid/ask spread of a foreign currency can be computed by which of the following formulae?

(A)Bid Rate – Ask Rate Ask Rate

(B)Ask Rate – Bid Rate Ask Rate

(C)Bid Rate – Ask Rate Bid Rate

(D)Ask Rate – Bid Rate Bid Rate

74. Match the items given in Column–I with most appropriate options given in Column–II

Column – I

(a) Conditions imposed by a Government in respect of foreign investment

(b) Information with commercial value

(c) Monopoly right granted by law

Column – II

(i) Patents

(ii) Intellectual Property Right

(iii) TRIMs

Codes:

	(a)	(b)	(c)
(A)	(iii)	(i)	(ii)
(B)	(iii)	(ii)	(i)
(C)	(ii)	(iii)	(i)
(D)	(ii)	(i)	(iii)

75. Match the following :

List – I (Statements)

I. Countries which follow a unified informal tariff but different external tariff.

II. Countries which follow a unified internal and external tariff system.

III. Countries which follow a unified internal and external tariff and allows free movement of factors of production.

IV. Countries which follow a unified internal and external tariff and allows free movement of factors of production plus having common economic and monitoring policy and common currency.

List – II (Terms)

i. Customs Union

ii. Common market

iii. Free trade area

iv. Economic union

Codes:

	I	II	III	IV
(A)	iii	i	iv	ii
(B)	iii	ii	iv	i
(C)	iii	ii	i	iv
(D)	iii	i	ii	iv

UGC- NET-MANAGEMENT-PAPER-III-JUNE 2013-ANSWER KEYS

1 B	16 C	31 A	46 D	61 B
2 A	17 B	32 B	47 B	62 B
3 B	18 D	33 B	48 A	63 A
4 D	19 D	34 C	49 C	64 A
5 C	20 C	35 B	50 B	65 C
6 C	21 C	36 C	51 A	66 B
7 A	22 D	37 C	52 D	67 C
8 D	23 B	38 D	53 D	68 D
9 B	24 B	39 A	54 D	69 C
10 D	25 A	40 D	55 C	70 A
11 B	26 B	41 C	56 A	71 A
12 B	27 D	42 A	57 A	72 A
13 B	28 B	43 D	58 C	73 B
14 D	29 B	44 A	59 C	74 B
15 C	30 A	45 B	60 C	75 D

---000---

UGC-NET-MANAGEMENT-PAPER-II-SEPTEMBER-2013

1. The sum of the value of all final goods and services produced within a country and net factor income from abroad is termed as

(A) GNP (B) Nominal GDP

(C) NNP (D) Real GDP

2. If a firm raises Rs.1,00,000 by the issue of debentures at 10%, repayable after 10 years, the rate of return that equates the present value of cash inflows with the present value of cash outflows is referred to as

(A) Explicit cost (B) Implicit cost

(C) Specific cost (D) Future cost

3. The major objective of economists to monopolies is

(A) lack of technological progress in such industries.

(B) the dangerous impact on democratic government.

(C) the inability in an industry where there is a single producer.

(D) the tendency to restrict output and charge higher price.

4. **Statement I :** Demand for acommodity refers to quantity of the commodity demanded at a certain price during any particular period of time.

Statement II : Contraction of demand is the result of increase in the price of the goods concerned.

(A) Both I & II are correct.

(B) Both I and II are incorrect.

(C) I is correct and II is incorrect.

(D) II is correct and I is incorrect.

5. Match the items given in List-I with most suitable options given in List-II.

List – I

(a) Rate of discount which equates the net present value to zero.

(b) Ratio of present value of cash inflows to the cash outflow.

(c) Percentage of annual net income earned on average fund invested in a project.

(d) Investment divided by annual net cash inflow.

List – II

(i) Payback period

(ii) Internal Rate of Return

(iii) Profitability Index

(iv) Average Rate of Return

Codes:

(a) (b) (c) (d)

(A) (iii) (ii) (iv) (i) (B) (iii) (ii) (i) (iv)

(C) (ii) (iii) (iv) (i) (D) (ii) (iii) (i) (iv)

6. The process through which individuals attempt to determine the causes behind others' behaviour is known as

(A) Perception (B) Attitude

(C) Attribution (D) Social identity theory

7. Which theory of human motivation focuses on personal perceptions of the performance process?

(A) Adam's Theory of Inequality

(B) McClelland's Need Theory

(C) Vroom's Expectancy Theory

(D) Alderfer's ERG Theory

8. Annual Reports, Balance Sheets, Brochures and Advertisements in organisational communication are the means to aim at

(A) Influencing (B) Image building

(C) Group building (D) Credibility building

9. Match the following :

List-I

a. Attitudes

b. Job Satisfaction

c. Prejudice

d. Stereo types

List-II

1. Beliefs that individuals possess certain characteristics because of their membership in certain groups.

2. Negative attitude toward the members of specific groups, based solely on the fact that they are members of those groups.

3. Positive or negative attitudes held by individuals toward their jobs.

4. Relatively stable clusters of feelings, beliefs and behavioural intentions toward specific objects, people or institutions.

Codes:

a b c d

(A) 1 2 3 4 (B) 2 3 4 1

(C) 3 4 1 2 (D) 4 3 2 1

10. Match the following:

List-I

a. Delegating

b. Situational theory

c. Grid training

d. Participative Leadership

List-II

1. A function of a situation wherein a leader is effective only when the style used to influence and alter the situation is appropriate.

2. Low nurturing and low regulating behaviour.

3. A function of a situation wherein a leader permits subordinates to take part in decision making and permit them a considerable degree of autonomy.

4. A multi step process designed to cultivate concern for people and concern for production.

Codes:

a b c d

(A) 1 2 3 4 (B) 2 1 4 3

(C) 3 2 4 1 (D) 4 3 1 2

11. On-the-job training methods are not based on

(A) Demonstration methods

(B) Interactive methods

(C) Vestibule Training methods

(D) Apprentice training method

12. Minimum wage means

(A) Wage sufficient to ensure the workman food, shelter, clothing, frugal comfort and provision for evil days.

(B) Wages paid in proportion to workman's work efficiency.

(C) A wage sufficient to satisfy the workman's basic needs.

(D) A sum of money paid under contract by an employer to a workman for services rendered.

13. Which of the following statement is true?

(A) Profit sharing is an agreement freely entered into by which the employees receive share fixed in advance from the organization's profits.

(B) An experiment in profit shares on a wide scale would therefore be definitely undertaking a voyage of an unchartered sea.

(C) Profit distribution under a profit sharing plan are used to fund employee retirement plans.

(D) All of the above.

14. Performance appraisal includes

(A) Check reviews done by the supervisors.

(B) review his performance in relation to the objectives and other behaviours.

(C) Promote employees for self appraisal.

(D) All of the above.

15. Match the following :

List-I

a. Human Resource Strategy

b. Compensation

c. Flexitime

d. Management by Objectives

List-II

1. A goal-directed approach in which workers and their supervisors set goals together for the upcoming appraisal period.

2. Time during which employees can choose not to be at work.

3. A legally required benefit that provides medical care, income continuation and rehabilitation expenses.

4. A firm's deliberate use of human resources to help it to gain or maintain an edge against its competitors.

Codes:

a b c d

(A) 1 2 3 4 (B) 4 3 2 1

(C) 2 3 4 1 (D) 3 4 1 2

16. In which case, The acquirer puts pressure on the management of the target company by threatening to make an open offer, the board capitulates straight away and agrees for settlement with the acquirer for change of control.

(A) Poison Put (B) Bear Hug

(C) Poison Pill (D) None of the above

17. Which of the following method of incorporation of risk in the capital budgeting decision framework is useful for situations in which decisions at one point of time also affect the decisions of the firm at some later date?

(A) Certainty Equivalent Approach

(B) Probability Distribution Approach

(C) Risk-adjusted Discount Rate Approach

(D) Decision-tree Approach

18. In which of the approach, the market value of the firm depends upon the EBIT and the overall cost of capital:

(A) Net Income Approach

(B) Net Operating Income Approach

(C) Modigliani-Miller Approach

(D) None of the above

19. Which is the assumption of Modigliani and Miller approach to cost of capital?

(A) The firms can be classified into homogeneous risk class.

(B) The capital markets are assumed to be perfect.

(C) All investors have the same expectations from a firm's net operating income which is necessary to evaluate the value of a firm.

(D) All of the above.

20. Match the following:

List – I (Functions of Finance)

a. Financial Statements

b. Administration of Tax

c. Internal Audit

d. Budgeting

List – II (Significance)

1. Check on Financial Activities

2. Reduction of Tax Liability

3. Allocation of Fund

4. Income Statement

Codes:

a b c d

(A) 1 2 3 4 (B) 4 3 2 1

(C) 4 2 1 3 (D) 2 3 4 1

21. A deliberate and careful choice of organization, product, price promotion, place strategies and policies best define the concept of:

(A) Marketing Mix

(B) Product Mix

(C) Market Penetration

(D) Market Segmentation

22. Rational motives in buying process are explained as

(A) Motives based on careful, logical reasoning and self acceptance.

(B) Motives based on sensual satisfaction, fear and entertainment.

(C) Activity buyer adopts to satisfy buying needs.

(D) All of the above.

23. Which of the following combination, according to hierarchy of effects model is correct?

(A) Awareness – Liking – Knowledge – Conviction – Preference – Purchase.

(B) Awareness – Knowledge – Liking – Preference – Conviction – Purchase.

(C) Awareness – Liking – Knowledge – Conviction –Purchase – Preference.

(D) Awareness – Preference – Knowledge – Liking – Preference – Purchase.

24. This consists of two lists of statements or terms and the candidate has to match an item in one list with an item in the other.

List – I (Statement)

I. Brands which are evaluated for the purchase decision.

II. Brands which are considered by the buyer for evaluation.

III. Brands which are disliked and avoided.

IV. Brands which the buyer is aware but is indifferent towards it.

List – II (Terms)

1. Consideration set

2. Evoked set

3. Inept set

4. Inert set

Codes:

I II III IV

(A) 2 3 1 4 (B) 1 2 3 4

(C) 2 1 3 4 (D) 2 1 4 3

25. "Marketing concept is the recognition on the part of management that all business decisions at the firm must be made in the light of customer needs and wants, hence that all marketing activities must be under one supervision and that all activities of a firm must be coordinated at the top in the light of market requirements." Who said it?

(A) Lazo and Carton (B) Schwartz G

(C) King RL (D) C.P. Mc Namara

26. Which one of the following is not a qualitative forecasting method?

(A) Educated guess

(B) Executive Committee Consensus

(C) Delphi method

(D) Linear regression method

27. **Statement I :** Mean (–X) chart do not give the desired result about process variability.

Statement II : Range (R) chart monitors process variability.

(A) Statement I is correct, but Statement II is false.

(B) Statement II is correct, but Statement I is false.

(C) Both Statements I and II are correct.

(D) Both Statements I and II are false.

28. Which one is not a part of control charts for attributes?

(A) P-chart (B) σ-chart

(C) np-chart (D) c-chart

29. There are different phases in a Operations Research Project. They are

(i) Research phase

(ii) Action phase

(iii) Judgement phase

The correct sequence of these phases is

(A) (i), (ii), (iii) (B) (iii), (i), (ii)

(C) (ii), (iii), (i) (D) (iii), (ii), (i)

30. The Graphical method can be used to solve":

(A) A Linear Programming Problem (LPP) with all integer data.

(B) A LPP with two decision variables.

(C) Any LPP.

(D) A transportation problem with two origins and two destinations.

31. A vendor can make a profit of ` 3,000 with a probability of 0.4 or make a loss of ` 1,000 with a probability of 0.6. What is his expected profit?

(A) ` 600 (B) ` 800

(C) ` 1,000 (D) ` 500

32. If the sample size is less than 50, which non parametric test can be used to test the independence of attributes?

(A) Chi-square test

(B) Fisher Irwin test

(C) Cochran Q test

(D) Kruskal Wallis test

33. Match the items given in List-I with most appropriate options given in List-II.

List – I

(a) Centroid Method

(b) Hierarchical Method

(c) Relationship between a single metric dependent and two or more independent variables

(d) The main and interactive effects of categorical variables on multiple dependent interval variables.

List – II

(i) Multiple Regression

(ii) Factor Analysis

(iii) MANOVA

(iv) Cluster Analysis

Codes:

(a) (b) (c) (d)

(A) (iv) (ii) (i) (iii) (B) (ii) (iv) (i) (iii)

(C) (ii) (iv) (iii) (i) (D) (iv) (iii) (i) (ii)

34. Identify the window not associated with SPSS.

(A) Editor (B) Syntax

(C) Output (D) Format Cells

35. Match the items given in Column-A with the items given in Column-B.

Column – A

(i) Pattern recognition

(ii) Data Scrubbing

(iii) Operational system

Column - B

(a) A process to upgrade the quality of the data before it is moved into a data warehouse.

(b) A system that is used to run the business in real time and is based on current data.

(c) A critical success factor in data mining of large data store.

Codes:

(a) (b) (c)

(A) (ii) (iii) (i) (B) (iii) (ii) (i)

(C) (i) (ii) (iii) (D) (ii) (i) (iii)

36. In BCG Matrix which division represents the organization's best long-run opportunities for growth and profitability?

(A) Question marks (B) Stars

(C) Cash Cows (D) Dogs

37. In a comprehensive strategy formulation framework which matrix reveals the relative attractiveness of alternative strategies and thus provides objective basis for selecting specific strategies.

(A) SPACE Matrix

(B) SWOT Matrix

(C) QSPM Matrix

(D) Competitive Profile Matrix (CPM)

38. Stage 2 of strategy formulation consists of

(A) EFE Matrix, the IFE Matrix and the Competitive Profile Matrix (CPM).

(B) SWOT Matrix, SPACE Matrix, BCG Matrix, the Internal- External (IE) Matrix, and the Grand Strategy Matrix.

(C) Quantitative Strategic Planning Matrix (QSPM).

(D) EFE Matrix, the IFE Matrix and Quantitative Strategic Planning Matrix (QSPM).

39. Match the following:

Term

(a) Strategy

(b) Vision

(c) Mission

(d) Objectives

Explanation

1. Enduring statements of purpose that distinguish one business from other simple firms.

2. Specific results that an organization seeks to achieve.

3. What do we want to become?

4. Means by which long term objectives will be achieved.

Codes :

a b c d

(A) 4 3 1 2 (B) 4 2 3 1

(C) 1 3 2 4 (D) 1 2 3 4

40. Match the following :

List – I

(a) Italian Culture

(b) American Culture

(c) Mexican Culture

(d) Japanese Culture

List – II

(i)Importance on group loyalty and consensus

(ii) Employment as workers of those who are agreeable, respectful and obedient rather than innovative, creative and independent.

(iii) Willing to do business with individuals they do not know.

(iv)A culture where in you do not soften up executives with praise before criticize.

Codes:

(a) (b) (c) (d)

(A) (i) (ii) (iii) (iv) (B) (iv) (iii) (ii) (i)

(C) (ii) (iii) (iv) (i) (D) (iii) (iv) (i) (ii)

41. An Entrepreneur who is dominated more by customs, religions, traditions and past practices and he is not ready to take any risk is called as:

(A) Drone Entrepreneur

(B) Adoptive Entrepreneur

(C) Fabian Entrepreneur

(D) Innovative Entrepreneur

42. "Poverty is an artificial creation. It does not belong to human civilization and we can change that and can make people come out of poverty through redesigning our institutions and policies." This preamble refers to:

(A) Women Entrepreneurship

(B) Corporate Entrepreneurship

(C) Social Entrepreneurship

(D) None of the above

43. Match the following:

List – I (Subject)

(a) Entrepreneurship

(b) Marketing

(c) Inventory Management

(d) HR Planning

List – II (Technique)

(i) Innovation

(ii) Promotion Mix

(iii) Reorder Level

(iv) Appraisals

Codes:

a b c d

(A) (i) (iii) (ii) (iv) (B) (i) (ii) (iii) (iv)

(C) (iv) (iii) (ii) (i) (D) (iv) (ii) (iii) (i)

44. _______ means identifying and imitating the best in the world at specific tasks and functions.

(A) Quality circle

(B) Outsourcing

(C) Bench marking

(D) Continuous Improvement

45. Match the following :

List – I

(a) Action planning

(b) Accountability

(c) Working the plan

(d) Reviewing the progress

List – I

(i) New Actions are taken and old habits are broken.

(ii) It is the periodic review of what has already been executed.

(iii) It is the art of delegation to implement a business plan.

(iv)Making decisions relating to the order in which the Business plan is implemented.

Codes:

(a) (b) (c) (d)

(A) (ii) (iii) (iv) (i)

(B) (iv) (iii) (i) (ii)

(C) (i) (iv) (iii) (ii)

(D) (iii) (iv) (ii) (i)

46. Which of the following duties is not a general duty of directors of a company?

(A) Duty of good faith

(B) Duty of care

(C) Duty to attend Board Meeting

(D) Duty not to delegate

47. The principles to be followed for corporate social responsibility are:

(A) involvement of stakeholders.

(B) maintaining transparency in reporting.

(C)independent verification of policies and outcome.

(D) All of the above.

48. Match the following :

List – I

(a) Value

(b) Unethical behaviour

(c) Indian ethos

(d) Environmental responsibility

List - II

(i) Aham Brahmasmi

(ii) Recycling Waste

(iii)Bribery

(iv) Trust worthiness

Codes:

(a) (b) (c) (d)

(A) (i) (iii) (ii) (iv)

(B) (iv) (iii) (i) (ii)

(C) (ii) (iii) (iv) (i)

(D) (i) (iii) (iv) (ii)

49. The obligation of an organisation behave in a ethical way is known as

(A) Knowledge about ethics

(B) Social responsibility of business

(C) Organisational behaviour

(D) Business without ethics

50. Identify the correct sequence of steps in a value identification process:

(i) Define the role of executive in leading the staff.

(ii) Learn about and discuss the power of shared values.

(iii) Obtain consensus that the leaders are committed to creating value based work place.

(iv) Provide written material the executives can share with their reporting staff.

Codes:

(A) (i), (ii), (iii) and (iv)

(B) (iv), (ii), (iii) and (i)

(C) (ii), (iii), (i) and (iv)

(D) (ii), (iii), (iv) and (i)

UGC-NET-MANAGEMENT-PAPER-II-SEPTEMBER-2013-ANSWER KEYS

Q01 A	Q11 B	Q21 A	Q31 A	Q41 C
Q02 A	Q12 C	Q22 A	Q32 B	Q42 C
Q03 D	Q13 D	Q23 B	Q33 B	Q43 B
Q04 A	Q14 D	Q24 B	Q34 D	Q44 C
Q05 C	Q15 B	Q25 B	Q35 A	Q45 B
Q06 C	Q16 B	Q26 D	Q36 B	Q46 C
Q07 C	Q17 D	Q27 C	Q37 C	Q47 D
Q08 B	Q18 B	Q28 B	Q38 B	Q48 B
Q09 D	Q19 D	Q29 B	Q39 A	Q49 B
Q10 C	Q20 C	Q30 B	Q40 B	Q50 C

---000---

UGC-NET-MANAGEMENT-PAPER-III-SEPTEMBER-2013

1. The elasticity of demand is greater than unity, when

(A) Percentage change in demand is equal to the percentage change in price.

(B) Percentage change in demand is more than the percentage change in price.

(C) Percentage change in demand is less than the percentage change in price.

(D) There is change in price.

2. GDP includes which of the following measures?

(A) The size of a population that must share a given output within one year.

(B) The negative externalities of the production process of a nation within one year.

(C) The total monetary value of all final goods and services produced within a nation within one year.

(D) The total monetary value of goods and services including barter transactions within a nation in one year.

3. If the equation $y = 5 + 0.6x$ was graphed, the

(A) Slope would be – 5

(B) Vertical intercept would be + 0.6

(C) Slope would be + 5

(D) Slope would be + 0.6

4. Match the following:

List – I

(a) The producers will offer more of a product at a higher price.

(b) The quantum that producers want to sell is equal to the quantum that consumers want to buy.

(c) The sensitivity of consumers to price changes.

(d) Percentage change in quantity demanded to percentage change in price.

List – II

(i) Market in equilibrium

(ii) Law of supply

(iii) Co-efficient of price elasticity of demand.

(iv) Price elasticity of demand

Codes:

(a) (b) (c) (d)

(A) (ii) (i) (iii) (iv) (B) (iv) (i) (ii) (iii)

(C) (ii) (iv) (iii) (i) (D) (ii) (i) (iv) (iii)

5. Statement I: The slope of an indifference curve is the Marginal Rate of Substitution in the consumption (MRSc), which is increasing.

Statement II: The slope of the budget line is ratio of the prices of two goods and is the Marginal Rate of Substitution in exchange (MRSe)

(A) Statement I and II are correct.

(B) Statement I is correct, but II is incorrect.

(C) Statements I and II are incorrect.

(D)Statement I is not correct, but IIis correct.

6. Forming a fixed opinion or attitude towards a single person or object is termed as:

(A) Perceptual defense (B) Stereo typing

(C) The Halo effect (D) The perceptual set

7. Which of the following best describes the theory X ?

(A) People are committed to their responsibilities.

(B) Motivation is a result of rational behaviour towards attaining goals.

(C) The perceived relationship between a given level of efforts and an expected performance.

(D) None of the above.

8. Hawthorne experiments were conducted at:

(A) Hawthorne Electric Company

(B) Western Electric Company

(C) General Electric Company

(D) Eastern Electric Company

9. Match the following:

OD Interventions

(a) OD Cube

(b) Consul cube

(c) Intervention families

(d) Four quadrants

Grouping Term Proposed by

(i) French and Bell

(ii) Freneh and Bell

(iii) Blake and Mouton

(iv) Schmuck and Miles

Codes:

(a) (b) (c) (d)

(A) (iv) (iii) (ii) (i) (B) (iii) (iv) (ii) (i)

(C) (ii) (i) (iii) (iv) (D) (i) (ii) (iv) (iii)

10. Match the following:

List-I

(a) Stability

(b) Strategy

(c) Synergy

(d) Span of control

List-I

(i) Number of subordinates that report to one supervisor.

(ii) The whole is greater than the sum of its parts.

(iii) Plans for the allocation of firm's scarce resources to reach identified goals in time.

(iv) Employees should not be moved frequently from one job to another

Codes:

(a) (b) (c) (d)

(A) (iv) (iii) (ii) (i) (B) (iii) (iv) (i) (ii)

(C) (ii) (iii) (iv) (i) (D) (i) (ii) (iii) (iv)

11. Role of Human Resource Manager is

(A) Advisory

(B) Mediator Role

(C) Representative Role

(D) All of the above

12. Which statement is true?

(A) Job analysis is a group of positions, that are similar as to kind and level of work.

(B) A promotion is the advancement of an employee to a better job better in terms of greater responsibilities, more prestige or status, greater skill and especially, increase rate of pay or salary.

(C) A promotion is the vertical transfer of an employee.

(D) All of the above

13. Job is defined as:

(A) Set of activities performed in the organization.

(B) Set of activities similar as to kind of work.

(C) Set of position similar as to nature and kind of work.

(D) None of these.

14. The benefit of paraphrasing in Employee Appraisal is that it:

(A) Suggests interest and active listening.

(B) Clarify and convey to the rater that you are listening actively.

(C) Shows that you are trying to understand the emotional aspect of the work place.

(D) All of the above.

15. An employee can be laid off when the organization has:

(A) Acquired labour more than the required.

(B) Purchased raw material more than the immediate required.

(C) Breakdown of machinery.

(D) All of the above.

16. Match the following:

List – I (Items of HRM)

(a) Human Resource Planning

(b) Selection

(c) Advancement

(d) Industrial relations

List – II (Features)

(i) Forecast man power needs based strategies of the trend.

(ii) Use the criteria and measures developed to match individual skills in the job requirements.

(iii) Promotion.

(iv) Amicable and harmonious working in the organization.

Codes:

(a)(b)(c)(d)

(A) (i) (ii) (iii) (iv) (B) (i) (iv) (iii) (ii)

(C) (iii) (i) (iv) (ii) (D) (iv) (i) (iii) (ii)

17. Which one of the following is a disadvantage of having expatriate employees to staff international subsidiaries?

(A) Brings cultural similarities with parent company.

(B) Gives employees a multinational orientation.

(C) Attempts to establish a foreign culture to the company.

(D) Provides broader global perspective.

18. Whistle Blowing is the situation wherein an employee

(A) Causes indiscipline in the organization.

(B) Discloses other employees' illegal immoral or illegitimate activities.

(C) Discloses the employer's illegal immoral or illegitimate activities.

(D) All of the above.

19. Distributive bargaining may be explained as

(A) Bargaining wherein both parties are willing to negotiate over wages, hours and conditions of employment.

(B) Bargaining that focuses on convincing the other party that the cost of disagreeing with the proposed terms would be very high.

(C) Bargaining that focuses on convincing the other party that the benefits of agreeing with the proposed terms would be very high.

(D) None of the above.

20. Match the following:

List – I

(a) Balancing Equity

(b) Internal Equity

(c) Individual Equity

(d) External Equity

List – II

(i) The perceived fairness of the pay structure within a firm.

(ii) The perceived fairness in pay relative to what other employers are paying for the same type of labour.

(iii) The perceived fairness in establishment of internal and external pay equity.

(iv)The perceived fairness of individual pay decisions.

Codes:

	(a)	(b)	(c)	(d)
(A)	(iii)	(iv)	(ii)	(i)

(B) (i) (ii) (iii) (iv)

(C) (ii) (iv) (i) (iii)

(D) (iv) (i) (iii) (ii)

21. Which of the below features is not wealth maximization objective of Financial Management?

(A) Considers both quantity and quality dimensions of benefits.

(B) Based on the concept of cash flows generated by the decision rather than accounting profit.

(C) Decision should be oriented to the maximization of profits.

(D) Focus is on the value to the owners or suppliers of equity capital.

22. Financial Breakeven Level of EBIT is one at which

(A) EPS is one (B) EPS is infinite

(C) EPS is zero (D) EPS is negative

23. Which of the following is not considered by Miller-Orr Model?

(A) Variability in cash requirement

(B) Cost of transaction

(C) Holding cash

(D) Total annual requirement of cash

24. If the minimum stock level and average stock level of material A are 4000 and 9000 units respectively, what is the Reorder quantity?

(A) 8000 units (B) 10,000 units

(C) 11,000 units (D) 9,000 units

25. According to Lintner Model, factors affecting dividend of current year are:

(A) DPS of previous year, EPS, target pay-out ratio and adjustment rate.

(B) EBIT, interest rate and retention ratio.

(C) P/E ratio, retention ratio and pay-out ratio.

(D) E/P ratio, pay-out ratio and rate of interest on it.

26. Given the sales volume, which of the following would lead to an increase in contribution margin?

(A) Variable cost remains same.

(B) Variable cost per unit decreases.

(C) Variable cost per unit increases.

(D) Fixed cost increase.

27. Vertical merger represents merger of firms

(A) engaged in the same line of business.

(B) at different stages of production in an industry.

(C) engaged in unrelated line of activities.

(D) All of the above.

28. A high debtors turnover ratio indicates

(A) low amount tied upon debtors

(B) increase in sales turnover

(C) efficient conversion of debtors into cash

(D) (A) & (C)

29. Match the following:

List – I (Statement)

I. Independent floating exchange rate.

II. Exchange rate depending entirely on market forces.

III. Floating exchange rate regime where the monetary authorities interfere in the foreign exchange market for stabilizing exchange rate.

IV. Non convertible paper currency.

List – II (Term)

1. Fiat money

2. Clean float

3. Managed float

4. Free float

Codes:

I II III IV

(A) 2 4 3 1 (B) 4 3 1 2

(C) 1 3 4 2 (D) 2 1 3 4

30. Projected cash flows change with changes in projected demand, price, cost of production, cost of capital, etc. All these changes are accommodated in a random manner by:

(A) Sensitivity Analysis

(B) Simulation Technique

(C) Decision - Tree

(D) None of the above

31. When a firm has diversified in unrelated products, it is called:

(A) Scramble diversification

(B) Related diversification

(C) Product mix

(D) Product line simplification

32. Which of the following condition is true about determinants and strengths of positioning strategy?

(A) There should be competition warranting positioning.

(B) The market segment to be served should be sizeable and profitable.

(C) The market segment should be able to effectively receive communication messages transmitted by the company.

(D) All of these.

33. Delphi method of estimating future demand for a product or service is associated with:

(A) Past sales analysis

(B) Expert opinion method

(C) Market test method

(D) Composite of sales force opinion

34. A method for deriving the utility values that consumers attach to varying levels of a product attribute is called

(A) product analysis

(B) conjunctive analysis

(C) conjoint analysis

(D) market price analysis

35. Two statements are given below :

Statement I: Opinion leaders who provide product related information to the buyer and assist him or her in buying is called market mover.

Statement II: Opinion leaders who understand the buyer's personal needs and use situations and aid the buyer is called purchase pal.

Choose the correct option about the statements from the options given below:

(A) Statement I alone is correct.

(B) Statement II alone is correct.

(C) Both statements are wrong.

(D) Both statements are correct.

36. Two statements are given below relating to the consumer brand selection model.

Statement I: As per disjunctive decision rule consumers set a minimum acceptable cut off level for each attribute and choose the first alternative that meets the minimum standard for all selected attributes.

Statement II: As per lexicographic decision rule consumers choose the best brand on the basis of its perceived most important attribute.

Choose the correct option about the statements from the options given below:

(A) Statement I alone is correct.

(B) Statement II alone is correct.

(C) Both statements are correct.

(D) Both statements are wrong.

37. Arrange the following stages in the industrial buying process in the sequential order :

1. General need description
2. Supplier search
3. Problem recognition
4. Performance review
5. Order route specification
6. Product specification
7. Proposal solicitation
8. Supplier selection

(A) 3-1-2-6-7-8-5-4

(B) 3-2-1-7-6-5-8-4

(C) 3-1-6-2-7-5-8-4

(D) 3-1-6-2-7-8-5-4

38. Match the following:

List – I (Statements)

(a) Attacking the weak spots of the competitor

(b) Avoiding the main competitor and attacking easier ones.

(c) Attacking the leader on several areas.

(d) Attacking the leader on its strong area.

List – II (Terms)

(i) Flank attack

(ii) Frontal attack

(iii) Encirclement attack

(iv) By Pass attack

Codes:

(a) (b) (c) (d)

(A) (i) (iv) (iii) (ii) (B) (i) (iii) (ii) (iv)

(C) (ii) (iii) (i) (iv) (D) (iii) (i) (ii) (iv)

39. Match the following:

List – I (Statements)

(a) A market situation in which many competitors offering undifferentiated products or services.

(b) A market situation in which many competitors offering differentiated products or services.

(c) A market situation in which a small number of large firms offering differentiated and standardized products or services.

(d) A market situation in which only one firm provides a certain products or services.

List – II (Terms)

(i) Pure monopoly

(ii) Oligopoly

(iii) Monopolistic competition

(iv) Pure competition

Codes:

(a)(b)(c)(d)

(A) (iv) (iii) (i) (ii) (B) (iv) (ii) (iii) (i)

(C) (iv) (iii) (ii) (i) (D) (iii) (iv) (ii) (i)

40. Which one of the three basic approaches used customarily explaining the Marketing System?

(A) Commodity, institutions and functional approach.

(B) Commodity, functional risks, management approach.

(C) Product, service mix, functional and institutional approach.

(D) None of the above.

41. Statement I: One of the key factors impacting on Production Managers is that the country's borders no longer provide protection from foreign imports due to globalization.

Statement II: To succeed in global competition, Production Management of Companies must make a commitment to innovate products and services with high quality at low prices.

(A) Both the statements are incorrect.

(B) Statement I is correct, but II is incorrect.

(C) Statement I is incorrect, but II is correct.

(D) Both statements are correct.

42. Positioning the production system means

(A) Selecting the type of product design.

(B) Selecting the type of production processing system.

(C) Selecting the type of finished good inventory policy for each product group.

(D) All of the above.

43. Which one is not a part of control charts for variables?

(A) –X-chart (B) R-chart

(C) σ-chart (D) C-chart

44. Match the following:

List – I

(a) Decision making under conditions of certainty.

(b) Decision making under conditions of risk.

(c) Decision making under conditions of uncertainty.

List – II

(i) When the outcomes are known but the probabilities of outcomes are not known.

(ii) When elements of decision problem are clear and also the outcomes of different alternatives are known.

(iii) When outcomes probabilities are known.

Codes:

(a)(b)(c)

(A) (i) (ii) (iii) (B) (ii) (iii) (i)

(C) (iii) (ii) (i) (D) (i) (iii) (ii)

45. Edwards Deming, one of the Quality Gurus, introduced a concept of cycle for continuous improvement of quality. The cycle consists of

(i) Act (ii) Plan

(iii) Do (iv) Check

The correct order of this cycle of activities is

(A) (i), (iii), (iv), (ii)

(B) (ii), (iv), (iii), (i)

(C) (ii), (iii), (iv), (i)

(D) (i), (ii), (iii), (iv)

46. Variable which has a strong contingent effect on the independent dependent variable relationship is referred to as:

(A) Extraneous variable

(B) Intervening variable

(C) Moderating variable

(D) None of the above

47. Coefficient of determination (R2) indicates

(A) percentage of variation in the dependent variable that can be explained by independent variable.

(B) Percentage of variation in the dependent variable that cannot be explained by independent variable.

(C) percentage variation in the independent variable that can be explained by dependent variable.

(D) Percentage variation in the independent variable that cannot be explained by the dependent variable.

48. If $\alpha = 0.05$ and $\beta = 0.10$, the power of that hypothesis test is:

(A) 0.15 (B) 0.90

(C) 0.85 (D) 0.95

49. Match the following:

List – A

(a) Connects a very large number of devices and spans across a dispersed geographical location covering many cities.

(b) Encrypted communication tunnels with access control and user authentication

(c) Physical or geometric arrangement of the network influenced by the physical connections of links and nodes.

(d) Local area network technology that sends communication through radio frequency signals.

List – B

(i) Topology

(ii) Ethernet

(iii) Wide Area Network

(iv) Virtual Private Network

Codes:

(a) (b) (c) (d)

(A) (iii) (i) (iv) (ii)

(B) (iv) (iii) (i) (ii)

(C) (iii) (iv) (ii) (i)

(D) (iii) (iv) (i) (ii)

50. From the statements given below, choose the correct answer.

Statement I: One of the important aspects of IT enabled services is value addition.

Statement II : ERP and CRM are examples for IT enabled services.

Codes:

(A) Statements I and II are correct.

(B) Statement I is correct, but II is incorrect.

(C) Statements I and II are incorrect.

(D) Statement I is incorrect, but II is correct.

51. Statement 1: The IE Matrix is similar to the BCG Matrix in that both tools involve plotting organisation divisions in a schematic diagram.

Statement 2 : The BCG Matrix requires more information about the divisions than the IE matrix.

(A) Statements 1 and 2 both are correct.

(B) Statements 1 and 2 both are incorrect.

(C) Statement 1 is correct, but statement 2 is incorrect.

(D) Statement 1 is incorrect, but statement 2 is correct.

52. Match the following :

List–I

(a) Individual within (Psychological)

(b) Group within (Normative)

(c) Individual outside (implied)

(d) Group outside (Social)

List–II

(i) Interpretations that third parties make regarding contractual terms.

(ii) Broad beliefs and obligations associated with society's culture.

(iii) Beliefs that individuals hold, regarding promises made, accepted and relied on between and another themselves.

(iv) The shared psychological contract that emerges when members of a social group/organization/ work unit hold.

Codes:

(a) (b) (c) (d)

(A) (i) (ii) (iii) (iv)

(B) (iii) (iv) (i) (ii)

(C) (ii) (iii) (iv) (i)

(D) (iv) (iii) (ii) (i)

53. Statement 1 : SWOT involves specifying the objectives of the business venture or project and identifying the internal and external factors that are favourable and unfavourable to achieve that objective.

Statement 2 : Setting the objectives should be done after the SWOT analysis has been performed.

(A) Both the statements are correct.

(B) Statement 1 is correct, but statement 2 is incorrect.

(C) Statement 1 is incorrect, but statement 2 is correct.

(D) Both the statements are incorrect.

54. The three disciplines of WTO agreements are

(A) International trade in goods, international transactions in services and protection of intellectual property rights.

(B) International trade in goods, international transaction in services and protection of interest of MNCs.

(C) International trade in goods, international transaction in services and protection of interest of P.S. units.

(D) International trade in goods, international transaction in services and protection of interest of Domestic Government.

55. Substitute question marks with appropriate terms :

Products Markets

Existing Products

New Products

Existing Market

1 – ? 2 – ?

New Market 3 – ? 4 – ?

Options:

(A) 1- Market development

2- Market penetration

3- Product development

4- Diversification

(B) 1-Market penetration

2-Product development

3-Market development

4-Diversification

(C) 1-Market development

2-Diversification

3-Market penetration

4-Product development

(D) 1-Market penetration

2-Product development

3-Diversification

4-Market development

56. Arrange the Entrepreneurial motivation factors on the basis of proper sequences.

(A) Need for achievement, Locus of control, vision, desire for independence, passion and drive.

(B) Locus of control, vision, desire for independence, passion, drive and need for achievement.

(C) Vision, desire for independence, passion, drive, locus of control and need for achievement.

(D) Desire for independence, need for achievement, locus of control, vision, passion and drive.

57. The main function of venture capitalist is to

(A) Provide funds to the steps necessary to establish the commercial viability of a new product, process or service.

(B) Provide funds at all stages of marketing of new product, process or service.

(C) Provide funds at all stages of production of a new product, process or a service.

(D) Provide funds at all stages of Research of a new product, process or a service.

58. An industrial unit, according to RBI, is sick if:

(A) incurred cash loss in the previous accounting year.

(B) likely to incur loss in the following year.

(C) current ratio is less than 1 : 1 with weak debt: equity ratio.

(D) All of the above.

59. SIDBI has been entrusted with the responsibility of:

(A) Providing financial assistance to all sectors.

(B) Developing medium and large scale industry.

(C) Providing incentives to medium scale industry.

(D) Developing and supporting small business.

60. Match the following:

List – I (Innovation)

(a) Paradigm innovation

(b) Position innovation

(c) Product innovation

(d) Process innovation

List – II (Refers to)

(i) Changes in the things which are organization offers.

(ii) Changes in the ways in which they are created and delivered.

(iii) Changes in 8the context in which the products/ services are introduced.

(iv) Changes in the underlying mental models which frame what the organization does.

Codes:

(a) (b) (c) (d)

(A) (iv) (iii) (i) (ii)

(B) (i) (ii) (iii) (iv)

(C) (iii) (iv) (ii) (i)

(D) (ii) (i) (iv) (iii)

61. A Business Organization deals with product/service and has relationship with stakeholder which is being considered a part of 'management discipline' is known as:

(A) Maximisation of Wealth

(B) Business Ethics

(C) Relationship Management

(D) Optimisation of Profits

62. Lawrence Kohlberg, in his six stage model of cognitive development, explains :

(A) Why people make different decisions in similar ethical situations?

(B) How people make decisions based on the stage of cognitive moral development?

(C) Both of the above.

(D) None of the above.

63. The Board of Directors can appoint

(i) Additional Director

(ii) Causal Director

(iii) Alternative Director

(iv) Nominee Director

(A) (i), (ii) and (iii)

(B) (ii), (iii) and (iv)

(C) (iii), (iv) and (i)

(D) (iv), (i) and (ii)

64. **Assertion (A):** The poor compliance to environmental regulations is attributed to tax enforcement despite regulatory framework.

Reasoning (R): The Government is not capable of enforcing full compliance.

(A) (A) is correct and (R) is the right explanation of (A).

(B) (A) and (R) both are correct, but (R) is not the right explanation of (A).

(C) (A) is correct, but (R) is not correct.

(D) Both (A) and (R) are incorrect.

65. Match the following:

List – I

(a) Work ethics

(b) Values

(c) Environmental responsibility of a business

(d) Corporate Social Responsibility

List – II

(i) includes taking care of issues like air and water pollution, toxic waste disposal etc.

(ii) is an organisation's obligation to benefit society in ways that transcend the prime business objectives of maximizing profit.

(iii) is a characteristic attitude of a group towards what constitutes the morality of work.

(iv) determine the overall personality of an individual and the organization that he is working for.

Codes:

(a) (b) (c) (d)

(A) (i) (ii) (iii) (iv)

(B) (iv) (iii) (ii) (i)

(C) (iii) (iv) (i) (ii)

(D) (ii) (i) (iv) (iii)

66. The degree to which the value of future cash transactions can be affected by exchange rate fluctuations is referred to as:

(A) Economic exposure

(B) Transaction exposure

(C) Translation exposure

(D) None of the above

67. Forward Premium or Discount can be computed by which of the following formulae?

(A) Spot rate – Forward rate Spot rate × 360

Future point in time

(B) Spot rate – Forward rate Forward rate ×360 Future point in time

(C) Forward rate – Spot rate Forward rate × 360 Future point in time

(D) Forward rate – Spot rate Spot rate × 360

Future point in time

68. Which of the following is not a product technology transfer?

(A) Collaboration in R and D.

(B) Transfer of product designs and technical specifications.

(C) Feed back on product performance.

(D) Provision of machinery and equipment to suppliers.

69. Stops involved in settling disputes under WTO are given below. Arrange them in correct order.

(i) Panel set up and appointment of panelists.

(ii) Final Report to WTO members.

(iii) Final Report to partners.

(iv) Consultations, mediations, etc.

(v)Adoption of Report by Dispute Settlement Body.

Codes:

(A) (i), (iv), (ii), (iii), (v)

(B) (iv), (i), (ii), (iii), (v)

(C) (iv), (i), (iii), (ii), (v)

(D) (i), (ii), (iii), (v), (iv)

70. From the statements given below, choose the correct answer :

Statement I: To become a global corporation, a firm passes through different stages, viz, capturing markets abroad, establishing joint venture/subsidiaries abroad, developing into MNCs and moving towards global mode of operation.

Statement II: Government support is not a pre-requisite for the successful globalization of the business.

(A) Statement I is correct and II is wrong.

(B) Statements I and II are correct.

(C) Statements I and II are wrong.

(D) Statement I is wrong, but II is correct.

71. The main function(s) of WTO is/are :

(A) To handle trade disputes constructively.

(B) To help promote peace among business community.

(C) To provide rules that make life easier for all people involved in Foreign trade.

(D) All of the above.

72. Which of the following transactions reflect economic exposure but not transaction exposure?

(A) A firm's imports/exports denominated in local currency.

(B) A firm's imports/exports denominated in foreign currency.

(C) Interest received from foreign investments.

(D) Interest owed on foreign funds borrowed.

73. Which of the following is the rate at which a banker is willing to buy foreign currency?

(A) Ask rate (B) Offer rate

(C) Bid rate (D) Spread rate

74. Euro dollars are:

(A) Currency (B) Deposits

(C) Bonds (D) Equity

75. When an Indian exporter avails post shipment credit in foreign currency, what is taken as the bench mark for the interest rate?

(A) Bench mark lending rate (B) MIBOR

(C) LIBOR (D) Indian Bank rate

UGC-NET-MANAGEMENT-PAPER-III-SEPTEMBER-2013-ANSWER KEYS

1 B	16 A	31 A	46 C	61 B
2 C	17 C	32 D	47 A	62 B
3 D	18 C	33 B	48 B	63 A
4 A	19 B	34 C	49 D	64 D
5 D	20 D	35 D	50 A	65 C
6 C	21 C	36 B	51 C	66 B
7 D	22 C	37 D	52 B	67 B
8 B	23 D	38 A	53 A	68 D
9 A	24 B	39 C	54 A	69 C
10 A	25 A	40 B	55 B	70 A
11 D	26 B	41 D	56 A	71 D
12 B	27 B	42 D	57 A	72 A
13 C	28 D	43 D	58 D	73 C
14 B	29 A	44 B	59 D	74 B
15 C	30 B	45 C	60 A	75 C

---000---

MH-SET-MANAGEMENT-PAPER-II-FEBRUARY-2013

1. During the 3rd stage of Law of variable proportions:

(A)MP is negative (B)AP is negative

(C)AP is rising (D)TP is constant

2. A firm is a price takes under:

(A)Monopoly

(B)Duopoly

(C)Monopolistic competition

(D)Perfect competition

3. Which of the following is not one of the six sectors considered by CSO while computing National Income?

(A)Primary Sector (B) Social Sector

(C)Foreign Sector (D) Secondary Sector

4. The root cause of the current European Crisis is:

(A)Currency crisis

(B)Unsustainable Sovereign Debt

(C)Stagflation

(D)Over heatedness

5. The law of Demand does not assume constancy of:

(A)Price of the concern commodity

(B) Price of other commodity

(C) Consumers income level

(D)Tastes and preferences

6. 'Hyrogliphs' essentially is:

(A)Picture language (B) Script

(C)Notations (D) Gestures

7. What can drive conflict?

(A)Environment

(B) Goals

(C)Unreasonable rules

(D)Angry people

8. Downward communication means:

(A)Transmission of ideas or information from executives to the subordinates.

(B) Transmission of information from manager to manager.

(C) Transmission of ideas or information from worker to worker.

(D) Transmission of ideas or information from worker to superior.

9. Morale largely depends on:

(A)Physical well-being

(B) Monetary well-being

(C) Mental well-being

(D) Sociological well-being

10. Need for achievement theory was put forth by:

(A) A. H. Maslow (B)F. Herzberg

(C)D. McClelland (D)Clayton Alderfer

11. Voluntary Retirement is operated as a part of:

(A)Promotion policy (B)Exit policy

(C)Deployment (D) Lockout

12. Referral system in HRM relates to:

(A)Referring a supplier by another supplier

(B) Referring a consultant for organizational development

(C) Referring a candidate for job by existing employee

(D)Referring a leader to lead employees.

13. Principle of Natural Justice in Domestic Enquiry ensures:

(A)Justice in time

(B)Justice through Advocate

(C)Opportunity given to the delique employee being heard

(D)Payment of subsistence allowance

14. Collective Bargaining is handled between:

(A)Employees and Employees

(B) Employees and Trade union

(C) Trade union and Advocate

(D) Employer and Employees

15. Which of the following describes the process by which individuals come to agreement?

(A)Negotiation (B) Avoidance

(C)Accommodation (D) Fighting actively

16. Market Model was proposed by:

(A)Harry Markowitz (B)P.Samuelson

(C)Philip Kotler (D)William Sharpe

17. If coupon rate=required rate, the value of the bond would be equal to its:

(A)par value (B)redumption value

(C)issued value (D)YTM

18. If r<k, the payout of dividend should be 100% according to:

(A)Modigliani-Miller (B)Walter

(C)Du-Pont (D)Ezra Solomen

19. Altman proposed a model of predicting:

(A)financial distress

(B)market failure

(C)high performance of firm

(D)insolvency of the firm

20. Present value of annuity is calculated by discounting it by:

(A)Cost of Capital (B)IRR

(C)Zero coupon rate (D)YTM

21. According to Kotler,………….is the easiest marketing mix element to adjust.

(A)Price (B)Channel

(C)Product features (D)Promotion

22. AIDA Model is used mainly for:

(A)Promotion Decision

(B)Product Decision

(C)Pricing Decision

(D)Redressal of Grievances

23. The process of turning marketing strategies into specific day-to-day,month-to-month actions is called:

(A)Analysis (B) Implementation

(C)Planning (D) Control

24. The first concept of marketing is:

(A)Selling Concept

(B)Relationship Marketing Concept

(C)Product concept

(D)Societal Marketing Concept

25. Which of the following is an example of impulse buying?

(A)Buying mutual funds

(B)Buying ice-creams

(C)Buying a car

(D)Buying a house

26. Negative inventory means:

(A)excess stock of materials

(B)material in transit

(C)no. of units we owe to customers

(D)no. of defectives

27. Statistical methods of quality control can:

(A)help to decide number of defectives

(B)prevent defects in products

(C)improve customer satisfaction

(D)determine process capability

28. Product mix is done on a single assembly line for the purpose of:

(A)reducing WIP inventory

(B)meeting varied choice of customers

(C)leveling workload and reducing idle time

(D)reduce cost per unit

29. Basis for production, planning and control is:

(A)Accurate demand estimate

(B)Capacity installed

(C)Need to beat competition

(D)Finance available

30. Operations Management will never be successful if they ignore:

(A)Govt. Rules (B) Latest Technology

(C)Demand Pattern (D) Quality of Goods

31. Which of the following is known as 'Information Superhighway'?

(A)Intra-net (B) Extra-net

(C)i-pad II (D)Internet

32. Power of a hypothesis test indicates:

(A)How fast the hypothesis gives answer

(B)How well the hypothesis is stated

(C)Probability of rejecting null hypothesis when it is false

(D)Probability of accepting null hypothesis when it is true

33. While editing the completed questionares the researcher does *not* check for:

(A)Consistency (B)Accuracy

(C)Homogenity (D)Brevity

34. Alternate Hypothesis for Ho:$\mu \leq 50$ is:

(A)$H_1:\mu \geq 50$ (B) $H_1:\mu = 50$

(C) $H_1:\mu>50$ (D) $H_1:\mu \neq 50$

35. Which of the following is *not* a qualitative research technique?

(A)Focus group (B) Survey technique

(C)Depth interview (D) Word association

36. Who of the following was instrumental in developing a framework for classifying countries based on the work-related values (Dimension of Cultures) that predominate in respective countries, globally?

(A)W.Chan Kin (B)Renee Monborgue

(C)G.Hofstede (D)C.K.Prahlad

37. Relying on the typology suggested by Michael Porter, business strategies could be classified into 3 types. Which of the following *does not* fit into their classification?

(A)Cost leadership (B) Focus

(C)Industry Attractiveness (D)Differentiation

38. Which of the following data is *not* required for competition analysis?

(A)Recorded data (B) Observable data

(C)Opportunistic data (D) In-House data

39. Which of the following is the *correct* sequence for strategy formulation?

(A)Mission→Objectives→Strategy→Policy

(B)Strategy →Vision → Mission → Budget

(C)Vision→ Mission→ Enivornmental Analysis → Budget

(D)Vision → Mission → Strategy → Budget

40. A survey of nearly 50 corporations in a variety of countries and industries found 3 most highly rated benefits of strategic management .Which of the following is not of those 3 benefits?

(A)Clearer sense of strategic vision for the firm

(B)Internationalism of strategy, vision and mission

(C)Sharper focus ofn what is strategically important

(D)Improved understanding of a rapidly changing environment

41. ....is the non-traditional source of finance for entrepreneurs.

(A)Bank Loan (B) Venture Capital

(C)Friends and Relatives (D) SIDBI

42. Who is the author of the book 'Innovation and Entrepreneurship'?

(A)Philip Kotler (B)Michael Porter

(C)Peter Drucker (D)C.K.Prahlad

43. Which of the following is not one of the four elements in innovation process?

(A)New Knowledge Creation

(B)Commercial Application

(C)Organizing Resources

(D)Analytical Planning

44. Which of the following is not a phase in business plan preparation?

(A)Setting business goals

(B)Locating Resources

(C)Analysing Competitions

(D)Developing the labour market

45. The entrepreneurial activity is most prevalent in:

(A)United States (B) Japan

(C)Germany (D) Great Britian

46. The elements of good corporate governance in India have been laid down by:

(A)ICSI (B)IOD

(C)ICWAI (D)ICAI

47. Which of the following is not a stakeholder in the CSR?

(A)Creditors (B)Enivornment

(C)Government (D)SEBI

48. Which of the following key force influences a person's ethics?

(A)Nationality

(B)Education

(C)Family influences

(D)Relationship of the firm to the employee.

49. A personality measure of the strength of a person's convictions is:

(A)locus of control (B)locus of value

(C)ego strength (D)bench strength

50. Greed is the cornerstone of human values under:

(A)Socialism (B)Capitalism

(C)Mixed economy (D)Racialism

MH-SET-MANAGEMENT-PAPER-II-FEB-2013- ANSWER KEYS

Q01 A	Q11 B	Q21 A	Q31 D	Q41 B
Q02 D	Q12 C	Q22 A	Q32 C	Q42 C
Q03 B	Q13 C	Q23 B	Q33 D	Q43 A
Q04 B	Q14 D	Q24 C	Q34 C	Q44 D
Q05 A	Q15 A	Q25 B	Q35 B	Q45 A
Q06 A	Q16 D	Q26 C	Q36 C	Q46 A
Q07 B	Q17 A	Q27 D	Q37 C	Q47 D
Q08 A	Q18 B	Q28 C	Q38 D	Q48 C
Q09 C	Q19 A	Q29 A	Q39 A	Q49 C
Q10 C	Q20 A	Q30 B	Q40 B	Q50 B

---000---

MH-SET-MANAGEMENT-PAPER-III-FEBRUARY-2013

1. Which of the following statements is true?

(A)MC is a subset of incremental cost

(B) Incremental cost is a subset of MC

(C) MC is a subset of sunk cost

(D) Sunk cost is a subset of incremental cost

2. In order to predict human behaviour, it is best to supplement your intuitive opinions with information derived in what fashion?

(A)Common sense

(B)Systematic inquiry

(C)Direct observation

(D)Organisational theory

3. ____________absolves the employer's liability under the Maternity Benefit Act and Workmen's Compensation Act.

(A)Employees Provident Fund Act, 1952

(B)Industrial Employment (Standing Order) Act, 1946

(C)Employee State Insurance Act, 1948

(D)Industrial Dispute Act, 1947

4. As per Pecking-Order theory, the first financing choice in order of preference is:.

(A)Retained earnings

(B)Non-convertible debt

(C)Preference shares

(D)Equity.

5. Identify the incorrect pair of "Strategy-Approach":

(A)Market Penetration-Increase number of users

(B)Market Development-Sell in new locations

(C)Product Development-Improve technology

(D)Diversification-Convince non-users to use the product

6. Study the following table about various methods of selective inventory control and answer the question at the end of the table:

Inventory Control Methods

(a)ABC Analysis

(b)XYZ classification

(c)VED Analysis

(d)FSN classification

Concepts

(i)Speed of movement of inventory

(ii)Combination of unit cost and consumption pattern

(iii)Unit cost of inventory

(iv)Criticality of inventory item

Which of the following indicates the correct match of the methods and the concepts?

Code:

	(a)	(b)	(c)	(d)
(A)	(i)	(ii)	(iii)	(iv)
(B)	(ii)	(iii)	(iv)	(i)
(C)	(iii)	(i)	(ii)	(iv)
(D)	(iv)	(i)	(iii)	(ii)

7. Organize the following in the correct sequence:

(1)Knowledge

(2)Business Intelligence

(3)Data

(4)Information

Choose the right option:

(A)(1),(2), (3),(4)

(B) (1),(4), (2),(3)

(C) (3),(4), (1),(2)

(D) (3),(4), (2),(1)

8. Which of the following is not a force in the Porters Five Forces Model?

(A)Bargaining Power of Buyers

(B) Bargaining Power of Suppliers

(C)Industry Rivalry

(D) Bargaining Power of Dealers

9. Which of the following is not among the thrust areas of policy for SSIs in India?

(A)Resources availability

(B)Rehabilitation of sick SSI units

(C)Timely and adequate credit availability

(D)Quality improvement support

10. On the basis of the statement given below, answer the following question:
Puffery in advertisement is:

(1)An exaggerated claim in an advertisement that is considered as illegal

(2) An exaggerated claim in an advertisement that is considered as legal

(3)Usage of claims like 'best', 'greatest', 'finest', for a product or service

(4)Based on the concept of 'Placebo Effect'

(A)Options (1) and (3) are correct

(B) Options (1) and (2) are correct

(C) Options (1) ,(3)and (4) are correct

(D) Options (2),(3) and (4) are correct

11. The process of deciding what positions the firm will have to fill is called:

(A)Recruitment (B) Selection

(C)Personnel Planning (D) Interviewing

12. Training evaluation criteria include all but:

(A)Reactions (B) Results

(C)Relevance (D) Behavior

13. Match the pair for the following and indicate the correct option:

List-I

(a)Constant growth

(b)Profitability index

(c)Modigliani-Miller approach

(d)Leveraged buyout

List-II

(i)Capital Budgeting Technique

(ii)Capital Structure Theory

(iii)Corporate Restructuring

(iv)Share valuation model

(A)(a)-(i),(b)-(ii), (c)-(iii),(d)-(iv)

(B) (a)-(ii),(b)-(iii), (c)-(iv),(d)-(i)

(C) (a)-(iii),(b)-(ii), (c)-(i),(d)-(iv)

(D) (a)-(iv),(b)-(i), (c)-(ii),(d)-(iii)

14. Why is international trade significant among countries?

(A)For promoting the world peace

(B)For decreasing cost of production

(C)For difference in the taste and preference among nations

(D)To earn foreign exchange

15. The component of an effective performance management process that explains each employees role in terms of his or her day-to-day work is called:

(A)Role clarification

(B)Goal alignment

(C)Developmental goal setting

(D)Direction sharing

16. Which concept shows the overall output generated at a given level of input?

(A)Cost function

(B)Production function

(C)Marginal rate of technical substitution

(D)Isocost

17. Balance Score Card emphasizes on:

(A)only the strategy

(B)the importance of measuring business performance

(C)critical incident method

(D)intellectual capital

18. Inputs to the selection process include all but:

(A)Job applicants

(B)Human resource planning

(C)Supervision

(D)Job analysis

19. Which of the following approaches to dividend valuation assumes a constant non-growing dividend stream?

(A)Constant growth model

(B)Variable growth model

(C)Zero growth model

(D) Gordon model

20. When a manager focuses on making whatever products are easy to produce, and then trying to sell them, that manager has a-----------------orientation.

(A)Marketing (B) Production

(C)Sales (D) Profit

21. Organize the following activities in production planning process in the correct order:

(1)Master Production Schedule

(2)Raw Material Purchase Orders

(3)Aggregate Production Planning

(4)Material Requirements Planning

Choose the right option:

(A)(3),(1), (2),(4)

(B) (3),(1), (4),(2)

(C) (4),(3), (2),(1)

(D) (1),(2), (3),(4)

22. The standard error of the mean will decrease:

(A)As the sample size increases

(B) As the sample standard deviation increases

(C)To a point and then remains constant

(D) As the sample size decreases

23. A dog division stands for:

(A)A low market growth rate but high market share

(B) A high market growth rate and high market share

(C) A high market growth rate and low market share

(D) A low market growth rate and low market share

24. What are the areas of primary focus for "Public Entrepreneurship"?Which deals with revitalization of government agencies?

(A)Creation, Innovation

(B)Customer, Creation

(C)Customer, Efficiency

(D)Innovation, Efficiency

25. Choose the correct option:
Performance Review System, that makes managers rate people on normal distribution curve:

(A)Is ethically correct

(B)Values the full development of peoples potential

(C)Creates misalignment between values and practices

(D)Increases productivity of employees

26. Which of the following techniques is least susceptible to personal biases?

(A)Rating scales (B) Check lists

(C)Forced choices (D) BARS

27. Based on the statement below select the correct answer:

Hybrid Systems:

(1)As similar in operations to the multiple channel system

(2)Are systems where channel members perform complementary services

(3)Are more verticle

(4)Improve level of performance

(A)Statements (1) and (3) are correct

(B) Statements (1) and (2) are correct

(C) Statements (2) and (4) are correct

(D) Options (2) and (3) are correct

28. Because personal selling is taking on a more prominent role in the corporate marketing mix, selling today:

(A) requires fewer and less intensive communication skills than previously

(B) has become a less attractive career for college graduates

(C)Involves more use of communications and computer technologies

(D)Places greater focus on short-term persuasion, with less emphasis on consultation and problem solving

29. Which is the correct sequence, if we arrange various sources of finance from costliest to cheapest in terms of their cost of capital?

(A)Equity, Retained earnings, Debt, Preference

(B) Retained earnings, Equity, Preference, Debt,

(C)Debt, Equity, Preference ,Retained earnings,

(D) Preference, Debt, Equity, Retained earnings

30. Which of the following is a non-DCF technique?

(A)PI (B)IRR

(C)NPV (D)ARR

31. Which theory considers the possibility of trade between two countries having the same factor endowment and consumer preference?

(A)Comparative advantage theory

(B)Heckscher-ohlin theory

(C)Imitation-gap theory

(D)Absolute advantage theory

32. Role playing is often used to:

(A)Change attitudes (B)Learn skills

(C)Change results (D)Model behaviour

33. A demand curve suggesting unitary elasticity throughout shall be:

(A)a rectangular hyperbola

(B)a straight line parallel to X-axis

(C)a straight line parallel to Y-axis

(D)a negatively sloping straight line of 45° angle

34. A common method of measuring attitudes is by using:

(A) in-depth interviews

(B) observing people's behaviour

(C)systematic differential scales

(D)a lie detector

35. Which of the following is not an enivornmental challenge facing human resources?

(A)Competition for scarce inputs

(B)Governmental rules and regulations

(C)Global competition

(D)Enivornmental activities

36. Assertion(A): Dividing a segment into sub-segments with a distinctive set of traits seeking a special combination of benefits

Reasoning(R): Godrej Company introduced Ezee to target the consumers who wanted mild washing detergent foe woolen clothes.

(A)Both (A) and (R) are correct and (R) is correct explanation of (A)

(B) Both (A) and (R) are correct but (R) is not the correct explanation of (A)

(C)(A) is correct but (R) is incorrect

(D) (A) is incorrect but (R) is incorrect

37. For a 't' distribution, increasing the sample size will affect **:**

(1) degrees of freedom

(2)the 't' ratio

(3)standard error of mean

Chose the correct option:

(A)(1)only (B)(2)only

(C)(3)only (D)(1),(2),and (3)

38. Which of the following sets of activities truly reflects the strategic implementation?

(A)Leadership implementation, Organizational restructuring, Quality monitoring

(B)Resource allocation, Quality monitoring, Management policies, Leadership implementation

(C) Organizational restructuring, Resource allocation, Management policies, Maintainence management

(D) Leadership implementation, Resource allocation, Management policies, Organizational restructuring

39. Which of the following sets of factors should entrepreneurs considers carefully before selecting a new project?

(A)Investment size, Location technology, Market conditions

(B)Investment size, competition, expertise, age, gender

(C)Investment size, Market condition, Gestation period, Expertise

(D)Investment size, Repayment capability, Availability of Loans, Profit margins

40. Which of the following is not a stakeholder of a company?

(A)Employee (B) Customer

(C)Competitors (D) Shareholder

41. Sabbatical means:

(A)Extra pay for not taking sick leave

(B)An extended leave of absence

(C)Benefits for time not worked

(D)Membership-based,non-financial rewards offered to attract and retain employees

42. The gap between what customers expect and what they receive when dealing with a firm is:

(A)Related to the price they paid for something,not its quality

(B)Always positive because the higher of the two values is counted first

(C)One measure of their satisfaction with a firm and its products

(D)Impossible to measure because it is subjective, not objective

43. Which is the correct equation that calculates P(Profit before tax) Assume seliing price per unit=Rs.S, variable cost per unit=Rs.V Number of units sold=U units and Total fixed costs=Rs. F.

(A)P=SV-F (B)P=U(S-V)-F

(C)P=FS-V (D)P=S(V-F)

44. The exports to countries belonging to erstwhile British empire is called:

(A)ASEAN (B) Commonwealth

(C)SAPTA (D) SAARC

45. Which of the following figures represents perfect negative correlation between price and sales of a particular product of a company?

(A)

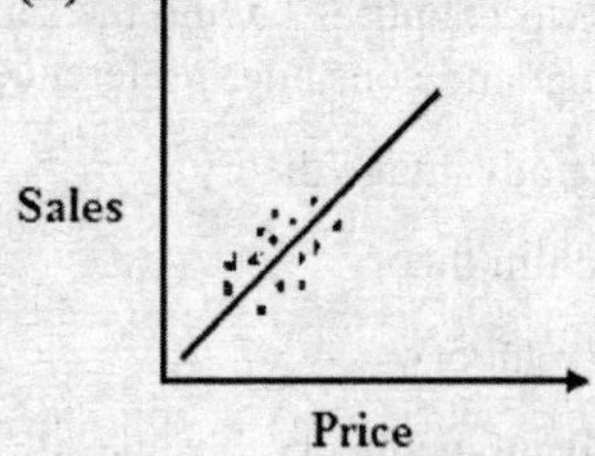

(B)

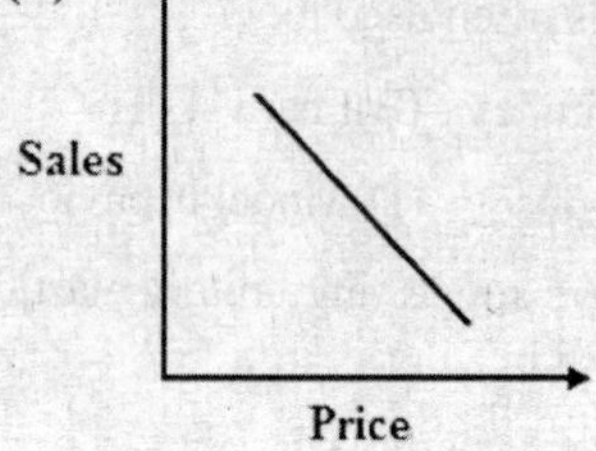

(C)

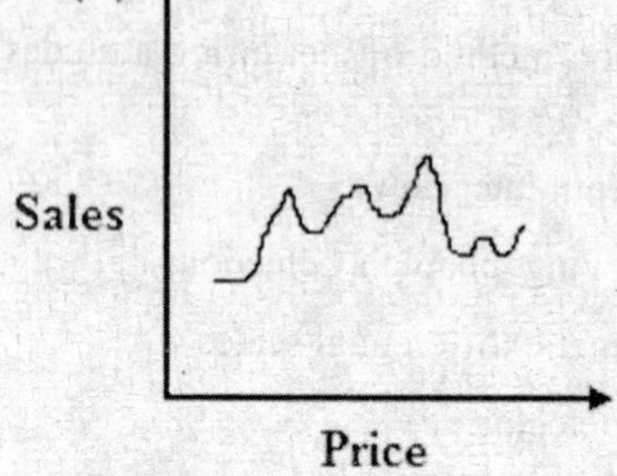

(D)

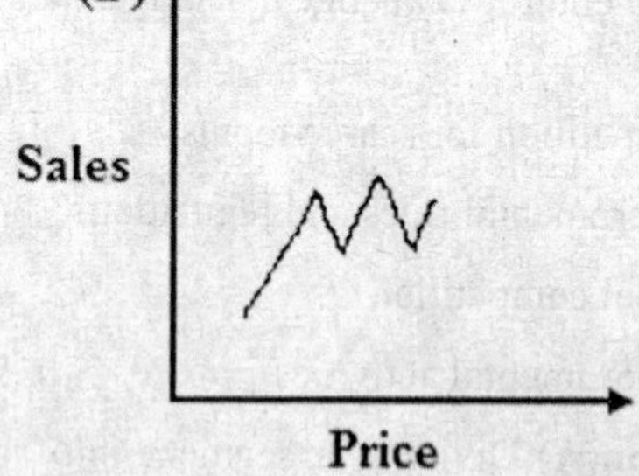

46. Penetration pricing of a product of a firm implies:

(A) low initial price followed by a high price

(B) high initial price followed by a low price

(C) moderate price of a product

(D) fluctuating price of a product

47. Which roles in a group-setting contribute to the socio-emotional bonding of a members and the group's overall success?

(A)facilitative or building role

(B)individualizing

(C)maintainence

(D)blocking

48. Match the correct options:

Graphic Rating Scale:

(A)Evaluation based on key incidents

(B)Rating in behavioural terms

(C)A scale that lists a number of traits and a range of performance for each

(D)Evaluation by ratee

49. Which of the following is not a hypothesis put forward to explain the rationale for issuing bonus shares and stock splits?

(A)Signalling hypothesis

(B)Trading range hypothesis

(C)Attention hypothesis

(D)Alternate hypothesis

50.……describes changes in an individual consumer behavior arising from experience

(A)Modeling (B)Perception

(C)Learning (D)Motivation

51. A problemcan be considered as Linear Programming Problem, if and only if it has:

(1)Objective function

(2)Constraints

(3)Alternative course of action

(4)Latest technology

(A) (1) only (B)(1) and (2)

(C)(1),(2) and (3) (D)(1),(2)and (4)

52. Management Information System usually:

(i)Provides managers with a generalized computing and telecommunication strategy fot problem solving

(ii)Serves managers interested in weekly,monthly and yearly results on various performance parameters

(iii)Performs and records daily routine transactions necessary for conducting business

(A)(i) Only (B) (ii) only

(C)(iii) Only (D) (i) and (ii)

53. Match the following:

Types of organization structure

(1)Functional

(2)Network

(3)Matrix

(4)Territorial

Characteristics

(a)Maximum use of limited functional resources

(b)Adopts to local conditions

(c)Simple communication

(d)More Agile and flexible

(A)(1)-(a),(2)-(c),(3)-(b),(4)-(d)

(B)(1)-(c),(2)-(d),(3)-(a),(4)-(b)

(C) (1)-(b),(2)-(a),(3)-(c),(4)-(d)

(D) (1)-(d),(2)-(b),(3)-(a),(4)-(c)

54. In which of the following types of ownership there is no distinction between the business entity and the owner(s):

(A)Company limited by shares

(B)The co-operative organization

(C)Proprietorship

(D)Joint stock company

55. Select the correct options:

Sarbanes-Oxley Act, 2002 emphasis on:

(A)Environmental Protection

(B)Work-life Balance

(C)Total quality Management

(D)Audit function and financial disclosures

56. Which of the following is not a "Public Relations Function"?

(A)Assess the correct reputation

(B)Audit C.S.R

(C)Conduct Positive image building activities

(D)Identify prospective customers

57. When there is an official increase in exchange rate of the Indian rupee, then it is called-----

(A)Appreciation (B) Deflation

(C)Depreciation (D) Revaluation

58. In case the company goes into liquidation, which of the following is repayable first?

(A)Equity capital

(B)Redeemable Preference Capital

(C)Cumulative preference capital

(D)Debentures

59. Which type of unemployment takes place in the economy when there is a business downward?

(A)Frictional unemployment

(B)Structural unemployment

(C)Cyclical unemployment

(D)Unstructured unemployment

60. Which is the part of every interpersonal relationship?

(A)Conflict (B) Love

(C)Stress (D) Communication

61. Match the correct options:

Suspension:

(A)Actual posting of an employee to a specific job

(B)Termination of the services of an employee

(C)Downward movement of an employee in the organizational hierarchy

(D)Prohibiting an employee from attending work and performing normal duties to him/her

62. The basic objective of financial management is:

(A)Maximization of profits

(B)Maximization of shareholder's wealth

(C)Ensuring financial discipline in the organization

(D)Ensuring returns to debenture-holders

63. Which of the following methods is the most appropriate measure for cost reduction investment projects with unequal lives?

(A)Equivalent annual cost

(B) Equivalent annual NPV

(C) Equivalent present value index

(D)Capital rationing

64. ....is defined as the difference between the benefits a customer sees from a market offering and the costs of obtaining those benefits.

(A)Profit margin (B) Surplus

(C)Customer value (D) Consumer surplus

65. Which of the following is not an application of Markov Analysis?

(A)Brand switching analysis

(B)Accounts receivables problem

(C)Optimal maintenance policy

(D)Product mix decisions

66. Match the following:

Types of Production System

(1)Job type

(2)Mass type

(3)Batch type

(4)Project type

Characteristics

(a)Stationery layout and Unique

(b)Functional Departments and Complicated Material Management

(c)Huge Volume and Standard Design

(d)Large Variety and Less Investment

Choose the correct option:

(A)(1)-(d),(2)-(c),(3)-(b),(4)-(a)

(B) (1)-(a),(2)-(b),(3)-(c),(4)-(d)

(C) (1)-(c),(2)-(d),(3)-(b),(4)-(a)

(D) (1)-(b),(2)-(a),(3)-(d),(4)-(c)

67. The number of telephone calls received per day to a particular telephone number can be best modeled by using the:

(A)Binomial distribution

(B)Uniform distribution

(C)Possion distribution

(D)Normal distribution

68. Fill in the blanks spaces:

Ultimately.........was replaced by the.......on Jan.1, 1995.

(A)G.A.T.T, W.T.O. (B) W.T.O, G.A.T.T

(C)G.A.T.S, W.T.O (D) I.M.F., G.A.T.T

69. "Franchising" is an example of:

(A)Imitiation strategy

(B)Innovation strategy

(C)Broadscope strategy

(D)Marketscope strategy

70. Choose the correct option:

Industrial Policy (1956) declared by the Government of India aimed at establishing:

(A)Capitalistic economy

(B)Socialistic pattern of society

(C)Mixed economy

(D)Democratic economy

71. An adult worker under the Factories Act,1948 is eligible for leave with wages @1 day for every ....days worked during the preceding year.

(A) 50 (B) 20

(C) 15 (D) 240

72. In strategic pricing process, there are various steps undertaken as under:

(i)selecting price method

(ii) selecting the final price

(iii)Studying the competitiors price

(iv)Estimating demand

(v)Selecting the pricing objective

(vi)Estimating cost

Select the correct sequence of steps from the following:

(A)(i)-(v)-(iii)-(ii)-(iv)-(vi)

(B) (v)-(iv)-(vi)-(iii)-(i)-(ii)

(C) (iv)-(iii)-(i)-(ii)-(vi)-(v)

(D) (ii)-(iii)-(v)-(vi)-(iv)-(i)

73. Assume the following facts:

−Risk free return (rf) =7.75%

−Beta (β) =2

−Expected return of investors(r)=16%

What will be the expected returns as per CAPM model?

(A) 4.125% (B) 16.00%

(C) 11.875% (D) 7.75%

74. How can the government of a country reduce its deficit in the BOP for arresting imports and stimulating exports?

(A)Depreciation (B) Deflation

(C)Devaluation (D) Inflation

75. Under the traditional distribution structure in International Marketing, which of the following controls a fixed supply of goods that are sold as high prices to a small group of customers?

(A)Exporter (B) Cartel

(C)Importer (D) Manufacturer

MH-SET-MANAGEMENT-PAPER-III-FEB-2013- ANSWER KEYS

Q1 A	Q16 B	Q31 C	Q46 A	Q61 D
Q2 B	Q17 B	Q32 A	Q47 C	Q62 B
Q3 C	Q18 C	Q33 A	Q48 C	Q63 A
Q4 A	Q19 C	Q34 B	Q49 D	Q64 C
Q5 D	Q20 B	Q35 A	Q50 C	Q65 D
Q6 B	Q21 B	Q36 A	Q51 C	Q66 A
Q7 C	Q22 A	Q37 D	Q52 B	Q67 C
Q8 D	Q23 D	Q38 D	Q53 B	Q68 A
Q9 B	Q24 C	Q39 A	Q54 C	Q69 A
Q10	Q25 C	Q40 C	Q55 D	Q70 B
Q11	Q26 D	Q41 B	Q56 D	Q71 B
Q12	Q27 C	Q42 C	Q57 A	Q72 B
Q13	Q28 C	Q43 B	Q58 D	Q73 C
Q14	Q29 B	Q44 B	Q59 C	Q74 C
Q15	Q30 D	Q45 B	Q60 A	Q75 B

---000---

AP-SET-MANAGEMENT-PAPER-II-2012

1. Product differentiation is a common feature of:

(A) Perfect Competition

(B) Monopoly

(C) Monopolistic Competition

(D) Oligopoly

2. In Growth Share Matrix Question Mark indicates

(A) High Business Growth-High Market Share

(B) High Business Growth-Low Market Share

(C) Low Business Growth-High Market Share

(D) Low Business Growth-Low Market Share

3. The Basic objective of Financial Management is

(A) Maximisation of Profit

(B) Maximisation of Shareholders Wealth

(C) Ensuring Financial discipline in the organisation

(D) None of the above

4. The EOQ inventory model attempts to minimize

(A) The number of items ordered

(B) The number of orders placed

(C) The total inventory costs

(D) The safety stock

5. Select the correct chronological arrangement of the following 'Acts'

1. Minimum Wages Act

2. Workmen's Compensation Act

3. Employee Provident Fund Act

4. Payment of Wages Act

(A) 4,3,2,1 (B) 1,4,3,2

(C) 2,4,1,3 (D) 2,4,3,1

6. Who is a Merchant Middleman?

(A) Stock Broker

(B) Commission Agent

(C) Retailer

(D) Selling Agent of a Company

7. Which of the following is alternatively called Corporate Venturing?

(A) Entrepreneurship

(B) Intrapreneurship

(C) A new product start-up

(D) Venture Capital

8. The following Company is in the news for violation of Corporate Governance through fraudulent practices

(A) Tata Chemicals Ltd.

(B) Reliance Industries Ltd.

(C) Hindustan Unilever Ltd.

(D) Satyam Computers Ltd.

9. Different types of Probability Distribution include

1. Binomial distribution

2. Poisson distribution

3. Normal distribution

4. Exponential distribution

(A) 1 and 2 only

(B) 1, 2 and 3 only

(C) 3 and 4 only

(D) 1, 2, 3 and 4

10. Organizational Behaviour is a

(A) Function of its consequences

(B) Study of character of people

(C) Study of team behavior

(D) Study of management behavior

11. Usually the demand for necessities is

(A) Highly elastic

(B) Highly inelastic

(C) Slightly elastic

(D) Slightly inelastic

12. Match the following :

List – A

(a) How do we succeed

(b) What Business should

(c) How does this unit

List – B

(i) Functional Strategy in this business?

(ii) Business Strategy we are in?

(iii) Corporate Strategy contributes?

(a) (b) (c)

(A) (i) (ii) (iii)

(B) (iii) (ii) (i)

(C) (i) (iii) (ii)

(D) (ii) (iii) (i)

13. A Bond can be issued at a premium, if

(A) Coupon rate is greater than required return

(B) Coupon rate is less than required return

(C) Coupon rate is equal to required return

(D) None of the above

14. The objective of Operations Management is to enhance the performance of an organization in terms of its

(A) Competitiveness

(B) Product quality

(C) Productivity

(D) Overall performance

15. Which of the following is not the principle of Trade Unionism?

(A) Unity is Strength

(B) Equal Pay for equal work

(C) Security of service

(D) Right to lock out

16. Hypothesis is tested in the following research design

(A) Exploratory and Descriptive

(B) Descriptive and Causal

(C) Causal and Exploratory

(D) Experimental and Exploratory

17. Which one of the following is not the reason for the sickness of Small Enterprise?

(A) Lack of Working Capital

(B) Lack of Market Demand

(C) Lack of Competition

(D) Lack of Raw Material

18. The Social Responsibility of a Business is important to

(A) Owners and Investors

(B) Employees

(C) Government

(D) All the above

19. Read the following statements and select the correct combination given there under:

Statement – 1: Linear Programming is a mathematical function.

Statement – 2: Transportation model is one of the part of Linear Programming.

(A) Statement 1 is true but 2 is not true

(B) Statements 1 and 2, both are true

(C) Statement 1 is not true but 2 is true

(D) Both the statements 1 and 2 are not true

20. Personality is determined by:

(A) Heredity

(B) Environment

(C) Situation

(D) All the three above.

21. If total cost function of a firm :

TC=1050+10Q2+8Q, find the marginal cost of the firm when the quantity produced is 15 units

(A) 105 (B) 225

(C) 308 (D) 247

22. Match the following :

List – I (Types of Strategies)

(a) Retrenchment strategy

(b) Combination strategy

(c) Stability strategy

(d) Growth strategy

List – II(Examples)

(i) Reduction

(ii)Filled / used

(iii)Maintain present course

(iv) PLC

(a)(b)(c)(d)

(A) (i) (ii) (iii) (iv)

(B) (iv) (ii) (i) (iii)

(C) (i) (iv) (iii) (ii)

(D) (iii) (i) (ii) (iv)

23. Match the following :

List – I

(a) Number of years required to recover the initial outlay is determined by

(b) A method which uses accounting information for evaluating proposed capital expenditure is

(c) Theoretically correct technique for selection of Investment project is

(d)A technique which ascertains a discount rate that equates the aggregate present values of net cash inflows with that of the aggregate present values of net cash outflows is

List –II

(i) NPV

(ii)Pay Back period

(iii)IRR

(iv)ARR

(a)(b)(c)(d)

(A) (i) (iii) (iv) (ii)

(B) (ii) (iv) (i) (iii)

(C) (i) (ii) (iv) (iii)

(D) (iii) (iv) (ii) (i)

24. The following is used for identifying the total resources required for meeting customers' requirements

(A) Capacity Planning

(B) Process Planning

(C) Inventory Management

(D) Master Production Schedule

25. What describes the tasks, duties and responsibilities of a Job?

(A) Job Analysis

(B) Job Enrichment

(C) Job Description

(D) Job Empowerment

26. Who defined Advertising as 'Any paid form of non-personal presentation and promotion of ideas, goods and services by an identified sponsor'?

(A) Philip Kotler

(B) Peter F. Drucker

(C) Mc Carthy

(D) American Marketing Association

27. Dynamic process of creating incremental wealth by individuals who assume the risks of equity, time and careers, to infuse resources with value for society is referred as

(A) Business Plan

(B) Venture Capital

(C) Business Opportunity

(D) Entrepreneurship

28. 'Ethics' is derived from 'Ethos', a Latin word, which means:

(A) Character

(B) Responsibility

(C) Integrity

(D) Morality

29. The regression lines cut each other at the point of:

(A) Average of X and Y

(B) Average of X only

(C) Average of Y only

(D) Median of X and Y

30. Learning means

(A) Relatively permanent change in the behavior of people

(B) Developing the skills

(C) Improving the knowledge

(D) Changing the habits

31. The average fixed cost curve of a firm is

(A) parallel to the horizontal axis

(B) parallel to the vertical axis.

(C) a 'U' shaped curve

(D) a downward sloping curve from left to right

32. The FOUR functions viz., R & D, Production, Marketing, Sales & Service, through which Value addition occurs, are referred to as

(A) Value added activities

(B) Value addition functions

(C) Primary activities

(D) Secondary activities

33. In terms of relative risk, which of the following is true?

(A) Debt is risky for investors, while equity is risky for firm

(B) Both debt and equity are risky for investors

(C) Both debt and equity are risky for firm

(D) Debt is risky for the firm, while equity is risky for investors

34. A Floor plan for determination and arranging the desired machinery and equipment of a Plant is referred to as:

(A) Plant Location

(B) Plant Lay-Out

(C) Product Design

(D) Process Planning

35. Which of the following is not a method of Performance Appraisal?

(A) 360^0Performance Appraisal

(B) Ranking Method

(C) Graphic Rating Scales Method

(D) Man Power Planning

36. From the following, the 4 Ps of marketing coined originally are:

1. Product 2. Price

3. Packaging 4. People

5. Promotion 6. Place

(A) 1, 2, 3 and 4 (B) 1, 2, 5 and 6

(C) 3, 4, 6 and 5 (D) 1, 2, 5 and 4

37. Small sample means

(A) Less than 10

(B) Less than 15

(C) Less than 20

(D) Less than 30

38. Which of the following is not Goal Conflict?

(A) Approach-Approach conflict

(B) Approach-Avoidance conflict

(C) Avoidance-Avoidance conflict

(D) Role ambiguity

39. 'Irrelevance concept of dividend' is proposed by:

(A) Walter (B) Gordon

(C) Modigliani and Miller (D) Laplace

40. Total Float is:

(A) $L_j - E_j - +$

(B) $E_j - E_i - +$

(C) $L_j - E_j$

(D) $E_j - L_i - +$

41. A system in which Unions and Management negotiate with each other to develop the work rules, under which Union members will work for a stipulated period of time, is referred to as

(A) Man Power Planning

(B) Career Planning

(C) Collective Bargaining

(D) Training and Development

42. Developing new products for new markets, is called:

(A) Market Penetration

(B) Diversification

(C) Product Development

(D) Market Development

43. The term 'Exchange Ratio' is used in

(A) Profitability Assessment

(B) Capital Structure

(C) Mergers and Acquisitions

(D) Leverages

44. Which of the following is a common cause of Machine Break down?

(A) Inadequate preventive maintenance

(B) Dirt, Oil and Chemicals accumulation

(C) Incorrect machine set-up

(D) All the above

45. In the process of generating a Pool of qualified candidates for a particular Job, the 1st step, the hiring process, is called

(A) Induction

(B) Selection

(C) Recruitment

(D) Training

46. FOB Pricing is:

(A) Price skimming

(B) Penetration pricing

(C) Psychological pricing

(D) Pricing in international trade

47. A transaction, where financial securities are issued against the cash flow generated from a pool of assets is called

(A) Securitization

(B) Credit Default swaps

(C) Credit Linked Notes

(D) Total return swaps

48. Read the following statements and select correct answer

Statement–1: Operations Research is useful for optimization of resources.

Statement–2: Operations Research does not determine the optimum replacement policies.

(A) Statements 1 and 2 are true

(B) Statement 1 is true but statement 2 is not true

(C) Statement 1 is not true but statement 2 is true

(D) Both statements 1 and 2 are not true

49. Match the following :

List – 1	**List – 2**
(Marketing Variables)	**(Qualities)**
(a) Product	(i) Shape
(b) Price	(ii) Advertising
(c) Promotion	(iii) Discounts
(d) Place	(iv)Layout of store

(a)(b)(c)(d)

(A) (i) (ii) (iii) (iv)

(B) (iii) (iv) (i) (ii)

(C) (iv) (iii) (ii) (i)

(D) (i) (iii) (ii) (iv)

50. The process of providing employees with specific skills or helping them correct deficiencies in their performance is called

(A) Counseling

(B) Motivation

(C) Recruitment and selection

(D) Training

AP-SET-MANAGEMENT-PAPER-II-2012-ANSWER KEYS

Q01 C	Q11 B	Q21 C	Q31 D	Q41 C
Q02 B	Q12 D	Q22 A	Q32 C	Q42 B
Q03 B	Q13 A	Q23 B	Q33 D	Q43 C
Q04 C	Q14 D	Q24 A	Q34 B	Q44 D
Q05 C	Q15 D	Q25 C	Q35 D	Q45 C
Q06 C	Q16 D	Q26 D	Q36 B	Q46 D
Q07 B	Q17 C	Q27 D	Q37 D	Q47 A
Q08 D	Q18 D	Q28 D	Q38 D	Q48 B
Q09 D	Q19 B	Q29 A	Q39 C	Q49 D
Q10 A	Q20 D	Q30 A	Q40 A	Q50 D

---000---

AP-SET-MANAGEMENT-PAPER-III-2012

1. Which objective of financial management considers the risk and time value of money?

(A) Profit Maximisation objective

(B) Wealth Maximisation objective

(C) Turnover Maximisation objective

(D) Growth Maximisation objective

2. A zero level channel refers to

(A) Personal selling (B) Direct Marketing

(C) Buying from a retailer (D) Advertising

3. Vestible training is provided

(A) in the class room (B) off the job

(C) in the training dept. (D) on the job

4. Marine cargo insurance refers to

(A) Surface Transport insurance

(B) Aviation insurance

(C) Sea Shipment insurance

(D) None of the above

5. Free cash flow means

(A) Cash available for financing incremental working capital

(B) Cash available for financing additional investment in plant and machinery

(C) Cash available for meeting financial flows like debt servicing, dividend payments etc.

(D) None of the above

6. Demarketing is done if one of the demand state is existing

(A) Negative demand (B) Latent demand

(C) Overfull demand (D) Irregular demand

7. Group Training means

(A) Sensitivity training

(B)Class room training

(C) Role playing

(D) Training conference

8. Which of the following is foreign investment?

(A) Equity (B) Debenture

(C) FDI (D) Government Bonds

9. A portfolio consisting of two risky securities can be made riskless i.e. θp=0, if

(A) the securities are perfectly positively correlated

(B) the securities are perfectly negatively correlated

(C) if the correlation ranges between 0 and 1

(D) none of the above

10. Market is defined as

(A) A place where buyers and sellers meet

(B) A place where goods are sold

(C) A place where goods are bought

(D) A set of actual and potential buyers of product

11. The foundations of MBO is

(A) Goal setting only

(B) Feedback only

(C) Participation only

(D) Goal setting, feedback, participation

12. Which of the following is not a trading block?

(A) SAARC (B) EU

(C) NAFTA (D) IMF

13. XYZ Co. Ltd. is operating in an industry in which the average rate of return on market portfolio is 10%. The beta coefficient of the company is computed as 1.75 and return on Government Security (risk free) is 6%. What will be the required rate of return on a stock of the company?

(A) 12.5 % (B) 13.0 %

(C) 12.9 % (D) 12.0 %

14. When a company introduced a new Product, to its surprise, an article appeared in a news paper about the good qualities of the product. This is referred to as:

(A) Advertising (B) Sales Promotion

(C) Publicity (D) Personal selling

15. Under Worker's Participation Scheme

(A) Workers participate in decision making process

(B) Workers get more benefits

(C) Workers increase productivity

(D) Workers decide their work themselves

16. GATT was signed in the year

(A) 1995 (B) 2005

(C) 1947 (D) 1952

17. Du Pont analysis was developed

(i) in 1920

(ii) by F. Donalson Brown

(iii) a mechanical engineer

(iv) in Du Pont corporation

The correct combination is

(A) (i) , (iii) and(iv)

(B) (i) and (iv)

(C) (ii),(iii) and (iv)

(D) (i) , (ii) and(iv)

18. Based on the customer value hierarchy, there are five product levels. Arrange them in lower value to higher value to the customer

1. Expected product 2. Basic product

3. Core product 4. Potential product

5. Augmented product

(A) 1, 2, 3, 4, 5 (B) 3, 2, 1, 5, 4

(C) 3, 4, 5, 2, 1 (D) 1, 5, 4, 3, 2

19. Collective Bargaining is:

(A) one party process (B) two party process

(C) multi party process(D) none of the above

20. Which one of the following is the function of Foreign Exchange Market?

(A) Transfer of purchasing power

(B) Minimising exchange rate risks

(C) Credit for international business

(D) All the above

21. To get book value per share, what numerator is divided by what denominator?

(i) Networth as numerator

(ii) Number of outstanding equity shares

as denominator

(iii) Value of outstanding equity shares

as numerator

(iv)Total assets as denominator

Choose the right combination

(A) (i) and (iii) (B) (i) and (ii)

(C) (ii) and (iv) (D) (iii) and (iv)

22. Arrange the following marketing concepts in an order, so that the last concept should mean "everything matters in marketing".

1. The selling concept

2. The marketing concept

3. The holistic marketing concept

4. The product concept

5. The production concept

(A) 1, 2, 3, 5, 4 (B) 5, 4, 3, 2, 1

(C) 5, 4, 1, 2, 3 (D) 1, 2, 5, 4, 3

23. Identify the element that is not a factor of limited success of collective bargaining in India

(A) Problems with Union

(B) Negotiation

(C) Legal problems

(D) Political Interference

24. Which of the following is not a export document?

(A) Bill of Lading (B) Export license

(C) Carting order (D) Duty drawback

25. Which of the following are considered as capital components for the purpose of computing weighted average cost of capital ?

I. Common stock & Preferred stock

II. Short term loans from Banks

III. Commercial Papers

IV. Long term Debt

Choose the right combination

(A) I and II (B) II, III and IV

(C) I and IV (D) I, II, III and IV

26. A company has broad choices to enter a foreign market. Arrange the strategies from lower level to higher level involvement:

1. Licensing 2. Direct exporting

3. Indirect exporting 4. Joint venture

5. Direct investment

(A) 3, 2, 1, 4, 5 (B) 1, 2, 3, 4, 5

(C) 5, 4, 3, 2, 1 (D) 4, 5, 1, 2, 3

27. Identify the one that is not a function of Industrial Relations

(A) Establishment of Workers and Managers Communication

(B) Establishment of Employees and Management rapport

(C) Ensure Trade Union Creative contribution

(D) To Improve Workers Strength

28. Which one of the following is a export promotion measure?

(A) Abolishing export duties

(B) Export subsidies

(C) Marketing incentives

(D) All of the above

29. Which of the following would increase company's debt ratio?

I. An increase in cost incurred while filing for bankruptcy

II. An increase in corporate tax rate

III. An increase in personal tax rate

IV. A decrease in firm's business risk

Choose the right combination

(A) I, II and III (B) II, III and IV

(C) II and IV (D) III and IV

30. Marketing Research involves the following three steps. Arrange them in a sequence to make it meaningful

1. Data collection

2. Systematic design

3. Analysis of data

(A) 1, 2, 3 (B) 1, 3, 2

(C) 2, 1, 3 (D) 3, 1, 2

31. Find the 'odd' in the 'Benefits of Strategic HR Planning'

(A) Encouragement of proactive in place of reactive behaviour

(B) Explicit communication of organization goals

(C) Identification of gaps in current situation and future vision

(D) Coping with the environment

32. The double entry system of record of all economic transactions between the residents of a country and the rest of the world carried out in a specific period of time is referred to as

(A) Balance of Trade

(B) Balance of Payments

(C) Current Account

(D) Capital Account

Based on the following information, answer the next three multiple choice questions: **33** to **35**.

A company is considering an investment proposal to install new milling controls at a cost of Rs. 50,000. The facility has a life expectancy of 5 years and no salvage value. The tax rate is 35%. Assume the firm uses straight line depreciation and the same is allowed for tax purposes. The estimated cash flows before depreciation and tax (CFBT) from the investment proposal are as follows

Year : 1 2 3 4 5

CFBT(Rs.)10,000,10,692,12,769,13,462, 20,385

PV @10% 0.909, 0.826, 0.751, 0.683, 0.621

33. Choose the Pay Back Period

(A) 4 years (B) 4.328 years

(C) 4.5 years (D) 4.75 years

34. Choose the Average rate of return

(A) 9% (B) 9.5%

(C) 10% (D) 11%

35. Choose the profitability index at 10% discount factor

(A) 0.875 (B) 0.970

(C) 0.958 (D) 0.978

36. Which of the following are consumer promotion tools?

1. Premium 2. Coupons 3. Samples

(A) 1 and 2 are true (B) 1 and 3 are true

(C) 2 and 3 are true (D) 1, 2 and 3 are true

37. Pricing a product will have certain objectives and they are

1. Attracting employees

2. Profit maximisation

3. Sales maximisation

(A) 1 and 2 are true (B) 1 and 3 are true

(C) 2 and 3 are true (D) 1, 2 and 3 are true

38. Conditions for existence of exchange potential

1. Existence of two parties

2. Something of value to offer to other party

3. Capability of communication and delivery on both parties

4. Liberty to accept or reject the exchange offer

(A) 1 and 2 should exist

(B) 2 and 3 should exist

(C) 3 and 4 should exist

(D) All the above should exist

Based on the following information, answer the next three multiple choice questions: **39** to **42**

Simuflite, a Texas Aviation Training Company, expected to whip the competition with Fas Trak, its Computer Based Training (CBT) curriculum for Corporate Pilots. Instead, the new venture sent Simuflite into a nosedive. In traditional ground-school training, Pilots ask questions and learn from 'War Stories' told by classmates and instructors. With Fas Trak, they sat in front of the computer for hours absorbing information. Their only interaction was tapping the computer screen to provide answers to questions, and that novelty wore off very quickly. Pilots grew bored with the CBT Ground-School.

39. Simuflite expected to combat competition with

(A) Curriculum Based Training

(B) Competition Based Training

(C) Combat Based Training

(D) Computer Based Training

40. Pilots in Ground-School training heard from their Classmates and Instructors

(A) Fiction Stories (B) War Stories

(C) Humour Stories (D) Love Stories

41. Pilots only interaction was with

(A) Instructors (B) Computers

(C) Classmates (D) Aero Engineers

42. CBT by Simuflite resulted in

(A) Higher sales (B) Lower sales

(C) High competition (D) Low competition

43. Which of the following is in correct sequence order?

Ministerial Conference of WTO

1. I Ministerial Conference

2. II Ministerial Conference

3. III Ministerial Conference

4. IV Ministerial Conference

Held in

a. Doha b. Seattle c. Singapore d. Geneva

1 2 3 4

(A) a c d b (B) d c b a

(C) b c a d (D) c d b a

44. Which one of the following is international credit rating agency

(A) IMF (B) World Bank

(C) Standard and Poor (D) WTO

45. Fifth Ministerial Conference of WTO was held in

(A) Doha (B) Singapore

(C) Mcxico (D) Seattle

46. Assertion (A): Optimal Capital Structure is the Capital structure at the level of debt, equity proportion, where the market value per share is maximum and cost of capital is minimum

Reason (R) : Earning per share multiplied by price-earning ratio gives market price per share.

(A) A is correct but R is wrong

(B) Both A and R are wrong

(C) Both A and R are correct

(D) A is wrong but R is correct

47. Qualities required for production concept

1. Products are widely available and inexpensive

2. Managers concentrate on high production efficiency and low cost

3. Mass distribution

4. All the above

(A) 1 and 2 are true (B) 2 and 3 are true

(C) 1 and 3 are true (D) All the above are true

48. Arrange the following as per the procedure of conducting domestic enquiry

1. Calling the employee for explanation.

2. Considering the explanation of the employee.

3. Issuing a show cause notice.

4. Holding a full fledged enquiry.

5. Considering the witness report, documents, etc.

6. Considering the enquiry report.

Write the correct sequence steps

(A) 1, 2, 3, 4, 5, 6 (B) 6, 1, 2, 3, 4, 5

(C) 5, 4, 3, 2, 1, 6 (D) 3, 2, 1, 5, 4, 6

49. Which one of the following is not an instrument of trade policy

(A) Tariffs (B) Subsidics

(C) Import Quotas (D) Letter of credit

50. Assertion (A): Venture capital is the capital to raise to invest in high risk projects.

Reason (R): ICICI was established to finance only venture capital projects.

(A) Both A and R are correct

(B) A is correct but R is wrong

(C) Both A and R are wrong

(D) A is wrong but R is correct

51. Match the following

List -1 (Authors)

a. William J.Stanton

b. Cundiff and Still

c. Mc Carthy

d. Philip Kotler

List -2 (Books)

1. Principles of Marketing
2. Basic Marketing
3. Sales Management
4. Fundamentals of Marketing

a b c d

(A) 1 2 3 4 (B) 4 3 2 1

(C) 2 3 1 4 (D) 3 2 4 1

52. Match the following Big Five Personality

List-I	**List-II**
(a) Extroversion	(i) Warm
(b) Agreeableness	(ii) Gregarious
(c) Conscientiousness	(iii) Stable
(d) Emotional stability	(iv) Imaginative
(e) Openness experience	(v) Planful

(a) (b) (c) (d) (e)

(A) (ii) (iii) (i) (v) (iv)

(B) (iii) (i) (ii) (iv) (v)

(C) (ii) (i) (v) (iii) (iv)

(D) (i) (iii) (iv) (v) (ii)

53. GATT was transformed into WTO in the year:

(A) 2001 (B) 1996

(C) 1995 (D) 2010

54. Assertion (A): Walter's and Gordon's models are applicable to firms in which all financing is done through retained earnings and with zero leverage.

Reason (R): The market price of the share, according to Gordon model is favourably effected with the increasing payment of dividends.

(A) Both A and R are correct

(B) Both A and R are wrong

(C) A is correct but R is wrong

(D) A is wrong but R is correct

55. Match the following

List – I

(a) Need

(b) Want

(c) Demand

List – II

(i) want supported by purchasing power

(ii) felt deprivation

(iii) expression for specific good

(a) (b) (c)

(A) (ii) (iii) (i)

(B) (i) (ii) (iii)

(C) (iii) (ii) (i)

(D) (i) (iii) (ii)

56. Match the following

a. Maslow	1. Expectancy theory
b. Herzberg	2. ERG theory
c. Vrooms	3. Need hierarchy
d. Alderfers	4. Hygiene theory

a b c d

(A) 3 1 4 2

(B) 3 4 1 2

(C) 3 2 4 1

(D) 2 4 3 1

57. To encourage domestic production or to protect the domestic producer from foreign competitors, government pays to domestic producer by reducing operations cost. Such payments are called

(A) Bill of Exchange (B) Foreign Exchange

(C) Bill of Lading (D) Subsidies

58. Arrange the components of current assets in the order of liquidity

I. Sundry Debtors

II. Bills Receivables

III. Inventories

IV. Cash and Bank

(A) IV, III, II and I (B) IV, II, I and III

(C) I, IV, II and III (D) III, II, IV and I

59. Match the following

List – I (Four Ps)	List – II (Four Cs)
(a) Product	1. Convenience
(b) Price	2. Communication
(c) Place	3. Customer Solution
(d) Promotion	4. Customer Cost

	(a)	(b)	(c)	(d)
(A)	3	1	4	2
(B)	3	4	1	2
(C)	1	2	3	4
(D)	4	3	2	1

60. Assertion (A): Employee Welfare enhances Industrial/ Organizational Productivity.

Reason (R): Welfare needs to be tackled on Statutory and Non-statutory basis.

(A) A is right and R is wrong

(B) A is wrong and R is right

(C) A and R are right

(D) A and R are wrong

61. Give the Acronym of ASEAN

(A) Association of South East Asian Nations

(B) Asian South East African Nations

(C) Association of South East American Nations

(D) Association of South East Ancient Nations

62. Match the following

List – I (Form of Dividend)

i. Cash Dividend

ii. Stock Dividend

iii. Bond Dividend

iv. Property Dividend

List- II (Feature)

a. Securities

b. Promissory notes

c. Liquidity

d. Bonus shares

i ii iii iv

(A) d b c a

(B) a c d b

(C) c d b a

(D) b a d c

63. Match the following

List-I (Companies)

a. Xerox

b. Columbia Pictures

c. Carrier

d. Missouri Pacific Railroad

List-II (Market definition)

1. We provide climate control in the home

2. We are a people and goods mover

3. We help improve office productivity

4. We market entertainment

a b c d

(A) 3 4 2 1 (B) 3 2 1 4

(C) 3 4 1 2 (D) 3 2 4 1

64. Write the steps in voluntary arbitration

1. The voluntary submission of dispute to an arbitrator

2. The subsequent attendance of witness and investigations

3. The enforcement of an award may not be necessary

(A) 3, 2, 1 (B) 2, 1, 3

(C) 1, 2, 3 (D) 3, 1, 2

65. Match the following:

List – I

i. The price at which instrument is traded.

ii. A contract that gives the holder the right but not the obligation.

iii. An agreement to buy or sell a security on a specified date for a specified price.

iv. The possibility of default by any one risk party to the transaction

List – II

a. Option

b. Forward Contract

c. Spot price

d. Counter party

i ii iii iv

(A) a c d b (B) b a c d

(C) c a b d (D) d c a b

66. 'Marketing Myopia' is coined by

(A) Philip Kotler (B) Al Ries

(C) Theodore Levith (D) Peter F. Drucker

67. Job Analysis involves

1. Developing training skills

2. Identifying Machine tools

3. Identification of the task to be performed by an individual

4. Determination of the materials and products.

Write the correct sequence of steps in Job Analysis

(A) 3, 2, 4, 1 (B) 3, 2, 1, 4

(C) 2, 3, 4, 1 (D) 2, 3, 1, 4

68. Match the following

List – I

i. The price of one currency expressed in terms of the currency of another country

ii. The difference between the Ask price and Bid price

iii. The rate of exchange of two currencies on the basis of rate exchange quotes of other pairs of currencies

iv. Rate of exchange of the day on which the transaction rate has taken place and of the day the transaction is executed

List – II

a. Spread

b. Spot rate

c. Cross

d. Exchange

Code:

i ii iii iv

(A) a c d b

(B) d a c b

(C) b c a d

(D) c b d a

69. Match the following

List-1 (Strategies)

a. Market penetration

b. Market development

c. Product development

d. Diversification

List- 2 (Market and Products)

1. New markets-new products.

2. New marketscurrent products

3. Current markets new products

4. Current marketscurrent

products

a b c d

(A) 4 3 2 1

(B) 1 2 3 4

(C) 3 2 4 1

(D) 4 2 3 1

70. Promotion means

1. Elevation to higher position.

2. Elevation to higher position with financial benefits.

3. Elevation to higher position with more power.

(A) 1 and 2 only (B) 1 and 3 only

(C) 2 and 3 only (D) All the above

71. Choose customer order processing in sequential order from the following

(A) Invoice raised, establish credit status, check credit limit, goods deliver, issue delivery note

(B) Issue delivery note, establish credit status, check credit limit, invoice raised, goods deliver

(C) Establish credit status, check credit limit, issue delivery note, goods deliver, invoice raised

(D) Check credit limit, invoice raised, establish credit status, issue delivery note, goods deliver

72. In marketing, needs are defined as

(A) primary needs

(B) physiological needs

(C) psychological needs

(D) any felt deprivations

73. Which of the following constitute manpower planning?

1. Determine human resource requirements both qualitatively and quantitatively.

2. Find the source of talented individuals.

3. Planning for the human resource needs of an organization.

4. Processing the right people.

(A) 1, 2 and 4 (B) 2 and 3

(C) 1 and 3 (D) 1, 2, 3 and 4

74. Choose the process of capital budgeting in a sequential order from the following

(A)Project evaluation, Project generation, Project selection and Project execution

(B)Project selection, project execution, project generation and project evaluation.

(C) Project generation, project evaluation, project selection and project execution.

(D) Project generation, project selection, project execution and project evaluation

75. Match the following

a. Strike	1. Employer
b. Lock out	2. Arbitrator
c. Adjudication	3. Employee
d. Arbitration	4. Courts

a b c d

(A) 3 2 4 1

(B) 3 1 4 2

(C) 3 4 1 2

(D) 3 1 2 4

AP-SET-MANAGEMENT-PAPER-III-2012-ANSWER KEYS				
Q01 B	Q16 C	Q31 D	Q46 C	Q61 A
Q02 B	Q17 D	Q32 B	Q47 D	Q62 C
Q03 B	Q18 B	Q33 B	Q48 A	Q63 C
Q04 C	Q19 B	Q34 A	Q49 D	Q64 C
Q05 C	Q20 D	Q35ALL	Q50 B	Q65 C
Q06 C	Q21 B	Q36 D	Q51 B	Q66 C
Q07 A	Q22 C	Q37 C	Q52 C	Q67 A
Q08 C	Q23 B	Q38 D	Q53 C	Q68 B
Q09 B	Q24 D	Q39 D	Q54 A	Q69 D
Q10 A	Q25 C	Q40 B	Q55 A	Q70 D
Q11 D	Q26 A	Q41 B	Q56 B	Q71 C
Q12 D	Q27 D	Q42 B	Q57 D	Q72 D
Q13 B	Q28 D	Q43 D	Q58 B	Q73 D
Q14 C	Q29 C	Q44 C	Q59 B	Q74 C
Q15 A	Q30 C	Q45 C	Q60 C	Q75 B

---000---

Bibliography

- P. Subba Rao(2012): *Essentials of Human Resource and Industrial Relations Text, Cases and Games,* Himalaya Publishing House -5th Revised edition.
- P. Subba Rao(2012): *Personnel and Human Resource Management,* Himalaya Publishing House -4th Revised edition.
- Garry Dessler and Biju Varkkey(2009): *Human Resource Management,* Pearson Prentice Hall - 11th edition.
- David A. Decenzo and Stephen P. Robbins (2001): *Human Resource Management,* John Wiley & Sons, Inc -6th edition.
- Harold Koontz and Heinz Weihrich (2004):*Essentials of Management,* Tata McGraw-Hill Publishing- 6th edition.
- Ruddar Datt and K.P.M. Sundharam(2004):*Indian Economy* S.Chand-49th Revised edition.
- John W. Newstrom and Keith Davis(1997):*Organizational Behaviour: Human Behaviour at work,* Tata McGraw-Hill Publishing- 10th edition.
- Suja R.Nair(2010):*Organizational Behaviour: Text and Cases,* Himalaya Publishing House -1st edition.
- C.B.Mamoria: *Personnel Management(Management of Human Resources)(1997),* Himalaya Publishing House -12th edition.
- S.C.Srivastava: *Industrial Relations and Labour Laws(2004),* Vikas publishing House Pvt.Ltd.- 4th revised edition.
- Wendell L. French and Cecil H.Bell, Jr:*Organization Development(2006),*Prentice –Hall of India Pvt .Ltd-6th edition.
- P.C.tripathi: *Personnel Management and Industrial Relations(1998) ,Sultan Chand and Sons* - 13th Revised edition.
- Aswathappa, K. (2005): *Human Resource and Personnel Management Text and Cases,* 4th edition
- ICFAI Center for Management Research, *"Introduction to Human Resource Management, 2004.*
- Nilesh S. Ugemuge and Moreshwar N.Kudkilwar(2013):*Human Resource Management, Industrial management and Labour Welfare for UGC-NET/SET*, Himalaya Publishing House.
- P. L. Mehta,*Managerial Economics*, Sultan Chand & Sons, New Delhi
- N. D. Vohra *Quantitative Techniques in Management*, (TMGH).
- S. Sudalaimuthu, S.Anthony Raj (2008),*Computer Application in Business*, Himalaya Publishing House.
- Kotler, Keller, Koshy, Jha ,*Marketing Management.*
- Kotler, Armstrong, Agnihotri, Haque ,*Principles of Marketing.*
- Kapil,*Financial Management,* Pearson Publication.
- Chary ,*Production & Operations Management.*
- R. P. Banerjee ,*Ethics in Business & Management,*Himalaya Publication.
- V S Ramaswami, S Namaumari,*Strategic Planning & Formulation of Corporate Strategy*, Macmillan Publication.
- Robert D Hisrich ,*Entrepreneurship* 6th edition., Tata McGraw-Hill.